MARITIME DELIMITATION AS A JUDICIAL PROCESS

Maritime Delimitation as a Judicial Process is the first comprehensive analysis of judicial decisions, state practice and academic opinions on maritime boundary delimitation. For ease of reading and clarity, it follows this three-stage approach in its structure.

Massimo Lando analyses the interaction between international tribunals and states in the development of the delimitation process, in order to explain rationally how a judicially created approach to delimit maritime boundaries has been accepted by states. Pursuing a practical approach, this book identifies disputed points in maritime delimitation and proposes solutions which could be applied in future judicial disputes. In addition, the book engages with the underlying theories of maritime delimitation, including the relationship between delimitation and delineation, the effect of third states' rights on delimitation and the manner in which each stage of the process influences the other stages.

Massimo Lando is Associate Legal Officer at the International Court of Justice, The Hague. He holds a doctorate from the University of Cambridge. He has published in leading journals, including the *International and Comparative Law Quarterly*, the *Leiden Journal of International Law* and the *Modern Law Review*. His published research focuses on the law of the sea, the law of provisional measures, as well as other issues of international dispute settlement, immunity, and the relationship between national and international law.

CAMBRIDGE STUDIES IN INTERNATIONAL AND COMPARATIVE LAW: 144

Established in 1946, this series produces high-quality, reflective and innovative scholarship in the field of public international law. It publishes works on international law that are of a theoretical, historical, cross-disciplinary or doctrinal nature. The series also welcomes books providing insights from private international law, comparative law and transnational studies which inform international legal thought and practice more generally. The series seeks to publish views from diverse legal traditions and perspectives, and of any geographical origin. In this respect it invites studies offering regional perspectives on core *problématiques* of international law, and in the same vein, it appreciates contrasts and debates between diverging approaches. Accordingly, books offering new or less orthodox perspectives are very much welcome. Works of a generalist character are greatly valued and the series is also open to studies on specific areas, institutions or problems. Translations of the most outstanding works published in other languages are also considered. After seventy years, Cambridge Studies in International and Comparative Law sets the standard for international legal scholarship and will continue to define the discipline as it evolves in the years to come.

Series Editors

Larissa van den Herik

Professor of Public International Law, Grotius Centre for International Legal Studies, Leiden University

Jean d'Aspremont

Professor of International Law, University of Manchester and Sciences Po Law School

A list of books in the series can be found at the end of this volume.

MARITIME DELIMITATION AS A JUDICIAL PROCESS

MASSIMO LANDO
International Court of Justice

CAMBRIDGE
UNIVERSITY PRESS

University Printing House, Cambridge CB2 8BS, United Kingdom

One Liberty Plaza, 20th Floor, New York, NY 10006, USA

477 Williamstown Road, Port Melbourne, VIC 3207, Australia

314-321, 3rd Floor, Plot 3, Splendor Forum, Jasola District Centre, New Delhi - 110025, India

79 Anson Road, #06-04/06, Singapore 079906

Cambridge University Press is part of the University of Cambridge.

It furthers the University's mission by disseminating knowledge in the pursuit of education, learning and research at the highest international levels of excellence.

www.cambridge.org
Information on this title: www.cambridge.org/9781108497398
DOI: 10.1017/9781108608893

© Cambridge University Press 2019

This publication is in copyright. Subject to statutory exception and to the provisions of relevant collective licensing agreements, no reproduction of any part may take place without the written permission of Cambridge University Press.

First published 2019

A catalogue record for this publication is available from the British Library

Library of Congress Cataloging in Publication data
Names: Lando, Massimo, 1989– author.
Title: Maritime delimitation as a judicial process / Massimo Lando, International Court Of Justice.
Description: Cambridge, United Kingdom ; New York, NY, USA : Cambridge University Press, 2019. | Series: Cambridge studies in international and comparative law ; 144 | Based on author's thesis (doctoral – University of Cambrdige, 2017) issued under title: Consistency in the international law of maritime delimitation : towards a set of common principles for the judicial establishment of maritime boundaries. | Includes bibliographical references and index.
Identifiers: LCCN 2019008394 | ISBN 9781108497398 (hardback)
Subjects: LCSH: Maritime boundaries.
Classification: LCC KZA1450 .L36 2019 | DDC 341.4/48–dc23
LC record available at https://lccn.loc.gov/2019008394

ISBN 978-1-108-49739-8 Hardback
ISBN 978-1-108-74005-0 Paperback

Cambridge University Press has no responsibility for the persistence or accuracy of URLs for external or third-party internet websites referred to in this publication, and does not guarantee that any content on such websites is, or will remain, accurate or appropriate.

CONTENTS

List of Figures   page xi
Foreword   xiii
Preface   xvii
Table of Cases   xx
Table of Treaties and Legislation   xxiv
List of Abbreviations   xxxii

1 Maritime Delimitation in the Time of International Tribunals   1

  I Maritime Boundaries and International Tribunals   1

  II Scope of the Book   2

  III Structure of the Book   5

2 Historical and Conceptual Framework   9

  I Rules and Processes in Maritime Delimitation   9

  II Historical Framework of Maritime Delimitation   10

    A Rules Governing Maritime Delimitation   10
      1 The 1930 League of Nations Codification Conference   10
      2 The 1958 Geneva Convention on the Continental Shelf   12
      3 The 1982 United Nations Convention on the Law of the Sea   15
    B Methods for Delimiting the EEZ and the Continental Shelf   17
      1 The primacy of relevant circumstances (1969–1993)   17

v

          2 The two-stage approach (1993–2009)   20
          3 The three-stage approach (2009–present)   21
    III Conceptual Framework of Maritime Delimitation   23
          A Maritime Delimitation as a Process   24
          B Objectivity and the Equitable Solution   26
          C Connection between Delimitation and the Basis of Title   30
    IV An Inevitable Development?   33

3 Relevant Coast and Relevant Area   34
    I An Essential Stage in the Delimitation Process   34
    II The Relevant Coast   37
          A The Land Dominates the Sea   37
                1 The delimitation of the maritime zones within 200 nautical miles   37
                2 The delimitation of the continental shelf beyond 200 nautical miles   41
          B Identifying the Relevant Coast   43
                1 The most distant base points as end-points of the relevant coast   44
                2 The approximation of the relevant coast by means of straight lines   48
                3 The coast of bays and inlets as part of the relevant coast   56
    III The Relevant Area   65
          A The Concept of the Relevant Area   65
                1 The elusive definition of the relevant area   65
                2 The 2018 *Costa Rica* v. *Nicaragua* judgment   69
          B The Direction of Coastal Projections   72
                1 The envelope of arcs as the implementation of radial projections   73
                2 The application of radial projections by international tribunals   76
          C The Limits of the Relevant Area   81
                1 The maximum extent of national jurisdiction under UNCLOS   81
                2 Pre-existing maritime boundaries   84
                3 Relevant areas generated by coasts facing the open sea   90

4   The delimitation of the continental shelf beyond 200 nautical
     miles   95

IV An Additional Stage in the Delimitation
   Process   98

4 Equidistance   102

 I Brief History of Equidistance   102

 II Legal Basis of Equidistance in Delimitation within 200
    Nautical Miles   104
    A Connection to the Basis of Title   104
       1 Basis of title over the EEZ   104
       2 Basis of title over the continental shelf within 200 nautical
         miles   105
    B Relationship between the Continental Shelf and the
      EEZ   109
       1 EEZ declarations, judicial approaches and recent
         studies   109
       2 Interpreting the relevant UNCLOS provisions   111
       3 Approach of states in bilateral delimitation
         treaties   116
    C Impact of Coastal Configuration   121
       1 The 2007 *Nicaragua* v. *Honduras* judgment   122
       2 The 2012 *Nicaragua* v. *Colombia* judgment   124
       3 Reconciling *Nicaragua* v. *Honduras* and *Nicaragua*
         v. *Colombia*   126

 III Equidistance and the Continental Shelf beyond 200
     Nautical Miles   128
     A The Bay of Bengal Cases and *Ghana/Côte d'Ivoire*   128
     B The Problem of the Basis of Title   130
        1 The Article 76 UNCLOS compromise   130
        2 Distance as an element of the basis of title   131
     C The Grey Area Issue   135
        1 The absence of legal basis under UNCLOS   135
        2 Grey areas and the EEZ-continental shelf
          relationship   140

 IV Constructing an Equidistance Line   143
    A Selection of Base Points   144
       1 The general principles of base point selection   144
       2 Low-tide elevations as base points   147
    B Islands, Base Points and 'Creeping Relevant
      Circumstances'   150

               1 Using islands as base points   150
               2 Avoiding 'creeping relevant circumstances'   154
            C Base Points and the Relevant Coast   156
               1 The relevant coast and the feasibility of an equidistance line   156
               2 Coastal instability and the feasibility of an equidistance line   161

      V A Common Approach to Equidistance   165

5 Relevant Circumstances   167

      I   A Dual Basis for Relevant Circumstances   167

      II The Basis of Title: Geographical Circumstances   168
            A Cut-Off Effect   168
            B Coastal Length Disparity   173
            C Islands   178
               1 Enclavement   178
               2 No effect   181
               3 Half effect   186
               4 Full effect   188
            D The Location and Direction of the Land Boundary Terminus   193

      III The Functions of Maritime Zones: Non-Geographical Circumstances   195
            A Access to Natural Resources   195
               1 The approach of states   196
               2 The approach of international tribunals   197
            B Navigation   201
            C Security   205

      IV Irrelevant Circumstances   210
            A Conduct   211
            B Rights of Third States   217
            C Geomorphology   221

      V Implications of the Judicial Approach to Relevant Circumstances   227
            A Identifying Relevant Circumstances   227
            B Weighing Relevant Circumstances   232
            C Adjusting a Provisional Equidistance Line   235
               1 The adjustment and the judicial function   236

2   The methods for adjusting an equidistance line   239

VI   Consistency in Evaluating Relevant Circumstances   245

6   Disproportionality   246

I   Disproportionality as the Final Stage of the Delimitation Process   246

II   A Note on Terminology   248

III   The Legal Basis of Disproportionality   252
   A   Proportionality as a Delimitation Method   252
   B   The Original Absence of a Legal Basis for Proportionality   253
   C   Disproportionality in Delimiting the Continental Shelf beyond 200 Nautical Miles   259

IV   Judicial Approaches to Disproportionality   260
   A   The Function of Disproportionality in the Delimitation Process   260
      1   The unclear function of proportionality: 1969–1992   261
      2   Disproportionality as a test of equitableness: 1993–present   263
   B   The Assessment of Disproportionality by International Tribunals   267
      1   Scope of application   267
      2   Disproportionality as a mathematical assessment   270
   C   The Impact of Coastal Configuration on Disproportionality   275

V   Disproportionality and Coastal Length Disparity   280
   A   The Functions of Disproportionality and Coastal Length Disparity   280
   B   Disproportionality and Coastal Length Disparity in the Jurisprudence   282
      1   Before the three-stage approach   282
      2   After the three-stage approach   286

VI   Disproportionality Re-Affirmed   288

7. States, International Tribunals and the Delimitation Process   290

  I Misgivings on the Delimitation Process as a Judicial Creation   290

  II International Tribunals as Lawmakers   291
      A Legal Basis of Judicial Law-making in Maritime Delimitation   292
          1 Lack of customary international law on the delimitation process   292
          2 Consequences of the vagueness of Articles 74 and 83 UNCLOS   294
      B Judicial Decisions as a Source of the Law of Maritime Delimitation   300
          1 Status of judicial decisions under Article 38 of the ICJ's Statute   301
          2 Relevance of *res judicata*   306

  III Approach of States   308
      A Maritime Delimitation Treaties   308
      B Statements on the Delimitation Process   310
          1 Statements in multilateral fora   311
          2 Pleadings before international tribunals   312
      C Compliance with Judicial Decisions Establishing Maritime Boundaries   317

  IV Interaction between States and International Tribunals   321

  V What Next for the Delimitation Process?   322

Appendix 1   324
Appendix 2   334
Bibliography   357
Index   383

FIGURES

3.1 The relevant coast in *Bangladesh/Myanmar*. Source: [2012] ITLOS Rep 60   page 51
3.2 The geography of the Gulf of Maine and the Bay of Fundy. Source: [1984] ICJ Rep 289   57
3.3 The relevant coast identified by the ICJ in *Black Sea*. Source: [2009] ICJ Rep 94   60
3.4 The 'area of overlapping claims' and the 'area of overlapping entitlements' in *Jan Mayen*. Source: [1993] ICJ Rep 45   68
3.5 The *Peru* v. *Chile* claim lines. Source: [2014] ICJ Rep 17   75
3.6 The general direction of the coast in *Nicaragua* v. *Honduras*. Source: [2007] ICJ Rep 750   78
3.7 The relevant area in *Nicaragua* v. *Colombia*. Source: [2012] ICJ Rep 687   85
3.8 The relevant area in *Costa Rica* v. *Nicaragua* in the Pacific Ocean. Source: ICJ, forthcoming   94
4.1 The grey areas in the Bay of Bengal Cases. Source: 167 ILR 172 © The Permanent Court of Arbitration   137
4.2 PS Rao's proposed boundary in *Bangladesh* v. *India*. Source: 167 ILR 208 © The Permanent Court of Arbitration   142
4.3 The relevant area as identified by the ICJ in *Nicaragua* v. *Colombia*. Source: [2012] ICJ Rep 687   158
5.1 Ukraine's proposed adjustment in *Black Sea*. Source: [2009] ICJ *Black Sea* – Rejoinder of Ukraine, Figure 7.3   238
5.2 The provisional equidistance line established in *Bangladesh/Myanmar*. Source: [2012] ITLOS Rep 77   242
5.3 The parties' proposed provisional equidistance lines in *Bangladesh/Myanmar*. Source: [2012] ITLOS Rep 75   243
6.1 Comparison of coastal length ratio and marine area ratio across delimitation cases. Source: Created by the author   272

FOREWORD

Since the 1969 judgments of the International Court of Justice (ICJ) in the *North Sea Continental Shelf* cases, and increasingly after the adoption of the 1982 United Nations Convention on the Law of the Sea (UNCLOS), maritime delimitation has been a very frequent subject of adjudication in cases brought before the ICJ, international arbitral tribunals and, during the last few years, the International Tribunal for the Law of the Sea (ITLOS). Although up to the end of the twentieth century such cases have been submitted to adjudication on the basis of special agreements, declarations of acceptance of the optional clause under Article 36, paragraph 2, of the ICJ's Statute and the Pact of Bogotá, there is no doubt that entry into force of the UNCLOS in 1994 has added considerably to the possibilities of adjudicating delimitation disputes. Under UNCLOS, a state party may submit delimitation disputes to an international court or tribunal unilaterally. As among the parties to UNCLOS, compulsory settlement thus applies to delimitation disputes. While such applicability may be derogated through a declaration made under Article 298, paragraph 1, of UNCLOS, only a relatively limited number of States parties have taken advantage of the possibility of making such a declaration. Indeed, since the beginning of the present century, practice shows various instances of delimitation cases brought unilaterally to adjudication under the dispute settlement provisions of UNCLOS.

While the UNCLOS dispute-settlement mechanism is relatively robust, its provisions concerning delimitation of the Exclusive Economic Zone and of the continental shelf are quite weak. Articles 74 and 83 are mostly procedural and only indicate that delimitation must achieve an equitable solution.

The tension between the weakness of the provisions on delimitation and the existence of multiple possibilities to submit delimitation disputes to adjudication is the starting point of this book by Dr Massimo Lando. He underscores that 'the jurisprudence of international tribunals on maritime delimitation may be a reaction to the inability of states to agree on a clear rule governing maritime delimitation', and that the tribunals' law-making function 'stems both from the impossibility for customary rules of international law to develop in maritime delimitation, and from the inability of states to agree on clear treaty rules governing delimitation'.

The book addresses the process of delimitation as developed by the jurisprudence of international courts and tribunals, stressing in particular the importance of the three-stage methodology adopted by the ICJ in the 2009 *Black Sea* delimitation case, and followed by the ICJ and other tribunals since then. The three stages (provisional equidistance line, relevant circumstances and adjustment of the equidistance line, check of disproportionality) provide the structure of the book and the order and subject of its main chapters. In examining each question the author presents clearly and precisely the evolution of the law of maritime delimitation as a product of judicial activity, underscoring that the three-stage delimitation process 'is not the outcome of inevitable development [...] [h]ad judges on international tribunals been different, or thought differently, we would likely be delimiting boundaries differently'. As underscored in the concluding chapter, while 'international tribunals remain the main developers of the delimitation process' states are not without a role, although a limited one, in particular 'sanctioning the delimitation process developed by international tribunals' by concluding treaties confirming the judicial approach and readily implementing judicial and arbitral decisions.

Dr Lando's main concern is not only to argue that decisions of international courts and tribunals play a role as both material and formal sources of international law, thus going beyond the 'subsidiary means for the determination of rules of law' mentioned in Article 38, paragraph 1 (d), of the ICJ's Statute. He is also concerned with the details of the delimitation process as international courts and tribunals have shaped it, not hesitating to put forward views on improvements that should be introduced and on defects that should be corrected.

As regards the possible improvements, Dr Lando correctly insists on the importance of the determination of the relevant coast and relevant area in the delimitation process. He underscores that such determination is preliminary to the first of the three stages in which the delimitation process is articulated. He concludes that identifying the relevant coast and the relevant area should be recognised as a 'full-fledged', additional first stage in maritime delimitation, arguing that this 'would increase transparency in the establishment of maritime borders'.

As far as defects are concerned, after a detailed analysis of the relationship between the continental shelf and the Exclusive Economic Zone in light of UNCLOS, the author focuses on the 'grey areas'. These are areas of the sea situated in the Exclusive Economic Zone of one state, and on the continental shelf beyond 200 nautical miles of another state, whose existence is the consequence of a boundary different from an equidistance line. He argues vigorously and provocatively that 'grey areas' do not have a legal basis in UNCLOS, and states that the approach followed in dealing with these areas in the ITLOS judgment and in the Annex VII arbitral tribunal's award in the Bay of Bengal delimitation cases is 'unconvincing'. He argues, *inter alia*, that in cases different from the ones concerning the Bay of Bengal, there may be need for recommendations of the Commission for the Limits of the Continental Shelf, that in those cases ITLOS and the arbitral tribunal considered to be unnecessary.

This fine book also contains a table of cases and a table of treaties and legislation, as well by two appendices and a bibliography. There is also a table which refers to the fifteen figures, mostly taken from judgments and awards, that appropriately complete the text. The first appendix lists the states that have proclaimed an Exclusive Economic Zone, those that have proclaimed a fishery zone and those having proclaimed other zones beyond twelve nautical miles. The second appendix lists the bilateral treaties establishing boundaries based on equidistance, the treaties based on a criterion other than equidistance, and those establishing some form of inter-state co-operation in the exploitation of natural resources. These tables and appendices show the broad basis of documents on which the book relies. This is confirmed by the bibliography, showing the author's familiarity with a vast literature not only in English, but also in French and Italian.

Dr Lando's book will appeal both to scholars and practitioners. Scholars will be attracted by the new light delimitation throws on international law-making and the theory of sources, as well as on new areas of the law of the sea, while practitioners will find an updated, informed and stimulating treatment of a subject that is often at the heart of international litigation.

Tullio Treves

Milan
November 2018

PREFACE

The scholar of international law and the expert in the settlement of international disputes should have at least a basic understanding of maritime delimitation in the Exclusive Economic Zone and in the continental shelf. Maritime disputes are among the most litigated cases before inter-state courts and tribunals, and they make up a field of law in which international judges have exercised considerable influence. The number of maritime disputes filed by states with international courts and tribunals has been steadily growing in the last decades, accompanied by the development of the methodology which such courts and tribunals apply in order to delimit maritime boundaries. The judgment of the International Court of Justice (ICJ) in *Maritime Delimitation in the Black Sea (Romania v. Ukraine)* is the latest landmark evolution in the law of maritime delimitation. That judgment systematised the delimitation process in a manner which has made it possible for other international courts and tribunals to adopt the same delimitation process as the standard approach to establish maritime boundaries. One could justifiably speak of a common law of maritime delimitation.

This study is dedicated to this common law of maritime delimitation. Although Articles 74 and 83 of the United Nations Convention on the Law of the Sea (UNCLOS) are the foundation on which the edifice of maritime delimitation stands, international courts and tribunals are considered to have made the very law of maritime delimitation which they themselves apply to settle maritime disputes. In their effort to create a clear and consistent body of law concerning maritime delimitation, international courts and tribunals have pursued consistency with their own previous decisions, accepting apparent deviations from the earlier jurisprudence when such deviations do not compromise the intellectual structure which they have previously built. However, maritime delimitation does not take place only by way of judicial process. More than two hundred treaties establishing maritime boundaries are currently in existence, whether in force or not. On the whole, the story of maritime delimitation is a story of success in the peaceful settlement of international disputes, whether such settlement may have been achieved by way of negotiation or by way of judicial process.

This study also wishes to achieve an additional objective. Scholars and practitioners in international law have surely heard, at least once in their professional life, the confident declaration, sometimes accompanied by a degree of hilarity manifested to one's audience, that there is no such thing as 'law' in maritime delimitation. This book intends to make the case for the opposite perspective. While there may not be much law if one limits oneself to UNCLOS and customary international law, the extensive maritime delimitation jurisprudence ought to be seen as a formal source of international law.

This book originates from a thesis submitted in September 2017 for the degree of Doctor of Philosophy at the University of Cambridge. I thank St Catharine's College, Cambridge, for electing me to the Jacobson Scholarship in International Law, and the Cambridge Commonwealth, European and International Trust for awarding me a Cambridge European Scholarship.

Professor Christine Gray supervised my doctoral research. Since our first meeting in St John's College on a rainy day of early October 2014, she has been a supportive presence in my academic and professional life. I am grateful both for the time and attention she has devoted to my scholarship, and for the support she has shown in respect of my endeavours both within and outside of Cambridge. Dr Philippa Webb and Dr Lorand Bartels examined my PhD thesis in November 2017, and gave valuable suggestions for turning it into this book. I would also like to thank Professor Tullio Treves, who first inspired me to read and write on international dispute settlement and law of the sea, and Judge James Crawford for having supervised my earlier research.

After my PhD, I served as an Associate Legal Officer at the ICJ. I was privileged to witness the preparation of the judgment of 2 February 2018 in *Maritime Delimitation in the Caribbean Sea and the Pacific Ocean (Costa Rica v. Nicaragua)*. I thank Judge Dalveer Bhandari for giving me the opportunity to work in his chambers. Within and outside the ICJ, I owe additional debts of gratitude to Judge Giorgio Gaja, Sir Christopher Greenwood, Judge *ad hoc* Charles Brower, and Professor Paolo Palchetti.

I am grateful to a number of other persons who, in different capacities, were present when this book was being written. In no particular order of precedence, they are: Mike Becker, Niccolò Ridi, Lorenzo Maniscalco, Eva Paloma Treves, Emilija Marcinkeviciute, Lan Nguyen, Daniel Peat,

PREFACE

Clara Rauchegger, Jessica Joly-Hébert, Vladyslav Lanovoy, Rose Cameron, Nina Grange, Anne Coulon, Asier Garrido-Muñoz, Bin Jiang, Kalaycia Clarke, Callum Musto, Sondre Torp Helmersen, Snjólaug Árnadóttir, Lucas Carlos Lima, Loris Marotti, Cameron Miles, Ghazala Kroes, Claire O'Connell and Kritika Sharma.

My research was made immensely easier by the assistance of expert librarians. I would like to thank David Wills, Lesley Dingle, Kathy Young, Kay Naylor and Clive Argent of the Squire Law Library at the Cambridge Law Faculty. I am also grateful to Cyril Emery, Corinne Fumé, Christelle Gianolio, Sanja Taslaman, and Artur Brodowicz of the Library of the International Court of Justice.

This book would not exist without the support of Finola O'Sullivan and Marianne Nield of Cambridge University Press. Finola believed in this project since the first time we discussed it on yet another rainy Cambridge day. Marianne was of great assistance during the publication process, patiently dealing with my many first-time author queries. Additional thanks are owed to Emma Collison, Anna Gardner and Mathivathini Mareesan.

I am fortunate to have a supportive, encouraging and nurturing family, my parents Bianca and Fabio and my sister Nicoletta. Since 2014, Michael and I have been accompanying each other through life, which for him has also meant patiently hearing about states, maritime boundaries and international courts and tribunals. I am grateful to all of them for being a source of inspiration and example.

Massimo Lando

The Hague
December 2018

TABLE OF CASES

(in reverse chronological order by jurisdiction)

International Court of Justice

Maritime Delimitation in the Caribbean Sea and the Pacific Ocean (Costa Rica
   v. Nicaragua) (Judgment) [2018] ICJ Rep 139   5, 23, 27, 35, 45, 47, 49, 54, 63, 69–72,
   76, 80, 87–8, 92–4, 100, 153, 155, 171, 188, 195, 220, 265, 281, 315
Alleged Violations of Sovereign Rights and Maritime Spaces in the Caribbean Sea
   (Nicaragua v. Colombia) (Counter-claims) [2017] ICJ Rep 289   56
Maritime Delimitation in the Indian Ocean (Somalia v. Kenya) (Preliminary
   Objections) [2017] ICJ Rep 3   29, 97–8, 139
Question of the Delimitation of the Continental Shelf between Nicaragua and
   Colombia beyond 200 Nautical Miles from the Nicaraguan Coast (Nicaragua
   v. Colombia) (Preliminary Objections) [2016] ICJ Rep 100   29, 96–7, 138
Alleged Violations of Sovereign Rights and Maritime Spaces in the Caribbean Sea
   (Nicaragua v. Colombia) (Preliminary Objections) [2016] ICJ Rep 3   320
Maritime Dispute (Peru v. Chile) (Judgment) [2014] ICJ Rep 3   2, 22, 28–9, 36, 66, 70,
   72, 74–5, 83, 90–3, 103, 145, 194–5, 216–7, 249, 265–7, 270–1, 281, 287, 316
Frontier Dispute (Burkina Faso/Niger) (Judgment) [2013] ICJ Rep 44   31–2
Territorial and Maritime Dispute (Nicaragua v. Colombia) (Judgment) [2012] ICJ Rep
   624   34–35, 40, 45–6, 48, 52, 66, 70, 79, 83–7, 89, 96–7, 103, 107, 121, 124–8, 145–7, 152,
   154, 156–61, 166, 171–3, 176, 179–80, 200, 209–10, 215–16, 220–1, 234, 236, 240–1, 244,
   250–1, 265–7, 270, 272–4, 277–8, 281, 287, 306, 315–6, 318, 320
Jurisdictional Immunities of the State (Germany v. Italy) (Judgment) [2012] ICJ Rep
   99   292–3
Maritime Delimitation in the Black Sea (Romania v. Ukraine) (Judgment) [2009] ICJ Rep
   61   1–2, 21–3, 27–9, 33, 34–6, 41, 48, 52, 56, 58–64, 66, 77, 79, 84, 86, 99, 103, 109, 121,
   125, 145–6, 149, 153–5, 160, 170, 176, 184–5, 200, 209–10, 214, 219–20, 231, 236, 238, 240,
   246–7, 249, 264–7, 270–1, 274–5, 278, 281–2, 311, 315–6, 321–2
Territorial and Maritime Dispute (Nicaragua v. Colombia) (Preliminary Objections)
   [2007] ICJ Rep 832   215

Territorial and Maritime Dispute between Nicaragua and Honduras in the Caribbean Sea (Nicaragua v. Honduras) (Judgment) [2007] ICJ Rep 659   20–1, 27–8, 39, 49, 72, 77–8, 121–8, 156, 160–6, 194, 214, 219–20, 264, 267–71, 314

Frontier Dispute (Benin/Niger) (Judgment) [2005] ICJ Rep 90   31

Land and Maritime Boundary between Cameroon and Nigeria (Cameroon v. Nigeria; Equatorial Guinea intervening) (Merits) [2002] ICJ Rep 303   20, 31, 39, 170, 196, 198, 213–4, 216, 219, 264, 266–7, 270–4, 282, 314, 318, 321

Maritime Delimitation and Territorial Questions between Qatar and Bahrain (Qatar v. Bahrain) (Merits) [2001] ICJ Rep 40   1–3, 20, 56, 66, 148–9, 152–5, 180, 183, 185–6, 188–9, 219, 231, 240, 264, 266–7, 270–1, 282, 314, 319

Maritime Delimitation between Greenland and Jan Mayen (Denmark v. Norway) (Judgment) [1993] ICJ Rep 38   20, 24, 40, 45–6, 48–9, 65–9, 71, 73, 134, 174–5, 190, 199–200, 206, 209–10, 212–13, 220, 227, 229, 232–4, 236, 246, 251, 260, 263–4, 266, 270–4, 278, 282–5, 287, 313–4, 318

Land, Island and Maritime Frontier Dispute (El Salvador/Honduras) (Application by Nicaragua per Permission to Intervene) [1990] ICJ Rep 92   220

Frontier Dispute (Burkina Faso/Mali) (Judgment) [1986] ICJ Rep 554   31

Continental Shelf (Libya/Malta) (Judgment) [1985] ICJ Rep 13   30, 40, 42, 45–6, 66, 89, 110, 114–16, 146, 150, 174, 188–9, 202, 206, 209–10, 217–21, 224, 227, 230, 236, 239, 249, 251, 257, 262–3, 270, 273, 277–8, 280, 282–5, 287, 313, 315, 318

Delimitation of the Maritime Boundary in the Gulf of Maine Area (Canada/USA) (Judgment) [1984] ICJ Rep 246   41, 49, 56–64, 66, 79, 110, 146, 173–4, 187–8, 191, 193, 197–200, 208, 212, 220, 240–1, 248, 251, 254, 262, 264, 270, 280, 282, 284–5, 287

Continental Shelf (Libya/Malta) (Application by Italy for Permission to Intervene) [1984] ICJ Rep 3   218, 307

Continental Shelf (Tunisia/Libya) (Judgment) [1982] ICJ Rep 18, 49, 58, 66, 81–2, 110, 165, 182–3, 185, 187, 191, 193, 195, 211, 220, 224–5, 235, 240, 262–3, 269–70, 284, 313, 318

Barcelona Traction, Light and Power Company, Limited (Belgium v. Spain) (Second Phase) [1970] ICJ Rep 3   307

North Sea Continental Shelf (Federal Republic of Germany/Denmark; Federal Republic of Germany/Netherlands) (Judgment) [1969] ICJ Rep 3   1, 7, 9, 14, 17, 23, 29, 33, 35, 37, 55, 103, 105–7, 167–9, 202, 207, 217, 221, 227, 229, 232, 235, 248, 252, 254–6, 258, 260–3, 270, 273–7, 292, 298, 313, 322–3

North Sea Continental Shelf (Federal Republic of Germany/Denmark; Federal Republic of Germany/Netherlands) (Joinder of Proceedings) [1968] ICJ Rep 9   14

Certain Expenses of the United Nations (Advisory Opinion) [1962] ICJ Rep 151   308

Fisheries (UK v. Norway) (Judgment) [1951] ICJ Rep 116   78

Reservations to the Convention on the Prevention and Punishment of the Crime of Genocide (Advisory Opinion) [1951] ICJ Rep 15   308

International Status of South-West Africa (Advisory Opinion) [1950] ICJ Rep 128   87

Interpretation of Peace Treaties (Advisory Opinion) [1950] ICJ Rep 65   308

Reparation for Injuries Suffered in the Service of the United Nations (Advisory Opinion) [1949] ICJ Rep 174   308

Permanent Court of International Justice

Interpretation of the Treaty of Lausanne (Advisory Opinion) PCIJ Series B No 12   119
Lotus (France v. Turkey) (Judgment) PCIJ Series A No 10   298

International Tribunal for the Law of the Sea

Delimitation of the Maritime Boundary between Ghana and Côte d'Ivoire in the Atlantic Ocean (Ghana/Côte d'Ivoire) (Judgment), Judgment of 23 September 2017– 3–4, 23, 29, 35, 42, 47, 90–1, 95, 98, 123, 126–8, 130, 164, 170, 194–6, 204, 214, 222, 259–60, 265, 269, 278–9 , 281, 312, 316, 319
Delimitation of the Maritime Boundary in the Bay of Bengal (Bangladesh/Myanmar) (Judgment) [2012] ITLOS Rep 4   1, 3, 22, 29, 35–6, 42, 44, 46, 48–9, 51–3, 66, 82, 84, 86, 90–1, 95, 100, 103, 128–30, 133–43, 146, 153–5, 160, 168–9, 172, 177, 184–6, 191, 214, 220–6, 234, 239–40, 242–3, 250, 259, 265–7, 270, 273, 278, 281, 311–12, 316
M/V Saiga (No. 2) (Saint Vincent and the Grenadines v. Guinea) (Judgment) [1999] ITLOS Rep 10   205

Arbitral Tribunals constituted under Annex VII UNCLOS

South China Sea Arbitration (Philippines v. China) (Merits) (2016) 170 ILR 180   150
Bay of Bengal Maritime Boundary Arbitration (Bangladesh v. India) (2014) 167 ILR 1   1, 3, 22–3, 28–9, 35, 41–2, 44, 47–9, 52, 66, 71, 77, 79, 80, 82, 84, 86, 95, 103, 128–9, 133–42, 146, 149, 151, 154–6, 164, 172, 177–8, 194–5, 200, 222–3, 225–6, 234, 239, 250, 259–60, 265–6, 270, 272–3, 278–9, 281, 316
Maritime Boundary Arbitration (Guyana v. Suriname) (2007) XXX RIAA 1   1, 3, 20, 27, 36, 66, 194, 202–3, 214, 241, 264, 270, 284, 314
Maritime Boundary Arbitration (Barbados v. Trinidad and Tobago) (2006) XXVII RIAA 147   20, 27, 66, 76, 170, 176, 189, 199, 214, 217, 249, 251, 264, 270, 272–3, 282–5, 287, 314

Ad hoc Arbitral Tribunals

Arbitration between Croatia and Slovenia under the Arbitration Agreement of 4 November 2009 (Croatia/Slovenia), Award of 29 June 2017   4
Arbitration between Newfoundland and Labrador and Nova Scotia (Newfoundland and Labrador/Nova Scotia) (Second Phase) (2002) 128 ILR 504   282

AD HOC ARBITRAL TRIBUNALS

Second Stage of the Proceedings between Eritrea and Yemen (Maritime Delimitation) (Eritrea/Yemen) (1999) XXII RIAA 335   20, 71, 82, 151–2, 154–5, 183, 185–6, 191, 218–19, 232, 240, 249, 264, 270, 278, 284

Delimitation of Maritime Areas between Canada and France (St. Pierre et Miquelon) (Canada/France) (1992) XXI RIAA 265   49, 62, 77–8, 170, 189–92, 198–9, 249, 260, 262–3, 270, 278, 284, 286

Delimitation of the Maritime Boundary between Guinea and Guinea-Bissau (Guinea/Guinea-Bissau) (1985) XIX RIAA 149   18, 39–40, 182–3, 185, 190, 193, 198–9, 208–10, 220, 240, 254, 262, 269–70

Dubai/Sharjah Border Arbitration (Dubai/Sharjah) (1981) 91 ILR 543   181–2, 185

Continental Shelf (France/UK) (1977) XVIII RIAA 3   19–20, 146–9, 178–82, 186–9, 191–2, 204–5, 207, 220, 227, 240–1, 261, 271, 283

Beagle Channel (Argentina/Chile) (1977) XXI RIAA 53   202, 241

Petroleum Development Ltd v. Sheikh of Abu Dhabi (1951) 18 ILR 144   105

Trail Smelter (USA v. Canada) (1941) III RIAA 1905   306

Grisbådarna (Norway/Sweden) (1909) XI RIAA 147   29, 199

TABLE OF TREATIES AND LEGISLATION

Multilateral Treaties

(in chronological order by date of adoption)

Declaration on the Maritime Zone (the 'Santiago Declaration') (18 August 1952), 1006 UNTS 325   74, 216
Convention on the Continental Shelf (29 April 1958), 499 UNTS 311   9, 12–4, 19–20, 102, 105–7, 114, 175, 181, 186, 197, 202, 204, 261–2, 311, 314
Convention on the Territorial Sea and the Contiguous Zone (29 April 1958), 516 UNTS 205   102
Vienna Convention on the Law of Treaties (23 May 1969), 1155 UNTS 331   86–8
United Nations Convention on the Law of the Sea (10 December 1982), 1833 UNTS 3   1–3, 5, 7–8, 9–10, 12–17, 20, 23, 25, 27–8, 32–3, 41–3, 52–5, 61, 66–7, 73, 81–3, 90, 96–8, 102–5, 107–8, 110–17, 120–1, 123, 128, 130–2, 134–6, 138–40, 144–7, 149–52, 155, 161–2, 165, 178–9, 188, 195–7, 203–6, 211, 216–7, 222–3, 231, 233–5, 237, 239–40, 244–5, 257–9, 276, 279, 288–9, 290, 292, 294, 298, 300, 311–12, 317, 321

Bilateral Treaties

(in chronological order by date of conclusion)

1971

Treaty between the Kingdom of Denmark and the Federal Republic of Germany concerning the Delimitation of the Continental shelf under the North Sea (28 January 1971), 857 UNTS 119   318
Treaty between the Kingdom of the Netherlands and the Federal Republic of Germany concerning the Delimitation of the Continental shelf under the North Sea (28 January 1971), 857 UNTS 142   318
Treaty between Australia and Indonesia Establishing Certain Seabed Boundaries (18 May 1971), 974 UNTS 308   116

1972

Treaty between Australia and Indonesia Establishing Certain Seabed Boundaries in the Area of the Timor and Arafura Seas, Supplementary to the Agreement of 18 May 1971 (9 October 1972), 974 UNTS 320   116

1977

Treaty on the Delimitation of Marine and Submarine Areas and Maritime Co-operation between Colombia and Costa Rica (17 March 1977), *Limits in the Seas No. 84*   87, 117

1978

Treaty between the German Democratic Republic and the Kingdom of Sweden on the Delimitation of the Continental Shelf (22 June 1978), 1147 UNTS 193   119

Treaty between Australia and Papua New Guinea concerning Sovereignty and Maritime Boundaries in the Torres Strait (18 December 1978), 1429 UNTS 207   116

1980

Treaty concerning Delimitation of Marine Areas and Maritime Co-operation between the Republic of Costa Rica and the Republic of Panama (2 February 1980), *Limits in the Seas No. 97*   69

Treaty between the USA (American Samoa) and New Zealand (Tokelau) on the Delimitation of the Maritime Boundary between Tokelau and the USA (2 December 1980), 1643 UNTS 251   117

1984

Treaty between Denmark and Sweden concerning the Delimitation of the Continental Shelf and Fishing Zones (9 November 1984), 1409 UNTS 445   119

1986

Agreement between the Great Socialist People's Libyan Arab Jamahiriya and the Republic of Malta implementing Article III of the Special Agreement and the Judgment of the International Court of Justice (10 November 1986), in JI Charney

and LM Alexander (eds.), *International Maritime Boundaries* (Martinus Nijhoff, 1993) vol. II, 1649   318
Treaty between India and Myanmar on the Delimitation of the Maritime Boundary in the Andaman Sea, in the Coco Channel and in the Bay of Bengal (23 December 1986), 1484 UNTS 172   120

1988

Agreement between the Libyan Arab Socialist People's Jamahiriya and the Republic of Tunisia to Implement the Judgment of the International Court of Justice in the Tunisia/Libya Continental Shelf Case (8 August 1988), in JI Charney and LM Alexander (eds.), *International Maritime Boundaries* (Martinus Nijhoff, 1993) vol. II, 1663   318
Treaty between the Solomon Islands and Australia Establishing Certain Sea and Seabed Boundaries (13 September 1988), (1988) 12 *LoSB* 19   117

1990

Agreement on Fisheries Enforcement (26 September 1990), 1852 UNTS 73   318

1992

Agreement between Albania and Italy for the Determination of the Continental Shelf of each of the two Countries (18 December 1992), (1994) 26 *LoSB* 54   120

1993

Exchange of Notes between France and the United Kingdom of Great Britain and Northern Ireland constituting an Agreement concerning the Creation and Delimitation of an Economic Zone around the Islands of Pitcairn, Henderson, Ducie and Oeno (17 December 1992 – 19 January 1993), 1772 UNTS 95   119
Treaty between Jamaica and Cuba on the Delimitation of the Maritime Boundary (12 November 1993), (1994) 26 *LoSB* 50   117

1995

Agreement between Denmark and Norway concerning the Delimitation of the Continental Shelf in the Area between Jan Mayen and Greenland and concerning the Boundary between the Fishery Zones in the Area (18 December 1995), 1903 UNTS 171   318

BILATERAL TREATIES xxvii

1997

Treaty between Australia and Indonesia Establishing an Exclusive Economic Zone Boundary and Certain Seabed Boundaries (14 March 1997), (1997) 36 ILM 1053   110, 116

Agreement between the United States of America and Niue on the Delimitation of a Maritime Boundary (13 May 1997), *Limits in the Seas No. 119*   117

2000

Treaty between Mexico and the United States on the Delimitation of the Continental Shelf in the Western Gulf of Mexico beyond 200 Nautical Miles (9 June 2000), (2001) 44 *LoSB* 71   226

Treaty between Saudi Arabia and Kuwait concerning the Submerged Area adjacent to the Divided Zone (2 July 2000), 2141 UNTS 251   120

2001

Treaty between Honduras and the United Kingdom of Great Britain and Northern Ireland concerning the Delimitation of the Maritime Areas between the Cayman Islands and Honduras (4 December 2001), (2002) 49 *LoSB* 60   117

2002

Timor Sea Treaty between the Government of East Timor and the Government of Australia (20 May 2002), 2258 UNTS 3   197

2004

Treaty between Australia and New Zealand Establishing certain Exclusive Economic Zone and Continental Shelf Boundaries (25 July 2004), 2441 UNTS 235   117

2005

Framework Agreement between the United Kingdom of Great Britain and Northern Ireland and the Kingdom of Norway concerning Cross-boundary Petroleum Co-operation, (4 April 2005), 2491 UNTS 3   197

Treaty between France and Madagascar on the Delimitation of Maritime Areas situated between La Réunion and Madagascar (14 April 2005), (2010) 71 *LoSB* 23   117

2006

Agreed Minutes on the Delimitation of the Continental Shelf beyond 200 Nautical Miles between the Faroe Islands, Iceland and Norway in the Southern Part of the Banana Hole in the Northeast Atlantic (20 September 2006), in DA Colson and RW Smith (eds.), *International Maritime Boundaries* (Martinus Nijhoff, 2011) vol. VI, 4532   226

2007

Treaty between Russia and Norway on Maritime Delimitation in the Varangerfjord Area (11 July 2007), (2008) 67 *LoSB* 42   118

Treaty between Mauritius and Seychelles on the Delimitation of the Exclusive Economic Zone (29 July 2008), (2009) 69 *LoSB* 106   117

2009

Exchange of Notes amending the Agreement between the United Kingdom of Great Britain and Northern Ireland and Norway Relating to the Delimitation of the Continental Shelf between the two countries (30 April 2009), UKTS No. 16 (2009)   118

Agreement between France and Barbados on the Delimitation of the Maritime Space between France and Barbados (15 October 2009), 2663 UNTS 163   226

Exchange of Notes between the United Kingdom of Great Britain and Northern Ireland and Denmark Confirming the Limits of the United Kingdom of Great Britain and Northern Ireland's Exclusive Economic Zone in the North Sea (22 October 2009), UKTS No. 1 (2010)   118

2010

Treaty between the Republic of Trinidad and Tobago and Grenada on the Delimitation of Marine and Submarine Areas (21 April 2010), 2675 UNTS 5   120, 310

Agreement between New Zealand and the Cook Islands concerning the Delimitation of the Maritime Boundaries between Tokelau and the Cook Islands (4 August 2010), (2014) 82 *LoSB* 54   120, 226

Treaty between the Russian Federation and the Kingdom of Norway concerning Maritime Delimitation and Co-operation in the Barents Sea and the Arctic Ocean (15 September 2010), 2791 UNTS 3   120, 309

Agreement between the State of Israel and the Republic of Cyprus on the Delimitation of the Exclusive Economic Zone (17 December 2010), (2011) 75 *LoSB* 27   117

2011

Exchange of Letters between the United Kingdom of Great Britain and Northern Ireland and the French Republic relating to the Delimitation of the Exclusive Economic Zone (20 April 2011), UKTS No. 19 (2014)   119

Agreement by Exchange of Notes of identical Content between the Republic of Peru and the Republic of Ecuador (2 May 2011), 2756 UNTS 223   118

Agreement between the Commonwealth of the Bahamas and the Republic of Cuba for the Delimiting Line between their Maritime Zones (3 October 2011), (2013) 79 *LoSB* 19   120

Agreement on the Delimitation of the Maritime Boundary between the Republic of Mozambique and the United Republic of Tanzania (5 December 2011), in C Lathrop (ed.), *International Maritime Boundaries* (Martinus Nijhoff, 2016) vol. VII, 4793   118

2012

Agreement between the Union of the Comoros and the Republic of Seychelles on the Delimitation of the Maritime Boundary of the Exclusive Economic Zone and the Continental Shelf in the Indian Ocean (17 February 2012), in C Lathrop (ed.), *International Maritime Boundaries* (Martinus Nijhoff, 2016) vol. VII, 5039   118

Maritime Delimitation Treaty between the Republic of Honduras and the Republic of Cuba (21 August 2012), (2017) 86 *LoSB* 35   117

Agreement between the Cook Islands and Kiribati concerning the Delimitation of Maritime Boundaries between the Cook Islands and Kiribati (29 August 2012), (2017) 85 *LoSB* 32   118

Agreement between the Cook Islands and Niue concerning the Delimitation of Maritime Boundaries between the Cook Islands and Niue (29 August 2012), (2014) 82 *LoSB* 51   118

Agreement between the Republic of Kiribati and the Republic of the Marshall Islands concerning Maritime Boundaries (29 August 2012), in C Lathrop (ed.), *International Maritime Boundaries* (Martinus Nijhoff, 2016) vol. VII, 4869   118

Agreement between the Republic of Kiribati and the Republic of Nauru concerning Maritime Boundaries (29 August 2012), in C Lathrop (ed.), *International Maritime Boundaries* (Martinus Nijhoff, 2016) vol. VII, 4881   118

Agreement between New Zealand and the Republic of Kiribati concerning the Delimitation of the Maritime Boundaries between Tokelau and Kiribati (29 August 2012), (2017) 90 *LoSB* 49   120, 226

Agreement between the Republic of the Marshall Islands and the Republic of Nauru concerning Maritime Boundaries (29 August 2012), in C Lathrop (ed.), *International Maritime Boundaries* (Martinus Nijhoff, 2016) vol. VII, 4915   118

2013

Agreement between Ireland and the United Kingdom of Great Britain and Northern Ireland Establishing a Single Maritime Boundary between the Exclusive Economic Zone of the two Countries and Parts of their Continental Shelves (28 March 2013), UKTS No. 21 (2014)   119

Exchange of Letters between the United Kingdom of Great Britain and Northern Ireland and the Kingdom of the Netherlands amending the Agreement relating to the Delimitation of the Continental Shelf under the North Sea between the two Countries of 6 October 1965 as amended by the Protocol of 25 November 1971 and the Exchange of Notes January and June 2004 (19 April 2013 – 3 July 2013), UKTS No. 20 (2014)   119

Exchange of Letters between the United Kingdom of Great Britain and Northern Ireland and the Kingdom of Belgium amending the Agreement relating to the Delimitation of the Continental shelf under the North Sea between the two Countries of 19 May 1991 as amended by Exchange of Letters of 21 March and 7 June 2005 (25 June 2013 – 12 August 2013), UKTS No. 14 (2016)   119

Treaty between the United States of America and the Republic of Kiribati on the Delimitation of Maritime Boundaries (6 September 2013), in C Lathrop (ed.), *International Maritime Boundaries* (Martinus Nijhoff, 2016) vol. VII, 4935   120

2014

Treaty between the United States of America and the Federated States of Micronesia on the Delimitation of a Maritime Boundary (1 August 2014), in C Lathrop (ed.), *International Maritime Boundaries* (Martinus Nijhoff, 2016) vol. VII, 4963   120

National Legislation

(in alphabetical order by state)

Bangladesh

Territorial Waters and Maritime Zones Act 1974, Act No. XXVI of 1974   55

Costa Rica

Decree 18581-RE of 14 October 1988   54

Honduras

Executive Decree No. PCM 007-2000 of 21 March 2000, (2000) 43 *LoSB* 96   162

Myanmar

Territorial Sea and Maritime Zones Law 1977, Law No. 3 of 9 April 1977, as amended by the State Peace and Development Council Law No. 8/2008 of 5 December 2008   55

Nicaragua

Act No. 205 of 19 December 1979 on the Continental Shelf and Adjacent Sea   121
Decree No. 33-2013 of 19 August 2013   54

Romania

Act concerning the Legal Regime of the Internal Waters, the Territorial Sea and the Contiguous Zone of Romania of 7 August 1990, (1991) 19 *LoSB* 9   61

Ukraine

Statute concerning the State Frontier of 4 November 1991, (1994) 25 *LoSB* 84   61

ABBREVIATIONS

AFDI	Annuaire Français de Droit International
African JICL	African Journal of International and Comparative Law
AJIL	American Journal of International Law
Asian JIL	Asian Journal of International Law
Australian YIL	Australian Yearbook of International Law
Austrian RIEL	Austrian Review of International and European Law
BYIL	British Yearbook of International Law
Chicago JIL	Chicago Journal of International Law
Chinese JIL	Chinese Journal of International Law
CJICL	Cambridge Journal of International and Comparative Law
CLJ	Cambridge Law Journal
CTS	Consolidated Treaty Series
EJIL	European Journal of International Law
GYIL	German Yearbook of International Law
IBA	International Bar Association
ICLQ	International and Comparative Law Quarterly
ICLR	International Community Law Review
IJMCL	International Journal of Marine and Coastal Law
IJECL	International Journal of Estuarine and Coastal Law
ILM	International Legal Materials
ILR	International Law Reports
JIDS	Journal of International Dispute Settlement
LJIL	Leiden Journal of International Law
LoSB	Law of the Sea Bulletin
LoSIC	Law of the Sea Information Circular
MPYUNL	Max Planck Yearbook of United Nations Law
NILR	Netherlands International Law Review
Netherlands YBIL	Netherlands Yearbook of International Law
ODIL	Ocean Development and International Law
OJLS	Oxford Journal of Legal Studies
RDI	Rivista di Diritto Internazionale
RGDIP	Revue Générale de Droit International Public
RHDI	Revue Hellénique de Droit International

RIAA	Reports of International Arbitral Awards
SRIEL	Swiss Review of International and European Law
UKTS	United Kingdom Treaty Series
UNTS	United Nations Treaty Series
US TIAS	Texts of International Agreements to which the United States is a party
VaJIL	Virginia Journal of International Law

1

Maritime Delimitation in the Time of International Tribunals

I Maritime Boundaries and International Tribunals

A considerable share of interstate disputes before international tribunals concerns the delimitation of maritime boundaries. However, the existing rules of international law fail to provide any clear guidance on how to establish maritime boundaries by way of judicial process. Both the rules of the 1982 United Nations Convention on the Law of the Sea (UNCLOS),[1] and the customary rules of international law on maritime delimitation,[2] are exceedingly indeterminate. The main deficiency of such rules is that they do not indicate any method for delimiting maritime boundaries.

International tribunals have grappled with maritime delimitation since the 1969 judgment in *North Sea Continental Shelf*.[3] Judicial decisions on delimitation, influenced by the works of the Third United Nations Conference on the Law of the Sea (UNCLOS III), constitute a significant body of jurisprudence shaping what is now considered to be the method for delimiting the continental shelf and the Exclusive Economic Zone (EEZ).[4] Since the International Court of Justice (ICJ or Court) handed down the *Black Sea* judgment in 2009, international tribunals have been delimiting the continental shelf and the EEZ using

---

[1] United Nations Convention on the Law of the Sea, 1833 UNTS 3. See Section III.A below.
[2] Ibid.
[3] *North Sea Continental Shelf (Federal Republic of Germany/Denmark; Federal Republic of Germany/Netherlands)* (Judgment) [1969] ICJ Rep 3, 51 [96].
[4] See *Maritime Delimitation and Territorial Questions between Qatar and Bahrain (Qatar v. Bahrain)* (Merits) [2001] ICJ Rep 40, 94 [176]; *Maritime Boundary Arbitration (Guyana v. Suriname)* (2007) XXX RIAA 1, 82 [295]-[296]; *Delimitation of the Maritime Boundary in the Bay of Bengal (Bangladesh/Myanmar)* (Judgment) [2012] ITLOS Rep 4, 42-3 [127]-[129]; *Bay of Bengal Maritime Boundary Arbitration (Bangladesh v. India)* (2014) 167 ILR 1, 111-14 [336]-[346].

a three-stage approach.[5] Academic writers have expressed different views on this approach and on its practical application. While some writers emphasised the creation of a uniform law of maritime delimitation, others underscored that international tribunals apply the three-stage approach inconsistently owing to the vagaries of each case.[6]

The introduction of the three-stage approach can be seen to have increased the consistency, predictability and certainty of maritime delimitation before international tribunals. Although the three-stage approach raises numerous issues requiring further elaboration, such issues do not seem to outweigh the benefits of a standard approach to delimitation. International tribunals pursue consistency in establishing maritime boundaries by means of the three-stage approach on four different levels: first, with the relevant conventional and customary rules of international law; second, with the basis of title over the continental shelf and the EEZ; third, with the function of such maritime zones; and fourth, with their own earlier delimitation jurisprudence. However, it does not follow that, by pursuing consistency, international tribunals actually achieve it. While this book emphasises the common principles applied across international tribunals in establishing maritime boundaries, it also focuses on the controversial issues stemming from the implementation of the three-stage approach. Section II outlines the scope of the book. Section III sets out the structure of this book.

II Scope of the Book

The scope of this book is limited to the delimitation of the EEZ and of the continental shelf, both within and beyond 200 nautical miles (nm). The delimitation of the territorial sea is excluded from the present enquiry. Three reasons justify this choice. First, the customary rule of international law on the delimitation of the territorial sea, codified in Article 15 UNCLOS,[7] is different from the customary rules of international law on the delimitation of the EEZ and of the continental shelf, respectively codified in Articles 74 and 83 UNCLOS.[8] Article 15

---

[5] Chapter 2, section II.B.3 below. See *Maritime Delimitation in the Black Sea (Romania v. Ukraine)* (Judgment) [2009] ICJ Rep 61, 101–103 [115]-[122].
[6] Chapter 2, section III.B below.
[7] *Qatar v. Bahrain* (n. 4) 94 [176].
[8] *Territorial and Maritime Dispute (Nicaragua v. Colombia)* (Judgment) [2012] ICJ Rep 624, 666 [114]; *Maritime Dispute (Peru v. Chile)* (Judgment) [2014] ICJ Rep 3, 65 [179].

UNCLOS[9] formulates a much more detailed rule than the one contained in Article 74 and 83 UNCLOS. Second, and as a consequence of the detailed rule contained in Article 15 UNCLOS, the method for delimiting the territorial sea is considered to be more firmly established than the method for delimiting the EEZ and the continental shelf.[10] Although international tribunals have recently shown some hesitation in applying the method for territorial sea delimitation, they did not seem to doubt that Article 15 UNCLOS requires the territorial sea to be delimited by means of a two-stage approach. Judicial uncertainties on territorial sea delimitation only concerned the practical implementation of this two-stage approach.[11]

Third, the method for delimiting the territorial sea is distinct from the method for delimiting the EEZ and the continental shelf. The two-stage approach for territorial sea delimitation requires international tribunals to draw a provisional equidistance line, and subsequently to adjust it should special circumstances so require.[12] International tribunals delimit the EEZ and the continental shelf in three stages: they draw a provisional equidistance line; they eventually adjust that line if relevant circumstances so require; and they assess the overall equitableness of that line by checking for the absence of gross disproportionality between the length of the relevant coasts and the marine areas found to appertain to each state.[13] According to some recent suggestions, these two methods are converging. In its 2017 judgment, the Special Chamber of the International Tribunal for the Law of the Sea (ITLOS or Tribunal) in *Ghana/Côte d'Ivoire* decided 'to use the same methodology for the

---

[9] Under Art. 15 UNCLOS, '[w]here the coasts of two States are opposite or adjacent to each other, neither of the two States is entitled, failing agreement between them to the contrary, to extend its territorial sea beyond the median line every point of which is equidistant from the nearest points on the baselines from which the breadth of the territorial seas of each of the two States is measured. The above provision does not apply, however, where it is necessary by reason of historic title or other special circumstances to delimit the territorial seas of the two States in a way which is at variance therewith.'

[10] MD Evans, 'Maritime Boundary Delimitation' in DR Rothwell et al. (eds.), *The Oxford Handbook of the Law of the Sea* (OUP, 2015) 254, 255-6; DR Rothwell and T Stephens, *The International Law of the Sea* 2nd edn (Hart, 2016) 431.

[11] M Lando, 'Judicial Uncertainties concerning Territorial Sea Delimitation under Article 15 of the United Nations Convention on the Law of the Sea' (2017) 66 *ICLQ* 589.

[12] See *Qatar v. Bahrain* (n. 4) 94 [176]; *Guyana v. Suriname* (n. 4) 82 [295]-[296]; *Bangladesh/Myanmar* (n. 4) 42-3 [127]-[129]; *Bangladesh v. India* (n. 4) 111-14 [336]-[346].

[13] Chapter 2, Section II.B.3 below.

delimitation of the Parties' territorial seas, exclusive economic zones and continental shelves within and beyond 200 nm'.[14] In its 2017 award, the *Croatia/Slovenia* arbitral tribunal commented that the ICJ applies a method for delimiting 'boundaries without distinguishing between its application to the territorial sea and its application beyond the territorial sea'.[15] Similarly, Kamto wrote that 'la Cour a développé la doctrine de la ligne unique de délimitation de toutes les zones maritimes ... aboutissant ainsi à une application par glissement ou translation de l'équidistance ou équidistance-circonstances spéciales dans la mer territoriale au plateau continental'.[16]

However, such suggestions are unpersuasive. The approach in *Ghana/ Côte d'Ivoire* was based on the Special Chamber's interpretation of the parties' submissions, 'to the effect that it should use the same delimitation methodology for the whole delimitation process, namely the methodology developed for the delimitation of exclusive economic zones and continental shelves'.[17] Therefore, *Ghana/Côte d'Ivoire* could not support the convergence on one methodology for delimiting all maritime zones. Concerning the *Croatia/Slovenia* arbitral award, the authorities cited by the tribunal do not support its blanket statement mentioned above,[18] and, as the tribunal's task was limited to delimiting the territorial sea, comments on the method for EEZ and continental shelf delimitation were unjustified.[19]

Furthermore, the special circumstances in territorial sea delimitation may be different from the relevant circumstances in EEZ and continental shelf delimitation. Relevant circumstances are only those factors having a connection either with the basis of title over the EEZ and the continental shelf, or with their function under international law.[20] However, both the basis of title and the function of the territorial sea are distinct

---

[14] *Delimitation of the Maritime Boundary between Ghana and Côte d'Ivoire in the Atlantic Ocean (Ghana/Côte d'Ivoire)* (Judgment), Judgment of 23 September 2017 [263].

[15] *Arbitration between Croatia and Slovenia under the Arbitration Agreement of 4 November 2009 (Croatia/Slovenia)*, Award of 29 June 2017 [1000].

[16] M Kamto, 'Considérations actuelles sur la méthode de délimitation maritime devant la Cour internationale de Justice. De charybde en Scylla?' in J Crawford et al. (eds.), *The International Legal Order: Current Needs and Possible Responses – Essays in Honour of Djamchid Momtaz* (Brill, 2017) 383, 405.

[17] *Ghana/Côte d'Ivoire* (n. 15) [259].

[18] M Lando, 'The *Croatia/Slovenia* Arbitral Award of 29 June 2017: Is there a Common Method for Delimiting All Maritime Zones under International Law?' (2017) 100 *RDI* 1184, 1186-7.

[19] *Croatia/Slovenia* (n. 16) [1103].

[20] Chapter 5 below.

from the basis of title and the function of the EEZ and of the continental shelf. Accordingly, special circumstances affecting territorial sea delimitation could be considered not to be identical to relevant circumstances in EEZ and continental shelf delimitation. Moreover, in his separate opinion appended to the ICJ's 2018 judgment in *Costa Rica v. Nicaragua*, Judge Robinson compellingly argued that the proper interpretation of UNCLOS requires international tribunals to distinguish the method for territorial sea delimitation on one hand, and the method for EEZ and continental shelf delimitation on the other hand.[21] Judge Robinson's assessment appears correct.

The distinction between the methods for delimiting the maritime zones within and beyond 12 nm counsels against discussing the two-stage approach alongside the three-stage approach. Therefore, this book focuses on the latter, also in view of their wider variety and of their more contentious character in current international law.

III Structure of the Book

This book is divided into seven chapters. Chapter One and Chapter Seven serve as introduction and conclusion. Chapter Two outlines the historical development of maritime delimitation, with reference both to the positive rules of international law on delimitation, and to the processes developed by international tribunals for implementing such rules. Moreover, Chapter Two discusses the conceptual development of maritime delimitation, by reference to the fundamental notions of the discipline.

Chapters Three to Five examine the components of the three-stage delimitation process. It may seem odd to dedicate *four* chapters to a study of the *three*-stage approach. However, discussing the delimitation process in three chapters would have conflated too many issues in the first of these three chapters, leading to a confusing and thus unsatisfactory discussion of the first stage of the delimitation process. Consequently, this book divides the first stage of delimitation into two parts: first, the identification of the relevant coast and of the relevant area; second, the establishment of an equidistance line.

---

[21] *Maritime Delimitation in the Caribbean Sea and the Pacific Ocean (Costa Rica v. Nicaragua); Land Boundary in the Northern Part of Isla Portillos (Costa Rica v. Nicaragua)* (Judgment) [2018] ICJ Rep 139, 250–61 (Separate Opinion Robinson).

The stages of the three-stage approach cannot be seen to be entirely independent of each other. Maritime delimitation must be understood as a process,[22] which entails that one stage of the delimitation process may considerably impact on a subsequent one. For example, the determination of the relevant coast and of the relevant area, which belongs in the first step of delimitation, greatly influences the disproportionality assessment at the last stage of delimitation. Nevertheless, for ease of exposition this book examines each stage of the delimitation process in turn.

Chapter Three analyses the identification of the relevant coast and of the relevant area. Regrettably, academic writers have not shown great interest in this issue,[23] although identifying the relevant coast and the relevant area has remarkable effects on all subsequent stages of delimitation. Chapter Three examines the connection between the relevant coast and the relevant area on one hand, and the basis of title over maritime zones on the other hand. It critiques the judicial methods for identifying the relevant coast and the relevant area. While building upon such methods, it examines some contentious aspects of the international tribunals' approach, making suggestions for improvement. Chapter Three argues that the identification of the relevant coast and of the relevant area should be considered a full-fledged stage in the delimitation process, additional to the three established stages of delimitation. If such a view were accepted, the delimitation process could be conceived as being constituted of four stages.

Chapter Four examines equidistance as the first stage of the three-stage delimitation process. Since commentators have already explored the multiple facets of equidistance, the discussion focuses on the most recent international jurisprudence. Chapter Four discusses the relationship between equidistance and the basis of title, and the impact of coastal configuration on equidistance. It also explores whether using equidistance in delimiting the continental shelf beyond 200 nm has a sound legal basis. Chapter Four concludes by analysing the methods for constructing an equidistance line, including the selection of base points.

Chapter Five discusses relevant circumstances as the second stage of the three-stage approach. Chapter Five argues that international tribunals have

---

[22] MD Evans, 'Maritime Boundary Delimitation: Where Do We Go From Here?' in D Freestone et al. (eds.), *Law of the Sea – Progress and Prospects* (OUP, 2006) 137, 145.
[23] A Oude Elferink, 'Relevant Coast and Relevant Area' in A Oude Elferink et al. (eds.), *Maritime Boundary Delimitation – The Case Law: is it Consistent and Predictable?* (CUP, 2018) 173; S Fietta and R Cleverly, *A Practitioner's Guide to Maritime Boundary Delimitation* (OUP, 2016) 45-52 and 595-602; Evans (n. 11) 267-8 and 270-2.

been deciding whether certain factors could be considered to be relevant circumstances pursuant to a dual 'title-function' basis. First, the basis of title could be seen to be the legal basis of geographical relevant circumstances. Second, the function of maritime areas could be seen to be the legal basis of non-geographical relevant circumstances. As a result, all factors unrelated either to the basis of title, or to the function of maritime areas, should be considered to be irrelevant circumstances. With respect to each individual relevant circumstance, Chapter Five shows that international tribunals have mostly decided later cases consistently with earlier decisions, contrary to what some academic authors have suggested.

Chapter Six is dedicated to disproportionality, the third stage of the delimitation process. Chapter Six argues that disproportionality was devoid of legal basis when the ICJ first mentioned it as a factor relevant to delimitation in *North Sea Continental Shelf*, but that it acquired a legal basis due to later developments. Chapter Six clarifies the function of disproportionality in the delimitation process, examines its assessment in the relevant cases, and discusses the impact that coastal configuration could have on it. Furthermore, it explores the relationship between disproportionality and the relevant circumstance of coastal length disparity. The literature has obliquely alluded to this issue, without ever addressing it.[24] Chapter Six criticises the views of certain commentators according to whom international tribunals should dispense with disproportionality in the delimitation process.[25] Although it may not play a major role in delimitation, disproportionality fulfils the important function of ensuring that boundaries achieve the equitable solution required under Articles 74 and 83 UNCLOS.

By way of conclusion, Chapter Seven considers the interaction between international tribunals and states in the development of the delimitation process. Chapter Seven argues that the delimitation process is a judicial creation, which stems both from the difficulty in the formation of customary rules of international law in respect of the delimitation process itself, and from the extreme vagueness of the rules on EEZ and continental shelf delimitation as codified in Articles 74 and 83 UNCLOS. In the context of maritime delimitation, the decisions of international tribunals constitute actual law-making, and are therefore a formal source

---

[24] MD Evans, *Relevant Circumstances and Maritime Delimitation* (OUP, 1989) 228; Y Tanaka, 'Reflections on the Concept of Proportionality in the Law of Maritime Delimitation' (2001) 16 *IJMCL* 433, 443.
[25] Evans (n. 23) 154-6.

of international law, which should not be seen to be precluded by the traditional notion of judicial decisions as mere 'subsidiary means for the determination of rules of law' in accordance with Article 38(1)(d) of the ICJ's Statute. Chapter Seven also argues that states have sanctioned the creation and development of the delimitation process by international tribunals in a number of ways. States accepted that international tribunals could exercise a law-making function by agreeing that Articles 74 and 83 UNCLOS would be drafted as remarkably indeterminate rules. States have also indirectly approved the judicial elaborations on maritime delimitation by establishing their agreed boundaries following certain principles or certain procedures, through their statements before international organisations and their pleadings before international tribunals, and through their attitude towards compliance with judicial decisions on maritime delimitation.

2

Historical and Conceptual Framework

I Rules and Processes in Maritime Delimitation

The development of maritime delimitation by international tribunals has been greatly influenced by the manner in which the positive rules of international law on maritime delimitation have evolved. States discussed issues of maritime delimitation for the first time at the 1930 League of Nations Codification Conference, but it was only with the adoption of the 1958 Geneva Conventions that rules on maritime delimitation were codified. However, in the subsequent Third United Nations Conference on the Law of the Sea (UNCLOS III) states rejected the rules on delimitation of the 1958 Geneva Conventions, at least as far as the continental shelf was concerned, in favour of more open-ended rules which were eventually codified in the 1982 United Nations Convention on the Law of the Sea (UNCLOS).[1] Such rules governed the delimitation of both the continental shelf and the Exclusive Economic Zone (EEZ), and only stated the objective which delimitation must achieve, without indicating the method for achieving such an objective. The states' change of approach marked by the adoption of UNCLOS was possibly influenced by the 1969 judgment of the International Court of Justice (ICJ or Court) in *North Sea Continental Shelf*, in which the Court found that the rule on the delimitation of the continental shelf contained in the 1958 Convention on the Continental Shelf (CCS)[2] was not part of customary international law, and that continental shelf delimitation was to be effected in accordance with equitable principles.

---

[1] 1833 UNTS 3.
[2] 499 UNTS 311.

Starting in the late 1970s, states began requesting international tribunals to delimit maritime boundaries with increasing frequency. Owing to the developments which had taken place between 1958 and UNCLOS III, international tribunals found themselves bound to apply a vague rule of international law under which maritime delimitation was to be effected in accordance with equitable principles. Over time, international tribunals developed a methodology for implementing such an indeterminate rule. Viewed from this perspective, one could see the development of the delimitation process as a product of the judicial elaboration which international tribunals undertook case after case. The methodology for maritime delimitation changed considerably over time. Nevertheless, changes to the methodology were independent of the rules on maritime delimitation, which have not been altered since 1982. Such changes appear to be attributable only to the international tribunals' own jurisprudence.

Section II of this chapter traces the historical development of maritime delimitation with respect both to the rules governing delimitation, and to the processes for implementing such rules. Section III discusses the conceptual development of maritime delimitation. Section IV concludes.

II Historical Framework of Maritime Delimitation

This section outlines the relevant rules of international law on maritime delimitation. In addition, it describes the development of the method for continental shelf and EEZ delimitation by international tribunals.

A Rules Governing Maritime Delimitation

The rules of international law on maritime delimitation have evolved considerably since the earliest discussion at the time of the League of Nations. This evolution resulted in the progressive dilution of the content of such rules.

1 The 1930 League of Nations Codification Conference

The earliest multilateral discussions on maritime delimitation took place at the 1930 League of Nations Codification Conference, which ultimately failed to adopt a treaty on the law of the sea.[3] Since at that time both the

---

[3] On the 1930 Conference, see League of Nations, *Acts of the Conference for the Codification of International Law held at The Hague from March 13th to April 12th 1930*. See also H Miller, 'The Hague Codification Conference' (1930) 24 *AJIL* 674.

continental shelf and the EEZ did not exist under international law, the 1930 Conference only dealt with the delimitation of the territorial sea around straits used for international navigation. The works of the 1930 Conference built upon the drafting of a number of bases for discussion, on which states would provide comments, and on the basis of which the committees would be expected to prepare the text of a treaty.[4] Basis for Discussion No. 16 on the regime of territorial waters provided that:

> [w]hen two States border on a strait which is not wider than twice the breadth of territorial waters, the territorial waters of each State extend in principle up to a line running down the centre of the strait; if the strait is wider, the breadth of the territorial waters of each State is measured in accordance with the ordinary rule.[5]

Basis for Discussion No. 16 seems to be the earliest reference to the equidistance method in relation to maritime delimitation. In their comments, states unanimously supported equidistance. For example, Germany stated that '[i]f the strait is so narrow that the territorial water zones overlap, the sovereign rights of each coastal State extend to the median line'.[6] Great Britain, to which India and New Zealand associated themselves,[7] commented that 'if the total width of the strait is less than six miles, the waters on either side will be territorial waters of the State to which the shore belongs up to midway between the two shores'.[8] Japan went as far as defining that the 'middle line measured from the two coasts' was to be understood as the rule.[9] A number of other states agreed or made comparable statements.[10]

Basis for Discussion No. 16 generated some debate within the Second Committee owing to a Swedish amendment. Sweden proposed to insert a clause under which '[w]hen States are already parties to a Convention, these rules shall not modify the limits of the territorial waters as resulting from the Convention'.[11] Sweden's representative explained that '[i]t would ... be quite illogical ... to bring about any

---

[4] In addition to the regime of territorial waters, the 1930 Conference focused on nationality and on the responsibility of states for damage done in their territory to the person or property of foreigners.
[5] S Rosenne, *League of Nations Conference for the Codification of International Law* (Oceana, 1975) vol. II, 277.
[6] Ibid. 273.
[7] Ibid. 275–6.
[8] Ibid. 275.
[9] Ibid. 276.
[10] Ibid. 274 (Australia); ibid. 274 (Denmark); ibid. 275 (France); ibid. 275 (Italy); ibid. 276 (Netherlands); ibid. 276 (Romania); ibid. 273 (South Africa); ibid. 277 (Sweden).
[11] Rosenne, *League of Nations Conference* (n. 5) vol. IV, 1397.

modification of existing frontiers between two or more States',[12] which justified 'avoid[ing] these expressions "in principle" "in general", etc'.[13] Great Britain and Yugoslavia agreed with Sweden,[14] while Norway commented that 'Basis for Discussion No 16 assumes – what is not necessarily true – that the breadth of the territorial waters is the same on both coasts. . . . Basis for Discussion No 16 would be more in place in a special Convention and is less suited to appear in a general Convention'.[15]

The plenary of the 1930 Conference did not comment on Basis for Discussion No. 16.[16] The records of the 1930 Conference suggest that there was consensus among states on equidistance being the appropriate method for delimiting the territorial sea around straits. Although the works of the 1930 Conference did not result in a treaty, they are useful to identify the early trends in the codification of rules on maritime delimitation.

2 The 1958 Geneva Convention on the Continental Shelf

The 1958 United Nations Conference on the Law of the Sea (UNCLOS I) resulted in the adoption of four treaties which also addressed issues of delimitation.[17] In preparation for UNCLOS I, the International Law Commission (ILC) conducted a six-year-long study, producing the 1956 Draft Articles discussed at the 1958 Conference.[18] Draft Article 72 provided that continental shelf boundaries shall be delimited by agreement between the states concerned, failing which the boundary shall be the line equidistant from the baselines from which the breadth of the territorial sea is measured, unless special circumstances require a boundary at variance therewith. The ILC's commentary to the 1956 Draft Articles explained that the concept of special circumstances was introduced as 'provision must be made for departures necessitated by

---

[12] Ibid. 1319.
[13] Ibid.
[14] Ibid.
[15] Ibid.
[16] Rosenne, *League of Nations Conference* (n. 5) vol. III, 752–6.
[17] By the time of UNCLOS I, the continental shelf was already an institution under international law. The foundational moment in continental shelf theory is the 1945 Proclamation by US President Harry Truman, see 'Proclamation by the President with respect to the Natural Resources of the Subsoil and Sea Bed of the Continental Shelf' (1945) 40 *AJIL Supplement* 45. For early debates on the legal character of the continental shelf, see H Lauterpacht, 'Sovereignty over Submarine Areas' (1950) 27 *BYIL* 376; H Waldock, 'The Legal Basis of Claims to the Continental Shelf' (1951) 36 *Transactions of the Grotius Society* 115.
[18] Report of the International Law Commission covering the work of its eighth session, UN Doc A/3159 (23 April–4 July 1956), *ILC Yearbook (1956)*, vol. II, 253.

II HISTORICAL FRAMEWORK OF MARITIME DELIMITATION

any exceptional configuration of the coast, as well as the presence of islands or of navigable channels'.[19] Individual members of the ILC linked both the equidistance method,[20] and the concept of special circumstances,[21] to the need that delimitation be equitable.

In the Fourth Committee of UNCLOS I, few states commented on the provision on continental shelf delimitation drafted by the ILC. Yugoslavia proposed to delete the reference to 'special circumstances' in favour of delimitation by strict equidistance.[22] By contrast, Venezuela wished to delete references to equidistance, as it argued that the continental shelf should only be delimited by agreement.[23] However, neither proposal was retained. At the UNCLOS I plenary, Draft Article 72 received sixty-three votes in favour, no vote against, and two abstentions.[24] Upon adoption of the 1958 Conventions, Draft Article 72 became Article 6 CCS. According to that provision:

(1) [w]here the same continental shelf is adjacent to the territories of two or more States whose coasts are opposite each other, the boundary of the continental shelf appertaining to such States shall be determined by agreement between them. In the absence of agreement, and unless another boundary line is justified by special circumstances, the boundary is the median line, every point of which is equidistant from the nearest points of the baselines from which the breadth of the territorial sea of each State is measured.

(2) Where the same continental shelf is adjacent to the territories of two adjacent States, the boundary of the continental shelf shall be determined by agreement between them. In the absence of agreement, and unless another boundary line is justified by special circumstances, the boundary shall be determined by application of the principle of equidistance from the nearest points of the baselines from which the breadth of the territorial sea of each State is measured.

Article 6 CCS distinguishes delimitation between states with opposite coasts, for which the boundary is 'the median line', from delimitation

---

[19] Ibid. 300.
[20] *ILC Yearbook (1953)*, vol. I, 127 [23] (Pal).
[21] *ILC Yearbook (1956)*, vol. I, 152 [28] (Fitzmaurice).
[22] Doc A/CONF.13/C.4/SR.31 (8 April 1958), *Official Records of the United Nations Conference on the Law of the Sea*, vol. VI, 91 [4] (Yugoslavia).
[23] Doc A/CONF.13/C.4/SR.10 (14 March 1958), *Official Records of the United Nations Conference on the Law of the Sea*, vol. VI, 21 [29] (Venezuela).
[24] Doc A/CONF.13/SR.9 (22 April 1958), *Official Records of the United Nations Conference on the Law of the Sea*, vol. II, 15.

between states with adjacent coasts, for which the boundary is 'the equidistance line'. However, the ICJ clarified that median and equidistance lines are based on the same principle.[25] Although states supported continental shelf delimitation by equidistance at UNCLOS I, the states' attitude towards equidistance changed in subsequent years, presumably owing to the ICJ's 1969 judgment in *North Sea Continental Shelf*. Although that judgment would be criticised both within the bench and in the literature,[26] it would greatly influence the works leading to the adoption of UNCLOS in 1982.

In 1967, Germany, Denmark and the Netherlands notified to the ICJ two identical special agreements introducing two cases, later joined.[27] Germany, Denmark and the Netherlands requested the Court to state '[w]hat principles and rules of international law are applicable to the delimitation as between the Parties of the areas of the continental shelf in the North Sea which appertain to each of them'.[28] The heart of the dispute was the applicability of Article 6 CCS. While Denmark and the Netherlands were parties to the CCS, Germany was not. Germany argued that, since it was not a party to the CCS and since Article 6 was not a customary rule of international law,[29] the equidistance principle under Article 6 was not binding on it. Denmark and the Netherlands contended that the equidistance principle was inherent in the definition of the continental shelf, and that Article 6 was a rule of customary international law.[30]

First, the Court found that 'at no time was the notion of equidistance as an inherent necessity of continental shelf doctrine entertained'.[31] Second, it held that 'if the [CCS] was not in its origins or inception declaratory of a mandatory rule of customary international law enjoining the use of the

---

[25] *North Sea Continental Shelf (Federal Republic of Germany/Denmark; Federal Republic of Germany/Netherlands)* (Judgment) [1969] ICJ Rep 3, 36 [57].
[26] See *North Sea Continental Shelf* (n. 25) 154 (Dissenting Opinion Koretsky); ibid. 171 (Dissenting Opinion Tanaka); ibid. 197 (Dissenting Opinion Morelli); ibid. 218 (Dissenting Opinion Lachs). See also E Lauterpacht, *Aspects of the Administration of International Justice* (CUP, 1991) 125; W Friedmann, 'The *North Sea Continental Shelf Cases*: A Critique' (1970) 64 *AJIL* 229; RY Jennings, 'The Limits of Continental Shelf Jurisdiction: Some Possible Implications of the *North Sea Case* Judgment' (1969) 18 *ICLQ* 819.
[27] *North Sea Continental Shelf (Federal Republic of Germany/Denmark; Federal Republic of Germany/Netherlands)* (Joinder of Proceedings) [1968] ICJ Rep 9.
[28] *North Sea Continental Shelf* (n. 25) 6–7.
[29] Reply of Germany (31 May 1968), 421 [75].
[30] Common Rejoinder of Denmark and the Netherlands (30 August 1968), 478 [39] and 511 [96].
[31] *North Sea Continental Shelf* (n. 25) 35 [55].

equidistance principle for the delimitation of continental shelf areas between adjacent States, neither has its subsequent effect been constitutive of such a rule'.[32] The Court identified the rules of international law on delimitation applicable to the parties, which required that:

> delimitation must be the object of agreement between the States concerned, and that such agreement must be arrived at in accordance with equitable principles. On a foundation of very general precepts of justice and good faith, actual rules of law are here involved which govern the delimitation of adjacent continent shelves . . .; in short, it is not a question of applying equity simply as a matter of abstract justice, but of applying a rule of law which itself requires the application of equitable principles.[33]

According to the Court, 'there is no legal limit to the considerations which States may take account of for the purpose of making sure that they apply equitable procedures'.[34] Equitable principles included factors such as 'the general configuration of the coasts of the Parties, as well as the presence of any special or unusual feature', 'the physical and geological structure, and natural resources, of the continental shelf areas involved', and 'the element of a reasonable degree of proportionality . . . between the extent of the continental shelf areas appertaining to the coastal State and the length of its coast measured in the general direction of the coastline'.[35]

3 The 1982 United Nations Convention on the Law of the Sea

At UNCLOS III, the delimitation of the continental shelf and of the EEZ was a highly contentious issue, with states divided between two different approaches. While certain states supported equidistance for delimiting both the continental shelf and the EEZ,[36] other states criticised equidistance as too rigid and preferred that boundaries be delimited pursuant

---

[32] Ibid. 45 [81].
[33] Ibid. 46-7 [87].
[34] Ibid. 50 [93].
[35] Ibid. 54 [101].
[36] *Report of the Committee on the Peaceful Uses of the Sea-bed and the Ocean Floor beyond the Limits of National Jurisdiction*, UN Doc A/9021(VOL. III)(SUPP) (1 January 1973) 43 (Malta), 78 (Australia and Norway), 111 (Japan); Doc A/CONF.62/C.2/L.25 (26 July 1974), *Official Records of the Third United Nations Conference on the Law of the Sea*, vol. III, 202 (Greece); Doc A/CONF.62/C.2/L.31/Rev.1 (16 August 1974), *Official Records of the Third United Nations Conference on the Law of the Sea*, vol. III, 211 (Japan); R Platzöder, *Third United Nations Conference on the Law of the Sea: Documents* (Oceana, 1986) vol. IX, 392 (Bahamas, Barbados, Canada, Colombia, Cyprus, Democratic Yemen, Denmark, Gambia, Greece, Guyana, Italy, Japan, Kuwait, Malta, Norway, Spain, Sweden, United Arab Emirates, United Kingdom, Yugoslavia), 399 (Peru), 448 (Israel), 448 and 451 (Mexico); R Platzöder, *Third United Nations Conference on the Law of the Sea:*

to equitable principles.[37] The UNCLOS negotiating texts suggest the states' effort to reconcile these opposing views. Under the 1975 Informal Single Negotiating Text and the 1976 Revised Single Negotiating Text, the EEZ and the continental shelf were both to be delimited by agreement on the basis of equitable principles, using the equidistance and the median line where appropriate; however, in delimiting the continental shelf states would also need to take into account all relevant circumstances.[38] The 1977 Informal Composite Negotiating Text assimilated the provision on EEZ delimitation to that on continental shelf delimitation, so that both maritime zones would be delimited by agreement on the basis of equitable principles, taking into account all relevant circumstances.[39]

The successive negotiating texts were prepared by the three committees of UNCLOS III. However, the states which received those negotiating texts could not agree to accept the provisions on delimitation as formulated by the Second Committee. Polarising negotiations resulted in the President of UNCLOS III drafting a new provision on delimitation in August 1981, only a few days before the release of the Draft Convention, which removed any reference to equidistance.[40] States accepted the President's text as a suitable compromise. The first paragraph of Articles 74 and 83 UNCLOS provides that:

Documents (Oceana, 1986) vol. IV, 316 (Cyprus), 317 (Greece), 319 (Spain), 320 and 467 (Canada).

[37] *Report of the Committee* (n. 36) 22 (Turkey); Doc A/CONF.62/C.2/L.14 (19 July 1974), *Official Records of the Third United Nations Conference on the Law of the Sea*, vol. III, 190-1 (Netherlands); Doc A/CONF.62/C.2/L.18 (23 July 1974), *Official Records of the Third United Nations Conference on the Law of the Sea*, vol. III, 195-6 (Romania); Doc A/CONF.62/C.2/L.28 (30 July 1974), *Official Records of the Third United Nations Conference on the Law of the Sea*, vol. III, 205 (Kenya and Tunisia); Doc A/CONF.62/C.2/L.74 (22 August 1974), *Official Records of the Third United Nations Conference on the Law of the Sea*, vol. III, 237 (France); Platzöder, *Third United Nations Conference* (n. 36) vol. IX, 402 (Algeria, Argentina, Bangladesh, Benin, Congo, France, Iraq, Ireland, Ivory Coast, Kenya, Liberia, Libya, Madagascar, Mali, Mauritania, Morocco, Nicaragua, Nigeria, Pakistan, Papua New Guinea, Poland, Romania, Senegal, Syria, Somalia, Turkey, Venezuela); Platzöder, *Third United Nations Conference* (n. 36) vol. IV, 318 (Ireland), 319 (Turkey), 390 (Morocco), 468 (Algeria, France, Iraq, Ireland, Libya, Morocco, Nicaragua, Papua New Guinea, Poland, Romania, Turkey).

[38] Doc A/CONF.62/WP.8/PART II (7 May 1975), *Official Records of the Third United Nations Conference on the Law of the Sea*, vol. IV, 162-3 (Arts. 61 and 70); Doc A/CONF.62/WP.8/Rev.1/PART II (6 May 1976), *Official Records of the Third United Nations Conference on the Law of the Sea*, vol. V, 164-5 (Arts. 62 and 71).

[39] Doc A/CONF.62/WP.10 (15 July 1977), *Official Records of the Third United Nations Conference on the Law of the Sea*, vol. VIII, 16-17 (Arts. 74 and 83).

[40] Platzöder, *Third United Nations Conference* (n. 36) vol. IX, 474.

[t]he delimitation of the exclusive economic zone [and of the continental shelf] between States with opposite or adjacent coasts shall be effected by agreement on the basis of international law, as referred to in Article 38 of the Statute of the International Court of Justice, in order to achieve an equitable solution.

As stated above, the ICJ declared such provisions to be part of customary international law. Articles 74 and 83 UNCLOS are highly indeterminate, being silent on the method for their implementation. The implementation of such indeterminate provisions would have likely posed some challenges for international tribunals. Presumably as a result of such indeterminacy, international tribunals developed a process for the delimitation of maritime boundaries by way of their jurisprudence.

Although states may request international tribunals to delimit maritime boundaries, Articles 74 and 83 UNCLOS seems to be clear in sanctioning the primacy of delimitation by agreement. The text of these two provisions states that maritime delimitation is to be effected in the first instance by agreement between the states concerned. International tribunals could delimit maritime boundaries only if such states failed to reach an agreement in accordance with international law. Therefore, before applying the methods for the implementation of Articles 74 and 83 UNCLOS,[41] international tribunals must ascertain whether two states have agreed, expressly or tacitly, on their maritime boundary. Lacking agreement, boundaries could be delimited by judicial process.

B Methods for Delimiting the EEZ and the Continental Shelf

International tribunals have gradually developed mechanisms for implementing Articles 74 and 83 UNCLOS. One may distinguish three time periods since the 1969 judgment in *North Sea Continental Shelf*, which correspond to three different methods for delimiting maritime boundaries by way of judicial process.

1 The primacy of relevant circumstances (1969–1993)

Between 1969 and 1993, international tribunals approached each delimitation case as a *unicum*. Lacking a delimitation method applicable in any

---

[41] Jia argued that the methods to implement Arts. 74 and 83 UNCLOS are entirely judge-made law. See BB Jia, 'International Case Law in the Development of International Law' (2015) 382 *Recueil des Cours* 175, 283-9.

given situation, maritime boundaries would be delimited pursuant to equitable principles. Under this approach, international tribunals would formulate the appropriate delimitation method on a case-specific basis, having taken into account all relevant circumstances. A central role was thus played by the concepts of equitable principles and relevant circumstances. In 1989, Evans argued that 'relevant circumstances are used in two ways within the delimitation process: they ameliorate the strict application of a chosen method, and they indicate what that method is to be'.[42] The 1985 arbitral award in *Guinea/Guinea-Bissau* illustrated this case-by-case approach. The Court of Arbitration stated that:

> [l]es facteurs et les méthodes [de délimitation] résultent de règles juridiques, bien que procédant de données physiques, mathématiques, historiques, politiques, économiques ou autres. Mais ils ne sont pas limités dans leur nombre et aucun d'entre eux n'est obligatoire pour le Tribunal, puisque chaque cas de délimitation est bien un *unicum* .... S'agissant des facteurs, le Tribunal doit les inventorier et les apprécier. Ils se déduisent des circonstances de l'espèce et singulièrement des caractéristiques propres à la région. Ces circonstances ne seront prises en considération par le Tribunal que quand celui-ci les jugera pertinentes en l'espèce. Elles sont de diverses natures. Elles ne se limitent pas aux données physiques, que celles-ci soient géographiques, géologiques ou géomorphologiques.[43]

In the 1982 *Tunisia/Libya* judgment, the ICJ similarly held that:

> [t]he result of the application of equitable principles must be equitable. This terminology, which is generally used, is not entirely satisfactory because it employs the term equitable to characterize both the result to be achieved and the means to be applied to reach this result. It is, however, the result which is predominant; the principles are subordinate to the goal. The equitableness of a principle must be assessed in the light of its usefulness for the purpose of arriving at an equitable result. It is not every such principle which is in itself equitable; it may acquire this quality by reference to the equitableness of the solution.[44]

The *Anglo/French Arbitration* was the only dispute in which a boundary was delimited using an apparently different approach, since Article 6

---

[42] MD Evans, *Relevant Circumstances and Maritime Delimitation* (OUP, 1989) 87.
[43] *Delimitation of the Maritime Boundary between Guinea and Guinea-Bissau (Guinea/Guinea-Bissau)* (1985) XIX RIAA 149, 182 [89].
[44] *Continental Shelf (Tunisia/Libya)* (Judgment) [1982] ICJ Rep 18, 59 [70].

CCS was applicable as between France and the UK.[45] On this basis, and on the basis of the parties' agreement, the Court of Arbitration delimited the English Channel using an equidistant boundary.[46] Owing to their location, the Channel Islands were awarded a 12-nm enclave,[47] while the presence of the Scilly Isles well out to sea determined the decision to give the Scilly Isles half effect in constructing the equidistance line in the Atlantic.[48]

Although the Court of Arbitration seemed simply to draw an equidistance line with some adjustments, a close reading of the award suggests differently. According to the Court of Arbitration, special circumstances entailed that:

> even under Article 6 the question whether the use of the equidistance principle or some other method is appropriate for achieving an equitable delimitation is very much a matter of appreciation in the light of the geographical and other circumstances. ... [E]ven under Article 6 it is the geographical and other circumstances of any given case which indicate and justify the use of the equidistance method as the means of achieving an equitable solution rather than the inherent quality of the method as a legal norm of delimitation.[49]

The Court of Arbitration pushed the meaning of Article 6 CCS, to deprive equidistance of its character as an obligatory delimitation method and to give primacy to special circumstances. Only lacking special circumstances would the Court of Arbitration have decided to delimit the boundary between France and the UK by equidistance.

The international tribunals' approach meant that such tribunals could choose to delimit a boundary using any method which they considered to be appropriate in the circumstances, at the expense of predictability and certainty. States would simply have no way of knowing how international tribunals would delimit a boundary between them. One could understand this approach by taking into account that the time from 1969 to the end of the 1980s marked the beginnings of delimitation by judicial process. Furthermore, the lack of rules of international law determining an applicable delimitation method may justify some experimentalism. Unable to codify clearer rules on delimitation, states deferred the

---

[45] *Continental Shelf (France/UK)* (1977) XVIII RIAA 3, 45 [70].
[46] Ibid. 52 [87].
[47] Ibid. 95 [202].
[48] Ibid. 116 [249].
[49] Ibid. 45-6 [70].

development of a delimitation method to international tribunals. Presumably, international tribunals did their best with the limited instruments at their disposal.

2 The two-stage approach (1993–2009)

The ICJ's judgment in *Jan Mayen* was the turning point at which international tribunals abandoned the case-by-case approach to delimitation. In that case, the Court established the maritime boundary between Greenland and Jan Mayen as two coincident boundaries, one for the continental shelf and one for Fishery Zone (FZ).[50] Although the applicable law was Article 6 CCS for the continental shelf and customary international law for the FZ,[51] the Court found that the delimitation method was the same for both maritime zones. Concerning the continental shelf, the Court stated that 'it is appropriate to begin by taking provisionally the median line between the territorial sea baselines, and then enquiring whether "special circumstances" require "another boundary line"'.[52] The Court found that the same method also applied to FZ delimitation.[53] In *Jan Mayen*, the ICJ applied a two-stage approach to delimitation: first, it drew a provisional equidistance line; second, it adjusted this equidistance line based on special circumstances in the continental shelf, and based on relevant circumstances in the FZ. The two-stage approach to delimitation was applied without much discussion in later cases in which UNCLOS was the applicable law, which included *Eritrea/Yemen*,[54] *Qatar v. Bahrain*,[55] *Cameroon v. Nigeria*,[56] *Barbados v. Trinidad and Tobago*[57] and *Guyana v. Suriname*.[58]

Between 1993 and 2009, only the 2007 judgment in *Nicaragua v. Honduras* appeared to cast doubt on the established character of the

---

[50] *Maritime Delimitation between Greenland and Jan Mayen (Denmark v. Norway)* (Judgment) [1993] ICJ Rep 38, 79-81 [90]-[93].
[51] Ibid. 57-8 [42]-[44].
[52] Ibid. 59-60 [49].
[53] Ibid. 61-2 [52]-[53].
[54] *Second Stage of the Proceedings between Eritrea and Yemen (Maritime Delimitation)* (Eritrea/Yemen) (1999) XXII RIAA 335, 365-6 [130]-[135].
[55] *Maritime Delimitation and Territorial Questions between Qatar and Bahrain (Qatar v. Bahrain)* (Merits) [2001] ICJ Rep 40, 94 [176].
[56] *Land and Maritime Boundary between Cameroon and Nigeria (Cameroon v. Nigeria; Equatorial Guinea intervening)* (Merits) [2002] ICJ Rep 303, 441 [288].
[57] *Maritime Boundary Arbitration (Barbados v. Trinidad and Tobago)* (2006) XXVII RIAA 147, 214-15 [242].
[58] *Maritime Boundary Arbitration (Guyana v. Suriname)* (2007) XXX RIAA 1, 95 [342].

two-stage approach. Nicaragua requested the Court to draw an angle-bisector, as coastal instability at the mouth of the River Coco precluded the identification of suitable base points for drawing an equidistance line,[59] whereas Honduras sought to prove that an agreed boundary existed running along the fifteenth parallel.[60] The Court rejected Honduras's argument,[61] and subsequently discussed the law on delimitation with respect to the territorial sea first,[62] and to the EEZ and continental shelf second.[63] The Court decided that equidistance was not appropriate owing to coastal instability and to the convexity of the coast around Cape Gracias a Dios. However, the Court failed clearly to distinguish between the delimitation of different maritime zones: while its reasoning only concerned the territorial sea, the angle-bisector boundary it drew also continued into the EEZ and continental shelf.[64] Possibly, the Court's decision was influenced by the parties' arguments. However, that decision constituted a departure from the two-stage approach, which had by then acquired the character of established method for delimiting the EEZ and the continental shelf.

3 The three-stage approach (2009-present)

The seminal 2009 *Black Sea* judgment developed the two-stage approach into a three-stage approach. Before 2009, the second stage of the delimitation process included a final test to evaluate the overall equitableness of the boundary by reference to the absence of gross disproportionality between the length of the relevant coasts and the marine areas found to appertain to each state. In *Black Sea*, the ICJ severed disproportionality from other relevant circumstances. It stated that '[w]hen called upon to delimit the continental shelf or [EEZs], or to draw a single delimitation line, the Court proceeds in defined stages'.[65] The Court found that:

> the first stage of the Court's approach is to establish the provisional equidistance line. ... The course of the final line should result in an equitable solution ... Therefore, the Court will at the next, second stage

---

[59] CR 2007/5, 15-18 [53]-[56] (Pellet); CR 2007/12, 53 (Argüello Gómez).
[60] CR 2007/9, 10-39 [1]-[57] (Sands).
[61] *Territorial and Maritime Dispute between Nicaragua and Honduras in the Caribbean Sea (Nicaragua v. Honduras)* (Judgment) [2007] ICJ Rep 659, 737 [258].
[62] Ibid. 739-41 [265]-[269].
[63] Ibid. 741 [270]-[272].
[64] Ibid. 742-5 [277]-[282].
[65] *Maritime Delimitation in the Black Sea (Romania v. Ukraine)* (Judgment) [2009] ICJ Rep 61, 101 [115].

22   HISTORICAL AND CONCEPTUAL FRAMEWORK

consider whether there are factors calling for the adjustment or shifting of the provisional equidistance line in order to achieve an equitable result. ... Finally, and at a third stage, the Court will verify that the line (a provisional equidistance line which may or may not have been adjusted by taking into account the relevant circumstances) does not, as it stands, lead to an inequitable result by reason of any marked disproportion between the ratio of the respective coastal lengths and the ratio between the relevant maritime area of each State by reference to the delimitation line.[66]

Curiously, the three-stage approach set out in *Black Sea* has been regarded since its inception as the established method for continental shelf and EEZ delimitation. In all post-2009 cases, international tribunals delimited boundaries pursuant to that approach.

In the 2012 *Bangladesh/Myanmar* judgment, the International Tribunal for the Law of the Sea (ITLOS or Tribunal) outlined the evolution of the three-stage approach,[67] and found that, to delimit the maritime boundary between Bangladesh and Myanmar, it would 'follow the three-stage approach, as developed in the most recent case law'.[68] Similarly, in the 2012 *Nicaragua v. Colombia* judgment the ICJ stated that '[t]he Court has made clear on a number of occasions that the methodology which it will normally employ when called upon to effect a delimitation between overlapping continental shelf and [EEZ] entitlements involves proceeding in three stages'.[69] In its 2014 award, the *Bangladesh v. India* arbitral tribunal went even further. Commenting on the method for delimiting the continental shelf and the EEZ, the arbitral tribunal stated that:

> two different, although interrelated, issues must be addressed. The first is whether a presumption exists in favour of the [three-stage approach] for the delimitation of the [EEZ] and the continental shelf within 200 nm. The second is the application of this method in this particular case.[70]

---

[66] Ibid. 101-103 [118]-[122].
[67] *Delimitation of the Maritime Boundary in the Bay of Bengal (Bangladesh/Myanmar)* (Judgment) [2012] ITLOS Rep 4, 65-6 [229]-[233].
[68] Ibid. 69 [240].
[69] *Territorial and Maritime Dispute (Nicaragua v. Colombia)* (Judgment) [2012] ICJ Rep 624, 695-6 [190]-[193]. See also *Maritime Dispute (Peru v. Chile)* (Judgment) [2014] ICJ Rep 3, 65 [180].
[70] *Bay of Bengal Maritime Boundary Arbitration (Bangladesh v. India)* (2014) 167 ILR 1, 112 [337].

The tribunal discussed whether there was a presumption in favour of applying the three-stage approach, and obliquely gave a positive answer. Since the vagueness of Articles 74 and 83 UNCLOS left the delimitation method 'to be determined through the mechanisms for the peaceful settlement of disputes',[71] the arbitral tribunal concluded that '[t]he ensuing ... case law constitutes ... an *acquis judiciaire*, a source of international law under article 38(1)(d) of the Statute of the International Court of Justice, and should be read into articles 74 and 83 [UNCLOS]'.[72] The two delimitation cases settled after 2014 were also decided by applying the three-stage approach.[73]

Nonetheless, the international tribunals' application of the three-stage approach is not mechanical. The ICJ held in *Black Sea* that the three-stage delimitation process is used 'unless there are compelling reasons that make [the drawing of an equidistance line] unfeasible in the particular case'.[74] Similarly, the *Bangladesh* v. *India* arbitral tribunal held that the three-stage approach 'is preferable unless ... there are "factors which make the application of the equidistance method inappropriate"'.[75] The three-stage delimitation process is currently regarded as the established method for EEZ and continental shelf delimitation. However, this does not mean that international tribunals apply the three-stage approach convincingly. There is much room for improvement.

III Conceptual Framework of Maritime Delimitation

Since *North Sea Continental Shelf*, maritime delimitation has been characterised by and associated to certain concepts which are closely connected to the international tribunals' elaboration on delimitation. These concepts cut across and inform the analysis of the delimitation process in the following chapters.

---

[71] Ibid. [339].
[72] Ibid.
[73] *Delimitation of the Maritime Boundary between Ghana and Côte d'Ivoire in the Atlantic Ocean (Ghana/Côte d'Ivoire)* (Judgment), Judgment of 23 September 2017 [360]; *Maritime Delimitation in the Caribbean Sea and the Pacific Ocean (Costa Rica v. Nicaragua); Land Boundary in the Northern Part of Isla Portillos (Costa Rica v. Nicaragua)* (Judgment) [2018] ICJ Rep 139, 190 [135] and 203 [168].
[74] *Black Sea* (n. 65) 101 [116].
[75] *Bangladesh v. India* (n. 70) 114 [345].

A   Maritime Delimitation as a Process

Maritime delimitation by way of the three-stage approach should be understood as a process. The character of delimitation as a process means that it should not be seen to be a single operation, through the application of which international tribunals establish maritime boundaries. In this sense, the three-stage approach appears to be similar to delimitation according to the two-stage approach, but different from the case-specific approach which international tribunals employed before *Jan Mayen*. Under the latter approach, international tribunals considered all relevant circumstances and, on that basis, chose the method, or combination of methods, which seemed appropriate for delimiting the maritime boundary concerned. Delimitation was approached as a single operation, namely the choice and subsequent implementation of a method suitable in the circumstances of each case.

Delimitation as a process entails that none of the stages of that process can be studied, or applied, in isolation. Decisions made in the earlier stages of the delimitation process influence the decisions in its later stages. The airtight distinction between stages of the delimitation process appears to be artificial. The identification of the relevant coast and of the relevant area determines the stretch of coast on which international tribunals select base points for drawing an equidistance line, and is likely decisive in establishing both the existence of marked coastal length disparity as a relevant circumstance, and the absence of disproportionality. The manner in which an equidistance line is established could influence the analysis of relevant circumstances, especially the effect which islands may have on the course of that equidistance line insofar as they are relevant circumstances. The division of maritime areas by the equidistance line, whether adjusted or not, is crucial in assessing disproportionality.

Although the character of maritime delimitation as a process means that the stages of that process are interconnected, it also means that it is feasible practically to apply that process without pre-empting at an earlier stage a decision belonging in a later stage. For instance, the identification of the relevant coast and of the relevant area ought to be separate from the disproportionality test. Similarly, selecting islands as base points could result in deciding on the effect of those islands at the first stage of the process, instead of making that decision at the second stage based on the correct consideration that islands could be potential

III CONCEPTUAL FRAMEWORK OF MARITIME DELIMITATION

relevant circumstances.[76] Conflating distinct stages of the delimitation process could adversely affect the states' perception of decisions establishing maritime boundaries, and might also impact on compliance. Following the *Nicaragua* v. *Colombia* judgment, the president of Colombia stated that the ICJ's decision was 'wrong and contradictory'.[77] In an address to the nation, President Santos also said that the Court 'cometió errores graves',[78] including not giving sufficient weight to 'circunstancias a las que se ha debido dar peso, tales como consideraciones de seguridad y acceso equitativo a los recursos naturales'.[79] Although Colombia's president did not fully list the inconsistencies and mistakes to which he referred, his address suggests that the issues with the Court's judgment related to the manner in which the Court had applied the delimitation process. Conversely, if international tribunals applied each stage in the delimitation process discretely, and did not pre-empt at an earlier stage decisions which belong in a later stage, the reasoning of decisions on maritime delimitation may be strengthened. As a consequence, states may perceive such decisions more positively, which could influence their attitudes towards compliance.

Understanding delimitation as a process also means that, whereas the process in itself pursues the achievement of an equitable solution in accordance with Articles 74 and 83 UNCLOS, each stage retains its internal objectives. As discussed below,[80] delimitation oscillates between ensuring a degree of objectivity and pursuing an equitable solution. The following chapters argue that the initial stages of the three-stage approach should aim at increasing objectivity in delimitation, while the later stages should ensure that the provisional line drawn based on objective methods achieves an equitable solution. Both identifying the relevant coast and the relevant area, and establishing a provisional equidistance line, are based on mathematical and geometrical methods which allow international tribunals to

---

[76] Chapter 4, Section IV.B below.
[77] 'UN Ruling Gives Colombia Islets But Nicaragua More Sea' (*BBC News*, 20 November 2012) www.bbc.com/news/world-latin-america-20391180.
[78] '"La Corte cometió errores graves": Santos' (El Espectador, 19 November 2012) www.elespectador.com/noticias/politica/corte-cometio-errores-graves-santos-articulo-387957.
[79] Ibid. The translation of the relevant parts of President Santos's address can be found at 'Boundary Disputes in Latin America: An Islet for a Sea' (*The Economist*, 8 December 2012) www.economist.com/node/21567986/all-comments.
[80] Section III.B.

approach them as objective operations, while at the same time relying on their earlier jurisprudence.[81] Adjusting equidistance lines based on relevant circumstances and the disproportionality test rests on a case-by-case appreciation of the peculiarities of a case by the international tribunal concerned. These stages of the delimitation process are not chiefly based on objective criteria, but rely on international tribunals to decide like cases alike. Reliance by international tribunals on their previous jurisprudence, which takes place in respect of all stages of the delimitation process, contributes to the creation of what could be seen to be a common law of maritime delimitation.[82]

The development of a common law of maritime delimitation would entail that the understanding of maritime delimitation as a process cuts across international tribunals. As the following chapters discuss, international tribunals are developing maritime delimitation as a uniform body of law, with respect both to each individual stage, and to the process as a whole. This development is also shown by the increasingly common citations to the jurisprudence of other international tribunals in maritime delimitation decisions.[83] Even the ICJ, traditionally reluctant to refer to the jurisprudence of other international tribunals, has followed this trend.[84] The presence of such citations in maritime delimitation decisions suggests that judges at least discuss the decisions of other international tribunals during the deliberation process, and are conceivably careful to treat like cases alike. States also appear to understand maritime delimitation as a process. Their submissions before international tribunals suggest that states have sanctioned the three-stage approach applied by international tribunals,[85] which includes the international tribunals' conception of delimitation as a process.

B Objectivity and the Equitable Solution

In delimiting maritime boundaries international tribunals tread a fine line between ensuring that the delimitation process achieves a predictable solution, and respecting the circumstances which may be peculiar to one

---

[81] Section III.C below.
[82] Chapter 7 below.
[83] E De Brabandere, 'The Use of Precedent and External Case Law by the International Court of Justice and the International Tribunal for the Law of the Sea' (2016) 15 *Law and Practice of International Courts and Tribunals* 24.
[84] For example, see *Costa Rica v. Nicaragua* (n. 73) 190 [135].
[85] Chapter 7, Section III.B.2 below.

particular case. Maritime delimitation by judicial process is a balance between objectivity on one hand, and the need to achieve the equitable solution required by Articles 74 and 83 UNCLOS on the other hand.

Academic writers largely welcome the development of a common method for maritime delimitation.[86] However, certain influential commentators remain critical with respect to the practical implementation of the delimitation process by international tribunals. In his annual commentary on the ICJ's activity, Thirlway discussed maritime delimitation issues on two occasions. In 1995, he warned his reader 'against entertaining any expectations that the jurisprudence [on delimitation] could be presented as a complete, orderly and coherent system',[87] adding that '"the rule of equity" has . . . produced the divergences and unpredictability of result to be expected from so broad and undefined a notion'.[88] In 2007, Thirlway made positive comments on the developments in maritime delimitation since 1995, writing that 'the process followed [for delimiting maritime boundaries] has become established'.[89] Nevertheless, he still commented that maritime delimitation was 'a leap to the sort of solution that looks and feels right on a basis of equitableness as fairness, followed by the construction of an intellectual process to support it'.[90] On balance, Thirlway's comments appear to be tepid.

Evans has become increasingly critical of the delimitation decisions handed down in the last decade. Writing in 2006 with respect to the cases pending at the time,[91] Evans cautioned that 'any judgments given in these cases should further clarify the relationship between equidistance and equitable principles'.[92] In 2015, Evans wrote that, although both the

---

[86] DR Rothwell and T Stephens, *The International Law of the Sea* 2nd edn (Hart, 2016) 427–31; P Couvreur, *The International Court of Justice and the Effectiveness of International Law* (Brill, 2017) 175; S Fietta and R Cleverly, *A Practitioner's Guide to Maritime Boundary Delimitation* (OUP, 2016) 584; K Neri, 'L'Arrêt de la Cour Internationale de Justice du 27 Janvier 2014 dans l'Affaire du Différend Maritime (Perou c. Chili)' (2014) 60 *AFDI* 91, 105; RR Churchill, 'Dispute Settlement under the UN Convention on the Law of the Sea: Survey for 2009' (2010) 25 *IJMCL* 457, 477–8; H Thirlway, 'The Law and Procedure of the International Court of Justice 1960-1989 – Supplement, 2007: Parts Four, Five and Six' (2007) 78 *BYIL* 17, 132.

[87] H Thirlway, 'The Law and Procedure of the International Court of Justice 1960–1989 – Part Six' (1994) 65 *BYIL* 1, 77.

[88] Ibid. 80.

[89] Thirlway (n. 86) 132.

[90] Ibid. 139.

[91] Evans referred to *Guyana* v. *Suriname, Barbados* v. *Trinidad and Tobago, Nicaragua* v. *Honduras, Nicaragua* v. *Colombia* and *Black Sea*.

[92] MD Evans, 'Maritime Boundary Delimitation: Where Do We Go From Here?' in D Freestone et al. (eds.), *Law of the Sea – Progress and Prospects* (OUP, 2006) 137, 140.

ITLOS and the ICJ endorsed the three-stage approach formulated in *Black Sea*, they 'went on to apply it in a fashion which ... casts doubt upon the weight to be given to equidistance in practice'.[93] Evans became more critical in 2016, when he stated that:

> [i]n 2009, the [ICJ] in the *Romania v Ukraine* (the *Black Sea* case) appeared to have put the final touches to an approach which it had been incrementally developing over the past ten years or so, during which it had been gradually whittling away at the uncertainties that had surrounded the subject for so long.... However, we should have had more faith in the capacities of international courts and tribunals to keep this most fecund field of controversy alive.[94]

Tanaka seems to be less critical than Evans, despite expressing some doubts concerning the ICJ's judgment in *Nicaragua* v. *Honduras*, which he called 'a major departure from the previous case law relating to maritime delimitations'.[95]

Churchill welcomed the methodological clarifications made by international tribunals in the early years of the twenty-first century.[96] Nevertheless, in his dispute settlement survey for 2014 he showed a degree of scepticism towards the decisions in *Peru* v. *Chile* and in *Bangladesh* v. *India*. With respect to the former, Churchill commented that 'the [ICJ's] judgment is intellectually unconvincing'.[97] With respect to the latter, he wrote that '[t]he application of the three-stage method by international courts and tribunals in recent cases has not always been entirely convincing, and the present case is no exception'.[98] The second comment does not relate solely to *Bangladesh* v. *India*, but seems to extend Churchill's criticism to previous cases.[99]

---

[93] MD Evans, 'Maritime Boundary Delimitation' in DR Rothwell et al. (eds.), *The Oxford Handbook of the Law of the Sea* (OUP, 2015) 254, 260.

[94] MD Evans, 'Maritime Boundary Delimitation: Whatever Next?' in J Barrett and R Barnes (eds.), *Law of the Sea – UNCLOS as a Living Treaty* (BIICL, 2016) 41, 41–2.

[95] Y Tanaka, 'Case concerning the Territorial and Maritime Dispute between Nicaragua and Honduras in the Caribbean Sea (8 October 2007)' (2008) 23 *IJMCL* 327, 338.

[96] RR Churchill, 'Dispute Settlement under the UN Convention on the Law of the Sea: Survey for 2006' (2007) 22 *IJMCL* 463, 475-8; RR Churchill, 'Dispute Settlement under the UN Convention on the Law of the Sea: Survey for 2007' (2008) 23 *IJMCL* 601, 622; RR Churchill, 'Dispute Settlement under in the Law of the Sea: Survey for 2006' (2013) 28 *IJMCL* 564, 573 and 606.

[97] RR Churchill, 'Dispute Settlement under in the Law of the Sea: Survey for 2014' (2015) 30 *IJMCL* 585, 636.

[98] Ibid. 616–17.

[99] A scholar has also recently voiced her concern with respect to the three-stage approach, criticised as 'fraught with subjectivity and, consequently, unpredictability'. Although

III CONCEPTUAL FRAMEWORK OF MARITIME DELIMITATION 29

One ought to take stock of the comments made by such and other learned writers. However, without either agreeing or disagreeing with their criticism fully, this book does not endorse a radically critical outlook on the delimitation process evolved since *North Sea Continental Shelf*. Although the decisions of international tribunals on maritime delimitation are not impeccable, they should be commended for the result of their work in clarifying the law of maritime delimitation. International tribunals have overcome the near-complete uncertainty of the early cases, and have developed a method that increases certainty and predictability in the delimitation process. While the cases have not always been cogently decided, an overall appraisal of delimitation cannot leave one insensitive to the great leaps forward which have taken place since 1969.

Futhermore, it appears to be the time for such an appraisal. Maritime boundaries have been established by judicial process for nearly half a century.[100] A decade has passed since the ICJ formulated the three-stage approach in *Black Sea*, during which international tribunals have established seven maritime boundaries,[101] and two delimitation disputes remain currently pending.[102] No comprehensive analysis of the three-stage delimitation process has been completed. The overall appraisal of the judicial delimitation process is principally accomplished by reference to international judicial decisions. However, state practice is examined in detail where relevant.

As its ultimate objective, this book intends to bring together the distinct approaches to issues of maritime delimitation which different international tribunals have adopted. Moreover, this book seeks to show that international tribunals can establish maritime boundaries by implementing each stage of the delimitation process in turn, without pre-empting at an earlier stage decisions that belong in a later stage. The feasibility of such an approach to maritime delimitation shows that international tribunals need not necessarily be seen to establish

---

there is merit to this argument, she only flags the problems of the three-stage approach without seemingly providing any solution. See F Olorundami, 'Objectivity versus Subjectivity in Maritime Boundary Delimitation' (2017) 32 *IJMCL* 36, 42.

[100] Or for more than a century, if one keeps score starting with the 1909 arbitral award in Grisbådarna. See *Grisbådarna (Norway/Sweden)* (1909) XI RIAA 147.

[101] *Black Sea, Bangladesh/Myanmar, Nicaragua v. Colombia, Peru v. Chile, Bangladesh v. India, Ghana/Côte d'Ivoire* and *Costa Rica v. Nicaragua*.

[102] *Question of the Delimitation of the Continental Shelf between Nicaragua and Colombia beyond 200 nautical miles from the Nicaraguan Coast (Nicaragua v. Colombia)*, filed 16 September 2013; *Maritime Delimitation in the Indian Ocean (Somalia v. Kenya)*, filed 28 August 2014.

a boundary first, and only subsequently find the legal justifications for their decision. One must distinguish between the first stage of that process on one hand, and the second and third stages of that process on the other. Identifying the relevant coast and the relevant area, and establishing a provisional equidistance line, should be approached as objective exercises. Conversely, adjusting the provisional equidistance line and the assessment of disproportionality ensure that the boundary achieves an equitable solution.[103] However, international tribunals have not always adhered to this understanding of delimitation, by making at an earlier stage considerations which belonged in a later stage of the process.

C Connection between Delimitation and the Basis of Title

One of the main themes of maritime delimitation, to which many a section of this book is devoted, is that maritime delimitation as a judicial process is governed by and has its legal foundation in the basis of title over the EEZ and the continental shelf. Each subsequent stage in the three-stage approach is fundamentally linked to the basis of title over these two maritime areas, which justifies the character of that stage as an integral part of the delimitation process. In its 1985 judgment in *Libya/Malta*, the ICJ stated that '[t]he legal basis of that which is to be delimited, and of entitlement to it, cannot be other than pertinent to that delimitation'.[104] However, the Court neither justified its statement, nor did it elaborate on it. Commentators wrote on the connection between delimitation and the basis of title before.[105] However, that connection was never explored in the context of the three-stage delimitation process. International tribunals have not explained why delimitation must be connected to the basis of title. The existing literature similarly leaves one wondering why title must be pertinent to delimitation.[106]

---

[103] In particular see Chapter 4, Section II.C below.
[104] *Continental Shelf (Libya/Malta)* (Judgment) [1985] ICJ Rep 13, 30 [27].
[105] See especially P Weil, *Perspectives du Droit de la Délimitation Maritime* (Pédone, 1988) 77.
[106] Judge Cot wrote that '[t]he relationship between entitlement and delimitation is not all that evident. Doctrine has largely ignored the issue, albeit a central one for the process of delimitation'. See J-P Cot, 'The Dual function of Base Points' in H Hestermeyer et al. (eds.), *Coexistence, Cooperation and Solidarity – Liber Amicorum Rüdiger Wolfrum* (Martinus Nijhoff, 2012) 807, 820.

Title could be defined as any fact or act constituting the foundation of a right under international law.[107] In and of themselves, facts or acts from which title originates have no legal relevance. However, such facts or acts acquire legal relevance by being invoked by a state as the basis for its rights under international law. Title is a necessary and sufficient condition for the assertion of a state's right under international law, and could result from the combination of multiple facts or acts, none of which could, taken in isolation, ground a state's right. While a number of facts or acts could be necessary for a state to assert a right, none of them would be sufficient by itself. This definition of title also applies to title over maritime zones, including the EEZ and the continental shelf.[108]

It is plausible that the link between title and maritime delimitation was inspired by the connection between title and land boundary demarcation. A basic tenet of land boundary demarcation is the paramountcy of title in identifying parcels of territory to be attributed to a state. For instance, title could stem from a treaty of cession or from *uti possidetis juris*. However, if title does not afford a solid basis for the attribution of territory, a state can invoke its prolonged display of authority *à titre de souverain*, known as *effectivités*. While the relationship between title and *effectivités* was not entirely clear until recently, leading commentators supported the primacy of the former.[109] In the 2005 *Benin/Niger* judgment, a Chamber of the ICJ held that 'pre-eminence is to be accorded to legal title over effective possession as a basis of sovereignty',[110] and linked this statement to the demarcation of the boundary between the parties, since '[t]o determine the course of the ... boundary at the critical date it is necessary to examine first the legal titles relied on by the Parties, with any *effectivités* being considered only on a confirmatory or subsidiary basis'.[111] The ICJ confirmed this decision in its 2013 *Burkina Faso/Niger* judgment, stating that '[w]hile an *effectivité* may enable an obscure or ambiguous legal title to be interpreted, it cannot contradict the applicable title',[112] and that 'the *effectivités* as

---

[107] M Kohen, *Possession Contestée et Souveraineté Territoriale* (PUF, 1997) 128.
[108] See also Chapter 4, Section II.A below.
[109] M Kohen, 'La Relation Titre/Effectivités dans le Contentiex Territorial à la Lumière de la Jurisprudence Récente' (2004) 108 *RGDIP* 561; R O'Keefe, 'Legal Title versus Effectivités: Prescription and the Promise and Problem of Private Law Analogies' (2011) 13 *ICLR* 147.
[110] *Frontier Dispute (Benin/Niger)* (Judgment) [2005] ICJ Rep 90, 120 [47].
[111] Ibid. 143 [128].
[112] *Frontier Dispute (Burkina Faso/Niger)* (Judgment) [2013] ICJ Rep 44, 79 [78]. See also *Cameroon v. Nigeria* (n. 56), 415 [223]; *Frontier Dispute (Burkina Faso/Mali)* (Judgment) [1986] ICJ Rep 554, 586–7 [63].

established at the critical date may serve to compensate for the absence of a legal title or to complete a defective title'.[113] Title would thus be paramount because it defines the territorial scope of sovereignty through the establishment of boundaries.

This reasoning also applies to maritime delimitation. However, the continental shelf and the EEZ are not to be assimilated to territory. Sovereignty over maritime areas only exists in respect of the territorial sea,[114] while a state's jurisdiction over the continental shelf and the EEZ only includes sovereign rights for exploring and exploiting natural resources.[115] Since states have rights over the continental shelf and EEZ, such rights must be based on a legal title circumscribing their geographical scope. Similarly to territorial sovereignty, the geographical scope of sovereign rights over the continental shelf and EEZ could be seen as a function of title. Title provides a legal basis for rights over maritime areas, and, by implication, also limits the geographical extent of such rights. This is the reason why delimitation methods should be connected to the basis of title over maritime areas. In particular, equidistance as the starting point of the three-stage approach is consistent with the basis of title over the EEZ and the continental shelf.[116] However, title is not the only criterion governing delimitation. As with *effectivités* in land boundary demarcation, considerations other than title could be relevant in delimiting maritime boundaries.[117]

Nevertheless, title remains the main foundation on which the three-stage delimitation process rests. As the following chapters argue, each stage of the delimitation process is connected with the basis of title, which is the legal basis for considering those stages as part of the process itself. Additionally, the basis to title indicates the practical methods for identifying the relevant coast and the relevant area, and for drawing a provisional equidistance line. In this second function, the basis of title ensures that the initial stages of the delimitation process rest on an objective basis, from which objective methods for their implementation stem. The basis of title has a twofold *raison d'être* in the delimitation process: it constitutes the legal basis for each stage of the process, and it contributes to ensure objectivity and certainty by guiding the initial stages of that process.

---

[113] *Burkina Faso/Niger* (n. 112) 84 [98].
[114] Art. 2 UNCLOS.
[115] Arts. 56 and 77 UNCLOS.
[116] Chapter 4, Sections II–III below.
[117] Chapter 5 below.

IV An Inevitable Development?

The manner in which the delimitation process has developed was not inevitable. Since international tribunals have been the drivers of this development, their decisions have largely determined the formulation and application of the delimitation process. For example, nothing requires disproportionality to be the final stage of the delimitation process, also considering that both states and commentators used to conceive it as a delimitation method in its own right.[118] However, in *North Sea Continental Shelf* the ICJ stated that 'a reasonable degree of proportionality' is a result which delimitation based on equitable principles ought to bring about.[119] Presumably, this statement led states to plead proportionality as one of the relevant circumstances based on which international tribunals would determine the appropriate delimitation method under the circumstances. International tribunals subsequently included proportionality as a relevant circumstance capable of justifying the adjustment of a provisional equidistance line. As states largely argued that proportionality indicated the overall equitableness of a boundary, in *Black Sea* the ICJ recognised disproportionality as the final stage of the delimitation process.

The existence and the place of each stage within the delimitation process is the result of judicial decisions, which either took stock of common positions of states appearing in maritime disputes, or were simply seen to be the most appropriate means to achieve the equitable solution required by UNCLOS and customary international law. The three-stage delimitation process is not the outcome of an inevitable development, but the result of judicial elaborations over the years. Had judges on international tribunals been different, or thought differently, we would likely be delimiting boundaries differently.

---

[118] Chapter 6, Section III.A below.
[119] *North Sea Continental Shelf* (n. 25) 52 [98].

3

Relevant Coast and Relevant Area

I An Essential Stage in the Delimitation Process

In its 2009 *Black Sea* judgment, the International Court of Justice (ICJ or Court) stated that 'the task of delimitation consists in resolving the [states party's] overlapping claims by drawing a line of separation between the maritime areas concerned'.[1] Although the Court's definition of maritime delimitation could be regarded as uncontroversial, the term 'overlapping' seems to raise a number of issues. 'Overlapping' means that maritime boundaries can only be delimited, whichever the dispute settlement method, when the states' claims over maritime areas overlap. Therefore, this is a condition absent which there cannot be delimitation.

Writing in 2015, Evans correctly noted that the ICJ's *Black Sea* definition is not entirely accurate, since, according to the Court, what must 'overlap' are the 'claims' of the states concerned over maritime areas. It is more precise to say that delimitation aims at delimiting the 'overlapping entitlements' of neighbouring states. As Evans put it, 'just because a State claims that it has an entitlement does not mean that it does'.[2] However, there is a close connection between 'claims' and 'entitlement', since states 'claim' maritime areas to which they believe to be 'entitled' under international law. The difference between 'claims' and 'entitlement' concerns the standard applied for their identification. While 'claims' are *subjectively* identified by a coastal state, the existence and extent of maritime

---

[1] *Maritime Delimitation in the Black Sea (Romania v. Ukraine)* (Judgment) [2009] ICJ Rep 61, 89 [77]. The Court repeated the statement verbatim in *Territorial and Maritime Dispute (Nicaragua v. Colombia)* (Judgment) [2012] ICJ Rep 624, 674–5 [141].

[2] MD Evans, 'Maritime Boundary Delimitation' in DR Rothwell et al. (eds.), *The Oxford Handbook of the Law of the Sea* (OUP, 2015) 254, 261.

I AN ESSENTIAL STAGE IN THE DELIMITATION PROCESS   35

'entitlement' results from an *objective* determination by the international tribunal requested to delimit a maritime boundary.

The states' maritime entitlements are a function of distance from the coast, which is the basis of title over maritime areas.[3] This manner of generating maritime entitlements is expressed by the principle 'the land dominates the sea',[4] under which maritime entitlements are generated by the seaward projections of a state's coast. The objective identification by international tribunals of overlapping maritime entitlements is thus connected with the existence of a coast, whose seaward projections overlap with the seaward projections of a neighbouring state's coast. The coast of neighbouring states whose projections overlap is called 'relevant coast'. The area of overlapping entitlements generated by the relevant coast is part of the 'relevant area'.[5] Beyond being useful for ascertaining the existence of overlapping entitlements as a precondition for delimitation, the relevant coast and the relevant area are also important in all subsequent stages of the delimitation process: in constructing an equidistance line, in assessing relevant circumstances, and in relation to disproportionality.[6]

Starting with the ICJ's *Black Sea* judgment, international tribunals have, with limited exceptions, dedicated consecutive sections of their judgments to identifying the relevant coast and the relevant area. This was the case in *Black Sea, Nicaragua v. Colombia, Bangladesh v. India, Ghana/Côte d'Ivoire* and *Costa Rica v. Nicaragua*.[7] In *Bangladesh/ Myanmar*, the International Tribunal for the Law of the Sea (ITLOS or Tribunal) devoted one section of its judgment only to identifying the

---

[3] Chapter 4, Section II.A discusses title over the continental shelf within 200 nm and the EEZ. Chapter 4, Section III.B analyses the basis of title over the continental shelf beyond 200 nm, arguing that distance from the coast is one of the basis of title's two components.

[4] *North Sea Continental Shelf (Federal Republic of Germany/Denmark; Federal Republic of Germany/Netherlands)* (Judgment) [1969] ICJ Rep 3, 51 [96]. See also S Touzé, 'Affaire relative à la Délimitation Maritime en Mer Noire (Roumanie c. Ukraine): Une Clarification Didactique de la Règle de l'Équidistance-Circonstances Pertinentes' (2009) 55 *AFDI* 221, 229.

[5] The terminological issues of the notions of 'relevant coast' and 'relevant area' are addressed in Sections II and III below.

[6] See Chapters 4, 5 and 6 below.

[7] *Black Sea* (n. 1) 89-100 [77]-[114]; *Nicaragua v Colombia* (n. 1) 674-86 [140]-[166]; *Bay of Bengal Maritime Boundary Arbitration (Bangladesh v. India)* (2014) 167 ILR 1, 89-103 [277]-[311]; *Delimitation of the Maritime Boundary between Ghana and Côte d'Ivoire in the Atlantic Ocean (Ghana/Côte d'Ivoire)* (Judgment), Judgment of 23 September 2017 [361]-[386]; *Maritime Delimitation in the Caribbean Sea and the Pacific Ocean (Costa Rica v. Nicaragua); Land Boundary in the Northern Part of Isla Portillos (Costa Rica v. Nicaragua)* (Judgment) [2018] ICJ Rep 139, 181-7 [108]-[122] and 208-14 [177]-[185].

relevant coast, while the relevant area was discussed in the section on disproportionality.[8] In *Peru* v. *Chile*, the ICJ did not include any section on the relevant coast or the relevant area. According to the Court, the existence of an agreed boundary up to 80 nautical miles (nm) from Chile's coast made it difficult to identify the relevant coast and the relevant area.[9] One may expect that future decisions will include parts specifically discussing the relevant coast and the relevant area.

The international tribunals' attention to these issues requires their appraisal as elements of the delimitation process. However, academic commentators have not written much on this subject. Writing on proportionality, Tanaka only briefly mentioned the relevant coast and the relevant area.[10] Evans wrote on these issues on at least two occasions, but his discussion mainly concerned the relevant coast and the relevant area as relevant circumstances or within the disproportionality test.[11] Fietta and Cleverly[12] and Oude Elferink[13] authored the latest contributions to this topic.

This chapter argues that international tribunals are developing a common approach to identifying the relevant coast and the relevant area in the delimitation process. However, there are numerous unresolved problems stemming from this judicial approach. Section II concerns the relevant coast. Section III discusses the relevant area. By way of conclusion, Section IV suggests that identifying the relevant coast and the relevant area should be seen as a full-fledged stage in the delimitation process.

---

[8] *Delimitation of the Maritime Boundary in the Bay of Bengal (Bangladesh/Myanmar)* (Judgment) [2012] ITLOS Rep 4, 56–9 [185]–[205] and 123–6 [477]–[499]. Before *Black Sea*, the same approach as ITLOS was taken in the 2007 *Guyana v. Suriname* arbitral award. See *Maritime Boundary Arbitration (Guyana v. Suriname)* (2007) XXX RIAA 1, 95–7 [343]–[352] and 109 [392].

[9] *Maritime Dispute (Peru v. Chile)* (Judgment) [2014] ICJ Rep 3, 69 [193]. While paragraphs 24–176 are devoted to establishing the existence of an agreed boundary between the parties and the starting point of that agreed boundary, paragraphs 177–95 are the only ones dedicated to tracing the maritime boundary beyond 80 nm.

[10] Y Tanaka, 'Reflections on the Concept of Proportionality in the Law of Maritime Delimitation' (2001) 16 *IJMCL* 433, 461.

[11] Evans (n. 2) 267–72; MD Evans, 'Maritime Boundary Delimitation: Where Do We Go From Here?' in D Freestone et al. (eds.), *The Law of the Sea – Progress and Prospects* (OUP, 2006) 137, 152–6.

[12] S Fietta and R Cleverly, *A Practitioner's Guide to Maritime Boundary Delimitation* (OUP, 2016) 45–52 and 595–602.

[13] A Oude Elferink, 'Relevant Coast and Relevant Area' in A Oude Elferink et al. (eds.), *Maritime Boundary Delimitation – The Case Law: is it Consistent and Predictable?* (CUP, 2018) 173.

II The Relevant Coast

This section examines the link between the relevant coast and the basis of a state's title over maritime areas. It analyses the international tribunals' approach to identifying the relevant coast, offering some ideas on how the relevant coast could be identified in order to make the delimitation process more transparent and consistent with the basis of title.

A The Land Dominates the Sea

The principle according to which 'the land dominates the sea' means that a state cannot exercise any rights over maritime areas if it does not have a coast, and expresses distance from the coast as the basis of title over maritime zones within 200 nm.

1 The delimitation of the maritime zones within 200 nautical miles

The coast is the element through which a state can assert maritime rights under international law. With respect to the coast's capacity to generate maritime entitlements, in *North Sea Continental Shelf* the ICJ held that:

> [t]he doctrine of the continental shelf is a recent instance of encroachment on maritime expanses which, during the greater part of history, appertained to no-one. ... [T]he land dominates the sea; it is consequently necessary to examine closely the geographical configuration of the coastlines of the countries whose continental shelves are to be delimited. ... [S]ince the land is the legal source of the power which a State may exercise over territorial extensions to seaward, it must first be clearly established what features do in fact constitute such extensions.[14]

It is regarded as uncontroversial that the origin of a state's maritime jurisdiction over the Exclusive Economic Zone (EEZ) and the continental shelf within 200 nm is the geographical fact of having a coast abutting the sea.[15] The coast is essential to delimitation, since it generates maritime entitlements that, by overlapping with those of a neighbouring state, are the necessary and sufficient precondition for establishing a line separating them. However, the entire coast of a state may not be pertinent to delimitation. As the precondition to delimitation is the existence of *overlapping* entitlements, only the coast generating entitlements

---

[14] *North Sea Continental Shelf* (n. 4) 51 [96].
[15] This issue is less uncontroversial with respect to the continental shelf beyond 200 nm, as discussed in Chapter 4, Section III.B below.

overlapping with those of a neighbouring state is relevant to delimitation. Identifying the relevant coast is an exercise which is difficult to separate from the identification of the relevant area. However, there exist aspects relating to the relevant coast that are peculiar to its identification.[16]

Identifying the relevant coast requires international tribunals to select a stretch on the coast of the states concerned as being relevant. Upon identifying this stretch of coast, international tribunals attribute a numerical value to it, which expresses its length. This numerical value is important in the later stages of the delimitation process: it is useful both to establish whether coastal length disparity could be a relevant circumstance, and to assess the absence of disproportionality. However, Weil explained that there is no mathematical relationship between the length of the relevant coast and the maritime areas generated by it.[17] Fietta and Cleverly took Weil's explanation further, stating that 'coastal length is not a legal basis of title'.[18] However, using a numerical value to express coastal lengths is not inconsistent with the basis of title, so long as evaluating that numerical value in relation to relevant circumstances and disproportionality in the second and third stages of the delimitation process remains an approximate comparison between coastal lengths. What would be inconsistent with the basis of title is to require that the smallest disparity in coastal length determine the adjustment of an equidistance line. Since stretches of coast of the same length do not necessarily generate the same extent of maritime entitlements, comparing coastal length should be done only approximately.[19] Although Fietta and Cleverly may have certain misgivings about the role of the relevant coast in delimitation, especially concerning the effects of the international tribunals' calculation of coastal length, one should agree that the relevant coast nonetheless has a central function in delimitation as an element of the basis of title over maritime areas.

Consistency with the basis of title requires international tribunals to identify the relevant coast only along the coast of the states between which a boundary is to be delimited, to the exclusion of the coast of third states. Only the coast of the states between which a boundary is to be delimited generates overlapping maritime entitlements, thus requiring delimitation. The relevant coast has a function in establishing equidistance boundaries, as it is on that coast that base points are selected to

---

[16] Section III below.
[17] P Weil, *Perspectives du Droit de la Délimitation Maritime* (Pédone, 1988) 77.
[18] Fietta and Cleverly (n. 12) 609.
[19] See Chapter 5, Section II.B, and Chapter 6.

construct a provisional equidistance line.[20] The relevant coast also has a function in establishing angle-bisector boundaries, which are obtained by bisecting the angle formed by the lines approximating the general direction of the parties' relevant coast.[21]

In this perspective, the *Guinea/Guinea-Bissau* arbitral award could be criticised for having considered the coast of third states to be relevant.[22] The Court of Arbitration found that taking into account not only the parties' coast, but also the entire West African coast, would ensure an equitable solution.[23] It decided that, beyond Alcatraz island, the boundary would follow 'une direction correspondant *grosso modo* à la perpendiculaire à la ligne unissant la pointe des Almadies au cap Shilling'.[24] The Court of Arbitration considered that such a boundary would be 'susceptible d'être insérée équitablement dans les délimitations actuelles de la région ouest-africaine et dans ses délimitations futures telles qu'on peut raisonnablement les imaginer en recourant à des principes équitables et d'après les hypothèses les plus vraisemblables'.[25] However, in selecting as relevant the coast from Almadies Point to Cap Shilling, the Court of Arbitration did not consider that the coast of third states would not generate maritime entitlements pertinent to the delimitation between Guinea and Guinea-Bissau, and that, as a consequence, the coast of third states should not have contributed to establishing the boundary requested by the parties. Moreover, if the angle-bisector had been drawn only by reference to the coast of the parties, the resulting boundary would have plausibly been different.

Differently from *Guinea/Guinea-Bissau*, in *Cameroon v. Nigeria* the ICJ rejected Cameroon's contention that 'account should be taken of the

---

[20] On the construction of an equidistance line, see Chapter 4, Section IV below.
[21] In *Nicaragua v. Honduras*, the Court first identified the parties' relevant coast, and, second, it bisected the angle formed by the lines approximating the relevant coast. See *Territorial and Maritime Dispute between Nicaragua and Honduras in the Caribbean Sea (Nicaragua v. Honduras)* (Judgment) [2007] ICJ Rep 659, 745–9 [283]–[298].
[22] *Guinea/Guinea-Bissau* was decided before the introduction of a standard delimitation process (Chapter 2, Section II.B above). Therefore, in its respect one cannot strictly speak of the identification of the relevant coast as pertaining to a particular stage of the delimitation process.
[23] *Delimitation of the Maritime Boundary between Guinea and Guinea-Bissau (Guinea/Guinea-Bissau)* (1985) XIX RIAA 149, 189 [108]. See M-C Aquarone, 'The 1985 Guinea/Guinea-Bissau Maritime Boundary Case and its Implications' (1995) 26 *ODIL* 413.
[24] *Guinea/Guinea-Bissau* (n. 23) 190 [111].
[25] Ibid. 189 [109].

coastline of the Gulf of Guinea from Akasso (Nigeria) to Cap Lopez (Gabon) in order to delimit Cameroon's maritime boundary with Nigeria'.[26] According to the Court, 'the maritime boundary between Cameroon and Nigeria can only be determined by reference to points on the coastlines of these two States and not of third States'.[27] The ICJ's approach is more consistent with the basis of title than the one of the Court of Arbitration in *Guinea/Guinea-Bissau*. In any case, the latter approach is unique to *Guinea/Guinea-Bissau*, since no other international tribunal has ever considered the coast of third states as being part of the relevant coast.

Consistency with the basis of title also requires that the entire coast generating overlapping entitlements be relevant to delimitation. This principle is in turn premised on the principle under which a state's coast projects radially, or, in other words, in all directions.[28] For example, in *Nicaragua v. Colombia* a number of Colombian islands faced Nicaragua's mainland. The ICJ considered the entire coast of Colombia's islands to be relevant, as it generated entitlements overlapping with those generated by Nicaragua's mainland.[29] Although Judge Abraham criticised the Court for the manner in which it delimited the boundary, he seemed to agree that entire coast of Colombia's islands was relevant.[30] Similarly, in *Libya/Malta* the island of Malta faced Libya's mainland. However, the ICJ considered that only Malta's southern coast was relevant,[31] which is *prima facie* inconsistent with the solution adopted in *Nicaragua v. Colombia*. However, the two cases can be seen to be different. In *Libya/Malta* the presence of Italy's maritime entitlements north of Malta prevailed over Libya's entitlements in the same area, while in *Nicaragua v. Colombia* no other state had maritime entitlements east of Colombia's islands and within 200 nm of Nicaragua's mainland. The *Libya/Malta* and *Nicaragua v. Colombia* judgments are also consistent with the decision in *Jan Mayen*. In *Jan Mayen*, the parties' coasts lay more than 200 nm apart, which justified not considering Jan Mayen's eastern coast as relevant.[32]

---

[26] *Land and Maritime Boundary between Cameroon and Nigeria (Cameroon v. Nigeria; Equatorial Guinea intervening)* (Merits) [2002] ICJ Rep 303, 442 [291].
[27] Ibid.
[28] Weil (n. 17) 68. The direction of coastal projections is discussed in Section III.B below.
[29] *Nicaragua v Colombia* (n. 1) 679–80 [150]–[154];
[30] Ibid. 736 [24]-[25] (Separate Opinion Abraham).
[31] *Continental Shelf (Libya/Malta)* (Judgment) [1985] ICJ Rep 13, 49–50 [67]–[68].
[32] *Maritime Delimitation in the Area between Greenland and Jan Mayen (Denmark v. Norway)* (Judgment) [1993] ICJ Rep 38, 47–8 [18]–[21].

II THE RELEVANT COAST   41

In *Bangladesh v. India*, neither India nor Bangladesh argued that the coast of India's Andaman Islands was relevant. However, the arbitral tribunal held that the projections of the Andaman Islands' coast overlapped with the projections of Bangladesh's coast, and thus considered 'the western coast of the northern half of the island chain' as relevant.[33] In *Bangladesh v. India*, the tribunal decided *motu proprio* that part of the Andaman coast was relevant, which shows its quest for consistency with the basis of title independently of the parties' arguments. Including the coastline of marine bays and inlets within the relevant coast is more controversial, as in relation to the Bay of Fundy in *Gulf of Maine* and to Karkinits'ka Gulf in *Black Sea*.[34]

2 The delimitation of the continental shelf beyond 200 nautical miles

A controversial issue is whether the identification of the relevant coast, and therefore of overlapping coastal projections, is a precondition to delimiting the continental shelf beyond 200 nm. While the basis of title over the EEZ and the continental shelf within 200 nm is distance from the coast, the function of distance from the coast as the basis of title over the continental shelf beyond 200 nm is still debated. For a state to be entitled to sovereign rights beyond 200 nm, international law requires that there be a physical continental margin extending beyond 200 nm from its coast. The existence of that continental margin must be established in accordance with paragraphs 4–8 of Article 76 of the United Nations Convention on the Law of the Sea (UNCLOS).[35] Although the basis of title over the continental shelf beyond 200 nm also incorporates a geomorphological element, the continental shelf's physical existence beyond 200 nm is not in and of itself sufficient for a state to be entitled to sovereign rights beyond 200 nm.[36] Without a coast, there is no continental shelf, and therefore no sovereign rights beyond 200 nm. Accordingly, coastal projections play a role alongside geomorphology, as part of the basis of title over the continental shelf beyond 200 nm. Identifying the relevant coast is thus also important in delimitation beyond 200 nm, as recognised by international tribunals.

---

[33] *Bangladesh v. India* (n. 7) 100–102 [303]–[304].
[34] Section II.B.3 below.
[35] 1833 UNTS 3.
[36] The basis of title over the continental shelf beyond 200 nm is discussed in more detail in Chapter 4, Section III.B below

In *Bangladesh/Myanmar*, ITLOS found that '[n]ot every coast generates entitlements to a continental shelf extending beyond 200 nm'.[37] Implicit in ITLOS's statement was that the coast, and thus its projections, generates maritime entitlements beyond 200 nm. ITLOS's view appears consistent with the notion that under international law there is a single continental shelf.[38] The *Bangladesh v. India* tribunal made similar considerations.[39] *Ghana/Côte d'Ivoire* produced the clearest statement of this approach. The Special Chamber took the view that:

> since there is only one continental shelf, it does not see a basis for distinguishing between projections within 200 nm and those beyond. Accordingly, the coasts of the two Parties are relevant, irrespective of whether an overlap occurs within 200 nm of both coasts, beyond 200 nm of both coasts, or within 200 nm of one and beyond 200 nm of another coast.[40]

However, there appear to be reasons more compelling than the rather simplistic one adopted in the cases mentioned above. In *Libya/Malta*, the ICJ accepted that the basis of title over the EEZ and over the continental shelf within 200 nm is distance from the coast.[41] However, whether distance from the coast is the basis of title over the continental shelf beyond 200 nm is still a matter of contention.[42] As stated above, for a state to be entitled to sovereign rights beyond 200 nm, international law requires that there be a physical continental margin extending beyond 200 nm from its coast, whose existence must be established in accordance with paragraphs 4–8 of Article 76 UNCLOS.

Although the basis of title over the continental shelf beyond 200 nm also incorporates a geomorphological element, the continental shelf's physical existence beyond 200 nm is not in and of itself sufficient for a state to be entitled to sovereign rights beyond 200 nm. Without a coast,

---

[37] *Bangladesh/Myanmar* (n. 8) 114 [439].
[38] Ibid. 96 [361].
[39] *Bangladesh v. India* (n. 7) 99 [299].
[40] *Ghana/Côte d'Ivoire* (n. 7) [373].
[41] The basis of title over the EEZ and over the continental shelf within 200 nm is discussed in more detail in Chapter 4, Section II.A below. The basis of title over the continental shelf beyond 200 nm is discussed in more detail in Chapter 4, Section III.B below.
[42] B Kunoy, 'A Geometric Variable Scope of Delimitations: The Impact of a Geological and Geomorphological Title to the Outer Continental Shelf' (2006) 11 *Austrian RIEL* 49; N Marques Antunes, 'Entitlement to Maritime Zones and their Delimitation – In the Doldrums of Uncertainty and Unpredictability' in A Oude Elferink et al. (eds.), *Maritime Boundary Delimitation – The Case Law: is it Consistent and Predictable?* (CUP, 2018) 62, 66–9.

there is no continental shelf, and therefore no sovereign rights beyond 200 nm. Moreover, under Article 76(5) the points on the continental shelf's outer limit, defined according to paragraph 4, 'either shall not exceed 350 [nm] from the baselines from which the breadth of the territorial sea is measured or shall not exceed 100 [nm] from the 2,500 metre isobath'. Article 76(6) also provides that 'on submarine ridges, the outer limit of the continental shelf shall not exceed 350 [nm] from the baselines from which the breadth of the territorial sea is measured'. Both paragraphs 5 and 6 of Article 76 UNCLOS define the maximum extent of a state's rights over the continental shelf beyond 200 nm by reference to distance from the territorial sea baselines, which, under ordinary circumstances, coincide with the coast.[43] It emerges from a reading of the relevant provisions of UNCLOS that distance from the coast plays a role alongside geomorphology as the basis of title over the continental shelf beyond 200 nm. This would suggest that the identification of the relevant coast should also be seen to be an element of the delimitation process for establishing maritime boundaries in the continental shelf beyond 200 nm. This view is further confirmed by the fact that, according to a recent study, paragraphs 5–6 of Article 76 UNCLOS could be considered to be part of customary international law,[44] and, as a consequence, also bind states which are not parties to UNCLOS.

As the basis of title over the EEZ and the continental shelf within 200 nm, and as an element of the basis of title over the continental shelf beyond 200 nm, the relevant coast is central in delimiting all such maritime zones. International tribunals have recognised the centrality of the relevant coast, but have been more uncertain in identifying the relevant coast in practice.

B Identifying the Relevant Coast

Although international tribunals agree on the definition of the relevant coast, a number of problematic issues arise concerning the identification of that coast in practice. This section, devoted to the analysis of these

---

[43] Under Art. 5 UNCLOS, '[e]xcept where otherwise provided in this Convention, the normal baseline for measuring the breadth of the territorial sea is the low-water line along the coast'. The most common exception to the ordinary baseline along the coast is the so-called straight baselines envisaged under Art. 7 UNCLOS. On straight baselines and the relevant coast, see Section II.B.2 below.

[44] KA Baumaert, 'The Outer Limits of the Continental Shelf under Customary International Law' (2017) 111 *AJIL* 827, 857.

issues, discusses suggestions made by scholars and approaches adopted by international tribunals in that respect.

1 The most distant base points as end-points of the relevant coast

A stretch of coast is relevant to delimitation if its seaward projections overlap with the seaward projections of another state's coast. This definition seems to convey an objective standard for determining which part of a state's coast is relevant. However, identifying the relevant coast does not appear to be entirely objective. With little discussion, international tribunals typically justify their decisions only by stating that the seaward projections of the coast identified as relevant overlap with the seaward projections of a neighbouring state's coast also identified as relevant.

In determining Bangladesh's relevant coast, the *Bangladesh v. India* tribunal justified its decision by reference to the parties' agreement that the entire coast was relevant.[45] With respect to India's relevant coast, the tribunal redundantly found 'the Indian coast to be relevant to the extent that its projection generates any overlap with the projection generated by the coast of Bangladesh'.[46] It subsequently specified which parts of India's coast were relevant.[47] Similarly, in *Bangladesh/Myanmar*, ITLOS first held that 'the whole of the coast of Bangladesh is relevant for delimitation purposes, generating projections seaward that overlap with projections from the coast of Myanmar'.[48] ITLOS then found that 'the coast of Myanmar from its land boundary terminus with Bangladesh to Cape Negrais is to be regarded as Myanmar's relevant coast',[49] since 'the coast of Myanmar from the terminus of its land boundary with Bangladesh to Cape Negrais does ... generate projections that overlap projections from Bangladesh's coast'.[50] International tribunals seem to conceal their circular reasoning on the identification of the relevant coast both behind the reiteration of the definition of relevant coast, and behind the statement that its identification is objective. However, international tribunals ought to set forth more fully the legal bases on which the identification of the relevant coast rests.

---

[45] *Bangladesh v. India* (n. 7) 93 [285]–[286].
[46] Ibid. 99 [299].
[47] Ibid. 99–102 [299]–[305].
[48] *Bangladesh/Myanmar* (n. 8) 59 [201].
[49] Ibid. 59 [203].
[50] ibid.

II THE RELEVANT COAST

If delimitation takes place between adjacent states, both states' relevant coast begins at the land boundary terminus, thus the issue is to identify the end-points of their relevant coast.[51] Finding the relevant coast's end-points is similarly an issue between opposite states, especially if the coasts abut the open sea, as in *Jan Mayen*, and not an enclosed or semi-enclosed sea, as in *Nicaragua v. Colombia*.[52] Scholars suggested that base points could be used to identify the extreme points of the parties' relevant coast.[53] Writing extra-judicially, Judge Cot stated that base points 'may be used to calculate the respective length of the relevant coasts of the parties'.[54] Moreover, according to Evans:

> [t]he use of equidistance will spawn a number of points which control the generation of that line seaward. The relevant coastal lengths are, in effect, the distance from the land boundary to the most distant controlling points in each direction, a point made by the Court in the *Libya/Malta* and the *Jan Mayen* cases. Any coastline beyond these points is, for the purposes of generating the delimitation line, irrelevant.[55]

Evans's argument raises a number of issues. Evans seems to suggest that, in *Libya/Malta* and *Jan Mayen*, the ICJ held that the relevant coast was to be specifically identified by reference to the most distant base points.

However, these judgments do not seem to support this inference. In *Libya/Malta*, the Court stated that the equidistance line was to be controlled 'only by points between Ras il-Qaws and Benghisa Point on the southwestern coast of the island of Malta'.[56] Nothing was said on the relevant coast itself, as the Court simply selected the base points for constructing the equidistance line. In *Jan Mayen*, the Court noted that:

> the selection of points G and H, which define the extent of the Greenland coastline used by Denmark for comparison with the length of the coast of

---

[51] *Costa Rica v. Nicaragua* presented a so far unique situation, in which an international tribunal found the relevant coast to be split in two separate segments. See *Costa Rica v. Nicaragua* (n. 7) 210 [181].

[52] In the latter scenario, the existence of shorter coastlines and established boundaries with third states will generally indicate the extreme points of the parties' relevant coast.

[53] On base points and the construction of an equidistance line, see Chapter 4, Section IV below.

[54] J-P Cot, 'The Dual Function of Base Points' in H Hestermeyer et al. (eds.), *Coexistence, Cooperation and Solidarity – Liber Amicorum Rüdiger Wolfrum* (Martinus Nijhoff, 2012) 807, 808.

[55] Evans, 'Maritime Boundary Delimitation: Where Do We Go From Here?' (n. 11) 154. For a critique of using base points in order to identify the relevant coast, see also Oude Elferink (n. 13) 193–6.

[56] *Libya/Malta* (n. 31) 51 [70].

> Jan Mayen, is not arbitrary. Point H is the point on the Greenland coast which determines, in conjunction with the appropriate point on the northern tip of Jan Mayen (point E), the equidistance line at its point of intersection with the Danish 200-mile line (point A). Similarly, point G is the point on the Greenland coast which determines, in conjunction with the southern tip of Jan Mayen (point F), the equidistance line at its point of intersection (point D) with the 200-mile line claimed by Iceland which the Parties have agreed to be the southern limit of the delimitation requested of the Court.[57]

Similarly to *Libya/Malta*, in *Jan Mayen* the Court did not state that the relevant coast ran between the most distant base points. In both cases, the geography of the delimitation area suggested that the most distant base points could be used as the end-points of the relevant coast. However, nothing would have prevented the ICJ from choosing different base points to draw the equidistance line. The Court was compelled to choose the end-points of the relevant coast as base points both by the relationship of oppositeness between Libya and Malta and between Greenland and Jan Mayen, and by the small size of Malta and Jan Mayen in comparison with, respectively, Libya and Greenland.

Evans's argument seems unconvincing also in the light of the more recent cases. In *Nicaragua v. Colombia* the ICJ decided that Nicaragua's entire Caribbean coast was relevant, except for a short stretch near Punta de Perlas.[58] At the same time, it held that the equidistance line would be controlled, on Nicaragua's side, by two base points on Little Corn Island and Great Corn Island, which did not coincide with the extreme points of Nicaragua's relevant coast. In *Bangladesh/Myanmar* ITLOS decided that 'the whole of the coast of Bangladesh is relevant for delimitation purposes'.[59] ITLOS 'measured [Bangladesh's coast] in two straight lines':[60]

> the first line from a point on Bangladesh's coast on Mandabaria Island near the land boundary terminus with India, which was used by Myanmar as a base point (ß2) for the construction of its proposed equidistance line..., to a point on Kutubdia Island [and] [t]he second line... from the said point on Kutubdia Island to the land boundary terminus with Myanmar in the Naaf River.[61]

---

[57] *Jan Mayen* (n. 32) 47–8 [20].
[58] *Nicaragua v. Colombia* (n. 1) 678 [145].
[59] *Bangladesh/Myanmar* (n. 8) 59 [201].
[60] Ibid.
[61] Ibid. 59 [202].

On Myanmar's side, ITLOS determined that 'the coast of Myanmar from its land boundary terminus with Bangladesh to Cape Negrais is to be regarded as Myanmar's relevant coast'.[62] When selecting the base points for constructing the equidistance line, ITLOS chose the end-point of Bangladesh's relevant coast, identified as ß2. However, ITLOS did not choose Cape Negrais, the extreme point of Myanmar's relevant coast, as a base point.[63] The *Bangladesh v. India* tribunal made a similar decision in selecting neither end-point of either party's relevant coast as a base point to construct the equidistance line.[64] Neither the Special Chamber in *Ghana/Côte d'Ivoire*, nor the ICJ in *Costa Rica v. Nicaragua*, identified the relevant coast based on the base points for constructing the provisional equidistance line.[65]

The end-points of the relevant coast need not necessarily be the most distant base points to construct an equidistance line. The relevant coast is the one that generates maritime entitlements overlapping with those of a neighbouring state. Nothing in this definition suggests that the end-points of the parties' relevant coasts must be used to establish an equidistance line. While they could be used for that purpose, international tribunals follow a number of principles in choosing appropriate base points to trace an equidistance line, none of which is that the extreme points of the parties' relevant coasts are necessarily appropriate.[66] Moreover, arguing that base points determine the relevant coast puts the cart before the horses. In judicial decisions on maritime delimitation, the selection of base points is a step that follows the identification of the relevant coast.[67] Logically, it appears that selecting which part of a state's coast generates maritime entitlements which, by overlapping with the maritime entitlements of another state, raise the need for delimitation, should precede the first step of the process by means of which a boundary is established. From this perspective, base points may only be selected on

---

[62] Ibid. 59 [203].
[63] Ibid. 73 [266].
[64] *Bangladesh v. India* (n. 7) 93 [285]–[286], 99–102 [299]–[305] and 120 [365]–[366]. On India's side, the arbitral tribunal added one more base point for the construction of the equidistance line beyond 200 nm, but this point did not coincide with the extreme point of India's relevant coast. See ibid. 156–8 [459]–[463].
[65] *Ghana/Côte d'Ivoire* (n. 7) [372]–[380]; *Costa Rica v. Nicaragua* (n. 7) 184 [111]–[114] and 210 [179]–[181].
[66] Chapter 4, Section IV below.
[67] Ibid.

an already-identified relevant coast. It would be erroneous to choose the appropriate base points and, by reference to them, identify the relevant coast. It is the construction of an equidistance line that is a function of the relevant coast, not the reverse.

The issue arises as to why it is conceivable that international tribunals should select the most distant points controlling an equidistance line as the end of a relevant coast. The reason seems to be eminently pragmatic. International tribunals delimit boundaries following the parties' written and oral arguments, in which states indicate which base points they consider to be appropriate for constructing an equidistance line. However, as held by the ICJ in *Black Sea*, '[i]n ... the delimitation of the maritime areas involving two or more States, the Court should not base itself solely on the choice of base points made by one of those Parties'.[68] By contrast, '[t]he Court must, when delimiting the continental shelf and [EEZ], select base points by reference to the physical geography of the relevant coasts'.[69] While international tribunals may be persuaded by the parties' arguments to select certain base points instead of others, they retain a measure of discretion in that regard. Such discretion should be exercised with a view to respecting the logic of the delimitation process, which requires the construction of an equidistance line to follow the identification of the relevant coast.

2   The approximation of the relevant coast by means of straight lines

The objectivity deficit in determining the relevant coast also emerges in the international tribunals' tendency sometimes to approximate its length by means of straight lines drawn between points on the coast. International tribunals carry out this approximation prior to establishing an equidistance line, and while this operation does not take place in all cases, it is not uncommon. In *Black Sea* and in *Nicaragua v. Colombia*, the ICJ did not approximate the length of the relevant coast, but calculated its length along its natural configuration.[70] Conversely, in cases such as *Jan Mayen*, *Bangladesh/Myanmar* and *Bangladesh v. India*, international tribunals did not follow the coast's natural configuration, but calculated its length by reference to straight lines approximating the general direction of the coast. For example, in *Bangladesh/Myanmar*

---

[68] *Black Sea* (n. 1) 108 [137].
[69] Ibid.
[70] *Nicaragua v. Colombia* (n. 1) 681 (map); *Black Sea* (n. 1) 94 (map).

ITLOS held that '[t]o avoid difficulties caused by the complexity and sinuosity of [Bangladesh's] coast, it should be measured in two straight lines'. Accordingly, ITLOS traced such lines:

> [f]rom a point on Bangladesh's coast on Mandabaria Island near the land boundary terminus with India ... to a point on Kutubdia Island .... The second line extends from the said point on Kutubdia Island to the land boundary terminus with Myanmar in the Naaf River.[71]

With reference to Myanmar's relevant coast, ITLOS found that:

> Myanmar's relevant coast should also be measured by two lines so as to avoid difficulties caused by the sinuosity of the coast and to ensure consistency in measuring the respective coasts of the Parties. The first line is measured from the land boundary terminus in the Naaf River to Bhiff Cape and the second line from this point to Cape Negrais.[72]

The *Bangladesh v. India* arbitral tribunal adopted ITLOS's approach. First, it decided that Bangladesh's relevant coast was to be approximated using the same lines ITLOS had traced in *Bangladesh/Myanmar*;[73] second, it found that India's relevant coast ran along four straight lines connecting the land boundary terminus, a point near the city of Balasore, Maipura Point, Devi Point and Sandy Point.[74]

International tribunals exercise a large measure of discretion both in deciding whether to approximate the relevant coast, and how to effect that approximation. Consequently, the result of exercising such discretion does not always yield consistent results. For example, in *Costa Rica v. Nicaragua* the ICJ found that '[s]ince in the Pacific Ocean the coast of Costa Rica is characterized by a certain degree of sinuosity ... the Court considers it appropriate to identify the relevant coast of both Parties by means of straight lines'.[75] However, Costa Rica's Pacific coast appears to be much

---

[71] *Bangladesh/Myanmar* (n. 8) 59 [202].
[72] Ibid. 59 [204].
[73] *Bangladesh v. India* (n. 7) 93 [285]–[286].
[74] Ibid. 99–102 [299]–[305]. Other cases in which international tribunals approximated the parties' relevant coasts using straight lines are *Continental Shelf (Tunisia/Libya)* (Judgment) [1982] ICJ Rep 18, 91 [131]; *Delimitation of the Maritime Boundary in the Gulf of Maine Area (Canada/USA)* (Judgment) [1984] ICJ Rep 246, 335-6 [221]; *Delimitation of Maritime Areas between Canada and France (St. Pierre et Miquelon) (Canada/France)* (1992) XXI RIAA 265, 279–282 [24]–[35]; *Jan Mayen* (n. 32) 47-8 [20]; *Nicaragua v. Honduras* (n. 21) 749 [296]–[298]; *Costa Rica v. Nicaragua* (n. 7) 210 [179]–[181].
[75] *Costa Rica v. Nicaragua* (n. 7) 210 [179]. The Court found it unnecessary to approximate the parties' Caribbean coast by means of straight lines, see ibid. 184 [114].

less sinuous than the coasts of Bangladesh and of Myanmar. Moreover, while numerous islands and low-tide elevations fringing the coasts of Bangladesh and Myanmar make it arduous to measure the relevant coast along its natural configuration, hardly any islands exist off the Pacific coast of Costa Rica. The Court's choice to approximate the parties' relevant coast in the Pacific Ocean by using straight lines does not seem consistent with earlier decisions, and thus remains unpersuasive.

Fietta and Cleverly wrote that 'the questions of the measurement of relevant coastal lengths ... is a classic intractable mathematical problem to which there is no correct answer'.[76] The reason for this assessment is that 'the length depends on the scale of measurement: as the scale becomes larger, the coast becomes more detailed, more sinuous, and longer'.[77] Such comments convey that approximating the relevant coast finds its basis not in law, but in the international tribunals' necessity to grapple with the technical aspects of delimitation.

From a legal perspective, approximating the relevant coast raises two main problems. First, approximating is an inherently subjective exercise. The approximation of the relevant coasts prior to establishing an equidistance line could be compared to the approximation of the relevant coasts in drawing an angle-bisector boundary. Establishing an angle-bisector emphasises subjectivity in delimitation, as it requires the complexity of a coast to be reduced to a single straight line.[78] The same could be said of approximating the relevant coasts of two states party to a delimitation case. The subjectivity in approximating the relevant coast would also affect the subsequent stages of the delimitation process. Because coastal length disparity as a relevant circumstance entails comparing the length of the parties' relevant coast,[79] approximating the parties' coast could have a great impact on whether comparing coastal lengths shows a marked disparity on the basis of which an equidistance line could be adjusted. Disproportionality also entails comparing the length of the relevant coasts. Approximating their length by using straight lines could impact on the result of a disproportionality test as the third stage of the delimitation process.[80]

[76] Fietta and Cleverly (n. 12) 51.
[77] Ibid.
[78] With reference to the approximation of the coasts in drawing an angle-bisector line, Cottier wrote that '[i]dentifying the straight lines on each state's coast calls for the exercise of judgment in assessing the actual coastal geography'. See T Cottier, *Equitable Principles of Maritime Boundary Delimitation* (CUP, 2015) 192.
[79] Coastal length disparity as a relevant circumstance is discussed in Chapter 5, Section II.B below.
[80] Disproportionality is discussed in Chapter 6 below.

II THE RELEVANT COAST

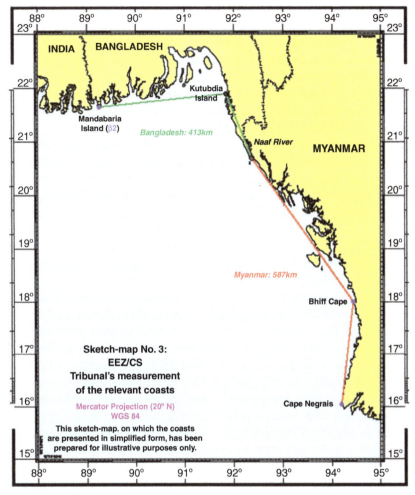

Figure 3.1   The relevant coast in *Bangladesh/Myanmar*
Source: [2012] ITLOS Rep 60

Second, the relevant coast is defined as the coast whose seaward projections overlap with the seaward coastal projections of another state. Approximating the relevant coast to straight lines seems to contradict this definition. The coast itself, and not straight lines connecting a number of points on such a coast, generates maritime entitlements that, by overlapping with those of a neighbouring state, require delimitation. In order to ensure consistency with the basis of title, the relevant coast should be measured by reference to the low-water mark, following and not discounting its natural configuration. Applying such a method for measuring the length of the relevant coast entails varying degrees of difficulty for international tribunals, depending on the complexity of the coast. If the coast is relatively smooth, international tribunals can easily measure its length along the low-water line. International tribunals could use a high-scale map, as it could adequately portray the coast's limited sinuosity. This was the case in *Black Sea* and in *Nicaragua* v. *Colombia*, in which the ICJ did not approximate the coast using straight lines.

By contrast, if the coast has numerous indentations, measuring its length becomes more difficult, and high-scale maps might be insufficient. In *Bangladesh/Myanmar* and *Bangladesh* v. *India*, the coast of the parties, or at least part of it, was deeply indented and cut into. In such cases, international tribunals are in the awkward position of having to choose between using small-scale maps, which ensures the accurate measurement of the relevant coast but might be time-consuming, or approximating the relevant coast, which seems to lower consistency with the basis of title but is less time-consuming.

A solution could be to identify the relevant coast by reference to straight baselines. As explained above, the approximation of the relevant coast is likely to take place when a coast is indented and cut into. However, in the presence of such a coast, Article 7 UNCLOS allows a state to establish a straight-baseline system. Under Article 7(1) UNCLOS, '[i]n localities where the coastline is deeply indented and cut into, or if there is a fringe of islands along the coast in its immediate vicinity, the method of straight baselines joining appropriate points may be employed in drawing the baseline from which the breadth of the territorial sea is measured'. Where straight baselines are in place, the breadth of the territorial sea is measured from points on such baselines, and the waters landward of such baselines are subject to the regime of internal waters.[81] Straight baselines thus become a state's 'legal coast', by reference to which the outer limits of all maritime zones are drawn,[82] as opposed to its 'natural coast', which follows the coastline in all its indentations. In the delimitation process, international tribunals establish coastal projections by reference to the 'natural coast'. However, straight baselines could be considered to be the legal representation of a state's coast, provided that the conditions for their establishment are met.

---

[81] This could be inferred from Art. 7(3) UNCLOS, under which 'the sea areas lying within the lines must be sufficiently closely linked to the land domain to be subject to the regime of internal waters'. See also VD Degan, 'Internal Waters' (1986) 17 *Netherlands YBIL* 3, 4.
[82] Arts. 3, 57 and 76 UNCLOS.

II THE RELEVANT COAST 53

Where straight baselines are in place, it is their seaward projection that generates maritime entitlements. Consequently, straight baselines could be considered to be the relevant coast for the purposes of delimitation. This solution could apply in the case of a river delta or in any other case in which the coastline is unstable. In accordance with Article 7(2) UNCLOS:

> [w]here because of the presence of a delta and other natural conditions the coastline is highly unstable, the appropriate points [to establish straight baselines] may be selected along the furthest seaward extent of the low-water line and ... the straight baselines shall remain effective until changed by the coastal State in accordance with this Convention.

Since Bangladesh had established straight baselines in 1974[83] and Myanmar in 1977,[84] ITLOS could have approximated the relevant coast by reference to straight baselines in *Bangladesh/Myanmar*, instead of effecting that approximation by means of its own straight lines. However, Bangladesh's objection to Myanmar's straight baselines could have been a reason against using such straight lines to approximate Myanmar's relevant coast.[85] States have objected to the drawing of straight baselines only on twenty-four occasions,[86] and only four of

---

[83] Territorial Waters and Maritime Zones Act 1974, Act No. XXVI of 1974; Notification No LT – I/3/74 of the Ministry of Foreign Affairs (13 April 1974).
[84] Territorial Sea and Maritime Zones Law 1977, Law No. 3 of 9 April 1977 (Annex), as amended by the State Peace and Development Council Law No. 8/2008 of 5 December 2008.
[85] Note verbale concerning the baselines of Myanmar (6 July 2009), (2009) 70 *LoSB* 61.
[86] Statement by Thailand on the Vietnamese claims concerning the so-called historical waters and the drawing of baselines (22 November 1985), (1986) 7 *LoSB* 111–12; Note verbale from Senegal concerning Act No. 2 of 1985 of Guinea-Bissau (2 April 1986), (1986) 8 *LoSB* 24; Note from Singapore on the Vietnamese claims concerning the so-called historical waters and the drawing of baselines (5 December 1986), (1987) 9 *LoSB* 53–54; Protest by the USA with respect to the straight baselines of the Democratic People's Republic of Korea (4 January 1990), (1990) 15 *LoSB* 8; Protest by the USA with respect to the straight baselines of Iran (11 January 1994), (1994) 25 *LoSB* 101–103; Démarche of Germany on behalf of the European Union concerning provisions of Iranian national law not compatible with international law of the sea (11 December 1994), (1996) 30 *LoSB* 60; Note verbale from Germany on behalf of the European Union concerning the straight baselines of Thailand (23 December 1994), (1995) 28 *LoSB* 31; Objections by Vietnam to the statement of 15 May 1996 by the People's Republic of China on the baselines from which the breadth of China's territorial sea is measured (6 June 1996), (1996) 32 *LoSB* 91; Note verbale from Qatar concerning the Act on the Marine Areas of the Islamic Republic of Iran in the Persian Gulf and the Sea of Oman (20 August 1996), (1996) 32 *LoSB* 89–90; Protest by India to the baselines of Pakistan (24 February 1997), (1997) 34 *LoSB* 46; Note from the USA in response to the note of 30 November 1999 from Iran (6 April 2000), (2000) 43 *LoSB* 105–6; Letters from Guatemala concerning the baselines of Honduras (15 June and 23 August 2000), (2000) 12 *LoSIC* 37; Note verbale from Nicaragua concerning the baselines of Honduras

these took place between states later parties to a judicial dispute on maritime delimitation. It appears likely that objections to the establishment of straight baselines would have limited consequences on the approximation of the relevant coast in future cases.

Using straight baselines could have been a feasible approach in *Costa Rica v. Nicaragua*, yet one which the ICJ did not adopt. Costa Rica had objected to Nicaragua's straight baselines in the Caribbean,[87] which could justify the Court's decision to measure the Caribbean relevant coast along its natural configuration. Conversely, since Nicaragua had not challenged Costa Rica's straight baselines in the Pacific Ocean,[88] the Court could have used such baselines to approximate Costa Rica's relevant coast. Nevertheless, Nicaragua never established straight baselines in the Pacific Ocean. One could doubt that Nicaragua's Pacific coast would have met the requirements for straight baselines under Article 7 UNCLOS. If the Court had used Costa Rica's straight baselines in order to approximate its relevant coast in the Pacific, it could not have done the same with respect to Nicaragua's relevant coast in the Pacific. Approximating the relevant coast by reference to straight baselines appears to be feasible only provided that both states have established a straight baseline system, and that neither state has objected to the straight baseline system established by the other state. If such conditions are not satisfied, it seems advisable for international tribunals to measure the relevant coast along its natural configuration.

Fietta and Cleverly are sceptical of using straight baselines to identify the relevant coast. According to them, '[s]traight-line coastal fronts are not to

---

(20 June 2000), (2000) 12 *LoSIC* 37; Note verbale from El Salvador concerning the baselines of Honduras (21 June 2000), (2000) 12 *LoSIC* 37; Statement by India on the baselines of Pakistan (22 May 2001), (2001) 46 *LoSB* 90; Note from Bangladesh concerning the baselines of Myanmar (6 July 2009), (2009) 70 *LoSB* 61; Note from Saudi Arabia concerning the baselines of the United Arab Emirates (9 August 2009), (2010) 71 *LoSB* 47; Note from the United Arab Emirates concerning the baselines of Saudi Arabia (17 November 2011), (2012) 78 *LoSB* 32; Note from the Pakistan concerning the baselines of India (6 December 2011), (2012) 78 *LoSB* 33; Note from Iran concerning the baselines of Saudi Arabia (14 August 2012), (2013) 80 *LoSB* 36; Letter from Costa Rica concerning the baselines of Nicaragua in the Caribbean Sea (23 October 2013), (2014) 83 *LoSB* 42; Letter from Colombia concerning the baselines of Nicaragua in the Caribbean Sea (1 November 2013), (2014) 83 *LoSB* 45; Note from Iran concerning the baselines of Iraq (3 August 2015), (2017) 89 *LoSB* 47; Note from Djibouti concerning the baselines of Somalia (31 January 2017), (2017) 93 *LoSB* 22.

[87] Letter from Costa Rica concerning the baselines of Nicaragua in the Caribbean Sea (23 October 2013), (2014) 83 *LoSB* 42. Nicaragua established straight baselines in Decree No. 33-2013 of 19 August 2013.

[88] Costa Rica established straight baselines in Decree 18581-RE of 14 October 1988.

be confused with artificial constructs such as straight or, especially, archipelagic baselines',[89] since '[i]n identifying the length of a relevant coast ... it is the lengths of the physical coastlines that are key'.[90] This argument is persuasive in relation to archipelagic baselines. Article 47 UNCLOS sets forth a number of requirements for establishing archipelagic baselines, making them a completely artificial construct.[91] In particular, Article 47(2) UNCLOS states that archipelagic baselines should not in principle be longer than 100 nm, which suggests that they are likely not to reflect the geography of the region in which an archipelago is situated.

However, the same cannot be said of straight baselines. Article 7(3) UNCLOS provides that '[t]he drawing of straight baselines must not depart to any appreciable extent from the general direction of the coast'. This means that, in establishing straight baselines, coastal states must pay heed to the general direction of the coast, ensuring that straight baselines reflect that direction. In approximating the relevant coast, international tribunals pursue the same objective. In *North Sea Continental Shelf*, the ICJ stated that the proportionality test requires the comparison between the length of the parties' relevant coast 'measured in the general direction of the coastline'.[92] Although a legal construct, straight baselines could not be said to be wholly artificial, owing to their close relationship with the general direction of the coast. Therefore, they could be used when necessary in order to identify the relevant coast in a delimitation dispute.

Using straight baselines to identify the relevant coast would increase both consistency with the basis of title, and transparency in the delimitation process. The international tribunals' discretion in the approximation of the relevant coast would be limited by the existence of straight baselines already established by the states concerned. However, this solution relies on coastal states establishing straight baselines in conformity with UNCLOS. Under Article 7 UNCLOS, it is the coastal state that may establish straight baselines, while international tribunals may only decide whether the circumstances in which a state established straight baselines

---

[89] Fietta and Cleverly (n. 12) 599.
[90] Ibid.
[91] Under Art. 47(1) and 47(2) UNCLOS, '(1) [a]n archipelagic State may draw straight archipelagic baselines joining the outermost points of the outermost islands and drying reefs of the archipelago provided that within such baselines are included the main islands and an area in which the ratio of the area of the water to the area of the land, including atolls, is between 1 to 1 and 9 to 1. (2) The length of such baselines shall not exceed 100 [nm], except that up to 3 per cent of the total number of baselines enclosing any archipelago may exceed that length, up to a maximum length of 125 [nm].'
[92] *North Sea Continental Shelf* (n. 4) 54 [101(D)(3)].

justified their establishment. In *Qatar v. Bahrain*, Bahrain contended that it was a 'multiple-island State characterized by a cluster of islands off the coast of its main islands',[93] and, accordingly, it was 'entitled to draw a line connecting the outermost islands and low-tide elevations'.[94] The Court found that 'it would be going too far, however, to qualify [such islands] as a fringe of islands along the coast',[95] and therefore held that 'Bahrain is not entitled to apply the method of straight baselines'.[96] The ICJ is also due to decide on the lawfulness of Nicaragua's straight baselines in the Caribbean Sea, as a result of having declared Colombia's fourth counter-claim admissible in its 2017 order in *Alleged Violations of Sovereign Rights and Maritime Spaces in the Caribbean Sea*.[97]

3 The coast of bays and inlets as part of the relevant coast

The lack of objectivity in identifying the relevant coast also emerges in the international tribunals' approach to deciding whether the coast of bays and inlets should be considered to be relevant. This issue specifically arose for decision in *Gulf of Maine* and *Black Sea*.

In *Gulf of Maine*, a Chamber of the ICJ discussed 'whether the Bay of Fundy should be considered to be a part of the Gulf of Maine or whether this bay should be regarded as a closed bay, considered as though it were sealed off by a straight line'.[98] Discussing the disparity in length between the Canadian and US coast, the Chamber held that the US relevant coast ran 'from the elbow of Cape Cod to Cape Ann, from Cape Ann to Cape Elizabeth and from the latter to the international boundary terminus'.[99] The Chamber found that Canada's relevant coast stretched:

> from the ... international boundary to the point on the New Brunswick coast off which there cease to be any waters in the bay more distant than 12 miles from a low-water line ..., then from that point across to the corresponding point on the Nova Scotian coast ..., thence to Brier Island, and from there to Cape Sable.[100]

---

[93] *Maritime Delimitation and Territorial Questions between Qatar and Bahrain (Qatar v. Bahrain)* (Judgment) [2001] ICJ Rep 40, 103 [211].
[94] Ibid.
[95] Ibid. 103 [214]–[215].
[96] Ibid.
[97] *Alleged Violations of Sovereign Rights and Maritime Spaces in the Caribbean Sea (Nicaragua v. Colombia)* (Counter-claims) [2017] ICJ Rep 289, 314–15 [82(A)(4)].
[98] *Gulf of Maine* (n. 74) 268 [31].
[99] Ibid. 336 [221].
[100] Ibid.

II THE RELEVANT COAST

However, with respect to Canada's relevant coast the Chamber added that:

> the fact that the two coasts opposite each other on the Bay of Fundy are both Canadian is not a reason to disregard the fact that the Bay is part of the Gulf of Maine, nor a reason to take only one of these coasts into account for the purpose of calculating the length of the Canadian coasts in the delimitation area. There is no justification for the idea that if a fairly substantial bay opening on to a broader gulf is to be regarded as a part of it, its shores must not all belong to the same State.[101]

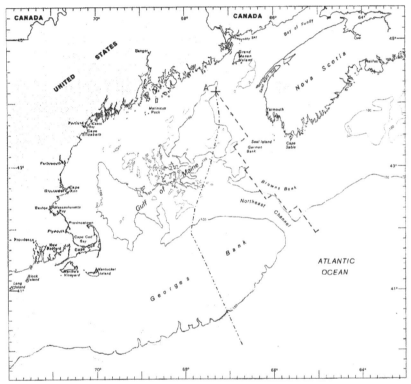

Figure 3.2 The geography of the Gulf of Maine and the Bay of Fundy
Source: [1984] ICJ Rep 289

According to the Chamber, there was no reason not to consider the Bay of Fundy's coast to be relevant. The Chamber compared the Bay of Fundy to the Gulf of Gabes, whose entire coast the ICJ had considered to be

[101] Ibid.

relevant two years earlier in *Tunisia/Libya*.[102] However, this does not seem to support the Chamber's finding to consider only part of the Bay of Fundy's coast to be relevant. It would seem that, since the entire Tunisian coast along the Gulf of Gabes was seen to be relevant, the same should have been done with respect to the Bay of Fundy. The Chamber assimilated the case of the Bay of Fundy to that of the Gulf of Gabes, yet made different findings from those made by the Court in *Tunisia/Libya*.

In his separate opinion, Judge Schwebel criticised the Chamber for holding that the coast of the Bay of Fundy was relevant. By including the Bay of Fundy's coast up to the point where the Bay only contains waters within 12 nm of the low-water mark, the Chamber '[did] not show why this is a determinative ... consideration'.[103] Moreover, Canada had explained that it viewed the Bay of Fundy as Canadian internal waters, which, according to Judge Schwebel, would suggest that it should not be included within the relevant coast.[104] The Bay of Fundy's coast should have thus not been considered to be relevant, and a closing line should have been drawn either from Point Lepreau or from St. John on New Brunswick's coast, to Brier Island in Nova Scotia. The closing line should have been included in the relevant coast. Judge Schwebel gave a number of reasons for his conclusion: first, the Bay of Fundy's coasts did not face the Gulf of Maine, but each other; second, for that reason 'the extension of the remaining, interior segments of the coasts of the Bay of Fundy cannot overlap the extension of the coasts of the United States in the Gulf of Maine area or the area of delimitation in any consequential measure';[105] third, 'to do otherwise and to give full weight to a feature which in this case is so distorting in a calculation of proportionality would be inequitable'.[106]

In *Black Sea*, the problem concerned whether the coast of Karkinits'ka Gulf, situated in Ukraine, was part of the relevant coast. Romania argued that 'the coastline of the Karkinits'ka Gulf, immediately north of the Crimean Peninsula, should not be counted as a relevant coast',[107] since 'such projections as are made by this northern coast are in fact overtaken

---

[102] ibid. The Chamber referred to *Tunisia/Libya* (n. 74) 91 [131].
[103] *Gulf of Maine* (n. 74) 354 (Separate Opinion Schwebel).
[104] Ibid.
[105] Ibid. 355–6.
[106] Ibid.
[107] *Black Sea* (n. 1) 95 [91].

II THE RELEVANT COAST

by the westward projections of the Ukrainian coast from Cape Tarkhankut to Cape Sarych'.[108] Conversely, Ukraine maintained that 'its entire south-facing coast generates "a 200 nautical mile continental shelf/EEZ entitlement that extends well south of the parallel of latitude of the Romanian/Bulgarian border", i.e., projecting into the area subject to delimitation with Romania'.[109]

The Court recalled the two principles governing the identification of the relevant coast: first, 'the land dominates the sea'; second, 'the coast, in order to be considered as relevant for the purpose of the delimitation, must generate projections which overlap with projections from the coast of the other Party'.[110] The Court then immediately held that it:

> cannot accept Ukraine's contention that the coasts of Karkinits'ka Gulf form part of the relevant coast. The coasts of this gulf face each other and their submarine extension cannot overlap with the extensions of Romania's coast. The coasts of Karkinits'ka Gulf do not project in the area to be delimited. Therefore, these coasts are excluded from further consideration by the Court. The coastline of Yahorlyts'ka Gulf and Dnieper Firth is to be excluded for the same reason.[111]

The Court drew a line between Cape Priboiny, in Crimea, to a point east of Zaliznyy port, as the closing line of Karkinits'ka Gulf. The Court, refrained from including:

> this line in the calculation of the total length of the Ukrainian relevant coasts, as the line 'replaces' the coasts of Karkinits'ka Gulf which, again, do not themselves project on the area to be delimited and thus do not generate any entitlement to the continental shelf and the [EEZ] in that area.[112]

No individual opinions were appended to the *Black Sea* judgment. The ICJ's decision in respect of Karkinits'ka Gulf was different from the treatment of the Bay of Fundy in *Gulf of Maine*. In the latter, the Chamber decided that part of the Bay of Fundy's coast was relevant. The Court's approach in *Black Sea* is more similar to the one taken by Judge Schwebel in his separate opinion in *Gulf of Maine*.

---

[108] Ibid.
[109] Ibid. 96 [95].
[110] Ibid. 97 [99].
[111] Ibid. 97 [100].
[112] Ibid.

Figure 3.3 The relevant coast identified by the ICJ in *Black Sea*
Source: [2009] ICJ Rep 94

Neither *Gulf of Maine* nor *Black Sea* are persuasive with respect to the identification of the relevant coast. Canada and Ukraine considered, respectively, the Bay of Fundy and Karkinits'ka Gulf to be internal waters. While Ukraine never explicitly argued that Karkinits'ka Gulf was part of its internal waters, it had deposited with the UN Secretary-General a list of co-ordinates of points to be connected by straight baselines.[113] Since Points 9 and 10 established its closing line, Karkinits'ka Gulf would fall within Ukraine's internal waters. Similarly, straight baselines also closed Yahorlyts'ka Gulf and Dnieper Firth, whose coasts the Court determined not to be relevant.[114]

Owing to Karkinits'ka Gulf being closed by a straight baseline, and thus being part of Ukraine's internal waters, the Court rightly excluded its coast from the relevant coast. However, the Court did not seem justified in excluding the closing line of Karkinits'ka Gulf from the relevant coast. Straight baselines should be considered to be part of the relevant coast, since they are a state's 'legal coast' if the conditions set out in Article 7 UNCLOS are met.[115] Consequently, straight baselines should be deemed to generate coastal projections, which justifies including them in the relevant coast.[116] The Court had not identified the closing line of Karkinits'ka Gulf as a straight baseline, which might explain its decision not to include it in the relevant coast. However, the fact that Ukraine had a straight baseline system in place should have determined the Court's decision to include the closing line of Karkinits'ka Gulf in Ukraine's relevant coast.

In *Gulf of Maine*, Canada stated that it 'maintient pour des raisons historiques son droit de traiter les eaux de la baie de Fundy comme des eaux intérieures'.[117] However, Canada admitted that it had never adopted 'des lignes de base droites pour délimiter la baie de Fundy à cet effet'.[118] The Bay of Fundy's situation was more complex than that of Karkinits'ka Gulf in *Black Sea*, as Canada had never drawn a straight baseline separating the Bay of Fundy from the Gulf of Maine.[119] The Chamber could

---

[113] 'List of the Geographical Co-ordinates of the Points defining the Position of the Baselines for Measuring the Width of the Territorial Waters, Economic Zone and Continental Shelf of the Black Sea', (1998) 36 *LoSB* 49. Ukraine's government identified such co-ordinates pursuant to Art. 5 of the Statute concerning the State Frontier of 4 November 1991, (1994) 25 *LoSB* 84. Romania established straight baselines in the Act concerning the Legal Regime of the Internal Waters, the Territorial Sea and the Contiguous Zone of Romania of 7 August 1990, (1991) 19 *LoSB* 9. Neither state objected to the other state's straight baselines.
[114] *Black Sea* (n. 1) 97 [100].
[115] Section II.B.2 above.
[116] Ibid.
[117] *Delimitation of the Maritime Boundary in the Gulf of Maine Area (Canada/USA)*, vol VII, Oral Proceedings (concluded), 133 (Malintoppi).
[118] Ibid.
[119] To date, Canada has not drawn a straight baseline across the Bay of Fundy.

not have relied on pre-existing straight baselines, including them as part of Canada's relevant coast. However, the Chamber could have used the closing line drawn by Canada for fishery purposes.[120] Judge Schwebel's views seem consistent with the Bay of Fundy's character as internal waters. However, he reached a convincing decision for unconvincing reasons, as did the Chamber in *Gulf of Maine* and the Court in *Black Sea*.

Neither the Chamber in *Gulf of Maine*, nor the Court in *Black Sea*, took into account the internal waters character of the Bay of Fundy and Karkinits'ka Gulf as decisive in identifying the relevant coast. Assuming that neither the Bay of Fundy, nor Karkinits'ka Gulf were internal waters, the decisions in *Gulf of Maine* and in *Black Sea* would be problematic nonetheless. Excluding the coasts of the Bay of Fundy and of Karkinits'ka Gulf from the relevant coast was based, both in *Gulf of Maine* and in *Black Sea*, on their seaward projections not overlapping with those of the other state party to the dispute. However, this reason is unpersuasive. Coasts generate maritime entitlements radially, not frontally,[121] which means that '[l]a projection de la souveraineté territoriale à travers l'ouverture côtière s'effectue dans toutes les directions'.[122] Conversely, frontal projection entails that 'les côtes se projettent uniquement dans la direction à laquelle elles font face, c'est-à-dire perpendiculairement à la direction générale de la façade maritime, et cette projection s'effectue sur la largueur correspondant à la largueur de la façade maritime'.[123] As discussed below, international tribunals seem consistent in upholding the principle of radial projection.[124]

However, in *Black Sea* the Court found that '[t]he coasts of this gulf face each other and their submarine extension cannot overlap with the extensions of Romania's coast'.[125] This finding appears to conflict with the radial projection principle. The Court emphasised that the coasts of Karkinits'ka Gulf 'face each other', thus implicitly meaning that the projections of such coasts overlap only with each other and not with

---

[120] *Gulf of Maine*, Oral Proceedings (n. 117) 133.
[121] Radial projections and frontal projections are discussed in more detail in Section III.B below.
[122] Weil (n. 17) 68.
[123] *St. Pierre et Miquelon* (n. 74) 304 [9] (Dissenting Opinion Weil).
[124] Section III.B below. The only case in which an international tribunal adopted frontal projections was *St. Pierre et Miquelon*.
[125] *Black Sea* (n. 1) 97 [100].

II THE RELEVANT COAST

those of Romania's coast. It would have been consistent with the radial projection principle to consider the coast of Karkinits'ka Gulf to be relevant. The Court referred to the same reason to exclude the coast of Nicoya Gulf from the Pacific relevant coast in *Costa Rica* v. *Nicaragua*, in which the Court noted that 'the coasts of Nicoya Gulf face each other'.[126] The Court's decision was correct, since the radial projections of Nicaragua's coast would not have generated entitlements inside Nicoya Gulf. However, the reason adduced by the Court is unconvincing for the same reasons which make the Court's approach to the coast of Karkinits'ka Gulf in *Black Sea* unconvincing.

Similarly to *Black Sea*, the Chamber's finding in *Gulf of Maine* that only part of the coast of the Bay of Fundy was relevant is not in full accordance with the principle of radial projection. While in *Gulf of Maine* the Chamber apparently upheld the principle of radial projection by recognising that part of the Bay of Fundy's coast was relevant, it did not find that entire coast to be relevant. The Chamber should have found that the entire coast of the Bay of Fundy was relevant, since the entitlements generated by it overlapped with the entitlements generated by the US coast. The Chamber drew a distinction: on one hand, it identified an inner part of the Bay of Fundy, whose coast only generated entitlements to a territorial sea and were thus not relevant to delimiting the EEZ and continental shelf; on the other hand, it identified an outer part of the Bay of Fundy, whose coasts were more than 24 nm apart and generated EEZ and continental shelf entitlements, and were thus relevant.[127] However, this distinction seems artificial. Although it relies on the frontal projection principles, it is inconsistent with that very principle, as it does not recognise that the north-western coast of the Bay of Fundy generated frontal maritime entitlements overlapping with those generated by the US coast. Moreover, a point on a coast generates maritime entitlements both within and beyond 12 nm.

The same could be said with respect to the treatment of Karkinits'ka Gulf in *Black Sea*. Differently from *Gulf of Maine*, in *Black Sea* the Court did not distinguish between an inner and an outer part of Karkinits'ka Gulf. Perhaps, the Court excluded the northern and southern coasts of Karkinits'ka Gulf because their maritime entitlements overlapped primarily with each other, and thus cancelled each other out and became irrelevant to the delimitation with Romania. However, this reasoning

---

[126] *Costa Rica* v. *Nicaragua* (n. 7) 210 [181].
[127] *Gulf of Maine* (n. 74) 336 [211].

does not seem justified. Presumably, the Court noticed that, if the coast of Karkinits'ka Gulf had been considered to be relevant, the coast of Ukraine would have considerably increased in length. This would have made it more difficult not to find a marked coastal length disparity, which might have required adjusting the equidistance line at relevant circumstances stage.[128] Yet, the Court should avoid pre-empting the finding that a marked coastal length disparity may or may not exist by selecting only certain parts of the coast as relevant before even plotting an equidistance line. In order to respect the logic of the three-stage delimitation process, international tribunals should assess coastal length disparity, a relevant circumstance, only after they have objectively identified the relevant coast and the relevant area, and after they have established an equidistance line.

Nor should the Court exclude the coast of marine inlets from being relevant because other segments of coast considered to be relevant subsume the coastal projections of such inlets. In *Black Sea*, this argument was suggested by Romania, which contended that the coastal projections of Karkinits'ka Gulf were 'overtaken by the westward projections of the Ukrainian coast from Cape Tarkhankut to Cape Sarych'.[129] If this line of argument were accepted, one could convincingly contend that the relevant coast could, in certain cases, be reduced to a single point. Pursuant to the radial projection principle, a single point on a state's coast generates maritime entitlements within a 200-nm radius. Accepting that a stretch of coast is not relevant because its projections are 'overtaken' by the projections of other stretches of coast would entail that a single point could create the entirety of a state's maritime entitlements. This is especially true of enclosed and semi-enclosed seas, such as the Black Sea or the Caribbean Sea. This argument is clearly incorrect, as it would nullify the function of the coast as the origin of maritime entitlements.

One could argue that excluding part of the coast from being relevant, especially if the coast is the one of marine inlets, could be necessary to achieve an equitable solution under Articles 74 and 83 UNCLOS. Judge Schwebel's third reason to exclude the Bay of Fundy's coast from the relevant coast was that 'to do otherwise and to give full weight to a feature which in this case is so distorting in a calculation of proportionality would be inequitable'.[130] However, this argument is unpersuasive.

---

[128] On relevant circumstances, see Chapter 5 below.
[129] *Black Sea* (n. 1) 95 [91].
[130] *Gulf of Maine* (n. 74) 356 (Separate Opinion Schwebel).

The three-stage approach to delimitation allows international tribunals to assess the equitableness of an equidistance line at its second and third stages, by reference to relevant circumstances and to the absence of disproportionality.[131] These two stages allow international tribunals to consider whether an equidistance line is equitable: first, the existence of great coastal length disparity is an established relevant circumstance; second, the disproportionality test entails a comparison between the length of the relevant coast and the relevant area allocated to each state. The three-stage approach gives international tribunals adequate scope to take stock of the relationship between the relevant coasts, and to adjust an equidistance line on account of a marked disparity between them. It is thus unsound to pre-empt such adjustments by excluding parts of relevant coasts at the start of the delimitation process.

III The Relevant Area

This section analyses the concept of the relevant area, and examines the identification of the relevant area with reference to the direction of coastal projections and to the limit of the relevant area which can be derived from existing rules of international law.

A *The Concept of the Relevant Area*

This section discusses whether international tribunals have produced an established definition of 'relevant area', and the impact of coastal configuration on the judicial determination of the relevant area.

1 The elusive definition of the relevant area

The relevant area is connected to the relevant coast, which is the section of two neighbouring states' coast whose seaward projections overlap.[132] Similarly, the relevant area should be the maritime space where the entitlements generated by the relevant coast overlap. However, the

---

[131] The ICJ stated that relevant circumstances are 'every particular fact or of the case which might suggest an adjustment or shifting of the median line provisionally drawn', and that the 'aim in each and every situation must be to achieve "an equitable result"'. See *Jan Mayen* (n. 32) 62 [54]. Concerning disproportionality, the ICJ held that '[a] final check for an equitable outcome entails a confirmation that no great disproportionality of maritime areas is evident by comparison to the ratio of coastal lengths'. See *Black Sea* (n. 1) 103 [122].

[132] Section II.A above.

international tribunals' jurisprudence is unclear as to whether the relevant area only covers two states' overlapping entitlements, or whether it is larger, also encompassing spaces where no entitlements overlap. International tribunals have named the maritime spaces in which delimitation takes place in various ways: 'area of overlapping potential entitlement',[133] 'area of overlapping entitlements',[134] 'area of overlap of the extensions of the territories of the two Parties',[135] 'area of overlapping claims'[136] and 'area of overlapping projections'.[137] International tribunals have also mentioned the 'relevant area',[138] as well as the 'delimitation area'.[139]

There are discrepancies in the international tribunals' understanding of the concept of relevant area. For instance, ITLOS found it to be 'the area of overlapping entitlements of the Parties that is relevant to this delimitation'.[140] In *Nicaragua v. Colombia*, the ICJ stated that the relevant area comprises 'that part of the maritime space in which the potential entitlements of the parties overlap'.[141] On one hand, the ICJ saw the relevant area as defined by the overlap between the parties' *potential* maritime entitlements, which may be seen as a reference to the parties' claims. On the other hand, ITLOS understood the relevant area to be defined by the overlap between the parties' *actual* maritime entitlements.

In *Jan Mayen*, the ICJ suggested that there exist three different marine areas within the wider area within which maritime boundaries are to be delimited: the area of overlapping claims, the area of overlapping entitlements and the relevant area.[142] While each is a distinct concept designating distinct marine areas, nothing prevents two or all three of these areas from coinciding. After *Jan Mayen*, international tribunals seem not to

---

[133] *Nicaragua v. Colombia* (n. 1) 678 [145]; *Jan Mayen* (n. 32) 47 [19].
[134] *Bangladesh/Myanmar* (n. 8) 105 [397].
[135] *Tunisia/Libya* (n. 74) 62 [75].
[136] *Maritime Boundary Arbitration (Barbados v. Trinidad and Tobago)* (2006) XVII RIAA 147, 214 [239]; *Jan Mayen* (n. 32) 47 [18].
[137] *Bangladesh v. India* (n. 7) 97 [295].
[138] Ibid. 102-103 [306]-[311]; *Peru v. Chile* (n. 9) 69 [193]; *Nicaragua v. Colombia* (n. 1) 682-6 [155]-[166]; *Bangladesh/Myanmar* (n. 8) 123 [477]; *Black Sea* (n. 1) 99-100 [110]-[114]; *Guyana v. Suriname* (n. 8) 109 [392]; *Jan Mayen* (n. 32) 47 [20]; *Libya/Malta* (n. 31) 51 [70]; *Gulf of Maine* (n. 74) 185 [323]; *Tunisia/Libya* (n. 74) 82 [114].
[139] *Bangladesh/Myanmar* (n. 8) 87 [323]; *Black Sea* (n. 1) 100 [113]; *Qatar v. Bahrain* (n. 94) 91 [169]; *Gulf of Maine* (n. 74) 272-8 [39]-[59].
[140] *Bangladesh/Myanmar* (n. 8) 123 [477].
[141] *Nicaragua v. Colombia* (n. 1) 683 [159].
[142] *Jan Mayen* (n. 32) 47-8 [18]-[21].

have employed this tripartite distinction explicitly in their judicial decisions.

The notions of area of overlapping claims and of area of overlapping entitlements are largely self-explanatory. The former designates the marine area in which the claims of the two parties overlap. Consequently, its limits are defined based on the parties' claimed boundaries: the area enclosed between the boundary proposed by one state and the boundary proposed by the other state denotes the area of overlapping claims. The latter is the marine area in which the entitlements generated by the coasts of neighbouring states overlap. Its existence is the precondition to delimitation.[143] Entitlements over marine areas are generated by land territory abutting the sea, as a radial function of distance from the coast.[144] The area of overlapping entitlements may be larger than the area of overlapping claims, as in most instances states do not, or cannot, claim a boundary extending to 200 nm from their coast *vis-à-vis* another state. In *Jan Mayen*, the area of overlapping claims was enclosed between Greenland's 200-nm EEZ limit, Denmark's claimed boundary, and the median line, Norway's claimed boundary.[145] The area of overlapping entitlements was enclosed between Greenland and Jan Mayen's 200-nm EEZ limit, representing the furthest reach of the neighbouring states' EEZ entitlements under international law.[146] However, the ICJ found that the relevant area in *Jan Mayen* extended all the way to the respective coasts of the parties.[147]

As *Jan Mayen* shows, the relevant area could be larger than the other two, since there may be marine spaces over which the states concerned have neither overlapping claims, nor overlapping entitlements, but which are nonetheless germane to the delimitation process.[148] International tribunals have never explained the reason why such marine areas are relevant to delimitation. However, the reason plausibly relates to the factors coming into play in delimitation. First, although constructing equidistance lines requires international tribunals to use the states' coast as a reference point,[149] the coast does not necessarily border the area of

---

[143] *Black Sea* (n. 1) 89 [77].
[144] Chapter 4, Section II.A below.
[145] *Jan Mayen* (n. 32) 47 [18].
[146] Art. 57 UNCLOS.
[147] *Jan Mayen* (n. 32) 47–8 [20].
[148] The relevant area 'is not the same as the area of overlapping claims'. See Fietta and Cleverly (n. 12) 600.
[149] Chapter 4, Section IV below.

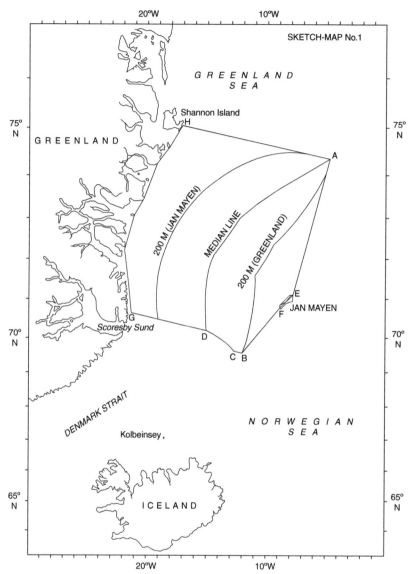

Figure 3.4 The 'area of overlapping claims' and the 'area of overlapping entitlements' in *Jan Mayen*
Source: [1993] ICJ Rep 45

overlapping claims or the area of overlapping entitlements. For example, in *Jan Mayen* the coast of neither state directly bordered the area in which the parties' claims or entitlements overlapped. Second, certain relevant circumstances could relate to the area where neither claims nor entitlements overlap.[150]

The concept of relevant area appears to be elusive. The definition of relevant area lacks the objectivity which seems to characterise the notion of area of overlapping claims and of area of overlapping entitlements. The cases tend to convey that the relevant area is simply whatever an international tribunal deems it to be in a given dispute, taking into account the geographical peculiarities of the case. In the three-stage approach, determining the relevant area is probably as subjective as adjusting the provisional equidistance line based on the existing relevant circumstances.[151] Owing to the absence of a clear notion of relevant area, international tribunals exercise a degree of discretion in determining what the relevant area is, based on the geographical features of each particular dispute.

2 The 2018 *Costa Rica* v. *Nicaragua* judgment

However, the ICJ's 2018 judgment in *Costa Rica* v. *Nicaragua* might be the beginning of a new approach which could clarify the definition of the relevant area. In that judgment, the Court decided that both the relevant area in the Caribbean Sea, and the relevant area in the Pacific Ocean, corresponded to the area of overlapping entitlements between the parties. In respect of the Caribbean Sea, the Court identified the relevant area after having decided on the effect of the existing treaties concluded by or with third states such as Colombia and Panama. The Court found that '[s]ince the maritime space appertaining to third States cannot be identified in the present proceedings, it is impossible for the Court to calculate precisely the part of the relevant area of each Party'.[152] The Court relied on the notional extension of the equidistance line established by the 1980 Costa Rica–Panama treaty[153] for identifying the relevant area.[154]

Although the Court did not express the method used to identify the Caribbean relevant area, its graphic representation suggests that the relevant area corresponded to the area of overlapping entitlements generated by the radial projections of the parties' coast. The Court approached the identification of the relevant area in the Pacific Ocean

---

[150] This was the case of access to natural resources in *Jan Mayen*. See Chapter 5, Section III.A below.
[151] On adjusting a provisional equidistance line, see Chapter 5, Section V.C below.
[152] *Costa Rica* v. *Nicaragua* (n. 7) 201–2 [164].
[153] Treaty concerning Delimitation of Marine Areas and Maritime Co-operation between the Republic of Costa Rica and the Republic of Panama, *Limits in the Seas No. 97*.
[154] *Costa Rica* v. *Nicaragua* (n. 7) 201–2 [164].

in a comparable fashion. The Court found the relevant area to be 'bordered in the north by a line starting at Punta Cosigüina and perpendicular to the straight line approximating the general direction of Nicaragua's coast'.[155] However, differently from its reasoning in respect of the relevant area in the Caribbean Sea, the Court clearly stated that '[i]n the west and in the south, the relevant area is limited by the envelope of arcs marking the limits of the area in which the potential maritime entitlements of the Parties overlap'.[156] At first glance, it may seem that the area of overlapping entitlements in the Pacific Ocean should also extend to the maritime area south of the Nicoya Peninsula. However, it seems possible that the Court decided that the Nicoya Peninsula itself blocked the radial projections of Nicaragua's coast.

In respect of the relevant area both in the Caribbean Sea, and in the Pacific Ocean, the Court stated at the outset that the relevant area 'comprises'[157] or 'includes'[158] the area of overlapping potential entitlements, which appears consistent with the case-by-case approach favoured in earlier cases. The Court quoted from its own judgment in *Nicaragua v. Colombia*, in which it held that '[t]he relevant area *comprises* that part of the maritime space in which the potential entitlements of the parties overlap'.[159] However, the quoted passage is different in the French text of the judgment, according to which '[l]a zone pertinente *correspond* à la partie de l'espace maritime dans laquelle les droits potentiels des parties se chevauchent'.[160] While the French text of the *Nicaragua v. Colombia* judgment suggests that the relevant area and the area of overlapping entitlements are co-extensive, the English text implies that the former merely includes the latter. Although the English text of the *Nicaragua v. Colombia* judgment is authoritative, it does not preclude adopting the approach which the Court implemented in *Costa Rica v. Nicaragua*.

Identifying the relevant area as the area of overlapping entitlements increases the predictability of a stage in the delimitation process which could be perceived as being fraught with subjectivity.[161] If the Court's

---

[155] Ibid. 211 [184].
[156] Ibid.
[157] Ibid. 184 [115].
[158] Ibid. 211 [184].
[159] *Nicaragua v. Colombia* (n. 1) 683 [159] (emphasis added). See *Costa Rica v. Nicaragua* (n. 7) 184 [115].
[160] *Nicaragua v. Colombia* (n. 1) 683 [159] (emphasis added).
[161] While the Court could have taken a similar approach in *Peru v. Chile*, it decided not to do so.

approach in *Costa Rica* v. *Nicaragua* were followed in future cases, the tripartite distinction made in *Jan Mayen* could become a bipartite distinction between the area of overlapping claims and the relevant area, since the latter would correspond to the area of overlapping entitlements. Current cartographic methods allow the precise identification of the area in which the overlapping entitlements of the states concerned overlap. There seems to be good reason for international tribunals to follow in the ICJ's footsteps, and regularly identify the relevant area as the area in which the maritime entitlements of the parties overlap. Nevertheless, the geographical circumstances may vary significantly from case to case, which would seem to discourage a strict adherence to the Court's approach in *Costa Rica* v. *Nicaragua*. In order to account for the peculiarities of future cases, international tribunals could identify the relevant area as the area of overlapping entitlements only in principle, while deviating from this approach in appropriate, yet limited, circumstances. Such circumstances could include cases in which the states concerned have already agreed on part of their maritime boundary, and cases in which potential rights of third states make it difficult precisely to identify the area of overlapping entitlements.

Coastal configuration could also greatly influence the determination of the relevant area, as well as its relationship with the area of overlapping claims and the area of overlapping entitlements. The main distinction concerns delimitation between opposite coasts and delimitation between adjacent coasts. In the former, the relevant area is likely to be co-extensive with the area of overlapping entitlements, especially if the states concerned abut an enclosed or semi-enclosed sea, as in *Eritrea/Yemen*.[162] If opposite states do not abut an enclosed or semi-enclosed sea, the relevant area is likely to be larger than the area of overlapping entitlements, as in *Jan Mayen*.

Second, between adjacent coasts the relevant area is not always likely to coincide with the area of overlapping entitlements.[163] If adjacent coasts are concave, and there is hardly any marine space beyond the area of overlapping entitlements, the relevant area is likely to be determined by reference to the states' overlapping entitlements. This was the case in *Bangladesh* v. *India*. If adjacent coasts are convex, determining the

---

[162] *Second Stage of the Proceedings between Eritrea and Yemen (Maritime Delimitation)* (*Eritrea/Yemen*) (1999) XXII RIAA 335. In this case, the arbitral tribunal did not explicitly identify the relevant area.

[163] According to Fietta and Cleverly, 'in many cases of adjacency it may not be practicable to define the relevant coasts or areas'. See Fietta and Cleverly (n. 12) 50.

relevant area by reference to the area of overlapping entitlements is more difficult. This could have been the case if the ICJ had drawn an equidistance line instead of an angle-bisector in *Nicaragua v. Honduras*.

There are also cases in which, owing to the complexities of coastal geography, international tribunals refrained from clearly identifying the relevant area. In *Peru v. Chile*, the ICJ held that 'the existence of an agreed line running for 80 [nm] along the parallel of latitude presents it with an unusual situation',[164] as that line '[made] difficult, if not impossible, the calculation of the length of the relevant coasts and of the extent of the relevant area'.[165] However, there was another reason beyond the existence of an agreed line, which the Court did not mention, why determining the relevant area in *Peru v. Chile* was problematic. The parties faced the open Pacific Ocean, and both had coasts stretching far beyond the relevant coast. Therefore, there were no clear limits to a hypothetical relevant area. While it was possible objectively to determine both the area of overlapping claims and the area of overlapping entitlements, identifying the relevant area would have required the ICJ to determine its extent entirely subjectively. *Peru v. Chile* shows that, although determining the area of overlapping claims and the area of overlapping entitlements is in principle objective, in certain cases determining the relevant area can be a subjective exercise.[166] Although international tribunals have produced no established definition of 'relevant area', and despite the latest developments in *Costa Rica v. Nicaragua*, it does not follow that international tribunals have unlimited discretion in determining the relevant area. The limits to this discretion are discussed below.[167]

B The Direction of Coastal Projections

Owing to the subjectivity of determining the relevant area, Evans wrote that 'determining the relevant area for the purposes of delimitation ... remains unclear and controversial'.[168] However, the determination of the relevant area does not need to be an entirely discretionary exercise. Legal principles guide the identification of the relevant area by imposing a number of limits on the discretion of international tribunals. The first

---

[164] *Peru v. Chile* (n. 9) 69 [193].
[165] Ibid.
[166] Section III.C.3 below.
[167] Sections III.B and III.C below.
[168] Evans (n. 2) 270.

of such limits stems from the direction in which a coast generates maritime entitlements.

1 The envelope of arcs as the implementation of radial projections

Radial projections entail that a point on a coast generates entitlements along a radius equal in length either to the maximum extent of maritime jurisdiction permitted under international law, or to the seaward extent of maritime jurisdiction claimed by a state.[169] Authoritative commentators have stated that maritime jurisdiction does not project frontally, but in all directions.[170] Although the radial projection principle may sound like a postulate, there is a practical justification for preferring it to the frontal projection principle. Marston wrote about the hypothetical situation of:

> a square-shaped island in the middle of the open ocean. Frontal projection would give it four rectangular arms of maritime zones and no more. However, it is clear that such an island would also be entitled to the maritime space between the arms, constructed by arcs of circles centred on the island's corners and linked the extremities of each arm to the next.[171]

Marston's example is extreme, as there exists no 'square-shaped island in the middle of the open ocean'. Nevertheless, the frontal projection principle could excessively curtail the reach of the coastal states' maritime jurisdiction, especially if international tribunals approximated the relevant coast by means of straight lines, as has become common practice.[172] This result would be at odds with one of UNCLOS's overarching objectives, the extension seaward of the coastal states' maritime jurisdiction.[173]

The envelope of arcs method, also called arcs of circle method, entails that 'a series of arcs of radius ... 200 [nm] (for the EEZ or distance-based continental shelf limit) are drawn from all points on the baseline; the outermost envelope of which constitutes the [outer] limit'.[174] This

---

[169] Section II.A above.
[170] Weil (n. 17) 68; MD Evans, 'Less Than an Ocean Apart: The St. Pierre et Miquelon and Jan Mayen Islands and the Delimitation of Maritime Zones' (1994) 43 *ICLQ* 678, 685.
[171] G Marston, 'St. Pierre–Miquelon Arbitration: Canada–France Maritime Delimitation Award' (1993) 17 *Marine Policy* 155, 167.
[172] Section II.B.2 above.
[173] R-J Dupuy, 'La Mer sous Compétence Nationale' in R-J Dupuy and D Vignes (eds.), *Traité du Nouveau Droit de la Mer* (Bruylant, 1985) 219, 242–56.
[174] Fietta and Cleverly (n. 12) 46. As argued below, the EEZ incorporates the continental shelf within 200 nm upon its proclamation by the coastal state. See Chapter 4, Section II.B.

method is alternative to the *tracé parallèle*, under which 'the outer limit is drawn by moving the coastline, with all its sinousities, a constant distance seaward thus creating a territorial sea or EEZ limit that replicates the coastline'.[175] Envelopes of arcs allow coastal states to extend their jurisdiction beyond what the *tracé parallèle* would permit. By definition, envelopes of arcs express the radial projection principle.

The ICJ implicitly accepted the envelope of arcs method, and thus the radial projection principle, in *Peru v. Chile*. The ICJ was requested to decide whether the 1952 Santiago Declaration had established the maritime boundary between Peru and Chile, or whether that boundary should have been delimited *de novo*. Paragraph II of the Santiago Declaration provided that the signatories, Chile, Ecuador and Peru, had 'exclusive sovereignty and jurisdiction over the sea along the coasts of their respective countries to a minimum distance of 200 [nm] from these coasts'.[176] Paragraph IV added that:

> [i]f an island or group of islands belonging to one of the countries making the declaration is situated less than 200 [nm] from the general maritime zone belonging to another of those countries, the maritime zone of the island or group of islands shall be limited by the parallel at the point at which the land frontier of the States concerned reaches the sea.

Chile argued that paragraph IV established the maritime boundary between the parties as the parallel of latitude starting at the land boundary terminus.[177] Peru contended that the parties had not agreed on a boundary.[178] The Court found that there was an 80-nm tacitly agreed boundary extending along the parallel of latitude and starting at the land boundary terminus,[179] while between 80 nm and 200 nm the Court drew the boundary *de novo* using the three-stage approach.[180]

Chile argued that the parties' 1947 Proclamations identified the maritime zones under their jurisdiction by reference to geographical parallels. This implemented a *tracé parallèle* method, which would be evidence of the parties' agreed boundary.[181] However, the Court held that 'the utilization of such method is not sufficient to evidence a clear

---

[175] Fietta and Cleverly (n. 12) 46.
[176] Declaration on the Maritime Zone, 1006 UNTS 325.
[177] *Peru v. Chile* (n. 9) 16 [23].
[178] Ibid. 16 [22].
[179] Ibid. 58 [151].
[180] Ibid. 65–71 [177]–[195].
[181] Ibid. 19 [31].

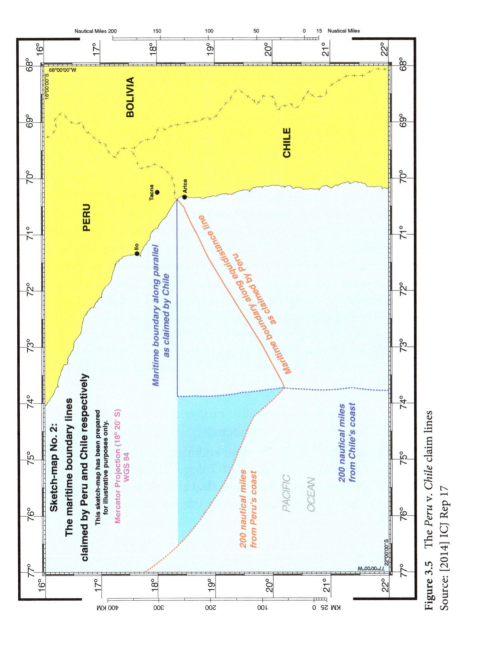

Figure 3.5 The *Peru* v. *Chile* claim lines
Source: [2014] ICJ Rep 17

intention of the Parties that their eventual maritime boundary would be a parallel'.[182] Moreover, in delimiting the boundary between 80 nm and 200 nm, the Court delineated the outer limits of the parties' EEZs using an envelope of arcs. Although Chile argued that the *tracé parallèle* proved the existence of an agreed boundary, the ICJ used the envelope of arcs method.

Moreover, Peru's second submission requested the Court to adjudge and declare that '[b]eyond the point where the common maritime border ends, Peru is entitled to exercise exclusive sovereign rights over a maritime area lying out to a distance of 200 [nm] from its baselines'.[183] Peru referred to the triangular area lying beyond 200 nm from Chile's coast. If the ICJ had upheld Chile's argument that there was a 200-nm agreed boundary, which party had jurisdiction in the outer triangle would have been uncertain. Peru's second submission is connected with the use of an envelope of arcs for delineating its EEZ's outer limits. The Court decided that, since 'it will proceed with the delimitation of the overlapping maritime entitlements of the Parties by drawing an equidistance line, Peru's second submission has become moot and the Court need not rule on it'.[184] In other words, the Court's decision to delimit the boundary between 80 and 200 nm as an equidistance line left the entire outer triangle under Peru's jurisdiction. This decision implicitly endorsed the envelope of arcs method, and radial projection as a result. The ICJ confirmed its implicit acceptance of radial projections in *Costa Rica v. Nicaragua*. Both in the Caribbean Sea, and in the Pacific Ocean, the Court's use of radial projections is shown by the shape of the relevant areas as identified by the Court, which relied on the envelope of arcs method.[185]

2 The application of radial projections by international tribunals

International tribunals have seldom endorsed radial projections explicitly. The *Barbados v. Trinidad and Tobago* tribunal stated that 'what matters is whether [coastal frontages] abut as a whole upon the disputed area by a radial or directional presence relevant to the delimitation'.[186]

---

[182] Ibid. 23 [40].
[183] Ibid. 12 [14].
[184] Ibid. 67 [189].
[185] *Costa Rica v. Nicaragua* (n. 7) sketch-maps 12 and 18 on pages 202 and 215.
[186] *Barbados v. Trinidad and Tobago* (n. 136) 236 [331].

III THE RELEVANT AREA

The *Bangladesh* v. *India* tribunal mentioned this statement with approval.[187] The acceptance of the radial projection principle is generally inferred from the graphic representations of the outer limits of maritime zones in delimitation decisions, or implicitly from such decisions' underpinnings. For example, in *Nicaragua* v. *Honduras*, the ICJ approximated the states' convex coasts to draw an angle-bisector. The general direction of the coast is also important in determining maritime entitlements under the frontal projection principle,[188] according to which coastal projections generate maritime entitlements along lines perpendicular to the general direction of the coast. If the Court had used frontal projections in *Nicaragua* v. *Honduras*, there would have been no area of overlapping entitlements, and therefore no need for delimitation.[189] The Court should be deemed to have thus endorsed the radial projection principle.

However, in *St. Pierre et Miquelon* the Court of Arbitration adopted the principle of frontal projection. In determining the maritime entitlements of the French islands, the Court of Arbitration stated that 'la France a pleinement droit à une projection frontale en mer, vers le sud, jusqu'à ce qu'elle atteigne la limite extérieure de 200 milles marins'.[190] As a result, it found that the French islands were entitled to a 200-nm maritime zone shaped as a long corridor.

Weil, the French-appointed arbitrator, wrote a strong dissenting opinion explaining his misgivings with respect to the Court of Arbitration's decision. According to Weil, 'la théorie de la projection frontale ... est contraire à la philosophie des projections maritimes et est démentie par la pratique des Etats et la jurisprudence'.[191] Weil wrote that:

> [u]ne projection maritime définie par une certaine distance de la côte ne s'effectue pas seulement dans une direction perpendiculaire à la direction générale du littoral et sur la largeur de ce littoral. Elle irradie dans toutes les directions, créant une enveloppe océanique autour de la façade côtière. En un mot, elle est radiale. Telle était déjà, à propos de la mer territoriale, la signification de la *cannon-shot rule*: le canon tire dans toutes les

---

[187] *Bangladesh* v. *India* (n. 7) 99 [300].
[188] *St. Pierre et Miquelon* (n. 74) 304 [9] (Dissenting Opinion Weil).
[189] Overlapping maritime entitlements are a precondition to delimitation. See *Black Sea* (n. 1) 89 [77]. In *Nicaragua* v. *Honduras*, the parties agreed that the disputed islands only generated entitlements to a territorial sea. See *Nicaragua* v. *Honduras* (n. 21) 749 [299].
[190] *St. Pierre et Miquelon* (n. 74) 290 [70].
[191] Ibid. 304 [8] (Dissenting Opinion Weil).

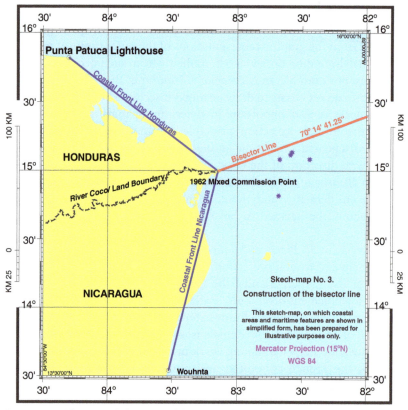

Figure 3.6 The general direction of the coast in *Nicaragua v. Honduras*
Source: [2007] ICJ Rep 750

directions, engendrant cette 'ceinture des eaux territoriales' .... Telle est aujourd'hui la règle pour la zone des 200 milles.[192]

Weil's views are consistent with the earlier jurisprudence.[193] In his dissenting opinion, Allan Gotlieb, the Canadian-appointed arbitrator, agreed with Weil.[194] Furthermore, Marston and Evans were sceptical of the decision to uphold the frontal projection principle.[195] *St. Pierre et*

---

[192] Ibid. 305 [11] (Dissenting Opinion Weil).
[193] The ICJ had already justified radial projection on the basis of the cannon-shot rule in *Anglo/Norwegian Fisheries*. See *Fisheries (UK v. Norway)* (Judgment) [1951] ICJ Rep 116, 129.
[194] *St. Pierre et Miquelon* (n. 74) 332 [35] (Dissenting Opinion Gotlieb).
[195] Marston (n. 171) 167; Evans (n. 170) 685–6.

III THE RELEVANT AREA

Miquelon should be seen as having taken a flawed approach to the issue of coastal projections, for being at odds with all other delimitation decisions.

International tribunals are generally consistent in endorsing the radial projection principle. However, there are cases in which they have not been entirely consistent in its application, such as *Gulf of Maine*, *Black Sea* and *Nicaragua v. Colombia*. First, in *Gulf of Maine* the application of the radial projection principle should have led the Chamber of the ICJ to decide that the entirety of the Bay of Fundy was part of the area of overlapping entitlements, and that the entirety of the Bay of Fundy's coast was part of the relevant coast.[196] Second, in *Black Sea* the Court should have included the waters of Karkinits'ka Gulf within the area of overlapping entitlements, and the Gulf's coast within the relevant coast, as required by radial projection.[197] Third, in *Nicaragua v. Colombia* the Court held that Nicaragua's coast near Punta de Perlas was not part of the relevant coast, since it faced 'due south and thus does not project into the area of overlapping potential entitlements'.[198] However, that coast generated entitlements overlapping with those of Colombia pursuant to the radial projection principle, and should have therefore been included in the relevant coast.

The reason for the international tribunals' not entirely consistent application of radial projection is likely to be pragmatic. In *Black Sea*, the ICJ excluded Karkinits'ka Gulf from the area of overlapping entitlements and from the relevant area because the projections of its coast overlapped with each other before meeting the projections of the Romanian coast.[199] The Chamber's reasoning in *Gulf of Maine* was similar.[200] However, neither decision acknowledged that the radial coastal projections of Karkinits'ka Gulf and of the Bay of Fundy overlapped with those of the Romanian and US coast.

The arbitral tribunal in *Bangladesh v. India* implicitly determined the relevant area by radial projections. However, *Bangladesh v. India* was the first case in which an international tribunal expressed the limits of radial

---

[196] Section II.B.3 above.
[197] Ibid.
[198] *Nicaragua v. Colombia* (n. 1) 678 [145]. In *Nicaragua v. Colombia*, the issue was the identification of the relevant coast. However, the ICJ's unpersuasive approach derived from the application of radial projection.
[199] See Section II.B.3 above.
[200] Ibid.

projections. In identifying the relevant coast, the arbitral tribunal observed that:

> a radial line drawn to the north-east from a point south of Sandy Point would also overlap with the projection of the coast of Bangladesh beyond 200 nm. In the Tribunal's view, there is a margin of appreciation in determining the projections generated by a segment of coastline and a point at which a line drawn at an acute angle to the general direction of the coast can no longer be fairly said to represent the seaward projection of that coast.[201]

Despite this comment, the arbitral tribunal did not exercise its margin of appreciation. Neither Bangladesh nor India had contended that India's relevant coast extended south of Sandy Point, at which point 'the overlapping projection extends in a nearly perpendicular line from [India's] coast'.[202] In his opinion appended to the award, Rao criticised the majority's statement since it 'is not part of the *aquis judiciare*'.[203]

One fails to understand why the arbitral tribunal made such a statement if it would not have been useful for deciding the case before it. Furthermore, that statement seems problematic in its vagueness. One wonders at what point an angle can 'no longer be fairly said to represent the seaward projection' of a state's coast.[204] Applying radial projections increases certainty and predictability in maritime delimitation, whereas admitting that a margin of appreciation exists in determining whether a radial projection can 'be fairly said to represent the seaward projection' of a coast re-introduces a subjective element. The exercise of this alleged margin of appreciation could effectively result in determining the relevant area, and the relevant coast, based on a method which may be called 'radial projection', while in fact it would be more correctly labelled 'frontal projection'. The *Bangladesh* v. *India* tribunal appeared implicitly to accept this possibility by admitting that 'the overlapping projection extends in a nearly perpendicular line from [India's] coast'.[205] The seaward projection of a segment of coast along a perpendicular line is nothing more than that segment's frontal projection. The vagueness and the potential consequences of the supposed margin of appreciation to which the *Bangladesh* v. *India* tribunal referred seem to be sufficiently

---

[201] *Bangladesh* v. *India* (n 7) 100 [302]. This statement was cited by the ICJ in *Costa Rica* v. *Nicaragua*. See *Costa Rica* v. *Nicaragua* (n. 7) 181 [108].
[202] *Bangladesh* v. *India* (n 7) 100 [302].
[203] Ibid. 190–1 [8] (Concurring and Dissenting Opinion of Dr PS Rao).
[204] Oude Elferink (n. 13) 198.
[205] *Bangladesh* v. *India* (n 7) 100 [302].

compelling reasons to doubt the appropriateness of accepting the existence of such a margin of appreciation. It does not appear reasonable to relinquish the level of certainty ensured by radial projections in the name of potentially unlimited discretion and lack of transparency in the delimitation process.

Excluding maritime spaces from the relevant area impacts on the achievement of an equitable solution under Articles 74 and 83 UNCLOS. By limiting the size of the relevant area, as well as by limiting the length of the relevant coast,[206] international tribunals might try to ensure that no disproportionality between these two parameters exists. However, in determining the relevant area international tribunals should not pre-empt decisions that belong in a later stage of the delimitation process. The means to ensure the achievement of an equitable solution are the adjustment of an equidistance line in the second and third stages of the delimitation process. In a similar way as determining the relevant coast, determining the relevant area should be conceived to be an objective exercise that, on one hand, is useful to achieving an equitable solution, while, on the other hand, logically precedes the phase at which international tribunals ensure that an equitable solution is achieved.[207]

C The Limits of the Relevant Area

In addition to the radial projection principle, other principles and rules of international law can contribute to limiting the international tribunals' discretion in the determination of the relevant area.

1 The maximum extent of national jurisdiction under UNCLOS

Determining the relevant area's extent should be premised on the identification of its limits. Such limits are imposed by UNCLOS and other rules of international law, such as the provisions of bilateral delimitation treaties. The inner limit of the relevant area is in principle the states' relevant coast. In *Tunisia/Libya*, the ICJ found that the relevant area would include part of Tunisia's internal waters, lying landward of its straight baselines. The Court discussed the relevant area with reference to proportionality, holding that proportionality 'is related to lengths of the coasts of the States concerned, not to straight baselines drawn round

---

[206] Section II.B above.
[207] The same argument is made concerning the relevant coast. See ibid.

those coasts'.[208] Therefore, it included Tunisia's internal waters within the relevant area.[209]

However, the ICJ's decision was inconsistent with the basis of title. Internal waters are an integral part of a coastal state's land territory.[210] International tribunals may decide to approximate the relevant coast by using straight lines following its general direction.[211] While this method is problematic, international tribunals tend to exclude areas landward of such straight lines from the relevant area. This was the case in *Bangladesh/Myanmar* and *Bangladesh v. India*. The exclusion of areas landward of the straight lines approximating the general direction of the coast is consistent with the basis of title, as such straight lines are the legal representation of the coast. Such straight lines also generate maritime entitlements, acting as a surrogate of the low-water line. It would be even more consistent with the basis of title if international tribunals used straight baselines established under Article 7 UNCLOS to identify the relevant coast, and, accordingly, the relevant area.[212]

The approach in *Bangladesh/Myanmar* and *Bangladesh v. India* had already been adopted in *Eritrea/Yemen*. For the purposes of proportionality, Eritrea was 'inclined to have [the general direction of the coast] follow the line of the mainland coast'.[213] However, the arbitral tribunal decided that '[t]here is ... no doubt that the "general direction" of the coast means that the calculation of the Eritrean coastal length should follow the outer circumference of the Dahlak group of islands'.[214] The arbitral tribunal then calculated the relevant area using the straight baselines established by Eritrea around the Dhalaks as the landward limit.

With respect to the outer limits of the relevant area, the overarching principle is that maritime spaces over which either state party to

---

[208] *Tunisia/Libya* (n. 74) 76 [104]. *Tunisia/Libya* was decided before the introduction of a standard delimitation method.

[209] Most writers did not criticise this approach. See MD Evans, *Relevant Circumstances and Maritime Delimitation* (OUP, 1989) 226-7; MB Feldman, 'The Tunisia-Libya Continental Shelf Case: Geographic Justice or Judicial Compromise?' (1983) 77 *AJIL* 219; LL Herman, 'The Court Giveth and the Court Taketh Away: An Analysis of the *Tunisia-Libya Continental Shelf* Case' (1984) 33 *ICLQ* 825. Ida criticised the ICJ's approach, see R Ida, 'The Role of Proportionality in Maritime Delimitation Revisited: The Origin and Meaning of the Principle from the Early Decisions of the Court' in N Ando et al. (eds.), *Liber Amicorum Judge Shigeru Oda* (Martinus Nijhoff, 2002) vol. II, 1037, 1042.

[210] Section II.B.2 above.

[211] Ibid.

[212] Ibid.

[213] *Eritrea/Yemen* (n. 162) 372 [166].

[214] Ibid.

a delimitation dispute is entitled under international law cannot be part of the relevant area. International tribunals have shown awareness of this constraint, as they generally respect two limits stemming from it. First, the relevant area cannot extend beyond the outer limits of national jurisdiction over maritime areas established by UNCLOS. Second, the relevant area cannot extend beyond existing maritime boundaries, whether established by treaty or by judicial process.[215]

UNCLOS rules limit the maximum extent of national jurisdiction over maritime areas. Article 57 UNCLOS states that '[t]he [EEZ] shall not extend beyond 200 [nm] from the baselines from which the breadth of the territorial sea is measured'. Similarly, under Article 76 UNCLOS:

> [t]he continental shelf of a coastal State comprises the seabed and subsoil of the submarine areas that extend beyond its territorial sea throughout the natural prolongation of its land territory to the outer edge of the continental margin, or to a distance of 200 [nm] from the baselines from which the breadth of the territorial sea is measured where the outer edge of the continental margin does not extend up to that distance.

National jurisdiction cannot extend beyond 200 nm with respect to the EEZ and, in some cases, to the continental shelf.[216] Consequently, the relevant area, as well as the area of overlapping entitlements and the area of overlapping claims, cannot encompass areas beyond the jurisdictional reach of the states party to a maritime dispute. The ICJ seemed conscious of this principle in *Peru v. Chile*. In that case, the Court found that the existence of an agreed boundary up to 80 nm from Chile's coast made 'difficult if not impossible, the calculation of the ... extent of the relevant area'.[217] Nevertheless, the Court did not seem to consider areas beyond 200 nm to be relevant to delimitation, as shown by its approach to Peru's second submission. Peru claimed to have sovereign rights in the outer triangle beyond 200 nm from Chile's coast, which the Court identified as including only areas within 200 nm from Peru's coast.

The Court made comparable findings in *Nicaragua v. Colombia*, in which it found that the relevant area comprised only the area of overlapping entitlements generated by the coast of the Nicaraguan mainland and the coast of the San Andrés Archipelago. The Court stated that:

> [t]he relevant area comprises that part of the maritime space in which the potential entitlements of the parties overlap. ... Nicaragua's coast, and the

---
[215] Section III.C.2 below.
[216] On the relevant area in cases of delimitation beyond 200 nm, see Section III.C.4 below.
[217] *Peru v. Chile* (n. 9) 69 [193].

Nicaraguan islands adjacent thereto, project a potential maritime entitlement across the sea bed and water column for 200 [nm]. That potential entitlement thus extends to the sea bed and water column to the east of the Colombian islands where, of course, it overlaps with the competing potential entitlement of Colombia derived from those islands. Accordingly, the relevant area extends from the Nicaraguan coast to a line in the east 200 [nm] from the baselines from which the breadth of Nicaragua's territorial sea is measured.[218]

In *Nicaragua v. Colombia*, the Court used the 200-nm outer limit of Nicaragua's EEZ as the limit of the relevant area. The Court could have decided to extend the relevant area west of Nicaragua's 200-nm EEZ limit, given the existence of Colombia's entitlement in that area. However, it decided not to, presumably owing to the semi-enclosed character of the Western Caribbean Sea and the likelihood that such an extension would encroach upon the maritime entitlements of third states.

2 Pre-existing maritime boundaries

The international tribunals' approach to whether relevant areas may extend beyond pre-existing boundaries is not entirely clear. In certain cases, international tribunals identified the relevant area as bordered by pre-existing boundaries. For instance, in *Nicaragua v. Colombia* the ICJ decided that the boundaries bilaterally agreed between Colombia, Panama and Costa Rica, the joint regime area instituted by Colombia and Jamaica, as well as the Nicaragua-Honduras boundary established by the ICJ itself five year prior, operated as limits of the relevant area. Similarly, the *Bangladesh v. India* tribunal recognised the Bangladesh–Myanmar boundary established by ITLOS as the easternmost limit of the relevant area.

However, in other cases international tribunals made different decisions, including maritime spaces over which third states had a claim in the relevant area.[219] This was the case in *Black Sea* and *Bangladesh/Myanmar*. In *Black Sea*, the parties held opposing views concerning the inclusion of certain marine spaces, called the south-western and south-eastern triangles, within the relevant area. The Court found that:

> [i]n both these triangles the maritime entitlements of Romania and Ukraine overlap. ... [I]n the south-western triangle, as well as in the small area in the western corner of the south-eastern triangle, entitlements of third parties may come into play. However where areas are included

[218] *Nicaragua v. Colombia* (n. 1) 683 [159].
[219] See Fietta and Cleverly (n. 12) 601.

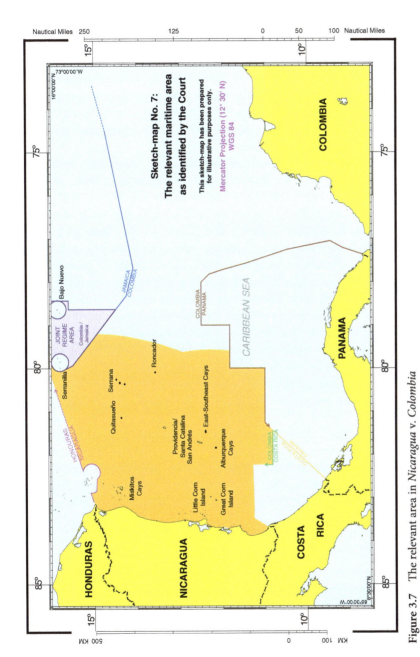

Figure 3.7 The relevant area in *Nicaragua v. Colombia*
Source: [2012] ICJ Rep 687

solely for the purpose of approximate identification of overlapping entitlements of the Parties to the case, which may be deemed to constitute the relevant area ..., third party entitlements cannot be affected. Third party entitlements would only be relevant if the delimitation between Romania and Ukraine were to affect them.[220]

ITLOS made similar findings in *Bangladesh/Myanmar*. According to ITLOS, '[t]he fact that a third party may claim the same maritime area does not prevent its inclusion in the relevant maritime area for purposes of the disproportionality test',[221] as '[t]his in no way affects the rights of third parties'.[222] ITLOS thus included within the relevant area marine spaces over which India had a claim.

The approach in *Nicaragua v. Colombia* and *Bangladesh v. India* appears consistent with the basis of title over maritime areas. When two states are either party to a delimitation treaty, or party to a delimitation case before an international tribunal, the establishment of boundaries entails one state's renunciation of its rights over the maritime entitlements falling on the other state's side of such boundaries. Therefore, in a dispute between two states, the existence of boundaries established between either state party and a third state precludes the existence of overlapping entitlements between the states party to the case. This absence of overlapping entitlements between the states party should decisively influence the identification of the relevant area, since including within it spaces over which third states have a clear entitlement under international law is inconsistent with the basis of title.

However, bilateral treaties only bind the states party to them under the *res inter alios acta* principle. Under Article 34 of the Vienna Convention on the Law of Treaties (VCLT), '[a] treaty does not create either obligations or rights for a third State without its consent'.[223] This provision would suggest that bilateral delimitation treaties with third states should have no effect on the judicial determination of the relevant area. This view is in principle correct. However, establishing a boundary, whether through treaty or judicial process, should be deemed to have effects for

---

[220] *Black Sea* (n. 1) 100 [114].
[221] *Bangladesh/Myanmar* (n. 8) 125 [494].
[222] Ibid.
[223] 1155 UNTS 331. Similar comments could be made in relation to the relative effect of international judicial decisions, see Art. 59 of the ICJ's Statute and Art. 33 of the ITLOS's Statute. According to Crawford, Art. 34 VCLT 'falls slightly short of expressing the customary rule, however: besides not *creating* obligations or rights, treaties cannot *infringe* the rights of third states without their consent'. See J Crawford, *Brownlie's Principles of Public International Law* 8th edn (OUP, 2012) 384.

states other than the parties to a treaty or to a case, which would be compelled to recognise a state's title over certain maritime spaces.

Treaties establishing boundaries create so-called 'objective regimes'. These are treaty regimes that 'characterize agreements that define the status of a state, a certain territory, or an international waterway by establishing a legal regime that is intended to be valid and binding *erga omnes*'.[224] In its counter-memorial in *Costa Rica* v. *Nicaragua*, Nicaragua mentioned objective regimes in relation to the 1977 Colombia–Costa Rica treaty.[225] Nicaragua referred to its 2010 oral submissions in the *Nicaragua* v. *Colombia* intervention proceedings, in which it had argued that 'Costa Rica's renunciation of entitlement to areas beyond the agreed boundary line in the 1977 treaty with Colombia is *erga omnes* as to other States',[226] since 'a treaty establishing a boundary gives birth to an objective situation, which becomes in a sense disconnected with the instrument that created it'.[227] Although in its counter-memorial Nicaragua did not explicitly invoke the objective regimes theory in identifying the relevant area, it implicitly relied on it by stating that 'areas that Costa Rica has previously recognized as Colombia cannot be part of the relevant area for the delimitation between Nicaragua and Costa Rica'.[228] Costa Rica responded that the objective regimes theory had not been sanctioned in the VCLT, and that, in any event, the Special Rapporteur of the International Law Commission (ILC) had not envisaged treaties establishing maritime boundaries as creating objective regimes.[229]

Although both Costa Rica and Nicaragua had based some of their arguments on the relevance of the 1977 Colombia–Costa Rica treaty on the objective regimes theory, the ICJ did not comment on such arguments. The Court recognised that, in establishing a maritime boundary, it may have to deal with areas over which third states may lay claim.[230] However, the Court stated that its:

---

[224] B Simma, 'The Antarctic Treaty as a Treaty Providing for an "Objective Regime"' (1986) 19 *Cornell International Law Journal* 189; P Cahier, 'Le Problème des Effets des Traités à l'égard des Etats Tiers' (1974) 143 *Recueil des Cours* 589. For Lord McNair's classic formulation of the objective regimes theory, see *International Status of South-West Africa* (Advisory Opinion) [1950] ICJ Rep 128, 153 (Separate Opinion McNair).
[225] Treaty on the Delimitation of Marine and Submarine Areas and Maritime Co-operation between Colombia and Costa Rica, *Limits in the Seas No. 84*. See Counter-memorial of Nicaragua (8 December 2015), 69 [3.24] and 135 [3.128].
[226] Ibid. 69 [3.24].
[227] CR 2010/16, 27 [32] (Reichler).
[228] Counter-memorial of Nicaragua (8 December 2015), 102 [3.78].
[229] CR 2017/9, 15 [14] (Kohen).
[230] *Costa Rica* v. *Nicaragua* (n. 7) 187 [123].

Judgment can refer to those claims, but cannot determine whether they are well founded. Conversely, a judgment rendered by the Court between one of the Parties and a third State or between two third States cannot per se affect the maritime boundary between the Parties. The same applies to treaties concluded between one of the Parties and a third State or between third States.[231]

The Court seems simply to have restated the effects of the principles of *res inter alios acta* and *res judicata*. However, in making its finding on the relevance of the 1977 Colombia–Costa Rica treaty, the Court observed that:

> the 1976 Treaty between Panama and Colombia involves third States and cannot be considered relevant for the delimitation between the Parties. With regard to the 1977 Treaty between Costa Rica and Colombia, there is no evidence that a renunciation by Costa Rica of its maritime entitlements, if it had ever taken place, was also intended to be effective with regard to a State other than Colombia.[232]

The Court's one-paragraph finding could be read as an oblique rejection of the objective regimes theory, at least in the realm of maritime delimitation. According to the Court, the key to the relevance of a treaty concluded with or between third states rests on the intention of the parties to that treaty for it to be effective with respect to states other than the parties themselves. However, the intention of the parties is a key element in the objective regimes theory, as explained below. Therefore, on closer analysis the Court's decision in *Costa Rica v. Nicaragua* does not necessarily imply a rejection of the objective regimes theory.

International tribunals have never resorted to the objective regimes theory to justify not identifying as part of the relevant area spaces to which third states are entitled under international law. The VCLT itself does not contain a rule on objective regimes. However, treaties establishing boundaries are considered to be classic examples of objective regimes.[233] Although, under strict legal principle, establishing boundaries neither

---

[231] Ibid.
[232] Ibid. 189 [134].
[233] First Report on the Law of Treaties by Sir Hersch Lauterpacht, Special Rapporteur, UN Doc A/CN.4/63 (24 March 1953), *ILC Yearbook (1963)*, vol. II, 139; Fifth Report on the Law of Treaties by Sir Gerald Fitzmaurice, Special Rapporteur, UN Doc A/CN.4/130 (21 March 1960), *ILC Yearbook (1960)*, vol. II, 92–4 [50]–[54]; Second Report on the Law of Treaties by Sir Humphrey Waldock, Special Rapporteur, UN Doc A/CN.4/156 and Add.1-3 (20 March, 10 April, 30 April and 5 June 1963), *ILC Yearbook (1963)*, vol. II, 76–7 [15]; Third Report on the Law of Treaties by Sir Humphrey Waldock, Special Rapporteur, UN Doc A/CN.4/167 and Add.1-3 (3 March, 9 June, 12 June and 7 July 1964), *ILC Yearbook (1964)*, vol. II, 26–34.

confers rights on third parties, nor imposes obligations on them, it has certain *erga omnes* effects. Although delimitation treaties and judicial decisions on delimitation are binding only *inter partes*, they also entail legal effects for third states, such as the need to respect the factual and legal situation stemming from the treaty or judicial decision. ILC Special Rapporteur Sir Gerald Fitzmaurice wrote that:

> [i]t is fairly clear, and needs no argument, that treaties containing clauses that take effect immediately and become 'executed', such as transfers of territory, are *ipso facto* 'good' against any third State, unless such State has itself a valid and relevant claim – e.g. to territory purported to be transferred by the treaty.[234]

In Fitzmaurice's view, the question is whether a state party to a dispute with a state that has concluded a delimitation treaty with a third state has 'itself a valid and relevant claim'. Especially in enclosed or semi-enclosed seas, more than two states are likely to have claims over the same maritime areas, as in *Libya/Malta* and in *Nicaragua v. Colombia*. However, claims over maritime areas, which are only potential entitlements, should be distinguished from actual entitlements over maritime areas. At least within 200 nm, consistency with the basis of title requires that the state entitled to rights over certain maritime areas be the state closest to which such maritime areas lie. Ascertaining entitlement could thus easily disqualify a state from having any entitlement over the maritime areas already delimited between a state with which it has a dispute and a third state.

According to ILC Special Rapporteur Sir Humphrey Waldock, the intention to create an objective regime is vital in order for an objective treaty regime to exist, since any state that 'expressly or impliedly assents to its creation or to its execution will be considered as having accepted the general provisions of that regime'.[235] It seems difficult to deny that treaties establishing boundaries are concluded 'with the intention to create in the general interest obligations and rights relating to a particular region'.[236] For example, once a boundary has been established, third states' vessels are expected to respect the domestic law of the state on whose side of the boundary they sail. States concluding a bilateral delimitation treaty could be deemed to have envisaged that their stipulations would affect third states. This would also apply to judicial decisions

---

[234] Fifth Report on the Law of Treaties by Sir Gerald Fitzmaurice (n. 233) 99 [74].
[235] Third Report on the Law of Treaties by Sir Humphrey Waldock (n. 233) 33 [21].
[236] Simma (n. 224) 194.

establishing boundaries. The objective regimes theory supports the view that marine spaces over which a state is entitled under a delimitation treaty or a judicial decision should be excluded from the area relevant to delimitation between other states. However, international tribunals never invoked this doctrine as a reason for limiting relevant area by reference to pre-existing boundaries.

3 Relevant areas generated by coasts facing the open sea

Determining the relevant area in cases where no clear limits are discernible, such as in the case of states facing the open ocean, could pose a challenge. International tribunals may not specify the limits of the relevant area either owing to the absence of existing boundaries with third states, as in *Bangladesh/Myanmar* and in *Ghana/Côte d'Ivoire*, or owing to the states having a long coastline generating maritime entitlements far beyond the area in which delimitation is to be effected, as in *Peru v. Chile*. In *Bangladesh/Myanmar*, ITLOS held that '[t]he southern limit of the relevant area will be marked by the parallel westward from Cape Negrais',[237] while 'the western limit of the relevant area is marked by a straight line drawn from point ß2 due south'.[238] The Special Chamber of ITLOS in *Ghana/Côte d'Ivoire* held that '[i]n the east, the relevant area is ... delimited by a line running due south starting from Cape Three Points until it reaches the outer limits of the continental shelf of Ghana',[239] and that 'in the west, the relevant area is delimited by a line running due south starting from Sassandra until it reaches the outer limits of the continental shelf as claimed by Côte d'Ivoire in its submission to the [Commission on the Limits of the Continental Shelf (CLCS)]'.[240] In *Peru v. Chile*, the 80-nm agreed boundary created an 'unusual situation', since '[t]he existence of that line would make difficult, if not impossible, the calculation of the length of the relevant coasts and of the extent of the relevant area'.[241] Evans commented that the ICJ 'seems to have just "thrown in the towel"' by not identifying the relevant area.[242]

---

[237] *Bangladesh/Myanmar* (n. 8) 115 [491].
[238] Ibid. 126 [495].
[239] *Ghana/Côte d'Ivoire* (n. 7) [383].
[240] Ibid. [384].
[241] *Peru v. Chile* (n. 9) 69 [193].
[242] MD Evans 'Maritime Boundary Delimitation: Whatever Next?' in J Barrett and R Barnes (eds.), *Law of the Sea – UNCLOS as a Living Treaty* (BIICL, 2016) 41, 65.

III THE RELEVANT AREA 91

Situations similar to *Bangladesh/Myanmar* and *Peru v. Chile* are complex. Nevertheless, it could be feasible for international tribunals to consider that in such cases the area of overlapping entitlements and the relevant area are co-extensive, since the former is the most objectively determinable area in which delimitation is to be effected. However, this was not ITLOS's approach in *Bangladesh/Myanmar*, where the relevant area extended further south than Bangladesh's 200-nm EEZ limit. The reason for ITLOS's decision could be linked to Bangladesh's claim over a continental shelf beyond 200 nm. However, it seems unpersuasive to express such a claim using a parallel running due west from Cape Negrais. Using a parallel of latitude is reminiscent of the *tracé parallèle* method for tracing the outer limits of maritime zones, which the ICJ implicitly rejected.[243] Moreover, if the relevant coast is oriented in a general north-south direction, the parallel of latitude could be seen to implement the frontal projection principle, which international tribunals also effectively rejected.[244]

ITLOS presumably employed meridian and parallels for practical reasons. An alternative to drawing a meridian as the western limit of the relevant area was to establish a hypothetical equidistance line between Bangladesh and India. This method would have ensured a higher consistency with the basis of title. However, it would have been also partially inaccurate since, at the time when ITLOS decided *Bangladesh/Myanmar*, it would have been impossible to predict how the delimitation case between Bangladesh and India would have been decided.

Comparable considerations apply to the Special Chamber's judgment in *Ghana/Côte d'Ivoire*. In that case, Ghana had concluded no delimitation treaty with Togo to the east, and Côte d'Ivoire had not agreed on its maritime boundary with Liberia to the west. The Special Chamber could have established hypothetical equidistance lines to supplement the absence of agreed relevant boundaries, and thus identify the eastern and western limits of the relevant area. However, the Special Chamber's decision that only a segment of the parties' coast constituted the relevant coast may have limited the use of drawing hypothetical boundaries with Liberia and Togo. The Special Chamber used meridians as the eastern and western limits of the relevant area.[245] Although the facts in *Ghana/ Côte d'Ivoire* were not identical to those in *Bangladesh/Myanmar*, using

[243] Section III.B above.
[244] Ibid. ITLOS did not identify Bangladesh's relevant coast as a perfect east-west line, nor did it approximate Myanmar's coast as a perfect north-south line.
[245] *Ghana/Côte d'Ivoire* (n. 7) [383]–[384].

meridians and parallels to identify the relevant area can be an expedient approach, which nonetheless retains a degree of unconvincing artificiality.

The main problem in *Peru v. Chile* was the presence of an 80-nm agreed boundary, which made it difficult to identify the relevant area. Let us assume that such agreed boundary did not exist, and that the ICJ were requested to delimit the entire boundary. While the 200-nm EEZ limit determined the western extension of the relevant area, the northern and southern limits were unclear as both states have a long coastline stretching far beyond a notional relevant area. Consistency with the basis of title would have required the Court to decide that the area of overlapping entitlements was co-extensive with the relevant area. However, that would have produced a southern and northern limit shaped as an arc of circle. To obviate this shortcoming, the Court could have drawn such limits as lines perpendicular to the general direction of the coast. This solution would have been possible owing to the clear north-south direction of Chile's coast and the southeast-northwest direction of Peru's coast. The exact position of such limits could have been calculated geometrically, by drawing two rectangles, one for each state, having the same area as the sector of circle created by the states' overlapping entitlements. In the alternative, the relevant area could have just been drawn as having envelope-of-arcs-shaped limits. Nonetheless, the ICJ's approach in *Costa Rica v. Nicaragua* showed that a relevant area could be identified as enclosed within an envelope of arcs.[246]

The existence of an 80-nm agreed boundary required the Court to discount part of the area considered relevant to delimitation. The area to discount could have been calculated by tracing two arcs of circle having an 80-nm radius. The first arc of circle, centred on Point A, identified the furthest point on Peru's coast generating entitlements overlapping with those of Chile within 80 nm of its coast. The second arc of circle, centred on the land boundary terminus, identified the furthest point on Chile's coast generating entitlements overlapping with those of Peru within 80 nm of its coast. While the Court drew the second arc of circle, it did not draw the first, which nevertheless was only useful to identify appropriate base points.[247] The sectors of circle identified by such arcs of circle determine the area to be discounted in delimitation between 80 and 200 nm. Any point lying beyond the limits of such arcs of circle would

---

[246] Section III.B.2 above.
[247] *Peru v. Chile* (n. 9) 66–7 [185].

III THE RELEVANT AREA 93

have been part of overlapping entitlements generated beyond 80 nm from Chile's coast.

In principle, if the limits of the relevant area are difficult to determine, international tribunals could, using radial projections, identify a relevant area corresponding to the area of overlapping entitlements. The limits of the relevant area would run along the envelope of arcs identifying the area of overlapping entitlements between the states concerned. Historically, international tribunals have not used this approach. While the ICJ could have used it in *Peru* v. *Chile*, it did not to do so for the reasons discussed above. However, in *Costa Rica* v. *Nicaragua* the Court applied this approach to determine the relevant area in the Pacific Ocean, where the parties' coasts faced the open sea. First, the Court stated that 'the relevant area ... includes the maritime spaces in which the potential entitlements generated by the coasts of the Parties overlap'.[248] Second, it held that:

> the relevant area is bordered in the north by a line starting at Punta Cosigüina and perpendicular to the straight line approximating the general direction of Nicaragua's coast . . .. In the west and in the south, the relevant area is limited by the envelope of arcs marking the limits of the area in which the potential maritime entitlements of the Parties overlap.[249]

The Court decided that the relevant area corresponded to the area of overlapping entitlements, which it identified using radial projections. The Court thus also determined the limits of the relevant area. As discussed above, it is possible that the Court's decision on the relevant area in the Pacific Ocean was influenced by other factors, especially the existence of the Nicoya Peninsula.[250] However, the fact remains that the Court identified the relevant area by exclusively relying on the application of radial projections. This approach could be employed again in similar cases in which states party to a delimitation case face the open sea. International tribunals rely on cartographic support in maritime delimitation cases, which makes it technically feasible to identify the area in which the maritime entitlements of the states concerned overlap, and thus the relevant area.

---

[248] *Costa Rica* v. *Nicaragua* (n. 7) 211 [184].
[249] Ibid.
[250] Section III.A.2 above.

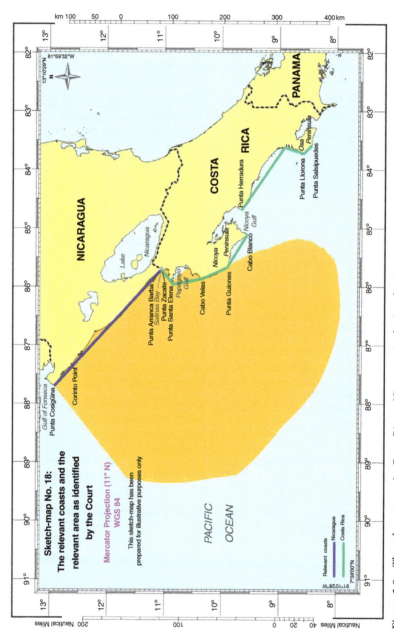

Figure 3.8 The relevant area in *Costa Rica v. Nicaragua* in the Pacific Ocean
Source: ICJ, forthcoming

4 The delimitation of the continental shelf beyond 200 nautical miles

A problematic issue concerns the limits of the relevant area in cases of continental shelf delimitation beyond 200 nm. Coastal projections generate maritime entitlements beyond 200 nm.[251] In *Bangladesh/Myanmar*, ITLOS did not use, as the relevant area's outer limit, the outer limits of the continental shelf claimed by the parties before the CLCS. Conversely, the *Bangladesh v. India* tribunal referred to the parties' submissions to the CLCS to establish the relevant area's outer limit. The arbitral tribunal found that '[t]o the south, the relevant area is bounded by the limit of Bangladesh's submission to the CLCS . . ., from the point where it intersects with the 200 nm limit from the coast of Myanmar to the point where it joins the 200 nautical mile line drawn from the coast of India'.[252]

The situation in *Ghana/Côte d'Ivoire* was different. On 5 September 2014, three months before the notification of the special agreement to submit the dispute to a Special Chamber of ITLOS, the CLCS had made a recommendation concerning the outer limits of Ghana's continental shelf beyond 200 nm.[253] Although Côte d'Ivoire's submission to the CLCS was pending at the time of the proceedings, Ghana accepted that Côte d'Ivoire also had an entitlement to a continental shelf beyond 200 nm.[254] As its main contention was that the boundary had to be established as an angle-bisector, Côte d'Ivoire did not explicitly identify the relevant area.[255] Ghana relied on the recommendation of the CLCS and on Côte d'Ivoire's pending submission in identifying the relevant area.[256] However, the Special Chamber's reasoning on the identification of the relevant area is non-existent. In a two-line paragraph, the Special Chamber only stated that '[i]n the south, the relevant area is delimited by the outer limits of the continental shelf of Ghana and those of the continental shelf claimed by Côte d'Ivoire'.[257]

---

[251] Chapter 4, Section III.B below.
[252] *Bangladesh v. India* (n. 7) 102–3 [309].
[253] UN Doc CLCS/85 (24 September 2014) 6–7 [25]–[27].
[254] ITLOS/PV.17/C23/3/Rev.1, 5 (Singh). At the time of the Special Chamber's judgment, Côte d'Ivoire's submission to the CLCS remained pending.
[255] Côte d'Ivoire argued that the proposed angle-bisector was equitable by reference to disproportionality between the parties' relevant coasts and the maritime areas appertaining to them. See Counter-memorial of Côte d'Ivoire (4 April 2016), 213–219 [8.41]–[8.53]; Rejoinder of Côte d'Ivoire (14 November 2016), 95–101 [3.57]–[3.65].
[256] Memorial of Ghana (4 September 2015), figure 5.6 following page 144; Reply of Ghana (25 July 2016), figure 3.10 following page 98.
[257] *Ghana/Côte d'Ivoire* (n. 7) [385].

Consistency with the basis of title would require delimitation beyond 200 nm to be effected only after the continental shelf's outer limits have been delineated pursuant to Article 76 UNCLOS. However, whether delineation must precede delimitation is a matter of controversy.[258] If this were the case, the outer limits of the continental shelf, and thus of the relevant area, would be established prior to delimitation. However, this does not seem to be the approach of international tribunals. Using the parties' CLCS submissions in order to determine the relevant area's limits is inadequate. Concerning marine areas within 200 nm, Evans wrote that 'just because a State claims that it has an entitlement does not mean that it does'.[259] This also applies to the continental shelf beyond 200 nm.

However, one might ask what international tribunals could conceivably do. Referring to overlapping entitlements beyond 200 nm as the limits of the relevant area seems unconvincing, since the existence and extent of such entitlements is certain only after the delineation of the continental shelf's outer limits pursuant to Article 76 UNCLOS.[260] The difficulty in determining the relevant area beyond 200 nm absent a clear and objective manner to determine the limits of the relevant area strongly suggests that international tribunals should delimit boundaries beyond 200 nm only after the delineation of the continental shelf's outer limits in accordance with Article 76 UNCLOS. The alternative to this solution is the international tribunals' exercise of a large measure of discretion in identifying the relevant area beyond 200 nm.

It might be conceivable for international tribunals to determine the limits of the relevant area beyond 200 nm by reference to the continental shelf's outer limits even before the CLCS's recommendation on delineation. In the 2016 *Nicaragua v. Colombia* preliminary objections judgment, the ICJ clarified that, in the earlier 2012 *Nicaragua v. Colombia* merits judgment, it had found that:

> [i]t is because ... Nicaragua had not yet submitted such information that the Court concluded ... that 'Nicaragua, in the present proceedings, has not established that it has a continental margin that extends far enough to

---

[258] Chapter 4, Section III.C below.
[259] Evans (n. 2) 261. Similarly, see X Liao, 'Evaluation of Scientific Evidence by International Courts and Tribunals in the Continental Shelf Delimitation Cases' (2017) 48 *ODIL* 136, 139.
[260] B Kunoy, 'The Delimitation of an Indicative Area of Overlapping Entitlement to the Outer Continental Shelf' (2012) 83 *BYIL* 61, 74–8. Other writers take a different view. See Chapter 4, section III.C below.

overlap with Colombia's 200-nautical-mile entitlement to the continental shelf, measured from Colombia's mainland coast'.[261]

According to the Court, if states wish to request international tribunals to delimit the continental shelf beyond 200 nm, they must file full submissions with the CLCS before the final decision on delimitation. International tribunals could have access to such submissions, whose scientific data they could assess without having to await the CLCS's recommendation under Article 76(8) UNCLOS. For instance, international tribunals could request expert opinions where allowed by their constitutive instruments, or refer the issue of determining maritime entitlements beyond 200 nm to the CLCS itself.[262]

This potential approach appears to be consistent with the view presumably expressed by the Court in the 2017 judgment on preliminary objections in *Somalia v. Kenya*. In deciding on Kenya's preliminary objections based on the 2009 Kenya-Somalia Memorandum of Understanding,[263] the Court stated that:

> [a] lack of certainty regarding the outer limits of the continental shelf, and thus the precise location of the endpoint of a given boundary in the area beyond 200 nautical miles, does not, however, necessarily prevent either the States concerned or the Court from undertaking the delimitation of the boundary in appropriate circumstances before the CLCS has made its recommendations.[264]

The Court stated that 'lack of certainty' does not prevent it from delimiting a boundary beyond 200 nm. However, that delimitation should be done 'in appropriate circumstances'. The Court did not elaborate on the character of such 'appropriate circumstances', but a recent commentator suggested that 'the conditions allowing the ITLOS and the Arbitral Tribunal in the Bay of Bengal Cases to overcome a hesitation to proceed to delimitation, that is, "absence of scientific uncertainty" or agreement, should inform the meaning of the "appropriate circumstances"

---

[261] *Question of the Delimitation of the Continental Shelf between Nicaragua and Colombia beyond 200 Nautical Miles from the Nicaraguan Coast (Nicaragua v. Colombia)* (Preliminary Objections) [2016] ICJ Rep 100, 131 [82].

[262] M Lando, 'Delimiting the Continental Shelf Beyond 200 Nautical Miles at the International Court of Justice: The *Nicaragua v Colombia* Cases' (2017) 16 *Chinese JIL* 137, 154–9. See also Liao (n. 259) 136.

[263] 2599 UNTS 35.

[264] *Maritime Delimitation in the Indian Ocean (Somalia v. Kenya)* (Preliminary Objections) [2017] ICJ Rep 3, 38 [94].

formula'.²⁶⁵ This case-by-case approach seems better to take stock of the existence of different scenarios in the delimitation of the continental shelf beyond 200 nm. While in some cases international tribunals can be reasonably certain that overlapping entitlements beyond 200 nm exist, in other cases such reasonable certainty may not exist. In either case international tribunals would be guided by scientific data, which constitute the only means to reach the 'absence of scientific uncertainty' necessary to proceed to delimitation beyond 200 nm.

However, even by assessing the scientific data provided to the CLCS, international tribunals could not delineate the continental shelf's outer limits, and thus establish the relevant area's limit beyond 200 nm. The continental shelf's outer limits are established by coastal states 'on the basis of' the CLCS's recommendations,²⁶⁶ without involving international tribunals. International tribunals may use the scientific data provided to the CLCS only to ascertain whether the states party to a case have continental shelf entitlements beyond 200 nm as a precondition to delimitation.²⁶⁷ However, ascertaining the existence of continental shelf entitlements beyond 200 nm does not entail that international tribunals could also establish the outer limits of the continental shelf, and thus of the relevant area beyond 200 nm. On this basis, international tribunals should await the delineation of the continental shelf's outer limits beyond 200 nm in order to ensure consistency with UNCLOS and with the basis of title.

IV An Additional Stage in the Delimitation Process

International tribunals have so far identified the relevant coast and the relevant area as a preliminary step in the delimitation process, preceding the drawing of an equidistance line at its first stage. The Special Chamber in *Ghana/Côte d'Ivoire* conceived of the identification of the relevant coast and of the relevant area as part of the first stage of delimitation, since it stated that '[t]he first step in the construction of the provisional equidistance line is to identify the Parties' coasts of which the seaward projection overlaps'.²⁶⁸ However, owing to its central function in delimitation, it seems desirable for the identification of the relevant coast

---

[265] G Vega-Barbosa, 'The Admissibility of Outer Continental Shelf Delimitation Claims Before the ICJ Absent a Recommendation by the CLCS' (2018) 49 *ODIL* 103, 112.
[266] Art. 76(8) UNCLOS.
[267] Lando (n. 262) 154–9.
[268] *Ghana/Côte d'Ivoire* (n. 7) [361]. On the first stage of delimitation, see Chapter 4 below.

and of the relevant area to be seen as a full-fledged first stage in delimitation. Since *Black Sea*, states have devoted entire parts of their written and oral submissions to the relevant coast and the relevant area. Similarly, international tribunals have devoted entire sections of their decisions to identifying the relevant coast and the relevant area. Acknowledging that such identification constitutes the first stage in the delimitation process would be nothing more than taking stock of a development which has already taken place in practice.

Writing in 2018, Evans argued that the relevant coast and the relevant area are mainly useful to establish the existence of a marked coastal length disparity at the second stage of the delimitation process, and to assess the absence of disproportionality at the third stage of that process. Evans added that, in *Black Sea*, the ICJ gave the relevant coast and the relevant area 'an additional *a priori* role at the very commencement' of the process.[269] However, according to him this decision was 'as remarkable as it is nonsensical',[270] since both the relevant coast and the relevant area have been 'routinely understood as being "relevant circumstances"'.[271] However, this view does not seem to be entirely justified based on the developments following the adoption of a standard delimitation process. Evans's observations would be correct if relevant circumstances had the function of indicating the appropriate delimitation method on a case-by-case basis. However, in the standard three-stage delimitation process relevant circumstances have the function of justifying the adjustment of a provisional equidistance line. In addition, the relevant coast and the relevant area have effects not only on the second and third stages of the process, but also on the first, since it is on the relevant coast that international tribunals select the appropriate base points for constructing a provisional equidistance line.[272] Understanding the identification of the relevant coast and of the relevant area as a classic relevant circumstance does not seem to be entirely convincing.

The recognition that identifying the relevant coast and the relevant area is a full-fledged stage in maritime delimitation would increase transparency in the establishment of maritime boundaries. Furthermore, it would avoid the inclination demonstrated both by

---

[269] MD Evans, 'Relevant Circumstances' in A Oude Elferink et al. (eds.), *Maritime Boundary Delimitation – The Case Law: Is It Consistent and Predictable?* (CUP, 2018) 222, 233.
[270] Ibid.
[271] Ibid.
[272] Chapter 4, Section IV.C below.

ITLOS in *Bangladesh/Myanmar*, and by the ICJ in respect of the Caribbean Sea in *Costa Rica* v. *Nicaragua*, potentially to defer the identification of the relevant area to the third and last stage of the delimitation process, the disproportionality test.[273] The ICJ identified the Caribbean relevant area at the stage of the disproportionality test because the section of the judgment in which it identified the relevant coast came before the section of the judgment in which it decided on the effect of the treaties with and between third states.[274] Had the Court examined the relevance of such treaties before identifying the relevant coast, it would have identified the relevant area before drawing a provisional equidistance line. The structure followed by the Court led to the same result which would have been reached if the relevance of treaties with and between third states had been examined before identifying the relevant coast. Nevertheless, this latter approach would have been more logical, since it would have avoided having a section of the judgment at paragraphs 115–122 entitled 'Relevant area' in which no relevant area was identified, while the Court actually identified the relevant area at paragraphs 163–164. Differently from *Costa Rica* v. *Nicaragua*, there did not seem to be any reason for ITLOS to identify the relevant area at the disproportionality stage in *Bangladesh/Myanmar*. These leaps in the logic of a maritime delimitation judgment could be avoided if international tribunals acknowledged that identifying the relevant coast and the relevant area constitutes the first, full-fledged stage of the delimitation process.

The identification of the relevant coast and of the relevant area is a complex operation, and, in carrying it out, a high number of considerations come into play. While this operation is governed by the basis of title, international tribunals exercise a measure of discretion in this regard. A sound method to identify the relevant coast and the relevant area is essential in the delimitation process: first, it is on the relevant coast that international tribunals select base points for constructing an equidistance line; second, it is within the framework of the relevant coast and of the relevant area that international tribunals ascertain the existence of relevant circumstances; third, disproportionality entails comparing the ratio of the relevant coast's length to the part of relevant area appertaining to each state.

---

[273] Chapter 6 below.
[274] *Costa Rica* v. *Nicaragua* (n. 7) 187 [120]–[121].

Identifying the relevant coast and the relevant area has important effects on maritime delimitation disputes. In order to enhance the predictability of the delimitation process, their identification should be achieved as objectively as possible. A connection with the basis of title facilitates the acquisition of a significant degree of objectivity in identifying the relevant coast and the relevant area. However, it seems difficult, and perhaps even undesirable, completely to remove the measure of discretion that international tribunals enjoy in this regard. The great variety of geographical settings in which delimitation could take place requires international tribunals to appreciate each case on its merits, especially in relation to the identification of the relevant area. This appreciation should respect the basis of title nonetheless, and not be exercised inconsistently with it.

4

Equidistance

I Brief History of Equidistance

Delimitation by equidistance entails the establishment of a boundary as a line every point of which is equidistant from the nearest points on the baselines from which the breadth of the territorial seas of the states concerned is measured. The 1930 League of Nations Codification Conference suggested equidistance as the method to delimit the territorial seas around international straits.[1] However, it was not until 1958 that equidistance would be codified as a rule of international law. Under Article 12 of the Convention on the Territorial Sea and the Contiguous Zone[2] and Article 6 of the Convention on the Continental Shelf (CCS),[3] the territorial sea and the continental shelf are delimited by equidistance, unless special circumstances require a boundary at variance therewith.[4] The United Nations Convention on the Law of the Sea (UNCLOS)[5] retained this solution for territorial sea delimitation.[6] However, the UNCLOS negotiations on continental shelf and EEZ delimitation saw states divided between 'two virtually irreconcilable approaches':[7] on one hand, delimitation by equidistance; on the other hand, delimitation pursuant to equitable principles. The result was a compromise provision drafted by the President of the Third United Nations Conference on the Law of the Sea (UNCLOS III),[8] which states subsequently incorporated

---

[1] Chapter 2, Section II.A.1 above.
[2] 516 UNTS 205.
[3] 499 UNTS 311.
[4] Chapter 2, Section II.A.2 above.
[5] 1833 UNTS 3.
[6] Art. 15 UNCLOS.
[7] MH Nordquist (ed.), *United Nations Convention on the Law of the Sea 1982 – A Commentary* (Martinus Nijhoff, 1993) vol. II, 801 and 954.
[8] R Platzöder, *Third United Nations Conference on the Law of the Sea: Documents* (Oceana, 1986) vol. IX, 474.

into UNCLOS. Conceivably, the earlier finding of the International Court of Justice (ICJ or Court) in *North Sea Continental Shelf* that equidistance was neither inherent in the concept of the continental shelf, nor a rule of customary international law,[9] influenced this outcome.

Articles 74 and 83 UNCLOS govern the delimitation of the Exclusive Economic Zone (EEZ) and of the continental shelf respectively.[10] As both provisions are remarkably vague, international tribunals are not compelled to use any pre-determined method to delimit the EEZ and the continental shelf, so long as the solution is equitable. However, international tribunals have elaborated on the equitable solution requirement, including by re-introducing equidistance as the starting point in the delimitation process.[11] The literature written in English has shown little interest in equidistance.[12] French-language writers have shown more interest, which is limited compared to the academic output on other delimitation-related topics nonetheless.[13] This limited interest could stem from the view, seemingly held by international tribunals, that equidistance is part of the established methodology for maritime delimitation.

While the function of equidistance may be well established, its application gives rise to a number of problems. This chapter explores the connection between equidistance and the basis of title over maritime zones, including with reference to the relationship between the EEZ and the continental shelf. Although this connection may raise some doubts with respect to the continental shelf beyond 200 nautical miles (nm), there are good reasons to overcome such doubts. Moreover, the configuration of the coast could affect the use of equidistance, as indicated by

---

[9] *North Sea Continental Shelf (Federal Republic of Germany/Denmark; Federal Republic of Germany/Netherlands)* (Judgment) [1969] ICJ Rep 3.

[10] The ICJ has declared both provisions to be part of customary international law. See *Maritime Dispute (Peru v. Chile)* (Judgment) [2014] ICJ Rep 3, 65 [179].

[11] See Chapter 2, Section II.B above. See *Maritime Delimitation in the Black Sea (Romania v. Ukraine)* (Judgment) [2009] ICJ Rep 61, 101 [116]; *Delimitation of the Maritime Boundary in the Bay of Bengal (Bangladesh/Myanmar)* (Judgment) [2012] ITLOS Rep 4, 67 [240]; *Territorial and Maritime Dispute (Nicaragua v. Colombia)* (Merits) [2012] ICJ Rep 624, 695 [191]; *Bay of Bengal Maritime Boundary Arbitration (Bangladesh v. India)* (2014) 167 ILR 1, 112–13 [341].

[12] In the last thirty years, only one article has appeared which specifically focuses on equidistance. See F Olorundami, 'The ICJ and its Lip-service to the Non-priority Status of the Equidistance Method of Delimitation' (2015) 4 *CJICL* 53.

[13] In the last thirty years, only two French-language works specifically concerned equidistance. See L Lucchini, 'Le Juge et l'Équidistance: Sense or Sensibility?' in F Alabrune et al. (eds.), *L'Etat Souverain dans le Monde d'Aujourd'hui – Mélanges en l'Honneur de Jean-Pierre Puissochet* (Pédone, 2008) 175; P Von Mühlendahl, *L'Équidistance dans la Délimitation des Frontières Maritimes* (Pédone, 2016).

the approach of international tribunals to constructing provisional equidistance lines.

Section II examines the legal basis of equidistance. Section III deals with equidistance in the delimitation of the continental shelf beyond 200 nm. Section IV analyses the construction of an equidistance line. Section V concludes.

II Legal Basis of Equidistance in Delimitation within 200 Nautical Miles

This section analyses the legal basis of equidistance as the starting point of delimitation in the three-stage approach, limited to the maritime areas within 200 nm. It discusses the connection between equidistance and the basis of title over the EEZ and the continental shelf, the relationship between the EEZ and the continental shelf, and the impact of coastal configuration on the drawing of an equidistance line.

A Connection to the Basis of Title

There is a widespread view that using equidistance in delimitation is grounded in the basis of title.[14] This section analyses the legal basis of this view, which international tribunals and academic writers have seldom tried to explain.[15]

1 Basis of title over the EEZ

The EEZ is not defined under UNCLOS with reference to the maritime spaces it covers. Article 56 UNCLOS only lists the sovereign rights of a coastal state in the EEZ. Paragraph 1 states that such rights relate to the exploration and exploitation of the natural resources of the seabed, subsoil and superjacent waters. Paragraph 3 provides that '[t]he rights set out in this article with respect to the seabed and subsoil shall be exercised in accordance with Part VI [on the continental shelf]'. Under Article 56, EEZ rights extend both to the water column, and to the seabed and subsoil.[16] Article 57 UNCLOS defines the EEZ's limit, providing that

---

[14] P Weil, *Perspectives du Droit de la Délimitation Maritime* (Pédone 1988) 220–221. See also Y Tanaka, *Predictability and Flexibility in the Law of Maritime Delimitation* (Hart 2006) 147–148.

[15] The notion of basis of title is set out in Chapter 2 Section III.C above.

[16] The relationship between the continental shelf and the EEZ is discussed in Section II.B below.

'[t]he [EEZ] shall not extend beyond 200 [nm] from the baselines from which the breadth of the territorial sea is measured'. There are two necessary, yet not sufficient, conditions for a state to assert sovereign rights in the EEZ: first, the state must have a coast, under the principle 'the land dominates the sea';[17] second, sovereign rights can be asserted only up to a distance of 200 nm from the coast. These two elements can be compounded into one, under which title over the EEZ is based on distance from a state's coast. Differently from the continental shelf, a state may enjoy EEZ rights only if it makes a declaration establishing an EEZ.[18]

2 Basis of title over the continental shelf within 200 nautical miles

Title over the continental shelf is more complex. From the 1945 Truman Proclamation[19] to the 1958 Geneva Conventions, the continental shelf debate centred on whether sovereign rights over it depended on occupation or existed *ipso jure* by virtue of a state having a coast.[20] The latter view prevailed, and the *ipso jure* principle was incorporated into Article 2(3) CCS, under which '[t]he rights of the coastal State over the continental shelf do not depend on occupation, effective or notional, or on any express proclamation'.[21] The states' acceptance of the *ipso jure* character of continental shelf rights only clarified that states need not either make a declaration asserting such rights, or perform acts of effective occupation. However, the *ipso jure* principle did not define the geographical scope of continental shelf rights.

Under Article 1 CCS, the continental shelf comprised 'the seabed and subsoil of the submarine areas adjacent to the coast but outside the area

---

[17] *North Sea Continental Shelf* (n. 9) 51 [96].
[18] D Attard, *The Exclusive Economic Zone in International Law* (OUP, 1987) 54–61. For a list of states which have declared an EEZ, see Appendix 1.
[19] Proclamation by the President with respect to the Natural Resources of the Subsoil and Sea Bed of the Continental Shelf (1945) 40 *AJIL Supplement* 45.
[20] According to Waldock, rights over the continental shelf depended on occupation, see H Waldock, 'The Legal Basis of Claims to the Continental Shelf' (1951) 36 *Transactions of the Grotius Society* 115. Lauterpacht, Oda and Colombos argued that rights over the continental shelf existed *ipso jure*, see H Lauterpacht, 'Sovereignty over Submarine Areas' (1950) 27 *BYIL* 376; S Oda, 'The Continental Shelf' (1957) 1 *Japanese Annual of International Law* 15; J Colombos, *The International Law of the Sea* 6th edn (Longman, 1967) 67–9 and 76. In favour of the *ipso jure* character of continental shelf rights, see also *Petroleum Development Ltd v. Sheikh of Abu Dhabi* (1951) 18 *ILR* 144, 156.
[21] This principle was subsequently incorporated into Art. 77 UNCLOS.

of the territorial sea, to a depth of 200 metres or, beyond that limit, to where the depth of the superjacent waters admits of the exploitation of the natural resources of the said areas'. The CCS defined the continental shelf by way of a double 'depth-exploitability' criterion. So long as a state was capable of exploiting the seabed and subsoil, sovereign rights could be asserted even beyond the geomorphological shelf. In its commentary to the 1956 Draft Articles, the International Law Commission (ILC) expressed the view that 'in no way ... the existence of a continental shelf, in the geographical sense as generally understood, is essential for the exercise of the rights of the coastal State as defined in these articles'.[22] Under the CCS, title over the continental shelf was based on two factors: the existence of a state's coast abutting the sea, and either the depth of the waters, or the exploitability of the seabed and subsoil. States criticised Article 1 CCS for the uncertainty stemming from the exploitability criterion.[23] To counter this uncertainty, Guatemala, the United Arab Republic and Yugoslavia had proposed to define the continental shelf as a function of a fixed distance from the coast. However, other states rejected such proposals.[24]

The ICJ commented on the basis of title in *North Sea Continental Shelf*, decided under customary international law.[25] Denmark and the Netherlands argued that the basis of title over the continental shelf was natural prolongation, called 'appurtenance' and understood in the sense of proximity to the coast, as embedded in the reference to 'adjacency'

---

[22] *ILC Yearbook (1956)*, vol. II, 297.

[23] Doc A/CONF.13/5 and Add. 1 to 4 (23 October 1957), *Official Records of the United Nations Conference on the Law of the Sea*, vol. I, 96 (Norway) and 105 (United Kingdom); Doc A/CONF.13/C.4/SR.4 (4 March 1958), *Official Records of the United Nations Conference on the Law of the Sea*, vol. VI, 4–5 (United Kingdom, China, Norway); Doc A/CONF.13/C.4/SR.8 (12 March 1958), *Official Records of the United Nations Conference on the Law of the Sea*, vol. VI, 12 (Turkey); Doc A/CONF.13/C.4/SR.10 (14 March 1958), *Official Records of the United Nations Conference on the Law of the Sea*, vol. VI, 19 (Pakistan) and 21 (Tunisia). See also A Matine-Daftary, 'Cours Abrégé sur la Contribution des Conférences de Genève au Développement Progressif du Droit International de la Mer' (1961) 102 *Recueil des Cours* 635, 659–60.

[24] Doc A/CONF.13/SR.8 (22 April 1958), *Official Records of the United Nations Conference on the Law of the Sea*, vol. II, 12 (Yugoslavia); Doc A/CONF.13/C.4/SR.12 (19 March 1958), *Official Records of the United Nations Conference on the Law of the Sea*, vol. VI, 27 (United Arab Republic); Doc A/CONF.13/C.4/SR.13 (20 March 1958), *Official Records of the United Nations Conference on the Law of the Sea*, vol. VI, 31 (Guatemala) and 32 (Yugoslavia).

[25] Germany was not a party to the CCS, therefore the ICJ's judgment examined the continental shelf as an institution under customary international law.

under Article 1 CCS.[26] Accordingly, the basis of title would require that, as a result of delimitation, each state be attributed the marine areas closer to its coast. The Court rejected this argument, and found that '[t]here seems ... to be no necessary, and certainly no complete, identity between the notions of adjacency and proximity'.[27] According to the Court, 'the notion of adjacency ... only implies proximity in a general sense, and does not imply any fundamental or inherent rule the ultimate effect of which would be to prohibit any State ... from exercising continental shelf rights in respect of areas closer to the coast of another State'.[28] The Court found that the basis of title over the continental shelf was natural prolongation, which did not entail proximity. Jennings suggested that the Court understood natural prolongation as the physical extension of the land territory into the sea, and that the Court's rejection of the identity between 'adjacency' and 'proximity' led it to rely on the connection between 'adjacency' and 'geographical appurtenance'.[29] According to Jennings, the Court understood title over the continental shelf to be the natural fact that the shelf constituted the basis on which a continent rested.

North Sea Continental Shelf greatly influenced the drafting of Article 76(1) UNCLOS, which the ICJ later declared to be part of customary international law.[30] Under that provision:

> [t]he continental shelf of a coastal State comprises the seabed and subsoil of the submarine areas that extend beyond its territorial sea throughout the natural prolongation of its land territory to the outer edge of the continental margin, or to a distance of 200 [nm] from the baselines from which the breadth of the territorial sea is measured where the outer edge of the continental margin does not extend up to that distance.

The impact of *North Sea Continental Shelf* is clear in the reference to 'natural prolongation'. Article 76 UNCLOS is the product of a compromise between two approaches.[31] On one hand, broad-shelf states sought recognition of a continental shelf extending as far seawards as nature

---

[26] Common Rejoinder of Denmark and the Netherlands (30 August 1968), 477–9 [39].
[27] *North Sea Continental Shelf* (n. 9) 30 [42].
[28] Ibid. 30–31 [42].
[29] R Jennings, 'The Limits of Continental Shelf Jurisdiction: Some Possible Implications of the *North Sea Case* Judgment' (1969) 18 *ICLQ* 819, 823–6.
[30] *Nicaragua v. Colombia* (n. 11) 666 [118].
[31] T McDorman, 'The Continental Shelf' in DR Rothwell et al. (eds.), *The Oxford Handbook of the Law of the Sea* (OUP, 2015) 181, 189–95.

would allow;[32] on the other hand, states having a narrow shelf argued for their right to a shelf extending to a fixed distance from the coast irrespective of geomorphology.[33] Under the compromise, all coastal states have rights over a continental shelf up to 200 nm from the coast. In addition, coastal states whose physical shelf protrudes into the sea further than 200 nm may claims sovereign rights up to the outer edge of the continental margin.[34] All UNCLOS negotiating texts retained this compromise,[35] finally adopted as Article 76 UNCLOS.

Under Article 76(1) UNCLOS, all coastal states have a continental shelf extending to 200 nm from their coasts. The parallel with the EEZ's maximum breadth is apparent.[36] As a result of this drafting, and limited to the continental shelf within 200 nm, Article 76(1) UNCLOS enshrines a basis of title constituted of two elements: a state must have a coast abutting the sea, and continental shelf rights can only be exercised up to a distance of 200 nm from the coast.[37] As with the EEZ, the basis of title over the continental shelf within 200 nm is distance from the coast.

By virtue of having the same basis of title, EEZ and continental shelf delimitation within 200 nm should be effected pursuant to the same method. Since title over the EEZ and continental shelf is distance from

---

[32] For example Argentina, Australia, Iceland and the United Kingdom. See also *Report of the Committee on the Peaceful Uses of the Sea-bed and the Ocean Floor beyond the Limits of National Jurisdiction*, UN Doc A/9021(VOL.III)(SUPP) (1 January 1973) 21 (Colombia, Mexico, Venezuela) and 74 (China).

[33] For example Chile and the West African states. See also Doc A/CONF.62/C.2/L.17 (23 July 1974), *Official Records of the Third United Nations Conference on the Law of the Sea*, vol. III, 195 (Nicaragua); Doc A/CONF.62/C.2/L.31/Rev.1 (16 August 1974), *Official Records of the Third United Nations Conference on the Law of the Sea*, vol. III, 211 (Japan); Doc A/CONF.62/86 (22 August 1979), *Official Records of the Third United Nations Conference on the Law of the Sea*, vol. XII, 69 (Group of Islamic States).

[34] This compromise solution was supported by various states. See *Report of the Committee* (n. 32) 78 (Australia, Norway) and 80 (Argentina); Doc A/CONF.62/L.4 (26 July 1974), *Official Records of the Third United Nations Conference on the Law of the Sea*, vol. III, 83 (Canada, Chile, Iceland, India, Indonesia, Mauritius, Mexico, New Zealand, Norway); Doc A/CONF.62/C.2/L.47 (8 August 1974), *Official Records of the Third United Nations Conference on the Law of the Sea*, vol. III, 224 (United States).

[35] Doc A/CONF.62/WP.8 (7 May 1975), *Official Records of the Third United Nations Conference on the Law of the Sea*, vol. IV, 162; Doc A/CONF.62/WP.8/Rev.1 (6 May 1976), *Official Records of the Third United Nations Conference on the Law of the Sea*, vol. V, 164; Doc A/CONF.62/WP.10 (15 July 1977), *Official Records of the Third United Nations Conference on the Law of the Sea*, vol. VIII, 16.

[36] The legal consequences of the EEZ's creation on the continental shelf are analysed in Section II.B below.

[37] The basis of title over the continental shelf beyond 200 nm is discussed in Section III.B below.

the coast, an area of continental shelf or EEZ should be attributed to the state whose coast is located closer to it. Therefore, the boundary between the EEZs and continental shelves of two neighbouring states is the line whose every point is located at the same distance from these states' coasts, which is the equidistance line. Equidistance ensures the highest degree of consistency with the basis of title. However, the need to achieve an equitable solution in delimitation is paramount, which suggests that equidistance should only be the starting point of delimitation. Equidistance lines could be either adjusted based on relevant circumstances,[38] or abandoned should 'compelling reasons' make it 'unfeasible' to establish them.[39] Moreover, although an equidistance line is based on geometric criteria, its establishment is closely linked to the selection of base points, which are points situated on the relevant coast from which every point of the boundary is equidistant. Selecting certain base points instead of others entails that equidistance lines follow a certain course instead of another. Therefore, the principles based on which international tribunals select base points greatly impact on EEZ and continental shelf delimitation.[40]

B Relationship between the Continental Shelf and the EEZ

While it is uncontroversial that distance from the coast is the basis of title over the EEZ, it could be argued that this is not as uncontroversial with respect to the continental shelf within 200 nm. Although equidistance should be the starting point for delimiting the EEZ, one could argue that it should not necessarily be the starting point for delimiting the continental shelf within 200 nm. However, the EEZ incorporates the continental shelf within 200 nm upon being proclaimed by a coastal state. In this perspective, equidistance, the delimitation method consistent with the basis of title over the EEZ, would also apply to the seabed and subsoil of the EEZ, which, prior to a state's proclamation of an EEZ, constitute the continental shelf.

1 EEZ declarations, judicial approaches and recent studies

Out of 151 coastal states, 124 have declared an EEZ, which makes the EEZ–continental shelf relationship a significant issue in delimitation.[41]

---

[38] Chapter 5 below.
[39] *Black Sea* (n. 11) 101 [116]. See Section II.C below.
[40] Section IV below.
[41] A list of EEZ declarations can be found in Appendix 1.

Individual judges and academic writers have elaborated on the relationship between the continental shelf and the EEZ, although interest in the topic has recently diminished.[42] While commentators stress the close link between the continental shelf and the EEZ, they tend to avoid giving a clear answer to the question concerning the relationship between these two maritime zones.

A recent study maintained that the continental shelf and the EEZ should be seen to be separate institutions.[43] However, the author seems to conceive the EEZ regime not to provide for the exercise of sovereign rights over the seabed and subsoil.[44] The argument in favour of a separation between the EEZ and the continental shelf chiefly rests on the existence of two delimitation treaties. Nevertheless, two delimitation treaties is a small number when compared to the approximately 200 agreements concluded by states to establish maritime boundaries. Moreover, the 1997 Australia–Indonesia treaty,[45] which is one of those two treaties, never entered into force, which may cast doubt on its use to support the argument for the separation of the continental shelf from the EEZ.

Another recent study touching upon the relationship between the EEZ and the continental shelf took a more nuanced view. According to the author, Article 56(3) UNCLOS should not be read in isolation.[46]

[42] See *Continental Shelf (Tunisia/Libya)* (Judgment) [1982] ICJ Rep 18, 157 (Dissenting Opinion Oda); *Delimitation of the Maritime Boundary in the Gulf of Maine Area (Canada/USA)* (Judgment) [1984] ICJ Rep 246, 360 (Dissenting Opinion Gros); *Continental Shelf (Libya/Malta)* (Judgment) [1985] ICJ Rep 13, 123 (Dissenting Opinion Oda). See also L Lucchini, 'Plaidoyer pour une Ligne Unique de Délimitation' in R Casado-Raigón and G Cataldi (eds.), *L'Evolution et l'Etat actuel du Droit International de la Mer – Mélanges offerts à Daniel Vignes* (Bruylant, 2009) 561; I Papanicolopulu, *Il confine marino: unità o pluralità?* (Giuffrè, 2005); S Kaye, 'The Use of Multiple Boundaries in Maritime Boundary Delimitation: Law and Practice' (1998) 19 *Australian YIL* 49; MD Evans, 'Delimitation and the Common Maritime Boundary' (1993) 64 *BYIL* 283; SP Sharma, 'The Single Maritime Boundary Regime and the Relationship between the Continental Shelf and the Exclusive Economic Zone' (1987) 2 *IJECL* 203; D McRae, 'The Single Maritime Boundary: Problems in Theory and Practice' in ED Brown and RR Churchill (eds.), *The UN Convention on the Law of the Sea: Impact and Implementation* (Law of the Sea Institute, 1987) 225; P Reuter, 'Une Ligne Unique de Délimitation des Espaces Maritimes' in *Mélanges Georges Perrin* (Diffusion Payot, 1984) 251.
[43] F Olorundami, 'Revisiting the *Libya/Malta* Decision and Assessing its Relevance (or otherwise) to the East China Sea Dispute' (2016) 15 *Chinese JIL* 717, 731-8.
[44] Ibid. 736.
[45] Treaty between Australia and Indonesia Establishing an Exclusive Economic Zone Boundary and Certain Seabed Boundaries, (1997) 36 *ILM* 1053.
[46] On Art. 56(3) UNCLOS, see Section II.B.2 below.

Although this provision links the continental shelf and the EEZ, these 'are still two distinct maritime zones',[47] since '[t]he EEZ regime does not cause the continental shelf regime to cease to exist, nor does the EEZ regime subsume the continental shelf regime'.[48] The author seems to conclude in favour of the separation of the EEZ and of the continental shelf in current international law, although she seems to express a degree of sympathy for the opposite view. However, the analysis of the relationship between the EEZ and the continental shelf requires one to assess UNCLOS provisions other than Article 56(3), as well as the approach which states have taken, especially by concluding delimitation treaties.

2 Interpreting the relevant UNCLOS provisions

The legal basis of the continental shelf's incorporation into the EEZ is Article 56 UNCLOS. Under Article 56(1) UNCLOS, in the EEZ a coastal state has 'sovereign rights for the purpose of exploring and exploiting, conserving and managing the natural resources, whether living or non-living, of the waters superjacent to the seabed and of the seabed and its subsoil'. Although Article 76(1) UNCLOS provides that the continental shelf comprises the seabed and subsoil extending to the outer edge of the continental margin, Article 56(1) UNCLOS defines a state's sovereign rights in the EEZ as including rights for the exploration and exploitation of the seabed and subsoil.

Article 56(3) UNCLOS, which links the continental shelf regime to the EEZ regime, suggests the incorporation of the former into the latter. Under Article 56(3), '[t]he rights set out in this Article with respect to the seabed and subsoil shall be exercised in accordance with Part VI'. Article 56(3) means that upon the EEZ's declaration under Part V UNCLOS, a state's sovereign rights over the resources of the EEZ's seabed and subsoil are governed by the provisions of Part VI UNCLOS on the continental shelf. In this perspective, one function of Article 56(3) would be to avoid repeating in Part V the provisions already contained in Part VI. Moreover, the rights over the EEZ's seabed and subsoil and over the continental shelf are identical in character, as UNCLOS provides for 'sovereign rights' in respect of both maritime zones.[49] This identity was conceivably aimed at overcoming the distinction between the EEZ's

---

[47] LN Nguyen, 'UNCLOS Tribunals and the Development of the Outer Continental Shelf Regime' (2018) 67 *ICLQ* 425, 450.
[48] Ibid.
[49] Arts. 56(1)(a) and 77(1) UNCLOS.

seabed and subsoil on one hand and the continental shelf on the other hand, promoting the amalgamation of the two zones.

The continental shelf's incorporation into the EEZ does not deprive the continental shelf regime of *effet utile*. As Part V UNCLOS does not contain any provision on non-living resources, Part VI UNCLOS still applies to the seabed and subsoil after the EEZ's proclamation. Moreover, similarly to the continental shelf regime, which exists *ipso facto* and *ab initio*,[50] the EEZ regime also has partial *ipso facto* character. That the EEZ must be proclaimed and the continental shelf exists *ipso facto* and *ab initio* does not have any legal impact on the seabed and subsoil, since states that have not declared an EEZ have sovereign rights over the seabed and subsoil in accordance with Part VI UNCLOS.[51] The argument that the EEZ cannot incorporate the continental shelf due to the *ipso facto* and *ab initio* character of the continental shelf regime is misconceived. EEZ rights over the seabed and subsoil also exist *ipso facto* and *ab initio*: they could be called 'continental shelf rights' before the EEZ's proclamation, and 'seabed and subsoil rights' after the EEZ's proclamation. While the label is different, their substance remains unchanged.

These views are supported by the drafting history of UNCLOS. The original 1972 Draft Articles on the EEZ stated, similarly to Article 56(1) UNCLOS, that '[t]he exercise of jurisdiction over the [EEZ] shall encompass all the economic resources of the area, living and non-living, either on the water surface or within the water column, or on the soil or sub-soil of the sea-bed and ocean floor'.[52] Certain 1973 Draft Articles on the patrimonial sea stated that '[i]n that part of the continental shelf covered by the patrimonial sea, the legal regime provided for the latter shall apply'.[53] Similarly, Malta proposed the creation of a single maritime zone under national jurisdiction, called 'national ocean space', extending to 200 nm from the coast, and which would cover the exploitation of both living and non-living resources.[54] In a proposal by a group of African states there was no reference to the continental shelf, while the EEZ

---

[50] Art. 77 UNCLOS.

[51] F Orrego-Vicuña, *The Exclusive Economic Zone: Regime and Legal Nature under International Law* (CUP, 1989) 71.

[52] *Report of the Committee on the Peaceful Uses of the Sea-bed and the Ocean Floor beyond the Limits of National Jurisdiction*, UN Doc A/8721(SUPP) (1 January 1972) 181 (Kenya).

[53] *Report of the Committee* (n. 32) 21 (Colombia, Mexico, Venezuela). 'Patrimonial sea' was a term used in the early stages of UNCLOS III to designate the EEZ.

[54] Ibid. 38–41 and 61–6. See also ibid. 87 (Algeria, Cameroon, Ghana, Ivory Coast, Kenya, Liberia, Madagascar, Mauritius, Senegal, Sierra Leone, Somalia, Sudan, Tunisia, Tanzania).

embraced sovereign rights over the marine resources of the water column, the seabed and the subsoil.[55] Narrow-shelf states were the main supporters of the incorporation of the continental shelf by the EEZ, as a means to limit the reach of the sovereign rights of broad-shelf states over the continental shelf.[56] Since UNCLOS provides that the outer limit of the continental shelf is the same as the outer limit of the EEZ, at least within 200 nm, the incorporation of the former into the latter may well have been an integral part of the Article 76 compromise.[57]

Other UNCLOS provisions appear to confirm the interpretation of Article 56 UNCLOS endorsing the continental shelf's incorporation into the EEZ. Articles 56(3) and 58(2) UNCLOS govern the relationship of the EEZ with other maritime zones, respectively the continental shelf and the high seas. Under Article 58(2), 'Articles 88 to 115 and other pertinent rules of international law apply to the [EEZ] in so far as they are not incompatible with this Part'. While Article 56(3) states that seabed and subsoil rights under the EEZ regime are exercised in accordance with Part VI, Article 58(2) is a compatibility clause, making the rules on the high seas applicable to the EEZ only if compatible with the EEZ regime. On one hand, Article 58(2) acknowledges the distinct characters of the high seas and of the EEZ. Since rights in the high seas may be incompatible with rights in the EEZ, there is no identity between the two regimes, with the latter being a *sui generis* zone distinct from the former.[58] On the other hand, Article 56(3) is not a compatibility clause, but a rule without exception under which the rights over the EEZ's seabed and subsoil are exercised in accordance with Part VI UNCLOS.

Article 60 UNCLOS concerns artificial islands, installations and structures in the EEZ, while Article 80 provides that 'Article 60 applies *mutatis mutandis* to artificial islands, installations and structures on the continental shelf'. The drafting history of Article 80 seems to confirm the states'

---

[55] Doc A/CONF.62/C.2/L.82 (26 August 1974), *Official Records of the Third United Nations Conference on the Law of the Sea*, vol. III, 240–1 (Gambia, Ghana, Ivory Coast, Kenya, Lesotho, Liberia, Libyan Arab Republic, Madagascar, Mali, Mauritania, Morocco, Senegal, Sierra Leone, Sudan, Tunisia, United Republic of Cameroon, United Republic of Tanzania, Zaire).

[56] V Marotta Rangel, 'Le Plateau Continental dans la Convention de 1982 sur le Droit de la Mer' (1985) 194 *Recueil des Cours* 269, 308–11.

[57] Section II.A.2 above.

[58] DR Rothwell and T Stephens, *The International Law of the Sea* 2nd edn (Hart, 2016) 86–8; J Crawford, *Brownlie's Principles of Public International Law* 8th edn (OUP, 2012) 276; RR Churchill and AV Lowe, *The Law of the Sea* (Manchester University Press, 1999) 165–166; Attard (n. 18) 61–7.

intention to incorporate the continental shelf into the EEZ. An earlier draft of Article 80 distinguished between artificial islands, installations and structures located within and beyond 200 nm. While the provision on artificial islands, installations and structures in the EEZ would apply *mutatis mutandis* to the shelf within 200 nm, beyond 200 nm only 'the provisions of paragraphs 2 through 6' of that provision would apply.[59] The continental shelf within 200 nm, in which the artificial islands, installations and structures regime would have been the same as in the EEZ, was seen as an integral part of the EEZ. Under another proposal Article 80 provided that 'Article 60 applies *mutatis mutandis* to artificial islands, installations and structures on the continental shelf beyond the economic zone'.[60] Under this proposal, the applicability of Article 60 only to the continental shelf beyond 200 nm conveyed that within 200 nm the EEZ would incorporate the continental shelf.

In *Libya/Malta*, Libya argued that Article 78(1) UNCLOS 'maintains the dissociation of the legal regime of the continental shelf, the sea-bed and subsoil, from the regime of the superjacent waters'.[61] Under Article 78(1), '[t]he rights of the coastal State over the continental shelf do not affect the legal status of the superjacent waters or of the air space above those waters'. However, Article 78(1) simply provides that, absent an express EEZ proclamation, the fact that a state enjoys *ipso facto* and *ab initio* sovereign rights over the continental shelf does not impair the character of the superjacent waters as high seas. This is supported by the fact that Article 78(1) derives from Article 3 CCS,[62] under which, according to the 1956 ILC Draft Articles, 'the rights of the coastal State over the continental shelf do not affect the legal status of the superjacent waters as high seas or of the airspace above'.[63] Article 78(1) UNCLOS falls short of precluding the incorporation of the continental shelf into the EEZ.

The ICJ endorsed the incorporation of the continental shelf into the EEZ in *Libya/Malta*, decided under customary international law shortly after the adoption of UNCLOS. While Libya and Malta agreed that the basis of title was relevant to delimitation, Libya argued that the basis of title was the geomorphological existence of the continental shelf, or

---

[59] Platzöder, *Third United Nations Conference* (n. 8), vol. XI, 503.
[60] Platzöder, *Third United Nations Conference* (n. 8), vol. IX, 378 (USSR).
[61] *Libya/Malta* (n. 42) 33 [32].
[62] MH Norquist, *The 1982 United Nations Convention on the Law of the Sea – A Commentary* (Martinus Nijhoff, 1993) vol. II, 906.
[63] *ILC Yearbook (1956)*, vol. II, 298.

natural prolongation, while Malta contended that the basis of title over the continental shelf was distance from the coast, at least within 200 nm.[64] Libya argued that equidistance was not necessary in continental shelf delimitation, while Malta reached opposite conclusions.

The ICJ stated that '[a]s the 1982 Convention demonstrates, the two institutions – continental shelf and [EEZ] – are linked together in modern law',[65] and added that:

> [s]ince the rights enjoyed by a State over its continental shelf would also be possessed by it over the sea-bed and subsoil of any [EEZ] which it might proclaim, one of the relevant circumstances to be taken into account for the delimitation of the continental shelf of a State is the legally permissible extent of the [EEZ] appertaining to that same State. This does not mean that the concept of the continental shelf has been absorbed by that of the [EEZ]; it does however signify that greater importance must be attributed to elements, such as distance from the coast, which are common to both concepts.[66]

The Court found that natural prolongation was still the basis of title over the continental shelf, but it had become a 'more complex and juridical concept ... in part defined by distance from the shore',[67] which entailed that 'the distance criterion must now apply to the continental shelf as well as to the [EEZ]'.[68] Therefore, 'whatever the geological characteristics of the ... sea-bed and subsoil, there is no reason to ascribe any role to geological or geophysical factors within that distance either in verifying the legal title of the States concerned or in proceeding to a delimitation as between their claims'.[69] Nonetheless, the Court rejected that equidistance must be the starting point for continental shelf delimitation. As it could fail to yield an equitable solution, equidistance was considered to be only one possible delimitation method.[70]

The Court was not wholly consistent in its reasoning. It premised the relevance of equidistance in continental shelf delimitation not on the basis of title, but on the impact that the development of the EEZ had on the continental shelf since UNCLOS III. However, after holding that the continental shelf within 200 nm has the same basis of title as the EEZ, the

---

[64] *Libya/Malta* (n. 42) 31–3 [29]–[32].
[65] Ibid. 33 [33].
[66] Ibid.
[67] Ibid.
[68] Ibid. 33 [34].
[69] Ibid. 35 [39].
[70] Ibid. 37 [43].

Court failed to draw the inference that equidistance was a necessary starting point for continental shelf, as well as EEZ, delimitation. Moreover, the Court stated that '[a]lthough there can be a continental shelf where there is no [EEZ], there cannot be an [EEZ] without a corresponding continental shelf'.[71] This appears incorrect under the current legal framework, under which one should conclude that the continental shelf is incorporated into the EEZ upon the latter's proclamation by a coastal state. If the former's incorporation into the latter is accepted, it follows that at no moment in time would the two maritime zones co-exist.

3 Approach of states in bilateral delimitation treaties

The approach of states to the EEZ–continental shelf relationship emerging from the existing bilateral delimitation treaties may help one understand Article 56(3) UNCLOS. States have delimited continental shelf and EEZ boundaries in two fashions: on one hand, using a single line or two coincident lines for each maritime zone; on the other hand, using two lines having distinct courses for each maritime zone. The latter option does not support the continental shelf's incorporation into the EEZ. The 1978 Torres Strait treaty and the 1972 and 1997 Australia–Indonesia treaties are the only cases of treaties delimiting distinct boundaries for the continental shelf and for the EEZ.[72] By contrast, states delimiting a single boundary or two coincident boundaries uphold the incorporation of the continental shelf into the EEZ. However, much depends on the language of each treaty. Treaties may only establish a boundary for one maritime zone, or result in a single boundary applicable to both the continental shelf and the EEZ. Moreover, treaties may extend an already existing boundary from one maritime zone to another. Out of almost 200 treaties establishing maritime boundaries beyond 12 nm, approximately three quarters of them have the effect of establishing single boundaries extending both to the water column, and to the seabed and subsoil.[73]

---

[71] Ibid. 33 [34].

[72] Treaty between Australia and Papua New Guinea concerning Sovereignty and Maritime Boundaries in the Torres Strait, 1429 UNTS 207; Treaty between Australia and Indonesia Establishing Certain Seabed Boundaries, 974 UNTS 308; Treaty between Australia and Indonesia Establishing Certain Seabed Boundaries in the Area of the Timor and Arafura Seas, Supplementary to the Agreement of 18 May 1971, 974 UNTS 320; Treaty between Australia and Indonesia Establishing an Exclusive Economic Zone Boundary and Certain Seabed Boundaries (1997) 36 *ILM* 1053.

[73] For a complete list of treaties establishing equidistance boundaries, see Appendix 2.

Certain treaties establish boundaries only dividing the EEZs of the states party. For example, the 2008 Mauritius–Seychelles treaty referred to '[t]he delimitation line between the exclusive economic zone of the Republic of Mauritius ... and the exclusive economic zone of the Republic of Seychelles'.[74] Similarly, the 2005 France–Madagascar treaty concerned 'the limit between the economic zone of the French Republic and the exclusive economic zone of the Republic of Madagascar'.[75] In such treaties, the states party intend to delimit all maritime zones in which they have overlapping entitlements.[76] Since Article 56 UNCLOS provides that the EEZ comprises the seabed and subsoil as well as the water column, the treaties referring to the EEZ only should be deemed to delimit the seabed and subsoil as well as the water column.

States may establish boundaries for the water column, the seabed and the subsoil by clearly specifying in their agreements that such boundaries extend both to the EEZ and to the continental shelf. While Article I(1) of the 2012 Cuba–Honduras treaty states that the parties agreed to establish 'the delimitation line of the exclusive economic zone of the Republic of Honduras and the Republic of Cuba',[77] Article I(2) immediately specifies that '[t]he delimitation line referred to in the preceding paragraph shall also serve as the boundary of the continental shelf between the Republic of Honduras and the Republic of Cuba'.[78] Using somewhat different

---

[74] Treaty between Mauritius and Seychelles on the Delimitation of the Exclusive Economic Zone, (2009) 69 *LoSB* 106.

[75] Treaty between France and Madagascar on the Delimitation of Maritime Areas situated between La Réunion and Madagascar, (2010) 71 *LoSB* 23.

[76] For other treaties delimiting only the EEZ, see Agreement between the State of Israel and the Republic of Cyprus on the Delimitation of the Exclusive Economic Zone, (2011) 75 *LoSB* 27; Treaty on Maritime Delimitation between Mexico and Honduras, (2007) 65 *LoSB* 33; Treaty between Honduras and the United Kingdom of Great Britain and Northern Ireland concerning the Delimitation of the Maritime Areas between the Cayman Islands and Honduras, (2002) 49 *LoSB* 60; Treaty between Jamaica and Cuba on the Delimitation of the Maritime Boundary, (1994) 26 *LoSB* 50; Treaty on the Delimitation of Marine and Submarine Areas and Maritime Co-operation between Colombia and Costa Rica, *Limits in the Seas No. 84*; Treaty between Australia and New Zealand Establishing certain Exclusive Economic Zone and Continental Shelf Boundaries, 2441 UNTS 235; Treaty between the US and Niue on the Delimitation of a Maritime Boundary, *Limits in the Seas No. 119*; Treaty between the Solomon Islands and Australia Establishing Certain Sea and Seabed Boundaries, (1988) 12 *LoSB* 19; Treaty between the US (American Samoa) and New Zealand (Tokelau) on the Delimitation of the Maritime Boundary between Tokelau and the US, 1643 UNTS 251.

[77] Maritime Delimitation Treaty between the Republic of Honduras and the Republic of Cuba, (2017) 86 *LoSB* 35.

[78] Ibid.

language, the 2012 Cook Islands–Kiribati treaty provides that '[t]he boundary between the exclusive economic zones and continental shelves of the Cook Islands and the Republic of Kiribati is a line of equidistance . . .'.[79] At times, states may include a reference to the maritime zones they intend to delimit in the preambles to their treaties. The preamble to the 2011 Mozambique–Tanzania treaty states that the parties intended 'to effect a precise and equitable delimitation of the common maritime boundary between their respective internal waters, territorial waters, exclusive economic zones and continental shelves'.[80] Similarly to treaties only establishing EEZ boundaries, treaties explicitly providing for boundaries extending both to the EEZ and to the continental shelf appear to convey the states' intention to unify the regime applicable to these two maritime zones.[81]

Treaties extending previous continental shelf boundaries to the EEZ also delimit single boundaries. This is the case of the 1987 Turkey–USSR treaty,[82] the 2007 Norway–Russia treaty,[83] the 2009 Denmark–UK treaty[84] and the 2009 Norway–UK treaty.[85] States may delimit a single

---

[79] Agreement between the Cook Islands and Kiribati concerning the Delimitation of Maritime Boundaries between the Cook Islands and Kiribati, (2017) 85 *LoSB* 32.

[80] Agreement on the Delimitation of the Maritime Boundary between the Republic of Mozambique and the United Republic of Tanzania, in C Lathrop (ed.), *International Maritime Boundaries* (Martinus Nijhoff, 2016) vol. VII, 4800.

[81] For other treaties explicitly mentioning both the EEZ and the continental shelf, see Agreement by Exchange of Notes of identical Content between the Republic of Peru and the Republic of Ecuador, 2756 UNTS 223; Agreement between the Cook Islands and Niue concerning the Delimitation of Maritime Boundaries between the Cook Islands and Niue, (2014) 82 *LoSB* 51; Agreement between the Republic of Kiribati and the Republic of the Marshall Islands concerning Maritime Boundaries, in Lathrop (n. 80), vol. VII, 4869; Agreement between the Republic of Kiribati and the Republic of Nauru concerning Maritime Boundaries, in Lathrop (n. 80), vol. VII, 4881; Agreement between the Republic of the Marshall Islands and the Republic of Nauru concerning Maritime Boundaries, in Lathrop (n. 80), vol. VII, 4915; Agreement between the Union of the Comoros and the Republic of Seychelles on the Delimitation of the Maritime Boundary of the Exclusive Economic Zone and the Continental Shelf in the Indian Ocean, in Lathrop (n. 80), vol. VII, 5039.

[82] Exchange of Notes constituting an Agreement on the Delimitation of the USSR and Turkish Economic Zone in the Black Sea, 1460 UNTS 135.

[83] Treaty between Russia and Norway on Maritime Delimitation in the Varangerfjord Area, (2008) 67 *LoSB* 42.

[84] Exchange of Notes between the United Kingdom of Great Britain and Northern Ireland and Denmark Confirming the Limits of the United Kingdom of Great Britain and Northern Ireland's Exclusive Economic Zone in the North Sea, UKTS No. 1 (2010).

[85] Exchange of Notes Amending the Agreement between the United Kingdom of Great Britain and Northern Ireland and Norway Relating to the Delimitation of the Continental Shelf between the two countries, UKTS No. 16 (2009).

II DELIMITATION WITHIN 200 NAUTICAL MILES 119

boundary by means of one treaty, yet effect the delimitation using two distinct provisions of that same treaty, as with the 1984 Denmark–Sweden treaty on the delimitation of their continental shelf and Fishery Zone (FZ).[86] While Articles 3–5 of that treaty define the co-ordinates of the boundary's turning points, Article 7 adds that '[t]he boundary line specified in Articles 3 to 5 shall also form the boundary line between the fishing zones of the two States'. Another example is the 1978 Sweden–GDR treaty: Articles 1–2 describe the course of the continental shelf boundary, while the protocol states that 'the boundary line as determined in Articles 1 and 2 ... shall also form the boundary line between the fishing zones of the two States'.[87] Treaties extending an earlier continental shelf boundary to the EEZ also suggest the unification of the regimes applicable to these two maritime zones.[88]

In addition to treaties identifying the maritime zones they delimit, certain treaties do not refer to any maritime zone in establishing boundaries. It seems reasonable to infer that the states concerned intended to establish all outstanding boundaries, in accordance with the principle under which it is 'natural that any article designed to fix a frontier should ... be so interpreted that the result of the application of its provisions in their entirety should be the establishment of a precise, complete and definitive frontier'.[89] Such a solution was adopted in the

[86] Treaty between Denmark and Sweden concerning the Delimitation of the Continental Shelf and Fishing Zones, 1409 UNTS 445.
[87] Treaty between the German Democratic Republic and Sweden on the Delimitation of the Continental Shelf, 1147 UNTS 193.
[88] For other treaties extending a continental shelf boundary to the EEZ, see Exchange of Letters between the United Kingdom of Great Britain and Northern Ireland and the French Republic relating to the Delimitation of the Exclusive Economic Zone, UKTS No. 19 (2014); Agreement between Ireland and the United Kingdom of Great Britain and Northern Ireland Establishing a Single Maritime Boundary between the Exclusive Economic Zone of the two Countries and Parts of their Continental Shelves, UKTS No. 21 (2014); Exchange of Letters between the United Kingdom of Great Britain and Northern Ireland and the Kingdom of the Netherlands amending the Agreement relating to the Delimitation of the Continental Shelf under the North Sea between the two Countries of 6 October 1965 as amended by the Protocol of 25 November 1971 and the Exchange of Notes January and June 2004, UKTS No. 20 (2014); Exchange of Letters between the United Kingdom of Great Britain and Northern Ireland and the Kingdom of Belgium amending the Agreement relating to the Delimitation of the Continental Shelf under the North Sea between the two Countries of 19 May 1991 as amended by Exchange of Letters of 21 March and 7 June 2005, UKTS No. 14 (2016); Exchange of Notes between France and the United Kingdom of Great Britain and Northern Ireland constituting an Agreement concerning the Creation and Delimitation of an Economic Zone around the Islands of Pitcairn, Henderson, Ducie and Oeno, 1772 UNTS 95.
[89] *Interpretation of the Treaty of Lausanne* (Advisory Opinion) PCIJ Series B No. 12, 20.

1986 India–Myanmar treaty,[90] whose Article I refers to '[t]he maritime boundary between Burma and India in the Andaman Sea and in the Coco Channel'. Article IV simply mentions the 'actual location at sea and on the sea-bed and on the continental shelf of the points specified in Articles I and II'. Similarly, Article 1 of the 2010 Norway–Russia treaty only refers to '[t]he maritime delimitation line between the Parties in the Barents Sea and the Arctic Ocean'.[91] General references to 'maritime boundaries' unaccompanied by clauses specifying which maritime zones such boundaries delimit have become increasingly common in recent years.[92] This development indicates that numerous states see the EEZ and the continental shelf to be governed by one legal regime.

There also exist treaties only establishing continental shelf boundaries, such as the 1992 Italy–Albania treaty and the 2000 Kuwait–Saudi Arabia treaty.[93] Currently, there are around fifty treaties delimiting only the continental shelf, but such treaties have become uncommon. The high number of treaties delimiting coincident boundaries for the continental shelf and the EEZ suggests that states implicitly acknowledge that the EEZ incorporates the continental shelf upon being proclaimed. If that were not the case, it would be difficult to explain why certain states agree that their treaties only delimit the EEZ. Similarly, it would be difficult to explain why states decide to extend previously established continental shelf boundaries to the EEZ.

The incorporation of the continental shelf into the EEZ has a firm legal basis under UNCLOS. The consequence is that, at least within 200 nm,

---

[90] Treaty between India and Myanmar on the Delimitation of the Maritime Boundary in the Andaman Sea, in the Coco Channel and in the Bay of Bengal, 1484 UNTS 172.

[91] Treaty between the Russian Federation and the Kingdom of Norway concerning Maritime Delimitation and Co-operation in the Barents Sea and the Arctic Ocean, 2791 UNTS 3.

[92] See Treaty between the Republic of Trinidad and Tobago and Grenada on the Delimitation of Marine and Submarine Areas, 2675 UNTS 5; Agreement between New Zealand and the Cook Islands concerning the Delimitation of the Maritime Boundaries between Tokelau and the Cook Islands, (2014) 82 *LoSB* 54; Agreement between the Commonwealth of the Bahamas and the Republic of Cuba for the Delimiting Line between their Maritime Zones, (2013) 79 *LoSB* 19; Agreement between New Zealand and the Republic of Kiribati concerning the Delimitation of the Maritime Boundaries between Tokelau and Kiribati, (2017) 90 *LoSB* 49; Treaty between the USA and the Republic of Kiribati on the Delimitation of Maritime Boundaries, in Lathrop (n. 80), vol. VII, 4935; Treaty between the USA and the Federated States of Micronesia on the Delimitation of a Maritime Boundary, in Lathrop (n. 80), vol. VII, 4963.

[93] Agreement between Albania and Italy for the Determination of the Continental Shelf of each of the two Countries, (1994) 26 *LoSB* 54; Treaty between Saudi Arabia and Kuwait concerning the Submerged Area adjacent to the Divided Zone, 2141 UNTS 251.

equidistance should be the starting point for delimiting the continental shelf and the EEZ, or, more accurately the EEZ.[94] Even if one doubted that distance from the coast could be the basis of title over the continental shelf within 200 nm, its incorporation into the EEZ should dispel such doubts. A problem could arise if one of two neighbouring states party to a delimitation case did not declare an EEZ, while the other one did. However, due to the small number of states without an EEZ, this issue is of limited practical significance. Moreover, states without an EEZ have been parties to delimitation cases, in which they were treated as having an EEZ. Nicaragua declared in 1979 that it would have a 200-nm territorial sea,[95] and yet was treated as having a 200-nm EEZ both in *Nicaragua v. Honduras* and in *Nicaragua v. Colombia*.[96]

C Impact of Coastal Configuration

Although equidistance is the starting point for delimitation, the need to achieve an equitable solution is paramount under UNCLOS. In *Black Sea*, the ICJ held that it would not abandon equidistance in delimitation between adjacent coasts unless 'compelling reasons' made it 'unfeasible' to draw an equidistance line.[97] In *Nicaragua v. Colombia*, the ICJ applied the 'compelling reasons–unfeasibility test' to opposite coasts.[98]

Two issues arise concerning the relationship between the equitable solution under UNCLOS and the 'compelling reasons–unfeasibility test', and the factors that could be a 'compelling reason' rendering it 'unfeasible' to draw an equidistance line. Tracing an equidistance line is based on geometric criteria using the relevant coast as a reference point. This suggests that both the application of the 'compelling reasons–unfeasibility test', and the achievement of an equitable solution, should be assessed based on coastal configuration. The ICJ discussed whether coastal configuration justified delimitation by a method other than equidistance in *Nicaragua v. Honduras* and in *Nicaragua v. Colombia*.

---

[94] While arguing for the incorporation of the continental shelf into the EEZ, this chapter retains the terminological distinction between 'continental shelf' and 'EEZ' for historical reasons.
[95] Act No. 205 of 19 December 1979 on the Continental Shelf and Adjacent Sea.
[96] Sections II.C.1 and II.C.2 below.
[97] *Black Sea* (n. 11) 101 [116]. The Court used 'equidistance' as shorthand for 'three-stage approach'.
[98] *Nicaragua v. Colombia* (n. 11) 695 [191].

1 The 2007 *Nicaragua* v. *Honduras* judgment

In *Nicaragua* v. *Honduras*, neither party requested the ICJ to delimit their boundary by equidistance. On one hand, Nicaragua asked the Court to establish the boundary as the bisector of the lines approximating the parties' coastal fronts, since 'the instability of the mouth of the River Coco at the Nicaragua-Honduras land boundary terminus ... would make fixing base points and using them to construct a provisional equidistance line unduly problematic'.[99] On the other hand, Honduras argued for a boundary following the fifteenth parallel, which it regarded as an adjusted equidistance line, and also acknowledged that 'the mouth of the River Coco "shifts considerably, even from year to year",[100] making it "necessary to adopt a technique so that the maritime boundary need not change as the mouth of the river changes"'.[101] The Court stated that 'the equidistance method does not automatically have priority over other methods of delimitation and, in particular circumstances, there may be factors which make the application of the equidistance method inappropriate'.[102]

The Court rejected equidistance based both on the impossibility of finding appropriate base points,[103] and on coastal geography. Concerning coastal geography, the Court made two main findings. First, 'Cape Gracias a Dios, where the Nicaragua-Honduras land boundary ends, is a sharply convex territorial projection abutting a concave coastline on either side to the north and south-west'.[104] Second, 'the sediment carried to and deposited at sea by the River Coco have caused its delta, as well as the coastline to the north and south of the Cape, to exhibit a very active morpho-dynamism',[105] which entailed that 'accretion at the Cape might render any equidistance line so constructed today arbitrary and unreasonable in the near future'.[106]

The latter consideration seems hardly capable of determining a decision not to use equidistance. Morpho-dynamism at Cape Gracias a Dios does not directly concern the current coastal configuration, since,

---

[99] *Territorial and Maritime Dispute between Nicaragua and Honduras in the Caribbean Sea (Nicaragua v. Honduras)* (Judgment) [2007] ICJ Rep 659, 741 [273].
[100] Ibid. 742 [274].
[101] Ibid.
[102] Ibid. 741 [272] (emphasis added).
[103] Base points and coastal instability are discussed in Section IV.C.2 below.
[104] *Nicaragua v. Honduras* (n. 99) 742 [277].
[105] Ibid.
[106] Ibid.

as conceived by the Court, it more specifically relates to the viability of selecting suitable base points.[107] Even accepting that it does, it is unsure how long it would take for sediment accretion to result in a coastline so distinct from the present as to justify a non-equidistant boundary. Moreover, an international tribunal should delimit a boundary based on the current geography, since predictions on how the coastline might exactly change could be speculative.

The former consideration could also be criticised. While it is true that Cape Gracias a Dios is a convex protrusion flanked by the concave coastlines of both Honduras and Nicaragua, the Court should have noted that Nicaragua's concave coast was balanced by Honduras's also concave coast. If one of the parties had a concave coast and the other a convex coast, an equidistance line would deflect towards the state with a concave coast, resulting in the cut-off of its coastal projections. However, if both coasts are concave, no such a risk exists. In *Nicaragua v. Honduras*, the general direction of the parties' coast did not appear compelling enough to warrant abandoning equidistance. From Cape Gracias a Dios, Nicaragua's coast proceeds southwards in a straight line for almost 80 km, while Honduras's coast runs north-westerly at a 45° angle for roughly 30 km. An equidistance line is not necessarily inequitable in this coastal configuration and, in fact, the Court never explicitly stated that it would be. Furthermore, nothing prevents international tribunals from drawing equidistance lines using base points located close to the land boundary terminus.[108] An equidistance line could also be subsequently adjusted pursuant to relevant circumstances.[109]

The Court's approach to equidistance in its relationship to coastal geography is not fully convincing, and was criticised by some of the judges. Judge Ranjeva discussed the Court's approach to Article 15 UNCLOS, arguing that the ICJ erroneously gave pre-eminence to special circumstances over equidistance in delimiting the territorial sea. According to Judge Ranjeva, under Article 15 UNCLOS 'the unstable nature of the coastlines does not, in itself, constitute a situation of impossibility giving rise to a legal vacuum such as to exclude the application of the general rule of the equidistance line'.[110] His remarks also apply

---

[107] See Section IV.C below.
[108] *Delimitation of the Maritime Boundary between Ghana and Côte d'Ivoire in the Atlantic Ocean (Ghana/Côte d'Ivoire)* (Judgment), Judgment of 23 September 2017 [393]–[401].
[109] See Chapter 5.
[110] *Nicaragua* v. *Honduras* (n. 99) 767 [7] (Separate Opinion Ranjeva).

to the continental shelf and EEZ, so long as they concern coastal instability as a function of coastal geography.[111] Judge *ad hoc* Torres Bernárdez stated that the convexity of Cape Gracias a Dios did not justify drawing a boundary other than equidistance.[112] Overall, the Court's reasoning in *Nicaragua* v. *Honduras* on the impact of coastal configuration seems dubious.

2 The 2012 *Nicaragua* v. *Colombia* judgment

In *Nicaragua* v. *Colombia*, Nicaragua's coast abutting the Caribbean Sea faced Colombia's San Andrés Archipelago. Nicaragua argued that delimitation was to be effected between the parties' mainland coasts and that Colombia's islands had to be enclaved,[113] while Colombia contended that the boundary had to be drawn by reference to Nicaragua's coast and the San Andrés Archipelago.[114] Although the Court held that '[t]he three-stage process is not ... to be applied in a mechanical fashion and ... will not be appropriate in every case to begin with a provisional equidistance/median line',[115] it found that the construction of an equidistance line was feasible. According to the Court:

> [t]he question is not whether the construction of such a line is feasible but whether it is appropriate as a starting-point for the delimitation. That question arises because of the unusual circumstance that a large part of the relevant area lies to the east of the principal Colombian islands and, hence, behind the Colombian baseline from which a provisional median line would have to be measured.[116]

However, the Court found that this 'unusual circumstance' pertained to the second stage of the delimitation process, and that it did not justify 'discarding the entire methodology and substituting an approach in which the starting-point is the construction of enclaves for each island, rather than the construction of a provisional median line'.[117]

Certain judges were critical of the Court. Judge Keith stated that the disproportion in coastal length demonstrated the impossibility of starting with a provisional equidistance line, even if it would subsequently be

---

[111] The impact of coastal instability on the choice of base points is addressed in Section IV. C.2 below.
[112] *Nicaragua* v. *Honduras* (n. 99) 818 [128] (Dissenting Opinion Torres Bernárdez).
[113] *Nicaragua* v. *Colombia* (n. 11) 694 [185]–[186].
[114] Ibid. 694–5 [187]–[189].
[115] Ibid. 695–6 [190]–[194].
[116] Ibid. 697 [195].
[117] Ibid.

adjusted. He added that establishing part of the boundary along parallels of latitude was not adjusting the equidistance line, but using different methods to achieve an equitable solution.[118] Similarly, Judge Xue wrote that '[m]ethodology cannot be pre-determined',[119] and doubted whether it was worth using the three-stage approach for the sake of using a standardised method.[120] Both judges seemed to favour a return to a case-by-case assessment of the suitable delimitation method, taking into account all relevant circumstances.

However, this view would lower the predictability of maritime delimitation that the three-stage approach endeavours to achieve. In addition, both judges denied that the Court had simply adjusted a provisional equidistance line, because the result of the purported adjustment was too far from it. Yet, nothing suggests that adjustments must be limited. The need to achieve an equitable solution could require a substantial shifting of an equidistance line.[121] The three-stage approach to delimitation is distinct from the two-stage approach to territorial sea delimitation, in which special circumstances are exceptions to equidistance entailing that boundaries should be as close to equidistance as possible.[122] This does not apply to the three-stage approach, in which relevant circumstances are not exceptions to equidistance, but an integral part of the delimitation process.

In *Nicaragua v. Colombia*, the ICJ employed an approach different from that in *Nicaragua v. Honduras*. In the latter, equidistance was a mere method, not to be applied if factors exist that make 'the application of the equidistance method inappropriate'.[123] By contrast, in the former the Court adopted the 'compelling reasons–unfeasibility test' formulated in *Black Sea*, which it seemed to understand as having the same function as the *Nicaragua v. Honduras* 'inappropriateness test'.[124] However, while it is one thing to say that it is 'inappropriate' to start with an equidistance line, it is a different thing to say that there must be 'compelling reasons' making it 'unfeasible' to start with equidistance.

---

[118] Ibid. 744 [9] (Declaration Keith).
[119] Ibid. 746 [2] (Declaration Xue).
[120] Ibid. 749 [9] (Declaration Xue).
[121] On the adjustment, see Chapter 5, Section V.C below.
[122] M Lando, 'Judicial Uncertainties concerning Territorial Sea Delimitation under Article 15 of the United Nations Convention on the Law of the Sea' (2017) 66 *ICLQ* 589.
[123] *Nicaragua v. Honduras* (n 99) 741 [272].
[124] Compare paragraphs 194 and 195 of the *Nicaragua v. Colombia* judgment.

3 Reconciling *Nicaragua v. Honduras* and *Nicaragua v. Colombia*

It seems possible to reconcile the two approaches. In *Nicaragua v. Colombia* there was no lack of appropriate base points to construct the equidistance line. The ICJ thus stated that '[t]he question is not whether the construction of [an equidistance] line is feasible but whether it is appropriate as a starting-point for the delimitation'.[125] Reading *Nicaragua v. Honduras* and *Nicaragua v. Colombia* together, it emerges that the Court linked the selection of base points to the 'compelling reasons–unfeasibility test', and the 'inappropriateness test' to coastal configuration against which the achievement of the 'equitable solution' must be assessed. While the 'compelling reasons–unfeasibility test' only relates to the feasibility of constructing the equidistance line, the 'inappropriateness test' relates to whether the equidistance line is capable of ensuring an 'equitable solution'. The two tests should be applied consecutively: first, the 'compelling reasons–unfeasibility test' ensures that the equidistance line can be drawn; second, the 'inappropriateness test' ensures that equidistance can be adjusted in order to achieve an equitable solution. Equidistance lines could always be drawn as a starting point, and later adjusted if they are inappropriate for achieving an equitable solution.

Regrettably, the Special Chamber of the International Tribunal for the Law of the Sea (ITLOS or Tribunal) in *Ghana/Côte d'Ivoire* seemed to conflate the two tests by stating that international jurisprudence confirms that the equidistance/relevant circumstances methodology should be used to delimit maritime boundaries 'in the absence of any compelling reasons that make it impossible or inappropriate to draw a provisional equidistance line'.[126] It appears that the Special Chamber could have exercised greater care in formulating the test on the basis of which international tribunals may decide that a maritime boundary should not be delimited by equidistance.

The construction of an equidistance line seems to be 'feasible' in the vast majority of cases, since appropriate base points are almost always identifiable. The 'compelling reasons–unfeasibility test' sets a high bar in order to show that an equidistance line cannot be constructed. In *Nicaragua v. Honduras*, the Court did not apply this high bar to assess the feasibility of an equidistance line. Nevertheless, the Court may have

---

[125] *Nicaragua v. Colombia* (n. 11) 697 [195].
[126] *Ghana/Côte d'Ivoire* (n. 108) [289].

been right in deciding that the coastal configuration made the use of equidistance 'inappropriate'. The 'inappropriateness test' must be seen as simply requiring an assessment of whether using the three-stage approach could achieve an 'equitable solution'. Moreover, it should not be applied too liberally, as this could affect the predictability of maritime delimitation. There are also cases in which drawing a strict equidistance line would be feasible, yet inappropriate due to coastal configuration. For instance, if the undelimited Guatemala–Honduras boundary were based on equidistance, it could result in the cut-off of the former's coastal projections. However, it does not follow that that and other boundaries should be delimited on the basis of a method at variance with equidistance.

The three-stage approach includes the means to adjust a strict equidistance line should it be inequitable. The *raison d'être* of its second and third stages is to allow international tribunals to adjust a strict equidistance line if using it as the boundary would be inequitable. If constructing the equidistance line is feasible, assessing whether that line is inappropriate in a given geographical setting is already included in the three-stage approach. There is thus no intrinsic reason why international tribunals should not use equidistance in delimiting maritime boundaries, except for the cases in which constructing an equidistance line is 'unfeasible' due to 'compelling reasons' relating to base point selection. In *Ghana/Côte d'Ivoire*, Côte d'Ivoire relied on several factors in order to justify the use of the angle-bisector method instead of equidistance, which included 'geographical considerations (location of base points, location of base points on Jomoro, instability of the coastline) as well as the interests of neighbouring States'.[127] The Special Chamber addressed each of these points in its judgment. However, one could doubt that this approach was convincing.

Ghana/Côte d'Ivoire raises the question as to whether there exist 'compelling reasons' other than the lack of appropriate base points making it 'unfeasible' to construct an equidistance line. The only 'compelling reasons' making the construction of an equidistance line 'unfeasible' must relate to the absence of an element necessary for that exercise. To draw an equidistance line, international tribunals must identify the parties' relevant coasts and subsequently select appropriate base points on that relevant coast.[128] The equidistance line results from the ensuing

---

[127] *Ghana/Côte d'Ivoire* (n. 108) [291].
[128] On the relevant coast, see Chapter 3, Section III above. Base points are discussed in Section IV below.

geometric exercise. The unfeasibility of constructing an equidistance line relates either to the identification of the relevant coast, or to the selection of appropriate base points. Since it is always possible to identify the relevant coast,[129] the issue is selecting appropriate base points.[130] Non-geographical factors could not be 'compelling reasons' making it 'unfeasible' to establish an equidistance line. Non-geographical factors may suggest that an equidistance line is inequitable, and thus relate not to the 'compelling reasons–unfeasibility test', but to the 'inappropriateness test'. Therefore, they cannot influence the feasibility of constructing an equidistance line.

III Equidistance and the Continental Shelf beyond 200 Nautical Miles

Using the three-stage approach to delimit the continental shelf beyond 200 nm raises problems owing to its reliance on equidistance as a starting point. The issues are whether equidistance is linked to the basis of title over the continental shelf beyond 200 nm, which warrants using it as a starting point for delimitation, and the creation of grey areas.

A The Bay of Bengal Cases and Ghana/Côte d'Ivoire

Bangladesh/Myanmar, Bangladesh v. India and *Ghana/Côte d'Ivoire* are the three cases in which international tribunals have delimited the continental shelf beyond 200 nm. In all cases, international tribunals applied the three-stage approach, including an equidistance line as a starting point.

Responding to ITLOS's question on the delimitation method beyond 200 nm, the parties in *Bangladesh/Myanmar* agreed that the delimitation should be effected in the same manner both within and beyond 200 nm.[131] ITLOS accepted this view, finding that 'article 83 [UNCLOS] addresses the delimitation of the continental shelf between States with opposite or adjacent coasts without any limitation as to area',[132] which meant that it 'applies equally to the delimitation of the continental shelf both within and beyond 200 nm'.[133] ITLOS held that

---

[129] Chapter 3, Section II.B above.
[130] Section IV below.
[131] *Bangladesh/Myanmar* (n. 11) 116 [452]–[453].
[132] Ibid. 117 [454].
[133] Ibid.

'the delimitation method to be employed in the present case for the continental shelf beyond 200 [nm] should not differ from that within 200 nm'.[134] Bangladesh invoked the 'most natural prolongation' argument and cut-off effect as relevant circumstances. ITLOS rejected the 'most natural prolongation' argument,[135] and held that the adjusted delimitation line drawn within 200 nm 'continues in the same direction beyond the 200-nm limit of Bangladesh until it reaches the area where the rights of third States may be affected'.[136]

ITLOS's application of the three-stage approach beyond 200 nm is unusual, since, strictly speaking, ITLOS did not establish an equidistance line. Instead, ITLOS examined the relevant circumstances existing beyond 200 nm, concluding that the already-adjusted equidistance line within 200 nm continued beyond Bangladesh's 200-nm EEZ limit along the same azimuth.[137] As ITLOS did not draw an equidistance line beyond 200 nm, the three-stage approach was applied only notionally. By contrast, the *Bangladesh v. India* tribunal first established the equidistance line both within and beyond 200 nm, and subsequently adjusted it in a single operation.[138]

Five arbitrators, three of whom were or had been ITLOS judges, decided *Bangladesh v. India*. An approach similar to that of *Bangladesh/Myanmar* could thus have been expected. Bangladesh's line was based on its prior contention that, within 200 nm, the maritime boundary should be the bisector of the 180° angle approximating the general direction of the parties' coast. Bangladesh argued that, at the 200-nm limit, the 180° bisector should start running along a 215° azimuth, roughly parallel to ITLOS's *Bangladesh/Myanmar* boundary.[139] India argued that the three-stage approach also applied to delimitation beyond 200 nm.[140] The tribunal accepted India's argument, and delimited the continental shelf beyond 200 nm starting with an equidistance line originating at the intersection of the parties' 200-nm limit, and continuing until it met the *Bangladesh/Myanmar* boundary. Subsequently, the tribunal found that the cut-off of Bangladesh's coastal projections,

---

[134] Ibid. 117 [455].
[135] Ibid. 118 [460].
[136] Ibid. 118 [461].
[137] Ibid. 87–9 [323]–[336].
[138] In *Bangladesh v. India* there was no express reference to the *modus operandi* adopted in *Bangladesh/Myanmar*.
[139] *Bangladesh v. India* (n. 11) 146–51 [440]–[448].
[140] Ibid. 151–6 [449]–[455].

already found to be a relevant circumstance within 200 nm,[141] required the adjustment of the equidistance line beyond 200 nm. Differently from *Bangladesh/Myanmar*, the arbitral tribunal adjusted the equidistance line, both within and beyond 200 nm, in a single operation.[142]

The Special Chamber in *Ghana/Côte d'Ivoire* adopted the same approach as the Bay of Bengal cases. According to the Special Chamber:

> there is only one single continental shelf. Therefore it is considered inappropriate to make a distinction between the continental shelf within and beyond 200 nm as far as the delimitation methodology is concerned.[143]

Both Ghana and Côte d'Ivoire had contended that the Special Chamber should have delimited the maritime boundary within and beyond 200 nm using the same method, while disagreeing as to what that method should have been.[144] Presumably, the Special Chamber limited itself to agreeing with the position expressed by both parties. The Special Chamber subsequently found that there was no need to adjust the delimitation line beyond 200 nm on account of relevant circumstances.[145]

B The Problem of the Basis of Title

The legal basis of equidistance in delimitation within 200 nm is the basis of title over the continental shelf and the EEZ.[146] However, the link between equidistance and the basis of title could seem dubious with regard to the continental shelf beyond 200 nm.

1 The Article 76 UNCLOS compromise

Article 76 UNCLOS resulted from a compromise at UNCLOS III between broad-shelf states and narrow-shelf states.[147] Article 76 recognises on one hand the rights of all coastal states over the seabed and subsoil up to 200 nm from their coast, and on the other hand that coastal states with a continental shelf physically extending beyond 200 nm can assert their rights up to the outer edge of the continental margin

---

[141] Ibid. 132–8 [400]–[421] and 157–61 [456]–[475].
[142] Ibid. 163–5 [476]–[480].
[143] *Ghana/Côte d'Ivoire* (n. 108) [526].
[144] Ibid. [522]–[525].
[145] Ibid. [527].
[146] Section II.A above.
[147] Section II.A.2 above.

determined through the procedures of paragraphs 4–8. Article 76 seems to divide the continental shelf in two parts, one within and one beyond 200 nm. Rights over the entire continental shelf exist *ipso facto* and *ab initio*.[148] While within 200 nm a state can exercise sovereign rights simply by virtue of having a coast and up to a certain distance from it, beyond 200 nm a state must prove the existence of a physical continental shelf in accordance with the provisions of paragraphs 4–8 of Article 76.

Such provisions create a complex procedure for delineating the outer limits of the continental shelf. Delineation requires a coastal state to make a submission to the Commission on the Limits of the Continental Shelf (CLCS), which delivers a recommendation on the basis of which the coastal state shall establish the continental shelf's outer limits.[149] The existence of a procedure to establish 'final and binding' outer limits for the continental shelf suggests that, although sovereign rights over the seabed and subsoil exist *ipso facto* and *ab initio*, they cannot be lawfully exercised until delineation. A state has no title to sovereign rights beyond 200 nm unless there is a physical continental margin whose existence has been ascertained by the CLCS pursuant to Article 76 UNCLOS. That states are entitled to exercise sovereign rights beyond 200 nm based on the *ipso facto* and *ab initio* character of such rights[150] appears to be a convenient fiction. Concerning delimitation, the question arises as to whether it is justified to use equidistance, and thus the three-stage approach, to delimit the continental shelf beyond 200 nm, given that the basis of title over it does not seem to depend on distance, but on geomorphology.

2 Distance as an element of the basis of title

It would be erroneous to believe, as it has been argued,[151] that distance from the coast is entirely unrelated to the basis of title over the continental shelf beyond 200 nm. Article 76(4)(a) UNCLOS sets forth two alternative, yet not mutually exclusive, methods for delineation. A state may delineate the continental shelf's outer limit 'by reference to the outermost fixed points at each of which the thickness of sedimentary

---

[148] Art. 77(3) UNCLOS.
[149] Art. 76(8) UNCLOS. On delineation, see BM Magnússon, *The Continental Shelf Beyond 200 Nautical Miles – Delineation, Delimitation and Dispute Settlement* (Martinus Nijhoff, 2015) 40–116.
[150] Art. 77 UNCLOS.
[151] B Kunoy, 'A Geometric Variable Scope of Delimitations: The Impact of a Geological and Geomorphological Title to the Outer Continental Shelf' (2006) 11 *Austrian RIEL* 49, 50.

rocks is at least 1 per cent of the shortest distance from such point to the foot of the continental slope'. Alternatively, a state may delineate the continental shelf's outer limit 'by reference to fixed points not more than 60 [nm] from the foot of the continental slope'. In both cases, '[t]he coastal State shall delineate the outer limits of its continental shelf . . . by straight lines not exceeding 60 [nm] in length, connecting fixed points, defined by coordinates of latitude and longitude'.[152] Both methods under Article 76(4)(a) include a distance element. Moreover, under Article 76(5) the points on the continental shelf's outer limit, defined according to paragraph 4, 'either shall not exceed 350 [nm] from the baselines from which the breadth of the territorial sea is measured or shall not exceed 100 [nm] from the 2,500 metre isobath'. Article 76(6) also provides that 'on submarine ridges, the outer limit of the continental shelf shall not exceed 350 [nm] from the baselines from which the breadth of the territorial sea is measured'.

Paragraphs 4–6 of Article 76 have in common that they only determine the maximum limits that the continental shelf of a coastal state could reach, doing so with reference to distance from the coast, from the foot of the continental slope,[153] or from the 2,500-metre isobath. Article 76 suggests that distance is not unrelated to the basis of title over the continental shelf beyond 200 nm. Distance is a necessary, yet not sufficient, element for determining the extent of a state's continental shelf rights beyond 200 nm. Under Article 76 UNCLOS, both the physical existence of a continental margin and distance are necessary to identify the geographical extent of continental shelf rights. However, neither is sufficient, which means that, as a result, they both contribute to defining the extent of a state's continental shelf rights. Consequently, they are both elements of the basis of title over the continental shelf beyond 200 nm, which entails that using equidistance as a delimitation method beyond 200 nm could be legally grounded in UNCLOS.

Distance as the basis of title over the EEZ follows from Article 57 UNCLOS, which fixes the EEZ's maximum breadth.[154] The fact that Article 57 sets a maximum breadth for a state's EEZ does not preclude the establishment of EEZs extending to less than 200 nm from the coast. Similarly, distance should be seen as an element of the basis of title over the continental shelf beyond 200 nm based on Article 76, which fixes its

---

[152] Art. 76(7) UNCLOS.
[153] Under Art. 76(4)(b) UNCLOS, 'the foot of the continental slope shall be determined as the point of maximum change in the gradient at its base'.
[154] Section II.A.1 above.

maximum breadth under international law. However, differently from Article 57, Article 76 does not always use the coast as a reference point from which to measure the continental shelf's maximum reach. This issue concerns the identification of the point with reference to which an equidistance line should be drawn. Article 76(5) mentions both distance from the coast and distance from the 2,500-metre isobath. Article 76(4) mentions the distance from the foot of the continental slope, yet this does not constitute a basis on which to determine the maximum limit of the continental shelf beyond 200 nm. If the outer limit established in accordance with Article 76(4) lay beyond the outer limit provided under Article 76(5), the latter would prevail. Consequently, it could not be said that the foot of the slope is part of the distance element of the basis of title over the continental shelf beyond 200 nm. However, it is relevant to its geomorphological element. Therefore, and differently from what certain authors argue,[155] the foot of the slope could not be used as a reference based on which to establish an equidistance line beyond 200 nm. That reference must be either the territorial sea baseline, or the 2,500-metre isobath.

The coast plays a central role with respect to delimitation beyond 200 nm, and it is on the coast that international tribunals should select appropriate base points for delimitation beyond 200 nm. In both *Bangladesh/Myanmar* and *Bangladesh v. India*, base points were chosen on the coast to construct the equidistance line beyond 200 nm. In the former case, ITLOS prolonged the boundary established within 200 nm, which entailed that the line on which the boundary beyond 200 nm was based had been drawn by reference to base points on the parties' coasts. In *Bangladesh v. India*, the arbitral tribunal drew the equidistance line beyond 200 nm using the base points for the equidistance line within 200 nm, adding a base point located at Devi Point on India's coast.[156]

Nevertheless, the question arises as to whether base points should be selected also or exclusively on the 2,500-metre isobath, given that

---

[155] B Kunoy, 'The Delimitation of an Indicative Area of Overlapping Entitlement to the Outer Continental Shelf' (2012) 83 *BYIL* 61, 72; B Kunoy, 'Establishment of the Outer Limits of the Continental Shelf: Is Crossing Boundaries Trespassing?' (2011) 26 *IJMCL* 313, 314–315; D Colson, 'The Delimitation of the Outer Continental Shelf between Neighboring States' (2003) 97 *AJIL* 91, 103; Ø Jensen, *The Commission on the Limits of the Continental Shelf – Law and Legitimacy* (Martinus Nijhoff, 2014) 145. See *contra* BM Magnússon, 'The Rejection of the Theoretical Beauty: The Foot of the Continental Slope in Maritime Boundary Delimitations Beyond 200 Nautical Miles' (2014) 45 *ODIL* 41.

[156] *Bangladesh v. India* (n. 11) 156–8 [459]–[463].

Article 76(5) UNCLOS mentions it in relation to the outer limits of the continental shelf. The answer should be in the negative. The 2,500-metre isobath is linked to the basis of title over the continental shelf beyond 200 nm, since it is also by reference to it that the continental shelf's maximum breadth is measured. However, the seawards projections of the 2,500-metre isobath do not generate continental shelf rights. The 2,500-metre isobath could be located beyond 200 nm from the coast. As its projections would presumably generate maritime entitlements in a seaward direction, there could be a gap between the 200-nm limit and the 2,500-metre isobath in which no maritime entitlements would exist. Conversely, coastal projections are able to generate continental shelf rights both within and beyond 200 nm. According to ITLOS, '[a] coastal State's entitlement to the continental shelf exists by the sole fact that the basis of entitlement, namely, sovereignty over the land territory, is present'.[157] Implicit in this holding is the statement that the coast is indispensable for entitlement to a continental shelf, within and beyond 200 nm. Since coastal projections generate entitlement to a continental shelf, it is by reference to the coast that the continental shelf should be delimited. Consequently, the base points for constructing an equidistance line beyond 200 nm should be placed on a state's coast, and not on the 2,500-metre isobath.

Applying the three-stage approach in the delimitation of the continental shelf beyond 200 nm seems grounded in, and therefore consistent with, the basis of title as codified under Article 76 UNCLOS.[158] This conclusion is consistent with the existence of a single continental shelf, implicit in Articles 76 and 83 UNCLOS, and confirmed by international tribunals.[159] It does not follow that geomorphological factors cannot influence delimitation beyond 200 nm, but simply that such factors cannot determine the use of a method other than the three-stage

---

[157] *Bangladesh/Myanmar* (n. 11) 107 [409].

[158] Although Elferink argued that the method for delimitation beyond 200 nm should be chosen on a case-by-case basis, having taken into account all relevant circumstances, his views are reminiscent of the outdated pre-*Jan Mayen* delimitation methodology. See A Oude Elferink, 'ITLOS's Approach to the Delimitation of the Continental Shelf beyond 200 Nautical Miles in the *Bangladesh/Myanmar* Case: Theoretical and Practical Difficulties' in R Wolfrum et al. (eds.), *Contemporary Developments in International Law – Essays in Honour of Budislav Vukas* (Martinus Nijhoff, 2016) 231, 245–8.

[159] *Bangladesh/Myanmar* (n. 11) 96 [361]; *Bangladesh v. India* (n. 11) 31 [77]. See also S Suarez, *The Outer Limits of the Continental Shelf – Legal Aspects of their Establishment* (Springer, 2008) 224.

approach. Delimitation based on geomorphology is connected to the basis of title, yet it conflicts with the existence of a single continental shelf, which suggests a single method for its delimitation.[160] By contrast, delimitation by equidistance has a connection to the basis of title, and it is also consistent with the principle of the single continental shelf, since it entails boundaries are delimited identically both within and beyond 200 nm.

C The Grey Area Issue

Although using equidistance to delimit the entire continental shelf is grounded in UNCLOS, the application of the three-stage approach beyond 200 nm could raise issues if the boundaries established were not strict equidistance lines. In the Bay of Bengal cases, the three-stage approach resulted in the creation of grey areas. These are maritime spaces situated both within a state's EEZ, and in a zone where another state claims a continental shelf beyond 200 nm. Grey areas stem from the establishment of boundaries that do not intersect the point at which the 200-nm limit of two neighbouring states' EEZs meet. While using strict equidistance avoids creating grey areas, adjusting an equidistance line based on relevant circumstances could result in grey areas. Since grey areas lack legal basis under UNCLOS, equidistance should be seen as the starting point for delimiting the continental shelf beyond 200 nm.

1 The absence of legal basis under UNCLOS

ITLOS and the *Bangladesh v. India* tribunal accepted that grey areas are natural by-products of delimitation. Yet, their legal basis under UNCLOS appears dubious, and their management problematic for the states concerned. Elferink wrote that the very name 'grey area' is due 'most likely because of the uncertainty of its legal status'.[161] When discussing the grey area in *Bangladesh/Myanmar*, ITLOS established that 'the boundary delimiting the area beyond 200 nm from Bangladesh but within 200 nm of Myanmar is a boundary delimiting the continental shelves of the Parties, since in this area only their continental shelves overlap'.[162] Consequently:

---

[160] Geomorphological factors as relevant circumstances are discussed in Chapter 5, Section IV.C below.
[161] A Oude Elferink, 'Does Undisputed Title to a Maritime Zone Always Exclude its Delimitation: The Grey Area Issue' (1998) *IJMCL* 143, 144.
[162] *Bangladesh/Myanmar* (n. 11) 120 [471].

in the area beyond Bangladesh's [EEZ] that is within the limits of Myanmar's [EEZ], the maritime boundary delimits the Parties' rights with respect to the seabed and subsoil of the continental shelf but does not otherwise limit Myanmar's rights with respect to the [EEZ], notably those with respect to the superjacent waters.[163]

ITLOS held that grey areas are envisaged '[u]nder the Convention' as a result of maritime delimitation.[164]

The *Bangladesh* v. *India* tribunal seemed to acknowledge that grey areas stem from the application of the three-stage approach by finding that a grey area 'will arise whenever the entitlements of two States to the continental shelf extend beyond 200 nm and relevant circumstances call for a boundary other than the equidistance line at or beyond the 200-nm limit in order to provide an equitable delimitation'.[165] The arbitral tribunal confirmed ITLOS's findings in *Bangladesh/Myanmar*, by holding that 'within the area beyond 200 nm from the coast of Bangladesh and within 200 nm of the coast of India, the boundary identified by the Tribunal delimits only the Parties' sovereign rights to explore the continental shelf ... however, the boundary does not otherwise limit India's sovereign rights to the [EEZ] in the superjacent waters'.[166] The combination of the *Bangladesh/Myanmar* and *Bangladesh* v. *India* boundaries created an area of overlap in which Bangladesh was entitled to a continental shelf beyond 200 nm, while India and Myanmar were both entitled to water column rights.

The approach of ITLOS and of the *Bangladesh* v. *India* tribunal seems unconvincing. UNCLOS does not mention grey areas, and the grey area issue was never raised during the UNCLOS negotiations. The lack of references to equidistance in Articles 74 and 83 UNCLOS might suggest that UNCLOS implicitly accepted that certain delimitation methods could lead to creating grey areas. However, UNCLOS only states that delimitation must achieve an 'equitable solution', not requiring a specific delimitation method to be applied. Grey areas stem from the three-stage approach, developed by international tribunals to implement UNCLOS's vague delimitation provisions. Moreover, both the considerable number of states pleadings for equidistance as the most suitable delimitation method, and the significant number of bilateral treaties delimiting

---

[163] Ibid. 121 [474].
[164] Ibid. 121 [475].
[165] *Bangladesh* v. *India* (n. 11) 169 [498].
[166] Ibid. 171 [505].

III EQUIDISTANCE AND THE CONTINENTAL SHELF

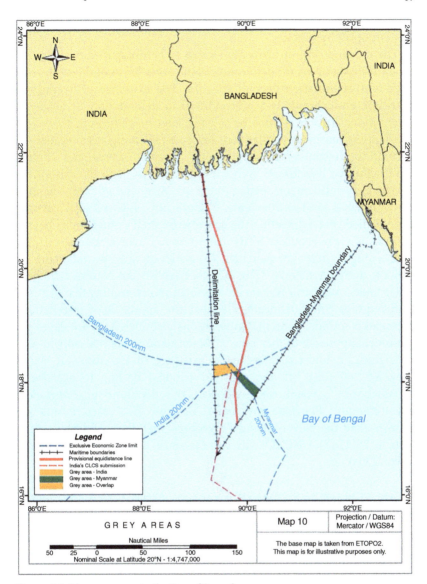

Figure 4.1 The grey areas in the Bay of Bengal cases
Source: 167 ILR 172 © The Permanent Court of Arbitration

equidistant boundaries,[167] suggest that a vast majority of coastal states prefers not to deal with the consequences of grey areas. Grey areas should

[167] Section II.B.3 above.

be seen as a by-product of delimitation neither envisaged at UNCLOS III, nor endorsed by states.

The creation of grey areas seems also to be unjustified based on the relationship between the delineation of the outer limits of the continental shelf and delimitation beyond 200 nm. The existence of overlapping maritime entitlements is a precondition to delimitation. In principle, international tribunals must be satisfied that neighbouring states have overlapping maritime entitlements before establishing any boundary. In relation to the continental shelf beyond 200 nm, international tribunals have delimited boundaries even without certainty as to the existence of overlapping entitlements, owing to the *ipso facto* and *ab initio* character of continental shelf entitlements.[168] Until now, international tribunals have denied that delineating the continental shelf's outer limits beyond 200 nm is a pre-requisite to its delimitation.[169] Nevertheless, certainty concerning entitlement can be fully achieved only by following the process under Article 76 UNCLOS to establish the continental shelf's outer limits. Academic writers are less unanimous, arguing that delimitation requires prior delineation,[170] that the approach of international tribunals is sound,[171] and that international tribunals have not developed a uniform approach to this issue.[172] Magnússon wrote that only in cases of 'significant uncertainty as to the existence of a continental margin [beyond 200 nm] will the court or tribunal decline to exercise its jurisdiction'.[173] Magnússon endorsed the decisions in *Bangladesh/Myanmar* and *Bangladesh v. India*. In these two cases, it was well known that the Bay of Bengal's geology met the conditions under Article 76(4)-(7) UNCLOS for the existence of a continental margin beyond 200 nm.

---

[168] Art. 77 UNCLOS. See *Bangladesh/Myanmar* (n. 11) 107 [408]-[409]; *Bangladesh v. India* (n. 11) 31 [77].

[169] *Bangladesh/Myanmar* (n. 11) 106-107 [406]-[411]; *Bangladesh v. India* (n. 11) 31-3 [74]-[83]; *Question of the Delimitation of the Continental Shelf between Nicaragua and Colombia beyond 200 Nautical Miles from the Nicaraguan Coast (Nicaragua v. Colombia)* (Preliminary Objections) [2016] ICJ Rep 100, 136-7 [105]-[114].

[170] B Kunoy, 'The Admissibility of a Plea to an International Adjudicative Forum to Delimit the Outer Continental Shelf Prior to the Adoption of Final Recommendations by the Commission on the Limits of the Continental Shelf' (2010) 25 *IJMCL* 237, 268.

[171] BM Magnússon, 'Is there a Temporal Relationship between the Delineation and the Delimitation of the Continental Shelf beyond 200 Nautical Miles?' (2013) 28 *IJMCL* 465.

[172] S Veierud Busch, 'The Delimitation of the Continental Shelf beyond 200 nm: Procedural Issues' in A Oude Elferink et al. (eds.), *Maritime Boundary Delimitation - The Case Law: is it Consistent and Predictable?* (CUP, 2018) 319.

[173] Magnússon (n. 171) 482.

III EQUIDISTANCE AND THE CONTINENTAL SHELF   139

However, the Bay of Bengal cases are exceptional.[174] At UNCLOS III, Sri Lanka showed that the formula for delineating the continental shelf's outer limits under Article 76 UNCLOS would be detrimental to the states abutting the Bay of Bengal. The geological peculiarities of the region entailed that, if Article 76 were applied to it, a great share of continental margin would not fall under the jurisdiction of the coastal states. UNCLOS III emphasised that, in the Bay of Bengal, both the thickness of the sedimentary rocks, and the location of the foot of the continental slope, would determine outer limits lying well beyond the maximum limits set in Article 76(5) UNCLOS.[175] The scientific evidence produced at UNCLOS III thus proved that the states abutting the Bay of Bengal were certainly entitled to a continental shelf beyond 200 nm. Therefore, the Final Act of the Conference recognised that a different system could be used to delineate the continental shelf's outer limits in the Bay of Bengal and in comparable areas.[176]

With respect to the Bay of Bengal, entitlement to a continental shelf beyond 200 nm was certain, while the only uncertain aspect was the exact location of the continental shelf's outer limit. Borrowing ITLOS's formula, with respect to the Bay of Bengal there was no 'significant uncertainty as to the existence of a continental margin' beyond 200 nm.[177] Therefore, the delimitation of the continental shelf beyond 200 nm in *Bangladesh/Myanmar* and *Bangladesh v. India* was in principle justified.

This conclusion does not necessarily apply to other cases in which states claim a continental shelf beyond 200 nm. In such cases, international tribunals should await the CLCS's recommendation, which would conclusively establish, based on scientific evidence, whether entitlement to a continental shelf beyond 200 nm exists. This position was apparently expressed by the ICJ in the 2017 judgment on preliminary objections in *Somalia v. Kenya*.[178] As the existence of overlapping entitlements beyond 200 nm is a precondition to delimitation, international tribunals should

---

[174] M Lando, 'Delimiting the Continental Shelf Beyond 200 Nautical Miles at the International Court of Justice: The *Nicaragua v. Colombia* Cases' (2017) 16 *Chinese JIL* 160–3.
[175] See the Figure 2 at R Mishra, 'The "Grey Area" in the Northern Bay of Bengal: A Note on a Functional Cooperative Solution' (2016) 47 *ODIL* 29, 31.
[176] Doc A/CONF.62/121 (27 October 1982), *Official Records of the Third United Nations Conference on the Law of the Sea*, vol. XVII, 148 (Annex II – Statement of Understanding concerning a Specific Method to be Used in Establishing the Outer Edge of the Continental Margin). See also MCW Pinto, 'Article 76 of the UN Convention on the Law of the Sea and the Bay of Bengal Exception' (2013) 3 *Asian JIL* 215.
[177] *Bangladesh/Myanmar* (n. 11) 115 [443].
[178] Chapter 3, Section III.C.4 above.

not delimit the continental shelf beyond 200 nm if there is 'significant uncertainty' concerning the existence of a continental margin beyond 200 nm. There was no 'significant uncertainty' in the Bay of Bengal cases. Whether there is 'significant uncertainty' in other cases depends on whether the CLCS has issued its recommendation. The effect for grey areas is that, if entitlement beyond 200 nm is 'significantly uncertain', delimitation could not take place, and thus no grey area could be created. This reasoning would disqualify the creation of grey areas in the vast majority of delimitation cases, but it would not have prevented the creation of grey areas in the Bay of Bengal cases.

2 Grey areas and the EEZ-continental shelf relationship

The EEZ-continental shelf relationship as one of incorporation of the latter into the former[179] excludes the lawfulness of grey areas. In *Bangladesh/Myanmar*, Bangladesh was entitled to a continental shelf beyond 200 nm, while in the same maritime area Myanmar was entitled to an EEZ. ITLOS held that Bangladesh would have jurisdiction over the seabed and subsoil, while Myanmar over the water column. A comparable decision was reached in *Bangladesh v. India*. However, if one accepts the incorporation of the continental shelf into the EEZ, the separation of jurisdiction in *Bangladesh/Myanmar* and *Bangladesh v. India* between seabed and subsoil on one hand and water column on the other hand would be legally groundless.

In *Bangladesh v. India*, Rao wrote a strong dissenting opinion in which he argued that '[t]he creation of a grey area is entirely contrary to law and the policies underlying the decision taken in UNCLOS to create the EEZ as one single, common maritime zone within 200 nm which effectively incorporates the regime of the continental shelf within it'.[180] According to Rao, 'the sovereign rights of a coastal State over the water column and the seabed and its subsoil are considered as two indispensable and inseparable parts of the coastal State's rights in the EEZ',[181] owing to rights over the seabed, subsoil and water column within 200 nm having distance from the coast as a common basis of title. Since entitlement to a continental shelf beyond 200 nm is based on the establishment of its outer limits under Article 76 UNCLOS, Rao stated that 'entitlement to the continental shelf beyond 200 nm . . . is not

---

[179] Section II.B above.
[180] *Bangladesh v. India* (n. 11) 199 [24] (Concurring and Dissenting Opinion of Dr PS Rao).
[181] Ibid. 203 [31] (Concurring and Dissenting Opinion of Dr PS Rao).

as absolute as the entitlement to the EEZ',[182] from which it followed that 'the entitlement to the EEZ takes priority over the entitlement to the continental shelf beyond 200 nm'.[183] Rao would have delimited a boundary intersecting the point where Bangladesh's EEZ limit met Myanmar's EEZ limit, as well as the point where India's EEZ limit met Myanmar's EEZ limit. Rao's proposed boundary would not have impacted on the grey area created in *Bangladesh/Myanmar*. However, it would have avoided the creation of another grey area in *Bangladesh v. India*, at the same time recognised Bangladesh's entitlement to a continental shelf beyond 200 nm.

One could counter-argue that Rao's solution resulted in the partial cut-off of Bangladesh's coastal projections beyond 200 nm. Nevertheless, while this observation may be correct, cut-off would not have been so marked as to outweigh the benefits of not creating a grey area. The equitable solution objective is paramount. The legal certainty promoted by the absence of a grey area would have achieved a solution more equitable than the one achieved by abating a limited cut-off effect and creating a grey area. This solution would also have been consistent with the relationship between the continental shelf and the EEZ.[184]

The EEZ–continental shelf relationship requires international tribunals to follow one simple principle. Maritime boundaries should clearly divide the areas in which two states exercise their rights under international law, from which it follows that certain states exercise their rights on one side of a boundary, and other states exercise their rights on the other side of a boundary. A different approach would unduly curtail one state's EEZ rights by allocating water column rights to that state, and seabed and subsoil rights to a neighbouring state. Partly curtailing a state's continental shelf rights in order to further legal certainty also appears more desirable than a solution that creates a grey area, in which the rights of two states remain uncertain.

By creating grey areas, international tribunals could be seen to abdicate their judicial function.[185] The international judicial function is not effectively exercised unless the final decision of interstate disputes constitutes their definitive settlement. If a grey area were created as a result of delimitation, the parties' dispute would not be fully settled. This was implicitly recognised in both Bay of Bengal cases. ITLOS stated that the

---

[182] Ibid. 207 [40] (Concurring and Dissenting Opinion of Dr PS Rao).
[183] Ibid.
[184] Section II.B above.
[185] *Bangladesh v. India* (n. 11) 205 [35] (Concurring and Dissenting Opinion of Dr PS Rao).

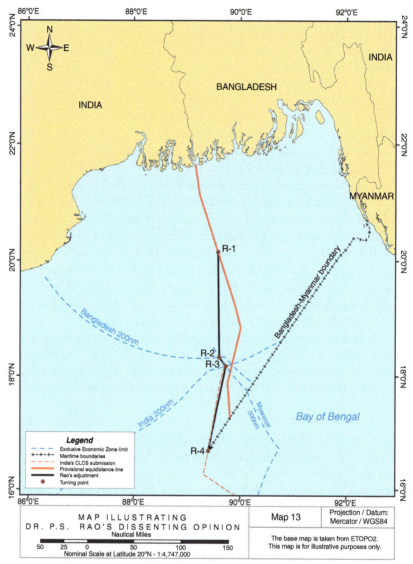

Figure 4.2 PS Rao's proposed boundary in *Bangladesh* v. *India*
Source: 167 ILR 208 © The Permanent Court of Arbitration

parties should promote the 'conclusion of specific agreements or the establishment of appropriate cooperative arrangements'.[186] Following the creation of grey areas in the Bay of Bengal, a commentator suggested

---

[186] *Bangladesh/Myanmar* (n. 11) 121 [476]. See also *Bangladesh* v. *India* (n. 11) 171 [508].

that Bangladesh, India and Myanmar should institute a joint development zone.[187]

Grey areas result from maritime boundaries not intersecting the point at which the parties' 200-nm limits meet, which is equidistant from the parties' coasts. The dubious lawfulness of grey areas is a reason for using equidistance to delimit the continental shelf beyond 200 nm, at least as a starting point. If equidistance were the starting point for delimitation beyond 200 nm, an equidistance line could depart from the point at which the parties' 200-nm limits meet, which entails that delimitation would need to be effected separately for the EEZ on one hand, and the continental shelf beyond 200 nm on the other hand. In *Bangladesh/Myanmar*, ITLOS approached delimitation beyond 12 nm in two phases: first by delimiting the boundary between 12 and 200 nm; second, by delimiting the boundary beyond 200 nm. ITLOS could be criticised for extending beyond 200 nm the boundary that had been previously delimited within 200 nm, thus creating a grey area.

To avoid this shortcoming, international tribunals could find that the endpoint of the boundary within 200 nm is the point at which the parties' 200-nm limits meet. Delimitation beyond 200 nm could thus start with a provisional equidistance line, to be adjusted if relevant circumstances so require, and also avoid grey areas. This methodology would allow a coherent application of the three-stage approach to delimit the continental shelf beyond 200 nm. While equidistance enhances legal certainty by avoiding the creation of grey areas, relevant circumstances afford some flexibility. Using the three-stage approach is justified in delimiting all maritime boundaries, and is capable of ensuring an equitable solution. By including equidistance as its starting point, the three-stage approach safeguards legal certainty, at the same time being based on the basis of a state's title over maritime areas, whether within or beyond 200 nm.[188]

IV Constructing an Equidistance Line

The selection of base points is essential in delimitation, as it determines the feasibility of drawing an equidistance line and influences the course of an equidistance line.[189] This section examines the principles

---

[187] Mishra (n. 175) 34.
[188] Sections II.A and III.B above.
[189] Writers have shown limited interest in the construction of an equidistance line. See P Weil, 'A propos la Double Fonction des Lignes et Points de Base dans le Droit de la

governing base point selection in delimitation both within and beyond 200 nm.

A Selection of Base Points

UNCLOS does not include clear rules governing the selection of base points for the purposes of delimitation. Although international tribunals have endeavoured to fill this gap, there remains a high degree of subjectivity in the selection of base points in practice.

1 The general principles of base point selection

Under Article 15 UNCLOS, an equidistance line is a line 'every point of which is equidistant from the nearest points on the baselines from which the breadth of the territorial seas of each of the two States is measured'.[190] The 'nearest points' mentioned in Article 15 are the base points. Although the territorial sea baseline coincides with the 'low-water line along the coast',[191] straight baselines can be used '[i]n localities where the coastline is deeply indented and cut into, or if there is a fringe of islands along the coast in its immediate vicinity'.[192] Under Article 13(2) UNCLOS, '[w]here a low-tide elevation is situated wholly or partly at a distance not exceeding the breadth of the territorial sea from the mainland or an island, the low-water line on that elevation may be used as the baseline for measuring the breadth of the territorial sea'. Such low-tide elevations could thus be valid base points. Since the territorial sea baseline is also used to measure the breadth of the continental shelf and EEZ,[193] an equidistance line delimiting such maritime zones uses base points located on the territorial sea baseline.

For archipelagic states, base points are located on the archipelagic baseline, as '[t]he breadth of the territorial sea, ... the [EEZ] and the

---

Mer' in EG Bello and BA Ajibola (eds.), *Essays in Honour of Judge Taslim Olawale Elias* (Martinus Nijhoff, 1992) 145; J-P Cot, 'The Dual function of Base Points' in H Hestermeyer et al. (eds.), *Coexistence, Cooperation and Solidarity – Liber Amicorum Rüdiger Wolfrum* (Martinus Nijhoff, 2012) 807; S Fietta and R Cleverly, *A Practitioner's Guide to Maritime Boundary Delimitation* (OUP, 2016) 55–65; Von Mühlendahl (n. 13) 270–81.

[190] Art. 15 UNCLOS.
[191] Art. 5 UNCLOS.
[192] Art. 7 UNCLOS.
[193] Arts. 57 and 76 UNCLOS.

continental shelf shall be measured from archipelagic baselines drawn in accordance with article 47 [UNCLOS]'.[194] Archipelagic baselines are comparable to territorial sea baselines. Article 11 UNCLOS provides that '[f]or the purpose of delimiting the territorial sea, the outermost permanent harbour works which form an integral part of the harbour system are regarded as forming part of the coast', while '[o]ff-shore installations and artificial islands shall not be considered as permanent harbour works'. Except for Articles 11 and 15, UNCLOS does not elaborate on the methods for identifying base points. Conceivably, any point on the baseline could be used to draw an equidistance line.

International tribunals have endeavoured to fill UNCLOS's gaps by formulating criteria for selecting base points suitable to construct an equidistance line. In *Black Sea*, the ICJ suggested that the figure formed by the line connecting all appropriate base points must reflect the general direction of the parties' coast.[195] The Court stated that base points are 'protuberant coastal points' and 'the most seaward points' on the coast,[196] confirming this statement in subsequent cases.[197] This principle is consistent with Article 11 UNCLOS, which qualifies the 'outermost permanent harbour works which form an integral part of the harbour system' as valid base points. Therefore, base points are salient points on a coast, such as land protrusions into the sea, islands located in the immediate vicinity of the coast, or low-tide elevations within 12 nm of the territorial sea baseline. Base points should not be situated excessively far from the coast.

In *Black Sea*, the Court stated that base points must be 'appropriate', which suggests that, besides finding that base points are the 'most seaward points of the two coasts', international tribunals must also assess whether they are 'appropriate'. However, the Court did not specify what makes base points 'appropriate'.[198] By stating that only certain points on the coast are 'appropriate' for constructing an equidistance line, the Court suggested that base points are selected on a case-by-case basis. This approach emphasises a subjective element in the selection of base

---

[194] Art. 48 UNCLOS.
[195] *Black Sea* (n. 11) 105 [127].
[196] Ibid. 101 [117].
[197] *Nicaragua v. Colombia* (n. 11) 698–700 [200]–[204]; *Peru v. Chile* (n. 10) 67 [185].
[198] Writing extra-judicially, Judge Cot seemed to accept that base point selection could rest on the discretion of international tribunals. See Cot (n. 189) 817–19.

points. However, certain judicial decisions have elaborated on the criteria governing the selection of base points.

For example, in *Gulf of Maine* the Chamber of the ICJ held that base points should not coincide with 'tiny islands, uninhabited rocks or low-tide elevations',[199] as placing base points on such maritime features could markedly distort an equidistance line. While it may be clear whether maritime features are uninhabited, it could be less clear whether islands are 'tiny'.[200] The real question is at what distance from the coast maritime features cease to be appropriate base points. International tribunals have considered maritime features to be appropriate base points so long as they lie within the 12-nm territorial sea. This was the case of Eddystone Rock in the *Anglo/French Arbitration*, Serpents' Island in *Black Sea*, and Moore Island, Mandrabaria/Clump Island and Putney Island in *Bangladesh v. India*.[201] Although there are limited exceptions to this principle, they appear to be based on pertinent geographical concerns.

For instance, in *Bangladesh/Myanmar* ITLOS used St Martin's Island as a base point for territorial sea delimitation, discounting it for delimitation beyond 12 nm since 'the selection of a base point on St. Martin's Island would result in a line that blocks the seaward projection from Myanmar's coast'.[202] In *Nicaragua v. Colombia*, the ICJ used as base points several islands situated beyond Nicaragua's territorial sea, the likely reason being that, in the narrow stretch between the San Andrés Archipelago and Nicaragua's mainland, using base points on the Mosquito Coast could have determined a provisional equidistance line too close to Nicaragua's coast to be equitable.[203] If either discounting islands in the territorial sea, or using islands beyond the territorial sea, as base points, international tribunals act in the pursuit of an equitable solution. Nevertheless, this approach could be seen to be problematic. The equitable solution is ensured by the second and third stage of the

---

[199] *Gulf of Maine* (n. 42) 329 [201].
[200] Von Mühlendhal wrote that even maritime features with an area of several hundred square kilometres could not be classified as islands if not able to sustain human habitation or an economic life of their own in accordance with Art. 121(3) UNCLOS. See P Von Mühlendhal, 'Tiny Land Features in Recent Maritime Delimitation Case Law' (2016) 31 *IJMCL* 1, 5.
[201] *Continental Shelf (France/UK)* (1977) XVIII RIAA 3, 74 [143]–[144]; *Black Sea* (n. 11) 109–10 [147]; *Bangladesh v. India* (n. 11) 84–8 [250]–[269] and 118–20 [353]–[367]. See also Section IV.A.2 below.
[202] *Bangladesh/Myanmar* (n. 11) 73 [265]. See also the ICJ's decision on Filfla in *Libya/Malta* (n. 42) 48 [64].
[203] *Nicaragua v. Colombia* (n. 11) 638 [21] and 699 [201].

delimitation process, while drawing an equidistance line should be an objective operation in which equitable solution considerations are not involved. The choice of base points in *Nicaragua* v. *Colombia* was thus problematic.

2 Low-tide elevations as base points

A persistent issue concerns using low-tide elevations as base points.[204] Article 13(1) UNCLOS defines a low-tide elevation as 'a naturally formed area of land which is surrounded by and above water at low tide but submerged at high tide'. Article 7 UNCLOS states that straight baselines cannot be drawn to and from low-tide elevations, unless either 'lighthouses or similar installations which are permanently above sea level have been built on them', or 'the drawing of baselines to and from such elevations has received general international recognition'. UNCLOS says nothing on whether low-tide elevations could be used as base points.

According to Murphy, 'while low-tide elevations ... can play a role in the establishment of baselines ..., it is not necessarily the case that they can be used as base points when delimiting overlapping maritime zones with another State'.[205] However, he did not further elaborate on this statement. Bowett and Tanaka suggested that if low-tide elevations are integrated into a system of straight baselines under Article 7 UNCLOS, they can also be used as base points.[206] However this view is not confirmed by the cases. In the *Anglo/French Arbitration*, a contentious point was whether Eddystone Rock, a maritime feature located 8 nm off Plymouth's coast, was a low-tide elevation, and whether, as a low-tide

---

[204] On low-tide elevations, see R Lavalle, 'The Rights of States over Low-Tide Elevations: A Legal Analysis' (2014) 29 *IJMCL* 457; R Lavalle, 'Not Quite a Sure Thing: The Maritime Areas of Rocks and Low-Tide Elevations Under the UN Law of the Sea Convention' (2004) 19 *IJMCL* 43; E Doussis, 'Îles, Îlots, Rochers et Hauts-Fonds Découvrants' in *Le Processus de Délimitation Maritime – Étude d'un Cas Fictif* (Pédone, 2004) 134; G Guillaume, 'Les Hauts-Fonds Découvrants en Droit International' in *La Mer et Son Droit – Mélanges Offerts à Laurent Lucchini et Jean-Pierre Quéneudec* (Pédone, 2003) 287; P Weil, 'Les Hauts-Fonds Découvrants dans la Délimitation Maritime' in N Ando et al. (eds.), *Liber Amicorum Shigeru Oda* (Martinus Nijhoff, 2002) vol. I, 307; G Marston, 'Low-Tide Elevations and Straight Baselines' (1972-73) 46 *BYIL* 405.

[205] SD Murphy, 'International Law relating to Islands' (2016) 386 *Recueil des Cours* 9, 175.

[206] DW Bowett, 'Islands, Rocks, Reefs, and Low-Tide Elevations in Maritime Boundary Delimitations' in JI Charney and LM Alexander, *International Maritime Boundaries* (Martinus Nijhoff, 1991) vol. I, 131, 149; Y Tanaka, 'Low-Tide Elevations in International Law of the Sea: Selected Issues' (2006) 20 *Ocean Yearbook* 189, 207–8. Bowett supported his argument by reference to six maritime delimitation treaties. However, the paucity of treaties relied upon shows that states have not developed a widely accepted approach in this matter.

elevation, it could be used as a base point to draw an equidistance line. Eddystone Rock was not part of the UK's straight-baseline system.[207] The Court of Arbitration did not clarify the status of Eddystone Rock, and found that it could be used as a base point. This decision was not based on its status as an island or a low-tide elevation, but on France's acceptance of both its use by the UK in establishing the latter's fishery limits, and its relevance in delimiting the 1971 median line in the English Channel.[208]

Qatar v. Bahrain also presented a number of maritime features whose status as islands was controversial. The parties agreed that Fasht ad Dibal was a low-tide elevation. The Court determined that Qit'at al Jaradah was an island, but refrained from determining the status of Fasht al Azm.[209] On using low-tide elevations to construct an equidistance line, the Court stated that:

> [w]hen a low-tide elevation is situated in the overlapping area of the territorial sea of two States, whether with opposite or with adjacent coasts, both States in principle are entitled to use its low-water line for the measuring of the breadth of their territorial sea. The same low-tide elevation then forms part of the coastal configuration of the two States. ... For delimitation purposes the competing rights derived by both coastal States from the relevant provisions of the law of the sea would by necessity seem to neutralize each other.[210]

A state's right to use low-tide elevations as base points would be neutralised if low-tide elevations were situated in an area of overlapping claims,[211] which seems to assume that such a right subsists if low-tide elevations are situated in the territorial sea of only one state.

However, this inference is hardly supported by the rest of the Court's reasoning. The ICJ neither stated whether certain features used as base points were low-tide elevations, nor did it use base points on features explicitly identified as such. Nonetheless, the Court stated that Fasht al Azm could have provided base points only if it had been considered to be part of the island of Sitrah,[212] which seems to entail that if it were not part of that island, and therefore a low-tide elevation, it could not be a base

---

[207] *Anglo/French Arbitration* (n. 201) 67 [125].
[208] Ibid. 73–4 [142]–[143].
[209] *Maritime Delimitation and Territorial Questions between Qatar and Bahrain (Qatar v. Bahrain)* (Merits) [2001] ICJ Rep 40, 98–100 [190]–[200].
[210] Ibid. 101 [202].
[211] See MD Evans, 'Case concerning *Maritime Delimitation and Territorial Questions between Qatar and Bahrain (Qatar v. Bahrain)*' (2002) 51 ICLQ 709, 716.
[212] *Qatar v. Bahrain* (n. 209) 104 [216].

point. Neither *Qatar v. Bahrain*, nor the *Anglo/French Arbitration*, clarified whether low-tide elevations could be base points in delimitation.

Bangladesh v. India raised similar issues. While not rejecting the use of low-tide elevations as base points, Bangladesh disputed the existence of some base points that India had located on certain low-tide elevations.[213] To verify the existence of such low-tide elevations, the arbitral tribunal held a site visit in the delimitation area. In the award, the tribunal found that from Article 13 UNCLOS it does not follow that low-tide elevations are 'appropriate base points',[214] and that 'base points located on low-tide elevations do not fit the criteria elaborated by the [ICJ] in the *Black Sea* case and confirmed in more recent cases'.[215] With respect to the territorial sea, the arbitral tribunal held that '[i]f alternative base points situated on the coastline of the parties are available, they should be preferred to base points located on low-tide elevations'.[216] The arbitral tribunal confirmed this interpretation by not using low-tide elevations as base points in continental shelf and EEZ delimitation.[217]

Becker and Rose wrote that '[i]t is conceivable that the failure to establish during the site visit whether New Moore/South Talpatty Island is a [low-tide elevation] prompted the Tribunal to select a legal rule that avoided the issue'.[218] While Becker and Rose may be correct, the tribunal's approach does not contradict the approach in the *Anglo/French Arbitration* and in *Qatar v. Bahrain*, as in those two cases international tribunals refrained from deciding whether low-tide elevations could be appropriate base points. *Bangladesh v. India* is also consistent with Articles 7 and 13 UNCLOS. Since these provisions are silent on low-tide elevations as base points, the tribunal chose one of two possible readings. The cases suggest that low-tide elevations are not appropriate base points, apart from situations in which either no other appropriate base point could be identified on the mainland, or low-tide elevations are integrated into a straight baseline system under Article 13(1) UNCLOS. So long as maritime features generate maritime entitlements, they can be used as a base point to construct an equidistance line. This is not the case for low-tide elevations, which, as the arbitral tribunal in the 2016 *South*

---

[213] *Bangladesh v. India* (n. 11) 69 [196].
[214] Ibid. 86 [260].
[215] Ibid. 86 [261].
[216] Ibid. 87 [262].
[217] Ibid. 119 [360]–[362].
[218] MA Becker and C Rose, 'Investigating the Value of Site Visits in Inter-State Arbitration and Adjudication' (2017) 8 *JIDS* 219, 239.

China Sea Arbitration stated, are '[neither] entitled to a territorial sea, [nor] entitled to an [EEZ] or continental shelf'.[219]

B Islands, Base Points and 'Creeping Relevant Circumstances'

Provided that the criteria for their identification are met, base points could in principle be situated on islands. While international tribunals generally decide on the effect of islands at the second stage of the delimitation process, deciding to place a base point on an island could move the decision on that island's effect to the first stage.[220] One could justifiably speak of 'creeping relevant circumstances', whose existence could negatively affect transparency in the delimitation process.[221]

1 Using islands as base points

Murphy seemed to accept this approach, as he wrote that 'when constructing the provisional equidistance line at the first stage, the tribunal may decide to disregard certain islands at the outset, rather than drawing a strict equidistance line and then adjusting for those islands at the second stage'.[222] Fietta and Cleverly argued that the choice of base points could be seen as an additional stage in the delimitation process.[223] The relevant decisions can be divided into three categories: cases in which islands were deemed, implicitly or explicitly, to be an integral part of the relevant coast; cases in which boundaries were to be delimited between a mainland coast and islands under a different state's sovereignty; and cases in which boundaries were to be delimited between two mainland coasts.

---

[219] *South China Sea Arbitration (Philippines v. China) (Merits)* (2016) 170 ILR 180, 326 [308]. The *South China Sea* tribunal said nothing on low-tide elevations as base points for delimitation. On the merits award, see R Le Bœuf, 'Différend en Mer de Chine Méridionale (Philippines c. Chine) – Sentence arbitrale du 12 juillet 2016' (2016) 62 *AFDI* 159; VP Cogliati-Bantz, 'The South China Sea Arbitration (The Republic of the Philippines v. The People's Republic of China)' (2016) 31 *IJMCL* 759.
[220] On islands as relevant circumstances, see Chapter 5, Section II.C.
[221] This section focuses on disputes in which international tribunals drew a provisional equidistance line as a starting point. The ICJ's judgment in *Libya/Malta* is not discussed, since it was handed down at a time when international tribunals still chose the delimitation method case-by-case.
[222] Murphy (n. 205) 174.
[223] Fietta and Cleverly (n. 189) 575–83.

Islands have been used as base points when seen as an integral part of the coast, as in *Eritrea/Yemen*. According to the arbitral tribunal, the Dhalaks, a 'tightly knit group of islands and islets ... of which the larger islands have a considerable population, [were] a typical example of a group of islands that forms an integral part of the general coastal configuration'.[224] Consequently, the sea inside that island system constituted Eritrean internal waters. The Dhalaks satisfied the conditions under Article 7 UNCLOS for the application of a straight baseline system, which entailed that the base points for the equidistance line could be placed on such baselines.[225] Concerning Yemen's islands of al-Tayr and al-Zubayr, the tribunal held that they were not appropriate base points, owing, *inter alia*, to their 'position well out to sea'.[226] However, the tribunal found that the Yemeni islands of Kamaran, Uqban and Kutama were part of 'a "fringe system" of the kind contemplated by article 7 [UNCLOS], even though Yemen does not appear to have claimed it as such',[227] and decided to place base points on them.

By using the Dhalaks, Kamaran, Uqban and Kutama as base points, the tribunal seemingly awarded them full effect as islands. However, this assessment of the award appears incorrect. The tribunal's main finding was that all those islands were an integral part of Eritrea's and Yemen's coasts, which superseded their character as islands. Therefore, the tribunal did not decide on their effect by placing base points on them, as the base points were seen as being on the parties' mainland coasts. There were no 'creeping relevant circumstances' in *Eritrea/Yemen*, as the decision on base points did not entail the decision as to the effect of any island. The same must be said of any other case in which an island group is deemed to be an integral part of the coast. The *Bangladesh* v. *India* tribunal also considered islands as base points, and found that Mandarbaria/Clump Island, New Moore Island and Bhanganduni Island were appropriate base points to delimit all maritime zones.[228] Neither party argued that those islands were relevant circumstances, thus the tribunal did not consider them as such. Given the location of the islands used as base points, it is likely that the tribunal implicitly considered them to be integral parts of the coast.

---

[224] *Second Stage of the Proceedings between Eritrea and Yemen (Maritime Delimitation) (Eritrea/Yemen)* (1999) XXII RIAA 335, 367 [139].
[225] Ibid. 367 [140]–[141].
[226] Ibid. 368 [147].
[227] Ibid. 369 [150]–[152].
[228] *Bangladesh* v. *India* (n. 11) 88 [268]–[269] and 120 [365]–[366].

Delimitation has also been effected between a mainland coast and islands under another state's sovereignty. In *Nicaragua v. Colombia*, the ICJ had little choice in selecting the base points on Colombia's relevant coast, which was only that of the islands of San Andrés, Providencia, Santa Catalina, and the maritime features of Albuquerque Cays, East-southeast Cays, Roncador and Serrana.[229] The Court placed Colombia's base points on San Andrés, Providencia, Santa Catalina and Albuquerque Cays, while Nicaragua's base points were located on Edinburgh Reef, Muerto Cay, Miskitos Cays, Ned Thomas Cay, Roca Tyra, Little Corn Island and Great Corn Island.[230] Islands were not discussed as relevant circumstances during the second stage of delimitation.[231] Nonetheless, the Court held that the marked coastal length disparity justified shifting the entire equidistance line eastwards. As a result, and before conducting the disproportionality test, the Court held that Nicaragua's base points must be given a weight of 3:1 *vis-à-vis* Colombia's base points.[232]

In *Nicaragua v. Colombia* there existed no question of 'creeping relevant circumstances'. The Court had no choice but to place base points on Colombia's islands, and the weighting of such base points took place in the second stage of the delimitation process on account of the marked coastal length disparity. The Court did not attribute effect to any island while plotting the equidistance line, doing so at a later phase, consistently with the logic of the three-stage approach. Similarly to *Eritrea/Yemen*, the *modus operandi* in *Nicaragua v. Colombia* could be of general application: mainland-to-island delimitation gives international tribunals limited discretion in locating appropriate base points. Therefore, this scenario does not raise a 'creeping relevant circumstances' issue. Yet, 'creeping relevant circumstances' would exist if an international tribunal, while locating base points, decided not to consider as base points either certain islands, or certain low-tide elevations within the territorial sea of those islands.

Delimitation has also been effected between mainland coasts off which a number of islands are situated. In *Qatar v. Bahrain*, numerous islands lay within the delimitation area, which could be used as base points to plot an equidistance line. The ICJ clarified that the islands off Bahrain's coast did not constitute a 'fringe of islands' in accordance with Article 7 UNCLOS.[233] As Bahrain could not use straight baselines, the islands

---

[229] *Nicaragua v. Colombia* (n. 11) 679–80 [151]–[152].
[230] Ibid. 699 [201]–[203].
[231] Ibid. 700–7 [205]–[228].
[232] Ibid. 709–10 [233]–[234].
[233] *Qatar v. Bahrain* (n. 209) 103–4 [214]–[215].

around it were not an integral part of its coast. The Court examined the effect of the islands on which base points were located at the second stage of the delimitation process. For example, Qit'at Jaradah was found to be a 'very small island, uninhabited and without any vegetation',[234] which could have a disproportionate effect on the equidistance line if given full effect as a base point.[235] In *Qatar v. Bahrain*, the ICJ first identified base points on certain islands, and only subsequently examined their effect on the boundary. Before determining the status of Fasht al Azm, the Court drew two equidistance lines, one accounting for Fasht al Azm as a low-tide elevation, and the other considering Fasht al Azm as part of the island of Sitrah.[236] This expedient allowed the Court to select appropriate base points while leaving the decision on the effect of the features on which such base points were located to a later phase. As a result, the Court avoided treating islands as 'creeping relevant circumstances'.

In *Black Sea*, the ICJ found that Tsyganka Island was an appropriate base point on Ukraine's coast, implicitly seeing that feature to be an integral part of the relevant coast.[237] Conversely, Serpents' Island lay isolated 20 nm off Ukraine's coast. However, '[t]o count Serpents' Island as a relevant part of the coast would amount to grafting an extraneous element onto Ukraine's coastline'.[238] Therefore, Serpents' Island was not used as a base point[239] and was later examined as a relevant circumstance. The Court decided that Serpents' Island could not determine the adjustment of the equidistance line since its maritime entitlements were subsumed by those generated by Ukraine's mainland coast.[240] Following the same approach, in *Costa Rica v. Nicaragua* the ICJ placed base points on the Corn Islands,[241] but later examined them as relevant circumstances and decided to give them half effect.[242] ITLOS adopted a similar approach in *Bangladesh/Myanmar*. In delimiting the continental shelf and EEZ, ITLOS decided that St. Martin's Island could not be a base

---

[234] Ibid. 104–9 [219].
[235] Ibid. The ICJ's reasoning concerning Fasht al Jarim is comparable, see ibid. 114–15 [245]–[248].
[236] Ibid. 104 [216].
[237] *Black Sea* (n. 11) 101 [116].
[238] Ibid. 109–10 [149].
[239] Ibid.
[240] Ibid. 122–3 [187].
[241] *Maritime Delimitation in the Caribbean Sea and the Pacific Ocean (Costa Rica v. Nicaragua); Land Boundary in the Northern Part of Isla Portillos (Costa Rica v. Nicaragua)* (Judgment) [2018] ICJ Rep 139, 191 [139]–[140].
[242] Ibid. 196 [153]–[154].

point,[243] and later in the judgment considered whether St. Martin's Island could be a relevant circumstance.[244]

2 Avoiding 'creeping relevant circumstances'

Using islands as base points could be an exercise in 'creeping relevant circumstances'. Islands are not 'creeping relevant circumstances' if they are found to be part of the coast, as in *Bangladesh* v. *India* and *Eritrea/Yemen*, and if boundaries are to be delimited between a mainland coast and islands under another state's sovereignty, as in *Nicaragua* v. *Colombia*. If delimitation takes place between two mainland coasts, international tribunals may decide on the effect of islands in establishing an equidistance line at the first stage of the delimitation process. It is in this scenario that islands could become 'creeping relevant circumstances'.

'Creeping relevant circumstances' only exist in respect of islands that, in addition to being potential base points, are also potential relevant circumstances.[245] Selecting islands as base points could also be based on the islands' unlikelihood, or impossibility, to be relevant circumstances. The parties' arguments could indicate whether an island could be a relevant circumstance. Otherwise, in drawing equidistance lines international tribunals could refer to the substantive criteria used to determine whether islands are relevant circumstances.[246] However, this latter method would conflate the first and second phases of the three-stage approach, and therefore seems unsound. In delimitation between mainland coasts, international tribunals have used a common approach to islands as base points. Both the ICJ in *Qatar* v. *Bahrain* and *Black Sea*, and ITLOS in *Bangladesh/Myanmar*, determined first whether islands could be base points, and only later what their effect as relevant circumstances would be. While in *Qatar* v. *Bahrain* two distinct equidistance lines were traced and compared, in *Black Sea* and in *Bangladesh/Myanmar* only one equidistance line was drawn. Although international tribunals have not yet treated islands as 'creeping relevant circumstances' in EEZ and continental shelf delimitation, they have recently delimited the territorial sea by inverting the phases of the two-stage approach,

---

[243] *Bangladesh/Myanmar* (n. 11) 73 [265].
[244] Ibid. 86 [316]–[319].
[245] On islands as relevant circumstances, see Chapter 5, Section II.C below.
[246] Ibid.

resulting in the unconvincing determination of the effects of islands before drawing a provisional equidistance line.[247]

There are two ways to avoid deciding the effect of islands in establishing an equidistance line. International tribunals could draw multiple equidistance lines, each taking into account different effects for the islands concerned. Deciding which equidistance line is preferable should take place at the second phase of the three-stage approach, in which islands are examined as relevant circumstances. The ICJ used this solution in *Qatar v. Bahrain*, although it is unclear whether the *raison d'être* concerned avoiding 'creeping relevant circumstances'. Alternatively, the same island could be considered twice in delimitation, both as a base point in the first phase, and as a relevant circumstance in the second phase.[248] This was the approach adopted in *Black Sea*, *Bangladesh/Myanmar*, and *Costa Rica v. Nicaragua*. This approach appears feasible given the different function that islands have in the first and second stage of the delimitation process: on one hand, islands are instruments in constructing an equidistance line; on the other hand, the islands' geographical position could justify shifting an equidistance line. In order for such a solution to be workable, the same islands must be considered both as base points, and as relevant circumstances, and their effect should be determined only in the latter phase. However, this method is not entirely convincing, as it seems impossible completely to avoid decisions on the effect of islands when selecting them as base points. Should an international tribunal reject a state's suggestion that an island be selected as a base point, that rejection could be seen as a decision of no effect.

A third possible solution, not explicitly adopted by international tribunals, is never to place base point on islands unless they are deemed to be an integral part of the relevant coast, as in *Bangladesh v. India* and *Eritrea/Yemen*. The cases show that islands have sometimes been considered to be an integral part of the relevant coast, either when they are included into straight baselines under Article 7 UNCLOS, or when they lie entirely within 12 nm of the territorial sea baseline. The former criterion was used in *Eritrea/Yemen*, to find that the Dhalaks were an integral part of Eritrea's coast. The latter criterion could be inferred from *Black Sea*, in which the ICJ decided that Serpents' Island was not a part of Ukraine's coast due to lying 20 nm from that coast. Coastal states exercise

---

[247] Lando (n. 174) 617–18.
[248] Fietta and Cleverly (n. 189) 56.

sovereignty in the territorial sea, which may justify considering islands lying within it as part of the coast.

However, in *Nicaragua* v. *Colombia* the ICJ did not seem to accept that base points should not be placed on islands unless they are an integral part of the coast. The Court used Little Corn Island and Great Corn Island as base points, despite them being situated at 26 nm from Nicaragua's coast.[249] The Court's decision was presumably determined by the need to prevent the establishment of a provisional boundary too close to Nicaragua's mainland coast, with a view to achieving an equitable solution. The selection of Little Corn Island and Great Corn Island as base points could be seen to be a consequence of the peculiar coastal geography. Nonetheless, this does not appear to be a sufficiently compelling reason to justify placing base points on those islands instead of on Nicaragua's mainland coast.

The solution never to place base points on islands seems to be the most suitable one, as it would not require international tribunals to trace multiple equidistance lines and would ground placing of base points on islands in a more objective criterion. Moreover, such an approach would prevent the selection of base points from being an exercise in 'creeping relevant circumstances'.

C Base Points and the Relevant Coast

Base points must be located on the relevant coast, since the relevant coast generates the maritime entitlements that base points are useful to delimit.[250] However, the application of this principle is not always straightforward. Issues could arise concerning the selection of base points on the relevant coast, as in *Nicaragua* v. *Colombia*, and coastal instability could affect base point selection, as in *Nicaragua* v. *Honduras* and *Bangladesh* v. *India*.

1 The relevant coast and the feasibility of an equidistance line

In *Nicaragua* v. *Colombia*, Nicaragua requested the ICJ to trace a boundary between the parties' mainland coasts. This would have resulted in

---

[249] *Nicaragua* v. *Colombia* (n. 11) 638 [21]. Evans criticised the ICJ's decision to place base points on Little Corn Island and Great Corn Island. See MD Evans, 'Maritime Boundary Delimitation: Whatever Next?' in J Barrett and R Barnes (eds.), *Law of the Sea – UNCLOS as a Living Treaty* (BIICL, 2016) 41, 61.

[250] *Nicaragua* v. *Colombia* (n. 11) 695 [191]. The identification of the relevant coast is discussed in Chapter 3, Section II.B above.

a boundary delimiting the continental shelf beyond 200 nm from its own mainland coast, yet within 200 nm from Colombia's coast. Nicaragua also requested the Court to enclave Colombia's islands, as they lay on the wrong side of a mainland-to-mainland equidistance line. Colombia requested the Court to delimit the boundary as an equidistance line between the Mosquito Coast and the San Andrés Archipelago.[251]

The Court found Nicaragua's request for continental shelf delimitation beyond 200 nm to be admissible despite being a new request with respect to the one submitted in the application.[252] However, the Court refused to uphold it 'since Nicaragua ... has not established that it has a continental margin that extends far enough to overlap with Colombia's 200-nautical-mile entitlement to the continental shelf, measured from Colombia's mainland coast'.[253] The Court found that:

> there can be no question of determining a maritime boundary between the mainland coasts of the Parties, as these are significantly more than 400 [nm] apart. There is, however, an overlap between Nicaragua's entitlement to a continental shelf and [EEZ] extending to 200 [nm] from its mainland coast and adjacent islands and Colombia's entitlement to a continental shelf and [EEZ] derived from the islands over which ... Colombia has sovereignty.[254]

Upon both parties' suggestion, the Court accepted that Nicaragua's relevant coast was its 'entire mainland coast'.[255] The parties held opposing views on Colombia's relevant coast: while Nicaragua argued that only the west-facing coast of Colombia's islands was relevant, Colombia contended that the entirety of its islands' coast was relevant, since 'islands radiate maritime entitlement in all directions'.[256] According to the Court, '[s]ince the area of overlapping potential entitlements extends well to the east of the Colombian islands, ... it is the entire coastline of these islands, not merely the west-facing coasts, which has to be taken into account'.[257] The Court found the relevant area to extend east of the San Andrés Archipelago up to the 200-nm limit from the baselines from which Nicaragua's territorial sea is measured.[258]

---

[251] *Nicaragua v. Colombia* (n. 11) 670–1 [133]–[135].
[252] Ibid. 662–5 [104]–[112].
[253] Ibid. 669 [129]. See Lando (n. 174) 143–6.
[254] *Nicaragua v. Colombia* (n. 11) 670 [132].
[255] Ibid. 678 [145].
[256] Ibid. 678–9 [146]–[149].
[257] Ibid. 680 [151].
[258] Ibid. 683 [159].

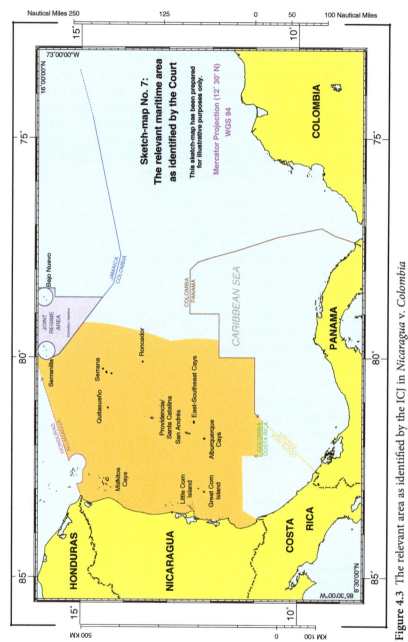

Figure 4.3 The relevant area as identified by the ICJ in *Nicaragua v. Colombia*
Source: [2012] ICJ Rep 687

IV CONSTRUCTING AN EQUIDISTANCE LINE

Subsequently, the Court discussed whether the three-stage approach was 'appropriate' in the geographical situation, 'because of the unusual circumstance that a large part of the relevant area lies to the east of the principal Colombian islands and, hence, behind the Colombian baseline from which a provisional median line would have to be measured'.[259] The Court found that this aspect did not make it inappropriate to draw an equidistance line, but that it could be 'a relevant circumstance requiring adjustment or shifting of the provisional median line'.[260] As it found it appropriate to draw an equidistance line, the Court selected appropriate base points, by determining 'which coasts are to be taken into account and, in consequence, what base points are to be used in the construction of the line'.[261]

Judge Abraham criticised this approach in his separate opinion.[262] Judge Abraham wrote that starting with an equidistance line was 'virtually impossible' since 'the overlapping does not only occur . . . in the area to the west of the Colombian islands and to the east of the Nicaraguan coast',[263] but also 'in the areas to the north, east and south of the Colombian islands – and even between them'.[264] The existence of overlapping entitlements around the San Andrés Archipelago was not a relevant circumstance, but 'a fundamental defect which deprives the line of its alleged "median" character'.[265] According to Judge Abraham, 'in order to perform its designated function in the delimitation process, a median line must take into account all the "relevant coasts" of the States present, that is to say, all the coasts which generate the projections creating the overlapping entitlements which make the delimitation necessary'.[266]

The problem in *Nicaragua* v. *Colombia* is that the Court seemed to determine the relevant coasts twice. While the Court first decided that Nicaragua's whole coast and the Colombian islands' whole coast was relevant in the delimitation process, it later held that selecting appropriate base points 'requires the Court to determine which coasts are to be taken into account'.[267] The latter statement does not seem correct, and

---

[259] Ibid. 697 [195].
[260] Ibid. 697 [196].
[261] Ibid. 698 [200].
[262] Judge Keith also criticised the Court for reasons comparable to those formulated in more detail by Judge Abraham. See ibid. 743-5 [9]-[12] (Declaration Keith).
[263] Ibid. 736 [25] (Separate Opinion Abraham).
[264] Ibid.
[265] Ibid. 737 [27] (Separate Opinion Abraham).
[266] Ibid. 737 [28] (Separate Opinion Abraham).
[267] Ibid. 698 [200].

could perhaps be attributed to awkward drafting. Presumably, the Court intended to say that it would select appropriate base points on the parties' coasts that faced each other, as the only viable option given the geographical setting. Judge Abraham did not address this question, and his criticism does not seem entirely convincing. Judge Abraham based his views on the Court's identification of the relevant area as extending up to the 200-nm limit from Nicaragua's coast. However, his statement that 'a median line must take into account all the "relevant coasts"' does not do justice to the effect that coastal geography could have on delimitation. Moreover, it does not seem supported by earlier cases. In *Bangladesh/ Myanmar* ITLOS did not locate base points on the entire coast in delimiting the continental shelf and the EEZ. Similarly, in *Black Sea* the Court did not select any base point along a long stretch of Ukraine's relevant coast between the Danube delta and Cape Tarkhankut.[268]

The position of Colombia's islands within Nicaragua's EEZ entails that, with respect to the relevant area east of the San Andrés Archipelago, the Court was required to decide which state had claims prevailing over those of the other. The Court decided that, in the east, Colombia's islands generated maritime entitlements prevailing over those of Nicaragua, subject to the need to avoid cutting off Nicaragua's coastal projections as much as possible. This was implicit in the Court's statement that it would select base points only on the western coast of Colombia's islands. Judge Abraham may have been correct in stating that the equidistance line drawn by the Court 'is only "median" with respect to one part of the "relevant area" to delimit'.[269] Judge Abraham argued that a 'true' median line would have also lain east of Colombia's islands. However, such a median line would have been unfeasible given the lack of a Nicaraguan coast east of Colombia's islands.

Judge Abraham also stated that a median line was 'inappropriate' owing to the impossibility to find appropriate base points on the entire relevant coast. However, the 'inappropriateness' of drawing an equidistance line is unrelated to the selection of base points.[270]

---

[268] *Black Sea* (n. 11) 105–10 [127]–[149].
[269] *Nicaragua v. Colombia* (n. 11) 738 [31] (Separate Opinion Abraham).
[270] Section IV.A above. It is possible that Judge Abraham used the term 'inappropriate' with the same meaning used by the Court in *Nicaragua v. Honduras*, as discussed and compared to the 'compelling reasons-unfeasibility' test in Section II.C above. In the original version of his separate opinion, written in French, he refers to the equidistance line as 'inappropriée', thus using the same word used by the Court in *Nicaragua v. Honduras*. See *Nicaragua v. Colombia* (n. 11) 737 [30] (Separate Opinion Abraham); *Nicaragua v. Honduras* (n. 99) 741 [272].

Judge Abraham linked base point selection, governed by the 'compelling reasons–unfeasibility test', to the 'inappropriateness test', which relates to the impact of coastal geography on delimitation, and is subsumed by the second phase of the three-stage approach.[271] Judge Abraham's criticism could have been more persuasive if he had referred to the 'compelling reasons–unfeasibility test' as a reason not to establish an equidistance line. Nonetheless, there is nothing under the current law of maritime delimitation that requires international tribunals to select base points on the entire relevant coast. Base points for constructing an equidistance line must be 'appropriate', which entails that they should be chosen in the light of the geographical setting of a case. This may require international tribunals to disregard part of the relevant coast as source of potential base points.

Moreover, the Court rightly found that the presence of overlapping entitlements east of Colombia's islands could be a relevant circumstance.[272] Geographical factors should relate to the basis of title over maritime areas to qualify as relevant circumstances,[273] as is the case with respect to the factor to which the Court referred. The Court's allusion to relevant circumstances could be seen to refer to the cut-off of Nicaragua's coast, which the Court subsequently found to warrant adjusting the equidistance line.[274] The Court's decision on the use of the three-stage approach and the construction of an equidistance line at its first phase seems consistent with earlier delimitation cases.

2 Coastal instability and the feasibility of an equidistance line

States have argued that coastal instability could be a 'compelling reason' making it 'unfeasible' to construct an equidistance line, thus justifying using a delimitation method other than the three-stage approach. On this issue, the ICJ and an arbitral tribunal constituted under Annex VII UNCLOS reached different conclusions.

In *Nicaragua* v. *Honduras*, Nicaragua contended that:

> the instability of the mouth of the River Coco at the Nicaragua-Honduras land boundary terminus, combined with the small and uncertain nature of the offshore islands and cays north and south of the 15th parallel, would

---

[271] Section II.C.3 above.
[272] *Nicaragua* v. *Colombia* (n. 11) 697 [196].
[273] Chapter 5 below.
[274] *Nicaragua* v. *Colombia* (n. 11) 703–4 [215].

make fixing base points and using them to construct a provisional equidistance line unduly problematic.[275]

Honduras agreed that 'the mouth of the River Coco "shifts considerably, even from year to year", making it "necessary to adopt a technique so that the maritime boundary need not change as the mouth of the river changes"'.[276] However, Honduras did not refer to base point selection to justify departing from equidistance, mentioning instead that instability at the mouth of the River Coco could rapidly make an equidistance line obsolete.

The ICJ stated that 'geographical and geological difficulties are further exacerbated by the absence of viable base points claimed or accepted by the Parties themselves at Cape Gracias a Dios'.[277] The Decree on Honduras's territorial sea baselines identified a Point 17, which, according to the 1962 Mixed Commission's decision,[278] coincided with the thalweg of the River Coco.[279] However, the Court held that Point 17 'is no longer in the mouth of the River Coco and cannot be properly used as a base point'.[280] The Court also noted that Nicaragua had not yet deposited with the United Nations Secretary-General the list of co-ordinates identifying its territorial sea baselines.[281] In addition, Nicaragua and Honduras still disputed 'sovereignty over the islets formed near the mouth of the River Coco and the establishment of "[t]he extreme common boundary point on the coast of the Atlantic"'.[282]

The Court's reasoning for not drawing an equidistance line in *Nicaragua v. Honduras* is not entirely clear. Referring to coastal instability as 'further exacerbat[ing]' the complex coastal configuration suggests that the main reason to depart from equidistance was the convexity of the relevant coast.[283] Although the Court used coastal instability as an

---

[275] *Nicaragua v. Honduras* (n. 99) 741 [273].
[276] Ibid. 742 [274].
[277] Ibid. 743 [278]. See also Section II.C.1 above.
[278] See Letter dated 30 October 1963 from the Chairman of the Inter-American Peace Committee addressed to the Secretary-General of the United Nations, UN Doc S/5452 (7 November 1963) 6.
[279] Executive Decree No. PCM 007-2000 of 21 March 2000, (2000) 43 *LoSB* 96.
[280] *Nicaragua v. Honduras* (n. 99) 743 [278].
[281] Ibid. Under Art. 16(2) UNCLOS '[t]he coastal State shall give due publicity to [charts showing the territorial sea baselines or lists] of geographical coordinates and shall deposit a copy of each such chart or list with the Secretary-General of the United Nations'.
[282] *Nicaragua v. Honduras* (n. 99) 743 [279].
[283] However, it was argued that this factor was not 'compelling' enough to justify abandoning equidistance. See Section II.C.1 above.

additional reason justifying not drawing an equidistance line, its reasoning remains unpersuasive. The Court stated that Point 17 was not found at the mouth of the River Coco any longer, but it could have selected the missing base point itself. Furthermore, the Court found it difficult to select appropriate base points owing to the sovereignty dispute over the islets around the mouth of the River Coco. Nevertheless, Nicaragua and Honduras could have decided not to incorporate these unspecified islets within the territorial sea baseline on which the base points to construct the equidistance line should be identified. Even if these islets were on the territorial sea baseline, nothing compelled the Court to use them as base points.

If considerable changes at the mouth of the River Coco would make an equidistance line obsolete, the same should be said of the angle-bisector line chosen by the Court. Between states with adjacent coasts, the construction of both an equidistance line and an angle-bisector line uses the states' land boundary terminus as a reference point. In *Nicaragua v. Honduras*, the Court traced the boundary as a bisector of the angle formed by the lines approximating the general direction of the parties' coasts, and thus heavily relied on the location of the parties' land boundary terminus. Although the Court refused to select base points owing to coastal instability, it identified the land boundary terminus as the point established by the 1962 Mixed Commission, which the Court defined as the point where 'the Parties' coastal fronts meet'.[284] Referring to that point is inaccurate, since it does not reflect the geographical reality in 2007, when the Court delimited the boundary. An equidistance line constructed in 2007 by reference to base points selected in 2007 might have become obsolete years into the future. However, a bisector drawn in 2007 by reference to a land boundary terminus established in 1962 was obsolete from the start.

Coastal instability with respect to base point selection was also discussed in *Bangladesh v. India*. Bangladesh argued for the application of the angle-bisector method instead of the three-stage approach, since the instability of the Bay of Bengal's coast made it impossible to select appropriate base points for constructing the equidistance line.[285] Alternatively, Bangladesh contended that coastal instability was a relevant circumstance determining the adjustment of the equidistance

---

[284] *Nicaragua v. Honduras* (n. 99) 748 [294].
[285] *Bangladesh v. India* (n. 11) 109 [328]–[329].

line.[286] The arbitral tribunal rejected Bangladesh's first argument, deciding to use the three-stage approach.[287] The tribunal also found that:

> only the present geophysical conditions are of relevance. Natural evolution, uncertainty and lack of predictability as to the impact of climate change on the marine environment, particularly the coastal front of States, make all predictions concerning the amount of coastal erosion or accretion unpredictable. Future changes of the coast, including those resulting from climate change, cannot be taken into account in adjusting a provisional equidistance line.[288]

The tribunal rejected the claim that coastal instability could determine the adjustment of an equidistance line.[289]

The Special Chamber in *Ghana/Côte d'Ivoire* adopted an approach similar to that of the *Bangladesh v. India* tribunal. Concerning Côte d'Ivoire's argument that coastal instability made it impossible to select suitable base points for constructing an equidistance line, the Special Chamber found that it was 'not convinced ... that the relevant coasts of Ghana and Côte d'Ivoire are unstable, such that it is difficult or impossible to identify appropriate base points'.[290] The Special Chamber's statement seems to be based on the consideration that the parties' coasts were not unstable as a matter of fact. The Special Chamber did not make a general statement, such as in *Bangladesh v. India*, limiting itself to deciding only for the purposes of the case before it.

Differently from *Nicaragua v. Honduras*, the *Bangladesh v. India* tribunal and the Special Chamber in *Ghana/Côte d'Ivoire* rejected that coastal instability could justify a departure from equidistance. Probably, the *Bangladesh v. India* tribunal was influenced by the site visit, during which it established whether the base points indicated by the parties existed. The tribunal refused to use low-tide elevations as base points,[291] and decided to construct the equidistance line by reference to base points located on islands which it apparently considered to be an integral part of the relevant coast. The tribunal emphasised that delimitation is exclusively based on the geographical realities prevailing at the time when the boundary is established, consistently with the ICJ's

---

[286] Ibid. 121 [372]–[379].
[287] Ibid. 114 [346].
[288] Ibid. 132 [399].
[289] Ibid.
[290] *Ghana/Côte d'Ivoire* (n. 108) [318].
[291] Section IV.A.2 above.

jurisprudence before *Nicaragua v. Honduras*.[292] Accordingly, coastal instability cannot be a 'compelling reason' making it 'unfeasible' to trace an equidistance line. Since delimitation depends on the existing geographical reality, coastal instability is also unrelated to the 'inappropriateness' of using an equidistance line. Moreover, coastal instability is a geographical factor unrelated to the basis of title over maritime areas, which disqualifies it as a relevant circumstance.[293]

V A Common Approach to Equidistance

The use of equidistance as a starting point for the three-stage approach to maritime delimitation is grounded in UNCLOS. Equidistance is linked to the basis of title over the maritime areas within 200 nm.[294] Moreover, equidistance is also linked to the basis of title over the continental shelf beyond 200 nm.[295] In addition to the connection to the basis of title, the use of equidistance within 200 nm is also premised on the EEZ–continental shelf relationship. The need to avoid creating grey areas, which appear to be unlawful under UNCLOS, further supports the use of equidistance beyond 200 nm. Nevertheless, equidistance should not be applied mechanically, since delimitation pursues the overriding objective to achieve an equitable solution, taking into account the coastal configuration. Only 'compelling reasons' making it 'unfeasible' to select appropriate base points could justify not starting delimitation with an equidistance line. However, although such appropriate base points may exist, it may be 'inappropriate' to draw an equidistance line as a starting point owing to the peculiar coastal configuration.[296]

The international tribunals' approach to equidistance seems to have been faithful to the existing rules of international law, as well as consistent with the basis of title over maritime zones. International tribunals have adopted a common approach to constructing equidistance lines, including with regard to the selection of base points. The principles governing the selection of base points are grounded in UNCLOS, and locating base points on islands need not necessarily be an exercise

---

[292] *Tunisia/Libya* (n. 42) 54 [61].
[293] The legal basis for identifying relevant circumstances is examined in Chapter 5.
[294] Section II.A above.
[295] Section III.B above.
[296] Section II.C above.

in 'creeping relevant circumstances'.[297] Uncertainty in base point selection could arise both owing to the coastal configuration, as in *Nicaragua v. Colombia*, and owing to coastal instability, as in *Nicaragua v. Honduras*. However, such uncertainty does not seem entirely unjustified.

[297] Section IV.B above.

5

Relevant Circumstances

I A Dual Basis for Relevant Circumstances

Under the three-stage approach, an equidistance line could lead to inequitable results. Relevant circumstances are the means through which international tribunals can remedy the inequitableness of an equidistance line. The International Court of Justice (ICJ or Court) mentioned relevant circumstances for the first time in *North Sea Continental Shelf*, in which it held that the 'delimitation [of the continental shelf] is to be effected by agreement in accordance with equitable principles, and taking account of all the relevant circumstances'.[1] In this chapter, 'factors' designates features that are potential relevant circumstances, while 'relevant circumstances' designates the factors that international tribunals have deemed actually to require the adjustment of an equidistance line. 'Factors' could be seen as the raw material, while 'relevant circumstances' as their legal qualification.

The interest of international tribunals and academic writers in relevant circumstances has recently diminished owing to the adoption of a standard delimitation method. Relevant circumstances are examined in less detail in recent decisions on delimitation, which instead focus on determining the relevant coast and the relevant area, and on establishing the provisional equidistance line. Despite this decreased interest, there is a degree of continuity in the judicial assessment of relevant circumstances over time.

The argument of this chapter is threefold. First, relevant circumstances are identified based on two criteria: the basis of title over maritime areas,

---

[1] *North Sea Continental Shelf (Federal Republic of Germany/Denmark; Federal Republic of Germany/Netherlands)* (Judgment) [1969] ICJ Rep 3, 53 [101(C)(1)].

and the function of maritime zones under international law. Their combination is called the dual 'title-function' basis. Second, international tribunals have achieved a high degree of consistency both in identifying relevant circumstances, and in assessing their impact on a provisional equidistance line. Third, although each delimitation case has its peculiarities, in later cases international tribunals have assessed similar factors consistently with their assessment in earlier cases.

Section II examines the relevant circumstances relating to the basis of title. Section III discusses the relevant circumstances linked to the function of maritime zones. Section IV analyses factors that have not been identified as relevant circumstances owing to the absence of any connection either to the basis of title, or to the function of maritime zones. Section V discusses the approach of international tribunals to identifying relevant circumstances, weighing relevant circumstances, and adjusting a provisional equidistance line. Section VI concludes.

II The Basis of Title: Geographical Circumstances

This section addresses relevant circumstances connected with the basis of title. As the basis of title over the continental shelf and the Exclusive Economic Zone (EEZ) is distance from the coast,[2] such circumstances are geographical in character. International tribunals have treated relevant circumstances similarly in similar cases, which has resulted in an appreciable degree of consistency with the approach taken in earlier delimitation decisions.

A Cut-Off Effect

Since *North Sea Continental Shelf*, international tribunals have regarded as sacrosanct the principle under which when a boundary 'produces a cut-off effect on the maritime entitlement of one of those States, as a result of the concavity of the coast, then an adjustment of that line may be necessary in order to reach an equitable result'.[3] When a boundary encroaches upon the maritime entitlements of a neighbouring state, a relevant circumstance warrants the adjustment of that boundary. In *Bangladesh/Myanmar*, the International Tribunal for the Law of the Sea

---

[2] Chapter 4, Sections II.A and III.B above.
[3] *Delimitation of the Maritime Boundary in the Bay of Bengal (Bangladesh/Myanmar)* (Judgment) [2012] ITLOS Rep 4, 81 [292].

(ITLOS or Tribunal) found that 'concavity *per se* is not necessarily a relevant circumstance',[4] but that 'when an equidistance line drawn between two States produces a cut-off effect on the maritime entitlement of one of those States, ... then an adjustment of that line may be necessary in order to reach an equitable result'.[5] This situation takes place where coasts are adjacent and concave.[6]

International tribunals have upheld cut-off as a relevant circumstance in continental shelf and EEZ delimitation since *North Sea Continental Shelf*. In that case, Germany argued that the configuration of its coast, enclosed in a concavity between the Danish and Dutch coasts, rendered a strict equidistance boundary inequitable. Germany stated that:

> in the case of a concave or recessing coast ..., the effect of the use of the equidistance method is to pull the line of the boundary inwards, in the direction of the concavity. Consequently, where two such lines are drawn at different points on a concave coast, they will, if the curvature is pronounced, inevitably meet at a relatively short distance from the coast, thus ... 'cutting off' the coastal State from the further areas of the continental shelf outside of and beyond this triangle.[7]

The ICJ accepted Germany's argument. The Court considered that it was 'unacceptable ... that a State should enjoy continental shelf rights considerably different from those of its neighbours merely because in the one case the coastline is roughly convex in form and in the other it is markedly concave'.[8] Delimitation must respect the principle of non-encroachment, under which delimitation must 'leave as much as possible to each [state] all those parts of the continental shelf that constitute a natural prolongation of its land territory into and under the sea'.[9]

In *St. Pierre et Miquelon*, the Court of Arbitration implicitly upheld non-encroachment as a relevant circumstance in continental shelf and EEZ delimitation. The French islands of St. Pierre and Miquelon are located off the coast of Newfoundland. Canada and France agreed that the coastal projection of St. Pierre and Miquelon towards the high seas would cut off Newfoundland's coastal projections, but that 'une certaine amputation est

---

[4] *Bangladesh/Myanmar* (n. 3) 81 [292].
[5] Ibid.
[6] *North Sea Continental Shelf* (n. 1) 17 [8].
[7] Ibid.
[8] Ibid. 50 [91].
[9] Ibid. 53 [101(C)(1)].

peut-être inhérente à toute délimitation'.[10] The Court of Arbitration decided that the French islands were entitled to a full 200-nautical-mile southward coastal projection, 'quand bien même cette extension provoquerait quelque empiétement sur certaines projections canadiennes vers le large'.[11] The Court of Arbitration seemed concerned with avoiding cutting off Canada's coastal projections. However, it found that Canada's contention that St. Pierre and Miquelon should have been enclaved 'n'est pas équitable car elle nie aux îles tout espace maritime au-delà des espaces qui lui sont déjà reconnus comme mer territoriale'.[12] The reason for this decision was that enclaving the French islands would have cut off their coastal projections.[13] This case established a link between cut-off and enclavement of islands.[14] The Court of Arbitration seemed to formulate a principle under which the need to avoid cut-off is a relevant circumstance overriding the enclavement of islands. Enclaving an island curtails their maritime entitlements. However, the need to avoid cut-off protects such entitlements from being curtailed. If one accepts that cut-off prevails over enclavement, it would also aim to ensure that islands are awarded the fullest extent of maritime entitlements under international law.

In later decisions, international tribunals confirmed that cut-off can be a relevant circumstance. However, in *Cameroon v. Nigeria*,[15] *Barbados v. Trinidad and Tobago*,[16] *Black Sea*[17] and *Ghana/Côte d'Ivoire*[18] international tribunals found that the cut-off of the states' coastal projections did not warrant adjusting the equidistance line, as it was not serious enough to render the equidistance line inequitable. The cases indicate that international tribunals adjust an equidistance line only if it inequitably cuts off a significant portion of a state's coastal

---

[10] *Delimitation of Maritime Areas between Canada and France (St. Pierre et Miquelon) (Canada/France)* (1992) XXI RIAA 265, 289 [67].
[11] Ibid. 290 [68].
[12] Ibid.
[13] MD Evans, 'Less Than an Ocean Apart: The St. Pierre and Miquelon and Jan Mayen Islands and the Delimitation of Maritime Zones' (1994) 43 *ICLQ* 678, 681.
[14] On enclavement of islands, see Section II.C.1 below.
[15] *Land and Maritime Boundary between Cameroon and Nigeria (Cameroon v. Nigeria; Equatorial Guinea intervening)* (Merits) [2002] ICJ Rep 303, 445–446 [297].
[16] *Maritime Boundary Arbitration (Barbados v. Trinidad and Tobago)* (2006) XXVII RIAA 147, 243 [375].
[17] *Maritime Delimitation in the Black Sea (Romania v. Ukraine)* (Judgment) [2009] ICJ Rep 61, 127 [201].
[18] *Delimitation of the Maritime Boundary between Ghana and Côte d'Ivoire in the Atlantic Ocean (Ghana/Côte d'Ivoire)* (Judgment), Judgment of 23 September 2017 [421]–[426].

II THE BASIS OF TITLE: GEOGRAPHICAL CIRCUMSTANCES 171

projections. Some degree of cut-off is inherent in delimitation, as the essence of the process is to delimit overlapping maritime entitlements.

The 2018 judgment in *Costa Rica v. Nicaragua* was the first case in which, in order to remedy the cut-off of a state's coastal projections, a feature other than an island was given half effect. This was the case of the Santa Elena Peninsula, part of the Pacific coast of Costa Rica. The Court constructed the provisional equidistance line also using base points on the Santa Elena Peninsula.[19] However, the Court observed that 'the base points placed on the Santa Elena Peninsula control the course of the provisional equidistance line from the 12-nautical-mile limit of the territorial sea up to a point located approximately 120 nautical miles from the coasts of the Parties'.[20] The result was that 'the effect of the Santa Elena Peninsula on the provisional equidistance line results in a significant cut-off of Nicaragua's coastal projections'.[21] The Court decided that giving half effect to the Santa Elena Peninsula would abate cut-off and contribute to achieving an equitable solution.[22]

In the 2012 *Nicaragua v. Colombia* judgment, the ICJ found for the first time that cut-off could be a relevant circumstance between states with opposite coasts. The delimitation area was characterised by Nicaraguan and Colombian islands lying opposite each other in close proximity to Nicaragua's mainland coast. Colombia requested the Court to draw a median-line boundary between the islands, stating that '[g]iven that there is a substantial maritime area lying between the San Andrés Archipelago and the Nicaraguan islands and cays ..., there is no risk of the equidistance line producing a "cut off" effect or unduly encroaching on the maritime areas appertaining to either Party'.[23] However, Nicaragua replied that 'Colombia has produced a line that not only cuts across Nicaragua's coastal front, but runs almost perfectly perpendicular to the seaward projection of that coast for its entire length',[24] which was 'the ultimate in cut-off effect'.[25] According to the Court:

---

[19] *Maritime Delimitation in the Caribbean Sea and the Pacific Ocean (Costa Rica v. Nicaragua); Land Boundary in the Northern Part of Isla Portillos (Costa Rica v. Nicaragua)* (Judgment) [2018] ICJ Rep 139, 214–16 [188].
[20] Ibid. 218 [193].
[21] Ibid.
[22] Ibid. 218 [194].
[23] Counter-memorial of Colombia (11 November 2008), 411 [9.86].
[24] CR 2012/10, 39–40 [37] (Reichler).
[25] Ibid.

[t]he effect of the provisional median line is to cut Nicaragua off from some three quarters of the area into which its coast projects. Moreover, that cut-off effect is produced by a few small islands which are many nautical miles apart. . . . The Court therefore concludes that the cut-off effect is a relevant consideration which requires adjustment or shifting of the provisional median line in order to produce an equitable result.[26]

The Court also found that 'any adjustment or shifting of the provisional median line must not have the effect of cutting off Colombia from the entitlements generated by its islands in the area to the east of those islands'.[27]

In *Bangladesh/Myanmar*, ITLOS found cut-off to be a relevant circumstance in delimitation beyond 200 nautical miles (nm).[28] According to Bangladesh, a strict equidistance boundary would mean that 'Bangladesh is "shelf-locked"; that is, cut off entirely from the outer continental shelf beyond 200 [nm]'.[29] Myanmar did not reject the existence of cut-off, arguing that 'a cut-off effect is never inequitable as such',[30] since '[i]t is if it produces an inequitable result with regard to the coastal geography, which Bangladesh has failed to show specifically'.[31] ITLOS simply held that '[h]aving considered the concavity of the Bangladesh coast to be a relevant circumstance for the purpose of delimiting the [EEZ] and the continental shelf within 200 nm, . . . this relevant circumstance has a continuing effect beyond 200 nm'.[32] The *Bangladesh v. India* tribunal adopted the same approach as ITLOS.[33]

The decisions that cut-off could be a relevant circumstance beyond 200 nm could be criticised, as coastal projections could be seen not to be linked to the basis of title over the continental shelf beyond 200 nm.[34] However, while one could agree that the basis of title over the continental shelf beyond 200 nm is not only distance from the coast but also the physical existence of a continental margin, it is difficult to accept the

---

[26] *Territorial and Maritime Dispute (Nicaragua v. Colombia)* (Merits) [2012] ICJ Rep 624, 703–4 [215].
[27] Ibid. 704 [216].
[28] ITLOS previously held that the Bay of Bengal's concavity was a relevant circumstance within 200 nm. See *Bangladesh/Myanmar* (n. 3) 80–2 [290]–[297].
[29] Reply of Bangladesh (15 March 2011), 144 [4.82].
[30] ITLOS/PV.11/10/Rev.1, 3 (Forteau).
[31] Ibid.
[32] *Bangladesh/Myanmar* (n. 3) 118 [461].
[33] *Bay of Bengal Maritime Boundary Arbitration (Bangladesh v. India)* (2014) 167 ILR 1, 134 [408].
[34] B Kunoy, 'The Delimitation of an Indicative Area of Overlapping Entitlement to the Outer Continental Shelf' (2012) 83 *BYIL* 61, 62.

II THE BASIS OF TITLE: GEOGRAPHICAL CIRCUMSTANCES 173

irrelevance of coastal projections. The coast is a necessary element for a state to assert sovereign rights over the continental shelf beyond 200 nm. Although not sufficient, the presence of a coast, coupled with the existence of a physical shelf beyond 200 nm, is the basis of title over the continental shelf beyond 200 nm. Distance from the coast plays an important role with respect to title over the continental shelf beyond 200 nm.[35] Coastal projections contribute to defining entitlements beyond 200 nm, which justifies treating cut-off as a relevant circumstance beyond 200 nm.

Cut-off is a relevant circumstance in delimiting the EEZ and the continental shelf, both within and beyond 200 nm. International tribunals approach the treatment of cut-off similarly in respect of all maritime areas. As the ICJ held in *Nicaragua* v. *Colombia*, cut-off applies to the situation of opposite coasts as well as between adjacent coasts. The application of cut-off as a relevant circumstance irrespective of coastal relationship is consistent with the basis of title being common to all maritime zones.

B *Coastal Length Disparity*

The disparity between the relevant coasts is not to be confused with disproportionality. Coastal length disparity, a relevant circumstance, could by itself determine the adjustment of an equidistance line. Disproportionality, the final step of the three-stage approach, is a test for the overall equitableness of the boundary, and is assessed by comparing the coastal length ratio to the marine area ratio after an equidistance line has eventually been adjusted.[36]

Gulf of Maine was the first decision in which coastal length disparity impacted on the course of the boundary. Canada and the USA requested a Chamber of the ICJ to delimit their maritime boundary in the Gulf of Maine, starting from a point, indicated in their special agreement, lying at 39 nm from the land boundary terminus.[37] Discussing the applicable delimitation criteria, the Chamber listed 'the criterion whereby ... the appropriate consequences may be drawn from any inequalities in the

---

[35] Chapter 4, Section III.B.2 above.
[36] See Y Tanaka, *The International Law of the Sea* 2nd edn (CUP, 2015) 210–13. Chapter 6, Section V below examines the relationship between disproportionality and coastal length disparity.
[37] *Delimitation of the Maritime Boundary in the Gulf of Maine Area (Canada/USA)* (Judgment) [1984] ICJ Rep 246, 318 [171].

extent of the coasts of two States into the same area of delimitation'.[38] The Chamber decided to split the boundary in three segments to be separately determined.[39] In the second segment the coasts were found to be opposite each other, yet the Chamber stated that tracing a strict median line 'would be to cling to a very superficial view of the matter'.[40] The Chamber found that 'it is ... impossible to disregard the circumstance ... that there is a difference in length between the respective coastlines of the two neighbouring States which border on the delimitation area',[41] and thus 'reaffirm[ed] the necessity of applying to the median line as initially drawn a correction which ... will pay due heed to the actual situation'.[42]

In *Libya/Malta*, the Court shifted the entire boundary on account of the marked difference between the parties' coastal lengths. Under the special agreement, the dispute concerned 'the delimitation of the area of the continental shelf which appertains to ... Malta and the area of continental shelf which appertains to [Libya]'.[43] The parties' coasts were opposite each other, and stood in a 8:1 ratio in Libya's favour.[44] According to the Court, it was necessary 'to attribute the appropriate significance to that coastal relationship'.[45] The Court held that 'it is first necessary to determine which are the coasts which are being contemplated'.[46] After having calculated the length of the parties' relevant coasts, the Court decided, 'to ensure the achievement of an equitable solution, that the delimitation line between the areas of continental shelf appertaining respectively to the two Parties, be adjusted so as to lie closer to the coasts of Malta'.[47] The Court shifted the boundary northwards by 18 minutes of latitude, which in its view achieved an equitable solution.[48]

Coastal length disparity featured prominently in *Jan Mayen*. Denmark requested the ICJ to delimit the single maritime boundary between

---

[38] Ibid. 313 [157].
[39] Ibid. 331 [207]–[208].
[40] Ibid. 334 [217].
[41] Ibid. 334 [218].
[42] Ibid. The Chamber seemed to understand this operation as a proportionality test, despite treating it as an equitable criterion of delimitation. See T McDorman et al., 'The Gulf of Maine Boundary: Dropping Anchor or Setting a Course?' (1985) 9 *Marine Policy* 90, 97.
[43] Special Agreement for the Submission to the International Court of Justice of a Continental Shelf Dispute (1982) 21 *ILM* 972, Art. I.
[44] *Continental Shelf (Libya/Malta)* (Judgment) [1985] ICJ Rep 13, 50 [68].
[45] Ibid. 49 [66].
[46] Ibid. 49 [67].
[47] Ibid. 51 [71].
[48] Ibid. 51–3 [72]–[73].

II THE BASIS OF TITLE: GEOGRAPHICAL CIRCUMSTANCES

Greenland and the Norwegian island of Jan Mayen. However, Norway objected to a single maritime boundary, requesting the Court to draw two distinct boundaries, one for the continental shelf and one for the Fishery Zone (FZ).[49] Since there existed two strands of applicable law, Article 6 of the Convention on the Continental Shelf (CCS)[50] for the continental shelf and customary international law for the FZ, the Court acceded to Norway's request.[51] Nevertheless, the Court examined special circumstances under Article 6 CCS and relevant circumstances under customary international law jointly.[52] It found that the case before it was one 'in which the relationship between the length of the relevant coasts and the maritime areas generated by them by application of the equidistance method is so disproportionate that it has been found necessary to take this circumstance into account in order to ensure an equitable solution'.[53] However, the Court conflated proportionality with relevant circumstances by stating that:

> [i]t is not a question of determining the equitable nature of a delimitation as a function of the ratio of the lengths of the coasts in comparison with that of the areas generated by the maritime projection of the points of the coast ... [y]et the differences in length of the respective coasts of the Parties are so significant that this feature must be taken into consideration during the delimitation operation.[54]

The Court found that:

> [t]he disparity between the lengths of coasts ... constitutes a special circumstance within the meaning of Article 6, paragraph 1, of the 1958 Convention. Similarly, as regards the fishery zones, the Court is of the opinion, in view of the great disparity of the lengths of the coasts, that the application of the median line leads to manifestly inequitable results.[55]

The Court upheld that disparity in coastal length could be both a special circumstance under Article 6 CCS, and a relevant circumstance under

---

[49] *Maritime Delimitation in the Area between Greenland and Jan Mayen (Denmark v. Norway)* (Judgment) [1993] ICJ Rep 38, 56–7 [41].
[50] 499 UNTS 311.
[51] *Jan Mayen* (n. 49) 57–8 [44].
[52] Ibid. 62 [56].
[53] Ibid. 67 [65].
[54] Ibid. 68 [68]. See RR Churchill, 'The Greenland-Jan Mayen Case and its Significance for the International Law of Maritime Boundary Delimitation' (1994) 9 *IJMCL* 1, 20–21; E Decaux, 'Affaire de la délimitation maritime dans la région située entre le Groenland et Jan Mayen (Danemark c. Norvège)' (1993) 39 *AFDI* 495, 505–7.
[55] *Jan Mayen* (n. 49) 68–9 [68].

customary international law. The Court confirmed such findings in *Nicaragua* v. *Colombia*, emphasising that 'it is normally only where the disparities in the lengths of the relevant coasts are substantial that an adjustment or shifting of the provisional line is called for'.[56] It then found that a 8.2:1 coastal length ratio in Nicaragua's favour was 'undoubtedly a substantial disparity ... that ... requires an adjustment or shifting of the provisional line'.[57] The arbitral tribunal in *Barbados* v. *Trinidad and Tobago* made comparable comments.[58]

The ICJ also found that disparity in coastal length could be a relevant circumstance in delimitation between adjacent coasts. In *Cameroon* v. *Nigeria*, the parties' coastlines were adjacent.[59] The Court found that the 1971 Yaoundé II Declaration and the 1975 Maroua Declaration were binding treaties delimiting the maritime boundary between Cameroon and Nigeria up to point G, located in the EEZ.[60] Therefore, the Court traced the maritime boundary from point G. Cameroon identified 'the disparity between the length of its coastline and that of Nigeria ... as a relevant circumstance that justifies shifting the delimitation line towards the north-west'.[61] The Court found that 'whichever coastline of Nigeria is regarded as relevant, the relevant coastline of Cameroon ... is not longer than that of Nigeria',[62] and that '[t]here is therefore no reason to shift the equidistance line in favour of Cameroon on this ground'.[63] However, it acknowledged that 'a substantial difference in the lengths of the parties' respective coastlines may be a factor to be taken into consideration in order to adjust or shift the provisional delimitation line'.[64]

Similarly to *Cameroon* v. *Nigeria*, in *Black Sea* Romania's coast 'is an adjacent coast with regard to the Ukrainian coast lying to the north, and it is an opposite coast to the coast of the Crimean Peninsula'.[65] The Court held that '[w]here disparities in the lengths of coasts are particularly marked, the Court may choose to treat that fact of geography as a relevant circumstance that would require some adjustments to the

[56] *Nicaragua* v. *Colombia* (n. 26) 702 [210].
[57] Ibid. 702 [211].
[58] *Barbados* v. *Trinidad and Tobago* (n 16) 234–5 [327].
[59] Ibid. 330 [30].
[60] *Cameroon* v. *Nigeria* (n. 15) 445–6 [297].
[61] Ibid. 446 [300].
[62] Ibid. 446–7 [301].
[63] Ibid.
[64] Ibid.
[65] *Black Sea* (n. 17) 93 [88].

II THE BASIS OF TITLE: GEOGRAPHICAL CIRCUMSTANCES 177

provisional equidistance line'.[66] However, it found that the coastal length disparity between Romania and Ukraine was not marked enough to justify shifting the equidistance line.[67]

The international tribunals' findings concerning coastal length disparity are consistent with the link between the character of a factor as a relevant circumstance and the basis of title over the continental shelf and the EEZ. Differently from cut-off,[68] international tribunals have never found that coastal length disparity was a relevant circumstance in the delimitation of the continental shelf beyond 200 nm. However, similarly to cut-off, coastal length disparity is closely linked to the basis of title over the continental shelf beyond 200 nm. Cut-off was considered a relevant circumstance in *Bangladesh/Myanmar* and *Bangladesh v. India*. In the same perspective, international tribunals might consider coastal length disparity to be a relevant circumstance in future disputes on delimitation beyond 200 nm.

Whether considering coastal length disparity as a relevant circumstance in delimitation beyond 200 nm would stand up to scrutiny could depend on whether coasts are opposite or adjacent. If coasts are opposite, the entire boundary to be delimited could be located beyond 200 nm from the coast of one state. This is similar to the situation in the dispute between Nicaragua and Colombia pending before the ICJ. As distance from the coast is an element of the basis of title over the continental shelf beyond 200 nm, coastal length disparity could in principle be a relevant circumstance.

If coasts are adjacent, adjusting an equidistance line owing to coastal length disparity within 200 nm may *ipso facto* determine an adjustment beyond 200 nm. International tribunals could either adjust the equidistance line separately within and beyond 200 nm, or adjust the entire equidistance line in a single operation. ITLOS adopted the former method with respect to a cut-off-based adjustment in *Bangladesh/Myanmar*. Having found that cut-off required it to shift the equidistance line within 200 nm, ITLOS declared that cut-off had 'a continuing effect beyond 200 nm'.[69] Conceivably, ITLOS was compelled to find that cut-off was a relevant circumstance beyond 200 nm. To find otherwise would have meant that, once it reached the EEZ's 200-nm limit, the adjusted line within 200 nm should have made an abrupt detour along that limit to

---
[66] Ibid. 116 [164].
[67] Ibid. 117–18 [168].
[68] Section II.A above.
[69] *Bangladesh/Myanmar* (n. 3) 87–9 [323]–[336] and 118 [461].

reach the point where the provisional equidistance line for delimitation beyond 200 nm would have originated. In *Bangladesh v. India*, the tribunal opted for the former method, examining all relevant circumstances, both within and beyond 200 nm, before adjusting the provisional equidistance line in a single operation.[70] Although this method allows international tribunals not to be constrained, in adjusting equidistance lines beyond 200 nm, by adjustments effected within 200 nm, it might render it difficult to distinguish the bases for adjusting a line within and beyond 200 nm. This problem has not yet arisen, as both ITLOS and the *Bangladesh v. India* tribunal found that cut-off was a relevant circumstance both within and beyond 200 nm.

C Islands

Although determining the effect of islands on delimitation might be contentious,[71] international tribunals have developed a consistent approach to it. The following sections discuss enclavement, no effect, half effect and full effect as methods to determine the effect of islands on maritime delimitation.

1 Enclavement

Enclaving an island under a state's sovereignty within the maritime spaces of another state may be appropriate for islands 'on the wrong side' of the median line.[72] The Channel Islands are the classic case. In the *Anglo/French Arbitration*, France and the UK had opposite coasts of comparable length, which called for a median-line delimitation.[73] However, the Channel Islands lay within the Bay of Granville, which placed them on the French side of a median line.[74] The Court of Arbitration noted that the Channel Islands had 'a considerable population and a substantial agricultural and commercial economy',[75] and were 'territorial and political units which have their own separate existence,

---

[70] *Bangladesh v. India* (n. 33) 121–39 [371]–[424] and 158–65 [465]–[480].
[71] T Cottier, *Equitable Principles of Maritime Boundary Delimitation* (CUP, 2015) 635; DP O'Connell, *The International Law of the Sea* (OUP, 1984) vol. II, 717. Under Art. 121(1) UNCLOS an island is 'a naturally formed area of land, surrounded by water, which is above water at high tide'.
[72] MD Evans, *Relevant Circumstances and Maritime Delimitation* (OUP, 1989) 149.
[73] *Continental Shelf (France/UK)* (1977) XVIII RIAA 3, 88 [182].
[74] See S Fietta and R Cleverly, *A Practitioner's Guide to Maritime Boundary Delimitation* (OUP, 2016) 196–9.
[75] *Anglo/French Arbitration* (n. 73) 88 [184].

II THE BASIS OF TITLE: GEOGRAPHICAL CIRCUMSTANCES 179

and which are of a certain importance in their own right separately from the United Kingdom'.[76] The Court of Arbitration rejected the UK's contention that the Channel Islands should be treated as a state, since the UK conducted the islands' foreign relations and was, more generally, the 'responsible authority'.[77] The Court of Arbitration stated that '[t]he presence of these British islands close to the French coast, if they are given full effect in delimiting the continental shelf, will manifestly result in a substantial diminution of the area of continental shelf which would otherwise accrue to the French Republic'.[78] Such a situation was 'a circumstance creative of inequity and calling for a method of delimitation that in some measure redresses the inequity'.[79]

The Court of Arbitration decided that France's continental shelf entitlements could not encroach upon the 12-nm territorial sea around the Channel Islands. It therefore held that the solution was:

> to enclose [the Channel Islands] in an enclave formed, to their north and west, by the boundary of the 12-mile zone just described by the Court and, to their east, south and south-west by the boundary between them and the coasts of Normandy and Brittany ...[80]

The Court of Arbitration's decision was determined by the fact that the Channel Islands were 'on the wrong side' of the median line. Political, economic and demographic status only contributed to determining the breadth of the Islands' maritime entitlements.[81]

In *Nicaragua* v. *Colombia*, Nicaragua submitted that, if the ICJ found that Colombia had sovereignty over the islands of San Andrés, Providencia and Santa Catalina, it should enclave such islands within a 12-nm territorial sea, since Colombia's islands were 'on the wrong side' of the median line between the two state's mainland coasts.[82] The Court recalled that under Article 121 of the United Nations Convention on the Law of the Sea (UNCLOS)[83] islands generate the same maritime entitlements as mainland territory, regardless of size, population or economic

---

[76] Ibid.
[77] Ibid. 89 [186].
[78] Ibid. 93 [196].
[79] Ibid.
[80] Ibid. 95 [202]. The Court of Arbitration had previously found itself without jurisdiction to delimit the territorial sea boundary between the Channel Islands and France, see ibid. 24 [21].
[81] Ibid. 89 [187].
[82] *Nicaragua* v. *Colombia* (n. 26) 636 [17].
[83] 1833 UNTS 3.

importance.[84] Similarly to the *Anglo/French Arbitration*, the ICJ held that:

> the overlap is between the territorial sea entitlement of Colombia derived from each island and the entitlement of Nicaragua to a continental shelf and [EEZ]. The nature of those two entitlements is different. ... [A] coastal State possesses sovereignty over the sea bed and water column in its territorial sea ... By contrast, coastal States enjoy specific rights, rather than sovereignty, with respect to the continental shelf and [EEZ].[85]

The Court did not settle the status of Albuquerque Cays, East-southeast Cays, Roncador, Serrana, Serranilla and Bajo Nuevo. Their maritime entitlements were found to be subsumed by those generated by San Andrés, Providencia and Santa Catalina, whose island status was undisputed. Concerning the low-tide elevations of Quintasueño, the Court decided that it would be enclaved within its 12-nm territorial sea.[86]

According to the Court, 'if each island were to be given an enclave of 12 [nm], ... the effect would be to cut off Colombia from the substantial areas to the east of the principal islands, where those islands generate an entitlement to a continental shelf and [EEZ]'.[87] The Court distinguished this case from the *Anglo/French Arbitration*, in which enclavement took place in a delimitation between mainland coasts. In *Nicaragua v. Colombia*, delimitation was between Nicaragua's mainland and Colombia's islands.[88] The Court rejected Nicaragua's enclavement argument, finding it equitable to give the Colombian islands one-quarter effect *vis-à-vis* Nicaragua's base points. In the *Anglo/French Arbitration*, enclavement was only considered viable as delimitation was between two mainland coasts, while the Channel Islands were located on France's side of the equidistance line. The ICJ upheld this approach in *Nicaragua v. Colombia* by refusing to enclave San Andrés, Providencia and Santa Catalina, thus also ensuring that the maritime entitlements of such islands were not cut off.

---

[84] *Maritime Delimitation and Territorial Questions between Qatar and Bahrain (Qatar v Bahrain)* (Merits) [2001] ICJ Rep 40, 97 [185]. See also MD Evans, 'Case concerning Maritime Delimitation and Territorial Questions between Qatar and Bahrain (*Qatar v. Bahrain*)' (2002) 51 *ICLQ* 709, 717; B Kwiatkowska, 'The Qatar v. Bahrain Maritime Delimitation and Territorial Questions Case' (2002) 33 *ODIL* 227, 244.
[85] *Nicaragua v. Colombia* (n. 26) 690 [177].
[86] Ibid. 692-3 [181]-[183].
[87] Ibid. 708 [230].
[88] Ibid. 708-9 [231].

II THE BASIS OF TITLE: GEOGRAPHICAL CIRCUMSTANCES   181

The Channel Islands' status as dependencies of the British Crown also justified enclavement in the *Anglo/French Arbitration*.[89] The UK argued that the Channel Islands 'are part neither of the [UK] nor of the Colonies but have for several hundred years been direct dependencies of the Crown; they have their own legislative assemblies, fiscal and legal systems, Courts of law and systems of local administration, as well as their own coinage and postal service'. The UK added that 'although [the UK] assumes responsibility for the foreign relations of the Channel Islands, they are in effect "island States enjoying an important degree of political, legislative, administrative and economic independence of ancient foundation"'.[90] The Court of Arbitration accepted that the Channel Islands 'enjoy a very large measure of political, legislative, administrative ... autonomy',[91] but, based on their defence arrangements and the ratification process of the CCS with respect to them, the Court of Arbitration found that it 'must treat the Channel Islands only as islands of the [UK], not as semi-independent States entitled in their own right to their own continental shelf'.[92]

Conceivably, the Court of Arbitration discussed political status because the UK had raised it. The main reason for enclaving the Channel Islands was their position 'on the wrong side' of the median line in a mainland-to-mainland delimitation. Political status simply reinforced a decision made on geographical grounds, consistently with the basis of title. While an island's effect should be decided based on physical geography, nothing prevents international tribunals from relying on human geography to support their conclusions. This practice also applies to decisions of no effect and full effect.[93] Human geography is not a relevant circumstance. Its function in respect of islands is to confirm decisions reached on other grounds.

2 No effect

Awarding no effect entails that islands are considered inexistent for the purposes of delimitation. *Dubai/Sharjah* was the first case of no

---

[89] *Anglo/French Arbitration* (n. 73) 88 [184]. See Evans (n. 72) 166. Bowett criticised the decision on political status, as the weight the Court of Arbitration attached to such a factor was unclear. See DW Bowett, 'The Arbitration between the United Kingdom and France concerning the Continental Shelf Boundary in the English Channel and South-Western Approaches' (1978) 49 *BYIL* 1, 17.
[90] *Anglo/French Arbitration* (n. 73) 84 [171].
[91] Ibid. 88 [184].
[92] Ibid. 89 [186].
[93] Sections II.C.2 and II.C.4 below.

effect.[94] Abu Musa was an island lying 35 nm from the parties' coasts, sovereignty over which was disputed between Sharjah and Iran and whose effect in delimitation was equally disputed.[95] The Court of Arbitration found that Abu Musa was entitled to a full territorial sea.[96] However, it also held that:

> to allow to the island of Abu Musa any entitlement to an area of the continental shelf of the [Persian] Gulf beyond the extent of its belt of territorial sea would indeed produce a distorting effect upon neighbouring shelf areas. The application of equitable principles here ... must lead to no effect being accorded to the island of Abu Musa for the purpose of plotting median or equidistance shelf boundaries ...[97]

Awarding Abu Musa full effect would have added 133.8 square nm to Sharjah's maritime entitlements, which 'would have produced a disproportionate and exaggerated entitlement to maritime space as between the Parties ...'.[98]

In *Tunisia/Libya*, the Court did not dwell on Jerba's effect. It simply held that '[t]he practical method for the delimitation to be expounded by the Court ... is ... such that, in the part of the area to be delimited in which the island of Jerba would be relevant, there are other considerations which prevail over the effect of its presence'.[99] Differently from the UK in the *Anglo/French Arbitration*, Tunisia did not contend that Jerba was to be treated as a separate island state, and the ICJ did not consider human geography in deciding on Jerba's effect. Commenting on *Tunisia/Libya*, Evans suggested that '[t]he size and position of features can only be relevant if the result of applying the practical method will be influenced by their size and position'.[100] Yet, this reasoning seems circular. It seems more correct to state that *Tunisia/Libya* is unpersuasive due to the Court's obscure reasoning on Jerba's effect, which did not specify the criteria governing the decision in that regard.

Guinea/Guinea-Bissau seemed to build upon *Tunisia/Libya*. The Court of Arbitration distinguished three categories of islands in the

---

[94] The *Dubai/Sharjah Arbitration* was held between two federal constituent subdivisions of the United Arab Emirates.
[95] See DW Bowett, 'The Dubai/Sharjah Boundary Arbitration of 1981' (1995) 65 *BYIL* 103, 130.
[96] *Dubai/Sharjah Border Arbitration (Dubai/Sharjah)* (1981) 91 ILR 543, 674.
[97] Ibid. 677.
[98] Ibid.
[99] *Continental Shelf (Tunisia/Libya)* (Judgment) [1982] ICJ Rep 18, 64 [79].
[100] Evans (n. 72) 146.

11 THE BASIS OF TITLE: GEOGRAPHICAL CIRCUMSTANCES 183

delimitation area, the third of which was designated as 'îlots éparpillés ... dont certains peuvent compter pour l'établissement des lignes de base et entrer dans les eaux territoriales'.[101] The Court of Arbitration deemed such islets not to be part of Guinea-Bissau's coast,[102] and held that 'les îles pertinentes ne doivent pas entrer en compte sous la forme du total obtenu par l'addition des pourtours de chacune d'elles, mais à titre d'éléments déterminant la direction générale de l'ensemble du littoral du pays considéré'.[103] The Court of Arbitration considered that the 'îlots éparpillés' could not be given effect because they did not determine the general direction of Guinea-Bissau's coast. Moreover, it decided to depart from equidistance, as an equidistance line would have left Guinea's island of Alcatraz on Guinea-Bissau's side of the boundary.[104] Similarly to *Tunisia/Libya*, in *Guinea/Guinea-Bissau* islands were a factor in choosing a delimitation method, yet, similarly to *Tunisia/Libya*, the reasoning in *Guinea/Guinea-Bissau* remains unclear.

In *Eritrea/Yemen*, a contentious point concerned the effect of certain islands, including Yemen's al-Tayr and al-Zubayr. According to the arbitral tribunal, '[t]hese islands do not constitute a part of Yemen's mainland coast',[105] and 'their barren and inhospitable nature and their position well out to sea ... mean that they should not be taken into consideration in computing the boundary-line between Yemen and Eritrea'.[106] Therefore, 'both the single island of al-Tayr and the island group of al-Zubayr should have no effect upon the median line international boundary'.[107] The reasoning in *Eritrea/Yemen* differed from the previous cases in that the size and position of al-Tayr and al-Zubayr were considered not in choosing the applicable delimitation method, but as a circumstance impacting on an already chosen delimitation method.

The ICJ adopted a similar approach in *Qatar v. Bahrain*, in which islands were considered only after the Court had drawn an equidistance line. The position, size, population and economy of islands were considered in choosing their effect. Although islands were mainly situated in the parties' territorial sea, Fasht al Jarim, 'a sizeable maritime feature

---

[101] *Delimitation of the Maritime Boundary between Guinea and Guinea-Bissau (Guinea/Guinea-Bissau)* (1985) XIX RIAA 149, 184 [95].
[102] Ibid. 184 [97].
[103] Ibid.
[104] Ibid. 187 [103].
[105] *Second Stage of the Proceedings between Eritrea and Yemen (Maritime Delimitation) (Eritrea/Yemen)* (1999) XXII RIAA 335, 368 [147].
[106] Ibid.
[107] Ibid. 368 [148].

partly situated in the territorial sea of Bahrain',[108] was relevant in establishing the continental shelf boundary. The Court found that it was 'a remote projection of Bahrain's coastline in the Gulf area, which, if given full effect, would "distort the boundary and have disproportionate effects"'.[109] It also stated that:

> such a distortion, due to a maritime feature located well out to sea and of which at most a minute part is above water at high tide, would not lead to an equitable solution ... In the circumstances of the case considerations of equity require that Fasht al Jarim should have no effect in determining the boundary line in the northern sector.[110]

The ICJ made comparable considerations in *Black Sea* with respect to Serpents' Island, located 20 nm off Ukraine's coast. The Court first decided that it could not use Serpents' Island as a base point to plot the equidistance line, as it 'cannot be taken to form part of Ukraine's coastal configuration'.[111] At the second stage of delimitation, the Court ascertained 'whether the presence of Serpents' Island in the maritime delimitation area constitutes a relevant circumstance calling for an adjustment of the provisional equidistance line'.[112] Given its geographical position, the Court found that:

> any continental shelf and [EEZ] entitlements possibly generated by Serpents' Island could not project further than the entitlements generated by Ukraine's mainland coast because of the southern limit of the delimitation area as identified by the Court ... Further, any possible entitlements generated by Serpents' Island in an eastward direction are fully subsumed by the entitlements generated by the western and eastern mainland coasts of Ukraine itself.[113]

The Court did not decide on whether Serpents' Island should be given any effect, since its maritime entitlements were incorporated into those generated by Ukraine's mainland coast. However, the Court's reasoning seemed to have been guided by the geographical position of Serpents' Island with regard to Ukraine's coast.

The effect of St. Martin's Island, which lay at 6.5 nm from the land boundary terminus, was central in *Bangladesh/Myanmar*. Bangladesh

---

[108] Ibid. 114 [245].
[109] Ibid. 114–15 [247].
[110] Ibid. 115 [248].
[111] *Black Sea* (n. 17) 110 [149].
[112] Ibid. 122 [186].
[113] Ibid. 122 [187].

underscored that 'this island ... supports a permanent population of 7,000 residents', 'it receives more than 360,000 tourists annually', and 'fishing is the most significant economic activity on the island'.[114] According to ITLOS:

> the effect to be given to an island in the delimitation of the maritime boundary in the [EEZ] and the continental shelf depends on the geographic realities and the circumstances of the specific case. There is no general rule in this respect. Each case is unique and requires specific treatment, the ultimate goal being to reach a solution that is equitable.[115]

ITLOS subsequently found that 'because of its location, giving effect to St. Martin's Island in the delimitation of the [EEZ] and the continental shelf would result in a line blocking the seaward projection from Myanmar's coast in a manner that would cause an unwarranted distortion of the delimitation line'.[116] ITLOS based its decision to give no effect to St. Martin's Island on geographical considerations, as giving St. Martin's Island full effect would have cut off Myanmar's maritime entitlements. *Bangladesh/Myanmar* suggests that international tribunals do not determine the effect of islands in isolation, since other relevant circumstances could have an impact on that determination.

Geography plays a key role in decisions to give no effect to islands. In *Tunisia/Libya*, the ICJ did not explicitly find that Jerba was to be given no effect, but it discussed geography before making a decision to discount Jerba's effect.[117] In *Guinea/Guinea-Bissau*,[118] *Eritrea/Yemen*[119] and *Black Sea*,[120] international tribunals considered that the islands concerned could not be seen to be part of the coast, and therefore gave them no effect. In *Dubai/Sharjah*, the arbitral tribunal held that giving Abu Musa full effect would have distorted the boundary to Dubai's detriment.[121] The ICJ made similar comments in respect of Fasht al Jarim in *Qatar v. Bahrain*.[122] Finally, in *Bangladesh/Myanmar*, ITLOS found that giving St. Martin's Island full effect would have cut off Myanmar's coastal

---

[114] Memorial of Bangladesh (1 July 2010), 16–17 [2.18].
[115] *Bangladesh/Myanmar* (n. 3) 86 [317].
[116] Ibid. 86 [318]–[319].
[117] *Tunisia/Libya* (n. 99) 63–4 [79].
[118] *Guinea/Guinea-Bissau* (n. 101) 184–5 [97].
[119] *Eritrea/Yemen* (n. 106) 368 [147].
[120] *Black Sea* (n. 17) 109–10 [149].
[121] *Dubai/Sharjah* (n. 96) 677.
[122] *Qatar v. Bahrain* (n. 84) 104–9 [219] and 114–15 [247]–[248].

projections.[123] Beyond physical geography, decisions to give no effect to islands at times also refer to factors of human geography, as in *Eritrea/Yemen*[124] and *Qatar v. Bahrain*.[125] Human geography seems to be a criterion for international tribunals to confirm decisions of no effect made on the basis of physical geography. *Bangladesh/Myanmar* also indicates that decisions of no effect could follow from reasoning *a contrario*, namely that giving a certain island full effect would result in an inequitable solution. This suggests that the effect of islands could be determined based on whether awarding full effect would cut off a neighbouring state's coastal projections.

3 Half effect

International tribunals have given islands half effect in four cases. In the *Anglo/French Arbitration*, the Scilly Isles were the British coast's westernmost point, lying in the Atlantic Ocean at 31 nm from Cornwall. The French island of Ushant, France's westernmost point, lay at 14 nm from Brittany. According to the Court of Arbitration, '[t]he effect of the presence of the Scilly Isles west-south-west of Cornwall is to deflect the equidistance line on a considerably more south-westerly course than would be the case if it were to be delimited from the baseline of the English mainland'. Therefore, '[t]he question [was] whether, in the light of all the pertinent geographical circumstances, that fact amounts to an inequitable distortion of the equidistance line ...'.[126] The Court of Arbitration stated that:

> the further projection westwards of the Scilly Isles, when superadded to the greater projection of the Cornish mainland westwards beyond Finistère, is of much the same nature for present purposes, and has much the same tendency to distortion of the equidistance line, as the projection of an exceptionally long promontory, which is generally recognized to be one of the potential forms of 'special circumstance'.[127]

The Court of Arbitration treated the Scillies as a special circumstance under Article 6 CCS and, although neither party explicitly requested it, gave them half effect by bisecting the angle formed by the two lines taking full and no account of the islands.[128] The fact that the Scillies lay

---

[123] *Bangladesh/Myanmar* (n. 3) 86 [318]–[319].
[124] *Eritrea/Yemen* (n. 106) 368 [147].
[125] *Qatar v. Bahrain* (n. 84) 104–9 [219] and 114–15 [247]–[248].
[126] *Anglo/French Arbitration* (n. 73) 113 [243].
[127] Ibid. 114 [244].
[128] Ibid. 117 [251].

11 THE BASIS OF TITLE: GEOGRAPHICAL CIRCUMSTANCES   187

at half Ushant's distance from Brittany may have determined this decision.[129] The Court of Arbitration gave half effect to the Scillies also because they were 'offshore islands situated outside the territorial sea of the mainland'.[130]

The ICJ used the half-effect technique in *Tunisia/Libya* in respect of the Kerkennah Islands, described as formations 'constituting by their size and position a circumstance relevant for the delimitation, and to which the Court must therefore attribute some effect'.[131] The Court identified the general direction of the Tunisian coast as a line drawn between the most westerly point of the Gulf of Gabes and Ras Kaboudia, whose bearing was of approximately 42° to the meridian.[132] If the islands were considered as part of the Tunisian coast, the line drawn from the most westerly point of the Gulf of Gabes seaward of the Kerkennahs would have a bearing of 62° to the meridian. The Court held that 'to cause the delimitation line to veer even as far as to 62°, to run parallel to the island coastline, would ... amount to giving excessive weight to the Kerkennahs'.[133] The ICJ decided that the boundary should follow a line bisecting the angle formed by the two lines at 42° and 62° bearing to the meridian and starting at the most westerly point of the Gulf of Gabes. Although the ICJ commented on the size and population of the Kerkennahs, it seems that, as in the *Anglo/French Arbitration*, the reason for awarding them half effect was their location and their impact on the boundary should they be given full effect.

In *Gulf of Maine*, Seal Island was under Canadian sovereignty and lay off the coast of Nova Scotia. It was 'some two-and-a-half miles long, [rose] to a height of some 50 feet above sea level, and [was] inhabited all the year round'.[134] According to the Chamber of the ICJ, 'as a result of its situation off Cape Sable, only some nine miles inside the closing line of the Gulf, the island occupies a commanding position in the entry to the Gulf'.[135] As a protrusion of Cape Sable into the Gulf of Maine, Seal Island was thus similar to the Scilly Isles in the *Anglo/French Arbitration*. The Chamber held that 'it would be excessive to treat the coastline of Nova

---

[129] Bowett (n. 89) 12.
[130] *Anglo/French Arbitration* (n. 73) 117 [251]. Ushant was deemed to be within France's territorial sea, see ibid. 115 [248].
[131] *Tunisia/Libya* (n. 99) 88–9 [128].
[132] The position of the most westerly point of the Gulf of Gabes was also determined, see ibid. 87 [124].
[133] Ibid. 89 [128].
[134] *Gulf of Maine* (n. 37) 337 [222].
[135] Ibid.

Scotia as transferred south-westwards by the whole of the distance between Seal Island and that coast'.[136] It therefore decided 'to give the island half effect'.[137] Although not stated in the judgment, Seal Island's effect on the median line would have been inequitable owing to its location at the entry of the Gulf of Maine. Giving Seal Island half effect was determined by geography, as in previous cases.

The latest case where half effect was awarded to an island was *Costa Rica v. Nicaragua*. In constructing the provisional equidistance line in the Caribbean Sea, the ICJ decided to give full effect to the Corn Islands, which lay at approximately 26 nm from Nicaragua's coast, by selecting them as base points.[138] However, Costa Rica argued that the position of the Corn Islands well out to sea justified an adjustment of the provisional equidistance line.[139] The Court agreed with Costa Rica, and observed that the Corn Islands 'are situated at about 26 nautical miles from the mainland coast and their impact on the provisional equidistance line is out of proportion to their limited size'.[140] According to the Court, 'given their limited size and significant distance from the mainland coast, it is appropriate to give them only half effect'.[141] Similarly to the *Anglo/French Arbitration* and *Gulf of Maine*, in *Costa Rica v. Nicaragua* the guiding principle for the Court was the location of the Corn Islands with respect to the mainland coast of the state exercising sovereignty over them.

4   Full effect

International tribunals have given full effect to islands in three categories of cases: first, in respect of island states; second, when islands lie far from their mainland, off the coast of another state; and third, when islands were considered part of a mainland coast.

Island states have been consistently given full effect in maritime delimitation. Article 121 UNCLOS provides that all islands in principle generate identical maritime entitlements, without distinction based on an island's status as a state.[142] In *Libya/Malta*, the ICJ held that:

---

[136] Ibid.
[137] Ibid.
[138] *Costa Rica v. Nicaragua* (n. 19) 191 [139]–[140].
[139] Ibid. 195 [151].
[140] Ibid. 196 [153].
[141] Ibid. 196 [154].
[142] L Lucchini and M Vœlckel, *Droit de la Mer* (Pédone 1990) vol. I, 339–42. The ICJ declared Art. 121 UNCLOS to be part of customary international law, see *Qatar v. Bahrain* (n. 84) 97 [185].

Malta being independent, the relationship of its coasts with the coasts of its neighbours is different from what it would be if it were a part of the territory of one of them. ... [I]t might well be that the sea boundaries in this region would be different if the islands of Malta did not constitute an independent State, but formed a part of the territory of one of the surrounding countries.[143]

The Court suggested that the maritime entitlements of island states are more resilient vis-à-vis those of islands under another state's sovereignty, and that island states should be given the fullest extent of maritime jurisdiction. Other cases in which island states were given full effect are *Qatar v. Bahrain*[144] and *Barbados v. Trinidad and Tobago*.[145] From the perspective of their maritime entitlements, island states are assimilated to mainland states.

Islands have also been given full effect when they lie far from their mainland and close to another state's coast.[146] In *St. Pierre et Miquelon*, Canada argued that the French islands should be enclaved within their 12-nm territorial sea. However, the Court of Arbitration found that Canada's solution was inequitable 'car elle nie aux îles tout espace maritime au-delà des espaces qui lui sont déjà reconnus comme mer territoriale'.[147] According to the Court of Arbitration, '[u]ne extension limitée de l'enclave au-delà de la mer territoriale dans ce secteur occidental répondrait dans une certaine mesure à l'attente raisonnable par la France d'un titre au-delà de l'étroite bande de mer territoriale, quand bien même cette extension provoquerait quelque empiétement sur certaines projections canadiennes vers le large'.[148] With respect to the delimitation in the southern sector, since the French islands faced the Atlantic Ocean the tribunal held that 'la France a pleinement droit à une projection frontale en mer ... jusqu'à ce qu'elle atteigne la limite extérieure de 200 milles marins'.[149] The Court of Arbitration found that there existed no reason to limit France's maritime entitlements, and gave full effect to St. Pierre's and Miquelon's entitlements in the

---

[143] *Libya/Malta* (n. 44) 42 [53].
[144] Bahrain's status was discussed in connection with straight baselines, see *Qatar v. Bahrain* (n. 84) 103 [210]–[214].
[145] In *Barbados v. Trinidad and Tobago*, no comment was made on the maritime entitlements of island states.
[146] See R O'Keefe, 'Palm-Fringed Benefits: Island Dependencies in the New Law of the Sea' (1996) 45 *ICLQ* 408, 417–19.
[147] *St. Pierre et Miquelon* (n. 10) 290 [68].
[148] Ibid.
[149] Ibid 290 [70].

southern sector. However, *St. Pierre et Miquelon* is criticisable for using frontal projections, resulting in the creation of a south-facing maritime corridor as wide as the islands' southern relevant coast.[150]

Jan Mayen presented a similar situation. Denmark argued that 'Jan Mayen falls into the category of islands which may be depicted as ... islands lying so far from their parent mainland that they are situated on the "wrong side" of an equidistance line measured between the respective mainlands *in casu* Greenland and Norway'.[151] According to Denmark, comparing the length of Greenland's coast and of Jan Mayen's coast suggested that 'giving full effect to Jan Mayen (i.e., a median line delimitation) would entail an entirely unreasonable and inequitable distortion of the division of the maritime area between Greenland and Jan Mayen'.[152] However, the ICJ held that:

> [t]he coast of Jan Mayen, no less than that of eastern Greenland, generates potential title to the maritime areas recognized by customary law, i.e., in principle up to a limit of 200 miles from its baselines. To attribute to Norway merely the residual area left after giving full effect to the eastern coast of Greenland would run wholly counter to the rights of Jan Mayen and also to the demands of equity.[153]

The Court rejected the argument that, since Jan Mayen was an island distant from Norway's mainland, less than full effect should be given to it. The ICJ adopted the *St. Pierre et Miquelon* approach, with the only difference that the ICJ did not apply frontal projections and upheld that Jan Mayen generated radial coastal projections.

Islands are also given full effect when they are considered to be part of a state's coast. In *Guinea/Guinea-Bissau*, the Bijagos were a cluster of island located between 2 and 37 nm from Guinea-Bissau's coast.[154] Discussing the general configuration of the coast, the Court of Arbitration found that 'il faut intégrer les îles pertinentes, c'est-à-dire les îles côtières et l'archipel des Bijagos'.[155] The Court of Arbitration thus considered the Bijagos to be an integral part of Guinea-Bissau's coast. It did not trace a boundary based on equidistance, therefore one could not strictly speak of effect of islands. However, if the Court of Arbitration had

---

[150] Chapter 3, Section III.B above.
[151] Reply of Denmark (31 January 1991), 109 [299].
[152] Memorial of Denmark (31 July 1989), 97 [301].
[153] *Jan Mayen* (n. 49) 69 [70].
[154] *Guinea/Guinea-Bissau* (n. 101) 184 [95].
[155] Ibid. 185 [98].

II THE BASIS OF TITLE: GEOGRAPHICAL CIRCUMSTANCES   191

opted for an equidistance line, the Bijagos would have been given full effect as part of Guinea-Bissau's coastline.

Similarly, in *Eritrea/Yemen* the tribunal defined the Dhalaks as 'a typical example of a group of islands that forms an integral part of the general coastal configuration'.[156] It followed that 'the baseline of the territorial sea will be found somewhere at the external fringe of the island system'.[157] The arbitral tribunal gave the Dhalaks full effect, since 'the western base points to be employed on this part of the Eritrean coast shall be on the low-water line of certain of the outer Dahlak islets'.[158] The cases show that international tribunals consider islands to be part of a state's coast when they are located within that state' territorial sea either entirely or partially. In the latter case, to be part of the coast islands must form an archipelago seen as a single geographical entity, part of which lies within a state's territorial sea.

The jurisprudence suggests that full effect is given to island states, isolated islands far from the mainland and islands deemed part of a state's coast. In all three situations, the criterion is eminently geographical, as international tribunals examine the position of an island in relation to the state's mainland under whose sovereignty it falls. Decisions in favour of half effect were also based on geographical considerations. In the *Anglo/French Arbitration*,[159] *Tunisia/Libya*[160] and *Gulf of Maine*[161] it was held that a decision of full effect would have distorted the boundary by curtailing the maritime entitlements of one of the states concerned.

Additionally to the geographical criterion, international tribunals have examined human geography in their decision to give full effect to islands. An important human geography aspect is political status of territory. In *St. Pierre et Miquelon*, Canada contended that 'le statut de dépendance politique des îles françaises par rapport à la France métropolitaine est un facteur justifiant des droits maritimes moins étendus que si ces îles constituaient un Etat insulaire indépendant'.[162] However, the Court of Arbitration found that:

---

[156] *Eritrea/Yemen* (n. 106) 367 [139].
[157] Ibid.
[158] Ibid. 368 [146]. ITLOS made comparable considerations in *Bangladesh/Myanmar*, yet in that case St. Martin's Island was considered in the context of territorial sea delimitation and was thus not a relevant circumstance. See *Bangladesh/Myanmar* (n. 3) 47 [149]–[152].
[159] *Anglo/French Arbitration* (n. 73) 114 [244].
[160] *Tunisia/Libya* (n. 99) 89 [128].
[161] *Gulf of Maine* (n. 37) 337 [222].
[162] *St. Pierre et Miquelon* (n. 10) 285 [48].

rien ne permet de soutenir que l'étendue des droits maritimes d'une île dépend de son statut politique. Aucune distinction n'est faite à cet égard par l'article 121, paragraphe 2, de la convention de 1982 sur le droit de la mer ni par les dispositions correspondantes des conventions de 1958 sur la mer territoriale et la zone contiguë et sur le plateau continental.[163]

St. Pierre et Miquelon seemed to make a decision different from the one in the *Anglo/French Arbitration*, in which the Channel Islands were enclaved.[164] However, the two cases state the same legal principle in different ways. They both upheld that all islands are entitled to full maritime jurisdiction under international law. What differs between the two cases is the solution. While in *St. Pierre et Miquelon* the islands were given full effect because they lay far from France's mainland, in the *Anglo/French Arbitration* the Channel Islands were enclaved based on their vicinity to the coast of both parties. This is confirmed by the statement in *St. Pierre et Miquelon* that what cannot depend on an island's political status is 'l'étendue des droits maritimes'.

Both *St. Pierre et Miquelon* and the *Anglo/French Arbitration* were decided on their facts by applying the same legal principles. While political status does not affect the entitlement of islands to their maritime zones, it could affect the effect of islands in a given case.[165] Moreover, international tribunals evaluate political status in connection with the islands' geographical location. On one hand, if the islands were situated far from one of the parties' mainland, they would be given full effect. On the other hand, if the islands lay near the mainland of the parties, they would not be given full effect. However, political status, similarly to economic importance and population, only confirms decisions of full effect already reached on geographical grounds. This approach appears consistent with the basis of title over maritime zones. While the decision on an island's effect is taken on geographical bases, nothing prevents an international tribunal from strengthening its decision by reference to other reasons. Considering human geography in full-effect decisions mirrors its consideration in no-effect decisions.

---

[163] Ibid. 285 [49].
[164] Section II.C.1 above.
[165] According to Murphy, 'the political status of the island as part of its State is not regarded as significant'. See SD Murphy, 'International Law relating to Islands' (2016) 386 *Recueil des Cours* 9, 175.

D The Location and Direction of the Land Boundary Terminus

International tribunals have found the location of the land boundary terminus to be a relevant circumstance. Since the position of the land boundary terminus determines the length of the relevant coast, and thus influences the maritime areas generated by such a coast, it can be seen to be connected to the basis of title. Although this factor pertains to delimitation between both adjacent and opposite coasts, it has so far been found to be a relevant circumstance only in the former scenario. In *Tunisia/Libya*, Libya contended that, by virtue of the 1910 treaty between the Bey of Tunis and the Ottoman Emperor, its boundary with Tunisia should continue 'in the northward direction of the land frontier'.[166] The Court rejected this argument, and held that:

> [b]oth Parties have agreed in recognizing the relevance of the land boundary starting point; this only reinforces the significance of Ras Ajdir as a basic point of reference. In this sense the Court believes that the 1910 Convention constitutes a relevant circumstance for the delimitation of the continental shelf between the two Parties.[167]

The ICJ found the 1910 treaty identifying the location of the land boundary terminus to be a relevant circumstance. The Court also held that 'the concept of prolongation of the general direction of the land boundary [is] ... [a] relevant criteri[on] to be taken into account in selecting a line of delimitation calculated to ensure an equitable solution'.[168] The Court deemed that both the land boundary terminus and the land boundary's direction were relevant circumstances in choosing the delimitation method.[169] The Court subsequently drew a boundary at a bearing of 26° to the meridian, which was the land boundary's approximate direction. The Court of Arbitration in *Guinea/Guinea-Bissau* cited *Tunisia/Libya* with approval, finding that the maritime boundary would start from the land boundary terminus identified as 'un point du thalweg du Cajet situé à l'embouchure de cette rivière, entre les îles Cataque et Tristâo'.[170]

In *Gulf of Maine*, both parties referred to the direction of their land boundary. The United States contended that Nova Scotia's protrusion south of the land boundary 'is aberrant to the general geographical

---
[166] *Tunisia/Libya* (n. 99) 66 [85].
[167] Ibid.
[168] Ibid. 85 [120].
[169] See *contra* Evans (n. 72) 161.
[170] *Guinea/Guinea-Bissau* (n. 101) 187–8 [106].

relationship between the Parties',[171] and that the equidistance line pleaded by Canada 'ignores the location of the international land boundary between the Parties'.[172] According to the United States, '[t]he principal international boundary extends from the Pacific Ocean to the Atlantic Ocean in a generally west-to-east direction'.[173] Canada conceded that the Canada–United States land boundary runs due east from Strait Juan de Fuca to the Lake of the Woods. However, it stated that from the Lake of the Woods 'the 6,416-kilometre boundary does not run in an east-west direction',[174] but 'it takes on a southerly orientation as it passes through Lake Superior, Lake Huron, Lake St. Clair and into Lake Erie ...'.[175] If a segment of the land boundary were relevant to maritime delimitation, it should be the southerly boundary between Maine and New Brunswick.[176] The Chamber did not comment on these arguments, and did not consider the land boundary's direction to be a relevant circumstance.

The land boundary's direction declined in importance with the development of a standard delimitation method. Subjectivity in identifying the land boundary's direction might have contributed to this decline. Yet, the location of the land boundary terminus remained a factor capable of requiring the adjustment of an equidistance line. In *Guyana* v. *Suriname* and in *Nicaragua* v. *Honduras*, the land boundary terminus was discussed by the parties, but was not declared to be a relevant circumstance. In *Guyana* v. *Suriname*, the arbitral tribunal found that the land boundary terminus had been fixed by the parties' agreement.[177] In *Nicaragua* v. *Honduras*, the ICJ found that the boundary should start 3 nm out to sea for reasons relating to coastal instability.[178] The starting point of the maritime boundary was also considered in *Peru* v. *Chile*. However, in that case the issue was not the identification of the land boundary terminus, which had been fixed in the 1929 Treaty of Lima, but 'to ascertain whether the Parties have agreed to any starting-point of their maritime boundary'.[179] The Special Chamber in *Ghana/Côte d'Ivoire* had

---

[171] Counter-memorial of the United States (28 June 1983), 126–7 [301]–[302].
[172] Ibid.
[173] Memorial of the United States (27 September 1982), 9 [20].
[174] Memorial of Canada (27 September 1982), 53 [81].
[175] Ibid.
[176] Ibid. 55 [86].
[177] *Maritime Boundary Arbitration (Guyana* v. *Suriname)* (2007) XXX RIAA 1, 86 [307].
[178] *Territorial and Maritime Dispute between Nicaragua and Honduras in the Caribbean Sea (Nicaragua* v. *Honduras)* (Judgment) [2007] ICJ Rep 659, 755–6 [306]–[311].
[179] *Maritime Dispute (Peru* v. *Chile)* (Judgment) [2014] ICJ Rep 3, 62 [163]. Only in *Bangladesh* v. *India* did the location of the land boundary terminus determine the

to settle the same issue which the ICJ had settled in *Peru v. Chile*, which, however, did not entail considering the location of the land boundary terminus as a relevant circumstance.[180] In *Costa Rica v. Nicaragua*, two main issues concerned the starting point of the land boundary and the starting point of the maritime boundary. However, neither was treated as a relevant circumstance in delimiting the EEZ and the continental shelf.

The cases indicate that the location of the land boundary terminus could be a relevant circumstance. While in *Tunisia/Libya* this factor was useful in choosing a delimitation method, its role changed with the evolution of a standard delimitation methodology. In the three-stage approach, the land boundary terminus is in principle a factor capable of justifying the adjustment of an equidistance line, although it has so far never had such an impact.

III The Functions of Maritime Zones: Non-Geographical Circumstances

Judicial decisions suggest that the legal basis for the relevance of non-geographical circumstances is the function of maritime zones under international law. The continental shelf and the EEZ were both created for exploring and exploiting natural resources,[181] and could also both be said to relate to navigation and security.[182] This section analyses the international tribunals' approach to non-geographical relevant circumstances. As with geographical relevant circumstances, international tribunals have achieved a good degree of consistency in assessing circumstances linked to the functions of maritime zones.

A Access to Natural Resources

The continental shelf and the EEZ concern the exploration and exploitation of natural resources. It is imprecise to say that 'economic factors' are relevant circumstances, as in delimitation international tribunals take into account 'access to natural resources'. In the relevant cases, the issue

---

adjustment of an equidistance line, but only in relation to territorial sea delimitation. See *Bangladesh v. India* (n. 33) 89 [273]–[274].
[180] *Ghana/Côte d'Ivoire* (n. 18) [344]–[357].
[181] Arts. 56 and 77 UNCLOS.
[182] Sections III.B and III.C below.

was neither the existence nor the extent of economically exploitable resources in the area to be delimited, but access to such resources.

1 The approach of states

Neighbouring states request international tribunals to establish their maritime boundaries because natural resources exist, or are thought to exist, in maritime areas over which they both assert sovereign rights under international law. It is not uncommon for judicial decisions to describe that both parties have granted concessions for the exploration and exploitation of petroleum resources in the area to be delimited.[183]

While in their pleadings before international tribunals states generally refrain from stating that the motivation behind maritime boundary litigation may relate to natural resources, they appear to be more forthcoming in other quarters. For example, in a 2014 letter to the United Nations Secretary-General concerning the pending maritime dispute with Kenya, Somalia protested:

> the continuing activities of oil companies under license to Kenya in maritime zones claimed by the Somali Republic, and in disputes between the two States, which are in contravention of Article 74(3), Article 83(3) and Article 300 of UNCLOS. The Somali Republic condemns these activities and urges all parties involved in such activities to immediately cease and desist from them.[184]

Similarly, speaking at the Sixth Committee of the United Nations General Assembly, Myanmar stated that UNCLOS:

> established the underlying principle and mechanism for maritime boundary delimitation, but it did not suggest that oil and gas deposits should be regulated as a shared natural resource. While State practice in that area varied, no one could deny that the State had the sovereign right to explore and exploit the natural resources, including oil and gas, that were located within its land and maritime territory.[185]

States have also demonstrated their interest in securing access to natural resources by concluding treaties which, instead of delimiting a maritime boundary, establish rules for the joint development of marine

---

[183] *Cameroon v. Nigeria* (n. 15) 437–9 [282]–[283]; *Ghana/Côte d'Ivoire* (n. 18) [146]–[150] and [163].

[184] Letter dated 4 February 2014 from the Minister of Foreign Affairs and International Cooperation addressed to the Secretary-General, (2017) 84 *LoSB* 105 [10].

[185] UN Doc A/C.6/64/SR.21 (22 December 2009) 2 [4].

resources.[186] Treaties establishing such zones are likely to contain detailed rules on the rights and obligations of the states party, such as in the case of the 2002 Timor Sea treaty[187] and the 2005 Norway–UK Framework Agreement.[188]

Presumably owing to the states' interest in maritime resources, the International Law Commission (ILC) had already considered resource-related factors with respect to continental shelf delimitation. The commentary to the 1956 ILC Draft Articles stated that exercising jurisdiction over coastal fisheries for the purposes of stock conservation and coastal population subsistence 'may reflect problems and interests which deserve recognition in international law'.[189] The ILC's remarks that resource-related factors could be considered in continental shelf delimitation could stem from the acknowledgement that such factors are linked to the function of the continental shelf under international law.[190] However, neither the 1958 CCS, nor the 1982 UNCLOS, explicitly refer to natural resources in relation to the delimitation of the EEZ and of the continental shelf. Neither states nor the ILC have expressed views concerning the manner in which access to natural resources may affect the judicial delimitation of maritime boundaries. International tribunals thus formulated a standard of their own.

2 The approach of international tribunals

Although fishing activity was a central issue in the 1909 *Grisbådarna* arbitral award, that decision only concerned the delimitation of the territorial sea. The first case in which access to natural resources was argued to be a factor relevant in delimiting the maritime zones beyond 12 nm was *Gulf of Maine*. In that case, Georges Bank was 'the real subject

---

[186] V Becker-Weinberg, *Joint Development of Hydrocarbon Deposits in the Law of the Sea* (Springer, 2014). For a list of treaties establishing joint development zones, see Appendix 2.

[187] Timor Sea Treaty between the Government of East Timor and the Government of Australia, 2258 UNTS 3.

[188] Framework Agreement between the United Kingdom of Great Britain and Northern Ireland and the Kingdom of Norway concerning Cross-boundary Petroleum Co-operation, 2491 UNTS 3.

[189] Draft Articles on the Law of the Sea with Commentaries, *ILC Yearbook (1956)*, vol. II, 293.

[190] See P Weil, *Perspectives du Droit de la Délimitation Maritime* (Pédone, 1988) 274; C Hurst, 'The Continental Shelf' (1949) 34 *Transactions of the Grotius Society* 153, 158; 'Text of the Proposals of the Committee on Rights to the Sea-bed and its Subsoil' in International Law Association, *Report of the Forty-fourth Conference* (Cambrian News, 1952) 133, 135.

of the dispute ... from the viewpoint of the potential resources of the subsoil and also, in particular, that of fisheries that are of major economic importance'.[191] According to the Chamber:

> [i]t might well appear that other circumstances ought properly to be taken into consideration in assessing the equitable character of the result produced by [the third] portion of the delimitation line, which is destined to divide the riches of the waters and shelf of [Georges] Bank between the two neighbouring countries. These other circumstances may be summed up by what the Parties have presented as the data provided by human and economic geography, and they are thus circumstances which, though in the Chamber's opinion ineligible for consideration as criteria to be applied in the delimitation process itself, may ... be relevant to assessment of the equitable character of a delimitation first established on the basis of criteria borrowed from physical and political geography.[192]

The Chamber did not see resource-related factors as criteria indicating the appropriate delimitation method, but found them to indicate whether the boundary was 'radically inequitable, that is to say, ... likely to entail catastrophic repercussions for the livelihood and economic well-being of the population of the countries concerned'.[193] The Chamber tested the boundary's overall equitableness against resource-related factors, in a manner similar to the role of disproportionality in the three-stage approach.[194] However, the Chamber lacked a clear legal basis for ascribing this function to resource-related factors.

Nevertheless, *Guinea/Guinea-Bissau* and *St. Pierre et Miquelon* upheld the decision in *Gulf of Maine*. In *Guinea/Guinea-Bissau*, the Court of Arbitration did not mention *Gulf of Maine* explicitly, while referring to economic factors in the last section of the award. First, it established the course of the boundary;[195] second, it examined proportionality;[196] third, it analysed resource-related factors.[197] The boundary's equitableness was assessed against two elements, proportionality and resource-related factors. However, the Court of Arbitration held that proportionality 'doit intervenir dans l'évaluation des facteurs qui entrent en ligne de compte pour arriver à un résultat équitable'.[198] Proportionality was thus not an

---

[191] *Gulf of Maine* (n. 37) 340 [232].
[192] Ibid.
[193] Ibid. 342 [237]. See also McDorman (n. 42) 101.
[194] Chapter 6 below.
[195] *Guinea/Guinea-Bissau* (n. 101) 190 [111].
[196] Ibid. 192–3 [118]–[120].
[197] Ibid. 193–4 [121]–[122].
[198] Ibid. 192 [118].

overall test of equitableness, but a relevant circumstance indicating the appropriate delimitation method. The award is not entirely clear, as the part on proportionality followed the description of the boundary. *Guinea/Guinea-Bissau* is nonetheless consistent with *Gulf of Maine* in treating proportionality as a relevant circumstance and resource-related factors as part of an overall test of equitableness.

St. Pierre et Miquelon is comparable to *Guinea/Guinea-Bissau*, as the Court of Arbitration described the course of the boundary before analysing resource-related factors.[199] However, differently from *Guinea/Guinea-Bissau* in *St. Pierre et Miquelon* the Court of Arbitration cited the 'catastrophic repercussions test' explicitly.[200] With respect to fisheries, it found that '[d]ans la présente affaire, les faits soumis au Tribunal indiquent que la démarcation envisagée n'aura pas d'incidence radicale sur la composition actuelle de la pêche dans la région'.[201] Concerning mineral resources, the Court of Arbitration held that it 'n'a aucune raison de considérer que les éventuelles ressources minérales ont une incidence sur la délimitation'.[202] Resource-related considerations were thus used to verify the boundary's equitableness. Moreover, differently from *Guinea/Guinea-Bissau* the Court of Arbitration in *St. Pierre et Miquelon* verified the boundary's equitableness also based on proportionality.[203] *St. Pierre et Miquelon* appears to mark the transition between the *Gulf of Maine* jurisprudence, under which resource-related factors were an test of overall equitableness, to the later jurisprudence, under which resource-related factors were a relevant circumstance justifying the adjustment of an equidistance line.

Since in *Jan Mayen* the ICJ established an equidistance line as the starting point of delimitation, the Court's understanding of the 'catastrophic repercussions test' changed. Concerning access to fisheries, the *Barbados v. Trinidad and Tobago* tribunal stated that 'tribunals have not altogether excluded the role of this factor but, as in *Gulf of Maine*, have restricted its application to circumstances in which catastrophic results might follow from the adoption of a particular delimitation line'.[204] The 'catastrophic repercussions test' was used to assess whether resource-related factors justified adjusting an equidistance line, and not as an

---

[199] *St. Pierre et Miquelon* (n. 10) 289–91 [66]–[74].
[200] Ibid. 294 [84].
[201] Ibid. 294 [85].
[202] Ibid. 296 [89].
[203] Ibid. 296–7 [92]–[93].
[204] *Barbados v. Trinidad and Tobago* (n. 16) 214 [241].

equitableness test. The finding that 'Barbados has not succeeded in demonstrating that the results of past or continuing lack of access by Barbados fisherfolk to the waters in issue will be catastrophic' appeared in a part of the award that began by stating that '[a] provisionally drawn equidistance line is ... subject to adjustment to take account of relevant circumstances'.[205] The tribunal took stock of the link between inequitableness and the 'catastrophic repercussions test': only if the boundary caused catastrophic repercussions would it render an equidistance line inequitable, justifying the treatment of resource-related factors as relevant circumstances. This understanding of the 'catastrophic repercussion test' was upheld in the most recent cases.[206]

Jan Mayen is the only post-1969 case in which resource-related factors directly impacted the course of a boundary. The ICJ quoted the 'catastrophic repercussions test', and specified that the issue in *Jan Mayen* was 'whether any shifting or adjustment of the median line, as [FZ] boundary, would be required to ensure equitable access to the capelin fishery resources for the vulnerable fishing communities concerned'.[207] The Court concluded that 'the median line is too far to the west for Denmark to be assured of an equitable access to the capelin stock'.[208] While in *Gulf of Maine* the Chamber established a single boundary, in *Jan Mayen* the Court drew two separate boundaries. The FZ's function is to extend a coastal state's jurisdiction over marine living resources. By virtue of the functional relationship with the FZ, the Court found that access to fisheries was a relevant circumstance with respect to FZ delimitation. By contrast, the continental shelf boundary was adjusted on account of coastal length disparity.[209] *Jan Mayen* shows that resource-related factors could justify adjusting an equidistance line.

In *Jan Mayen*, the Court referred to the 'catastrophic repercussions test' with approval, while developing its role with respect to the earlier jurisprudence. *Jan Mayen* transformed the 'catastrophic repercussions test' from an equitableness test to the test indicating whether access to natural resources warrants adjusting an equidistance line. The impact of resource-related factors is still assessed by reference to the 'catastrophic repercussions test'. What changed over time is not the test itself, but its

---

[205] Ibid. 221-2 [265] and [267].
[206] *Black Sea* (n. 17) 125-6 [198]-[199]; *Nicaragua v. Colombia* (n. 26) 706 [223]; *Bangladesh v. India* (n. 33) 138-9 [422]-[424]; *Ghana/Côte d'Ivoire* (n. 18) [452]-[453].
[207] *Jan Mayen* (n. 49) 71-2 [75].
[208] Ibid. 72 [76].
[209] Ibid.

function in delimitation. Although states have shown, directly and indirectly, that resource-related factors may be the reasons for litigating maritime disputes, international tribunals have adopted a restrictive approach to the impact that such factors could have on the adjustment of a provisional equidistance line as relevant circumstances. On this basis, the international tribunals' approach could be criticised as indifferent to the real concerns of states, yet not for having been consistent in upholding their restrictive approach to resource-related factors. Presumably, the adoption of that approach may have also been determined by the difficulty to formulate a possibly objective standard on the basis of which provisional equidistance lines could be adjusted in order to ensure access to natural resources. One could thus understand the reasons for adopting a standard which, being restrictive, shields international tribunals from having to make potentially difficult decisions on the adjustment of provisional equidistance lines. Furthermore, decisions to adjust equidistance lines in order to ensure access to natural resources may conceivably entail wide-ranging consequences on the economies of the states concerned.

B Navigation

Early in the ILC's debates on the territorial sea, Special Rapporteur François suggested that 'cases were not infrequent where the line of delimitation had to be drawn through the estuary of a river whose navigable channel did not follow the median line, and the line of delimitation would therefore present serious inconveniences; the Commission might consider that it was necessary to provide for cases of that kind'.[210] Mr Zourek, who was also arguing that the equidistance line was not always an adequate rule for territorial sea delimitation, stated that '[t]he most that could be done was to ... say that the principle of equidistance applied to cases where the requirements of shipping ... did not call for the application of another method'.[211] With respect to the continental shelf, the 1951 ILC Report to the United Nations General Assembly affirmed that '[n]avigation and fishing must be considered as primary interests, so that ... [f]or example, in narrow channels essential for navigation, the claims of navigation should have priority over those of exploitation'.[212] Similarly, the 1953 ILC Draft Articles stated that,

---

[210] *ILC Yearbook (1952)*, vol. I, 180 [3].
[211] *ILC Yearbook (1954)*, vol. I, 103 [16].
[212] *ILC Yearbook (1951)*, vol. II, 142.

although equidistance was the rule for continental shelf delimitation, 'provision must be made for departures necessitated by ... the presence of ... navigable channels'.[213] These remarks indicate that navigational factors were conceived by the ILC as a potential special circumstance in both territorial sea and continental shelf delimitation.[214]

International tribunals have explicitly recognised navigation as a relevant circumstance only in territorial sea delimitation.[215] In *North Sea Continental Shelf*, the ICJ did not mention navigation as a relevant circumstance. Only Judge Padilla Nervo wrote, in his separate opinion, that navigable channels could be a special circumstance under Article 6 CCS.[216] Similarly, while Libya argued for the relevance of navigation in continental shelf delimitation,[217] the ICJ's judgment in *Libya/Malta* did not comment on it. Conversely, in *Beagle Channel* and *Guyana v. Suriname* navigation was discussed in relation to territorial sea delimitation. In *Beagle Channel*, the Court of Arbitration delimited the territorial sea between Argentina and Chile guided 'by mixed factors of appurtenance, coastal configuration, equidistance, and also of convenience, navigability, and the desirability of enabling each Party so far as possible to navigate in its own waters'.[218] In its brief reasoning on maritime delimitation, Annex IV to the *Beagle Channel* award confirmed that the boundary 'is in principle a median line, adjusted in certain relatively unimportant respects for reasons of local configuration or of better navigability for the Parties'.[219]

In *Guyana v. Suriname*, navigational arguments were made in connection with territorial sea delimitation up to 3 nm. Guyana contended that the *Beagle Channel* award meant that 'any deviation from the median

---

[213] *ILC Yearbook (1953)*, vol. II, 216 [82]. See also Draft Articles on the Law of the Sea with Commentaries (n. 189) 300. Special Rapporteur François believed that 'many of the special considerations which were involved in delimiting the territorial sea, particularly questions of navigation and fishing interests, were irrelevant in delimiting the continental shelf'. See *ILC Yearbook (1953)*, vol. I, 129 [55].
[214] MW Mouton, 'The Continental Shelf' (1954) 85 *Recueil des Cours* 343, 420.
[215] ED Brown, 'The *Anglo-French Continental Shelf Case*' (1979) 16 *San Diego Law Review* 461, 493.
[216] *North Sea Continental Shelf* (n. 1) 93 (Separate Opinion Padilla Nervo).
[217] Memorial of Libya (26 April 1983), 154–5 [9.10]; Counter-memorial of Libya (26 October 1983), 55–6 [2.80] and 144 [6.08].
[218] *Beagle Channel (Argentina/Chile)* (1977) XXI RIAA 53, 146 [110].
[219] Ibid. 216 [4]. See also M Shaw, 'The Beagle Channel Arbitration Award' (1978) 6 *International Relations* 415, 431; J Barboza, 'The Beagle Channel Dispute: Reflections of the Agent of Argentina' (2014) 13 *Chinese JIL* 147, 167.

line based on navigational concerns need be minor'.[220] The tribunal rejected such an argument, finding that 'special circumstances of navigation may justify deviation from the median line'.[221] However, it later held that the parties had agreed on the boundary up to 3 nm.[222] Although an agreed boundary existed in *Guyana v. Suriname*, the tribunal confirmed that navigation could be a special circumstance in territorial sea delimitation. State practice confirms the international tribunals' view, as the only treaty clearly establishing a boundary on navigational grounds only delimited the territorial sea.[223]

The impact of navigation on delimitation within 12 nm is consistent with the territorial sea's function. Although the territorial sea is under a coastal state's sovereignty, the exercise of that sovereignty is qualified by the third states' right that their vessels enjoy innocent passage. Under Article 17 UNCLOS, 'ships of all States ... enjoy the right of innocent passage through the territorial sea'.[224] Based on the customary right of innocent passage, Colombos argued that, in the territorial sea, a state possesses 'a right of jurisdiction or qualified sovereignty'.[225] Sovereignty in the territorial sea 'may not be so extended as to allow exclusive rights of use as in the case of ownership since the application of absolute proprietary rights over the territorial sea might inevitably lead to unacceptable consequences'.[226] Rothwell and Stephens adopted this view, while admitting that sovereignty over the territorial sea remains 'relatively unfettered with respect to core areas of state interest'.[227] Evans correctly wrote that '[c]onceptually speaking, navigation has little to do with the continental shelf'.[228] Moreover, a state has no sovereignty over the EEZ, in which

---

[220] *Guyana v. Suriname* (n. 177) 85 [305].
[221] Ibid.
[222] M Lando, 'Judicial Uncertainties concerning Territorial Sea Delimitation under Article 15 of the United Nations Convention on the Law of the Sea' (2017) 66 ICLQ 589, 594.
[223] Protocol Note between the Federal Republic of Germany and the German Democratic Republic concerning the Boundary in Lübeck Bay, *Limits in the Seas No. 74*.
[224] Under Art. 19 UNCLOS, passage is innocent 'so long as it is not prejudicial to the peace, good order or security of the coastal State'. This rule is said to be part of customary international law, see V Lowe, 'Uniform Interpretation of the Rules of International Law Governing Innocent Passage' (1991) 6 IJECL 73.
[225] J Colombos, *The International Law of the Sea* 6th edn (Longman, 1967) 91.
[226] Ibid.
[227] DR Rothwell and T Stephens, *The International Law of the Sea* 2nd edn (Hart, 2016) 75. See also R-J Dupuy, 'La Mer sous Compétence Nationale' in R-J Dupuy and D Vignes (eds.), *Traité du Nouveau Droit de la Mer* (Bruylant, 1985) 219, 228–31.
[228] Evans (n. 72) 179.

foreign ships enjoy freedom of navigation.[229] In the EEZ, coastal states have no duty to ensure that foreign ships enjoy innocent passage. The EEZ is a functional maritime zone whose *raison d'être* is to allow a coastal state to explore and exploit the natural resources of the water column, the seabed and the subsoil. EEZ rights under UNCLOS have no express connection with navigation.

The only continental shelf delimitation case in which navigation was invoked as a special circumstance was the *Anglo/French Arbitration*.[230] Both parties mentioned navigation as a special circumstance under Article 6 CCS. While France pleaded to retain a continuous link between the eastern and western parts of the English Channel, the UK sought to maintain a direct link between the maritime areas generated by its mainland and by the Channel Islands. The Court of Arbitration held that 'the weight of such considerations in this region is ... somewhat diminished by the very particular character of the English Channel as a major route of international maritime navigation serving ports outside the territories of either of the Parties'.[231] It added that '[t]hey may support and strengthen, but they cannot negative, any conclusions that are already indicated by the geographical, political and legal circumstances of the region'.[232]

It is in principle correct to say that navigation could impact on continental shelf delimitation. However, it is unclear how the 'very particular character of the English Channel as a major route of international maritime navigation' could affect the character of navigation as a special circumstance. There seems to be hardly any connection between navigation as a special circumstance and the fact that foreign vessels sail through the English Channel. Navigation by foreign vessels could not determine navigation's character as a relevant circumstance in continental shelf delimitation, as this would open the door to claims unrelated to the parties' navigational rights. In principle, the navigational rights of third states should not have any impact on delimitation. Navigation was not a relevant factor in later continental shelf delimitations, as Evans acknowledged.[233]

---

[229] Arts. 56, 58 and 87 UNCLOS.
[230] Access to the port of Abidjan was discussed in *Ghana/Côte d'Ivoire*, but the Special Chamber treated it in the context of cut-off, and not as a relevant circumstance in its own right. See *Ghana/Côte d'Ivoire* (n. 18) [426].
[231] *Anglo/French Arbitration* (n. 73) 90 [188].
[232] Ibid.
[233] Evans (n. 72) 183.

Although the *Anglo/French Arbitration*'s reasoning is not entirely convincing, navigation could affect continental shelf and EEZ delimitation.[234] Numerous UNCLOS provisions seem to suggest the relevance of navigation. With respect to the EEZ, Article 58(1) UNCLOS provides that 'all States ... enjoy, subject to the relevant provisions of this Convention, the freedoms referred to in article 87 of navigation and overflight'. Article 60(4) UNCLOS states that, in relation to artificial islands, installations and structures, '[t]he coastal State may, where necessary, establish reasonable safety zones around such artificial islands, installations and structures in which it may take appropriate measures to ensure the safety ... of navigation ...'. Moreover, under Article 60(7) '[a]rtificial islands, installations and structures and the safety zones around them may not be established where interference may be caused to the use of recognized sea lanes essential to international navigation'.

Concerning the continental shelf, Article 78(2) UNCLOS states that '[t]he exercise of the rights of the coastal State over the continental shelf must not infringe or result in any unjustifiable interference with navigation and other rights and freedoms of other States as provided for in this Convention'. Article 60 UNCLOS on artificial islands, installations and structures applies *mutatis mutandis* to the continental shelf pursuant to Article 80 UNCLOS. Moreover, hot pursuit, which 'may be undertaken when the competent authorities of the coastal State have good reason to believe that the ship has violated the laws and regulations of that State', applies both to the continental shelf and to the EEZ by virtue of Article 111(2) UNCLOS.[235] These provisions suggest that, in the continental shelf and EEZ, coastal states have rights and duties concerning navigation. Accordingly, navigation could in principle affect the delimitation of such maritime zones.

C Security

Van Bynkershoek famously wrote that 'imperium terrae finit ubi finit armorum potestas', from which it followed that the territorial sea extends

---

[234] D Attard, *The Exclusive Economic Zone in International Law* (OUP, 1987) 269.
[235] For example, *M/V Saiga (No. 2)* was a case in which the right of hot pursuit had been allegedly lawfully exercised in the EEZ. However, ITLOS found that his was not the case, since 'no laws or regulations of Guinea applicable in accordance with the Convention were violated by the *Saiga*'. See *M/V Saiga (No. 2) (Saint Vincent and the Grenadines v. Guinea)* (Judgment) [1999] ITLOS Rep 10, 57–61 [139]–[152].

only as far as the state can display its military power.[236] Colombos stated that the territorial sea 'is justified by the necessity of defence and security of the littoral state',[237] and that a state's 'right of jurisdiction must not go beyond what is necessary for their protection and security'.[238] More recent literature corroborates such a view.[239] Concerning the continental shelf, the 1945 Truman Proclamation stated that 'self-protection compels the coastal nation to keep close watch over activities off its shores which are of the nature necessary for utilization of these resources'.[240] Apart from setting out the legal framework for exploring and exploiting natural resources, the foundational document of the continental shelf doctrine re-affirmed the coastal states' need to exercise maritime jurisdiction for security purposes. In this perspective, the continental shelf is similar to the territorial sea.

Although the ICJ has accepted the existence of a link between the continental shelf doctrine and the states' security interests,[241] the primary function of the continental shelf under UNCLOS is 'exploring it and exploiting its natural resources'.[242] The EEZ is no exception. Kenya's 1972 Draft Articles on the EEZ provided that '[a]ll States have a right to determine the limits of their jurisdiction over the seas adjacent to their coasts beyond a territorial sea of 12 miles in accordance with the criteria which take into account their own geographical, geological, biological, ecological, economic and national security factors'.[243] The *raison d'être* of the EEZ is economic, since in the EEZ coastal states have 'sovereign rights for the purpose of exploring and exploiting, conserving and managing the natural resources, whether living or non-living, of the waters superjacent to the seabed and of the seabed and its subsoil'.[244] Nevertheless, these reasons do not justify the outright rejection of the link between

---

[236] C Van Bynkershoek, *Quaestionum Juris Publici Libri Duo* (Clarendon, 1930) vol I, 59. Similarly, see H Grotius, *De Jure Belli ac Pacis* (W Whewell ed., CUP, 1853) vol. I, 267.
[237] J Colombos, 'Territorial Waters' (1924) 9 *Transactions of the Grotius Society* 89, 90–91.
[238] Ibid.
[239] P Weil, 'Des Espaces Maritimes aux Territoires Maritimes: Vers un Conception Territorialiste de la Délimitation Maritime' in *Le Droit International au Service de la Paix, de la Justice et du Développement – Mélanges Michel Virally* (Pédone, 1991) 501, 505; Rothwell and Stephens (n. 227) 76; V Lowe, *International Law* (OUP, 2007) 152.
[240] United States, Proclamation by the President with Respect to the Natural Resources of the Subsoil and Sea Bed of the Continental Shelf (1946) 40 *AJIL Supplement* 45.
[241] *Libya/Malta* (n. 44) 42 [51]; *Jan Mayen* (n. 49) 74–5 [81].
[242] Art. 77(1) UNCLOS.
[243] *Report of the Committee on the Peaceful Uses of the Sea-bed and the Ocean Floor Beyond the Limits of National Jurisdiction*, UN Doc A/8721 (SUPP) (1 January 1972) 180.
[244] Art. 56(1)(a) UNCLOS.

security on one hand, and the continental shelf and the EEZ on the other hand.

Security interests are connected to the continental shelf and the EEZ. First, Kenya's 1972 Draft Articles cited above specifically mentioned that the EEZ's outer limits would be established also based on 'national security factors'.[245] Second, states recurrently invoked security arguments in delimitation cases. In *North Sea Continental Shelf*, the ICJ did not mention security as a relevant circumstance in continental shelf delimitation. However, in the *Anglo/French Arbitration*, France contended that not enclaving the Channel Islands 'would involve severing the continental shelf of France in the Channel into two separate zones',[246] and, '[i]n consequence, ... the vital interests of the French Republic in the security and defence of its territory could not fail to be put in doubt'.[247] The UK replied that 'security, defence and navigational considerations ... may equally be urged in favour of a continuous continental shelf between its mainland and the Channel Islands for the defence of which the [UK] is responsible'.[248]

Similarly to navigation, the Court of Arbitration held that security did not exercise 'a decisive influence on the delimitation of the boundary',[249] as it 'may support and strengthen, but ... cannot negative, any conclusions that are already indicated by the geographical, political and legal circumstances of the region'.[250] The Court of Arbitration suggested that security could be a special circumstance in continental shelf delimitation, and that, short of determining the course of a boundary, it could only support a decision made on other grounds. This is confirmed by the Court of Arbitration's decision to enclave the Channel Islands owing to 'the predominant interest of the French Republic in the southern areas of the English Channel'.[251] According to the Court of Arbitration, security did not influence the course of the boundary due to the 'very particular character of the English Channel as a major route of international maritime navigation'.[252] Although this statement is unclear,[253] it suggests that the *Anglo/French Arbitration* was decided on its facts, and thus does

---

[245] *Report of the Committee* (n. 243) 180.
[246] *Anglo/French Arbitration* (n. 73) 80 [161].
[247] Ibid.
[248] Ibid. 85 [175].
[249] Ibid. 90 [188].
[250] Ibid.
[251] Ibid.
[252] Ibid.
[253] Section III.B above.

not state a principle of general application. However, it accepted that security might be a relevant circumstance in continental shelf delimitation.

In *Gulf of Maine*, the United States made a twofold security argument. First, common defence arrangements between Canada and the United States suggested a boundary running southeast through Browns Bank.[254] Second, the scale of defence activities undertaken by the United States in the Gulf of Maine exceeded that of Canada's activities.[255] The Chamber found that 'common defence arrangements, may require an examination of valid considerations of a political and economic character',[256] and that the criteria to delimit the Canada–United States boundary 'are essentially to be determined in relation to what may be properly called the geographical features of the area'.[257] Concerning the second US argument, the Chamber held that 'the respective scale of activities connected with ... defence ... cannot be taken into account as a relevant circumstance'.[258] The Chamber gave pre-eminence to neutral criteria common to both the EEZ and continental shelf,[259] among which security interests were also included. The Chamber did not dismiss the influence of security in delimitation, simply rejecting the US argument which specifically concerned common arrangements with Canada and the parties' relative scale of activity. *Gulf of Maine* did not reject that security could be a relevant circumstance, as the decision was limited to the parties' comparative scale of defence activities.

In *Guinea/Guinea-Bissau*, the Court of Arbitration followed the lead of the ICJ Chamber. It held that it 'n'est pas sans intérêt, bien qu'il convienne de souligner que ni la zone économique exclusive, ni le plateau continental ne sont des zones de souveraineté'.[260] The Court of Arbitration found that 'les implications que [la sécurité] aurait pu avoir sont déjà résolues par le fait que, dans la solution qu'il a dégagée, le Tribunal a tenue à ce que chaque Etat contrôle les territoires maritimes situés en face de ses côtes et dans leur voisinage'.[261] According to the Court of Arbitration, owing to the EEZ and continental shelf not being

---

[254] Memorial of the United States (27 September 1982) 46–7 [131]–[132].
[255] *Gulf of Maine* (n. 37) 340–1 [233].
[256] Ibid.
[257] Ibid. 278 [59].
[258] Ibid. 342 [237].
[259] Ibid. 327 [194].
[260] *Guinea/Guinea-Bissau* (n. 101) 194 [124].
[261] Ibid.

'zones de souveraineté', security is less important as a relevant circumstance than as a special circumstance. However, the tribunal did not explicitly exclude a role for security in continental shelf and EEZ delimitation.[262]

In *Libya/Malta*, the ICJ stated that '[s]ecurity considerations are of course not unrelated to the concept of the continental shelf'.[263] It decided that the great distance between Libya and Malta was an 'important consideration when deciding whether, and by how much, a median line boundary can be shifted without ... approaching so near to one coast as to bring into play other factors such as security'.[264] The Court confirmed the relevance of security in continental shelf delimitation, linking it to distance from the coasts. However, the Court did not explain why shifting the boundary northwards did not impinge on Malta's security. The Court made comparable comments in *Jan Mayen*. The Court held that the statement in *Libya/Malta* 'that "security considerations are of course not unrelated to the concept of the continental shelf", constituted a particular application, to the continental shelf ... of a general observation concerning all maritime spaces'.[265] In *Jan Mayen*, the Court unequivocally stated that security concerns are common to the delimitation of all maritime zones.

Later cases confirm the Court's statement. In *Black Sea*, Romania contended that Ukraine's proposed boundary compromised its security by running too close to its coast.[266] Romania's argument evoked the *Libya/Malta* statement connecting security and a boundary's distance from the coast. The Court repeated that 'the legitimate security considerations of the Parties may play a role in determining the final delimitation line'.[267] Moreover, since '[t]he provisional equidistance line determined by the Court fully respects the legitimate security interests of either Party',[268] the Court held that 'there is no need to adjust the line on the basis of this consideration'.[269] In *Nicaragua v. Colombia*, both parties advanced security arguments.[270] However, the Court found that such arguments actually related to the parties' conduct. Reiterating its

---

[262] Evans (n. 72) 176–7.
[263] *Libya/Malta* (n. 44) 42 [51].
[264] Ibid. 342 [73].
[265] *Jan Mayen* (n. 49) 75 [81].
[266] *Black Sea* (n. 17) 127–8 [202]–[203].
[267] ibid 128 [204].
[268] Ibid.
[269] Ibid.
[270] *Nicaragua v. Colombia* (n. 26) 705 [221].

Libya/Malta decision, the Court also stated that 'legitimate security concerns might be a relevant consideration if a maritime delimitation was effected particularly near to the coast of a State'.[271]

No boundary has ever been adjusted based on security considerations. International tribunals only state that a boundary is equitable as it also respects the parties' security concerns, which casts doubts on the actual role of security in delimitation. Moreover, it is unclear how international tribunals would adjust a provisional equidistance line on account of security concerns. One should agree with Evans that '[i]t is neither possible nor necessary to devise any general rules on these points'.[272] However, there are three features common to the relevant cases.

First, international tribunals have been consistent in holding that security could be a relevant circumstance in delimitation. Second, since *Libya/Malta* security has been associated with a boundary's distance from the coast.[273] Yet, the bar for a boundary to threaten a state's security, and thus become a relevant circumstance, is high. For example, although in *Nicaragua* v. *Colombia* the San Andrés Archipelago lay at only 100 nm from Nicaragua's coast,[274] the Court still found that the boundary would not be close enough to either state's coast to require adjustment based on security considerations. Third, the reference to 'zones de souveraineté' in *Guinea/Guinea-Bissau* could suggest that security interests would be threatened only if a boundary unduly curtailed a state's entitlement to the territorial sea. This is too restrictive an interpretation, since security does not seem only to relate to territorial sea delimitation. Nevertheless, since the territorial sea is the maritime zone most closely linked to security, international tribunals are likely to be more sensitive to security issues in territorial sea delimitation that in continental shelf or EEZ delimitation.

IV Irrelevant Circumstances

International tribunals have consistently rejected that factors unrelated either to the basis of title, or to the function of maritime zones, required the adjustment of an equidistance line. The lack of any connection between such factors and the dual 'title-function' basis justifies the label

---

[271] Ibid. 706 [222].
[272] Evans (n. 72) 177.
[273] This was the case in *Guinea/Guinea-Bissau*, *Jan Mayen*, *Black Sea* and *Nicaragua v. Colombia*.
[274] *Nicaragua* v. *Colombia* (n. 26) 637 [19].

of 'irrelevant circumstances'. However, states continue pleading irrelevant circumstances before international tribunals, while academic writers seemingly take for granted that factors mentioned by states in their pleadings could lead to adjusting an equidistance line.

A Conduct

Under general international law, state conduct could be evidence of existing international agreements, including maritime delimitation agreements. However, there is a difference between the function of conduct before and after UNCLOS's entry into force in 1994. Before 1994, the prevailing view was that the appropriate delimitation method was identified on a case-by-case basis taking into account all relevant circumstances.[275] Conduct was thus evidence of an agreement *on the applicable delimitation method*. However, since 1994 international tribunals have applied a standard delimitation method, in the context of which conduct cannot be evidence of the appropriate delimitation method. However, it can be evidence of an agreed boundary, consistently with Articles 74 and 83 UNCLOS, which provide that maritime boundaries are primarily delimited by agreement. Under UNCLOS, conduct is evidence of an agreement *on the boundary itself*. The jurisprudence confirms this difference between the pre-UNCLOS and post-UNCLOS functions of conduct.

In *Tunisia/Libya*, the ICJ rejected that parties had agreed on their boundary,[276] but found that there nonetheless existed a line established by Italy, Libya's former colonial power, as the maritime boundary with French Tunisia.[277] This line became a *modus vivendi* between Tunisia and Libya.[278] The Court held that 'the respect for the tacit *modus vivendi* ... could warrant its acceptance as a historical justification for the choice of the method for the delimitation of the continental shelf'.[279] Although the Court established that the boundary's first segment followed a line of 26° at the meridian, it stated that it was not:

> making a finding of tacit agreement between the Parties ... The aspect now under consideration ... is what method of delimitation would ensure an equitable result; and it is evident that the Court must take into account

[275] See Evans (n. 72) 217–24.
[276] *Tunisia/Libya* (n. 99) 68 [90] and 69 [92].
[277] Ibid. 70 [93]–[94].
[278] Ibid.
[279] Ibid. 70–1 [95].

whatever indicia are available of the line or lines which the Parties themselves may have considered equitable or acted upon as such.[280]

The Court clarified that, by considering the *modus vivendi* between former colonial powers, it was ascertaining 'what method of delimitation would ensure an equitable result', not the existence of a binding agreement establishing the boundary. A *modus vivendi* argument was also made in *Gulf of Maine*. Canada argued that the conduct of the United States could be considered in three fashions:

> first, as evidence of genuine acquiescence in the idea of a median line as the boundary between the respective maritime jurisdictions . . .; secondly, as an indication . . . of the existence of a *modus vivendi* or of a *de facto* boundary . . .; and, thirdly and lastly, as mere indicia of the type of delimitation that the Parties themselves would have considered equitable.[281]

Canada aimed at establishing the existence not of an agreed boundary, but of an agreed method for the delimitation of a boundary. However, the Chamber of the ICJ held that the conduct of the United States did not support Canada's arguments.[282]

Jan Mayen was a turning point in the international tribunals' attitude towards conduct in delimitation. Norway contended that a boundary with Denmark had already been established by the parties' recognition of the median line as the binding delimitation method, which in practice meant that the parties had agreed on a median-line boundary.[283] The Court rejected this argument.[284] Denmark further argued that 'the conduct of the Parties is a highly relevant factor in the choice of the appropriate method of delimitation where such conduct has indicated some particular method as being likely to produce an equitable result'.[285] Denmark relied on the delimitation treaty between Norway and Iceland, contending that the acceptance that Iceland would have a full 200-nm EEZ obligated Norway to accept the same *vis-à-vis* Denmark. The Court stated that in:

> maritime delimitation, international law does not prescribe . . . the adoption of a single method for the delimitation of the maritime spaces on all

---

[280] Ibid. 84 [118].
[281] *Gulf of Maine* (n. 37) 304 [128].
[282] Ibid. 310–11 [148], [150] and [152].
[283] *Jan Mayen* (n. 49) 48–56 [22]–[40].
[284] Ibid.
[285] Ibid. 75 [82].

sides of an island, or for the whole of the coastal front of a particular State, rather than, if desired, varying systems of delimitation for the various parts of the coast. The conduct of the parties will in many cases therefore have no influence on such a delimitation.[286]

Denmark's contention concerned Norway's conduct with regard to Iceland, a third state, which could not bind Denmark as *res inter alios acta*. With respect to Denmark's argument, the Court held that conduct would in many cases have no influence on the choice of the method likely to produce an equitable result.[287] The Court did not mention the parties' conduct in connection with the adjustment of the equidistance line. Initially, it discussed whether there was an agreed boundary,[288] and only subsequently delimited the boundary using a two-stage approach, in the context of which no reference was made to conduct as a relevant circumstance. The Court thus accepted that conduct could neither indicate the applicable delimitation method, as argued by Denmark, nor determine the adjustment of an equidistance line. Therefore, in delimitation conduct can only be evidence of an international agreement establishing a boundary.

In *Cameroon* v. *Nigeria*, the Court confirmed that conduct is evidence of a boundary agreement. The Court addressed Cameroon and Nigeria's oil concessions as an aspect of conduct, finding that:

> although the existence of an express or tacit agreement between the parties on the siting of their respective oil concessions may indicate a consensus on the maritime areas to which they are entitled, oil concessions and oil wells are not in themselves to be considered as relevant circumstances justifying the adjustment or shifting of the provisional delimitation line. Only if they are based on express or tacit agreement between the parties may they be taken into account.[289]

The ICJ dismissed oil-related practice as a relevant circumstance, and held that it could only be evidence of an 'express or tacit agreement between the parties'. However, the Court's statement is not entirely clear. One wonders whether the 'express or tacit agreement between the parties'

---

[286] Ibid. 77 [86].
[287] While Churchill suggested that the Court accepted the relevance of conduct as a relevant circumstance, Decaux and Politakis suggested that the Court wrongly excluded the relevance of the parties' conduct. See Churchill (n. 54) 24; Decaux (n. 54) 510–11; GP Politakis, 'The 1993 Jan Mayen Judgment: the End of Illusions?' (1994) 41 *NILR* 1, 15–16.
[288] *Jan Mayen* (n. 49) 53–6 [33]–[40].
[289] *Cameroon* v. *Nigeria* (n. 15) 447–8 [304].

pertains to the maritime boundary or to the location of oil concessions themselves. The Court's phrasing suggests that granting oil concessions was based on an agreement between the parties, which in turn suggests that in *Cameroon v. Nigeria* the Court upheld that conduct is evidence of an agreed boundary in its own right, and not a relevant circumstance.

The ICJ's statement in *Cameroon v. Nigeria* was cited with approval in *Barbados v. Trinidad and Tobago*.[290] However, in that case the arbitral tribunal rejected Barbados's claim that the centuries-old traditional fishing by Barbadian fisherfolk was a relevant circumstance in delimiting its boundary with Trinidad and Tobago, since 'the weight of evidence ... does not sustain its contention that its fisherfolk have traditionally fished for flyingfish off Tobago for centuries'.[291] The tribunal did not state whether fishing patterns were a relevant circumstance. In all later cases, international tribunals treated conduct as evidence of an agreed boundary, and not as evidence of the equitable character of a delimitation method.[292] The adoption of this approach was especially clear in *Ghana/Côte d'Ivoire*. The Special Chamber decided that the parties' conduct fell short of proving the existence of a tacitly agreed maritime boundary.[293] However, Ghana had argued that conduct could have also been a relevant circumstance justifying the adjustment of the provisional equidistance line. The Special Chamber observed that:

> Ghana's argument that the same conduct constitutes a relevant circumstance requiring the adjustment of the provisional equidistance line to conform to the 'customary equidistance boundary' appears to be an attempt to revive a tacit maritime boundary that was rejected by the Special Chamber by circumventing the high standard of proof required for the existence of a tacit agreement. The Special Chamber considers that accepting such argument would, in effect, undermine its earlier finding on the existence of a tacit agreement.[294]

Ghana/Côte d'Ivoire should be read as the recognition that conduct is to be considered only as the means through which neighbouring states may tacitly agree on their maritime boundaries. However, pleading conduct as a relevant circumstance would simply re-formulate the argument for

---

[290] *Barbados v. Trinidad and Tobago* (n. 16) 241 [364].
[291] Ibid. 221 [266].
[292] *Guyana v. Suriname* (n. 177) 108 [390]; *Nicaragua v. Honduras* (n. 178) 734–7 [252]–[258]; *Black Sea* (n. 17) 82–9 [55]–[76]; *Bangladesh/Myanmar* (n. 3) 35–42 [88]–[125].
[293] *Ghana/Côte d'Ivoire* (n. 18) [211]–[228].
[294] Ibid. [478].

a tacitly agreed boundary by labelling the same evidence using the different legal category of relevant circumstances.

However, the ICJ has recently found that conduct could, in exceptional cases, be a relevant circumstance determining the adjustment of an equidistance line. In the 2007 *Nicaragua* v. *Colombia* judgment on preliminary objections, the Court found that Nicaragua and Colombia had not agreed on their maritime boundary.[295] However, at the merits phase Colombia argued that it had 'for many decades regulated fishing activities, conducted scientific exploration and conducted naval patrols throughout the area to the east of the 82nd meridian, whereas there is no evidence of any significant Nicaraguan activity there until recent times'.[296] Nicaragua replied that 'Colombia's case ... amounts in practice to an attempt to resurrect its argument that the 1928 Treaty established a maritime boundary along the 82nd meridian, a theory which the Court rejected'.[297]

In the 2012 merits judgment, '[t]he Court [understood] Colombia to be advancing a different argument, namely that the conduct of the Parties east of the 82nd meridian constitutes a relevant circumstance in the present case, which suggests that the use of the provisional median line as a line of delimitation would be equitable'.[298] Colombia seemed to argue that conduct should indicate the applicable delimitation method. However, the Court held that it could not 'consider that the conduct of the Parties in the present case is so exceptional as to amount to a relevant circumstance which itself requires it to adjust or shift the provisional median line'.[299] The Court recognised that '[w]hile it cannot be ruled out that conduct might need to be taken into account as a relevant circumstance in an appropriate case, the jurisprudence of the Court and of arbitral tribunals shows that conduct will not normally have such an effect'.[300] However, in these statements the Court conflated two distinct issues. In deciding on Colombia's contention, the Court should have stated that conduct does not indicate the applicable delimitation method. Instead, the Court only referred to conduct as a relevant circumstance, despite having previously stated that Colombia had not pleaded conduct

---

[295] *Territorial and Maritime Dispute (Nicaragua* v. *Colombia)* (Preliminary Objections) [2007] ICJ Rep 832, 869 [120].
[296] *Nicaragua* v. *Colombia* (n. 26) 704 [217].
[297] Ibid. 704 [218].
[298] Ibid. 705 [220].
[299] Ibid.
[300] Ibid.

as a relevant circumstance. Nicaragua also contended that Colombia's argument was not about relevant circumstances, but was an attempt to revive the agreed boundary argument that had failed in 2007. Moreover, the statement that conduct could be considered to be a relevant circumstance in exceptional cases is inconsistent with the dual 'title-function' basis, as well as with the Court's own earlier jurisprudence. *Nicaragua v. Colombia* is unpersuasive with respect to the decision on conduct.

The 2014 *Peru v. Chile* judgment confirms that conduct is evidence of an agreed boundary, and not a relevant circumstance. The dispute concerned whether the 1952 Santiago Declaration[301] established the Peru–Chile maritime boundary as a line running along the parallel of latitude passing through the parties' land boundary terminus. At the outset, the Court stated that '[i]n order to settle the dispute before it, the Court must first ascertain whether an agreed maritime boundary exists'.[302] The Court did not mention Articles 74 and 83 UNCLOS, or the role of agreement in those provisions. Instead, it leaped into discussing the national and international instruments relevant to ascertaining whether the parties had agreed on their boundary. Possibly, the Court did not mention Articles 74 and 83 UNCLOS as they had not been written when the Santiago Declaration entered into force in 1952. Strictly speaking, *Peru v. Chile* could be said not directly to clarify the role of agreement in the three-stage approach.

The Court found that the agreed boundary between Peru and Chile extended along a parallel only for 80 nm, and delimited the boundary beyond 80 nm under UNCLOS, as the law in force in 2014.[303] The Court, '[h]aving concluded that an agreed single maritime boundary exists between the Parties, ... will ... determine the course of the maritime boundary from that point on'.[304] The Court found the segment of the boundary up to 80 nm to be established under an international agreement between Peru and Chile. This agreement was found to stem from the parties' conduct. Conduct thus was the basis for the agreed segment of the Peru–Chile boundary. This agreed segment was not established

---

[301] Declaration on the Maritime Zone, 1006 UNTS 325.
[302] *Peru v. Chile* (n. 179) 16 [24].
[303] Although Peru was not a party to UNCLOS, the Court found Arts. 74 and 83 UNCLOS to be customary international law. See ibid. 65 [179].
[304] ibid. 65 [177]. The Court's finding were controversial, as shown by the strong Joint Dissenting Opinion of Judges Xue, Gaja, Bhandari and Judge *ad hoc* Orrego-Vicuña. See ibid., 100.

under UNCLOS, but under general international law. However, the UNCLOS drafters intended for Articles 74 and 83 to embody the rule of general international law, expressed in *North Sea Continental Shelf*, that maritime boundaries are primarily established by agreement. Therefore, *Peru* v. *Chile* could be seen to indicate the function of conduct for establishing maritime boundaries under UNCLOS.

There seem to be two reasons for rejecting conduct as a relevant circumstance: first, Articles 74 and 83 UNCLOS clearly state that delimitation is to be effected by agreement, lacking which international tribunals could establish a boundary *de novo*; second, the absence of a connection to the basis of title. Moreover, if conduct were seen to be a relevant circumstance in the three-stage approach, it could be considered both as evidence of an agreed boundary, and, after it has been ascertained that it is not evidence of an agreed boundary, as a relevant circumstance for adjusting an equidistance line. If conduct were said not to be evidence of an agreed boundary, considering it to be a relevant circumstance would re-introduce it through the back door. The cases seem to confirm such views. International tribunals have rejected that, under Articles 74 and 83 UNCLOS, conduct justifies adjusting an equidistance line. Conversely, they have stated that arguments about conduct were actually arguments about other factors, such as access to natural resources. This was the case in *Cameroon* v. *Nigeria* and *Barbados* v. *Trinidad and Tobago*. In such cases, the relevant circumstance concerned is not conduct, but access to natural resources, which could be considered a relevant circumstance in the three-stage approach.[305]

B Rights of Third States

In delimitation cases, states have addressed third states' rights in a twofold manner. On one hand, third states have requested to intervene in delimitation proceedings; on the other hand, states have pleaded third party interests as relevant circumstances, which international tribunals have always rejected. Since the first issue is not directly related to the application of the three-stage approach, it is not examined in detail.

In *Libya/Malta*, the ICJ discussed Italy's claims in the delimitation area. The Court had already addressed this issue in the 1984 intervention

---

[305] Section III.A above.

proceedings, in which Italy had applied to intervene.[306] The Court dismissed Italy's request, finding that intervention's 'implementation must in principle be effected within the scope of the Special Agreement [between Libya and Malta]'.[307] The Court denied Italy's application because the Libya–Malta special agreement did not endow it with jurisdiction to decide a dispute involving Italy. At the merits stage, both Libya and Malta argued that:

> the Court should not feel inhibited from extending its decision to all areas which, independently of third party claims, are claimed by the Parties to this case, since if the Court were to exclude any such areas as are the subject of present or possible future claims by a third State it would in effect be deciding on such claims without jurisdiction to do so.[308]

The Court found that the special agreement only granted jurisdiction to delimit the areas appertaining to the parties, without covering areas over which third states may have a better title. Accordingly, the Court limited its decision to areas where there was no third-party claim.[309] The Court held that '[a] decision limited in this way ... signifies ... that the Court has not been endowed with jurisdiction to determine what principles and rules govern delimitations with third States, or whether the claims of the Parties outside that area prevail over the claims of those third States in the region'.[310] Although the Court had previously denied Italy's request for intervention, it exercised its jurisdiction only over the areas where Italy had no claims, thus granting what Italy had sought by applying to intervene.[311]

Similarly, in *Eritrea/Yemen* the determination of the northern and southern ends of the boundary could have impinged on Saudi Arabia's and Djibouti's rights.[312] The tribunal simply held that:

> [it] has the competence and the authority according to the Arbitration Agreement to decide the maritime boundary between the two Parties. But it has neither competence nor authority to decide on any of the

---

[306] *Continental Shelf (Libya/Malta)* (Application by Italy for Permission to Intervene) [1984] ICJ Rep 3.
[307] Ibid. 24 [38].
[308] *Libya/Malta* (n. 44) 25 [20].
[309] Ibid. 25 [21].
[310] Ibid. 26 [21].
[311] E Jouannet, 'L'impossible Protection des Droits des Tiers par la Cour Internationale de Justice dans les Affaires de Délimitation Maritime' in *La Mer et son Droit – Mélanges offerts à Laurent Lucchini et Jean-Pierre Quéneudec* (Pédone, 2003) 315, 325.
[312] *Eritrea/Yemen* (n. 106) 344 [44]–[46].

IV IRRELEVANT CIRCUMSTANCES

boundaries between either of the two Parties and neighbouring States. It will therefore be necessary to terminate either end of the boundary line in such a way as to avoid trespassing upon an area where other claims might fall to be considered.[313]

Following *Libya/Malta*, the *Eritrea/Yemen* tribunal found that it could not extend the boundary into the area in which Saudi Arabia and Djibouti could have entitlements.

In the *Qatar* v. *Bahrain* decision on the territorial sea boundary, the Court found that 'it cannot fix the boundary's southernmost point, since its definitive location is dependent upon the limits of the respective maritime zones of Saudi Arabia and of the Parties'.[314] Concerning the EEZ and continental shelf boundary, the Court did not establish the tripoint with Iran. The Court held that '[t]he boundary shall ... follow [an] adjusted equidistance line until it meets the delimitation line between the respective maritime zones of Iran on the one hand and of Bahrain and Qatar on the other'.[315] Similarly to the previous cases, the Court reasoned that its jurisdiction only covered the dispute between the parties before it. Similarly, in *Cameroon* v. *Nigeria* the Court stated that it cannot '... decide upon legal rights of third States not parties to the proceedings',[316] and that, 'in fixing the maritime boundary between Cameroon and Nigeria, the Court must ensure that it does not adopt any position which might affect the rights of Equatorial Guinea and Sao Tome and Principe'.[317]

Both *Nicaragua* v. *Honduras* and *Black Sea* raised the issue of the boundary's endpoint. In *Nicaragua* v. *Honduras*, the Court recalled that it could not decide on third states' rights lacking consent from the third states concerned.[318] Discussing Colombia's rights in the region, it found that they could not be affected by the delimitation between Nicaragua and Honduras.[319] The Court did not identify the boundary's endpoint, simply stating that it could extend east of the eighty-second meridian without prejudicing third states' rights.[320] The Court made comparable comments in *Black Sea*, where the boundary followed 'the equidistance

---

[313] Ibid. 366 [136].
[314] *Qatar* v. *Bahrain* (n. 84) 109 [221].
[315] Ibid. 115 [249].
[316] *Cameroon* v. *Nigeria* (n. 15) 421 [238].
[317] Ibid.
[318] *Nicaragua* v. *Honduras* (n. 178) 756 [312].
[319] Ibid. 758–9 [315]–[317].
[320] Ibid. 759 [319].

line in a southerly direction until the point beyond which the interests of third States may be affected'.[321] The Court held that it would consider the delimitation agreements with third states only in its decision on the boundary's endpoint,[322] thus implicitly rejecting that delimitation treaties with third states could justify adjusting the boundary, and, as a result, rejecting Romania's contention that such agreements were a relevant circumstance.[323]

At the merits stage of *Nicaragua v. Colombia*, the ICJ considered whether the agreements between Colombia and Costa Rica, Jamaica and Panama imposed 'limits upon the action which the Court can take in the present case, because of the requirement that the Court respect the rights of third States'.[324] The Court found that 'as Article 59 of the Statute ... makes clear, ... a judgment of the Court is not binding on any State other than the parties to the case'.[325] The ICJ inferred the irrelevance of third states' rights from Article 59 of the ICJ's Statute, which is linked to the Court's consensual jurisdiction.[326] ITLOS adopted the same reasoning in *Bangladesh/Myanmar* with reference to Article 33(2) of its Statute.[327]

Establishing boundaries without an end-point aims to avoid impinging on third states' rights. Recently, international tribunals have established several open-ended boundaries, such as in *Nicaragua v. Honduras, Black Sea, Bangladesh/Myanmar* and *Costa Rica v. Nicaragua*, marking a difference with earlier cases. International tribunals identified the boundaries' end-points in the *Anglo/French Arbitration, Gulf of Maine, Libya/Malta* and *Jan Mayen*, while leaving the end-point unspecified in *Tunisia/Libya* and *Guinea/Guinea-Bissau*. Open-ended boundaries suggest that third states' rights could be considered to be relevant circumstances in maritime delimitation. Nevertheless, this is not entirely correct for two reasons. First, the role of relevant circumstances is to determine the adjustment of an equidistance line. However, leaving a boundary open-ended does not amount to adjusting it. Second, the rationale for establishing open-ended boundaries is to prevent judicial decisions from

---

[321] *Black Sea* (n. 17) 129 [209].
[322] Ibid. 120 [177].
[323] Ibid. 120 [178].
[324] *Nicaragua v. Colombia* (n. 26) 707 [226].
[325] Ibid. 707 [228].
[326] *Land, Island and Maritime Frontier Dispute (El Salvador/Honduras)* (Application by Nicaragua per Permission to Intervene) [1990] ICJ Rep 92, 133 [95].
[327] *Bangladesh/Myanmar* (n. 3) 97 [366]–[367].

affecting the rights of non-parties to a dispute. International judicial decisions could be handed down and bind only states that have consented to the exercise of jurisdiction in a particular dispute. The *raison d'être* of open-ended boundaries is inherently jurisdictional, and is unrelated to third states' rights being relevant circumstances.

The cases suggest that third states' rights are not relevant circumstances in maritime delimitation. International tribunals consistently reject the relevance of such factors on jurisdictional grounds, based on the binding effect of international decisions only between the parties to a dispute. In 1995, Evans argued that maritime delimitation 'is about as bilateral an issue as it is possible to have'.[328] The bilateral character of delimitation has been recognised by long-standing international jurisprudence, which has consistently, although implicitly, acknowledged that third-party interests have no place in the delimitation process.[329] Third states' rights could not be considered to be relevant circumstances, which can also be explained by the absence of a connection either with the basis of title, or with the function of maritime areas.

C Geomorphology

Since the continental shelf originated as a physical concept, in early delimitation cases states and international tribunals tended to discuss factors such as natural prolongation, geology and geomorphology.[330] Since the ICJ's judgment in *Libya/Malta*, international tribunals have rejected that such factors are relevant in delimitation.[331] Geomorphological factors are categorised as 'irrelevant circumstances' because international tribunals have so far rejected their relevance in delimitation. However, while the irrelevance of geomorphology is

---

[328] MD Evans, 'Intervention, the International Court of Justice and the Law of the Sea' (1995) 48 *RHDI* 73, 90. See also, C Chinkin, *Third Parties in International Law* (OUP, 1993) 162.

[329] See Weil (n. 190) 268–72.

[330] *North Sea Continental Shelf* (n. 1) 51 [95]. See Draft Articles on the Law of the Sea with Commentaries (n. 189) 297; Proclamation by the President (n. 240) 45. See also H Lauterpacht, 'Sovereignty over Submarine Areas' (1950) 27 *BYIL* 376, 423–4; J Crawford and T Viles, 'International Law on a Given Day' in J Crawford (ed.), *International Law as an Open System* (Cameron May, 2002) 69, 73.

[331] *Libya/Malta* (n. 44) 34–6 [36]–[40]; *Nicaragua v. Colombia* (n. 26) 703 [214]; *Bangladesh/Myanmar* (n. 3) 87 [322]. See Ø Jensen, 'Maritime Boundary Delimitation Beyond 200 Nautical Miles: The International Judiciary and the Commission on the Limits of the Continental Shelf' (2015) 84 *Nordic Journal of International Law* 580, 589–604.

accepted with respect to the maritime zones within 200 nm, the question is still open concerning the continental shelf beyond 200 nm. Title over the continental shelf beyond 200 nm is not only distance from the coast, but also the physical existence of a continental margin comprising 'the seabed and subsoil of the shelf, the slope and the rise'.[332] The basis of title over the continental shelf beyond 200 nm is linked to geomorphology. This suggests that geomorphological factors could be regarded to be relevant circumstances in delimiting the continental shelf beyond 200 nm.

International tribunals found the appropriate method for delimitation beyond 200 nm to be the three-stage approach.[333] In *Bangladesh/Myanmar*, the first case on continental shelf delimitation beyond 200 nm, ITLOS put a question to the parties on the applicable delimitation method. Bangladesh replied that Article 83 UNCLOS did not distinguish between delimitation within and beyond 200 nm, adding that '[t]he merits of any method of delimitation in this context ... can only be judged on a case-by-case basis'.[334] Myanmar agreed.[335] ITLOS decided that 'the delimitation method to be employed in the present case for the continental shelf beyond 200 [nm] should not differ from that within 200 nm'.[336] The reason for ITLOS's decision was that '[t]his method is rooted in the recognition that sovereignty over the land territory is the basis for the sovereign rights and jurisdiction of the coastal State with respect to both the [EEZ] and the continental shelf'.[337] The *Bangladesh v. India* tribunal and the Special Chamber in *Ghana/Côte d'Ivoire* also adopted the three-stage approach to delimit the continental shelf beyond 200 nm.[338]

International tribunals did not consider geomorphology to be a relevant circumstance. In *Bangladesh/Myanmar*, ITLOS plotted a provisional equidistance line as a starting point, and later analysed relevant circumstances. According to Bangladesh, 'the relevant circumstances in the delimitation of the continental shelf beyond 200 nm include the geology and geomorphology of the seabed and subsoil, because entitlement beyond 200 nm depends entirely on natural

---

[332] Art. 76(3) UNCLOS.
[333] Chapter 4, Section III above.
[334] *Bangladesh/Myanmar* (n. 3) 116 [452].
[335] Ibid. 116 [453].
[336] Ibid. 117 [455].
[337] Ibid.
[338] *Bangladesh v. India* (n. 33) 158 [465]; *Ghana/Côte d'Ivoire* (n. 18) [263].

prolongation while within 200 nm it is based on distance from the coast'.[339] Bangladesh argued that a relevant circumstance was the fact that Bangladesh's shelf beyond 200 nm was the 'most natural prolongation',[340] while 'Myanmar's natural prolongation only extends to the subduction zone which marks the boundary between the Indian and Burmese Plates'.[341]

ITLOS rejected this contention because it had already determined that the parties possessed overlapping entitlements beyond 200 nm.[342] Bangladesh's argument entailed that, by having the 'most natural prolongation', it had better title over areas beyond 200 nm than Myanmar. ITLOS's rejection of the 'most natural prolongation' argument was thus based on considerations unrelated to relevant circumstances and linked to the basis of title. ITLOS's statement seems to confirm that there must be a link between relevant circumstances and the basis of title. However, ITLOS's reasoning does not indicate whether geomorphological factors could in principle be considered to be relevant circumstances in delimitation beyond 200 nm.

Following ITLOS's rejection of the 'most natural prolongation' argument, in *Bangladesh* v. *India* Bangladesh accepted that 'neither Party is entitled to claim a superior entitlement based on geological or geomorphological factors in the overlapping area'.[343] The arbitral tribunal adjusted the provisional equidistance line within and beyond 200 nm as a single operation.[344] The tribunal did not comment on geomorphology as a relevant circumstance, presumably because neither party had raised the issue.

In *Bangladesh/Myanmar*, ITLOS correctly stated that title over the continental shelf beyond 200 nm is sovereignty over land. However, this statement is imprecise, as it does not fully describe the basis of title over the continental shelf as codified by Article 76(1) UNCLOS. Under Article 76(1), the basis of title over the continental shelf beyond 200 nm is the combination of two elements, the physical existence of a continental margin and distance from the coast.[345] Geomorphology

---

[339] *Bangladesh/Myanmar* (n. 3) 118 [457].
[340] Memorial of Bangladesh (1 July 2010), 106 [7.32].
[341] Ibid.
[342] *Bangladesh/Myanmar* (n. 3) 118 [460].
[343] *Bangladesh* v. *India* (n. 33) 146 [439].
[344] Ibid. 163–5 [476]–[480].
[345] Chapter 4, Section III.B above. The fact that geomorphology is a component of the basis of title could render the application of the three-stage approach to delimitation beyond 200 nm dubious.

could be a relevant circumstance only should it have a link with this basis of title.

Geomorphology concerns the configuration of the marine seabed and subsoil, and encompasses factors such as the presence of a trench or a furrow and the existence of a subduction zone between tectonic plates. Generally, states and international tribunals have referred to geomorphological factors as being facts of nature evidencing a discontinuity in the seabed, such as the Tripolitanian Furrow in *Tunisia/Libya*[346] and the 'rift zone' in *Libya/Malta*.[347] It appears more appropriate to speak of 'geomorphological discontinuities', instead of 'geomorphological factors'. Geomorphological discontinuities would be linked to the basis of title over the continental shelf beyond 200 nm, and they should thus be treated as relevant circumstances. However, this raises some legal and practical issues, which could justify the international tribunals' reluctance to accept that geomorphological discontinuities are relevant circumstances.

Geomorphology as the basis of title over the continental shelf beyond 200 nm conflicts with the existence of a single continental shelf under international law. Article 76 UNCLOS suggests that the continental shelf is a single entity, and that no distinction exists between the shelf within and beyond 200 nm. Similarly, Article 83 UNCLOS does not indicate that delimitation should be effected differently within and beyond 200 nm.[348] In order to have a single basis of title for a single continental shelf, it would appear necessary to distinguish between states not having a shelf extending beyond 200 nm and states that do. For the former, the only basis of title over the continental shelf would be distance from a state's coast, and for the latter the only basis of title would be the physical presence of a continental shelf. Supporting this view, Huang and Liao wrote that 'only if a state's natural continental margin is narrower than 200 miles does the distance criterion come into operation'.[349] However, this view does not have any legal basis in Article 76 UNCLOS. Moreover, it entails that factors typically regarded by international tribunals to be relevant circumstances, such as coastal length disparity, could in some cases be seen not to be relevant circumstances in continental shelf

---

[346] *Tunisia/Libya* (n. 99) 57 [66].
[347] *Libya/Malta* (n. 44) 34 [36].
[348] *Bangladesh/Myanmar* (n. 3) 96 [361]; *Bangladesh v. India* (n. 33) 31–2 [77].
[349] L Huang and X Liao, 'Natural Prolongation and Delimitation of the Continental Shelf Beyond 200 nm: Implications of the *Bangladesh/Myanmar* Case' (2014) 4 *Asian JIL* 281, 284.

delimitation because they would be unrelated to the geomorphological basis of title over a continental shelf extending beyond 200 nm.

There would be significant problems if a dispute arose between a state whose shelf does not extend beyond 200 nm, for which the basis of title would be distance, and a state whose shelf extends beyond 200 nm, for which the basis of title would be geomorphology. With respect to the former, factors that could be relevant circumstances should be related to distance. Conversely, with respect to the latter, factors that could be relevant circumstances should be related to geomorphology. However, the link between the basis of title and relevant circumstances would require accepting that neither geographical nor geomorphological circumstances would be applicable in delimiting the boundary in such a situation, by virtue of not being common to both bases of title. This conclusion seems impractical, as there would be no applicable relevant circumstances, and contradicts the jurisprudence affirming the relevance of geographical circumstances in delimitation beyond 200 nm. Both *Bangladesh/Myanmar* and *Bangladesh v. India* found that cut-off was a relevant circumstance beyond 200 nm, although both states had a continental shelf beyond 200 nm. The existence of two distinct bases of title, depending on whether the continental shelf extends beyond 200 nm, is unconvincing. It seems more appropriate to uphold the single shelf theory, accepting that relevant circumstances should be the same within and beyond 200 nm, although this may diminish the impact of geomorphology as the basis of title beyond 200 nm.

Supposing that geomorphological discontinuities could be relevant circumstances, the question arises concerning how their effects would be weighed against the effects of geographical circumstances, such as cut-off. Let us imagine that a trench or a furrow were located, beyond the 200-nm limit, broadly parallel to the coast of a state party to a delimitation case.[350] If a boundary beyond 200 nm were drawn along that feature, it would cut off the coastal projections of the state in front of which the features lies, contradicting the decisions in *Bangladesh/Myanmar* and *Bangladesh v. India* that cut-off must be abated also beyond 200 nm.[351] This scenario shows that it may be challenging to uphold both geographical and geomorphological circumstances, and could explain the

---

[350] In *Tunisia/Libya*, the Tripolitanian Furrow lay parallel to Libya's coast. Tunisia argued that the boundary should have followed its course. However, *Tunisia/Libya* concerned only continental shelf delimitation within 200 nm. See *Tunisia/Libya* (n. 99) 55–6 [63]–[64].

[351] Section II.A above.

international tribunals' reluctance to accept that geomorphological discontinuities are relevant circumstances in delimitation beyond 200 nm.

Considering geomorphological factors to be relevant circumstances is also inconsistent with state practice. In the Bay of Bengal cases, neither India nor Myanmar asked the international tribunals concerned to adjust the equidistance line based on geomorphological discontinuities. In *Bangladesh* v. *India*, Bangladesh abandoned its 'most natural prolongation' argument, which had failed in *Bangladesh/Myanmar*. Moreover, treaties do not establish boundaries beyond 200 nm following geomorphological discontinuities. The only treaty in force delimiting the continental shelf beyond 200 nm, signed by Mexico and the United States in 2000, establishes a strict equidistant boundary.[352] The 2006 Denmark–Iceland–Norway joint statement, which is not a binding treaty, disregarded the potential existence of geomorphological discontinuities.[353] In their 2009 treaty, Barbados and France delimited their boundaries up to 200 nm based on strict equidistance, and also agreed that, if in the future they should claim a continental shelf beyond 200 nm, the equidistance line established within 200 nm shall extend beyond 200 nm.[354] The 2010 Cook Islands–New Zealand treaty and the 2012 Kiribati–New Zealand treaty followed a different system, since they both provided that, should the boundary need to be extended beyond the EEZ, 'that line shall be extended by agreement in accordance with international law'.[355] This wording suggests that the states party will have to negotiate additional agreements on the delimitation of their boundary beyond 200 nm. Nevertheless, such agreements seem likely simply to extend the equidistance line which both the 2010 and the 2012 treaties established.

---

[352] Treaty between Mexico and the United States on the Delimitation of the Continental Shelf in the Western Gulf of Mexico beyond 200 Nautical Miles, (2001) 44 *LoSB* 71.

[353] Agreed Minutes on the Delimitation of the Continental Shelf beyond 200 Nautical Miles between the Faroe Islands, Iceland and Norway in the Southern Part of the Banana Hole in the Northeast Atlantic, in DA Colson and RW Smith (eds.), *International Maritime Boundaries* (Martinus Nijhoff, 2011) vol. VI, 4532.

[354] Agreement between France and Barbados on the Delimitation of the Maritime Space between France and Barbados, 2663 UNTS 163.

[355] Agreement between New Zealand and the Cook Islands concerning the Delimitation of the Maritime Boundaries between Tokelau and the Cook Islands, (2014) 82 *LoSB* 54; Agreement between New Zealand and the Republic of Kiribati concerning the Delimitation of the Maritime Boundaries between Tokelau and Kiribati, (2017) 90 *LoSB* 49.

There are difficulties in considering that geomorphological discontinuities could be relevant circumstances, although they are linked to the basis of title over the continental shelf beyond 200 nm. The notion that the continental shelf beyond 200 nm has a basis of title different from the basis of title within 200 nm is problematic. There have been only two cases concerning delimitation beyond 200 nm, which suggests that the international tribunals' views are likely to develop further.

V   Implications of the Judicial Approach to Relevant Circumstances

International tribunals have developed a consistent approach to relevant circumstances grounded in the dual 'title-function' basis. This section discusses the implications of this approach in three respects: the identification of relevant circumstances, the weighing of relevant circumstances and the adjustment of the boundary.

A   Identifying Relevant Circumstances

In *North Sea Continental Shelf*, the ICJ expressed the view that 'there is no legal limit to the considerations which States may take account of for the purpose of making sure that they apply equitable procedures'.[356] Although this statement concerns factors that states may take into account in negotiating maritime boundaries, the Court itself also read it as applicable to judicial disputes.[357] However, international tribunals have gradually limited the list of relevant circumstances, both explicitly and implicitly. The extensive maritime boundary litigation allows one to re-think the criteria for the identification of relevant circumstances. Evans, Weil and Tanaka wrote on this issue, but their conclusions have not been confirmed by later judicial decisions.

Writing in 1989, Evans maintained that relevant circumstances have two functions in the delimitation process: to 'ameliorate the strict application of a chosen method' and to 'indicate what that method is to be'.[358] Relevant circumstances thus operate at all stages of delimitation.[359] According to Evans, each relevant circumstance could be associated to

---

[356] *North Sea Continental Shelf* (n. 1) 50 [93].
[357] *Libya/Malta* (n. 44) 40 [48]. See *contra*, *Anglo/French Arbitration* (n. 73) 115 [245]; *Jan Mayen* (n. 49) 63 [57].
[358] Evans (n. 72) 87.
[359] ibid.

one of the four stages of delimitation, which he called 'stage association'.[360] Since the stages of the delimitation process are hierarchical, 'the potential relevance of a factor or a circumstance to a later stage in the process will be affected by the relevance of factors at an earlier stage'. Evans called this process 'association between the roles'.[361] 'Stage association' and 'association between the roles' would limit conflicts between relevant circumstances, and assign a relative weight to all relevant factors.[362] Evans's framework is problematic since relevant circumstances do not indicate the appropriate delimitation method any more, their appreciation being limited to the second stage of the delimitation process.

In 1991, Evans further argued that there existed two bases on which to restrict the catalogue of circumstances: first, the link to the basis of title; second, factors relating to the circumstances of the case, such as geographical factors and the parties' conduct.[363] While one could agree with Evans's argument in respect of the former, the same cannot be said for the latter. Geographical factors could themselves be relevant circumstances, and it would be circular to say that the list of relevant circumstances is limited by relevant circumstances themselves. Moreover, the parties' conduct could not determine the relevance of a circumstance, since conduct is only evidence of an agreement under Articles 74 and 83 UNCLOS.[364] The existence of agreement is ascertained before any factors could be identified as relevant circumstances in the second stage of delimitation. Evans concluded that 'the framework of analysis commonly resorted to fails to give guidance concerning what a relevant circumstance might be'.[365] Evans's ideas may have been convincing in relation to delimitation as understood in 1991. However, they do not persuade under the current legal framework.[366]

---

[360] The four delimitation stages according to Evans are: the identification of the area in dispute; the identification of the appropriate method of delimitation; the application of the practical method; and the assessment of the equitability of the result. See ibid. 87–9.
[361] Ibid.
[362] Ibid. 90–1.
[363] MD Evans, 'Maritime Delimitation and Expanding Categories of Relevant Circumstances' (1991) 40 *ICLQ* 1, 17–26.
[364] Section IV.A above.
[365] Evans (n. 363) 30.
[366] More recently, Evans wrote on relevant circumstances, but did not appear to suggest any manner in which such circumstances could be identified. See MD Evans, 'Relevant Circumstances' in A Oude Elferink et al. (eds.), *Maritime Boundary Delimitation – The Case Law: Is It Consistent and Predictable?* (CUP, 2018) 222, 247–60.

V IMPLICATIONS OF THE JUDICIAL APPROACH

In 1988, Weil criticised the Court's statement in *North Sea Continental Shelf* on the unlimited number of relevant circumstances.[367] According to Weil, only factors connected to the basis of title could be relevant circumstances.[368] However, Weil's view, which posited a relationship between relevant circumstances and the basis of title, cannot account for all the factors that international tribunals have found to be relevant circumstances. For instance, in *Jan Mayen* the ICJ shifted the FZ boundary in order to facilitate Denmark's access to capelin fisheries.[369] Access to natural resources does not concern the basis of title over maritime areas.[370] Weil's approach could be useful to explain why a number of factors could be relevant circumstances, yet it fails to provide a comprehensive framework.

In 2006, Tanaka suggested three criteria to identify relevant circumstances in the two-stage delimitation process applied at the time of his writing. First, relevant circumstances cannot 'run counter to the legal title of distance'; second, relevant circumstances are factors having 'geographically inequitable results when the equidistance method is resorted to'; third, relevant circumstances are only factors 'affect[ing] the rights over the maritime spaces involved'.[371] Tanaka accepted that a link to the basis of title could limit the number of relevant circumstances. Tanaka's second criterion is unconvincing. Relevant circumstances provide a legal justification for adjusting an equidistance line. Stating that factors could be relevant circumstances if they rendered an equidistance line inequitable overlooks that the function of relevant circumstances is not to render a line inequitable, but to remedy its inequitableness. Moreover, this criterion does not seem to be helpful in identifying relevant circumstances, since, instead of limiting the list of potential relevant circumstances, it could expand it. Any factor rendering an equidistance line inequitable could be a relevant circumstance, which reminds one of the open-ended list of relevant circumstances under *North Sea Continental Shelf*.

However, Tanaka emphasised a problem with the notion of relevant circumstances. Relevant circumstances provide both a benchmark against which international tribunals assess whether an equidistance

---

[367] *North Sea Continental Shelf* (n. 1) 50 [93].
[368] Weil (n. 190) 229.
[369] *Jan Mayen* (n. 49) 71–2 [75]–[76].
[370] Section III.A above.
[371] Y Tanaka, *Predictability and Flexibility in the Law of Maritime Delimitation* (Hart, 2006) 336–7.

line is inequitable, and the means to remedy inequitableness. The factors that could be relevant circumstances in a given case could be either related or unrelated to the dual 'title-function' basis. If the latter, they could not determine the adjustment of an equidistance line, although such a line could appear inequitable due to their presence. If the former, they could determine the adjustment of an equidistance line as relevant circumstances. Tanaka's second criterion entails that certain factors indicating that an equidistance line is inequitable could be relevant circumstances despite being unrelated to the dual 'title-function' basis. This conclusion contradicts long-standing international jurisprudence. Moreover, a 'factor' becomes a 'relevant circumstance' only when it has determined that an equidistance line is inequitable. Before then it is only a 'factor', a natural incident lacking legal significance.

Tanaka's third criterion seems to be connected to the functional basis of non-geographical relevant circumstances. However, Tanaka did not specify which relevant circumstances, geographical or non-geographical, would have the function of maritime zones as their legal basis. Tanaka also argued that factors such as conduct could be relevant circumstances, while whether security could be regarded to be a relevant circumstance remained obscure.[372] However, conduct has no link to the dual 'title-function' basis, while security is related to the *raison d'être* of both the continental shelf and the EEZ.[373] While Tanaka seemed correctly to suggest a functional criterion for identifying relevant circumstances, his conclusions do not seem fully consistent with his views.

Evans, Weil and Tanaka did not provide a fully convincing framework to identify relevant circumstances. However, one can explain the identification of relevant circumstances by reference to the dual 'title-function' basis. In *Libya/Malta*, the ICJ established a close link between the basis of title over maritime areas on one hand, and relevant circumstances on the other. According to the Court:

> [t]hat the questions of entitlement and of definition of continental shelf, on the one hand, and of delimitation of continental shelf on the other, are not only distinct but are also complementary is self-evident. The legal basis of that which is to be delimited, and of entitlement to it, cannot be other than pertinent to that delimitation.[374]

The Court also added that:

---

[372] Ibid. 298–9 and 313–14.
[373] Section III.C and IV.A above.
[374] *Libya/Malta* (n. 44) 30 [27].

although there is assuredly no closed list of considerations, it is evident that only those that are pertinent to the institution of the continental shelf as it has developed within the law, and to the application of equitable principles to its delimitation, will qualify for inclusion. Otherwise, the legal concept of continental shelf could itself be fundamentally changed by the introduction of considerations strange to its nature.[375]

International tribunals are unanimous in accepting geographical factors as the bedrock of delimitation.[376]

Various geographical factors have been considered to be relevant circumstances. Coastal length disparity relates to the basis of title insofar as '[t]he title of a State to the continental shelf and to the [EEZ] is based on the principle that the land dominates the sea through the projection of the coasts or the coastal fronts'.[377] Similarly, cut-off relates to the basis of title since it prevents the maritime entitlements of a state from being inequitably curtailed by the maritime entitlements of another state. Islands are also connected to the basis of title, as their coasts generate maritime entitlements under Article 121 UNCLOS. In *Qatar v. Bahrain*, the ICJ stated 'islands, regardless of their size, in this respect enjoy the same status, and therefore generate the same maritime rights, as other land territory'.[378] An island's character as a relevant circumstance could require that its maritime entitlement be limited in order to achieve an equitable solution. UNCLOS does not attribute distinct maritime entitlements to islands and to mainland states. However, an island's political status could support a finding on the effect of such an island reached on geographical grounds. The location of the land boundary is also a function of the basis of title, as it determines the starting point of a state's coast, and thus contributes to defining the extent of its maritime entitlements.

Nevertheless, the basis of title cannot account for all factors that international tribunals have found to be relevant circumstances. Navigation, access to natural resources and security have no direct relation to the basis of title. However, a functional relationship links the continental shelf and the EEZ to such factors.[379] The international

---

[375] Ibid. 40 [48].
[376] Section II above.
[377] *Black Sea* (n. 17) 89 [77].
[378] *Qatar v. Bahrain* (n. 84) 97 [185].
[379] Fietta and Cleverly suggested that '[t]he particular characteristics of the territorial sea can give rise to further special considerations that would not so readily apply in the continental shelf and EEZ'. See Fietta and Cleverly (n. 74) 107.

tribunals' approach suggests that the relevant circumstances unrelated to the basis of title are linked to the functions of the continental shelf and of the EEZ. Moreover, since *Eritrea/Yemen* international tribunals have established maritime boundaries not as a single exercise, but separately for the maritime zones within and beyond 12 nm, which upholds the functional connection between each maritime zone and the relevant circumstances relating to it.

The dual 'title-function' basis can also explain why certain factors have not been considered to be relevant circumstances. The cases show that international tribunals have not treated conduct and third-party interests, which are unrelated to either the basis of title or the function of maritime zones, as relevant circumstances. Geomorphology's character as a relevant circumstance is unclear. While it is linked to the basis of title over the continental shelf beyond 200 nm, international tribunals are reluctant to regard it as a relevant circumstance. The international tribunals' future decisions on delimitation beyond 200 nm might clarify this matter.

B   Weighing Relevant Circumstances

In *North Sea Continental Shelf*, the ICJ stated that 'more often than not it is the balancing-up of all ... considerations that will produce this result rather than reliance on one to the exclusion of all others'.[380] The Court added that '[t]he problem of the relative weight to be accorded to different considerations naturally varies with the circumstances of the case'.[381] In most delimitation disputes, states argue that multiple relevant circumstances exist. International tribunals are thus requested to determine their relative weight in order to adjust an equidistance line. This process is the 'weighing' of relevant circumstances, through which international tribunals measure the impact of each relevant circumstance on an equidistance line, with the aim of achieving an equitable solution.

The subjectivity of the weighing process has generated judicial and academic criticism. In *Jan Mayen*, Judge Schwebel commented on the effect of access to capelin fisheries on the adjustment of the equidistance line, lamenting that '[i]f what is lawful in maritime delimitation by the Court is what is equitable, and if what is equitable is as variable as the weather of The Hague, then this ... may be as defensible and desirable as

---

[380] *North Sea Continental Shelf* (n. 1) 50 [93].
[381] Ibid. 50 [93].

another'.[382] Similarly, Evans wrote that weighing relevant circumstances is a matter left to the international tribunals' discretion exercised 'within an ambit set not by external constraints, but by the [tribunal] itself'.[383]

The dual 'title-function' basis helps international tribunals in the weighing of relevant circumstances by excluding all factors that are irrelevant to delimitation, and that should thus not be considered in the weighing process. Moreover, the dual 'title-function' basis also helps an international tribunal to identify the circumstances that only pertain to one maritime zone, thus excluding them from being considered in the delimitation of other maritime zones. A special circumstance in territorial sea delimitation is not necessarily a relevant circumstance in continental shelf and EEZ delimitation. Tanaka suggested that there is a hierarchy of circumstances. Geographical circumstances are considered first, while non-geographical circumstances are considered only at the verification stage, when international tribunals verify that the boundary achieves an equitable solution.[384] However, the three-stage approach does not envisage the analysis of non-geographical circumstances at the verification stage, which only requires a disproportionality assessment.[385] Furthermore, hierarchy between circumstances lacks legal basis. International tribunals consider all relevant circumstances to be on the same plane, which suggests that, within the second stage of delimitation, no relevant circumstance is hierarchically superior to another.

Delimitation cannot be reduced to a mechanical exercise, in which international tribunals apply well-defined criteria to establish a boundary. If this were the case, there would be no reason to request international tribunals to adjudicate maritime boundary disputes. It is precisely because solving such disputes is complex that states trigger third-party dispute settlement. Moreover, maritime delimitation is not declaratory but constitutive. International tribunals do not discover pre-existing boundaries, but they establish them *de novo*.[386] In delimiting maritime boundaries international tribunals do not set out to find a 'right answer', but they endeavour to find an equitable solution pursuant to Articles 74 and 83 UNCLOS. To establish maritime boundaries, international tribunals follow a delimitation process, which may lead different

---

[382] *Jan Mayen* (n. 49) 120 (Separate Opinion Schwebel).
[383] Evans (n. 363) 29.
[384] Tanaka (n. 371) 348.
[385] On disproportionality, see Chapter 6 below.
[386] Weil (n. 190) 48–50.

tribunals to different solutions, all legally acceptable and equitable under UNCLOS. So long as international tribunals follow the various stages of the delimitation process, they will reach one of the legally acceptable solutions.

Establishing an equidistance line is a geometric exercise, which could be seen to have a pre-determined outcome. By contrast, relevant circumstances provide flexibility in delimitation, as on their basis international tribunals can adjust an equidistance line. International tribunals retain a degree of discretion in assessing the impact of relevant circumstances in maritime delimitation. Should only one relevant circumstance exist, international tribunals need not weigh it against any other relevant circumstance. While international tribunals are requested to assess the impact of various factors on delimitation, their decisions show that typically only one factor qualifies as a relevant circumstance requiring the boundary to be adjusted. For example, in *Bangladesh/Myanmar* the only relevant circumstance determining the shifting of the provisional equidistance line was cut-off.[387] Where adjustment is required by more than one circumstance, it is generally in connection with distinct maritime areas, and the boundary of each area is thus shifted based on only one circumstance. The *Bangladesh* v. *India* tribunal adjusted the equidistance line in the territorial sea based on the location of the land boundary terminus, while the equidistance line beyond 12 nm was adjusted based on cut-off.[388]

On occasion, international tribunals are required to weigh multiple factors. However, in this case international tribunals typically proceed in phases. First, they adjust the provisional equidistance line based on one relevant circumstance, which already results in an adjusted line. Second, they further adjust that line on account of another relevant circumstance. This process takes place for all subsequent relevant circumstances.

Nicaragua v. *Colombia* exemplifies this process. First, the Court shifted the provisional equidistance line eastwards to abate the effect of coastal length disparity. Second, the Court decided that the boundary should run eastwards along two parallels of latitude, starting at the northernmost point of the provisional equidistance line and at the easternmost point of the 12-nm arcs of circle around East-Southeast Cays. This reduced the cut-off of Nicaragua's coastal projections.[389] Even if multiple relevant

---

[387] Section II.A above.
[388] Section II.A and II.D above.
[389] *Nicaragua* v. *Colombia* (n. 26) 709–13 [232]–[237].

circumstances existed, no weighing process actually takes place. The impact of multiple relevant circumstances is assessed in turn, and the adjustment of an equidistance line takes place in subsequent phases, each resulting in the adjustment of the provisional equidistance line based on one relevant circumstance.

At present, the weighing process is not an issue arising in practice. The prevailing, although implicit, view among international tribunals is that all relevant circumstances contribute to adjusting a provisional equidistance line. A weighing process would be required if multiple relevant circumstances determined the adjustment of an equidistance line in a single operation. This may have been the correct view in the cases before boundaries were delimited by way of the two-stage, later three-stage, approach, in which the holistic consideration of all relevant circumstances would indicate the applicable delimitation method. In fact, international tribunals only mentioned the 'weighing' of relevant circumstances in three cases: *North Sea Continental Shelf*,[390] *Tunisia/Libya*[391] and *Jan Mayen*.[392] The reference to the weighing process in *Jan Mayen* could be seen to be an oddity, as in that case the ICJ delimited the maritime boundary by means of a two-stage approach, and not by choosing a delimitation method having taken into account all relevant circumstances. However, as *Jan Mayen* was the first application of the two-stage approach, the Court's reference to the weighing of relevant circumstances could be considered to be a remnant of the earlier approach. Since 1993, international tribunals have not explicitly mentioned the weighing of relevant circumstances. The weighing process is not an operation with which international tribunals currently concern themselves.

C Adjusting a Provisional Equidistance Line

A complex issue connected to relevant circumstances is how to adjust an equidistance line in practice. While negotiated boundaries could achieve whatever solution the states concerned deem suitable, delimitation by judicial process could not establish inequitable boundaries, as Articles 74 and 83 UNCLOS limit the international tribunals' discretion by requiring

---

[390] *North Sea Continental Shelf* (n. 1) 50 [93].
[391] *Tunisia/Libya* (n. 99) 44 [38].
[392] *Jan Mayen* (n. 49) 63 [58].

that delimitation achieve an equitable solution. Nevertheless, it is difficult to identify *a priori* how to effect an equitable adjustment.

1 The adjustment and the judicial function

In their individual opinions, certain judges have criticised the subjectivity of the adjustment operation. In *Libya/Malta*, Judge Oda stated that there was 'no convincing ground whatsoever for shifting the delimitation line along a meridian which in essence bears no geographical relation to Libya and Malta'.[393] In *Jan Mayen*, Judge Schwebel compared the equitable adjustment of an equidistance line to the variable weather of The Hague.[394] More recently, Judges Abraham, Keith and Xue criticised the adjustment in *Nicaragua v. Colombia* for being arbitrary.[395]

Despite this well-founded criticism, a degree of arbitrariness seems inescapable in assessing how relevant circumstances impact on an equidistance line in practice. In adjusting an equidistance line, international tribunals may find guidance in the parties' pleadings, in which the states concerned both indicate the factors to which they attach particular importance, and suggest whether and how to adjust an equidistance line. For example, in *Black Sea* Romania argued that 'the existing geographical background and relevant circumstances [did] not [justify] any further adjustment of the equidistant/median line'.[396] Conversely, Ukraine contended that 'it would ... be necessary to adjust the provisional line, account being taken ... in particular of the very marked disparity between coastal lengths'.[397] On this basis, Ukraine suggested that the:

> adjustment can be realized through a shifting of the provisional line in a south-westerly direction up to a line starting from Point 1 at 45°05'21"N; 30°02'27"E (... labelled Point A of the provisional equidistance line), and passing through Point 2 at 44°54'00"N; 30°06'00"E, and then following the azimuth 156 until Point 3 at 43°20'37"N; 31°05'39"E ... From Point 3, the line continues along the same azimuth until it reaches a point where the interests of third States potentially will come into play. No terminal point can therefore be indicated for that line, which ends with an arrow.[398]

---

[393] *Libya/Malta* (n. 44) 138 [25] (Dissenting Opinion Oda).
[394] *Jan Mayen* (n. 49) 120 (Separate Opinion Schwebel).
[395] *Nicaragua v. Colombia* (n. 26) 735–9 [22]–[33] (Separate Opinion Abraham); ibid. 744 [9] (Declaration Keith); ibid. 747–9 [5]–[9] (Declaration Xue).
[396] Memorial of Romania (19 August 2005), 239.
[397] Counter-memorial of Ukraine (19 May 2006), 238 [9.26].
[398] Ibid. 238–9 [9.26].

While the parties' arguments could inspire international tribunals, they could not limit them. In maritime delimitation, international tribunals have jurisdiction to apply the indeterminate delimitation rules under UNCLOS and customary international law. They could thus be seen to have the power to exercise discretion to achieve an equitable solution, which does not require them necessarily to uphold the parties' requests.

Nonetheless, international tribunals seem to have an interest in the implementation of their delimitation decisions,[399] which could justify seriously considering the parties' arguments on the adjustment. In relation to the ICJ, Hernández wrote that '[i]n the international legal order, with no centralized judicial authority and a lack of enforcement mechanisms for judicial decisions, a judgment's authority is even more content dependent, as its authority is tightly intertwined with the reasons given in its support'.[400] Kennedy similarly stated that the Court crafts 'its decisions to enhance its legitimacy and pull towards compliance'.[401]

If a judicially established boundary strikes a balance between the lines suggested by the parties, such parties may likely be more willing to implement the judicial decision establishing that boundary. In adjusting an equidistance line, international tribunals may seem to relinquish their judicial function and approach that of a policy-maker. The adjustment of an equidistance line could be seen to be the judicial function's vanishing point in maritime delimitation. While the principal function of international tribunals is to settle international disputes peacefully, the exercise of the judicial function is fully successful when a dispute is not only settled, but also when the states legally bound to comply with a judicial decision have done so. The adjustment of an equidistance line is an instrument to establish a boundary that is not only in accordance with the applicable law, but also with which the states concerned would comply. Based on her assessment of the delimitation decisions up to 2005, Klein wrote that '[t]he typical tactic is for States to submit maximalist claims . . . and [international tribunals] are left the task of devising a compromise position between these claims to achieve an "equitable

---

[399] See JS Warioba, 'Monitoring Compliance with and Enforcement of Binding Decisions of International Courts' (2001) 5 *MPYUNL* 41; P Couvreur, *The International Court of Justice and the Effectiveness of International Law* (Brill, 2017) 79.

[400] GI Hernández, *The International Court of Justice and the Judicial Function* (OUP, 2014) 99.

[401] D Kennedy, 'The *Nuclear Weapons* Case' in L Boisson de Chazournes and P Sands (eds.), *International Law, the International Court of Justice and Nuclear Weapons* (CUP, 1999) 462, 464.

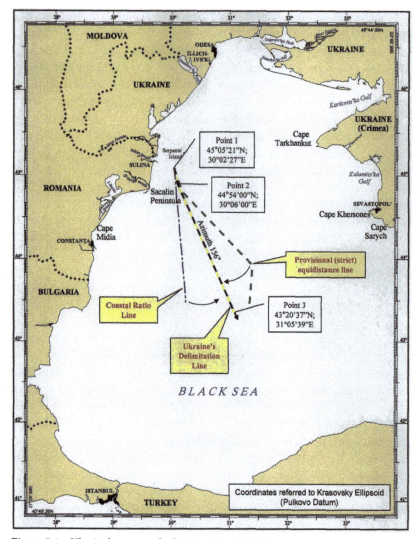

Figure 5.1 Ukraine's proposed adjustment in *Black Sea*
Source: [2009] ICJ *Black Sea* – Rejoinder of Ukraine, Figure 7.3

result'".[402] A reading of the existing delimitation decisions gives the impression that international tribunals endeavour to find equitable solutions capable of reconciling the parties' requests, with the implicit purpose of promoting compliance with their judicial decisions.

[402] N Klein, *Dispute Settlement in the UN Convention on the Law of the Sea* (CUP, 2005) 254.

2 The methods for adjusting an equidistance line

International tribunals have used different methods to adjust equidistance lines. For example, international tribunals have shifted entire equidistance lines closer to the coast of one of the parties. In *Libya/Malta*, the ICJ 'decided that the equitable boundary line is a line produced by transposing the median line northwards through 18' of latitude'.[403] Moreover, international tribunals have deflected part of the provisional equidistance line from a point with specific co-ordinates. In *Bangladesh/Myanmar* ITLOS determined that 'the adjustment of the provisional equidistance line should commence at point X with coordinates 20°03'32.0"N, 91°50'31.8"E, where the equidistance line begins to cut off the southward projection of the coast of Bangladesh'.[404] ITLOS subsequently found that 'any plausible adjustment of the provisional equidistance line would not differ substantially from a geodetic line starting at an azimuth of 215°'.[405] The *Bangladesh v. India* tribunal similarly decided that, from a point with co-ordinates 21°07'44.8"N, 89°13'56-5"E, 'the adjusted line ... within and beyond 200 nm is a geodetic line with an initial azimuth of 177°30'00" until this line meets with the maritime boundary established by [ITLOS] to delimit the [EEZ] and the continental shelf between Bangladesh and Myanmar'.[406]

The issue arises concerning whether determining that islands should have reduced effect amounts to adjusting an equidistance line.[407] Determining the effect of islands could be a 'creeping circumstance' if performed when selecting the base points to draw an equidistance line. This practice is unsound, as it conflates operations pertaining to different phases of the three-stage delimitation process. International tribunals should refrain from placing base points on islands, in order for it to be determined at the second stage of delimitation.[408] Pursuant to Article 121 UNCLOS, islands generate both maritime entitlements up to 200 nm, and continental shelf entitlements beyond 200 nm if the Article 76 UNCLOS conditions are satisfied. Reducing the effect of islands curtails such maritime entitlements, and could thus be seen to amount to adjusting an equidistance line.

---

[403] *Libya/Malta* (n. 44) 52 [73].
[404] *Bangladesh/Myanmar* (n. 3) 88 [331].
[405] Ibid. 89 [334].
[406] *Bangladesh v. India* (n. 33) 163 [478].
[407] Murphy seems implicitly to accept that reducing the effect of islands amounts to adjusting a provisional equidistance line. See Murphy (n. 165) 182.
[408] Chapter 4, Section IV.B above.

In this perspective, a third method for adjusting the equidistance line is to reduce the effect of islands. This has been done in a number of cases.[409] The Court of Arbitration decided to enclave the Channel Islands in the *Anglo/French Arbitration*. Half effect was awarded to the Scilly Isles in the *Anglo/French Arbitration*, to the Kerkennah Islands in *Tunisia/Libya*, and to Seal Island in *Gulf of Maine*. Moreover, international tribunals awarded no effect to Abu Musa in *Dubai/Sharjah*, to the so-called 'îlots éparpillés' in *Guinea/Guinea-Bissau*, to al-Tayr and al-Zubayr in *Eritrea/Yemen*, to Fasht al Jarim in *Qatar* v. *Bahrain*, to Serpents' Island in *Black Sea*, and to St. Martin's Island in *Bangladesh/Myanmar*.

In *Nicaragua* v. *Colombia*, the ICJ adjusted the provisional equidistance line using a combination of two methods. First, it shifted the entire equidistance line eastwards on account of coastal length disparity, drawing 'a line each point on which is three times as far from the controlling base point on the Nicaraguan islands as it is from the controlling base point on the Colombian islands'.[410] This decision seemed to find a balance between half effect and no effect. Second, to avoid cutting off Nicaragua's coastal projections the Court traced two lines along parallels of latitude starting from the northernmost point of the already-shifted boundary and from the easternmost point on the 12-nm envelope of arcs around East-Southeast Cays.[411]

Nicaragua v. *Colombia* raised the problematic issue as to whether the adjustment of a provisional equidistance line should be limited. The Court held that the three-stage approach 'does not preclude very substantial adjustment to ... the provisional line in an appropriate case, nor does it preclude the use of enclaving in those areas where the use of such a technique is needed to achieve an equitable result'.[412] However, Judge Keith wrote that '[t]he latitudinal lines to the east and the starting-point for the southern one ... can find no possible justification in terms of any shifting of a provisional median line lying between the Colombian islands and the Nicaraguan coast'.[413] Concerning the enclaving of Quintasueño and Serrana and the latitudinal lines, Judge Xue stated that '[i]t is hard to justify them as "adjustment of" or "shifting from" the provisional median line', if the latter does not mean total departure'.[414]

Judge Abraham also maintained that the latitudinal lines cannot be regarded 'as a mere "adjustment" or even "shifting" of the provisional

---

[409] Section II.C above.
[410] *Nicaragua* v. *Colombia* (n. 26) 710 [234].
[411] Ibid. 713 [237].
[412] Ibid. 697 [197].
[413] Ibid. 744 [9] (Declaration Keith).
[414] Ibid. 748 [8] (Declaration Xue).

line',[415] since 'those lines are actually entirely unrelated to the provisional line'.[416] According to Judge Abraham, 'the Court terms an "adjustment" or "shift" a process which does not really merit being termed as such'.[417] Among academic writers, Evans criticised the Court's approach. Concerning the Court's statement that adjustment need not be minor, Evans commented that 'this reduces the provisional equidistance line to a cipher, something to be adopted, amended or abandoned as the circumstances suggest'.[418] Evans suggested that this *modus operandi* 'is really nothing new at all in the idea that the appropriate method should be determined in the light of the relevant circumstances of the case, this being the approach taken way back in 1984 in the *Gulf of Maine* case'.[419]

The criticism against *Nicaragua v. Colombia* does not seem entirely justified. *Nicaragua v. Colombia* is consistent with an earlier statement in *Guyana v. Suriname*. Guyana argued that the *Beagle Channel* award suggested that in territorial sea delimitation deviation from the median line should be minor. The arbitral tribunal rejected this contention, finding that '[t]he *Beagle Channel* tribunal's statement that there was little deviation from the strict median line was merely descriptive; it was not prescribing that any deviation from the median line based on navigational concerns need be minor'.[420] In territorial sea delimitation, deviation from the equidistance line need not be minor. Yet, territorial sea boundaries should be as close to an equidistance line as possible, having considered all special circumstances.[421] If the *Guyana v. Suriname* statement is correct in territorial sea delimitation, for which Article 15 UNCLOS requires boundaries to be delimited by equidistance, it is *a fortiori* correct in continental shelf and EEZ delimitation, for which Articles 74 and 83 UNCLOS only require the achievement of an equitable solution.

The treatment of islands in delimitation also suggests that adjustments need not be minor. Although reducing the effect of islands could be seen to be a substantial adjustment, it is difficult to dispute that it is an adjustment nonetheless. If islands are enclaved, the resulting equidistance line deviates considerably with respect to the situation in which full effect is given to such islands. In the *Anglo/French Arbitration*, if the Channel Islands had not been enclaved, the equidistance line would have taken a turn

---

[415] Ibid. 738 [32] (Separate Opinion Abraham).
[416] Ibid.
[417] Ibid. 738 [33] (Separate Opinion Abraham).
[418] MD Evans, 'Maritime Boundary Delimitation: Whatever Next?' in J Barrett and R Barnes (eds.), *Law of the Sea - UNCLOS as a Living Treaty* (BIICL, 2016) 41, 60.
[419] Ibid.
[420] *Guyana v. Suriname* (n. 177) 85 [305].
[421] Art. 15 UNCLOS. See Lando (n. 222) 605–10.

southwards in the boundary's central segment. However, enclavement determined an equidistance line running in an east-west direction.

Enclaving islands is inconsistent with the principle that adjustments should be minor. Awarding no effect to islands has a result similar to enclavement, as it may determine a substantial adjustment of an equidistance line. In *Bangladesh/Myanmar*, ITLOS gave no effect to St. Martin's Island in delimiting the boundary beyond 12 nm.

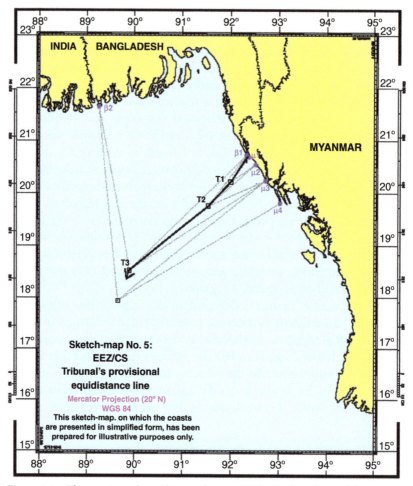

Figure 5.2 The provisional equidistance line established in *Bangladesh/Myanmar*
Source: [2012] ITLOS Rep 77

V IMPLICATIONS OF THE JUDICIAL APPROACH

However, if St. Martin's Island had been given full effect, as Bangladesh had argued,[422] the boundary would have taken a noticeably different course.

The view that the adjustment of an equidistance line must be minor seems unconvincing, and does not account for the considerable adjustments that

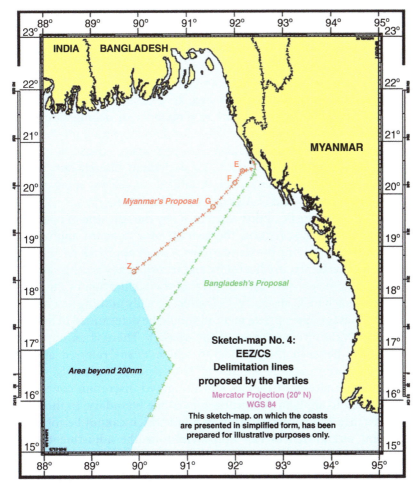

Figure 5.3 The parties' proposed provisional equidistance lines in *Bangladesh/Myanmar*
Source: [2012] ITLOS Rep 75

---

[422] *Bangladesh/Myanmar* (n. 3) 82–4 [298]–[308].

reducing the effect of islands may have on the course of maritime boundaries. Moreover, there seems to be no legal basis to argue that the adjustment of a provisional equidistance should be limited. Articles 74 and 83 UNCLOS simply require that delimitation achieve an equitable solution. This objective could require international tribunals substantially to adjust provisional equidistance lines.

The three-stage approach attempts to find the difficult balance between the equitable solution requirement under UNCLOS and the need for predictability. International tribunals ensure that the latter is achieved by using equidistance at the first stage of delimitation, and the former is ensured by adjusting the equidistance line should relevant circumstances so require. Equidistance, or a variant closely resembling it, is an equitable solution in the vast majority of delimitation cases. Nevertheless, achieving an equitable solution may require international tribunals to adjust an equidistance line more incisively, as in *Nicaragua v. Colombia*. The international tribunals' discretionary adjustment of equidistance lines renders it difficult to achieve complete certainty, predictability and transparency in delimitation.

Nevertheless, the flexibility introduced by the adjustment operation neither removes nor reduces the benefits of a standard approach to delimitation. Applying the standard three-stage approach ensures that a degree of certainty, predictability and transparency is achieved. One could not agree entirely with Evans that the application of the three-stage approach in *Nicaragua* v. *Colombia* 'is really nothing new at all in the idea that the appropriate method should be determined in the light of the relevant circumstances of the case'.[423] There is an important distinction between the method to which Evans referred and the three-stage approach as applied in *Nicaragua v. Colombia*. In the former, international tribunals had unlimited discretion concerning the method to apply in delimiting a maritime boundary. In the latter, equidistance is a necessary starting point which cannot be foregone. Relevant circumstances can only determine the adjustment of an equidistance line, and not the adoption of an entirely different delimitation method. The adjustment of an equidistance line can be substantial so long as its effect remains that of modifying the line established at the first stage of delimitation, and not of determining the adoption of a delimitation method other than the three-stage approach.

[423] Evans (n. 418) 60.

VI Consistency in Evaluating Relevant Circumstances

International tribunals have reached a degree of consistency in evaluating relevant circumstances at the second stage of the delimitation process. The identification of the factors capable of being relevant circumstances could be seen to be based on the link between such factors and either the basis of title, or the function of maritime zones. Factors unrelated both to the basis of title, and to the functions of maritime zones, have not been treated as relevant circumstances. In addition, the decisions of international tribunals show that like circumstances are treated in a like manner, which ensures consistency with the earlier jurisprudence on delimitation.

The weighing of relevant circumstances should be regarded as a non-issue. International tribunals do not weigh relevant circumstances in order to adjust an equidistance line by way of a single operation. Each relevant circumstance determines an adjustment of the provisional equidistance line, and the boundary's overall adjustment is thus divided into as many adjustments as there are relevant circumstances. The real question is how the adjustment is effected, and whether it must be minor. The need to achieve an equitable solution under UNCLOS entails that the adjustment is discretionary. However, what limits international tribunals in effecting the adjustment is that they must take the equidistance line as its starting point. Adjustments need not be minor. Whether they are so is determined by the peculiarities of the case, which in turn influence the methods to abate the inequitableness of an equidistance line. Substantial adjustments of equidistance lines appear consistent with Articles 74 and 83 UNCLOS, as well as with the need to ensure a degree of certainty, predictability and transparency in applying the three-stage approach. While in most cases substantial adjustments are not necessary, there could be cases in which, in order to achieve an equitable solution, an equidistance line ought to be considerably adjusted.

6

Disproportionality

I Disproportionality as the Final Stage of the Delimitation Process

Upon reaching the last stage of the delimitation process, international tribunals have already determined the relevant coast and the relevant area,[1] constructed an equidistance line,[2] and might have adjusted that line based on relevant circumstances.[3] International tribunals should approach both determining the relevant coast and the relevant area, and drawing an equidistance line, as objective exercises contributing to the achievement of an equitable solution only indirectly.[4] By contrast, adjusting the provisional equidistance line both based on relevant circumstances, and based on disproportionality, specifically aims at achieving an equitable solution. Whereas relevant circumstances are the chief means for ensuring that an inequitable equidistance line may be made into an equitable boundary, disproportionality is a final test for the overall equitableness of the solution.

In *Black Sea*, the International Court of Justice (ICJ or Court) explained that disproportionality requires international tribunals to verify that the line emerging from the previous stages of the delimitation process:

> does not ... lead to an inequitable result by reason of any marked disproportion between the ratio of the respective coastal lengths and the ratio between the relevant maritime area of each State by reference to the

---

[1] Chapter 3 above.
[2] Chapter 4 above.
[3] Chapter 5 above. See also *Maritime Delimitation in the Black Sea (Romania v. Ukraine)* (Judgment) [2009] ICJ Rep 61, 101 [118].
[4] The ICJ stated that equidistance is *prima facie* equitable. See *Maritime Delimitation in the Area between Greenland and Jan Mayen (Denmark v. Norway)* (Judgment) [1993] ICJ Rep 38, 66 [64].

delimitation line .... A final check for an equitable outcome entails a confirmation that no great disproportionality of maritime areas is evident by comparison to the ratio of coastal lengths.[5]

There has so far never been a case in which international tribunals found that a boundary failed to satisfy the disproportionality test. One could thus doubt the practical impact of disproportionality on the delimitation process. It has been argued that international tribunals should dispense with disproportionality altogether. Evans wrote that there is an:

> option which deserves serious contemplation: to accept that proportionality should no longer play any formal role in the process of maritime boundary delimitation conducted on the basis of international law. It does not fit and it does not help. So why do it?[6]

Tanaka is more cautious. He stated that 'the important role of proportionality appears to be well established in the case law',[7] and that 'the only realistic road to progress is to attempt to objectify the application of proportionality by devising a method or methods of identification and calculation of the relevant coasts and areas'.[8] Apart from sporadic considerations in some case commentaries, academic writers have rarely taken an interest in disproportionality.[9]

---

[5] *Black Sea* (n. 3) 103 [122].
[6] MD Evans, 'Maritime Boundary Delimitation: Where Do We Go From Here?' in D Freestone et al. (eds.), *Law of the Sea – Progress and Prospects* (OUP, 2006) 137, 156.
[7] Y Tanaka, 'Reflections on the Concept of Proportionality in the Law of Maritime Delimitation' (2001) 16 *IJMCL* 433, 461.
[8] ibid. The same ideas are expressed in Y Tanaka, *Predictability and Flexibility in the Law of Maritime Delimitation* (Hart, 2006) 161–83.
[9] Y Tanaka, 'The Disproportionality Test in the Law of Maritime Delimitation' in A Oude Elferink et al. (eds.), *Maritime Boundary Delimitation – The Case Law: is it Consistent and Predictable?* (CUP, 2018) 291; J-H Paik, 'The Role of Proportionality in Maritime Delimitation: State of the Jurisprudence' in HP Hestermeyer et al. (eds.), *Coexistence, Cooperation and Solidarity – Liber Amicorum Rüdiger Wolfrum* (Martinus Nijhoff, 2012) 199; R Ida, 'The Role of Proportionality in Maritime Delimitation Revisited: The Origin and Meaning of the Principle from the Early Decisions of the Court' in N Ando et al. (eds.), *Liber Amicorum Judge Shigeru Oda* (Martinus Nijhoff, 2002) vol. II, 1037; G Jaenicke, 'The Role of Proportionality in the Delimitation of Maritime Zones' in A Bos and H Siblesz (eds.), *Realism in Law-Making – Essays on International Law in Honour of Willem Riphagen* (Martinus Nijhoff, 1986) 51. Writings not exclusively dealing with proportionality include: P Weil, *Perspectives du Droit de la Délimitation Maritime* (Pédone, 1988) 250–60; MD Evans, *Relevant Circumstances and Maritime Delimitation* (OUP, 1989) 224–31; T Cottier, *Equitable Principles of Maritime Boundary Delimitation* (CUP, 2015) 541–59; S Fietta and R Cleverly, *A Practitioner's Guide to Maritime Boundary Delimitation* (OUP, 2016) 602–9.

This chapter explores these questions by analysing the approach of international tribunals to disproportionality. First, this chapter argues that proportionality stemmed from a conceptual mistake made by the ICJ in *North Sea Continental Shelf*. Second, it shows that the assessment of disproportionality in the cases is generally consistent with the basis of title. Third, it analyses the relationship between coastal length disparity as a relevant circumstance and disproportionality, arguing that the former and the latter are both useful components of the three-stage approach.

Section II clarifies the terminology used in this chapter. Section III examines the legal basis of disproportionality. Section IV discusses the judicial approach to disproportionality. Section V examines the relationship between coastal length disparity and disproportionality. Section VI concludes.

II A Note on Terminology

International tribunals have referred to the operation taking place at the third stage of the delimitation both as 'proportionality', and as 'disproportionality'. The question arises as to whether this difference in terminology entails a distinction in the practical assessment carried out at the third stage of delimitation.[10] The relevant decisions show that the use of the two distinct terms 'proportionality' and 'disproportionality' does not appear to correspond to two distinct manners of carrying out the operation at the third stage of the delimitation process.

The Chamber of the ICJ in *Gulf of Maine* was the first to use the word 'disproportion' in the context of comparing coastal length and maritime areas. The Chamber stated that:

> maritime delimitation can certainly not be established by a direct division of the area in dispute proportional to the respective lengths of the coasts belonging to the parties in the relevant area, but it is equally certain that a substantial disproportion to the lengths of those coasts that resulted from a delimitation effected on a different basis would constitute a circumstance calling for an appropriate correction.[11]

It appears to be the Chamber's view that, when comparing the length of the relevant coasts to the maritime areas appertaining to each party,

---

[10] See C Sun, 'Comments on the Three-stage Approach of Maritime Delimitation' in MH Nordquist et al. (eds.), *Challenges of the Changing Arctic – Continental Shelf, Navigation, and Fisheries* (Martinus Nijhoff, 2016) 613, 629–31 and 635.

[11] *Delimitation of the Maritime Boundary in the Gulf of Maine Area (Canada/USA)* (Judgment) [1984] ICJ Rep 246, 323 [185].

II A NOTE ON TERMINOLOGY

international tribunals check for the lack of 'substantial disproportion'. However, the Chamber conflated two distinct concepts in this passage, which casts doubts on its reasoning.[12] In *Libya/Malta*, the ICJ spoke of both proportionality and disproportion. The Court found that 'there is certainly no evident disproportion in the areas of shelf attributed to each of the Parties respectively such that it could be said that the requirements of the test of proportionality as an aspect of equity were not satisfied'.[13] The Court seemed to establish a link between proportionality and disproportionality, as the lack of 'evident disproportion' entailed that the proportionality test was satisfied.

The Court of Arbitration in *St. Pierre et Miquelon* made a statement which followed the ICJ's decision in *Libya/Malta*. It held 'qu'il n'y a certainement pas disproportion entre les espaces relevant de chacune des Parties',[14] and that, as a consequence, 'les exigences du test de proportionnalité, en tant qu'aspect de l'équité, ont été satisfaites'.[15] Similarly, the *Eritrea/Yemen* arbitral tribunal conducted what it called the 'test of proportionality'[16] by assessing that 'the line or delimitation it has decided upon results in no disproportion'.[17] The same took place in *Barbados v. Trinidad and Tobago*, in which the arbitral tribunal held that it would 'examine the outcome in the light of proportionality',[18] only to find that what it had to assess was whether the delimitation line traced would 'avoid gross disproportion in the outcome of the delimitation'.[19]

The ICJ took a different approach in *Black Sea*. In that case, the Court did not find that proportionality was satisfied by the absence of disproportion, but assessed whether 'the result thus far arrived at ... does not lead to any significant disproportionality by reference to the respective coastal lengths and the apportionment of areas that ensue'.[20] The Court later upheld this approach in *Peru v. Chile*,[21] which the International

---

[12] Section IV.A.1 below.
[13] *Continental Shelf (Libya/Malta)* (Judgment) [1985] ICJ Rep 13, 55 [75].
[14] *Delimitation of Maritime Areas between Canada and France (St. Pierre et Miquelon) (Canada/France)* (1992) XXI RIAA 265, 297 [93].
[15] Ibid.
[16] *Second Stage of the Proceedings between Eritrea and Yemen (Maritime Delimitation) (Eritrea/Yemen)* (1999) XXII RIAA 335, 372.
[17] Ibid. 373 [168].
[18] *Maritime Boundary Arbitration (Barbados v. Trinidad and Tobago)* (2006) XXVII RIAA 247, 243 [376].
[19] Ibid. 244 [376].
[20] *Black Sea* (n. 3) 129 [210].
[21] *Maritime Dispute (Peru v. Chile)* (Judgment) [2014] ICJ Rep 3, 69–71 [192]–[194].

Tribunal for the Law of the Sea (ITLOS or Tribunal) also adopted. In *Bangladesh/Myanmar*, ITLOS assessed 'whether the adjusted equidistance line ... caused a significant disproportion by reference to the ratio of the length of the coastlines of the Parties and the ratio of the relevant maritime area allocated to each Party'.[22] The *Bangladesh v. India* tribunal followed suit.[23]

Nicaragua v. Colombia is instructive in relation to the supposed distinction between proportionality and disproportionality. Discussing the third stage of delimitation, the Court stated that:

> it is not applying a principle of strict proportionality. Maritime delimitation is not designed to produce a correlation between the lengths of the Parties' relevant coasts and their respective shares of the relevant area. . . . The Court's task is to check for a significant disproportionality. What constitutes such a disproportionality will vary according to the precise situation in each case, for the third stage of the process cannot require the Court to disregard all of the considerations which were important in the earlier stages.[24]

Subsequently, the Court considered that:

> its task, at this third stage, is not to attempt to achieve even an approximate correlation between the ratio of the lengths of the Parties' relevant coasts and the ratio of their respective shares of the relevant area. It is, rather, to ensure that there is not a disproportion so gross as to 'taint' the result and render it inequitable. Whether any disproportion is so great as to have that effect is not a question capable of being answered by reference to any mathematical formula but is a matter which can be answered only in the light of all the circumstances of the particular case.[25]

The Court mentioned both proportionality and disproportionality, stating that the third stage of the delimitation process cannot entail disregard for the considerations made in the earlier stages. According to the Court, the aim of the third stage of delimitation is to establish that there is no 'disproportion so gross as to "taint" the result and render it inequitable'.[26]

---

[22] *Delimitation of the Maritime Boundary in the Bay of Bengal (Bangladesh/Myanmar)* (Judgment) [2012] ITLOS Rep 4, 126 [497].

[23] *Bay of Bengal Maritime Boundary Arbitration (Bangladesh v. India)* (2014) 167 ILR 1, 146–69 [438]–[497].

[24] *Territorial and Maritime Dispute (Nicaragua v. Colombia)* (Judgment) [2012] ICJ Rep 624, 715 [240].

[25] Ibid. 716 [242].

[26] Ibid.

II A NOTE ON TERMINOLOGY

The Court seemed to suggest that assessing proportionality entails an active function by international tribunals to ensure the existence of a correlation between the parties' respective portion of the relevant area and the length of their respective relevant coasts. Conversely, the Court suggested that disproportionality requires international tribunals to assess the relationship between the length of the relevant coast and the marine areas appertaining to each state more flexibly, as only gross disproportion could taint the boundary ensuing from the second stage of the delimitation process.

However, judicial decisions suggest that international tribunals have approached the third stage of the delimitation process in the same manner across all cases by comparing coastal length ratios to marine area ratios. While international tribunals have not calculated mathematical ratios in all cases, they have always done so since introducing the three-stage approach.[27] The international tribunals' method for assessing proportionality does not appear to differ from the method for assessing disproportionality. This suggests that resorting to distinct terms to designate the third stage of the delimitation process does not necessarily mean that international tribunals carry out different operations depending on the terminology in use.

The absence of disproportionality seems to entail the existence of at least some degree of proportionality. International tribunals have consistently held that proportionality does not require the mathematical apportionment of maritime areas based on coastal length ratios.[28] In *Libya/Malta*, the ICJ stated that in assessing proportionality the Court makes a 'broad assessment of the equitableness of the result'.[29] However, in *Nicaragua v. Colombia* the ICJ for the first time linked proportionality to mathematical apportionment. If mathematical apportionment were the essence of proportionality, the Court would have been correct in stating that, at the third stage of the delimitation process, it should check not for proportionality, but for the lack of disproportionality. However, in this manner the Court misconstrued the proportionality test as one requiring exact mathematical correspondence between coastal length ratios and marine area ratios. Both proportionality and disproportionality entail a flexible assessment of coastal length ratios and marine area ratios. There seems to be no

---

[27] Section IV.B.2 below.
[28] *Gulf of Maine* (n. 11) 323 [185]; *Jan Mayen* (n. 4) 68 [68]; *Barbados v. Trinidad and Tobago* (n. 18) 243–4 [376].
[29] *Libya/Malta* (n. 13) 55 [75].

difference between designating the third stage of the delimitation process as 'proportionality' or 'disproportionality'.

Following the terminology currently employed by international tribunals, this chapter designates the third stage of the delimitation process as the disproportionality test. When discussing specific cases, this chapter follows the terminology used in those cases.

III The Legal Basis of Disproportionality

The meaning of disproportionality evolved over time, which affected its legal basis under international law. The following sections examine this evolution.

A Proportionality as a Delimitation Method

Disproportionality is not a creation of *North Sea Continental Shelf*. The earliest reference to proportionality is in a 1946 article by FA Vallat on the Truman Proclamation.[30] Vallat wrote that the Truman Proclamation 'says that the [continental shelf] boundary is to be determined "in accordance with equitable principles"', but at the same time '[i]t does not say ... what these equitable principles are'.[31] He considered what these 'equitable principles' could be, and listed, among others, equidistance and the drawing of a line perpendicular to the coast.[32] However, Vallat concluded that '[p]erhaps the most equitable solution would be to divide the submarine area outside territorial waters among the contiguous states in proportion to the length of their coast lines'.[33] Vallat gave no reason for this comment.

In 1952, De Azcárraga criticised Vallat's theory of continental shelf delimitation by proportionality, stating that '[l]a mejor solución para evitar los posibles conflictos es ... la de concertar acuerdos particulares entre los Estados que compartan la misma plataforma'.[34] However, he did not explain the reasons for opposing proportionality. De Azcárraga made comparable comments in his report to the 1952 Conference of the

---

[30] Proclamation by the President with respect to the Natural Resources of the Subsoil and Sea Bed of the Continental Shelf (1945) 40 *AJIL Supplement* 45.
[31] FA Vallat, 'The Continental Shelf' (1946) 23 *BYIL* 333, 336.
[32] Ibid.
[33] Ibid.
[34] JL de Azcárraga, *La Plataforma Submarina y el Derecho Internacional – La Zona Nerítica Epijurisdiccional* (Instituto Francisco de Vitoria, 1952) 206.

International Bar Association (IBA), specifying that delimitation by proportionality could be unsuitable as it was founded on mathematical speculation.[35] Vallat also presented a report to the 1952 IBA Conference, which did not refer to continental shelf delimitation by proportionality. Instead, it stated that 'the definition of the boundary should be decided by agreement between the littoral States'.[36] Possibly convinced by De Azcárraga's criticism, Vallat seemed to abandon his view that proportionality could be helpful in establishing continental shelf boundaries.

The International Law Commission (ILC) did not discuss proportionality in the works culminating in the 1958 Geneva Conventions. Under Draft Article 7 of 1951:

> [t]wo or more States to whose territories the same continental shelf is contiguous should establish boundaries in the area of the continental shelf by agreement. Failing agreement, the parties are under the obligation to have the boundaries fixed by arbitration.[37]

In respect of this provision, De Azcárraga stated in 1953 that, when states bordered the same gulf, '[l]a répartition des plateaux faite, proportionnellement à la longueur des côtes des Etats intéressés ... peut donner une mauvaise solution parce qu'elle est basée sur la spéculation mathématique'.[38] De Azcárraga maintained the idea previously expressed in his 1952 IBA report.

Vallat, De Azcárraga and the ILC saw proportionality as a method for continental shelf delimitation. In this perspective, their view of the function of proportionality is distinct from the function of disproportionality under the three-stage approach, in which it is part of a process, and thus only one of several considerations.

B *The Original Absence of a Legal Basis for Proportionality*

The shift from proportionality as a standalone delimitation method to proportionality as one of many considerations in the delimitation process

---

[35] JL de Azcárraga, 'Cuestionario relativo a la "Plataforma Continental"' in International Bar Association, *Fourth International Conference of the Legal Profession (Madrid, July 16-23, 1952) – Summary of Proceedings and Resolutions adopted by the Conference* (Martinus Nijhoff, 1954) 281, 285.
[36] FA Vallat, 'Continental Shelf' in International Bar Association (n. 35) 286, 292.
[37] Report of the International Law Commission on its Third Session, UN Doc A/1858 (16 May–27 July 1951), in *ILC Yearbook (1951)*, vol. II, 143.
[38] Fourth Report on the Regime of the High Seas, UN Doc A/CN.4/60 (19 February 1953), in *ILC Yearbook (1953)*, vol. II, 27.

took place in *North Sea Continental Shelf*. In its written submissions, Germany argued that:

> [t]he coastal State's privilege of exploiting adjacent submarine areas rests upon the geographical-geological connection of these areas with the coast. Therefore, the degree of the natural connection of the land territory with the submarine areas adjoining the coast should be regarded as the decisive factor in measuring the share of each of the State which surround a shallow sea. In the case of the North Sea this would mean that the share of each coastal State should be measured by the length of its North Sea coastline.[39]

Germany's argument was that the three states party had coasts comparable in length, entitling them to comparable shares of maritime jurisdiction in the North Sea. Denmark and the Netherlands opposed such arguments, and contended that by mentioning proportionality Germany '[moved] out of the realm of existing rules and principles of international law into the field of arbitrary constructions'.[40] Similarly to Vallat and De Azcárraga, all parties understood proportionality as a criterion the application of which would result in the establishment of a complete boundary.

For the Court, proportionality was one of various factors to be taken into account in establishing an agreed maritime boundary. The Court held that the principles and rules of international law governing continental shelf delimitation require that it 'be effected by agreement in accordance with equitable principles, and taking account of all the relevant circumstances'.[41] According to the Court, relevant factors included:

> a reasonable degree of proportionality which a delimitation effected according to equitable principles ought to bring about between the extent of the continental shelf appertaining to the States concerned and the lengths of their respective coastlines, – these being measured according to their general direction in order to establish the necessary balance between States with straight, and those with markedly concave

---

[39] Memorial of Germany (21 August 1967), 77 [78]. Germany referred to Vallat's 1946 article in its written pleadings.
[40] Common Rejoinder of Denmark and the Netherlands (30 August 1968), 468 [26].
[41] *North Sea Continental Shelf (Federal Republic of Germany/Denmark; Federal Republic of Germany/Netherlands)* (Judgment) [1969] ICJ Rep 3, 53 [101(C)(1)]. The ICJ's approach was confirmed in *Gulf of Maine* (n. 11) 290 [81]; *Delimitation of the Maritime Boundary between Guinea and Guinea-Bissau (Guinea/Guinea-Bissau)* (1985) XIX RIAA 149, 182 [89].

III THE LEGAL BASIS OF DISPROPORTIONALITY

or convex coasts, or to reduce very irregular coastlines to their truer proportions.[42]

The Court stated that there existed various methods capable of ensuring consistency with proportionality, and said that '[t]he choice and application of the appropriate technical methods would be a matter for the parties'.[43] One of such methods, called 'principle of the coastal front, consists in drawing a straight baseline between the extreme points at either end of the coast concerned, or in some cases a series of such lines'.[44]

Two individual opinions expressed additional views on proportionality. On one hand, Judge ad hoc Sørensen stated that there was no 'basis for maintaining that the respective areas of the continental shelf should be proportionate to the length of the coasts of the States concerned'.[45] On the other hand, Judge Bustamante y Rivero wrote that:

> [t]he concept, already examined, of 'natural prolongation' of the land territory of the coastal State implies, as an obvious logical necessity, a relationship of *proportionality* between the length of the coastline of the land territory of a State and the extent of the continental shelf appertaining to such land territory. Parallel with this, so far as concerns inter-State relations, the conclusion is inescapable that the State which has a longer coastline will have a more extensive shelf.[46]

These opposing views show that the Court's decision to include proportionality as a factor to be taken into account in continental shelf delimitation was not uncontroversial.

The ICJ's decision seems to be inconsistent with the underlying principles of the *North Sea Continental Shelf* judgment, which has so far remained unnoticed. In discussing the argument that equidistance was applicable *a priori*, the Court examined the basis of title over the continental shelf. The Court found that:

> [s]ubmarine areas do not really appertain to the coastal State because – or not only because – they are near it. They are near it of course; but this would not suffice to confer title ... What confers the *ipso jure* title which international law attributes to the coastal State in respect of its continental shelf, is the fact that the submarine areas concerned may be deemed to be actually part of the territory over which the coastal State already has

---

[42] *North Sea Continental Shelf* (n. 41) 52 [98].
[43] Ibid.
[44] Ibid.
[45] Ibid. 255 (Dissenting Opinion Sørensen).
[46] Ibid. 58–59 (Separate Opinion Bustamante y Rivero).

> dominion, – in the sense that, although covered with water, they are a prolongation or continuation of that territory, an extension of it under the sea.[47]

According to the ICJ, the basis of title was the physical existence of a continental shelf adjacent to a state's coast.[48] This is confirmed by the Court's rejection of the argument that equidistance was applicable *a priori* by virtue of being inherent in the definition of the continental shelf.[49] If the Court had accepted that argument, it would have also accepted its premise that the basis of title over the continental shelf is distance from the coast. The Court rejected that argument, and therefore its premise.

However, proportionality is linked to distance, and not to natural prolongation. As expressed by the Court in paragraph 98 of the *North Sea Continental Shelf* judgment, proportionality compares 'the extent of the continental shelf appertaining to the States concerned and the lengths of their respective coastlines'.[50] The underlying idea, which is nonetheless misleading, is that coastal fronts of equal length generate equal maritime entitlements through their coastal projections up to a certain distance from the coast.[51] This conflicts with the Court's statement that distance is not the basis of title, as a state is entitled to continental shelf jurisdiction because of a physical shelf protruding into the sea. The concept of natural prolongation is geomorphological in character and does not entail that the coast generates maritime entitlements, since the extent of continental shelf entitlements depends on the shape of the seabed and subsoil. On this basis, proportionality cannot be seen as a circumstance relevant to delimitation. Proportionality is inconsistent with the basis of title over the continental shelf expressed by the Court in 1969.

Upon its introduction into the maritime delimitation discourse, proportionality had no legal basis under international law. One could thus disagree with Cottier's statement that 'the foundations of proportionality in maritime boundary law are fairly clear'.[52] Although lacking a legal basis in 1969, proportionality acquired one in subsequent years. This

---

[47] Ibid. 31 [43].
[48] Jennings explained that 'prolongation can only be identified by reference to physical fact, making geomorphological or perhaps geological considerations paramount'. See RY Jennings, 'The Limits of Continental Shelf Jurisdiction: Some Possible Implications of the North Sea Case Judgment' (1969) 18 *ICLQ* 819, 823.
[49] *North Sea Continental Shelf* (n. 41) 32 [46].
[50] Ibid. 52 [98].
[51] As discussed in Section IV.B below, equal coastal fronts do not generate equal maritime entitlements.
[52] Cottier (n. 9) 543. Cottier does not elaborate on this statement in more detail.

III THE LEGAL BASIS OF DISPROPORTIONALITY

development is especially due to the creation of the Exclusive Economic Zone (EEZ) at the Third United Nations Conference on the Law of the Sea (UNCLOS III), which had a strong impact on the doctrine of the continental shelf.[53] The ICJ recognised this evolution in *Libya/Malta*. In its 1985 judgment, the Court stated that '[a]s the 1982 Convention demonstrates, the two institutions – continental shelf and [EEZ] – are linked together in modern law'.[54] The Court found it 'incontestable that ... the institution of the [EEZ], with its rule on entitlement by reason of distance, is shown by the practice of States to have become a part of customary law'.[55] It followed that, 'for juridical and practical reasons, the distance criterion must now apply to the continental shelf as well as to the [EEZ]'.[56] Crucially, the Court held that:

> [t]his is not to suggest that the idea of natural prolongation is now superseded by that of distance. What it does mean is that where the continental margin does not extend as far as 200 miles from the shore, natural prolongation, which in spite of its physical origins has throughout its history become more and more a complex and juridical concept, is in part defined by distance from the shore, irrespective of the physical nature of the intervening sea-bed and subsoil.[57]

Although it held that natural prolongation was not rendered obsolete by distance, the Court admitted that it was qualified by it, at least within 200 nautical miles (nm). Later cases confirmed that under the United Nations Convention on the Law of the Sea (UNCLOS),[58] distance was the basis of title over both the EEZ and the continental shelf within 200 nm.[59]

Owing to these developments, proportionality acquired a more solid legal basis in the delimitation process. Under UNCLOS, maritime entitlements are generated and their extent defined not by the land territory's protrusion into the sea, but by the 200-nm seaward projection of the coast. This applies to both the EEZ and the continental shelf within 200 nm.[60] Therefore, at least within 200 nm, using proportionality in delimitation is grounded in the basis of title. Whether the connection to

---

[53] Chapter 4, Section II.A and II.B above.
[54] *Libya/Malta* (n. 13) 33 [33].
[55] Ibid. 33 [34].
[56] Ibid.
[57] Ibid.
[58] 1833 UNTS 3.
[59] Chapter 4, Section II.A above.
[60] Arts. 57 and 76(1) UNCLOS. The question of the continental shelf beyond 200 nm is discussed below.

the basis of title requires that proportionality be considered in delimitation is a different matter.[61]

Proportionality had no legal basis under international law at the time of *North Sea Continental Shelf*. This raises the question of whether the ICJ had any reason to include proportionality as a factor to be taken into account in delimitation. In its 1969 judgment, the Court wrote of 'a reasonable degree of proportionality which a delimitation effected according to equitable principles ought to bring about between the extent of the continental shelf appertaining to the States concerned and the lengths of their respective coastlines'.[62] The key terms in the Court's statement are 'reasonable', 'equitable' and 'ought to'. Such words all convey ideas of fairness and even-handedness. The Court might thus have accepted the relevance of proportionality in delimitation on account of its fair and even-handed character. However, these ideas are also reminiscent of natural law doctrines.[63] Commenting on *North Sea Continental Shelf*, Friedmann wrote that:

> it is possible to argue that the extension of a continental shelf should be broadly proportionate to the extension of the coastal territory from which it extends. But to regard this – as the Court appears to do – as a kind of natural law, is to succumb to the same fallacies that vitiate so many theories of natural law: to elevate a particular system of values into an absolute. The Court ... accepts the universality of the doctrine of the continental shelf as an extension of territorial sovereignty. But it is not only disturbing to find the majority treating this novel extension of national sovereignty as a kind of natural law principle but also to see it go even further and regard the proportionality between the area of the continental shelf and the size of the coastal state to which it belongs as an evident correction of 'unnatural' formations of coastlines.[64]

Although the Court might have been right to accept proportionality as a factor in delimitation because of its fair and even-handed character, Friedmann made a persuasive case against proportionality for being a concept lacking a basis in positive law, while being a product of natural law concepts such as fairness and equity. However, such reservations were overcome by UNCLOS's adoption of distance as the basis of title

---

[61] Sections IV and V below.
[62] *North Sea Continental Shelf* (n. 41) 52 [98].
[63] HLA Hart, *The Concept of Law* (3rd ed, OUP 2012) 193–200; R Dworkin, *Law's Empire* (Hart 1998) 35–37.
[64] W Friedmann, 'The North Sea Continental Shelf Cases – A Critique' (1970) 64 *AJIL* 229, 237.

over the continental shelf, which endowed proportionality with a basis in positive law.

C Disproportionality in Delimiting the Continental Shelf beyond 200 Nautical Miles

ITLOS, the *Bangladesh v. India* tribunal and the Special Chamber in *Ghana/Côte d'Ivoire* applied the three-stage approach, which included the disproportionality test, in delimiting boundaries beyond 200 nm.[65] However, disproportionality could be seen to lack a legal basis with respect to delimitation beyond 200 nm, as title over the continental shelf beyond 200 nm depends not only on distance, but also on geomorphology.

There is no continental shelf beyond 200 nm without the existence of a physical continental margin extending beyond that distance, ascertained pursuant to paragraphs 4–8 of Article 76 UNCLOS. However, distance plays a role in establishing the extent of continental shelf jurisdiction beyond 200 nm.[66] Establishing the existence of a physical continental margin is only the first step in determining the extent of state jurisdiction beyond 200 nm. The second step is linked to distance from the coast. Under Article 76(4)(a) UNCLOS, the method to delineate the continental shelf's outer limits refers to a maximum distance from the foot of the continental slope. Pursuant to Article 76(5), the continental shelf's outer limits 'shall not exceed 350 [nm] from the baselines from which the breadth of the territorial sea is measured or shall not exceed 100 [nm] from the 2,500 metre isobath'. Moreover, Article 76(6) provides that the outer limits of the continental shelf 'shall not exceed 350 [nm] from the baselines from which the breadth of the territorial sea is measured'.

Although coastal projections are not sufficient to endow a state with continental shelf entitlements beyond 200 nm, they play an important part in determining the extent of those entitlements. The basis of title over the continental shelf beyond 200 nm includes two elements: first, the existence of a geomorphological continental margin established in accordance with paragraphs 4–8 of Article 76 UNCLOS; second, distance

---

[65] *Bangladesh/Myanmar* (n. 22) 92–126 [341]–[499]; *Bangladesh v. India* (n. 23) 146–69 [438]–[497]; *Delimitation of the Maritime Boundary between Ghana and Côte d'Ivoire in the Atlantic Ocean (Ghana/Côte d'Ivoire)* (Judgment), Judgment of 23 September 2017 [533]–[538].
[66] Chapter 4, Section III.B above.

from a state's coast. Consequently, proportionality has a legal basis with respect to delimitation beyond 200 nm. From this perspective, ITLOS, the *Bangladesh v. India* tribunal and the Special Chamber in *Ghana/Côte d'Ivoire* were justified in applying disproportionality as part of the three-stage approach. However, one should agree with Evans that disproportionality should not be assessed unless it is clear where the continental shelf's outer limits lie.[67] Evans wrote that '[i]t is difficult to understand how even a disproportionality test ... can be applied to a situation in which the extent of what might be at issue between the parties is yet to be determined'.[68] Assessing disproportionality requires international tribunals to compare the parties' relevant area, which seems difficult without knowing where the outer limits of the continental shelf beyond 200 nm lie.[69]

Although lacking a legal basis at the time of *North Sea Continental Shelf*, subsequent developments endowed disproportionality with such a basis, justifying its use in the delimitation process. However, the existence of a legal basis for disproportionality does not necessarily entail that it must be a part of the delimitation process.

IV Judicial Approaches to Disproportionality

Disproportionality has changed over time, from a mere factor in boundary negotiations to a full-fledged stage of the delimitation process, as a result of the approach of international tribunals to the disproportionality test. This approach may also be influenced by coastal configuration.

A The Function of Disproportionality in the Delimitation Process

Similarly to its legal basis, disproportionality's function in maritime delimitation changed over time. International tribunals understood the role of disproportionality differently, depending on their approach to the delimitation process. Until the 1992 *St. Pierre et Miquelon* arbitral award, each case was treated as a *unicum*, and disproportionality would simply be one of several considerations suggesting the delimitation method appropriate in a given case. Starting with the 1993 *Jan Mayen* judgment,

---

[67] This issue is discussed in Section IV.C below.
[68] MD Evans, 'Maritime Boundary Delimitation: Whatever Next?' in J Barrett and R Barnes (eds.), *Law of the Sea – UNCLOS as a Living Treaty* (BIICL, 2016) 41, 76.
[69] The outer limits of the continental shelf beyond 200 nm could be used as the seaward limits of the relevant area in certain cases. See Chapter 3, Section III.C.4 above.

international tribunals have applied a standard delimitation method, in which disproportionality is a method for evaluating the overall equitableness of a boundary established by other means.

1   The unclear function of proportionality: 1969–1992

Until 1992, the international tribunals' approach to proportionality lacked consistency. Delimitation decisions were not entirely clear, and international tribunals understood proportionality as performing at least four different functions. First, proportionality was understood as a factor suggesting the practical method or methods to adopt in each case, operating on the same footing as other factors such as coastal configuration. In *North Sea Continental Shelf*, the ICJ held that 'delimitation is to be effected by agreement in accordance with equitable principles'.[70] Proportionality is thus one of multiple 'factors to be taken into account' in interstate negotiations, aimed at choosing the practical method or methods to draw the boundary.[71] The Court of Arbitration in *Guinea/ Guinea-Bissau* followed the ICJ's lead, holding that 'la proportionnalité doit intervenir dans l'évaluation des facteurs qui entrent en ligne de compte pour arriver à un résultat équitable',[72] as '[e]lle permet, combinée à tous les autres facteurs, de réaliser l'égalité des Etats concernés'.[73]

Second, proportionality was seen as a relevant circumstance, its function being to modify a provisional equidistance line. This was the case in the *Anglo/French Arbitration*. The *Anglo/French* arbitral tribunal did not consider proportionality as a mere factor in the choice of the practical delimitation method, as the ICJ had done in *North Sea Continental Shelf*, since both France and the UK were bound by Article 6 of the Convention on the Continental Shelf (CCS).[74] However, France had made a reservation to Article 6, under which it would not accept boundaries based on equidistance 'in areas where, in the Government's opinion, there are "special circumstances". . . that is to say: the Bay of Biscay, the Bay of Granville, and the sea areas of the Straits of Dover and of the North Sea off the French coast'.[75] The Court of Arbitration held that 'Article 6 is not applicable . . . to the extent that it is excluded by the French

---

[70] *North Sea Continental Shelf* (n. 41) 53–4 [101].
[71] Ibid.
[72] *Guinea/Guinea-Bissau* (n. 41) 192 [118].
[73] Ibid.
[74] 499 UNTS 311.
[75] *Continental Shelf (France/UK)* (1977) XVIII RIAA 3, 29 [33].

reservations',[76] but would otherwise be part of the applicable law. Since Article 6 CCS was part of the applicable law, equidistance was the compulsory delimitation method throughout the length of the disputed boundary. Proportionality could thus only be a special circumstance correcting the equidistance line. The Court of Arbitration found proportionality to be 'a factor to be taken into account in appreciating the effects of geographical features on the equitable or inequitable character of a delimitation, and in particular of a delimitation by application of the equidistance method'.[77]

Third, in *Gulf of Maine* the ICJ's Chamber spoke of proportionality in a completely different manner from that in *North Sea Continental Shelf*. In 1969, the Court held that proportionality entails comparing coastal length ratios to marine area ratios. However, in *Gulf of Maine* the Chamber mentioned proportionality in respect of coastal length ratio only. The Chamber stated that:

> a maritime delimitation can certainly not be established by a direct division of the area in dispute proportional to the respective lengths of the coasts belonging to the parties in the relevant area, but it is equally certain that a substantial disproportion to the lengths of those coasts that resulted from a delimitation effected on a different basis would constitute a circumstance calling for an appropriate correction.[78]

The Chamber conflated two distinct concepts: on one hand, coastal length disparity as a relevant circumstance; on the other hand, proportionality as a comparison between the coastal length ratio and marine area ratio. The former could be a relevant circumstance,[79] while only the latter is the concept of proportionality.

Fourth, international tribunals understood proportionality as a final test of the boundary's equitableness, as in *Tunisia/Libya*, *Libya/Malta* and *St. Pierre et Miquelon*. In *Tunisia/Libya*, the Court held that 'it is clearly not possible ... to apply [proportionality], by way of touchstone of equitableness, to the method or methods it may indicate, unless it can arrive at a reasonably clear conception of the extent of the areas on each side of the eventual line'.[80] The ICJ held that proportionality was 'applied'

---

[76] Ibid. 42 [62].
[77] Ibid. 57 [99].
[78] *Gulf of Maine* (n. 11) 323 [185].
[79] See Chapter 5, Section II.B above.
[80] *Continental Shelf (Tunisia/Libya)* (Judgment) [1982] ICJ Rep 18, 78 [108]. See also Evans (n. 9) 226–7.

to the chosen delimitation methods, suggesting that it would be considered after such methods would have already been identified. Consequently, proportionality could only be used as a means to evaluate the overall equitableness of those methods.

Libya/Malta displays inconsistency with respect to the role ascribed to proportionality. One on hand, the Court found that 'proportionality is one possibly relevant "factor", among several other factors ... "to be taken into account"', expressly citing *North Sea Continental Shelf*.[81] On the other hand, it held that this did not 'signify the rejection in principle of the applicability of the criterion of proportionality as a test of the equitableness of the result of a delimitation'.[82] This approach is unconvincing. Proportionality is either a factor to be taken into account in choosing the delimitation method, or the parameter to assess the equitableness of the chosen delimitation method. There seems to be no cogent reason why it should be both. The *St. Pierre et Miquelon* Court of Arbitration made findings comparable to *Tunisia/Libya*. Part XII of the award, entitled 'Vérification des résultats', used proportionality as a means to verify the equitableness of the boundary.[83] Moreover, the arbitral tribunal cited *Libya/Malta* with approval insofar as it clarified 'l'usage qu'il convient de faire de la proportionnalité en tant que moyen de vérifier l'équité'.[84]

2   Disproportionality as a test of equitableness: 1993–present

Since *Jan Mayen*, international tribunals have developed a uniform approach to disproportionality. Using a standard delimitation method allowed disproportionality to acquire a clearer role in the delimitation process. Beginning in 1993, proportionality was understood to be a relevant circumstance. However, it was seen to be a peculiar relevant circumstance, as it would function as a final test of equitableness. In *Jan Mayen*, the Court held that:

> [t]here are ... situations ... in which the relationship between the length of the relevant coasts and the maritime areas generated by them by application of the equidistance method, is so disproportionate that it has been found necessary to take this circumstance into account in order to ensure an equitable solution. The frequent references in the case-

---

[81] *Libya/Malta* (n. 13) 44 [57].
[82] Ibid. 46 [59].
[83] *St. Pierre et Miquelon* (n. 14) 296–7 [92]–[93].
[84] Ibid. 288 [63].

law to the idea of proportionality ... confirm the importance of the proposition that an equitable delimitation must ... take into account the disparity between the respective coastal lengths of the relevant area.[85]

Although innovative, *Jan Mayen* was not entirely clear, since, similarly to *Gulf of Maine*, the ICJ discussed proportionality and coastal length disparity jointly, blurring the distinction between them.

The ICJ did not discuss proportionality as a relevant circumstance in either *Qatar v. Bahrain* or *Cameroon v. Nigeria*,[86] presumably because states did not raise this question in the pleadings, and the parties' coasts were broadly comparable in length. Moreover, proportionality was not used in the delimitation process in *Nicaragua v. Honduras*, in which the ICJ established an angle-bisector boundary.[87] Consequently, it did not apply the two-stage approach, and did not discuss proportionality as a part of its second stage. The arbitral tribunals in *Eritrea/Yemen*, *Barbados v. Trinidad and Tobago* and *Guyana v. Suriname* dedicated some comments to proportionality. For instance, in *Barbados v. Trinidad and Tobago* the arbitral tribunal held that 'proportionality is a relevant circumstance to be taken into consideration in reviewing the equity of a tentative delimitation'.[88] Similarly, in *Guyana v. Suriname*, the arbitral tribunal first found that there did not exist 'any relevant circumstances in the continental shelf or [EEZ] which would require an adjustment to the provisional equidistance line'.[89] It then stated that it had 'checked the relevant coastal lengths for proportionality and comes up with nearly the same ratio of relevant areas ... as it does for coastal frontages'.[90] In both cases, proportionality was viewed as a relevant circumstance functioning as a final test of equitableness.

In *Black Sea*, the ICJ further clarified the role of disproportionality in the delimitation process. The Court held that disproportionality was more than a relevant circumstance, it was a means to 'check, *ex post facto*, on the equitableness of the delimitation line it has constructed'.[91]

---

[85] *Jan Mayen* (n. 4) 67 [65].
[86] *Maritime Delimitation and Territorial Questions between Qatar and Bahrain (Qatar v. Bahrain)* (Merits) [2001] ICJ Rep 40; *Land and Maritime Boundary between Cameroon and Nigeria (Cameroon v. Nigeria Equatorial Guinea intervening)* (Merits) [2002] ICJ Rep 303.
[87] *Territorial and Maritime Dispute between Nicaragua and Honduras in the Caribbean Sea (Nicaragua v. Honduras)* (Judgment) [2007] ICJ Rep 659, 746 [287].
[88] *Barbados v. Trinidad and Tobago* (n. 18) 237 [337].
[89] *Maritime Boundary Arbitration (Guyana v. Suriname)* (2007) XXX RIAA 1, 109 [392]. See also *Eritrea/Yemen* (n. 16) 372 [165].
[90] *Guyana v. Suriname* (n. 89) 109 [392].
[91] *Black Sea* (n. 3) 129 [213].

The Court distinguished relevant circumstances from disproportionality, stating that:

> the Court will verify that the line (a provisional equidistance line which may or may not have been adjusted by taking into account the relevant circumstances) does not ... lead to an inequitable result by reason of any marked disproportion between the ratio of the respective coastal lengths and the ratio between the relevant maritime area of each State ....[92]

Through disproportionality, international tribunals assess the equitableness of a boundary eventually adjusted based on relevant circumstances. In this perspective, it would be incoherent to consider disproportionality to be a relevant circumstance.

Comparable considerations were made by the ICJ in *Nicaragua v. Colombia*,[93] and *Costa Rica v. Nicaragua*,[94] by ITLOS in *Bangladesh/Myanmar*,[95] by the *Bangladesh v. India* tribunal,[96] and by the Special Chamber of ITLOS in *Ghana/Côte d'Ivoire*.[97] *Peru v. Chile* was an unusual case from the perspective of disproportionality. Although the ICJ applied the three-stage approach to delimit the boundary beyond 80 nm, it found that it could not properly identify the relevant coast and the relevant area.[98] Therefore, the Court engaged 'in a broad assessment of disproportionality', and concluded that 'no significant disproportion is evident, such as would call into question the equitable nature of the provisional equidistance line'.[99]

Isolating a third stage entirely devoted to disproportionality was plausibly determined by the need to rationalise the delimitation process. In *Black Sea*, the ICJ took stock of the earlier cases employing disproportionality as a final test of equitableness. The Court's decision in *Black Sea* to distinguish disproportionality from relevant circumstances presumably resulted from the Court's effort to systematise the delimitation process. The clarification of disproportionality's function in *Black Sea* entails an important effect. Before 2009, proportionality was a relevant

---

[92] Ibid. 103 [122].
[93] *Nicaragua v. Colombia* (n. 24) 715 [239].
[94] *Maritime Delimitation in the Caribbean Sea and the Pacific Ocean (Costa Rica v. Nicaragua); Land Boundary in the Northern Part of Isla Portillos (Costa Rica v. Nicaragua)* (Judgment) [2018] ICJ Rep 139, 198–201 [159]–[161].
[95] *Bangladesh/Myanmar* (n. 22) 126 [497].
[96] *Bangladesh v. India* (n. 23) 168 [492].
[97] *Ghana/Côte d'Ivoire* (n. 65) [533].
[98] *Peru v. Chile* (n. 21) 69 [193].
[99] Ibid. 69–71 [193]–[194]. *Peru v. Chile* is further discussed in Section IV.B below.

circumstance that international tribunals would consider only if raised by the parties in their pleadings. However, since 2009 disproportionality has become entrenched in the delimitation process, which means that international tribunals evaluate whether maritime boundaries meet the disproportionality test independently of the parties' arguments.

Based on the separation of disproportionality from other relevant circumstances, one may expect the parties' submissions concerning disproportionality to increase in clarity. For several years, international tribunals had blurred the line between proportionality on one hand, and coastal length disparity on the other hand. The reason for this blurring may also relate to the way in which the parties themselves framed their arguments, which often conflated the two concepts. For example, in *Jan Mayen* Denmark mentioned 'proportionality in the lengths of coasts',[100] and Norway similarly denoted proportionality as 'a factor based on the ratio of the lengths of the respective coasts'.[101] In *Qatar v. Bahrain*, Qatar referred to the 'disproportion between the respective lengths of the coasts of Qatar and Bahrain',[102] as did Bahrain.[103] In *Cameroon v. Nigeria*, Cameroon first mentioned proportionality between continental shelf areas and the length of the relevant coasts,[104] but subsequently referred to proportionality between the respective coasts of the parties.[105] Since *Black Sea*, international tribunals have refrained from conflating disproportionality with coastal length disparity, which may have contributed to guiding states in the formulation of their pleadings in later disputes, as shown by the absence, in the parties' submissions since *Black Sea*, of arguments conflating disproportionality with coastal length disparity.[106]

---

[100] Memorial of Denmark (31 July 1989), 106 [338].
[101] Counter-memorial of Norway (11 May 1990), 190 [680].
[102] Memorial of Qatar (30 September 1996), 281 [12.33].
[103] Memorial of Bahrain (30 September 1996), 273 [631].
[104] Memorial of Cameroon (16 March 1995), 547 [5.106].
[105] Ibid. 554 [5.121].
[106] For *Nicaragua v. Colombia*, see Reply of Nicaragua (18 September 2009), 96-8 [3.57]-[3.61]; Rejoinder of Colombia (18 June 2010), 304-11 [8.66]-[8.75]. For *Bangladesh/Myanmar*, see Memorial of Bangladesh (1 July 2010), 92-4 [6.75]-[6.78]; Counter-memorial of Myanmar (1 December 2010), 155-63 [5.145]-[5.153]; Reply of Bangladesh (15 March 2011), 103-11 [3.165]-[3.198]; Rejoinder of Myanmar (1 July 2011), 173-91 [6.63]-[6.91]. For *Peru v. Chile*, see Memorial of Peru (20 March 2009), 235-7 [6.69]-[6.75]; Reply of Peru (9 November 2010), 274 [5.15]. For *Bangladesh v. India*, see Memorial of Bangladesh (31 May 2011), 125-6 [6.124]-[6.128]; Counter-memorial of India (31 July 2012), 195-8 [6.108]-[6.113]; Reply of

Whether disproportionality is understood as a factor indicating, alongside others, the appropriate delimitation method, or whether it is understood as a final equitableness test, has no impact on its relationship with the basis of title. In both cases, disproportionality's legal basis is its connection with the basis of title over maritime areas. There is no inherent reason why disproportionality should indicate the appropriate method or check the equitableness of the result. It is the international tribunals' quest for consistency with their own previous jurisprudence, as well as their effort to systematise the delimitation process, which favours the latter function. Disproportionality plausibly acquired its current function in the three-stage delimitation process as a result of the international tribunals' decision to promote clarity and transparency in maritime delimitation.

B The Assessment of Disproportionality by International Tribunals

The issue arises concerning how international tribunals assess disproportionality as an element of the three-stage delimitation process in practice.

1 Scope of application

Since 1993, international tribunals have assessed disproportionality only where the boundary was to be established by means of the three-stage approach, or the two stage-approach before *Black Sea*.[107] In *Peru v. Chile*, the ICJ held that, at the third stage of the 'methodology [it] usually employs in seeking an equitable solution',[108] it would conduct 'a disproportionality test in which it assesses whether the effect of the line, as adjusted, is such that the Parties' respective shares of the relevant area are markedly disproportionate to the lengths of their relevant coasts'.[109] The Court borrowed this formula from previous decisions.[110] By contrast, in *Nicaragua v. Honduras* the ICJ found that 'the construction of an equidistance line from the mainland is not feasible',[111] and thus decided that

---

Bangladesh (31 January 2013), 125–8 [4.150]–[4.159] and 153–8 [5.59]–[5.74]; Rejoinder of India (31 July 2013), 185–9 [7.28]–[7.37].
[107] International tribunals did not conduct a proportionality test in *Qatar v. Bahrain* and *Cameroon v. Nigeria*, where the two-stage approach was employed. See Section IV.A above.
[108] *Peru v. Chile* (n. 21) 65 [180].
[109] Ibid.
[110] *Black Sea* (n. 3) 103 [122]; *Nicaragua v. Colombia* (n. 24) 696 [193]; *Bangladesh/Myanmar* (n. 22) 68 [240].
[111] *Nicaragua v. Honduras* (n. 87) 745 [283].

it would 'consider whether in principle some form of bisector of the angle created by lines representing the relevant mainland coasts could be a basis for the delimitation'.[112] In *Nicaragua v. Honduras*, the Court did not assess disproportionality. Once a bisector line was drawn, the Court took stock of the result.

However, one could doubt whether disproportionality only applies to boundaries delimited by way of the three-stage approach. The basis of title over maritime areas, which justifies using disproportionality in the three-stage approach, is not affected by the delimitation methods used by international tribunals.[113] From the perspective of the basis of title, nothing suggests that disproportionality should not, or could not, be used in delimitations based on the angle-bisector. The *raison d'être* of disproportionality is to ensure the equitable allocation of marine areas to states with different coastal lengths, and does not appear to be peculiar to the three-stage approach. In principle, an angle-bisector boundary should also achieve an equitable allocation of marine areas to be consistent with the basis of title. A state's entitlement over such areas is generated by the coast, the function of which is as central in the three-stage approach as it is in angle-bisector delimitations. The ICJ admitted that angle-bisectors approximate equidistance lines.[114] If disproportionality is useful to assess the equitableness of equidistance-based boundaries, it should also be useful to assess the equitableness of angle-bisector boundaries.

In *Nicaragua v. Honduras*, Nicaragua mentioned proportionality in connection with the equitableness of an angle-bisector boundary, arguing that '[t]he bisector method satisfies the criterion of proportionality in the geographical circumstances of the present case'.[115] In identifying the relevant coast, Nicaragua stated that '[t]hose coastal lengths are such that the bisector method … satisfies the criterion of proportionality'.[116] Moreover, Nicaragua also submitted 'that there is no disproportion in the maritime areas attributed to each of the Parties as a consequence of the use of the bisector method'.[117] Côte d'Ivoire also

---

[112] Ibid. 746 [287].
[113] Section III above.
[114] *Nicaragua v. Honduras* (n. 87) 746 [287].
[115] Reply of Nicaragua (13 January 2003), 193 [9.53].
[116] CR 2007/1, 59 [37] (Oude Elferink).
[117] CR 2007/5, 39–40 [64]–[66] (Brownlie). See also CR 2007/3, 35–7 [115]–[116] (Brownlie); CR 2007/12, 51–2 [63]–[66] (Brownlie).

made a similar argument in *Ghana/Côte d'Ivoire*, in order to show that the suggested angle-bisector boundary was equitable.[118]

Conversely, Honduras did not mention proportionality either in its written or in its oral submissions. However, the absence of references to proportionality is presumably not due to the conviction that it is inapplicable in angle-bisector delimitations. Honduras contended that the boundary should follow a parallel running due east from the point identified at the mouth of the River Coco by the 1962 Nicaragua-Honduras Mixed Commission.[119] It maintained that 'the *uti possidetis juris* principle ... is applicable to the maritime area off the coasts of Honduras and Nicaragua, and that the line of fifteenth parallel constitutes the line of maritime delimitation resulting from that application'.[120] Honduras thus made a historical argument, simply asking the ICJ to acknowledge a historical fact, and not requesting *de novo* delimitation. Accordingly, proportionality would not have supported Honduras's argument.

The Court of Arbitration in *Guinea/Guinea-Bissau* had recognised the pertinence of proportionality to angle-bisector delimitations. It drew the boundary beyond 12 nm west of Alcatraz as a 236° azimuth, perpendicular to the straight line joining Almadies Point to Cape Shilling.[121] The boundary thus bisected a 180° angle. The Court of Arbitration subsequently evaluated whether this angle-bisector boundary satisfied proportionality. In *Guinea/Guinea-Bissau*, proportionality was understood as a factor indicating the suitable delimitation method. Nevertheless, this did not prevent the tribunal from assessing an angle-bisector boundary through the lens of proportionality.[122] In its decision, the Court of Arbitration followed the ICJ's judgment in *Tunisia/Libya*. In *Tunisia/Libya*, the Court drew the second segment of the boundary as an angle-bisector, and later checked whether the boundary would cause a significant disproportion between the relevant coast and the relevant area.[123] Assessing proportionality in angle-bisector delimitations seems

---

[118] Counter-memorial of Côte d'Ivoire (4 April 2016), 213–19 [8.41]–[8.53]; Rejoinder of Côte d'Ivoire (14 November 2016), 96–101 [3.57]–[3.65].
[119] Counter-memorial of Honduras (21 March 2002), 150 [8.13].
[120] *Nicaragua v. Honduras* (n. 87) 727 [229].
[121] *Guinea/Guinea-Bissau* (n. 41) 190 [111]. These two points are in Senegal and Sierra Leone respectively.
[122] See Section IV.A above.
[123] *Tunisia/Libya* (n. 80) 89–91 [129]–[131].

consistent with the basis of title and with the *raison d'être* of disproportionality.

Disproportionality may sometimes seem not to be applicable owing to the difficulties in identifying the relevant coast and the relevant area. In *Tunisia/Libya*, the ICJ stated that 'it is clearly not possible for the Court to apply [proportionality] … to the method or methods it may indicate, unless it can arrive at a reasonably clear conception of the extent of the areas on each side of the eventual line'.[124] This was the case of *Peru v. Chile*, in which the ICJ held that the existence of an agreed 80-nm-long boundary 'would make difficult, if not impossible, the calculation of the length of the relevant coasts and of the extent of the relevant area, were the usual mathematical calculation of the proportions to be undertaken'.[125] One could also say that identifying the relevant area was problematic in *Nicaragua v. Honduras*. However, these arguments fail to persuade, as the relevant area can in principle be identified in all delimitation cases.[126]

2 Disproportionality as a mathematical assessment

In nine delimitation cases, international tribunals did not mathematically calculate coastal length ratios and marine area ratios.[127] In the other twelve cases, international tribunals numerically identified the ratios considered in the disproportionality test.[128] International tribunals have been more meticulous in mathematically assessing disproportionality after adopting a standard delimitation method. From *North Sea Continental Shelf* (1969) to *St. Pierre et Miquelon* (1992), international tribunals mathematically assessed proportionality in only two out of seven cases, while since *Jan Mayen* (1993) international tribunals have mathematically expressed coastal length ratios and marine area ratios in eight out of fourteen cases. Within this latter category, a further

---

[124] Ibid. 78 [108].
[125] *Peru v. Chile* (n. 21) 69 [193]. Peru argued that the boundary should be delimited *de novo*, and in this context assessed disproportionality. See Memorial of Peru (20 March 2009), 235–7 [6.69]–[6.75]; Reply of Peru (9 November 2010), 274 [5.15].
[126] Chapter 3, Section III above.
[127] *North Sea Continental Shelf, Anglo/French Arbitration, Gulf of Maine, Guinea/Guinea-Bissau, Libya/Malta, Qatar v. Bahrain, Cameroon v. Nigeria, Nicaragua v. Honduras, Peru v. Chile*.
[128] *Tunisia/Libya, St. Pierre et Miquelon, Eritrea/Yemen, Guyana v. Suriname, Black Sea, Bangladesh/Myanmar, Nicaragua v. Colombia, Bangladesh v. India*. In *Jan Mayen* and *Barbados v. Trinidad and Tobago*, the international tribunals concerned only explicitly mentioned coastal length ratios.

distinction exists between the cases applying the two-stage approach and the cases applying the three-stage approach. From *Jan Mayen* (1993) to *Nicaragua v. Honduras* (2007), mathematical calculations were made in four cases out of seven, while since *Black Sea* (2009) only one case in seven lacked a clear mathematical assessment. An increase in mathematical calculations of disproportionality is evident following the shift to a standard delimitation method, with a further increase following the introduction of the three-stage approach.

The function of disproportionality in the three-stage approach can explain this increase. While in the two-stage approach disproportionality was a relevant circumstance, it is a full-fledged stage in the three-stage approach, in the context of which international tribunals consider it irrespective of the parties' arguments.[129] The only case since 2009 in which disproportionality was not actually assessed is *Peru v. Chile*, but even in that case the ICJ stated that it conducted 'a broad assessment of disproportionality'.[130] Between 1993 and 2009, proportionality was not discussed in *Qatar v. Bahrain*, *Cameroon v. Nigeria* and *Nicaragua v. Honduras*. Proportionality was not a central issue in the parties' arguments in the first two cases, thus the ICJ only touched upon it. In the third case, the ICJ did not discuss proportionality because it delimited an angle-bisector boundary.

The move towards a standard delimitation process, followed by the clarification of the status of disproportionality as a full-fledged stage of that process, likely determined a more careful approach to disproportionality. International tribunals seem compelled to explain whether disproportionality is satisfied by reference to mathematical ratios, which states could perceive as increasing the objectivity of delimitation. However, there is little objectivity in the international tribunals' appraisal of disproportionality.

Figure 6.1 below shows a comparison between coastal length ratios and marine area ratios in the cases in which mathematical calculations were made. International tribunals formulate ratios in the form 1:x. '1' is the coastal length of the state with the shorter coast, while 'x' the coastal length of the state with the longer coast, expressed as a function of the coastal length of the state with the shorter coast. The graph's columns were obtained by dividing 1, representing the shorter coast, by the figure representing the longer coast. The higher the coastal length difference,

---

[129] Section IV.A.2 above.
[130] *Peru v. Chile* (n. 21) 69 [193].

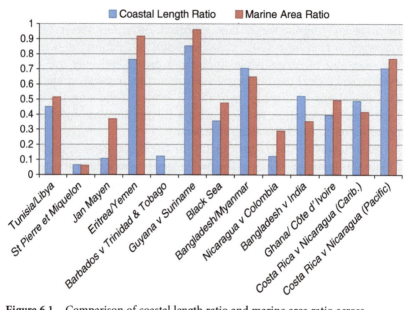

Figure 6.1 Comparison of coastal length ratio and marine area ratio across delimitation cases
Source: Created by the author

the shorter the blue column, while as coastal length difference decreases, the blue column becomes taller. This also applies to marine area ratios.[131] The greater the gap between the blue and the red columns, the greater the disparity between coastal length ratio and marine area ratio. Wider gaps between the taller red and blue columns indicate a less significant disparity between coastal length ratios and marine areas ratios. As the columns' height decreases, narrower gaps suggest more significant disparities. In most cases in which the disproportionality test was mathematically performed the disparity between the states' coastal length was marked. A value of 0.5 indicates that the coast of one state was double the length of the other state's coast. Including *Bangladesh* v. *India*, in which the coastal length ratio was 1:1.92, this situation occurred in nine cases,

---

[131] In *Jan Mayen* and *Barbados* v. *Trinidad and Tobago*, marine area ratios were not calculated, plausibly owing to the treatment of coastal length disparity as a relevant circumstance. See *Jan Mayen* (n. 4) 65–70 [61]–[71]; *Barbados* v. *Trinidad and Tobago* (n. 18) 233–6 [321]–[334]. Both cases were decided before the three-stage approach, in which disproportionality is always assessed. In *Nicaragua* v. *Colombia* the ICJ explicitly stated the *Jan Mayen* marine area ratio, which is used in Figure 6.1. See *Nicaragua* v. *Colombia* (n. 24) 717 [246].

IV JUDICIAL APPROACHES TO DISPROPORTIONALITY 273

which indicates that international tribunals usually deal with cases in which coastal length disparity seems to be significant.

The graph also shows that international tribunals have not sought mathematical accuracy in assessing disproportionality. While in most cases there seems to be a limited discrepancy between coastal length ratios and marine area ratios, there was no occasion in which the two values were identical. This should not surprise. International tribunals have admitted on various occasions that disproportionality is not a purely mathematical test.[132]

In assessing disproportionality, international tribunals do not seek to allocate marine areas based on the length of the states' respective coast, which is consistent with the view, expressed by the ICJ in *North Sea Continental Shelf*, that '[e]quity does not necessarily imply equality'.[133] Through disproportionality assessments, international tribunals seek to appraise whether the boundary established in the first two stages of the delimitation process is equitable. The ICJ clarified that this is 'a matter which can be answered only in the light of all the circumstances of the particular case',[134] since 'the third stage of the process cannot require the Court to disregard all of the considerations which were important in the earlier stages'.[135] Disproportionality should not be appraised in isolation from the other geographical and non-geographical relevant circumstances.

For instance, in *Nicaragua* v. *Colombia* there was a seemingly significant disproportion between coastal length ratio (1:8.2) and marine area ratio (1:3.44). The ICJ held that the boundary it had established pursued two objectives: first, preventing parts of either state's coastal projections from being cut off; second, avoiding that Colombia's islands be enclaved.[136] The Court concluded 'that, taking account of all the circumstances of the present case, the result achieved by the application of the line provisionally adopted ... does not entail such a disproportionality as to create an inequitable result'.[137] The Court found that there was no

---

[132] *Libya/Malta* (n. 13) 53 [74] *Jan Mayen* (n. 4) 69 [70]; *Barbados* v. *Trinidad and Tobago* (n. 18) 244 [376]; *Bangladesh/Myanmar* (n. 22) 123 [477]; *Nicaragua* v. *Colombia* (n. 24) 716 [242]; *Bangladesh* v. *India* (n. 23) 168 [492].
[133] *North Sea Continental Shelf* (n. 41) 49 [91]. See also *Libya/Malta* (n. 13) 39 [46]; *Cameroon* v. *Nigeria* (n. 86) 295 [445].
[134] *Nicaragua* v. *Colombia* (n. 24) 716 [242]. See also *Bangladesh* v. *India* (n. 23) 168 [492]; *Barbados* v. *Trinidad and Tobago* (n. 18) 244 [376]; *Jan Mayen* (n. 4) 69 [70]; *Libya/Malta* (n. 13) 53 [74].
[135] *Nicaragua* v. *Colombia* (n. 24) 715 [240].
[136] Ibid. 716 [244].
[137] Ibid. 717 [247].

disproportion since the boundary was equitable in the light of other geographical circumstances.[138]

Jan Mayen presented a situation similar to *Nicaragua v. Colombia*. The ICJ did not explicitly assess proportionality. However, the Court would have likely referred to it had it deemed the result to be inequitable. Presumably, the Court accepted that relevant circumstances justified a boundary ensuring that both Denmark and Norway had access to capelin fisheries.[139] Therefore, a non-geographical circumstance had a plausible effect on the Court's determination that, despite the great discrepancy between coastal length ratio and marine area ratio, proportionality was satisfied.

The issue arises as to the utility of expressing disproportionality as a function of mathematical ratios if such ratios do not determine, and have never so far determined, the adjustment of a boundary. This concerns the discretionary character of the disproportionality test developed in the jurisprudence. Writing extra-judicially, Judge Paik suggested that proportionality 'can override the result of [other equitable principles'] application as long as it finds the result inequitable'.[140] However, international tribunals seem to have taken the opposite approach. While a comparison of coastal length ratios and marine area ratios may strongly suggest that a boundary is inequitable, international tribunals tend to reverse such *prima facie* conclusions based on considerations concerning other relevant circumstances. Such circumstances are considered in the second stage of the delimitation process, and thus their effect on delimitation should not extend to the disproportionality test.

However, international tribunals have not always been consistent in this regard. In *Nicaragua v. Colombia*, the need to prevent cut-off and the enclavement of Colombia's islands outweighed the marked disproportion between coastal length ratio and marine area ratio.[141] Whether proportionality is satisfied is a matter for international tribunals to decide in exercising a degree of discretion. The ICJ confirmed this discretionary character of disproportionality assessments. In *Black Sea*, it stated that:

---

[138] Evans commented that '[i]f an outcome that awards one state an area which is over twice as great as the ratio between the relevant coastal lengths is not "disproportionate", what is?' See Evans (n. 68) 62.

[139] *Jan Mayen* (n. 4) 70-2 [73]-[76].

[140] Paik (n. 9) 207.

[141] Judge Keith wrote that there existed a 'gross disproportion' in Colombia's favour, yet agreed with the Court's findings that the need to avoid cut-off was paramount. See *Nicaragua v. Colombia* (n. 24) 744-5 [9] and [12] (Declaration Keith). See also ibid. 747 [4] (Declaration Xue).

various tribunals ... have drawn different conclusions over the years as to what disparity in coastal lengths would constitute a significant disproportionality which suggested the delimitation line was inequitable and still required adjustment. This remains in each case a matter for the Court's appreciation, which it will exercise by reference to the overall geography of the area.[142]

There seem to exist few limits to this discretion, which in principle justifies certain writers' criticism. Evans stated that the discretionary approach to the disproportionality test is not in keeping with the ICJ's approach in *Black Sea*, centred on mathematical calculations of coastal length and marine area ratios.[143] Tanaka wrote that '[b]oth the existence of a disproportion between coastal lengths and the extent of the adjustment of the provisional line were decided by judges in a discretionary manner'.[144]

However, such issues are not necessarily problematic. The three-stage approach endeavours to strike a balance between predictability and certainty on one hand, and flexibility on the other hand. The former are ensured by the objective identification of relevant coasts and of relevant areas, as well as by the geometrical establishment of equidistance lines. The latter is ensured by adjusting equidistance lines pursuant to relevant circumstances and disproportionality. The *raison d'être* of disproportionality is its very flexibility, which suggests that it should not be applied too rigidly. The real question is whether it serves any purpose in delimitation. Disproportionality has never determined the adjustment of a boundary, even in cases where one would have expected an adjustment owing to substantial disproportion.[145]

C   The Impact of Coastal Configuration on Disproportionality

When applying the three-stage approach, international tribunals automatically consider disproportionality, as an integral part of the delimitation process. However, some writers have argued both that assessing disproportionality in the delimitation process would be unsound since coasts having the same length do not necessarily generate the same maritime entitlements, and that disproportionality would only apply in

---

[142] *Black Sea* (n. 3) 129 [213].
[143] Evans (n. 68) 70.
[144] Tanaka (n. 7) 458.
[145] This matter is discussed in Section V below.

delimitation between adjacent coasts. However, these arguments are not fully convincing.

Weil is the main proponent of the first argument, according to which 'l'étendue d'une juridiction maritime, bien que commandée par la configuration côtière, n'est pas dans un rapport constant avec la longueur de la façade côtière'.[146] A coast generates different maritime entitlements depending on whether it runs in a mostly straight direction and without deep indentations, such as Nicaragua's Pacific coast, or on whether it is deeply indented, such as Norway's Atlantic coast. Weil argued that '[c]'est l'ouverture côtière dans son ensemble qui irradie en mer, et non pas une longueur côtière mesurée par l'arpenteur'.[147] According to Weil, the configuration of a state's coast has an impact on how international tribunals assess proportionality. He wrote that:

> [d]ès lors que le droit international, n'a pas accepté le principe d'une répartition des zones maritimes proportionnelles aux longueurs côtières, il ne pouvait pas accepter l'idée qu'entre Etats voisins la délimitation doive nécessairement refléter une comparaison des longueurs côtières mesurées au cordeau.[148]

Weil's view is in principle correct. However, his argument would be more persuasive if international tribunals actually measured coastal lengths by accounting for all existing indentations. International tribunals sometimes approximate the relevant coast by means of straight lines.[149] To ensure consistency with the basis of title, international tribunals ought to approximate the relevant coast by reference to straight baselines, which can be established by a coastal state if its coast is 'deeply indented and cut into'.[150] Both the international tribunals' approximation of the relevant coasts by means of straight lines, and the suggested reference to straight baselines, ensure that proportionality is assessed by reference to what Weil calls 'ouverture côtière'. Weil's criticism thus seems overstated.

According to the second argument, proportionality only applies between adjacent coasts. In 1979, Bowett wrote that:

> the proportionality factor might only be applied, or be meaningful, in the case of adjacent States . . . where the existence of a markedly concave or convex coastline will produce a cut-off effect if the equidistance principle

---

[146] Weil (n. 9) 77.
[147] Ibid.
[148] Ibid. 85.
[149] Art. 7 UNCLOS. See Chapter 3, Section II.B.2 above.
[150] Art. 7 UNCLOS.

is applied: that is to say, will allocate to one State shelf areas which in fact lie in front of, and are a prolongation of, the land territory of another.[151]

In *Libya/Malta*, Judge *ad hoc* Valticos adopted Bowett's views. According to Judge *ad hoc* Valticos, before *Libya/Malta* international tribunals used proportionality only where:

> the coasts concerned belonged to adjacent States, and their configurations were such as to carry a risk of encroachment or curtailment. The Court has itself pointed out that, in matters of delimitation, the position of opposite coasts is radically different from that of adjacent States .... The aim of proportionality, where *adjacent coasts* are concerned, is to avoid solutions which, in some instances, owing to the particular configuration of the coasts in question, may seem contrary to equity. Here, in my opinion, there are neither adjacent coasts nor any abnormal configuration, and no part should be played by proportionality.[152]

Bowett and Judge *ad hoc* Valticos's would confine proportionality's application only to cases in which coasts are adjacent, as the only case in which concave coastlines could determine cut-off.

However, this is not entirely correct. First, delimitation based on distance could curtail the entitlement of one state *vis-à-vis* another state even between opposite coasts. For example, in *Nicaragua v. Colombia* the ICJ found that a strict equidistance line would have cut off Nicaragua's coastal projections.[153] Second, nothing in the *North Sea Continental Shelf* judgment, which Judge *ad hoc* Valticos mentioned to support his view, conveys that the Court understood proportionality to be applicable solely between adjacent coasts. The ICJ accepted Germany's contention on the applicability of proportionality, which was explicitly based on Vallat's 1946 article.[154] Although Vallat had written of proportionality as a delimitation method, he had not limited its applicability depending on coastal configuration.

Both Tanaka, and Fietta and Cleverly, criticised the use of disproportionality between opposite coasts on geometrical bases. Referring to *Libya/Malta*, Tanaka wrote that the 'difference of coastal lengths [is] already reflected in the surfaces of the two zones separated by the median line'.[155] However, his argument unconvincingly conflates coastal length disparity and proportionality. That argument's persuasiveness also

---

[151] DW Bowett, *The Legal Regime of Islands in International Law* (Oceana, 1979) 164.
[152] *Libya/Malta* (n. 13) 110 [19] (Separate Opinion Valticos).
[153] *Nicaragua v. Colombia* (n. 24) 703–4 [215]–[216].
[154] Section III.A above.
[155] Tanaka (n. 7) 458–9.

depends on the shape of the relevant area. While it may be sound in relation to a trapezoidal relevant area, as in *Libya/Malta*, it may not be so in relation to a rectangular relevant area.

Fietta and Cleverly correctly wrote that 'lines have a square relationship with areas'.[156] They argued that disproportionality was originally only intended to abate cut-off, and that between opposite coasts cut-off is avoided by adjusting an equidistance line pursuant to the relevant circumstance of coastal length disparity.[157] However, disproportionality is not premised on a mathematical relationship between coastal length ratios and marine area ratios, nor should it be.[158] Moreover, the fact that between opposite coasts cut-off may be abated by shifting an equidistance line on account of coastal length disparity, a relevant circumstance, seems insufficient to conclude that disproportionality is not useful to test the equitableness of a boundary. Between opposite coasts, disproportionality ensures that adjusting an equidistance line at the second stage of the delimitation process based on coastal length disparity actually abated cut-off.[159] Limiting the applicability of disproportionality to delimitation between adjacent coasts is thus unpersuasive.

Another difficult question, which is still a matter of academic contention, is whether disproportionality should be employed in delimiting the continental shelf beyond 200 nm. ITLOS,[160] the *Bangladesh* v. *India* tribunal[161] and the Special Chamber in *Ghana/Côte d'Ivoire*[162] could be criticised for having assessed disproportionality in the delimitation of the continental shelf beyond 200 nm. Disproportionality is premised on the possibility to calculate mathematically, although not necessarily with full precision, the extent of the marine areas found to appertain to a state. Mathematical calculations are subsequently weighed against the geographical and non-geographical circumstances of a case, and thus do not necessarily determine further adjustments of a boundary. Since the adoption of the three-stage approach, international tribunals have made

---

[156] Fietta and Cleverly (n. 9) 604–5.
[157] Ibid. 607.
[158] Section IV.B above.
[159] Cottier also argued that, except for *Libya/Malta* and *Nicaragua* v. *Colombia*, international tribunals have not applied disproportionality in other opposite-coast delimitations. However, proportionality was also assessed in *St. Pierre et Miquelon*, *Jan Mayen*, *Eritrea/Yemen* and *Black Sea*. In *Black Sea*, the ICJ considered that Crimea's coast and Romania's coast were in a relationship of oppositeness. See *Black Sea* (n. 3) 93 [88].
[160] *Bangladesh/Myanmar* (n. 22) 125–6 [489]–[499].
[161] *Bangladesh* v. *India* (n. 23) 167–9 [490]–[497].
[162] *Ghana/Côte d'Ivoire* (n. 65) [533]–[538].

these calculations more frequently.[163] However, with respect to the continental shelf beyond 200 nm it is not always feasible to calculate the extent of the marine areas found to appertain to a state, unless the location of the continental shelf's outer limits is known. This is especially true between adjacent states. Although disproportionality's use is grounded in the basis of title over the continental shelf beyond 200 nm,[164] it may be inadvisable to employ it in delimitation beyond 200 nm before the continental shelf's outer limits are delineated.

Under Article 76 UNCLOS, delineating the continental shelf's outer limits requires a coastal state to file a submission with the Commission on the Limits of the Continental Shelf (CLCS). The CLCS delivers a recommendation 'on the basis' of which the coastal state unilaterally establishes the continental shelf's outer limits.[165] Until this procedure is completed, it is impossible to know exactly where the continental shelf's outer limits lie, and therefore to conduct a meaningful proportionality test beyond 200 nm. In the Bay of Bengal cases, both ITLOS and the *Bangladesh v. India* tribunal approximated the relevant area in order to be able to assess proportionality. While ITLOS employed two straight lines as the western and southern limits of the relevant area, the *Bangladesh v. India* tribunal used the continental shelf's outer limits as outlined in Bangladesh's submission to the CLCS. The task of the Special Chamber in *Ghana/Côte d'Ivoire* was easier, since the CLCS had already made its recommendation on the outer limits of Ghana's continental shelf. However, Côte d'Ivoire's submission to the CLCS was still pending at the time of the Special Chamber's judgment.

All three approaches lack precision. ITLOS's solution is inaccurate, as it cannot identify the continental shelf to which the parties were entitled beyond 200 nm. The *Bangladesh v. India* tribunal's approach is flawed as it assumed that the CLCS, in its future recommendation, would confirm the outer limits submitted by Bangladesh. The same issue arose in relation to the Special Chamber's approach, although limited to Côte d'Ivoire's continental shelf. Boundaries beyond 200 nm should not be delimited before the delineation of the continental shelf's outer limits, as prior to delineation there can be no certainty as to whether overlapping entitlements beyond 200 nm exist, and as to their exact location.[166] Avoiding delimitation beyond 200 nm before the continental shelf's

---
[163] Section IV.B above.
[164] Section III.C above.
[165] Art. 76(8) UNCLOS.
[166] Chapter 4, Section III.C above.

outer limits have been established would prevent issues as to whether it is appropriate to use disproportionality in that context.

V Disproportionality and Coastal Length Disparity

Coastal length disparity and disproportionality belong in distinct phases of the three-stage approach. While the former is a relevant circumstance at the second stage, the assessment of the latter constitutes the third stage. However, both require international tribunals to assess the ratio between the states' coastal lengths. One may question the utility of having two distinct elements of the delimitation process requiring international tribunals to assess the same aspect, namely coastal length ratio.

A *The Functions of Disproportionality and Coastal Length Disparity*

The relationship between disproportionality and coastal length disparity has hardly been mentioned in the literature. Evans discussed it with respect to *Gulf of Maine*, in which the Chamber did not use proportionality as a test for the overall equitableness of the result, relying on the 'catastrophic repercussions test' instead.[167] The Chamber held that verifying the equitableness of the result was unnecessary for the first two segments of the boundary, since:

> it would scarcely be possible to assess the equitable character of the delimitation there carried out on the basis of any other than the dominant parameters provided by the physical and political geography of the area. And it is precisely those parameters which served the Chamber as a guide in determining the parts of the line which are to take effect in this portion of the delimitation area.[168]

Evans interpreted this statement to mean that '[b]ecause the disproportion of the relevant coastal lengths is taken as a relevant circumstance affecting the implementation of the practical method, the question of assessing the proportionality of the result is no longer really necessary'.[169] Although Evans's reading appears plausible, the Chamber's statement is not entirely clear. Commenting on the ICJ's use of proportionality in *Libya/Malta*, Tanaka wrote that 'proportionality has played a double role as a factor for adjusting a provisionally drawn median line and as a test of

---

[167] *Gulf of Maine* (n. 11) 340–4 [232]–[241]. See chapter 5, Section III.A.2 above.
[168] *Gulf of Maine* (n. 11) 340 [231].
[169] Evans (n. 9) 228.

the equitableness of the result',[170] and that '[t]his double use of proportionality smacks of circular reasoning'.[171] However, neither Tanaka nor Evans explained their views further.

Costal length disparity and disproportionality have distinct functions in the three-stage approach. International tribunals treat the former as a relevant circumstance, capable of justifying the adjustment of an inequitable equidistance line. The latter is an overall test for the equitableness of the boundary. Moreover, although disproportionality requires re-assessing the ratio between the lengths of the states party's relevant coast, it also entails assessing the ratio between the marine areas allocated to each state. Both the functional difference, and the presence of the further component of marine area ratio, could warrant the use of both coastal length disparity and disproportionality in delimitation.

Furthermore, disproportionality has been applied in all delimitation cases decided by means of the three-stage approach.[172] Disproportionality could be assessed regardless of whether relevant circumstances had determined the adjustment of an equidistance line. In *Black Sea*, the ICJ found that no relevant circumstances justified adjusting the equidistance line, and later assessed whether that line satisfied disproportionality.[173] Similarly, in *Bangladesh/Myanmar*, *Bangladesh v. India*, *Ghana/Côte d'Ivoire* and *Costa Rica v. Nicaragua*, coastal length disparity did not determine an adjustment of the equidistance line. However, cut-off justified shifting the equidistance line in three of those cases.[174] *Nicaragua v. Colombia* was the only dispute decided by applying the three-stage approach in which an international tribunal adjusted the equidistance line based on coastal length disparity, and subsequently assessed disproportionality.[175] International tribunals do not necessarily consider both coastal length disparity and disproportionality in all delimitation cases. Therefore, the issue whether there are reasons not to assess disproportionality only arises if coastal length disparity has already determined the adjustment of the equidistance line.

---

[170] Tanaka (n. 7) 443.
[171] Ibid.
[172] Section IV.A above.
[173] *Black Sea* (n. 3) 112–30 [155]–[216].
[174] *Bangladesh/Myanmar* (n. 22) 80–2 [290]–[297] and 118 [461]–[462]; *Bangladesh v. India* (n. 23) 132–8 [400]–[421] and 160–1 [469]–[475]; *Ghana/Côte d'Ivoire* (n. 65) [533]–[538]; *Costa Rica v. Nicaragua* (n. 94) 218–20 [192]–[199] and 224 [202]–[204]. Although *Peru v. Chile* presented a situation similar to *Bangladesh/Myanmar* and *Bangladesh v. India*, the ICJ conducted no meaningful disproportionality test.
[175] *Nicaragua v. Colombia* (n. 24) 702 [209]–[211] and 715–17 [239]–[247].

As international tribunals always assess disproportionality in the three-stage approach, it is unconvincing only to refer to disputes decided by applying that approach in order to show that both coastal length disparity and disproportionality can and should be assessed in delimiting maritime boundaries. In pre-2009 disputes, both coastal length disparity and disproportionality were seen as relevant circumstances, appraised at the same stage of the delimitation process. The question is whether in such disputes international tribunals adjusted equidistance lines based on coastal length disparity and, at the same time, also assessed disproportionality.

B Disproportionality and Coastal Length Disparity in the Jurisprudence

International tribunals have adopted different approaches to the relationship between disproportionality and coastal length disparity, depending on whether the case in which the issue arose fell to be decided before or after the introduction of the three-stage delimitation process in *Black Sea*.

1 Before the three-stage approach

The arbitral tribunal in the 2002 *Newfoundland and Labrador/Nova Scotia Arbitration* found that 'in the cases where relative lengths of coasts have been treated as relevant circumstances ... the [ICJ] has not applied [proportionality], for reasons which appear to relate ... to the fact that the proportionality factor has already been taken into account in drawing the line'.[176] However, this statement is unpersuasive, as the arbitral tribunal wrongly conflated coastal length disparity with proportionality. Moreover, both earlier and later cases do not support the tribunal's assessment.

Coastal length disparity determined the adjustment of an equidistance line in *Gulf of Maine*,[177] *Libya/Malta*,[178] *Jan Mayen*[179] and *Barbados v. Trinidad and Tobago*.[180] However, in none of these cases was a proper

---

[176] *Arbitration between Newfoundland and Labrador and Nova Scotia (Newfoundland and Labrador/Nova Scotia) (Second Phase)* (2002) 128 ILR 504, 575 [5.17].
[177] *Gulf of Maine* (n. 11) 334–5 [218].
[178] *Libya/Malta* (n. 13) 48–53 [66]–[73].
[179] *Jan Mayen* (n. 4) 67–70 [65]–[71].
[180] *Barbados v. Trinidad and Tobago* (n. 18) 234–5 [327]–[328]. In *Qatar v. Bahrain* and *Cameroon v. Nigeria*, the ICJ concluded that coastal length disparity did not justify an adjustment of the equidistance line. See *Qatar v. Bahrain* (n. 86) 114 [241]–[243]; *Cameroon v. Nigeria* (n. 86) 446–7 [301].

proportionality test conducted. In *Libya/Malta*, the ICJ adopted an unclear position. The Court found that 'there is no reason of principle why the test of proportionality ... should not be employed to verify the equity of a delimitation between opposite coasts, just as well as between adjacent coasts'.[181] Nevertheless, it held that certain 'difficulties are particularly evident in the present case', relating to the identification of the relevant area.[182] In a seemingly contradictory manner, the Court subsequently stated that:

> it is possible for [the Court] to make a broad assessment of the equitableness of the result, without seeking to define the equities in arithmetical terms. The conclusion to which the Court comes in this respect is that there is certainly no evident disproportion in the areas of shelf attributed to each of the Parties respectively such that it could be said that the requirements of the test of proportionality as an aspect of equity were not satisfied.[183]

The Court performed no actual proportionality assessment because of the difficulty in identifying the relevant area.[184] It did not rely on having already shifted the provisional equidistance line northwards as a reason for not assessing proportionality.

In *Jan Mayen*, the ICJ conflated coastal length disparity with proportionality, and the Court ultimately assessed only the former, and not the latter.[185] The *Barbados* v. *Trinidad and Tobago* tribunal held that it would 'review the effects of the line of delimitation in the light of proportionality as a function of equity after having taken into account any other relevant circumstance'.[186] However, when purportedly assessing proportionality, the tribunal made no reference to the marine areas allocated to each party. Instead, it applied proportionality similarly to the *Anglo/French Arbitration*, as a means to establish whether certain maritime features have a 'disproportionate' effect on the boundary.[187] The arbitral tribunal found that:

> the deflection effected does not result in giving effect to the relevant coastal frontages in a manner that could itself be considered

---

[181] *Libya/Malta* (n. 13) 53 [74].
[182] Ibid.
[183] Ibid. 53–4 [75].
[184] See ibid. 132–4 [14]–[17] (Dissenting Opinion Oda); ibid. 181 and 186 (Dissenting Opinion Schwebel).
[185] Section IV.B.2 above.
[186] *Barbados* v. *Trinidad and Tobago* (n. 18) 237 [338].
[187] Section IV.A.1 above.

disproportionate .... The bending of the equidistance line reflects a reasonable influence of the coastal frontages on the overall area of delimitation, with a view to avoiding reciprocal encroachments which would otherwise result in some form of inequity.[188]

Neither *Jan Mayen* nor *Barbados* v. *Trinidad and Tobago* suggest that the reason for not assessing proportionality was that the boundary had already been adjusted as a result of coastal length disparity. *Gulf of Maine* is the only instance in which an international tribunal might have adduced the adjustment based on coastal length disparity as a reason not to assess proportionality.[189] However, the Chamber's statements in this respect are unclear. The individual opinions in the cases discussed above do not clarify whether coastal length disparity prevented proportionality from being meaningfully assessed. Only in *Libya/Malta* did Judge *ad hoc* Valticos express his reservations concerning 'the fact that ... the difference in the length of the coasts is taken into consideration both as a relevant circumstance and as a final check in the verification of the result'. However, he did not further elaborate on his view.[190]

In the pre-2009 cases, international tribunals assessed proportionality by reference to mathematical ratios, finding that it was met in *Tunisia/Libya*,[191] *St. Pierre et Miquelon*,[192] *Eritrea/Yemen*[193] and *Guyana* v. *Suriname*.[194] However, in none of these four cases did the international tribunals concerned adjust a boundary based on coastal length disparity. This indicates that, before 2009, international tribunals did one of two things: either they adjusted an equidistance line based on coastal length disparity, without meaningfully assessing proportionality at a later stage; or they did not adjust a boundary based on coastal length disparity, assessing proportionality by reference to mathematical ratios at a later stage, and finding that it was satisfied.

In his separate opinion in *Jan Mayen*, Judge Shahabuddeen suggested that 'there is no purpose in taking into account a disparity in coastal lengths in the process of effecting a delimitation unless the intention is that the disparity is to be reflected in the [continental shelf] rights of the

---

[188] *Barbados* v. *Trinidad and Tobago* (n. 18) 244 [379].
[189] Section V.A above.
[190] *Libya/Malta* (n. 13) 111 [20] (Separate Opinion Valticos).
[191] *Tunisia/Libya* (n. 80) 91 [131].
[192] *St. Pierre et Miquelon* (n. 14) 296–7 [92]–[93].
[193] *Eritrea/Yemen* (n. 16) 372 [165].
[194] *Guyana* v. *Suriname* (n. 89) 109 [392].

V DISPROPORTIONALITY AND COASTAL LENGTH DISPARITY 285

parties as assigned to them by the delimitation line'.[195] He specified that such rights are 'estimated ... by reference to the areal division accomplished by the line'.[196] Judge Shahabuddeen considered the appraisal of coastal length disparity as a relevant circumstance complementing the proportionality test. According to him:

> [u]nless, when taking account of a disparity in coastal lengths in the process of effecting a delimitation, one at the same time has an eye to the ultimate effect of the operation on the extent of the maritime areas which the delimitation will assign to each claimant, the disparity in coastal lengths will not have been realistically taken into account when effecting the delimitation. Conversely, ... where a disparity in coastal lengths has been realistically taken into account, any *ex post facto* test is unlikely to reveal anything inequitable in the result so far as proportionality between coastal lengths and continental shelf areas is concerned.[197]

According to Judge Shahabuddeen, '[t]hat [in *Jan Mayen*] the *ex post facto* test revealed no material disproportionality was not a miraculous coincidence; it was a logical consequence of account having been realistically taken of the disparity in coastal lengths in the process of delimitation'.[198]

Judge Shahabuddeen argued that while international tribunals did not say it explicitly, they assessed proportionality even in the cases in which the boundary had already been adjusted based on coastal length disparity. This explanation could be accepted in relation to *Jan Mayen*, since Judge Shahabuddeen sat on the ICJ when the case was decided. However, it seems more difficult to accept it in relation to *Libya/Malta* and *Gulf of Maine*, decided before Judge Shahabuddeen's time on the ICJ's bench. Similarly, Judge Shahabuddeen's view could not explain the decision in *Barbados* v. *Trinidad and Tobago*, decided thirteen years after *Jan Mayen*. It is also odd that international tribunals, when assessing coastal length disparity, would take into account the marine area ratio without saying it explicitly. There seems to be no rational reason for this *modus operandi*, since expressing marine area ratios would ground the international tribunals' decisions on delimitation in fuller and presumably more cogent reasoning.

Furthermore, Judge Shahabuddeen's explanation does not account for the cases in which no adjustment resulted from coastal length disparity,

---
[195] *Jan Mayen* (n. 4) 173 (Separate Opinion Shahabuddeen).
[196] Ibid.
[197] Ibid. 173–4.
[198] Ibid. 174.

and yet proportionality was found to have been satisfied. Judge Shahabuddeen wrote that lack of disproportionality 'was not a miraculous coincidence' in the cases where coastal length disparity determined the boundary's adjustment. This statement seemed to establish a causal connection between adjusting a boundary based on coastal length disparity and satisfying the proportionality test. It follows that in cases where no adjustment was made despite a great coastal length disparity, proportionality was satisfied only by coincidence. For example, in *St. Pierre et Miquelon* the disparity between the length of the parties' coast was considerable, since the coastal length ratio was of 1:15.3 in Canada's favour.[199] However, coastal length disparity did not lead to the adjustment of that boundary. Accepting Judge Shahabuddeen's views, one should conclude that proportionality was satisfied by mere chance. Judge Shahabuddeen's argument appears to be premised on the absence of rational decision-making by international tribunals in cases comparable to *St. Pierre et Miquelon*. However, one is or should be, reluctant to accept that decision-making by international tribunals could be irrational and guided by chance.

2   After the three-stage approach

The pre-2009 cases do not support the claim that the assessment, in the same dispute, of both coastal length disparity and disproportionality is legally or practically unsound. International tribunals never stated that disproportionality was satisfied as a result of having previously adjusted a boundary because of coastal length disparity. Moreover, satisfying disproportionality is independent of adjustments owed to coastal length disparity. Therefore, it does not seem that adjusting a boundary pursuant to coastal length disparity renders a disproportionality assessment redundant.

The three-stage approach strengthened the mutual independence of disproportionality and coastal length disparity. Disproportionality is an integral part of the three-stage approach. Being necessarily considered in all cases decided by means of the three-stage approach underscores its independence of any other relevant circumstance, including coastal length disparity. The necessary assessment of disproportionality may cause some issues. International tribunals could feel compelled to assess disproportionality, although the geographical complexity of a case might suggest that assessing disproportionality would be unsuitable, as in

---

[199] *St. Pierre et Miquelon* (n. 14) 281 [33].

Peru v. *Chile*. However, the issues with assessing disproportionality are unrelated to adjustments resulting from coastal length disparity, as they stem from the alleged problems in identifying the relevant coast and the relevant area.[200] Moreover, the function of disproportionality is different from that of coastal length disparity. While the latter is a check on the equitableness of a strict provisional equidistance line, the former is a check on the equitableness of an (eventually) adjusted provisional equidistance line. The three-stage approach emphasises this functional difference.

The assessment of disproportionality is also different from the assessment of coastal length disparity. The latter is an appreciation of whether there exists a marked disparity between the lengths of the relevant coasts. The former entails the appreciation of the relationship between coastal length ratio and marine area ratio, taking into account all the other circumstances of the case. These differences are evident in *Nicaragua* v. *Colombia*. The ICJ found the coastal length ratio to be 1:8.2 in Nicaragua's favour, and held that '[t]his is undoubtedly a substantial disparity and the Court considers that it requires an adjustment or shifting of the provisional line'.[201] On disproportionality, the Court decided whether the disproportion between a 1:8.2 coastal length ratio and a 1:3.44 marine area ratio was, 'in the circumstances of the present case, ... so great as to render the result inequitable'.[202] The Court held that the overriding need to prevent the cut-off of both states' coastal projections, and to prevent the enclavement of Colombia's islands, entailed that the existing disproportion did not render the boundary inequitable.[203]

In addition, the three-stage approach overcomes the problems arising from Judge Shahabuddeen's views. The three-stage approach avoids the surreptitious appreciation of marine area ratios.[204] Moreover, by rejecting the existence of a purported causal link between adjusting an equidistance line based on coastal length disparity and satisfying disproportionality, the three-stage approach avoids the semblance that disproportionality could be satisfied by chance. The three-stage approach could be seen to have clarified the once ambiguous relationship between coastal length disparity and disproportionality.

---

[200] See Chapter 3 above.
[201] *Nicaragua* v. *Colombia* (n. 24) 702 [211].
[202] Ibid. 716 [243].
[203] Ibid. 716–17 [244].
[204] As in *Gulf of Maine*, *Libya/Malta*, *Jan Mayen* and *Barbados* v. *Trinidad and Tobago*.

VI Disproportionality Re-Affirmed

Some writers argued that disproportionality should be removed from the delimitation process.[205] However, this argument fails to convince. Despite the initial lack of legal basis, disproportionality acquired such a basis as a result of the legal developments culminating with the adoption of UNCLOS. Disproportionality has a clear function in the three-stage delimitation process as a final test for the equitableness of a boundary. Other functions that disproportionality may have had prior to 2009 have been superseded. The views restricting disproportionality to delimitation between adjacent coasts are also unpersuasive. International tribunals have taken a number of approaches on disproportionality's assessment in the cases. Ultimately, this is a matter properly left to the international tribunals' own discretion. As to the relationship between disproportionality and coastal length disparity, assessing the latter does not make evaluating the former redundant. The three-stage approach clarified such a relationship, underlining the structural and functional differences that justify assessing disproportionality even in cases where coastal length disparity has already determined the adjustment of a provisional equidistance line.

Although certain commentators have made compelling arguments against using disproportionality in delimitation, their reservations ultimately relate to uncertainties in identifying the relevant coast and the relevant area. However, such uncertainties can be overcome.[206] Evans wrote that proportionality 'does not fit and ... does not help'.[207] This could be seen to be too sweeping a statement. The fact that international tribunals have always found that disproportionality was satisfied does not necessarily mean that it does not help. Conceivably, one should not expect disproportionality to play a revolutionary role in delimitation. Disproportionality has a more modest calling, as a final test to confirm that boundaries emerging from the first and second phases of the three-stage approach are equitable. Adjustments based on relevant circumstances already seek to remedy the inequitableness of provisional equidistance lines. Therefore, it could appear desirable that the boundaries resulting from these adjustments be equitable already. Disproportionality simply confirms that this is the case. Therefore, its function is to be a further benchmark ensuring the achievement of the equitable solution

---

[205] Section I above.
[206] Chapter 3 above.
[207] Evans (n. 6) 156.

required under Articles 74 and 83 UNCLOS. One should not simply dismiss disproportionality because it fulfils a limited function in maritime delimitation. In principle, disproportionality has a valuable part to play in the delimitation process, provided that international tribunals apply it consistently with the basis of title, with the function of maritime areas, and with their earlier jurisprudence.

7

States, International Tribunals and the Delimitation Process

I Misgivings on the Delimitation Process as a Judicial Creation

The jurisprudence of international tribunals on maritime delimitation may be a reaction to the inability of states to agree on a clear rule governing the establishment of maritime boundaries in the continental shelf and in the Exclusive Economic Zone (EEZ).[1] Despite the absence of such a rule, states have requested international tribunals to delimit maritime boundaries between them. However, the influence of states on the delimitation process extends beyond both their law-making function at the Third United Nations Conference on the Law of the Sea (UNCLOS III), and their role as parties in judicial disputes. States, as the main subjects of international law, have a function in sanctioning the delimitation process as developed by international tribunals. States create rules of international law, which are later applied by international tribunals. However, in maritime delimitation this process appears to have been inverted. States codified rules governing EEZ and continental shelf delimitation in Articles 74 and 83 of the United Nations Convention on the Law of the Sea (UNCLOS).[2] Nevertheless, the vagueness of such rules has determined an active role by international tribunals in shaping the judicial process for maritime delimitation.

International tribunals could be considered to be makers of the delimitation process. The legal basis of their law-making function stems both from the impossibility for customary rules of international law to develop in maritime delimitation, and from the inability of states to agree on clear treaty rules governing delimitation. Confronted with this

---

[1] Scovazzi wrote that Arts. 74 and 83 UNCLOS created obligations of a mere procedural character. See T Scovazzi, *Elementi di Diritto Internazionale del Mare* 3rd edn (Giuffrè, 2002) 63.
[2] 1833 UNTS 3.

normative void, international tribunals seem to have had little choice but to exercise a creative function, which, owing to their jurisprudence over half a century, has crystallised in the three-stage delimitation process. This creative function is connected with the character of international judicial decisions as formal sources of international law. While international tribunals may exercise a law-making function, states can either sanction the law developed through judicial elaboration, or oppose that development.

The approach of states towards the jurisprudence on maritime delimitation is key. One can assess this approach by reference to the manner in which states behave on the international plane, which includes their statements in international fora, maritime delimitation agreements, pleadings before international tribunals, and compliance with decisions establishing maritime boundaries. States seem to have influenced not only the acceptance of the delimitation process as formulated by international courts and tribunals, but also its very formulation, without explicitly or implicitly sanctioning the status of judicial decisions on the delimitation process as a source of international law. Concerning certain elements of that process, such as disproportionality, international tribunals have conceivably adopted the views expressed by states. The common idea that the delimitation process is entirely the product of judicial law-making is misconceived.

Section II considers the role of international tribunals as lawmakers in maritime delimitation. Section III analyses the approach of states to the three-stage delimitation process. Sections IV and V conclude.

II International Tribunals as Lawmakers

Judicial decisions are 'subsidiary means for the determination of rules of law', pursuant to Article 38(1)(d) of the Statute of the International Court of Justice (ICJ or Court). Scholars agree on the character of judicial decisions as material sources of international law.[3] However, there appears to exist a legal basis also to consider them to be a formal source of the law of maritime delimitation.

---

[3] The literature on sources of international law is extensive. For reference, see RY Jennings and A Watts, *Oppenheim's International Law* 9th edn (Longman, 1992) vol. I, 41–2; T Treves, *Diritto Internazionale – Problemi Fondamentali* (Giuffrè, 2005) 280–3; J Crawford, *Brownlie's Principles of Public International Law* 8th edn (OUP, 2012) 37–9; H Thirlway, *The Sources of International Law* (OUP, 2014) 117–19.

A Legal Basis of Judicial Law-making in Maritime Delimitation

The international tribunals' law-making function in maritime delimitation appears to be based both on the impossibility of the delimitation process becoming part of customary international law, and on the vagueness of Articles 74 and 83 UNCLOS.

1   Lack of customary international law on the delimitation process

Customary rules of international law are created by the joint presence of state practice and *opinio juris sive necessitatis*.[4] The existence of custom is thus ascertained through an inductive process. The recent work of the International Law Commission (ILC) on the identification of customary international law endorsed this view. ILC Special Rapporteur Sir Michael Wood proceeded on the basis that the identification of a rule of customary international law requires assessing both practice and the acceptance of that practice as law.[5] States supported the two-element approach in their comments to the ILC.[6] This support resulted in the ILC's Drafting Committee approving Conclusion 2 at its 2018 session, under which '[t]o determine the existence and content of a rule of customary international law, it is necessary to ascertain whether there is a general practice that is accepted as law (*opinio juris*)'.[7]

While the two-element approach to custom is well established, the relationship between the two elements and which evidence could prove their existence is more complex. The ILC Special Rapporteur stated that, in establishing the existence of a customary rule of international law, 'it is necessary to consider and verify the existence of each element separately',[8] which would require 'an assessment of different evidence for each element'.[9] Adhering to a purported rule does not prove that

---

[4] *North Sea Continental Shelf (Federal Republic of Germany/Denmark; Federal Republic of Germany/Netherlands)* (Judgment) [1969] ICJ Rep 3, 44 [77]; *Jurisdictional Immunities of the State (Germany v. Italy)* (Judgment) [2012] ICJ Rep 99, 122 [55].

[5] Second Report on the Identification of Customary International Law by Sir Michael Wood, Special Rapporteur, UN Doc A/CN.4/672 (22 May 2014) 7 [21]; Third Report on the Identification of Customary International Law by Sir Michael Wood, Special Rapporteur, UN Doc A/CN.4/682 (27 March 2015) 4 [13].

[6] Fifth Report on the Identification of Customary International Law by Sir Michael Wood, Special Rapporteur, UN Doc A/CN.4/717 (14 March 2018) 12 [28].

[7] Text of the Draft Conclusions as adopted by the Drafting Committee on Second Reading, UN Doc A/CN.4/L.908 (17 May 2018) 1.

[8] Third Report (n. 5) 5 [14].

[9] Ibid.

states feel compelled by a sense of legal obligation.[10] Therefore, state practice could not also be evidence of *opinio juris*. In *Jurisidictional Immunities of the State*, the ICJ appears to have taken a similar approach in analysing the customary character of the territorial tort exception to state immunity. The Court made a detailed analysis of state practice in the form of national legislation and court decisions,[11] while recognising that *opinio juris* is reflected:

> in particular in the assertion by States claiming immunity that international law accords them a right to such immunity from the jurisdiction of other states; in the acknowledgement, by States granting immunity, that international law imposes upon them an obligation to do so; and, conversely, in the assertion by States in other cases of a right to exercise jurisdiction over foreign States.[12]

This strict approach to identifying customary international law is problematic in maritime delimitation. States have produced a wealth of practice, especially in the form of maritime delimitation treaties.

However, such practice does not seem to be accompanied by the requisite *opinio juris*, ascertained based on distinct evidence. In the treaty texts, states do not justify on legal grounds the manner in which they have established a boundary. States simply agree that their boundary will follow a certain course, often identified by a set of co-ordinates. The negotiating history of such treaties is not public, making the use of the *travaux préparatoires* unfeasible to understand whether states delimited a boundary in a certain manner because of a sense of legal obligation. Nothing prevents states initially from following a course of conduct based on convenience,[13] yet convenience must evolve into a sense of legal obligation in order for that course of conduct to become customary international law.

Commentators wrote on the alternatives to the strict approach to finding evidence of state practice and *opinio juris*. Although implicitly, Klabbers appears to maintain that *opinio juris* can be derived from state practice.[14] Kirgis argued that custom could be seen to be on a sliding

---

[10] Second Report (n. 5) 58–9 [72]–[74].
[11] *Jurisdictional Immunities of the State* (n. 4) 130–4 [70]–[76].
[12] Ibid. 123 [55]. The Court considered such assertions to have been made by national courts, see ibid. 135 [77].
[13] M Mendelson, 'On the Quasi-Normative Effect of Maritime Boundary Agreements' in N Ando et al. (eds.), *Liber Amicorum Shigeru Oda* (Martinus Nijhoff, 2002) vol. II, 1069, 1077–83.
[14] J Klabbers, *International Law* 2nd edn (CUP 2017) 31–3.

scale: widespread and consistent practice would allow the identification of customary international law despite the paucity of *opinio juris*.[15] Alternatively, Talmon suggested that, in practice, the ICJ 'simply asserts the law as it sees fit'.[16] Using such techniques, international tribunals could rely on the extensive state practice on maritime delimitation and, either through deduction, or by assertion, state that certain delimitation methods are part of customary international law. However, it seems that no international tribunal has explicitly sanctioned any alternative to the classic two-element approach. Based on the ICJ's approach to identifying custom, it appears unrealistic to establish the existence of a customary rule of international law requiring international tribunals to use a delimitation method. Accordingly, the source of the rules of international law governing the delimitation process should be found elsewhere.

2   Consequences of the vagueness of Articles 74 and 83 UNCLOS

Judicial law-making is justified so long as the applicable law in a given case is sufficiently indeterminate so as not to provide for the manner in which specific rules of international law are practically to be applied.

Legal indeterminacy and the exercise of the international judicial function as a reaction to it are linked to the question of gaps in the law, and whether the existence of such gaps provides a legal justification to exercise judicial law-making. This issue is in turn linked to that of the completeness of international law. While the supporters of the completeness theory argue that judicial decisions have a vital role in developing the law, its detractors assume the possibility of *non liquet* and reject the gap-filling function of judicial decisions.[17]

---

[15] A Roberts, 'Traditional and Modern Approaches to Customary International Law: A Reconciliation' (2001) 95 *AJIL* 757, 758. See also F Kirgis, 'Custom on a Sliding Scale' (1987) 81 *AJIL* 146, 149; J Tasioulas, 'In Defence of Relative Normativity: Communitarian Values and the *Nicaragua* Case' (1996) 16 *OJLS* 85; J Kammerhofer, 'Uncertainty in the Formal Sources of International Law: Customary International Law and Some of its Problems' (2004) 15 *EJIL* 523, 542-6

[16] S Talmon, 'Determining Customary International Law: The ICJ's Methodology between Induction, Deduction and Assertion' (2015) 26 *EJIL* 417, 434.

[17] *Non liquet* refers to 'an insufficiency in the law: specifically, a finding by a court that the law does not permit a conclusion one way or the other concerning the issue in question'. See D Bodansky, '*Non Liquet* and the Incompleteness of International Law' in L Boisson de Chazournes and P Sands (eds.), *International Law, the International Court of Justice and Nuclear Weapons* (CUP, 1999) 153, 154.

Leading authors have supported the notion that a legal system cannot be complete. In the 1993 postscript to *The Concept of Law*, HLA Hart argued that:

> legal rules and principles identified in general terms by the criteria provided by the rule of recognition often have what I call frequently 'open texture', so that when the question is whether a given rule applies to a particular case the law fails to determine an answer either way and so proves partially indeterminate. Such cases are not merely 'hard cases', controversial in the sense that reasonable and informed lawyers may disagree about which answer is legally correct, but the law in such cases is fundamentally incomplete: it provides no answer to the questions at issue in such cases. They are legally unregulated and in order to reach a decision in such cases the courts must exercise the restricted law-making function which I call 'discretion'.[18]

Hart argues that judges having to apply 'open textured' legal provisions exercise a law-making function.[19] However, his argument appears somewhat contradictory. Although Hart stated that the law is incomplete, he approved of judicial law-making in the application of 'open textured' legal provisions. It seems that such law-making would eventually render the law complete. Hart's view is thus not entirely convincing.

Writing specifically on international law, Weil argued that:

> [r]egardless of the judicial and scholarly endeavors to affirm the completeness of international law, the truth of the matter is that international law is not complete. No legal order is, because there is not, cannot be, and should not be a rule at hand for every concrete or new situation.[20]

One could explain Weil's perspective based on his defence of classic legal positivism, which, in his view, is grounded in state consent as the basis for the creation of rules of international law.[21] However, state consent, although central, could be seen not to be the only basis for creating

---

[18] HLA Hart, *The Concept of Law* 3rd edn (OUP, 2012) 252. See also J Raz, 'Legal Reason, Sources and Gaps' in J Raz (ed.), *The Authority of Law* (OUP, 1979) 53. Hart's 'open texture' is classified by Bodansky as an 'epistemological gap in the law'. See Bodansky (n. 17) 154.

[19] Hart (n. 18) 135.

[20] P Weil, '"The Court Cannot Conclude Definitively..." *Non Liquet* Revisited' (1998) 36 *Columbia Journal of Transnational Law* 109, 118.

[21] P Weil, 'Le Droit International en Quête de son Identité' (1992) 237 *Recueil des Cours* 9, 66–81 and 177–9. Bodansky stated that '[i]f we assume that international law is based on consent, then the incompleteness of international law should not be surprising'. See Bodansky (n. 17) 164.

rules of international law,[22] as Weil himself acknowledged.[23] That the international legal system cannot be complete because states must consent to all rules binding on them overlooks that certain rules are not created wholly on the basis of state consent.

Sir Gerald Fitzmaurice also took the view that international law is incomplete. He argued that the necessity for international tribunals to avoid *non liquet* suffers from difficulties including 'the postulate of the completeness of the legal order'.[24] According to him, *non liquet* itself indicates that international law is incomplete.[25] Fitzmaurice also argued that it would be impossible to accept the principle that international law is complete, while negating the law-making power of international tribunals: since gaps in the law manifestly exist, in order for international law to be complete one should accept the existence of judicial law-making.[26] Fitzmaurice's view may appear to be convincing. However, Fitzmaurice also discussed the means to avoid *non liquet*, stating that 'a *non-liquet* is something that need never occur if, by this, we mean that a decision can always be given "somehow"',[27] but only to conclude that 'the ability of a tribunal to avoid a *non-liquet* in no way involves that the legal order is necessarily "gapless"'.[28] According to Fitzmaurice, accepting that *non liquet* need never occur only postulates, without proving, the completeness of international law. Nevertheless, the jurisprudence of international tribunals indicates that *non liquet* does not occur.[29] An explanation of this jurisprudence may be that the exercise of the international judicial function is premised on the completeness of international law.

---

[22] N Petersen, 'The Role of Consent and Uncertainty in the Formation of Customary International Law' in BD Lepard (ed.), *Reexamining Customary International Law* (CUP, 2017) 111; S Besson, 'State Consent and Disagreement in International Law-Making: Dissolving the Paradox' (2016) 29 *LJIL* 289; N Krisch, 'The Decay of Consent: International Law in an Age of Public Goods' (2014) 108 *AJIL* 1; JI Charney and GM Danilenko, 'Consent and the Creation of International Law' in L Fisler Damrosch et al. (eds.), *Beyond Confrontation – International Law for the Post-Cold War Era* (Westview Press, 1995) 23; A Pellet, 'The Normative Dilemma: Will and Consent in International Law-making' (1988-1989) 12 *Australian YIL* 22.

[23] P Weil, 'Vers une Normativité Relative en Droit International?' (1982) 86 *RGDIP* 5.

[24] G Fitzmaurice, 'The Problem of *Non Liquet*: Prolegomena to a Restatement' in *Mélanges Offerts à Charles Rousseau – La Communauté Internationale* (Pédone, 1974) 89, 107.

[25] Ibid. 102.

[26] Ibid. 109.

[27] Ibid. 101.

[28] Ibid. 102.

[29] However, see *Legality of the Threat or Use of Nuclear Weapons* (Advisory Opinion) [1996] ICJ Rep 226, 266 [105(2)(E)].

The argument rejected by Fitzmaurice was one of Lauterpacht's justifications for the completeness of international law.[30] However, Lauterpacht inverted the cause and the effect in Fitzmaurice's argument, by viewing *non liquet* as the corollary of completeness, while rejecting completeness as the *a priori* explanation of *non liquet*.[31] However, Lauterpacht still regarded completeness as 'an *a priori* assumption of every legal system'.[32] According to him, international law was complete for two reasons. The completeness of international law found support in international judicial practice, in which *non liquet* never occurred.[33] In addition, *non liquet*, as a corollary of completeness, was a general principle of law under Article 38(1)(c) of the ICJ's Statute,[34] from which it followed that completeness could be justified by reference to a source of international law.[35] Lauterpacht rejected the view that international law has gaps, since international tribunals can decide cases based on general principles of law if they can make no decision based on treaties and customary international law. Moreover, Lauterpacht stated that, if certain situations were governed by a rule of international law without being specifically regulated owing to the defects of international law-making, judicial law-making aiming to overcome legal indeterminacy was a 'legitimate realization of the will of the legislator'.[36]

Lauterpacht's views are comparable to those held by Kelsen, who saw Article 38(1)(c) of the Court's Statute as justifying the completeness of international law,[37] and argued based on the 'logical argument' and the 'residual negative principle argument'. According to Kelsen:

---

[30] Stone did not support either the completeness or the incompleteness view, arguing that the question of *non liquet* cannot be solved through technical legal arguments, and that the opposing positions in the debate rested on 'meta-legal premises'. See J Stone, 'Non Liquet and the Function of Law in the International Community' (1959) 35 *BYIL* 124, 125–6.

[31] H Lauterpacht, 'Some Observations on the Prohibition of "*Non Liquet*" and the Completeness of the Law' in *Symbolae Verzijl* (Martinus Nijhoff, 1958) 196, 221.

[32] H Lauterpacht, *The Function of Law in the International Community* (OUP, 2011) 71–2.

[33] Lauterpacht (n. 31) 197.

[34] H Lauterpacht, *The Development of International Law by the International Court* (CUP, 1982) 165.

[35] Lauterpacht (n. 31) 200. See also R Dworkin, *Taking Rights Seriously* (Duckworth, 1977) 81–130; R Dworkin, 'On Gaps in the Law' in P Amselek and N MacCormick (eds.), *Controversies about Law's Ontology* (Edinburgh University Press, 1991) 84–90.

[36] Lauterpacht (n. 32) 79.

[37] H Kelsen, 'Théorie Générale du Droit International Public' (1953) 84 *Recueil des Cours* 1, 122.

> [d]ans un cas concret le droit international particulier, conventionnel ou coutumier, l'emporte sur le droit international général coutumier, mais en l'absence de droit international particulier, c'est le droit international général qui s'applique. Il est logiquement impossible que dans un cas d'espèce ni le droit conventionnel, ni le droit coutumier ne soit applicable. Le droit international existant peut toujours être appliqué, car il permet toujours de répondre à la question de savoir si un Etat ou un autre sujet du droit international est ou non obligé de se conduire d'une manière déterminée. S'il n'y a aucune norme du droit international conventionnel ou coutumier imposant l'obligation de se conduire d'une manière déterminée, le sujet est au point de vue du droit international juridiquement libre de se conduire comme bon lui semble.[38]

Kelsen based its argument on the principle under which that which is not prohibited is permitted.[39] However, the 'residual negative principle argument' is not fully persuasive in relation to maritime delimitation. Articles 74 and 83 UNCLOS do not appear to be either permissive or prohibitive in character, only stating that delimitation must achieve an equitable solution. Moreover, such rules could be derogated from if, in a delimitation treaty, the states concerned so agree.[40]

Lauterpacht's view that international law is complete as an explanation of the practice of international tribunals not to declare *non liquet* seems convincing for its pragmatism. Nevertheless, Lauterpacht's views ought to be taken a step further in respect of the judicial process of maritime delimitation. As the evolution of the delimitation process cannot be explained by reference to treaties, custom or general principles of law, the means to explain how international law is complete with reference to maritime delimitation has to be the exercise of the international judicial function.[41]

That international law is complete owing to the exercise of the international judicial function does not seem to be entirely correct. Exercising the judicial function to fill such gaps suggests that the international legal system is incomplete. It seems more appropriate to state that, rather than

---

[38] Ibid. 121.
[39] *Lotus (France v. Turkey)* (Judgment) PCIJ Series A No. 10, 18–19.
[40] *North Sea Continental Shelf* (n. 4) 42 [72].
[41] Hernández emphasised the link between the completeness theory and the international judicial function, by writing that '[t]he theory of completeness ... rests on two interrelated precepts: that the law can be applied by courts to resolve any dispute, and that it can be applied with progressive effects on the development of the legal order'. See GI Hernández, *The International Court of Justice and the Judicial Function* (OUP, 2014) 254. US Supreme Court Justice Benjamin Cardozo stated that the judge '... legislates only between gaps. He fills the open spaces in the law'. See B Cardozo, *The Nature of the Judicial Process* (Yale University Press, 1921) 113.

'complete', the international legal system is 'completed' through the exercise of the international judicial function in concrete cases. Admitting that international tribunals can decide cases even if the applicable law is indeterminate does not prove completeness but incompleteness, while envisaging a legal process intended to overcome that incompleteness. International law may be complete or incomplete at any given time. If a case in respect of which there is no clear applicable law comes before an international tribunal, international law temporarily loses the attribute of completeness, only to regain it upon the settlement of that case through the exercise of the international judicial function.

International tribunals themselves stated that maritime delimitation is carried out in accordance with international law. In this perspective, given the lack of a clear delimitation process formulated under a treaty or customary international law, judicial decisions not only settle maritime delimitation cases, but also formulate the delimitation process itself pursuant to which boundaries are delimited. The product of the exercise of the international judicial function in maritime delimitation cases is the creation of law, limited to the process that international tribunals apply in deciding those cases.[42] One could frame this issue in terms of 'permissive sources'. Hart wrote that:

> [w]here [a judge] considers that no statute or other formal source of law determines the case before him, [they] may base his decision on e.g. a text of the Digest, or the writings of a French jurist ... The legal system does not require [them] to use these sources, but it is accepted as perfectly proper that [they] should do so. They are therefore more than merely historical or causal influences since such writings are recognized as 'good reasons' for decisions. Perhaps we might speak of such sources as 'permissive' legal sources to distinguish them both from 'mandatory' legal or formal sources such as statute and from historical or material sources.[43]

Gardner interpreted this passage to mean that '[j]udges may make "judgments" among a finite number of permissive standards without a resort to any further extra-legal standards',[44] and that '[s]ince the only standards used in such a case are legal standards, there can be no question but that the law provides a complete answer to the case'.[45]

---

[42] One should agree with Hernández that '[j]udicial law-creation is the point of any theory of completeness, as it presumes the indispensability of the judicial function'. See Hernández (n. 41) 276.
[43] Hart (n. 18) 294.
[44] J Gardner, 'Concerning Permissive Sources and Gaps' (1988) 8 *OJLS* 457, 460-1.
[45] Ibid.

Judicial decisions could be a 'permissive source' allowing international tribunals to provide a complete answer to delimitation cases pursuant to legal standards.[46]

One may reach this conclusion also by reference to Siorat's tripartite distinction of gaps in the law. According to Siorat, gaps in the law could be 'obscurités', 'carences' and 'lacunae', which are different degrees of vagueness. 'Obscurités' exist if, in a given case, the meaning of a treaty or customary international law is doubtful.[47] 'Carences' entail that the applicable law results in a solution which is unsatisfactory for the states party to a dispute,[48] leading states to solve the dispute through diplomatic channels.[49] 'Lacunae' relate to cases in which neither custom, nor treaty, provides the clear legal rule to solve a pending dispute.[50] Notwithstanding his opposition to judicial law-making and his view that international law is incomplete,[51] Siorat admitted that the international judge has power to fill a 'lacuna'.[52] By contrast, in the case of 'obscurités' international tribunals simply interpret the legal rules concerned.[53] Since Articles 74 and 83 UNCLOS do not indicate the process for their implementation, they are 'lacunae'. By exercising a limited law-making function, international tribunals can fill such 'lacunae'.

B Judicial Decisions as a Source of the Law of Maritime Delimitation

The notion that international tribunals exercise a law-making function in respect of the delimitation process raises the issue of whether judicial decisions could be considered to be formal sources of international law.[54]

---

[46] On Gardner's interpretation of Hart, see B Bix, *Law, Language and Legal Indeterminacy* (OUP, 1993) 25.
[47] L Siorat, *Le Problème des Lacunes en Droit International* (LGDJ, 1958) 63.
[48] Ibid. 85.
[49] Ibid. 86–7.
[50] Ibid. 126.
[51] Ibid. 44 and 251.
[52] Ibid. 251.
[53] Ibid. 74–82.
[54] With varying degrees of nuance, certain writers considered judicial decisions to be more than mere material sources of international law. See M Sørensen, *Les Sources du Droit International* (Einar Munksgaard, 1946) 162; G Fitzmaurice, 'Some Problems Regarding the Formal Sources of International Law' in *Symbolae Verzijl* (Martinus Nijhoff, 1958) 153, 172–3; C Parry, *The Sources and Evidences of International Law* (Manchester University Press, 1965) 93; M Shahabuddeen, *Precedent in the World Court* (CUP, 1996) 76–7; Lauterpacht (n. 34) 21.

1 Status of judicial decisions under Article 38 of the ICJ's Statute

Article 38 of the ICJ's Statute is generally considered to be the classic formulation of the sources of international law.[55] The drafting history of that provision sheds light on the position of judicial decisions within those sources.

In 1920, the Council of the League created an Advisory Committee of Jurists having the task to prepare a draft for the Statute of the Permanent Court of International Justice (PCIJ), subsequently to be approved by the Council and the Assembly of the League. The Committee received a number of documents from governments concerning the law applicable by the PCIJ. Certain states proposed that the sources of law from which the PCIJ would derive the applicable rules in each case would not include judicial decisions.[56] Other states included judicial decisions within the sources of international law.[57] The Explanatory Note to the Draft of Clovis Bevilaqua, the Brazilian member of the Committee, stated that the PCIJ was to pronounce 'a successions of verdicts with a common purpose of establishing law and of conciliating interests justly and equitably, by creating an international Common Law ...'.[58] A common feature to all proposals was the absence of any reference, in the provisions on sources, to the binding force of the Court's decisions only as between the parties to a given case.[59]

The Committee began discussing sources of international law at its thirteenth meeting. According to the draft prepared by Baron Descamps, '[t]he following rules are to be applied by the judge in the solution of international disputes ... (4) international jurisprudence as a means for

---

[55] J d'Aspremont, 'The Idea of "Rules" in the Sources of International Law' (2014) 84 *BYIL* 103, 111.
[56] Permanent Court of International Justice, Advisory Committee of Jurists, *Documents Presented to the Committee Relating to Existing Plans for the Establishment of a Permanent Court of International Justice* (Van Langenhuysen, 1920) 129 (Germany) and 267 (Switzerland).
[57] Ibid. 179 (Denmark, Norway, Sweden), 205 (Denmark), 241 (Sweden), 301 (Denmark, Netherlands, Norway, Sweden and Switzerland), 325 (Denmark, Netherlands, Norway, Sweden and Switzerland).
[58] Ibid. 359. Bevilaqua wrote that his proposal was inspired by Article 7 of the Introduction to the 1916 Brazilian Civil Code, under which '[t]o cases, which are not dealt with here, the provisions for analogous cases, and in the absence of such, the general principles of law shall be applied'.
[59] Section II.B.2 below.

the application and development of law'.[60] Lord Phillimore and Root criticised the inclusion of judicial decisions, as rules of international law were created by states.[61] The two jurists later presented a joint draft, the Root–Phillimore Plan, under which the PCIJ was to apply '[t]he precedent of judicial decisions and the opinions of the publicists as means for the application and development of the law'.[62] While agreeing with Lord Phillimore and Root, Ricci-Busatti suggested keeping the reference to international decisions to avoid cases of *non liquet*.[63] Hagerup and Loder supported the draft, owing to the need for the PCIJ to avoid *non liquet* and develop an international jurisprudence.[64] Hagerup even proposed that the 'English principle of judge-made law should be adopted: before refusing to admit a claim because no positive law exists, the judge must seek to find analogies, precedents, etc.'[65]

The Drafting Committee presented a Draft Statute at the twenty-fifth meeting. Article 31 stated that the PCIJ would apply '(4) rules of law derived from judicial decisions and the teachings of the most highly qualified publicists of the various nations'.[66] De Lapradelle opposed paragraph 4 of Article 31, since '[l]aws, customs, and general principles of law could not be applied without reference to jurisprudence and teaching'.[67] Baron Descamps proposed to add to the draft of Article 31 the words '[a]s subsidiary means for the determination of rules of law', which the Committee retained.[68] At the thirty-first meeting, the Committee adopted Article 31.[69] Although the provision as adopted omitted the words 'rules of law arising from' in relation to judicial decisions, nothing in the proceedings of the Committee clearly indicates that the reason for this removal was opposition to judicial decisions as a source of international law. Moreover, at the thirty-first meeting Ricci-Busatti proposed to substitute 'de la détermination des règles de droit'

---

[60] Permanent Court of International Justice, Advisory Committee of Jurists, *Procès-Verbaux of the Proceedings of the Committee, June 16–July 24 1920, with Annexes* (Van Langenhuysen, 1920) 306 (Descamps).
[61] Ibid. 294 and 309–10 (Root), 295 and 584 (Phillimore).
[62] Ibid. 548.
[63] Ibid. 314 and 334 (Ricci-Busatti).
[64] Ibid. 294 (Loder), 296 (Hagerup).
[65] Ibid. 317 (Hagerup).
[66] Ibid. 567.
[67] Ibid. 584 (De Lapradelle).
[68] Ibid. (Descamps).
[69] Ibid. 648.

with 'd'interprétation juridique'.[70] The rejection of his proposal seems to suggest that the Committee understood judicial decisions as a formal source of international law.

Article 31 finally became Article 35 in the Draft-Scheme approved by the Committee and presented to the Council of the League for discussion.[71] The Committee's position seems to be that judicial decisions do not create law, but determine it. However, the difference appears to be one of degree and not of kind.[72] The Committee's Draft-Scheme could be read as allowing international tribunals to use judicial decisions as a formal source of international law, but, in order to balance a limited law-making function, judicial decisions may only be 'subsidiary means for the determination of rules of law'.[73] All avenues should be exhausted before using judicial decisions as the applicable law.

At its tenth session, the Council adopted a modified version of Article 35, under which the PCIJ could apply judicial decisions, but only subject to the provision of Article 57bis.[74] Article 57bis, added by the Council following a proposal by Léon Bourgeois, provided that the PCIJ's decisions would only bind the parties to a case. Article 57bis explicitly aimed to allow the development of the law and was linked to intervention before the PCIJ.[75] Article 57bis would ensure that if states exercised their right to intervene, they would be bound by the PCIJ's decision. The *raison d'être* of Article 57bis in Bourgeois's proposal was not to limit the precedential character of the PCIJ's decisions, but to ensure that the binding force of those decisions would be limited to the parties to a case, whether original or intervening. Argentina proposed

---

[70] Ibid. 655 (Ricci-Busatti).
[71] Ibid. 680.
[72] R Jennings, 'General Course on Principles of International Law' (1967) 121 *Recueil des Cours* 323, 341.
[73] According to the authoritative work on the ICJ, the expression 'determination of rules of law' indicates that judicial decisions, alongside the works of the most highly qualified publicists, only 'determine' applicable rules of international law, 'that is rules falling into any one of heads *(a), (b),* and *(c)*' of Article 38 of the ICJ's Statute. See M Shaw, *Rosenne's Law and Practice of the International Court 1920–2015* 5th edn (Martinus Nijhoff, 2015) vol. III, 1607. However, the distinction between 'determining' a rule of law and 'creating' such a rule could be justifiably considered not to be entirely clear, and perhaps even artificial.
[74] League of Nations, Permanent Court of International Justice, *Documents concerning the Action taken by the Council of the League of Nations under Article 14 of the Covenant and the Adoption by the Assembly of the Statute of the Permanent Court of International Justice* (Van Langenhuysen, 1920) 81.
[75] Ibid. 50.

a subsequent amendment to Article 35, according to which the PCIJ would apply '[j]udicial decisions, as against the State in which they have been delivered, if it is a Party to the dispute'.[76] Hagerup commented that Argentina's amendment would have 'the effect of excluding every possibility of considering the judgments as precedents building up law'.[77] Nonetheless, the amendment was finally rejected.[78] Article 35 as adopted by the Council became Article 38 of the Draft Statute presented to the Assembly of the League.[79] The Assembly adopted Chapter II of the Draft Statute, which included Article 38, without amendments.[80] The changes approved by the Council and Assembly did not seem to alter the essence of the provision drafted by the Advisory Committee of Jurists, which could suggest that judicial decisions could be formal sources of international law.

Issues of applicable law before the PCIJ emerged again in the lead-up to the 1945 San Francisco Conference. The 1944 Report of the Inter-Allied Committee on the Future of the Permanent Court of International Justice stated, with respect to Article 38, that:

> this provision is open to criticism and it would not be difficult to make suggestions for improving it; but on the whole the difficulties resulting from it do not seem to be of a sufficiently serious character to necessitate any change. It seems to have worked well in practice, and we consider that any attempt to alter it would cause more difficulties than it would solve.[81]

Concerning Article 59 of the PCIJ's Statute, the Inter-Allied Committee commented that:

> [t]he effect of [Article 59] has, in our opinion, sometimes been misinterpreted. What it means is not that the decisions of the Court have no effect as precedents for the Court or for international law in general, but that they do not possess the binding force of particular decisions in the relations between the countries who are parties to the Statute. The provision in question in no way prevents the Court from treating its own judgments as precedents, and indeed it follows from Article 38 ... that the Court's decisions are themselves 'subsidiary means for the determination of rules of law'.[82]

---

[76] Ibid. 68 (Argentina).
[77] Ibid. 145 (Hagerup).
[78] Ibid.
[79] Ibid. 211.
[80] Ibid. 255.
[81] Report of the Inter-Allied Committee on the Future of the Permanent Court of International Justice (1945) 39 *AJIL* Supplement 1, 20.
[82] Ibid.

At the Dumbarton Oaks Conference, states agreed that the PCIJ Statute should be the basis of the statute for a new international court.[83] Few states commented specifically on Article 38, some approving the text as it stood and others proposing limited changes.[84]

Based on the Dumbarton Oaks Proposals, a Committee of Jurists was requested to prepare a draft statute for the future international court, further to be considered at the San Francisco Conference. The Committee did not hold much discussion on Article 38, adopting it unanimously at its seventh meeting.[85] Despite some modifications, the substance of the provision remained unchanged.[86] At the San Francisco Conference, Commission IV on 'Judicial Organization' retained the proposal made by the Committee of Jurists, including the text of Article 38.[87] The San Francisco Conference approved the Draft Statute, subsequently annexed to the Charter of the United Nations and including what is now Article 38 of the ICJ's Statute.[88]

The San Francisco Conference endorsed the rule on sources drafted for the PCIJ by the Advisory Committee of Jurists of the League of Nations. Moreover, the Inter-Allied Committee's Report clarified that Article 59

---

[83] Doc 2 G/7(c) (31 October 1944), *Documents of the United Nations Conference on International Organization (San Francisco 1945)* vol. III, 123 (Mexico); Doc 2 G/7(d)(1) (31 October 1944), *Documents of the United Nations Conference on International Organization (San Francisco 1945)* vol. III, 206 (Venezuela); Doc 2 G/7(h)(i) (4 May 1945), *Documents of the United Nations Conference on International Organization (San Francisco 1945)* vol. III, 279 [5] (Costa Rica); Doc 2 G/7(j) (January 1945), *Documents of the United Nations Conference on International Organization (San Francisco 1945)* vol. III, 320 [3] (Netherlands); Doc 2 G/7(m), *Documents of the United Nations Conference on International Organization (San Francisco 1945)* vol. III, 351 [9] (Honduras); Doc 2 G/7(n), *Documents of the United Nations Conference on International Organization (San Francisco 1945)* vol. III, 359 (Norway); Doc 2 G/7(p) (1 May 1945), *Documents of the United Nations Conference on International Organization (San Francisco 1945)* vol. III, 411 [1] (Ecuador); Doc 2 G/14(r) (5 May 1945), *Documents of the United Nations Conference on International Organization (San Francisco 1945)* vol. III, 581 [11] (Bolivia).

[84] Doc 2 G/7(d)(1) (n. 83) 230 (Venezuela); Doc 2 G/7(p) (n. 83) 412 (Ecuador); Doc 2 G/14 (g)(2) (n. 83) 520 (Cuba).

[85] Doc Jurist 40 G/30 (13 April 1945), *Documents of the United Nations Conference on International Organization (San Francisco 1945)* vol. XIV, 257.

[86] Doc Jurist 47 G/36 (14 April 1945), *Documents of the United Nations Conference on International Organization (San Francisco 1945)* vol. XIV, 492–3.

[87] Chile proposed the only amendment, which did not touch the substance of Article 38. See Doc 253 IV/1/16 (12 May 1945), *Documents of the United Nations Conference on International Organization (San Francisco 1945)* vol. XIII, 493.

[88] Doc 1210 P/20 (27 June 1945), *Documents of the United Nations Conference on International Organization (San Francisco 1945)* vol. I, 627 and 630.

did not limit the value of the Court's decisions as precedents. Article 38 survived the Dumbarton Oaks Conference, the Committee of Jurists and the San Francisco Conference untouched in its substance. This provision would thus retain the same spirit as Article 38 PCIJ Statute, allowing for judicial decisions to be formal sources of international law, within limits. According to Article 38 of the ICJ's Statute itself, judicial decisions can be used only as subsidiary means for the determination of rules of law. Commentators consider that Article 38 does not institute a hierarchy between sources of international law.[89] However, the presence of the adjective 'subsidiary' in Article 38 suggests that at least one element of hierarchy exists, namely that judicial decisions should be applied as formal sources of international law only as a last resort, if no rule of international law exists in treaties, custom or general principles.

2 Relevance of *res judicata*

Under the principle of *res judicata*, judicial decisions settling disputes are final and binding only between the parties to those disputes, and cannot be re-litigated.[90] According to the ICJ, in order for *res judicata* to apply there must be identity of parties, object, legal grounds and the Court must not have settled the claim by way of an earlier judgment.[91]

The issue arises as to whether *res judicata* prevents states from relying, in later disputes, on the judicial formulations of legal principles as authority for such principles. The reference to Article 59 PCIJ Statute in the text of Article 38 resulted from the decision of a political organ, the Council of the League of Nations.[92] Moreover, the Council based its decision on reasons relating to intervention before the PCIJ, and not on precluding the precedential relevance of the PCIJ's decisions. The

---

[89] A Pellet, 'Article 38' in A Zimmermann et al. (eds.), *The Statute of the International Court of Justice – A Commentary* 2nd edn (OUP, 2012) 731, 841; M Akehurst, 'The Hierarchy of the Sources of International Law' (1974–1975) 47 *BYIL* 273.

[90] Art. 59 of the ICJ's Statute and Art. 33(2) of the ITLOS's Statute. See *Trail Smelter Arbitration (USA v. Canada)* (1941) III RIAA 1905, 1950. See also DW Bowett, 'Res Judicata and the Limits of Rectification of Decisions by International Tribunals' (1996) 8 *African JICL* 577; H Charlesworth, 'Law-making and Sources' in J Crawford and M Koskenniemi (eds.), *The Cambridge Companion to International Law* (CUP, 2012) 187, 196; L Condorelli, 'L'Autorité de la Décision des Juridictions Internationales Permanentes' in *La Juridiction Internationale Permanente – Colloque de Lyon* (Pédone, 1987) 277, 309.

[91] *Question of the Delimitation of the Continental Shelf between Nicaragua and Colombia beyond 200 Nautical Miles from the Nicaraguan Coast (Nicaragua v. Colombia)* (Preliminary Objections) [2016] ICJ Rep 100, 126 [59].

[92] See the comment of the tribunal in *Lighthouses (Greece/France)* (1956) XII RIAA 155, 194.

reference to Article 59 in the text of Article 38 should thus be understood by reference to intervention.[93] The ICJ Chamber in *El Salvador/ Honduras* held that 'a State which considers that its legal interest may be affected by a decision in a case has the choice, to intervene or not to intervene; and if it does not, proceedings may continue, and that State is protected by Article 59 of the Statute'.[94] Article 59 appears to safeguard the consensual basis of jurisdiction before the Court. This function does not necessarily entail that the principles underlying decisions in particular cases cannot be regarded as stating what international law is, but merely that the decision made by the Court only binds the states party and intervening third states.[95]

Article 59 could nonetheless be seen to preclude judicial decisions from being sources of international law, as under Article 38 of its Statute the Court shall apply judicial decisions only 'subject to the provisions of Article 59'. However, this preclusion appears to be limited in practice. The Court's decisions, as well as the decisions of both ITLOS and arbitral tribunals, are replete with citations from previous cases,[96] which is especially true for maritime delimitation judgments. In practice, the authority of international decisions does not seem to be limited to one dispute. According to Judge Jennings:

> the slightest acquaintance with the jurisprudence of [the ICJ] shows that Article 59 does by no manner of means exclude the force of persuasive precedent. So the idea that Article 59 is protective of third States' interests in this sense at least is illusory. ... [I]t would be unrealistic even in consideration of strict legal principle, to suppose that the effects of a judgment are thus wholly confined by Article 59.[97]

---

[93] Intervention is governed by Arts. 62–63 of the ICJ's Statute. Leading writers have underscored the relationship between Article 59 and intervention, see C Chinkin, *Third Parties in International Law* (OUP, 1993) 155–60; S Rosenne, 'Article 59 of the Statute of the International Court of Justice Revisited' in *Liber Amicorum Eduardo Jiménez de Aréchaga* (FCU, 1994) 1129, 1141; C Brown, 'Article 59' in A Zimmermann et al. (eds.), *The Statute of the International Court of Justice – A Commentary* 2nd edn (OUP, 2012) 1416, 1441; DW Grieg, 'Third Party Rights and Intervention before the International Court' (1991–1992) *VaJIL* 285, 325–7.

[94] *Land, Island and Maritime Frontier Dispute (El Salvador/Honduras)* (Application by Nicaragua for Permission to Intervene) [1990] ICJ Rep 92, 115 [54].

[95] See Report of the Inter-Allied Committee (n. 81) 20.

[96] Condorelli (n. 90) 307; Rosenne (n. 93) 1143–4.

[97] *Continental Shelf (Libya/Malta)* (Application by Italy for Permission to Intervene) [1984] ICJ Rep 3, 157 [27]–[28] (Dissenting Opinion Jennings). See also ibid. 134 [9]–[10] (Dissenting Opinion Schwebel); *Barcelona Traction, Light and Power Company, Limited (Belgium v. Spain)* (Second Phase) [1970] ICJ Rep 3, 163 [9] (Separate Opinion Jessup).

Similar comments apply to the statements made in advisory opinions,[98] which have contributed significantly to developing international law[99] despite lacking binding force.[100] It would appear odd not to ascribe a similar function to decisions in contentious cases, which are legally binding on the parties to those cases. Although this conclusion relates to the ICJ in the context of its Statute, it also applies to other international tribunals.

III   Approach of States

Similarly to the English common law,[101] the development and consistency of the law of maritime delimitation depends on the existence of a small group of judges within which consensus could coalesce around common approaches. Yet, the approach of states to this consensus is critical. As states are the principal makers of international law, one may expect international tribunals to have built the delimitation process on their suggestions.

A   Maritime Delimitation Treaties

Maritime delimitation treaties constitute a wealth of practice, but they could not be considered to convey the *opinio juris* of states.[102] Nevertheless, in establishing boundaries by treaty states resorted to methods similar to that applied by international tribunals in the three-stage delimitation process. Although not all treaties mention the methods to which states resort in delimitation by agreement, one could ascertain such methods based on the co-ordinates identifying the agreed boundaries. Comparing such boundaries with hypothetical equidistance lines between the states concerned shows that 161 treaties delimit boundaries based on equidistance.[103] It is relatively common for states to establish strict or simplified equidistance boundaries, as well as boundaries based on a modified equidistance line. The latter could be likened to boundaries established by judicial process by tracing an equidistance line and

---

[98] I Scobbie, '*Res Judicata*, Precedent and the International Court: A Preliminary Sketch' (1999) 20 *Australian YIL* 299, 312.
[99] See *Reparation for Injuries Suffered in the Service of the United Nations* (Advisory Opinion) [1949] ICJ Rep 174; *Reservations to the Convention on the Prevention and Punishment of the Crime of Genocide* (Advisory Opinion) [1951] ICJ Rep 15; *Certain Expenses of the United Nations* (Advisory Opinion) [1962] ICJ Rep 151.
[100] *Interpretation of Peace Treaties* (Advisory Opinion) [1950] ICJ Rep 65, 71.
[101] J Bell, 'Sources of Law' (2018) 77 *CLJ* 40, 52.
[102] Section II.A.1 above.
[103] Appendix 2.

subsequently adjusting it based on relevant circumstances. Conversely, sixty-two treaties establish boundaries at variance with equidistance.[104] Treaties establishing non-equidistance boundaries remain numerous even when compared to those establishing boundaries based on equidistance. Nevertheless, the latter constitute a noticeably strong majority.

Although the treaties establishing maritime boundaries based on equidistance could be a validation of the first two stages of the delimitation process, the same consideration does not necessarily seem to apply to the third stage, the disproportionality test. Nothing in the treaties appears to convey that states take into account the respective relevant coastal length relative to the maritime areas appertaining to them. The disproportionality test is a check for the overall equitableness of the boundary. Assuming that states would not agree to establish inequitable boundaries, it seems that, although no clear reference to disproportionality exists in the relevant treaties, the aims of that test would presumably be satisfied when boundaries are drawn by agreement.

Indications concerning the methodology used in delimitation treaties are rare. In their 2010 Joint Declaration concerning the Barents Sea Treaty,[105] the Foreign Ministers of Norway and the Russian Federation recommended:

> a delimitation line on the basis of international law in order to achieve an equitable solution. In addition to the relevant factors identified in this regard in international law, including the effect of major disparities in respective coastal lengths, they have taken into account the progress achieved in the course of long-standing negotiations between the parties in order to reach agreement. They recommend a line that divides the overall disputed area in two parts of approximately the same size.[106]

The bill presented before the Storting for ratifying that treaty also referred to the judicial delimitation process.[107] Although neither the

---

[104] Ibid. While certain states may have concluded treaties based on equidistance due to the CCS being in force between them, the CCS would have only applied to continental shelf delimitation, and, in any event, states would have been free to conclude treaties at variance with the delimitation method under the CCS.

[105] Treaty between the Russian Federation and the Kingdom of Norway concerning Maritime Delimitation and Co-operation in the Barents Sea and the Arctic Ocean, 2791 UNTS 3.

[106] Joint Statement on maritime delimitation and cooperation in the Barents Sea and the Arctic Ocean (27 April 2010) www.regjeringen.no/globalassets/upload/ud/vedlegg/folk erett/030427_english_4.pdf.

[107] Prop 43 S (2010–2011), Samtykke til ratifikasjon av overenskomst av 15 september 2010 mellom Norge og Russland om maritim avgrensning og samarbeid i Barentshavet og

joint declaration nor the bill stated that the parties had delimited the boundary following that process, it suggests that they took it into consideration in their negotiations.[108]

The 2010 Grenada–Trinidad and Tobago treaty[109] reportedly followed the recommendations made by a joint commission. The commission recommended that the boundary be delimited by identifying the relevant area, tracing a provisional equidistance line, and adjusting that line should relevant circumstances so require. Apparently, Grenada supported the unadjusted equidistance line, while Trinidad and Tobago argued for its adjustment. The commission finally recommended a boundary combining strict equidistance and adjustments owed to relevant circumstances.[110]

These two treaties show that states may draw their agreed boundaries on the basis of the three-stage approach, which entails an indirect sanction of the judicial evolution of the delimitation process. However, more explicit references to that process seem to be necessary to conclude that, by delimiting their maritime boundaries by agreement, states clearly approved the judicial development of the delimitation process. Nevertheless, maritime delimitation treaties contain a wealth of implicit references to individual stages of the process. These references can be read both in the establishment of boundaries as strict equidistance lines, and in the delimitation of boundaries as modified equidistance lines, the latter constituting indirect recognition that certain factors may require the adjustment of strict equidistance lines in order to reach an equitable solution.

B Statements on the Delimitation Process

Statements concerning maritime delimitation are relevant in assessing the position of states with respect to the three-stage approach. Additionally to statements made in multilateral fora, written and oral submissions made before international tribunals are significant.

Polhavet, 6 www.regjeringen.no/contentassets/ed3ebd062f4345508f7341c3079bda53/no/pdfs/prp201020110043000dddpdfs.pdf.
[108] T Henriksen and G Ulfstein, 'Maritime Delimitation in the Arctic: The Barents Sea Treaty' (2011) 42 *ODIL* 1, 6.
[109] Treaty between the Republic of Trinidad and Tobago and Grenada on the Delimitation of Marine and Submarine Areas, 2675 UNTS 5.
[110] C Mitchell, 'Report 2-31 – Treaty between the Republic of Trinidad and Tobago and Grenada on the Delimitation of Marine and Submarine Areas', in C Lathrop (ed.), *International Maritime Boundaries* (Martinus Nijhoff, 2016) vol. VII, 4711–13.

1 Statements in multilateral fora

The 2013 Report of the Meeting of the States Parties to UNCLOS includes a passage according to which:

> [s]everal delegations noted with appreciation the judgment rendered in case No. 16, the first boundary delimitation case handled by [ITLOS], which included delimitation of the continental shelf beyond 200 nautical miles. ... It was noted with satisfaction that the decision was consistent with existing jurisprudence relating to maritime boundary delimitation.[111]

Similarly, the 2012 Report stated that:

> [s]everal delegations underscored the expeditious manner in which [case No. 16] had been handled. Appreciation was expressed for the fact that the judgment of the Tribunal built on the existing maritime boundary delimitation case law. The two parties in the case expressed their satisfaction in relation to the judgment and stated that the decision was balanced and equitable.[112]

Before ITLOS decided *Bangladesh/Myanmar*, the 2008 Report conveyed that 'some delegations expressed the hope that more States would choose the Tribunal to adjudicate their maritime disputes, allowing the establishment of a set of precedents to be relied upon, particularly in the case of delimitation disputes'.[113]

The Reports cited above do not specify which states made the quoted comments. It is thus difficult to weigh whether such comments were made in the abstract, or by states which had a stake in the proceedings before ITLOS or before another international tribunal. Nonetheless, states appeared to appreciate ITLOS's reliance on the pre-existing jurisprudence on maritime delimitation, which could be read as an implicit sanction of that jurisprudence.

Individual states rarely speak directly on the delimitation process. A high-ranking Ukrainian official was reported to have stated that the *Black Sea* judgment 'was comprehensively justified by the Court from the point of view of ... the methods of delimitation they have developed in the course of lengthy practice'.[114] This statement can be read as a sanction by Ukraine of the three-stage approach. However, it is more

---

[111] UN Doc SPLOS/263 (8 July 2013) 5 [19].
[112] UN Doc SPLOS/251 (11 June 2012) 5 [26].
[113] UN Doc SPLOS/184 (21 July 2008) 20 [109].
[114] 'Ukrainian presidential aide says UN Court rejected most of Romania's arguments' (*BBC News*, 3 February 2009).

common for states to make indirect references to the delimitation process, and for this reason their significance could be difficult to assess. At a meeting of the Sixth Committee of the UN General Assembly in 2013, Myanmar referred to the recent judgment in *Bangladesh/Myanmar*, and stated that the boundary had been established 'peacefully and equitably' in accordance with international law 'thanks to the wisdom of ITLOS'.[115] Referring to the judgment in *Ghana/Côte d'Ivoire* at a 2017 Sixth Committee meeting, Ghana stated that 'it was gratifying that both countries had accepted the verdict in good faith and had made a joint declaration to that effect'.[116] While statements of this tenor fall short of expressing an explicit acceptance of the three-stage approach, they do not criticise it, either directly or indirectly. References to the 'wisdom' of ITLOS, the acceptance of judgments by the states concerned, and the recognition that international tribunals establish boundaries 'equitably' pursuant to international law, suggest that states implicitly accept the three-stage approach as the established method to implement Articles 74 and 83 UNCLOS.

The paucity of explicit endorsements of the delimitation process could be linked to the states' reluctance to make statements in the abstract, without it being necessary owing to a pending dispute in which they are involved. However, states could be seen to have sanctioned the three-stage approach implicitly by way of their statements. No statement could be found conveying a rejection of that approach, while, by contrast, certain states have praised international tribunals for delimiting boundaries pursuant to international law and consistently with the earlier delimitation jurisprudence. The Reports of the Meeting of the States Parties to UNCLOS contain statements which could be attributed to all states parties, and therefore reflect the position of such states with respect to the delimitation process. Nevertheless, caution is in order, since the Reports do not identify the states which made specific statements.

2 Pleadings before international tribunals

It is more likely for states publicly to express their view on the delimitation process in the context of concrete disputes to which they are parties before international tribunals. States could make explicit comments sanctioning the judicial development of the process as a whole, or

---

[115] UN Doc A/C.6/68/SR.7 (20 November 2013) 17 [78] (Myanmar). See also UN Doc A/C.6/67/SR.5 (31 December 2012) 13 [80] (Myanmar).
[116] UN Doc A/C.6/72/SR.6 (31 October 2017) 13 [114] (Ghana).

structure their arguments so as to follow the stages of the process. Although states likely make arguments which benefit their case, as a matter of law pleadings before international tribunals express the official position of states on the legal issues arising for decision in a given case to which they are a party.

Before the ICJ introduced the two-stage approach in *Jan Mayen*, states pleaded their case by reference to the *North Sea Continental Shelf* jurisprudence, according to which a maritime boundary must be established in accordance with equitable principles, having taken into account all relevant circumstances.[117] In *Tunisia/Libya*, the special agreement between the parties specifically requested the Court to determine:

> the principles and rules of international law which may be applied for the delimitation of the area of the continental shelf appertaining to ... Tunisia and the area of the continental shelf appertaining to [Libya] and, in rendering its decision, to take account of equitable principles and the relevant circumstances which characterize the area.[118]

Both states emphasised the task under the special agreement, which limited the Court to applying the delimitation method formulated in *North Sea Continental Shelf*.[119] Both in *Gulf of Maine*,[120] and in *Libya/Malta*,[121] the parties made their arguments on the same method.

As in *Jan Mayen* the Court applied the two-stage delimitation process for the first time, one may expect the parties to have argued for its application. However, Denmark argued for 'the use of a method whereby all relevant factors are weighed against each other'.[122] Norway contended that delimitation was to be effected in two stages, in which '[t]he first stage

---

[117] *North Sea Continental Shelf* (n. 4) 53 [101].
[118] *Continental Shelf (Tunisia/Libya)* (Judgment) [1982] ICJ Rep 18, 21 [2].
[119] Memorial of Tunisia (27 May 1980), 52 [2.19]; Memorial of Libya (30 May 1980), 456 [6]; Counter-memorial of Tunisia (1 December 1980), 57 [6.10]; Counter-memorial of Libya (2 February 1981), 286 [363]; Reply of Tunisia (15 July 1981), 50 [3.22]; Reply of Libya (15 July 1981), 143 (footnote 8).
[120] Memorial of the United States (27 September 1982), 5 [8]; Memorial of Canada (27 September 1982), 116 [278]; Counter-memorial of the United States (28 June 1983), 59–60 [123]; Counter-memorial of Canada (28 June 1983), 5 [10]; Reply of the United States (12 December 1983), 376 [4]; Reply of Canada (12 December 1983), 151 [1].
[121] Memorial of Malta (26 April 1983), 484 [233]; Memorial of Libya (26 April 1983), 110 [6.30]; Counter-memorial of Libya (26 October 1983), 24 [2.01]; Reply of Malta (12 July 1984), 198 [149]; Reply of Libya (12 July 1984), 25 [3.14].
[122] Reply of Denmark (31 January 1991), 165 [453]. See also CR 1993/2, 54 and 59 (Jiménez de Aréchaga); CR 1993/4, 9–11 (Bowett).

involves establishing a provisional or primary boundary which may be subject to modification in the light of certain relevant circumstances'.[123] Norway did not argue that at the first stage the Court should necessarily draw an equidistance line. In applying the two-stage approach, the Court was likely influenced both by Norway's arguments, and by Article 6 of the Convention on the Continental Shelf (CCS)[124] as part of the applicable law, under which the boundary in the continental shelf would be an equidistance line 'unless another boundary line is justified by special circumstances'. Therefore, the two-stage approach could be considered to be a judicial creation influenced by Norway's pleadings and Article 6 CCS being part of the applicable law.

After *Jan Mayen*, states tended to focus their pleadings on the applicability of the two-stage approach. In *Qatar v. Bahrain*, the parties agreed that the EEZ and continental shelf was to be delimited based on the two-stage approach.[125] Differently, in *Cameroon v. Nigeria*, Nigeria[126] and Equatorial Guinea[127] supported the two-stage approach, while Cameroon favoured the *ad hoc* determination of an appropriate delimitation method.[128] In *Barbados v. Trinidad and Tobago*, Barbados argued for delimitation using the two-stage approach,[129] and Trinidad and Tobago even structured its own Counter-memorial following the phases of the two-stage approach. In *Guyana v. Suriname*, Guyana requested the arbitral tribunal to apply the two-stage approach.[130] Suriname argued for an angle bisector owing to the inequitableness of equidistance,[131] or for an adjusted equidistance line,[132] which may implicitly acknowledge the two-stage approach as the established delimitation method at that time. *Nicaragua v. Honduras* stands alone as the sole case in which neither state requested the establishment of an equidistance line, instead arguing that

---

[123] Rejoinder of Norway (27 September 1991), 170 [576].
[124] 499 UNTS 311.
[125] Memorial of Bahrain (30 September 1996), 282 [650]; Counter-memorial of Qatar (31 December 1997), 187 [6.3]; Counter-memorial of Bahrain (31 December 1997), 201 [469]-[470]
[126] Rejoinder of Nigeria (4 January 2001) [12.23]; CR 2002/13, 59 [30] (Crawford).
[127] Written Statement of Equatorial Guinea (4 April 2001), 16 [38].
[128] Memorial of Cameroon (16 March 1995), 533 [5.44]-[5.75]; Reply of Cameroon (4 April 2000), 402-3 [9.51]-[9.52].
[129] Memorial of Barbados (30 October 2004), 2 [6]; Reply of Barbados (9 June 2005), 174 [95].
[130] Hearing Transcript (Day 1), 25-26 (Ramphal).
[131] Counter-memorial of Suriname (1 November 2005), 103 [6.47]-[6.48].
[132] Ibid. 99 [6.30].

delimitation methods must be chosen taking into account all relevant circumstances.[133]

In *Black Sea*, neither party argued for the application of a three-stage delimitation process, adhering to the two-stage approach as the established delimitation method.[134] The Court did not formulate the three-stage approach based on the arguments of either party. However, since *Libya/Malta* certain states identified disproportionality as the test for the overall equitableness of the boundary and the last stage of the delimitation process.[135] Therefore, the formulation of the three-stage approach seemed to have been influenced by the position which states expressed in their pleadings before the Court, and could not be attributed entirely to the Court's creativity.

After *Black Sea*, states reacted differently to the three-stage approach, although they all appeared ultimately to accept it as the established method for maritime delimitation. Costa Rica,[136] India[137] and Myanmar[138] expressly endorsed the three-stage approach in their pleadings. In *Nicaragua v. Colombia*, Nicaragua argued its case based on the two-stage approach in its 2003 Memorial,[139] but in the 2012 oral proceedings it criticised Colombia for not conducting the disproportionality test as the third stage of the delimitation process.[140] Consistently with this position, Nicaragua supported the three-stage approach in *Costa Rica v. Nicaragua*.[141]

---

[133] Memorial of Nicaragua (21 March 2001), 95 [21]; Counter-memorial of Honduras (21 March 2002), 63 [4.16] and 145 [7.42]; CR 2007/12, 53 (Argüello).

[134] Counter-memorial of Ukraine (19 May 2006), 156-7 [6.27]-[6.31]; Reply of Romania (22 December 2006), 189 [6.5]; CR 2008/18, 61 [6] (Crawford); CR 2008/20, 13 [8] (Pellet); CR 2008/26, 10-11 [42] (Quéneudec).

[135] Counter-memorial of Malta (26 October 1983), 345 [257]; Counter-memorial of Qatar (31 December 1997), 298-9 [8.103]-[8.105]; Counter-memorial of Trinidad and Tobago (30 March 2005), 47-60 [144]-[173]; Counter-memorial of Ukraine (19 May 2006), 241 [10.1]; Reply of Romania (22 December 2006), 296-302 [9.20]-[9.41]; CR 2008/18, 18 [10] (Aurescu); CR 2008/21, 53-68 [1]-[83] (Lowe); CR 2008/24, 17 [32] (Vassylenko); CR 2008/29, 45 [6]-[7] (Bundy).

[136] Memorial of Costa Rica (3 February 2015), 25-6 [2.44]-[2.47]; CR 2017/7, 36-7 [6] (Parlett).

[137] Counter-memorial of India (31 January 2013), 115-21 [6.5]-[6.16]; Hearing Transcript (Day 1), 21-3 [14]-[24] (Vahanvati); Hearing Transcript (Day 3), 252-3 [10] (Chadha); Hearing Transcript (Day 4), 388 [91] (Wood).

[138] Counter-memorial of Myanmar (1 December 2010), 99-100 [5.30]-[5.32]; ITLOS/PV.11/7/Rev.1, 6-7 (Pellet); ITLOS/PV.11/9/Rev.1, 4 (Pellet); ITLOS/PV.11/16/Rev.1, 10 (Wood).

[139] Memorial of Nicaragua (28 April 2003), 212-13 [3.50]-[3.51].

[140] CR 2012/10, 29-30 [8]-[11] (Reichler); CR 2012/14, 43 [8]-[9] (Reichler).

[141] CR 2017/11, 22 [3] (Reichler).

In *Peru v. Chile*, Peru's position similarly evolved from the pre-2009 written submissions to the post-2009 oral proceedings.[142] The change in the position of Nicaragua and Peru can plausibly be attributed to the formulation of the three-stage approach in *Black Sea*. In *Ghana/Côte d'Ivoire*, Ghana structured its Reply following the three stages of the delimitation process,[143] and argued that, if the Special Chamber rejected its principal argument for a tacitly agreed boundary, it should apply the three-stage approach.[144]

The states which did not argue for boundaries to be drawn following the three-stage approach recognised the established character of that approach nonetheless. Although Bangladesh argued for angle-bisectors both in *Bangladesh/Myanmar*[145] and *Bangladesh v. India*,[146] in the former it acknowledged that the three-stage approach was the established delimitation process,[147] and in the latter attempted to show that the three-stage approach was not applicable in the circumstances.[148] In *Nicaragua v. Colombia*, Colombia's position did not evolve similarly to that of Nicaragua. Colombia based its arguments on the two-stage approach both before and after *Black Sea*,[149] presumably because it maintained that disproportionality was inapplicable between opposite coasts.[150] In *Ghana/Côte d'Ivoire*, while Côte d'Ivoire's main contention was in favour of an angle-bisector, it alternatively requested the boundary to be drawn pursuant to the 'well-established jurisprudence' on the three-stage approach.[151] The pleadings of Bangladesh, Colombia and Côte d'Ivoire suggest that such states sanctioned the three-stage approach by expressly recognising its established character, by

---

[142] Memorial of Peru (20 March 2009), 198 [6.10]; CR 2012/27, 36 [8] (Bundy).
[143] Reply of Ghana (25 July 2016), 96–121 [3.46]-[3.103].
[144] Memorial of Ghana (4 September 2015), 144 [5.84]-[5.85]; ITLOS/PV.17/C23/1/Rev.1, 10 (Sands).
[145] Memorial of Bangladesh (1 July 2010), 86–91 [6.56]-[6.67]; ITLOS/PV.11/15/Rev.1, 1-15 (Crawford).
[146] Memorial of Bangladesh (31 May 2011), 115 [6.100]; Hearing Transcript (Day 2), 118–119 [128]-[129] (Akhavan).
[147] Memorial of Bangladesh (1 July 2010), 86–91 [6.56]-[6.67]; ITLOS/PV.11/15/Rev.1, 1-15 (Crawford).
[148] Hearing Transcript (Day 2), 160–89 [1]-[59] (Boyle).
[149] Counter-memorial of Colombia (11 November 2008), 385–6 [9.13]; Rejoinder of Colombia (18 June 2010), 198 [6.3]; CR 2012/11, 26 [26] (Crawford).
[150] CR 2012/17, 16 [9] (Crawford).
[151] Counter-memorial of Côte d'Ivoire (4 April 2016), 163 [7.1]; ITLOS/PV.17/C23/4/Rev.1, 6 (Pitron).

developing arguments aimed at showing its inapplicability in the circumstances, and by making alternative requests based on it.

Called upon to express their views on the delimitation process, states have shown a remarkable inclination to sanction earlier judicial developments. However, international tribunals did not operate in a vacuum. Both the formulation of the two-stage approach, and the separation of disproportionality from other relevant circumstances resulting in the formulation of the three-stage approach, built upon the contentions of states. Pleadings suggest that the judicial elaboration on the delimitation process was influenced, and possibly guided, by the views of certain states party to disputes before international tribunals. It would seem reductive to agree that the three-stage approach is an entirely judicial creation.

C Compliance with Judicial Decisions Establishing Maritime Boundaries

States are under an obligation to comply with judicial decisions in cases to which they are a party.[152] However, as compliance with such decisions may not be enforced, willingness to comply may reveal the attitude of certain states with respect to the delimitation process. Once international tribunals hand down judgments establishing maritime boundaries, some negotiation is necessary in order to implement them.[153] While the literature on the implementation of judicial decisions in international law is scant,[154] it is possible to reconstruct the states' attitude towards compliance with decisions establishing maritime boundaries.

Concluding a treaty has been a common method to implement decisions establishing maritime boundaries. The states concerned concluded delimitation agreements based on prior delimitation decisions in *North*

---

[152] See Art. 94(1) UN Charter and Art. 296 UNCLOS.
[153] M Shaw, *Rosenne's Law and Practice of the International Court 1920-2015* 5th edn (Martinus Nijhoff, 2015) vol. I, 197.
[154] A Huneeus, 'Compliance with Judgments and Decisions' in C Romano et al. (eds.), *The Oxford Handbook of International Adjudication* (OUP, 2014) 437; M Al-Qahtani, 'The Role of the International Court of Justice in the Enforcement of its Judicial Decisions' (2002) 15 *LJIL* 781; C Schulte, *Compliance with Decisions of the International Court of Justice* (OUP, 2004); A Azar, *L'Exécution des Décisions de la Cour Internationale de Justice* (Bruylant 2003) 99. On provisional measures, see M Lando, 'Compliance with Provisional Measures Indicated by the International Court of Justice' (2017) 8 *JIDS* 22.

Sea Continental Shelf,[155] Tunisia/Libya,[156] Libya/Malta[157] and Jan Mayen.[158] After *Gulf of Maine*, Canada and the United States concluded an agreement on fisheries, which took the line established by the Chamber of the ICJ as the boundary between them.[159] While this treaty did not specifically concern the establishment of a maritime boundary, it was a step in implementing a legal regime stemming from the 1984 *Gulf of Maine* judgment.[160]

In *Cameroon* v. *Nigeria*, the parties created an *ad hoc* commission with a mandate to determine the precise mechanisms through which to achieve compliance with the ICJ's 2002 judgment.[161] Nigeria frequently repeated its commitment to implementation before the Sixth Committee of the General Assembly.[162] The commission's work is ongoing, but the obstacles it faces appear mainly to concern the land portion of the boundary, not the maritime one.[163] The result of the commission's work could also be a treaty to be concluded by Cameroon and Nigeria,

---

[155] Treaty between the Kingdom of Denmark and the Federal Republic of Germany concerning the Delimitation of the Continental Shelf under the North Sea, 857 UNTS 119; Treaty between the Kingdom of the Netherlands and the Federal Republic of Germany concerning the Delimitation of the Continental Shelf under the North Sea, 857 UNTS 142.

[156] Agreement between the Libyan Arab Socialist People's Jamahiriya and the Republic of Tunisia to Implement the Judgment of the International Court of Justice in the Tunisia/Libya Continental Shelf Case, in JI Charney and LM Alexander (eds.), *International Maritime Boundaries* (Martinus Nijhoff, 1993) vol. II, 1663.

[157] Agreement between the Great Socialist People's Libyan Arab Jamahiriya and the Republic of Malta implementing Article III of the Special Agreement and the Judgment of the International Court of Justice, in Charney and Alexander (n. 156) vol II, 1649.

[158] Agreement between Denmark and Norway concerning the Delimitation of the Continental Shelf in the Area between Jan Mayen and Greenland and concerning the Boundary between the Fishery Zones in the Area, 1903 UNTS 171.

[159] Agreement on Fisheries Enforcement, 1852 UNTS 73.

[160] Schulte (n. 154) 178.

[161] M Kamto, 'Considérations actuelles sur l'inexécution des Décisions de la Cour internnationale de Justice' in TM Ndiaye and R Wolfrum (eds.), *Law of the Sea, Environmental Law and Settlement of Disputes – Liber Amicorum Judge Thomas A. Mensah* (Martinus Nijhoff, 2007) 215; L Boisson de Chazournes and A Angelini, 'Regard sur la Mise en Œuvre des Décisions de la Court internationale de Justice' (2016) 40 *L'Observateur des Nations Unies* 63, 73–4.

[162] UN Doc A/C.6/70/SR.6 (6 November 2015) 15 [82]; UN Doc A/C.6/69/SR.6 (19 November 2014) 12 [70]; UN Doc A/C.6/68/SR.8 (22 October 2013) 3 [10]; UN Doc A/C.6/67/SR.6 (5 December 2012) 7 [36].

[163] UN Doc A/C.6/60/SR.15 (18 November 2005) 11 [51]. See also C Paulson, 'Compliance with Final Judgments of the International Court of Justice since 1987' (2004) 98 *AJIL* 434, 439–452.

although this is not entirely clear. Similarly, in *Ghana/Côte d'Ivoire* the parties set up a joint commission for implementing the judgment of 23 September 2017, whose work seems to be still ongoing.[164]

Once international tribunals establish maritime boundaries, states frequently make statements relating to the implementation of the decisions concerned. For example, President Sebastian Piñera was reported to say that 'Chile would abide by the judgment' of 27 January 2014.[165] Similarly, at the Sixth Committee of the UN General Assembly Peru stated that the two states 's'engageaient à respecter l'arrêt de la Cour internationale de Justice'.[166] Two months after the ICJ handed down its judgment, Peru and Chile agreed on the co-ordinates identifying their maritime boundary, and Peru confirmed that it had amended three pieces of legislation to make them consistent with the Court's decision.[167] Costa Rica and Nicaragua made comparable statements concerning their commitment to complying with the ICJ's judgment of 2 February 2018,[168] as did Bangladesh and India in respect of the arbitral award of 7 July 2014.[169] Academic writers have reported that the parties committed to complying with the ICJ's judgment in *Qatar v. Bahrain*,[170] and the former ITLOS President Yanai stated at the UN General Assembly that both Bangladesh and Myanmar 'welcomed' the judgment of 14 March 2012.[171]

Nicaragua v. Colombia is the only case in which a party rejected a decision on maritime delimitation, including its implementation. On 19 November 2012, President Santos was reported declaring that Colombia could not accept the omissions, mistakes, excesses and

---

[164] 'Ghana and Ivory Coast Set Up Body to Implement Maritime Border Ruling' (*Reuters*, 17 October 2017) www.reuters.com/article/ghana-ivorycoast-boundary/ghana-and-ivory-coast-set-up-body-to-implement-maritime-border-ruling-idUSL8N1MS3MQ.

[165] 'Hague Border Verdict Set to Strengthen Peru, Chile Ties' (*Reuters*, 27 January 2014) www.reuters.com/article/us-chile-peru-court/hague-border-verdict-set-to-strengthen-chile-peru-ties-idUSBREA0Q1ER20140127.

[166] UN Doc A/C.6/68/SR.7 (20 November 2013) 4 [14].

[167] 'Coordenadas del límite marítimo con Chile se definen en actas' (*El Comercio*, 26 March 2014) https://elcomercio.pe/politica/gobierno/coordenadas-limite-maritimo-chile-definen-actas-304572.

[168] 'World Court Settles Nicaragua-Costa Rica Disputes' (*Havana Times*, 8 February 2018) www.havanatimes.org/?p=130515.

[169] 'Bangladesh Wins Maritime Dispute with India' (*The Hindu*, 9 July 2014) www.thehindu.com/news/national/bangladesh-wins-maritime-dispute-with-india/article6191797.ece.

[170] Schulte (n. 154) 239; Paulson (n. 163) 455.

[171] UN Doc A/67/PV.49 (10 December 2012) 18.

inconsistencies of the ICJ's judgment.[172] He stated that maritime boundaries are established by agreement, not 'via rulings uttered by the International Court of Justice', withdrawing Colombia from the Pact of Bogotá.[173] Although Colombia's attitude towards compliance may have been initially unclear,[174] on 26 November 2013 Nicaragua instituted proceedings against Colombia concerning 'violations of Nicaragua's sovereign rights and maritime zones declared by the Court's Judgment of 19 November 2012 and the threat of the use of force by Colombia in order to implement these violations'.[175] Nicaragua requested the Court to find that 'Colombia is bound to comply with the Judgment of 19 November 2012, wipe out the legal and material consequences of its internationally wrongful acts, and make full reparation for the harm caused'.[176] Colombia argued that it 'has never taken any decision not to comply with the Judgment' and that 'both its highest officials and its highest court ... have made it clear that the Judgment is binding under international law'.[177] The Court delivered its judgment on preliminary objections on 17 March 2016,[178] and the merits phase is currently pending.

However, Colombia's reasons for contesting the ICJ's 2012 judgment did not seem to stem from the application of the three-stage approach, but from the Court's decision not to recognise the eighty-second meridian as the maritime boundary with Nicaragua.[179] Colombia's reluctance to implement the 2012 judgment could not be seen to be a rejection of the three-stage delimitation process. Furthermore, in all other cases states committed to compliance by concluding a treaty based on the decision concerned, creating *ad hoc* bodies to oversee compliance, or

---

[172] 'Colombia rechaza delimitación marítima con Nicaragua' (*La Nación*, 19 November 2012) www.nacion.com/el-mundo/colombia-rechaza-delimitacion-maritima-con-nicaragua/542URAVFTBAXRCMECZ4X6YETL4/story/.

[173] 'Colombia leaves Pact recognizing UN court rulings' (*Reuters*, 28 November 2012) www.reuters.com/article/us-colombia-icj/colombia-leaves-pact-recognizing-u-n-court-rulings-idUSBRE8AR11Q20121128.

[174] 'Colombia and Nicaragua: Hot Waters' (*The Economist*, 29 November 2012) www.economist.com/americas-view/2012/11/29/hot-waters.

[175] Application instituting proceedings (26 November 2013), 4 [2].

[176] Ibid. 24 [22].

[177] Preliminary Objections of Colombia (19 December 2014), 22 [2.24]. See also CR 2015/22, 42 [12] (Reisman).

[178] *Alleged Violations of Sovereign Rights and Maritime Spaces in the Caribbean Sea (Nicaragua v. Colombia)* (Preliminary Objections) [2016] ICJ Rep 3.

[179] *Territorial and Maritime Dispute (Nicaragua v. Colombia)* (Judgment) [2012] ICJ Rep 624, 705 [219].

making statements on implementation. In *Cameroon v. Nigeria*, the federal structure of Nigeria was stated to be an obstacle to full compliance with the ICJ's 2002 judgment,[180] yet this does not appear to have affected the willingness of both parties to comply. The elevated compliance rate with decisions on maritime delimitation[181] does not appear to have been influenced by the process which international tribunals employed for establishing a boundary. Compliance with such decisions is high, irrespective of the three delimitation processes used by international tribunals.[182] Elevated compliance rates since 2009 suggest an indirect sanction by states of the delimitation process formulated in *Black Sea*. However, given that high compliance rates do not depend on the delimitation process used, one could predict that, should the delimitation process evolve in the future, states would likely sanction that evolution.

Writing on the ICJ, Paulson commented that there is no link between compliance and submitting a dispute by special agreement, and that, until 2004, states complied with all ICJ decisions establishing EEZ or continental shelf boundaries.[183] This assessment holds true with respect both to post-2004 cases, and to disputes decided by jurisdictions other than the ICJ. Conversely, states seem to implement decisions concerning land boundaries more reluctantly.[184] The reason for this difference in attitude towards boundary decisions could be linked to the different character between sovereignty over land and rights in the EEZ or continental shelf, which fall short of sovereignty.[185] Rights over the EEZ and continental shelf are also of considerably more recent making, while sovereignty over land dates much further back. Disputes over land sovereignty are likely to have a longer history, and appear generally to be more relatable to the general public than maritime boundary cases, which may entail a greater degree of politicisation.

IV Interaction between States and International Tribunals

The role of states in maritime delimitation disputes suggests that the view according to which international tribunals are the sole creators of the

---

[180] UN Doc A/C.6/65/SR.24 (1 December 2010) 3 [10].
[181] G Guillaume, 'De l'exécution des Décisions de la Cour internationale de Justice' (1997) 7 *SRIEL* 431, 436.
[182] Chapter 2, Section II.B above.
[183] Paulson (n. 163) 457.
[184] Ibid.
[185] Arts. 56 and 77 UNCLOS.

delimitation process is not entirely accurate. Certain decisions made by international tribunals in developing the delimitation process, such as the separation of disproportionality from other relevant circumstances, had already been suggested by states. Furthermore, the re-assertion by international tribunals of a central role for equidistance may have been both determined, and later confirmed, by the repeated establishment by states of maritime boundaries based on equidistance. International tribunals seem to have developed the delimitation process largely by taking stock of the approach adopted or legal arguments made by states.

However, international tribunals remain the developers of the delimitation process, and the makers of the three-stage approach. Although they may have formulated the delimitation process also by reacting to the states' approach to delimitation, without the assertion of a creative role by international tribunals maritime boundaries would still be conceivably delimited on a case-by-case basis. The states' decision at UNCLOS III to codify vague provisions on EEZ and continental shelf delimitation implicitly authorised international tribunals to assert a creative function in developing the delimitation process. Moreover, the two-element approach to the formation of customary international law entails that the delimitation process is likely never to become a rule of custom. In these circumstances, the international tribunals' decisions formulating the delimitation process should be considered to be formal sources of international law.

Moreover, states have sanctioned the delimitation process developed by international tribunals, both by concluding treaties which appear to confirm the judicial approach to delimitation, and by readily implementing decisions establishing maritime boundaries. The delimitation process was not developed by international tribunals in a vacuum. This development should be better conceived as having been determined by the continuous interaction between states and international tribunals. Should the delimitation process develop further, it is likely that any such development will take place as a consequence of this interaction.

V   What Next for the Delimitation Process?

The judicial elaboration of the delimitation process began in *North Sea Continental Shelf*. In *Black Sea*, the ICJ formulated the now-established three-stage approach to maritime delimitation. In the forty years between these two judgments, international tribunals have shaped and changed the delimitation process significantly, evolving it from a case-by-case

V WHAT NEXT FOR THE DELIMITATION PROCESS? 323

approach to a standard two-stage approach, and to the current three-stage delimitation process.[186] The delimitation jurisprudence of international tribunals could conceivably lead to further developments in the future.

The delimitation of the continental shelf beyond 200 nm has raised some complex issues of international law, which international tribunals have not settled yet. It seems likely that future developments will take place in relation to delimitation beyond 200 nm. The ICJ will likely address these issues in the pending case between Somalia and Kenya. Similarly, the pending ICJ dispute between Nicaragua and Colombia concerns the delimitation of the continental shelf beyond 200 nm, but also raises other questions, including that of the relationship between the continental shelf and the EEZ. Although the Court is traditionally reticent to make decisions unless they are strictly necessary, one could expect comments on such issues in the states' pleadings, and, presumably, in the Court's judgment itself and in the individual opinions.

It seems possible that international tribunals would recognise the importance of the identification of the relevant coast and of the relevant area in the delimitation process by separating their identification from the drawing of a provisional equidistance line, so as to become the first stage of EEZ and continental shelf delimitation. Although this separation would not be an unexpected development it would enhance the clarity of the delimitation process. Since *North Sea Continental Shelf*, international tribunals have endeavoured to rationalise the method for delimiting EEZ and continental shelf boundaries, in order to increase certainty in delimitation by way of judicial process. If international tribunals are further to develop the delimitation process, they are likely to do so in the pursuit of that same objective.

---

[186] Chapter 2, Section II.B above.

APPENDIX 1

List of States Which Have Proclaimed an EEZ (in alphabetical order by state)

State	Domestic Law Act	Breadth[1]
Angola	Law No. 21/92 of 28 August 1992, Art. 7	200 nm
Antigua and Barbuda	Maritime Areas Act 1982, Act No. 18 of 17 August 1982, Section 7	200 nm
Argentina	Act No. 23.968 of 14 August 1991, Art. 5	200 nm
Australia	Seas and Submerged Lands Act 1973, as amended by the Maritime Legislation Amendment Act 1994, Sections 10A–10C	200 nm
Bahamas	Act No. 37 of 1993, Section 8	200 nm
Bangladesh	Territorial Waters and Maritime Zones Act 1974, Act No. XXVI of 1974, Art. 5	200 nm
Barbados	Marine Boundaries and Jurisdiction Act 1978-3, 25 February 1978, Section 3	200 nm
Belgium	Act concerning the exclusive economic zone of Belgium in the North Sea, 22 April 1999, Art. 2	Specified by means of a list of co-ordinates
Belize	Maritime Areas Act 1992, of 24 January 1992, Section 6	200 nm
Brazil	Law No. 8.617 of 4 January 1993, Art. 6	200 nm
Brunei	Declaration on the Exclusive Economic Zone of 21 July 1993	200 nm
Bulgaria	Maritime Space, Inland Waterways and Ports Act, 28 January 2000, Art. 45	200 nm

[1] In cases in which states have not specified the breadth of their EEZ, it has been assumed that such states intended to extend their EEZ as far seawards as international law allows, i.e., 200 nm.

(*cont.*)

State	Domestic Law Act	Breadth
Cambodia	Decree of the Council of State of 13 July 1982, Art. 5	200 nm
Canada	Oceans Act of 18 December 1996 (An Act respecting the oceans of Canada, 18 December 1996), Section 13	200 nm
Cape Verde	Law No. 60/IV/92 of 21 December 1992, Art. 12	200 nm
Chile	Civil Code, Art. 596	200 nm
China	Exclusive Economic Zone and Continental Shelf Act, Art. 2	200 nm
Colombia	Act No. 10 of 4 August 1978, Art. 7	200 nm
Comoros	Law No. 82-005 of 6 May 1982, Art. 6	200 nm
Cook Islands	Territorial Sea and Exclusive Economic Zone Act, Act No. 16 of 14 November 1977, Art. 8	200 nm
Côte d'Ivoire	Law No. 77-926 of 17 November 1977, Art. 2	200 nm
Croatia	The Maritime Code 1994, Art. 33	200 nm
Cuba	Legislative Decree No. 2 of 24 February 1977, Art. 1	200 nm
Cyprus	The Exclusive Economic Zone and the Continental Shelf Act 2004 and 2014 (consolidated version), Section 2	200 nm
Denmark	Act No. 411 of 22 May 1996 on Exclusive Economic Zones, Art. 1	200 nm
Djibouti	Law No. 52/AN/78, Art. 12	200 nm
Dominica	Territorial Sea, Contiguous Zone, Exclusive Economic and Fishery Zones Act 1981, Act No. 26 of 25 August 1981, Section 5	200 nm
Dominican Republic	Act 66-07 of 22 May 2007, Art. 14	200 nm
DPR of Korea	Decree by the Central People's Committee establishing the Economic Zone of 21 June 1977	200 nm
Democratic Republic of the Congo	Act proclaiming an Exclusive Economic Zone along the Atlantic Coast, 4 November 1992	200 nm

(*cont.*)

State	Domestic Law Act	Breadth
Equatorial Guinea	Act No. 15/1984 of 12 November 1984, Art. 10	200 nm
Estonia	Law on the boundaries of the maritime tract, 10 March 1993, Art. 7	Limits set by agreement with neighbouring states
Fiji	Marine spaces Act 1977, Act No. 18 of 15 December 1977, as amended by the Marine Spaces (Amendment) Act 1978, Act No. 15 of 6 October 1978, Section 6	200 nm
Finland	Act on the Exclusive Economic Zone of Finland of 26 November 2004, Art. 1	Limits set by agreement with neighbouring states
France	Decrees Nos. 78-144, 78-146, 78-147 and 78-148 of 3 February 1978 (in respect of Reunion, Clipperton Island, Southern and Antarctic Territories, Tromelin, Glorieuses, Juan-de-Nova, Europa, Bassas-da-India)	200 nm
Gabon	Act No. 9/84, Arts. 1–2	200 nm
Germany	Proclamation of 25 November 1994 concerning the establishment of an exclusive economic zone of the Federal Republic of Germany, Section I	Specified by means of a list of co-ordinates
Ghana	Maritime Zones (Delimitation) Law 1986, Art. 5	200 nm
Grenada	Territorial Sea and Maritime Boundaries Act, 1989, Act No. 25 of 1989, Section 12	200 nm
Guatemala	Legislative Decree No. 20-76 of 9 June 1976, Art. 3	200 nm
Guinea	Decree No. 336/PRG of 30 July 1980, Art. 2	200 nm

(cont.)

State	Domestic Law Act	Breadth
Guinea-Bissau	Act No. 3/85 of 17 May 1985, Art. 3	200 nm
Guyana	Exclusive Economic Zone (Designation of Area) Order 1991, No. 19 of 1991, Art. 1	200 nm
Haiti	Declaration of 6 April 1977	200 nm
Honduras	Decree No. 921 of 13 June 1980 on the utilization of Marine Natural Resources, Art. 1	200 nm
Iceland	Law No. 41 of 1 June 1979, Art. 3	200 nm
India	The Territorial Waters, Continental Shelf, Exclusive Economic Zone and other Maritime Zones Act 1976, Section 7	200 nm
Indonesia	Act No. 5 of 18 October 1983, Art. 2	200 nm
Iran	Act on the Marine Areas of the Islamic Republic of Iran in the Persian Gulf and the Oman Sea 1993, Art. 14	200 nm
Ireland	Sea-Fisheries and Maritime Jurisdiction Act 2006 of 4 April 2006, Section 87	200 nm
Jamaica	The Exclusive Economic Zone Act 1991, Act No. 33 of 1991, Section 3	200 nm
Japan	Law on the Exclusive Economic Zone and the Continental Shelf, Law No. 74 of 1996, Art. 1	200 nm
Kenya	Presidential Proclamation of 28 February 1979, Art. 1	200 nm
Kiribati	Marine Zones (Declaration) Act 1983, Act No. 7 of 16 May 1983, Section 7	200 nm
Latvia	Law on Continental Shelf and Exclusive Economic Zone, 2 February 1993	Limits set by agreement with neighbouring states
Lebanon	Decree No. 6433 of 16 November 2011, Art. 1	200 nm

(cont.)

State	Domestic Law Act	Breadth
Liberia	Executive Order No. 48 of 10 January 2013, Section 5	200 nm
Libya	General People's Committee Decision No. 260 of 2009, Art. 1	200 nm
Lithuania	Resolution No. 1597 of 6 December 2004 on the Approval of the Limits of the Territorial Sea, Contiguous Zone, Exclusive Economic Zone and Continental Shelf	Limits defined by specific co-ordinates in Annex 2 to the resolution
Madagascar	Ordinance No. 85-013 of 16 September 1985, as amended by Law No. 85-013 of 11 December 1985, Art. 4	200 nm
Malaysia	Exclusive Economic Zone Act 1984, Act No. 311 of 1984, Section 3	200 nm
Maldives	Law No. 30/76 relating to the Exclusive Economic Zone of the Republic of Maldives of 5 December 1976, Art. 1	200 nm
Marshall Islands	Marine Zones (Declaration) Act 1984, Section 8	200 nm
Mauritania	Ordinance 88-120 of 31 August 1988, Art. 3	200 nm
Mauritius	Maritime Zones Act 2005, Art. 14	200 nm
Mexico	Federal Act relating to the Sea, 8 January 1986, Art. 46	200 nm
Micronesia	Code of the Federated States of Micronesia, Section 104	200 nm
Morocco	Act No. 1-81 of 18 December 1980, Art. 1	200 nm
Mozambique	Mozambique Council of Ministers Decree Law No. 31/76 of 19 August 1976, Art. 3	200 nm
Myanmar	Territorial Sea and Maritime Zones Law 1977, Law No. 3 of 9 April 1977, Section 17	200 nm

(*cont.*)

State	Domestic Law Act	Breadth
Namibia	Act No. 3 of 30 June 1990, Art. 4	200 nm
Nauru	Sea Boundaries Act 1997, Section 6	200 nm
Netherlands	Exclusive Economic Zone (Establishment) Act of 27 May 1999, Section 1	200 nm
New Zealand	Territorial Sea and Exclusive Economic Zone Act 1977, Act No. 28 of 26 September 1977 as amended by Act No. 146 of 1980, Section 9	200 nm
Nigeria	Decree No. 28 of 5 October 1978, Art. 1	200 nm
Niue	Territorial Sea and Exclusive Economic Zone Act 1996, Section 10	200 nm
Norway	Act No. 91 of 17 December 1976 relating to the Economic Zone of Norway, Paragraph 1	200 nm
Oman	Royal Decree of 10 February 1981, Arts. 4–5	200 nm
Pakistan	Territorial Waters and Maritime Zones of 22 December 1976, Section 6	200 nm
Panama	Decree Law No. 7 of 10 February 1998	200 nm
Philippines	Presidential Decree No. 1599 of 11 June 1978, Section 1	200 nm
Poland	Act concerning the maritime areas of the Polish Republic and the marine administration, 21 March 1991, Arts. 14–16	Limits set by agreement with neighbouring states
Portugal	Act No. 33/77 of 28 May 1977, Art. 2	200 nm
Republic of Korea	Exclusive Economic Zone Act, No. 5151 of 8 August 1996, Arts. 1–2	200 nm
Romania	Decree No. 142 of 25 April 1986 of the Council of State, Arts. 1–2	200 nm
Russian Federation	Federal Act on the Exclusive Economic Zone of the Russian Federation, Art. 1	200 nm

(cont.)

State	Domestic Law Act	Breadth
Samoa	Maritime Zones Act 1999, Act No. 18 of 25 August 1999, Section 19	200 nm
Saõ Tomé and Principe	Law No. 1/98, Art. 4	200 nm
Saudi Arabia	Royal Decree No. 6 of 18/1/1433 H, Arts. 12–16	Limits set by agreement with neighbouring states
Senegal	Act 87-27 of 18 August 1987, Art. 2	200 nm
Seychelles	Exclusive economic zone (No. 2) Order 1978	200 nm
Sierra Leone	The Maritime Zones (Establishment) Decree, 1996, Art. 8	200 nm
Singapore	Ministry of Foreign Affairs Press Release of 15 September 1980	Limits set by agreement with neighbouring states
Solomon Islands	The Delimitation of Marine Waters Act 1978, Act No. 32 of 21 December 1978, Section 6	200 nm
Somalia	Presidential Proclamation of 30 June 2014	200 nm
South Africa	Maritime Zones Act, No. 15 of 1994, Art. 7	200 nm
Spain	Act No. 15/1978 on the Economic Zone of 20 February 1978, Art. 1 (only in respect of the Atlantic coast)	200 nm
Sri Lanka	Presidential Proclamation of 15 January 1977, Paragraph 4	200 nm
Saint Kitts and Nevis	The Maritime Areas Act 1984, Section 9	200 nm
Saint Lucia	Maritime Areas Act 1984, Section 9	200 nm
Saint Vincent and the Grenadines	Maritime Areas Act 1983, Act No. 15 of 19 May 1983, Section 7	200 nm
State of Palestine	Declaration of the State of Palestine of 31 August 2015, Section 7	200 nm

(cont.)

State	Domestic Law Act	Breadth
Suriname	Law of 14 April 1978, Art. 3	200 nm
Sweden	Act on Sweden's economic zone of 3 December 1992, Art. 1	Limits set by agreement with neighbouring states
Syria	Law No. 28 of 8 November 2003, Art. 21	200 nm
Tanzania	Territorial Sea and Exclusive Economic Zone Act 1989, Art. 7	200 nm
Thailand	Royal Proclamation of 23 February 1981, Section 1	200 nm
Timor Leste	Law No. 7/2002, Art. 7	200 nm
Togo	Ordinance No. 24 of 16 August 1977	200 nm
Tonga	The Territorial Sea and Exclusive Economic Zone Act 1978, as amended by Act No. 19 of 1989, Section 9	200 nm
Trinidad and Tobago	Archipelagic Waters and Exclusive Economic Zone Act 1986, Section 14	200 nm
Tunisia	Act No. 50/2005 of 27 June 2005, Art. 1	200 nm
Turkey	Decree by the Council of Ministers No. 86/11264 of 17 December 1986, Art. 1 (only in respect of the Black Sea)	200 nm
Tuvalu	Maritime Zones Act 2012, Section 11	200 nm
United Arab Emirates	Declaration of the Ministry of Foreign Affairs of 25 July 1980, Sections 1–3	Limits set by agreement with neighbouring states
Ukraine	Law on the exclusive (marine) economic zone of 16 May 1995, Art. 2	200 nm
United Kingdom	Proclamation establishing an Exclusive Economic Zone (Pitcairn, Henderson, Ducie and Oeno Islands), Proclamation No. 1 of 1997	200 nm

(*cont.*)

State	Domestic Law Act	Breadth
United Kingdom	Exclusive Economic Zone Order 2013	200 nm
United States of America	Proclamation 5030 by the President of the United States of America of 10 March 1983	200 nm
Uruguay	Act 17.033 of 20 November 1998, Art. 4	200 nm
Vanuatu	Maritime Zones Act No. 6 of 2010, Section 9	200 nm
Venezuela	Act establishing an Exclusive Economic Zone along the coasts of the Mainland and Islands of 26 July 1978, Arts. 1-2	200 nm
Vietnam	Statement on the Territorial Sea, the Contiguous Zone, the Exclusive Economic Zone and the Continental Shelf of 12 May 1977, Section 3	200 nm
Yemen	Act No. 45 of 17 December 1977, Art. 13	200 nm

List of States Which Have Proclaimed a FZ[2] (*in alphabetical order by state*)

State	Domestic Law Act	Breadth
Algeria	Legislative Decree No. 94-13 of 28 May 1994, Art. 6	32 nm between the eastern border and Ras Ténès 52 nm between Ras Ténès and the western border
Palau	Palau National Code, Section 144	200 nm
Spain	Royal Decree 1315/1997 of 1 August 1997, Art. 1 (only in respect of the Mediterranean coast)	Up to the equidistance line with neighbouring states

[2] Where a state declared a FZ and subsequently an EEZ, the FZ is considered to have been superseded by the EEZ.

APPENDIX 1

List of States WHhich ave Proclaimed a Maritime Zone beyond 12 nm Other than an EEZ or a FZ (in alphabetical order by state)

State	Act No.	Denomination	Breadth
Benin	Decree No. 76-92, Art. 1	Territorial sea	200 nm
Cameroon	Act No. 74/16 of 5 December 1974, Art. 5	Territorial sea	50 nm
Congo	Ordinance No. 049/77 of 20 December 1977, Art. 2	Territorial sea	200 nm
El Salvador	Constitution of 13 December 1983, Art. 84	Territorial sea	200 nm
Italy	Law 61 of 8 February 2006, Art. 1 Presidential Decree No. 209 of 27 October 2011, Art. 2	Ecological Protection Zone	Specified by means of a list of co-ordinates
Nicaragua	Act No. 205 of 19 December 1979, Art. 2	Territorial sea	200 nm
Peru	Constitution of 29 December 1993, Art. 54	Territorial sea	200 nm
Slovenia	Ecological Protection Zone and Continental Shelf of the Republic of Slovenia Act 2005, Arts. 3–4	Ecological Protection Zone	Limits set by agreement with neighbouring states

APPENDIX 2

Bilateral Treaties establishing Boundaries based on Equidistance[1]
(in chronological order by date of conclusion)

1958
Frontier Agreement between Bahrain and Saudi Arabia (22 February 1958), 1733 UNTS 3

Protocol between the Polish People's Republic and the Union of Soviet Socialist Republics concerning the Delimitation of Polish and Soviet Territorial Waters in the Gulf of Gdansk of the Baltic Sea (18 March 1958), 340 UNTS 89

1964
Treaty between the Kingdom of the Netherlands and the Federal Republic of Germany concerning the Lateral Delimitation of the Continental Shelf in the vicinity of the Coast (1 December 1964), 550 UNTS 127

1965
Agreement between the United Kingdom of Great Britain and Northern Ireland and the Kingdom of Norway relating to the Delimitation of the Continental Shelf between the two Countries (10 March 1965), 551 UNTS 213

Agreement between Finland and the Union of Soviet Socialist Republics concerning the Boundaries of Sea Areas and of the Continental Shelf in the Gulf of Finland (20 May 1965), 566 UNTS 37

Agreement between the Kingdom of Denmark and the Federal Republic of Germany concerning the Delimitation in the Coastal Regions of the Continental Shelf of the North Sea (9 June 1965), 570 UNTS 95

Agreement between the Kingdom of the Netherlands and the United Kingdom of Great Britain and Northern Ireland relating to the Delimitation of the Continental Shelf under the North Sea between the two Countries (6 October 1965), *Limits in the Seas No. 10*

Agreement between Denmark and Norway relating to the Delimitation of the Continental Shelf (8 December 1965), 634 UNTS 75

---

[1] Where states agreed to depart from the strict equidistance line in order to compensate each other for ceding parts of maritime areas where they would have had jurisdiction under UNCLOS, it was concluded that the boundary is not based on equidistance.

1966
Agreement between the United Kingdom of Great Britain and Northern Ireland and the Kingdom of Denmark relating to the Delimitation of the Continental Shelf between the two Countries (3 March 1966), 592 UNTS 208

Agreement between the Kingdom of Denmark and the Kingdom of the Netherlands concerning the Delimitation of the Continental Shelf under the North Sea between the two Countries (31 March 1966), 604 UNTS 213

1967
Agreement concerning the Boundary of the Continental Shelf between Finland and the Soviet Union in the north-eastern Part of the Baltic Sea (5 May 1967), 640 UNTS 115

1968
Delimitation between Italy and Yugoslavia concerning the Delimitation of the Continental Shelf between the two Countries in the Adriatic Sea (8 January 1968), *Limits in the Seas No. 9*

Exchange of Letters constituting an Agreement amending the Agreement between Denmark and Norway of 8 December 1965 relating to the Delimitation of the Continental Shelf (24 April 1968), 643 UNTS 414

Agreement between Sweden and Norway concerning the Delimitation of the Continental Shelf (24 July 1968), 968 UNTS 240

Treaty between Poland and the German Democratic Republic concerning the Delimitation of the Continental Shelf in the Baltic Sea (29 October 1968), 768 UNTS 259

1969
Treaty between the Polish People's Republic and the Union of Soviet Socialist Republics concerning the Boundary of the Continental Shelf in the Gulf of Gdansk and the south-eastern part of the Baltic Sea (28 August 1969), 769 UNTS 81

Agreement concerning the Boundary Line dividing the Continental Shelf between Iran and Qatar (20 September 1969), 787 UNTS 171

Agreement between Malaysia and Indonesia on the Delimitation of the Continental Shelves between the two Countries (27 October 1969), *Limits in the Seas No. 1*

1971
Treaty between Australia and Indonesia Establishing Certain Seabed Boundaries (18 May 1971), 974 UNTS 308

Agreement concerning Delimitation of the Continental shelf between Iran and Bahrain (17 June 1971), 826 UNTS 233

Agreement between the Federal Republic of Germany and the United Kingdom of Great Britain and Northern Ireland relating to the Delimitation of the Continental Shelf under the North Sea between the two Countries (25 November 1971), 880 UNTS 185

Agreement between the Kingdom of Denmark and the United Kingdom of Great Britain and Northern Ireland relating to the Delimitation of the Continental Shelf between the two Countries (25 November 1971), 855 UNTS 208

Protocol between the United Kingdom of Great Britain and Northern Ireland and the Kingdom of the Netherlands amending the Agreement of 6 October 1965 relating to the Delimitation of the Continental Shelf under the North Sea between the two Countries (25 November 1971), UKTS No 130 (1972)

Agreement between the Kingdom of Thailand and the Republic of Indonesia relating to the Delimitation of a Continental Shelf Boundary between the two Countries in the northern Part of the Straits of Malacca and in the Andaman Sea (17 December 1971), 1103 UNTS 198

1972

Agreement between Canada and France on their Mutual Fishing Relations (27 March 1972), 862 UNTS 213

Exchange of Notes constituting an Agreement between Brazil and Uruguay on the Definitive Demarcation of the Sea Outlet of the River Chui and the Lateral Maritime Border (21 July 1972), 1120 UNTS 133

1973

Agreement between Australia and Indonesia concerning certain Boundaries between Papua New Guinea and Indonesia (12 February 1973), 975 UNTS 3

Treaty between Uruguay and Argentina concerning the Rio de la Plata and the corresponding Maritime Boundary (19 November 1973), 1295 UNTS 306

Agreement between the Kingdom of Denmark and Canada relating to the Delimitation of the Continental Shelf between Greenland and Canada (17 December 1973), 950 UNTS 151

1974

Agreement between Japan and the Republic of Korea concerning the Establishment of Boundary in the northern Part of the Continental Shelf adjacent to the two Countries (30 January 1974), 1225 UNTS 103

Convention between Spain and Italy on the Delimitation of the Continental Shelf between the two States (19 February 1974), 1120 UNTS 361

Exchange of Letters constituting an Agreement amending the Agreement between Denmark and Norway of 8 December 1965 relating to the Delimitation of the

Continental Shelf as amended by Exchange of Notes of 24 April 1968 (4 June 1974), 952 UNTS 390

Agreement between Sri Lanka and India on the Boundary in Historic Waters between the two Countries and Related Matters (26 June 1974 – 28 June 1974), 1049 UNTS 25

Agreement concerning Delimitation of the Continental Shelf between Iran and Oman (25 July 1974), 972 UNTS 273

Agreement between India and Indonesia relating to the Delimitation of the Continental Shelf Boundary between the two Countries (8 August 1974), 1208 UNTS 156

Offshore Boundary Agreement between Iran and Dubai (31 August 1974), *Limits in the Seas No. 63*

1976

Agreement between Sri Lanka and India on the Maritime Boundary between the two Countries in the Gulf of Manaar and the Bay of Bengal and Related Matters (23 March 1976), 1049 UNTS 43

Exchange of Notes constituting an Agreement on the Delimitation of the Exclusive Economic Zone of Mexico in the Sector adjacent to Cuban Maritime Areas (26 July 1976), 1390 UNTS 49

Treaty on the Delimitation of Marine and Submarine Areas and Related Matters between Colombia and Panama (20 November 1976), 1074 UNTS 221

Agreement between India and the Maldives on Maritime Boundary in the Arabian Sea and Related Matters (28 December 1976), *Limits in the Seas No. 78*

1977

Agreement between India and Indonesia relating to the Extension of the 1974 Continental Shelf Boundary between the two Countries in the Andaman Sea and the Indian Ocean (14 January 1977), 1208 UNTS 168

Agreement between the Hellenic Republic and the Italian Republic on the Delimitation of the respective Continental Shelf Areas of the two States (24 May 1977), 1275 UNTS 427

Agreement between the Republic of Haiti and the Republic of Cuba regarding the Delimitation of Maritime Boundaries between the two States (27 October 1977), in JI Charney and LM Alexander (eds.), *International Maritime Boundaries* (Martinus Nijhoff, 1993) vol. I, 551

Maritime Boundary Agreement between the United States of America and Cuba (16 December 1977), *Limits in the Seas No. 110*

1978

Agreement on the Delimitation of Marine and Submarine Areas and on Maritime Co-operation between Colombia and the Dominican Republic (13 January 1978), 1275 UNTS 363

Agreement on the Delimitation of the Maritime Boundaries between Colombia and Haiti (17 February 1978), 1155 UNTS 261

Maritime Boundary between the United States of America and Venezuela (28 March 1978), 1273 UNTS 25

Boundary Delimitation Treaty between the Republic of Venezuela and the Kingdom of the Netherlands (31 March 1978), 1140 UNTS 323

Treaty of Maritime Boundaries between the United States of America and the United Mexican States (Caribbean Sea and Pacific Ocean) (4 May 1978), 2143 UNTS 405

Treaty between the German Democratic Republic and the Kingdom of Sweden on the Delimitation of the Continental Shelf (22 June 1978), 1147 UNTS 193

Agreement between the Republic of India and the Kingdom of Thailand on the Delimitation of Seabed Boundary between the two Countries in the Andaman Sea (22 June 1978), *Limits in the Seas No. 93*

Agreement between Turkey and the Union of Soviet Socialist Republics concerning the Delimitation of the Continental Shelf between Turkey and the Union of Soviet Socialist Republics in the Black Sea (23 June 1978), 1247 UNTS 141

Treaty between Australia and Papua New Guinea concerning Sovereignty and Maritime Boundaries in the Torres Strait (18 December 1978), 1429 UNTS 207

Protocol Supplementary to the Agreement of 10 March 1965 between the United Kingdom of Great Britain and Northern Ireland and the Kingdom of Norway relating to the Delimitation of the Continental Shelf between the two Countries (22 December 1978), 1202 UNTS 362

1979

Treaty on the Delimitation of Marine and Submarine Areas between the Republic of Venezuela and the Dominican Republic (3 March 1979), in JI Charney and LM Alexander (eds.), *International Maritime Boundaries* (Martinus Nijhoff, 1993) vol. I, 577

Agreement on the Delimitation of the Continental Shelf in the Area between the Faeroe Islands and Norway and concerning the Boundary between the Fishery Zone near the Faeroe Islands and the Norwegian Economic Zone (15 June 1979), 1211 UNTS 168

Memorandum of Understanding on the Delimitation of the Continental Shelf Boundary between the two Countries in the Gulf of Thailand (24 October 1979), 1291 UNTS 250

1980

Convention between France (Wallis and Futuna) and Tonga on the Delimitation of Economic Zones (11 January 1980), 1183 UNTS 347

Treaty concerning Delimitation of Marine Areas and Maritime Co-operation between the Republic of Costa Rica and the Republic of Panama (2 February 1980), *Limits in the Seas No. 97*

Agreement regarding the Delimitation of the Areas of Finnish and Soviet Jurisdiction in the Field of Fishing in the Gulf of Finland and the northeastern Part of the Baltic Sea (25 February 1980), 1277 UNTS 7

Convention between France and Mauritius on the Delimitation of the French and Mauritian Economic Zones between the Islands of Reunion and Mauritius (2 April 1980), 1257 UNTS 62

Treaty between the United States of America and the Cook Islands on Friendship and Delimitation of the Maritime Boundary between the United States of American and the Cook Islands (11 June 1980), 1676 UNTS 223

Agreement between the Kingdom of Thailand and the Socialist Republic of the Union of Burma on the Delimitation of the Maritime Boundary between the two Countries in the Andaman Sea (25 July 1980), 1276 UNTS 447

Treaty between the USA (American Samoa) and New Zealand (Tokelau) on the Delimitation of the Maritime Boundary between Tokelau and the USA (2 December 1980), 1643 UNTS 251

Agreement between Indonesia and Papua New Guinea concerning the Maritime Boundary between Indonesia and Papua New Guinea and Co-operation on Related Matters (13 December 1980), in JI Charney and LM Alexander (eds.), *International Maritime Boundaries* (Martinus Nijhoff, 1993) vol. I, 1039

1981

Maritime Delimitation Treaty between Brazil and France in respect of French Guiana (30 January 1981), 1340 UNTS 7

Convention on Delimitation between France (Martinique) and Saint Lucia (4 March 1981), 1264 UNTS 426

1982

Agreement on Maritime Delimitation between Australia and France (New Caledonia, Chesterfield Islands) (4 January 1982), 1329 UNTS 107

Agreement between France and the United Kingdom of Great Britain and Northern Ireland relating to the Delimitation of the Continental Shelf in the Areas East of 30 Minutes West of the Greenwich Meridian (24 June 1982), 1316 UNTS 119

1983

Agreement between France and Fiji relating to the Delimitation of their Economic Zone (19 January 1983), 1597 UNTS 435

Convention on Maritime Boundaries between France (Tuamotu Archipelago) and the United Kingdom of Great Britain and Northern Ireland (Pitcairn, Henderson, Ducie, Oeno Islands) (25 October 1983), 1367 UNTS 181

1984

Treaty on the Delimitation of Marine and Submarine Spaces and Maritime Co-operation between Colombia and Costa Rica, additional to that signed in San José on 17 March 1977 (6 April 1984), 2139 UNTS 401

Treaty between Denmark and Sweden concerning the Delimitation of the Continental Shelf and Fishing Zones (9 November 1984), 1409 UNTS 445

1985

Agreement regarding the Delimitation of the Economic Zone, the Fishing Zone and the Continental Shelf in the Gulf of Finland and in the north-eastern Part of the Baltic Sea (5 February 1985), 1457 UNTS 261

Agreement between Costa Rica and Ecuador relating to the Delimitation of the Maritime Areas between Costa Rica and Ecuador (12 March 1985), in JI Charney and LM Alexander (eds.), *International Maritime Boundaries* (Martinus Nijhoff, 1993) vol. I, 819

Treaty between the People's Republic of Poland and the Union of Soviet Socialist Republics on the Delimitation of the Territorial Sea (Territorial Waters), the Economic Zone, the Fishery Zone and the Continental Shelf in the Baltic Sea (17 July 1985), in JI Charney and LM Alexander (eds.), *International Maritime Boundaries* (Martinus Nijhoff, 1993) vol. II, 2039

Exchange of Notes between Tuvalu and France constituting an Agreement concerning Provisional Maritime Delimitation between the Two Countries (6 August 1985 – 5 November 1985), 1506 UNTS 35

1986

Agreement between the Union of Soviet Socialist Republics and the Democratic People's Republic of Korea on the Delimitation of the Economic Zone and the Continental Shelf (22 January 1986), in JI Charney and LM Alexander (eds.), *International Maritime Boundaries* (Martinus Nijhoff, 1993) vol. I, 1145

Agreement between the Great Socialist People's Libyan Arab Jamahiriya and the Republic of Malta implementing Article III of the Special Agreement and the Judgment of the International Court of Justice (10 November 1986), in JI Charney and LM Alexander (eds.), *International Maritime Boundaries* (Martinus Nijhoff, 1993) vol. II, 1649

Convention between France and Italy on the Delimitation of Maritime Frontiers in the Area of the Strait of Bonifacio (28 November 1986), 1549 UNTS 123

Treaty between India and Myanmar on the Delimitation of the Maritime Boundary in the Andaman Sea, in the Coco Channel and in the Bay of Bengal (23 December 1986), 1484 UNTS 172

1987

Exchange of Notes constituting an Agreement on the Delimitation of the USSR and Turkish Economic Zone in the Black Sea (23 December 1986 – 6 February 1987), 1460 UNTS 135

Agreement on Maritime Delimitation between Dominica and France (7 September 1987), 1546 UNTS 305

1988

Treaty between the Solomon Islands and Australia Establishing Certain Sea and Seabed Boundaries (13 September 1988), (1988) 12 *LoSB* 19

Treaty between the Kingdom of Denmark and the German Democratic Republic on the Delimitation of the Continental Shelf and the Fishery Zones (14 September 1988), 1547 UNTS 295

1989

Agreement concerning the Delimitation of the Continental Shelf and Fishing Zones between the Kingdom of Sweden and the Polish People's Republic (10 February 1989), 1590 UNTS 361

1990

Exchange of Notes constituting an Agreement amending the Agreement between France and the United Kingdom of Great Britain and Northern Ireland relating to the Delimitation of the Continental Shelf in the Areas East of 30 Minutes West of the Greenwich Meridian of 24 June 1982 (21 March 1990 – 27 March 1990), 1581 UNTS 528

Agreement on Maritime Delimitation between the Cook Islands and France (3 August 1990), 1596 UNTS 391

Agreement between the French Republic and the Kingdom of Belgium on the Delimitation of the Continental Shelf (8 October 1990), 1728 UNTS 265

Agreement on Maritime Delimitation between France and the Solomon Islands (12 November 1990), 1591 UNTS 1990

1991

Agreement between France and the United Kingdom of Great Britain and Northern Ireland relating to the Completion of the Delimitation of the Continental Shelf in the Southern North Sea (23 July 1991), 1692 UNTS 295

1992

Agreement between Albania and Italy for the Determination of the Continental Shelf of each of the two Countries (18 December 1992), (1994) 26 *LoSB* 54

1993

Exchange of Notes between France and the United Kingdom of Great Britain and Northern Ireland constituting an Agreement concerning the Creation and Delimitation of an Economic Zone around the Islands of Pitcairn, Henderson, Ducie and Oeno (17 December 1992 – 19 January 1993), 1772 UNTS 95

Treaty on the Delimitation of the Maritime Frontier between the Republic of Cape Verde and the Republic of Senegal (17 February 1993), 1776 UNTS 305

Treaty on the Delimitation in the Caribbean of a Maritime Boundary relating to the US Virgin Islands and Anguilla (5 November 1993), 1913 UNTS 59

Treaty on the Delimitation in the Caribbean of a Maritime Boundary relating to Puerto Rico/US Virgin Islands and the British Virgin Islands (5 November 1993), 1913 UNTS 67

Treaty between Jamaica and Cuba on the Delimitation of the Maritime Boundary (12 November 1993), (1994) 26 *LoSB* 50

1994

Agreement between Jamaica and Cuba on the Delimitation of the Maritime Boundary between the two States (18 February 1994), (1997) 34 *LoSB* 64

1995

Agreement between Denmark and Norway concerning the Delimitation of the Continental Shelf in the Area between Jan Mayen and Greenland and concerning the Boundary between the Fishery Zones in the Area (18 December 1995), 1903 UNTS 171

1996

Agreement on Maritime Delimitation between France and the United Kingdom of Great Britain and Northern Ireland concerning Guadeloupe and Montserrat (27 June 1996), 2084 UNTS 65

Agreement on Maritime Delimitation between France and the United Kingdom of Great Britain and Northern Ireland concerning Saint Martin and Saint Barthelemy, on the one hand, and Anguilla on the other (27 June 1996), 2084 UNTS 71

Agreement between the Dominican Republic and the United Kingdom of Great Britain and Northern Ireland concerning the Delimitation of the Maritime Boundary between the Dominican Republic and the Turks and Caicos Islands (2 August 1996), in JI Charney and LM Alexander (eds.), *International Maritime Boundaries* (Martinus Nijhoff, 1998) vol. III, 2235

Agreement between Finland and Estonia on the Boundary of the Maritime Zones in the Gulf of Finland and on the Northern Baltic Sea (18 October 1996), 1964 UNTS 375

1997

Agreement between the United States of America and Niue on the Delimitation of a Maritime Boundary (13 May 1997), *Limits in the Seas No. 119*

Protocol between Turkey and Georgia on the Confirmation of the Maritime Boundaries between them in the Black Sea (14 July 1997), (2000) 43 *LoSB* 108

Treaty between the Republic of Lithuania and the Russian Federation on the Delimitation of the Exclusive Economic Zone and the Continental Shelf in the Baltic Sea (24 October 1997), (1999) 39 *LoSB* 26

Additional Protocol to the Agreement of 28 May 1980 between Norway and Iceland concerning Fishery and Continental Shelf Questions and the Supplementary Agreement derived therefrom of 22 October 1981 on the Continental Shelf in the Area between Jan Mayen and Iceland (11 November 1997), 2127 UNTS 227

Agreement between Turkey and Bulgaria on the Determination of the Boundary in the Mouth of the Rezovska/Mutludere River and Delimitation of the Maritime Areas between the two States in the Black Sea (4 December 1997), 2087 UNTS 5

1998

Agreement between the Government of the Kingdom of Sweden and the Government of the Republic of Estonia on the Delimitation of the Maritime Zones in the Baltic Sea (2 November 1998), 2474 UNTS 55

1999

Agreement between the Kingdom of Denmark together with the Home Government of the Faroe Islands, on the one hand, and the United Kingdom of Great Britain and Northern Ireland, on the other hand, relating to Maritime Delimitation in the Area between the Faroe Islands and the United Kingdom (18 May 1999), UKTS No. 22 (2014)

Treaty concerning the Delimitation of the Maritime Boundary between the Republic of Equatorial Guinea and the Democratic Republic of Saõ Tomé and Principe (26 June 1999), (2003) 50 *LoSB* 42

Agreement between Latvia and Lithuania on the Delimitation of the Territorial Sea, Exclusive Economic Zone and Continental Shelf in the Baltic Sea (9 July 1999), in JI Charney and RW Smith (eds.), *International Maritime Boundaries* (Martinus Nijhoff, 2002) vol. IV, 3107

2000

Treaty between Mexico and the United States on the Delimitation of the Continental Shelf in the Western Gulf of Mexico beyond 200 Nautical Miles (9 June 2000), (2001) 44 *LoSB* 71

Muscat Agreement on the Delimitation of the Maritime Boundary between the Sultanate of Oman and the Islamic Republic of Pakistan (11 June 2000), in JI Charney and RW Smith (eds.), *International Maritime Boundaries* (Martinus Nijhoff, 2002) vol. IV, 2809

Treaty between Saudi Arabia and Kuwait concerning the Submerged Area adjacent to the Divided Zone (2 July 2000), 2141 UNTS 251

2001

Agreement between France and Seychelles concerning Delimitation of the Maritime Boundary of the Exclusive Economic Zone and the Continental Shelf of France and of Seychelles (17 February 2001), 2162 UNTS 281

Agreement on Delimitation of the Maritime Border between the Gabonese Republic and the Democratic Republic of Saō Tomé and Principe (26 April 2001), (2003) 50 *LoSB* 65

Treaty between Honduras and the United Kingdom of Great Britain and Northern Ireland concerning the Delimitation of the Maritime Areas between the Cayman Islands and Honduras (4 December 2001), (2002) 49 *LoSB* 60

2002

Agreement between the United Republic of Tanzania and Seychelles on the Delimitation of the Maritime Boundary of the Exclusive Economic Zone and Continental Shelf (23 January 2002), 2196 UNTS 13

2003

Agreement between the Republic of Cyprus and the Arab Republic of Egypt on the Delimitation of the Exclusive Economic Zone (17 February 2003), 2488 UNTS 3

Agreement between France and New Zealand concerning the Delimitation of the Maritime Boundaries between Wallis and Futuna and Tokelau (30 June 2003), 2281 UNTS 123

Treaty on the Delimitation of the Maritime Frontier between the Islamic Republic of Mauritania and the Republic of Cape Verde (19 September 2003), (2004) 55 *LoSB* 32

2004

Exchange of Notes between the United Kingdom of Great Britain and Northern Ireland and the Kingdom of the Netherlands amending the Agreement of 6 October 1965 relating to the Delimitation of the Continental Shelf under the

North Sea between the two Countries as amended by the Protocol of 25 November 1971 (7 June 2004), UKTS No. 2 (2006)
Treaty between Australia and New Zealand Establishing certain Exclusive Economic Zone and Continental Shelf Boundaries (25 July 2004), 2441 UNTS 235

2005

Treaty between France and Madagascar on the Delimitation of Maritime Areas situated between La Réunion and Madagascar (14 April 2005), (2010) 71 *LoSB* 23
Treaty on Maritime Delimitation between Mexico and Honduras (18 April 2005), (2007) 65 *LoSB* 33
Treaty between the Republic of Estonia and the Russian Federation on the Delimitation of the Maritime Areas in the Gulf of Narva and the Gulf of Finland (18 May 2005), in DA Colson and RW Smith (eds.), *International Maritime Boundaries* (Martinus Nijhoff, 2011) vol. VI, 4567

2006

Agreement between the Kingdom of Norway on the one hand, and the Kingdom of Denmark together with the Home Rule Government of Greenland on the other hand, concerning the Delimitation of the Continental Shelf and the Fisheries Zones in the Area between Greenland and Svalbard (20 February 2006), 2378 UNTS 21
Palau-Federated States of Micronesia Boundary Treaty (5 July 2006), in DA Colson and RW Smith (eds.), *International Maritime Boundaries* (Martinus Nijhoff, 2011) vol. VI, 4348
Treaty between the Federated States of Micronesia and the Republic of the Marshall Islands concerning Maritime Boundaries and Cooperation on Related Matters (5 July 2006), in DA Colson and RW Smith (eds.), *International Maritime Boundaries* (Martinus Nijhoff, 2011) vol. VI, 4316
Treaty on the Maritime Boundary Delimitation between the Federal Republic of Nigeria and the Republic of Benin (4 August 2006), in DA Colson and RW Smith (eds.), *International Maritime Boundaries* (Martinus Nijhoff, 2011) vol. VI, 4256
Agreed Minutes on the Delimitation of the Continental Shelf beyond 200 Nautical Miles between the Faroe Islands, Iceland and Norway in the Southern Part of the Banana Hole in the Northeast Atlantic (20 September 2006), in DA Colson and RW Smith (eds.), *International Maritime Boundaries* (Martinus Nijhoff, 2011) vol. VI, 4532

2007

Agreement between the Republic of Lebanon and the Cypriot Republic Delimiting the Exclusive Economic Zone (17 January 2007), in DA Colson and RW Smith (eds.), *International Maritime Boundaries* (Martinus Nijhoff, 2011) vol. VI, 4445

Agreement between the Kingdom of Denmark together with the Government of the Faroes, on the one hand, and Iceland, on the other hand, relating to the Maritime Delimitation in the Area between the Faroe Islands and Iceland (1-2 February 2007), (2017) 85 *LoSB* 24

2008

Treaty between Mauritius and Seychelles on the Delimitation of the Exclusive Economic Zone (29 July 2008), (2009) 69 *LoSB* 106

2009

Agreement between the Hellenic Republic and the Republic of Albania on the Delimitation of their Respective Continental Shelf Areas and Other Maritime Zones to which they are entitled under International Law (27 April 2009), in DA Colson and RW Smith (eds.), *International Maritime Boundaries* (Martinus Nijhoff, 2011) vol. VI, 4462

Exchange of Notes amending the Agreement between the United Kingdom of Great Britain and Northern Ireland and Norway Relating to the Delimitation of the Continental Shelf between the two Countries (30 April 2009), UKTS No. 16 (2009)

Agreement between France and Barbados on the Delimitation of the Maritime Space between France and Barbados (15 October 2009), 2663 UNTS 163

Exchange of Notes between the United Kingdom of Great Britain and Northern Ireland and Denmark Confirming the Limits of the United Kingdom of Great Britain and Northern Ireland's Exclusive Economic Zone in the North Sea (22 October 2009), UKTS No. 1 (2010)

2010

Treaty between the Republic of Trinidad and Tobago and Grenada on the Delimitation of Marine and Submarine Areas (21 April 2010), 2675 UNTS 5

Agreement between New Zealand and the Cook Islands concerning the Delimitation of the Maritime Boundaries between Tokelau and the Cook Islands (4 August 2010), (2014) 82 *LoSB* 54

Treaty between the Russian Federation and the Kingdom of Norway concerning Maritime Delimitation and Co-operation in the Barents Sea and the Arctic Ocean (15 September 2010), 2791 UNTS 3

Agreement between the State of Israel and the Republic of Cyprus on the Delimitation of the Exclusive Economic Zone (17 December 2010), (2011) 75 *LoSB* 27

2011
Exchange of Letters between the United Kingdom of Great Britain and Northern Ireland and the French Republic relating to the Delimitation of the Exclusive Economic Zone (20 April 2011), UKTS No. 19 (2014)

Agreement between the Commonwealth of the Bahamas and the Republic of Cuba for the Delimiting Line between their Maritime Zones (3 October 2011), (2013) 79 *LoSB* 19

Agreement on the Delimitation of the Maritime Boundary between the Republic of Mozambique and the Union of the Comoros (5 December 2011), in C Lathrop (ed.), *International Maritime Boundaries* (Martinus Nijhoff, 2016) vol. VII, 5017

Agreement on the Delimitation of the Maritime Boundary between the United Republic of Tanzania and the Union of the Comoros (5 December 2011), in C Lathrop (ed.), *International Maritime Boundaries* (Martinus Nijhoff, 2016) vol. VII, 5059

2012
Agreement between the Union of the Comoros and the Republic of Seychelles on the Delimitation of the Maritime Boundary of the Exclusive Economic Zone and the Continental Shelf in the Indian Ocean (17 February 2012), in C Lathrop (ed.), *International Maritime Boundaries* (Martinus Nijhoff, 2016) vol. VII, 5039

Agreement between the Cook Islands and Kiribati concerning the Delimitation of Maritime Boundaries between the Cook Islands and Kiribati (29 August 2012), (2017) 85 *LoSB* 32

Agreement between the Cook Islands and Niue concerning the Delimitation of Maritime Boundaries between the Cook Islands and Niue (29 August 2012), (2014) 82 *LoSB* 51

Agreement between the Republic of Kiribati and the Republic of the Marshall Islands concerning Maritime Boundaries (29 August 2012), in C Lathrop (ed.), *International Maritime Boundaries* (Martinus Nijhoff, 2016) vol. VII, 4869

Agreement between the Republic of Kiribati and the Republic of Nauru concerning Maritime Boundaries (29 August 2012), in C Lathrop (ed.), *International Maritime Boundaries* (Martinus Nijhoff, 2016) vol. VII, 4881

Agreement between New Zealand and the Republic of Kiribati concerning the Delimitation of the Maritime Boundaries between Tokelau and Kiribati (29 August 2012), (2017) 90 *LoSB* 49

Agreement between the Republic of the Marshall Islands and the Republic of Nauru concerning Maritime Boundaries (29 August 2012), in C Lathrop (ed.), *International Maritime Boundaries* (Martinus Nijhoff, 2016) vol. VII, 4915

Agreement between the Tuvalu and Kiribati concerning their Maritime Boundaries (29 August 2012), (2014) 83 *LoSB* 37

2013

Exchange of Letters between the United Kingdom of Great Britain and Northern Ireland and the Kingdom of the Netherlands amending the Agreement relating to the Delimitation of the Continental Shelf under the North Sea between the two Countries of 6 October 1965 as amended by the Protocol of 25 November 1971 and the Exchange of Notes of January and June 2004 (19 April 2013 – 3 July 2013), UKTS No. 20 (2014)

Treaty between the United States of America and the Republic of Kiribati on the Delimitation of Maritime Boundaries (6 September 2013), in C Lathrop (ed.), *International Maritime Boundaries* (Martinus Nijhoff, 2016) vol. VII, 4935

2014

Agreement between the Republic of the Philippines and the Republic of Indonesia concerning the Delimitation of the Exclusive Economic Zone Boundary (23 May 2014), in C Lathrop (ed.), *International Maritime Boundaries* (Martinus Nijhoff, 2016) vol. VII, 4947

Treaty between the United States of America and the Federated States of Micronesia on the Delimitation of a Maritime Boundary (1 August 2014), in C Lathrop (ed.), *International Maritime Boundaries* (Martinus Nijhoff, 2016) vol. VII, 4963

Bilateral Treaties Establishing Boundaries Based on a Criterion other than Equidistance
(in chronological order by date of conclusion)

1957

Agreement between the Royal Norwegian Government and the Government of the Union of Soviet Socialist Republics concerning the Sea Frontier between Norway and the USSR in the Varangerfjord (15 February 1957), 312 UNTS 289

1960

Exchange of Letters between France and Portugal concerning the Territorial Sea and the Continental Shelf Boundary between Guinea-Bissau and Senegal (26 April 1960), *Limits in the Seas No. 68*

1968

Agreement concerning the Sovereignty over the Islands of Al-'Arabiyah and Farsi and the Delimitation of the Boundary Line separating the Submarine Areas between the Kingdom of Saudi Arabia and Iran (24 October 1968), 696 UNTS 195

1969
Agreement between Qatar and Abu Dhabi on the Settlement of Maritime Boundaries and Ownership of Islands (20 March 1969), 2402 UNTS 49

1971
Treaty between the Kingdom of Denmark and the Federal Republic of Germany concerning the Delimitation of the Continental shelf under the North Sea (28 January 1971), 857 UNTS 119

Treaty between the Kingdom of the Netherlands and the Federal Republic of Germany concerning the Delimitation of the Continental Shelf under the North Sea (28 January 1971), 857 UNTS 142

Agreement between the Republic of Tunisia and the Italian Republic concerning the Delimitation of the Continental Shelf between the two Countries (20 August 1971), 1129 UNTS 254

Agreement between the Republic of Indonesia, Malaysia and the Kingdom of Thailand relating to the Delimitation of the Continental Shelf Boundaries in the Northern Part of the Strait of Malacca (21 December 1971), *Limits in the Seas No. 81*

1972
Agreement between Sweden and Finland concerning the Delimitation of the Continental Shelf in the Gulf of Bothnia, the Bothnian Sea, the Aland Sea, and the northernmost Part of the Baltic Sea (29 September 1972), 987 UNTS 395

Treaty between Australia and Indonesia Establishing Certain Seabed Boundaries in the Area of the Timor and Arafura Seas, Supplementary to the Agreement of 18 May 1971 (9 October 1972), 974 UNTS 320

1974
Convention between France and Spain on the Delimitation of the Continental Shelves of the two States in the Bay of Biscay (29 January 1974), 996 UNTS 344

Agreement on the Delimitation of Boundaries between the Kingdom of Saudi Arabia and the United Arab Emirates (21 August 1974), 1733 UNTS 23

Convention demarcating the Land and Maritime Frontiers of Equatorial Guinea and Gabon (12 September 1974), 2248 UNTS 93

1975
The Maroua Declaration (1 June 1975), 1237 UNTS 319

Treaty fixing the Maritime Boundaries between the Republic of the Gambia and the Republic of Senegal (4 June 1975), *Limits in the Seas No. 85*

Agreement concerning Delimitation of Marine and Submarine Areas and Maritime Co-operation between Colombia and Ecuador (23 August 1975), 996 UNTS 239

Agreement between the Kingdom of Thailand and the Republic of Indonesia relating to the Delimitation of the Sea-bed Boundary between the two Countries in the Andaman Sea (11 December 1975), 1103 UNTS 214

1976

Agreement between Portugal and Spain on the Delimitation of the Continental Shelf (12 February 1976), in JI Charney and LM Alexander (eds.), *International Maritime Boundaries* (Martinus Nijhoff, 1993) vol. II, 1971

Convention concerning the State Frontier Line established between the Islamic Republic of Mauritania and the Kingdom of Morocco (14 April 1976), 1035 UNTS 119

Exchange of Notes constituting an Agreement on the Territorial Sea Boundary between Kenya and Tanzania (17 December 1975 – 9 July 1976), 1039 UNTS 147

1977

Treaty on the Delimitation of Marine and Submarine Areas and Maritime Cooperation between Colombia and Costa Rica (17 March 1977), *Limits in the Seas No. 84*

1980

Agreement between Iceland and Norway concerning Fishery and Continental Shelf Questions (28 May 1980), 2124 UNTS 225

Delimitation Treaty between France (Martinique and Guadeloupe) and Venezuela (17 July 1980), 1319 UNTS 219

1981

Agreement between Norway and Iceland on the Continental Shelf between Iceland and Jan Mayen (22 October 1981), 2124 UNTS 247

1984

Convention on Maritime Delimitation between the Government of the French Republic and the Government of His Serene Highness the Prince of Monaco (16 February 1984), 1411 UNTS 292

Treaty of Peace and Friendship between Chile and Argentina (29 November 1984), 1399 UNTS 102

1986

Treaty concerning Maritime Delimitation between the Republic of Colombia and the Republic of Honduras (2 August 1986), 2093 UNTS 291

1988

Agreement between the Kingdom of Sweden and the Union of Soviet Socialist Republics on the Delimitation of the Continental Shelf and of the Swedish

Fishery Zone and the Soviet Economic Zone in the Baltic Sea (18 April 1988), 1557 UNTS 282

Agreement between the Libyan Arab Socialist People's Jamahiriya and the Republic of Tunisia to Implement the Judgment of the International Court of Justice in the Tunisia/Libya Continental Shelf Case (8 August 1988), in JI Charney and LM Alexander (eds.), *International Maritime Boundaries* (Martinus Nijhoff, 1993) vol. II, 1663

Agreement between the United Kingdom of Great Britain and Northern Ireland and the Republic of Ireland concerning the Delimitation of Areas of the Continental Shelf between the two Countries (7 November 1988), 1564 UNTS 217

Agreement between the United Republic of Tanzania and Mozambique regarding the Tanzania/Mozambique Boundary (28 December 1988), in JI Charney and LM Alexander (eds.), *International Maritime Boundaries* (Martinus Nijhoff, 1993) vol. I, 893

1989

Treaty between Papua New Guinea and Solomon Islands concerning Sovereignty, Maritime and Seabed Boundaries between the two Countries, and Co-operation on Related Matters (25 January 1989), in JI Charney and LM Alexander (eds.), *International Maritime Boundaries* (Martinus Nijhoff, 1998) vol. III, 2323

Treaty between Poland and the German Democratic Republic on the Delimitation of the Sea Areas in the Oder Bay (22 May 1989), 1547 UNTS 283

1990

Treaty between Trinidad and Tobago and Venezuela on the Delimitation of Marine and Submarine Areas (18 April 1990), 1654 UNTS 293

Agreement between the United States of America and the Union of Soviet Socialist Republics on the Maritime Boundary (1 June 1990), (1990) 29 ILM 941

Treaty between Germany and Poland on the Confirmation of the Frontier between them (14 November 1990), 1708 UNTS 383

1991

Agreement between the United Kingdom of Great Britain and Northern Ireland and the Kingdom of Belgium relating to the Delimitation of the Continental Shelf between the two Countries (29 May 1991), UKTS No. 20 (1994)

1992

Protocol Supplementary to the Agreement between the United Kingdom of Great Britain and Northern Ireland and the Republic of Ireland concerning the Delimitation of Areas of the Continental Shelf between the two Countries of 7 November 1988 (8 December 1992), 1745 UNTS 472

1994

Agreement on the Delimitation of the Boundary between the Continental shelf and Fishery Zone of Finland and the Economic Zone of Sweden in the Åland Sea and the Northern Baltic Sea (2 June 1994), 1887 UNTS 229

1996

Agreement between Estonia and Latvia on the Maritime Delimitation in the Gulf of Riga, the Strait of Irbe and the Baltic Sea (12 July 1996), 1955 UNTS 345

Treaty between the Kingdom of the Netherlands and the Kingdom of Belgium on the Delimitation of the Continental Shelf (18 December 1996), 2051 UNTS 169

1997

Treaty between Australia and Indonesia Establishing an Exclusive Economic Zone Boundary and Certain Seabed Boundaries (14 March 1997), (1997) 36 ILM 1053

Agreement between the Kingdom of Thailand and the Socialist Republic of Viet Nam on the Delimitation of the Maritime Boundary between the two Countries in the Gulf of Thailand (9 August 1997), (1999) 39 *LoSB* 23

Additional Protocol to the Agreement of 18 December 1995 between Norway and Denmark concerning the Delimitation of the Continental Shelf in the Area between Jan Mayen and Greenland and the Boundary between the Fishery Zones in the Area (11 November 1997), 2100 UNTS 180

Agreement between the Kingdom of Denmark together with the Greenland Home Rule Government, on the one hand, and the Republic of Iceland, on the other hand, concerning the Delimitation of the Continental Shelf and the Fishery Zones in the Area between Greenland and Iceland (11 November 1997), 2074 UNTS 43

2000

International Border Treaty between the Republic of Yemen and the Kingdom of Saudi Arabia (12 June 2000), 2389 UNTS 203

Treaty between the Federal Republic of Nigeria and the Republic of Equatorial Guinea concerning their Maritime Boundary (23 September 2000), 2205 UNTS 325

Agreement between the People's Republic of China and the Socialist Republic of Viet Nam on the Delimitation of the Territorial Seas, Exclusive Economic Zones and Continental Shelves of the two Countries in Beibu Gulf/Bac Bo Gulf (25 December 2000), 2336 UNTS 179

2002

Agreement on Provisional Arrangements for the Delimitation of the Maritime Boundary between the Republic of Tunisia and the People's Democratic Republic of Algeria (11 February 2002), 2238 UNTS 197

Accord on the Delimitation of the Maritime Border between Angola and Namibia (4 June 2002), in DA Colson and RW Smith (eds.), *International Maritime Boundaries* (Martinus Nijhoff, 2005) vol. V, 3719

2003

Agreement between the Socialist Republic of Viet Nam and the Republic of Indonesia concerning the Delimitation of the Continental Shelf Boundary (26 June 2003), 2457 UNTS 155

Agreement on the Delimitation of the Maritime Boundary between the Sultanate of Oman and the Republic of Yemen (14 December 2003), 2309 UNTS 249

2005

Exchange of Notes between the United Kingdom of Great Britain and Northern Ireland and the Kingdom of Belgium amending the Agreement of 29 May 1991 relating to the Delimitation of the Continental Shelf under the North Sea between the two Countries (21 March 2005 – 7 June 2005), 2494 UNTS 83

2007

Treaty between Russia and Norway on Maritime Delimitation in the Varangerfjord Area (11 July 2007), (2008) 67 *LoSB* 42

2008

Joint Minutes on the Land and Maritime Boundaries to the Agreement of 4 December 1965 between the State of Qatar and the Kingdom of Saudi Arabia on the Delimitation of the Offshore and Land Boundaries (5 July 2008), 2575 UNTS 67

2009

Agreement between the United Republic of Tanzania and the Republic of Kenya on the Delimitation of the Maritime Boundary of the Exclusive Economic Zone and the Continental Shelf (23 June 2009), (2009) 70 *LoSB* 54

2011

Agreement by Exchange of Notes of identical Content between the Republic of Peru and the Republic of Ecuador (2 May 2011), 2756 UNTS 223

Agreement on the Delimitation of the Maritime Boundary between the Republic of Mozambique and the United Republic of Tanzania (5 December 2011), in C Lathrop (ed.), *International Maritime Boundaries* (Martinus Nijhoff, 2016) vol. VII, 4793

2012

Maritime Delimitation Treaty between the Republic of Honduras and the Republic of Cuba (21 August 2012), (2017) 86 *LoSB* 35

2013

Agreed Minutes on the Delimitation of the Continental Shelf beyond 200 Nautical Miles between Greenland and Iceland in the Irminger Sea (16 January 2013), in C Lathrop (ed.), *International Maritime Boundaries* (Martinus Nijhoff, 2016) vol. VII, 5259

Agreement between Ireland and the United Kingdom of Great Britain and Northern Ireland Establishing a Single Maritime Boundary between the Exclusive Economic Zone of the two Countries and Parts of their Continental Shelves (28 March 2013), UKTS No. 21 (2014)

Exchange of Letters between the United Kingdom of Great Britain and Northern Ireland and the Kingdom of Belgium amending the Agreement relating to the Delimitation of the Continental shelf under the North Sea between the two Countries of 19 May 1991 as amended by Exchange of Letters of 21 March and 7 June 2005 (25 June 2013 – 12 August 2013), UKTS No. 14 (2016)

Bilateral Treaties in relation to which it was not possible to determine whether they established Boundaries based on Equidistance

(in chronological order by date of conclusion)

1992

International Boundary Agreement between the Sultanate of Oman and the Republic of Yemen (1 October 1992), in DA Colson and RW Smith (eds.), *International Maritime Boundaries* (Martinus Nijhoff, 2005) vol. V, 3900

2001

Minutes of Meeting concerning Land Boundary Demarcation and Offshore Boundary Delimitation between Saudi Arabia and Qatar in Dawhat Salwa (21 March 2001), 2384 UNTS 318

Exchange of Notes between Ireland and the United Kingdom of Great Britain and Northern Ireland constituting an Agreement pursuant to Article 83, paragraph 3, of the United Nations Convention on the Law of the Sea 1982 on the Provisional Delimitation of an Area of the Continental Shelf (18 October 2001 – 31 October 2001), 2309 UNTS 21

2014

Agreement between Lithuania and Sweden on the Delimitation of the Exclusive Economic Zones and the Continental Shelf in the Baltic Sea (10 April 2014), (2017) 92 *LoSB* 16

Agreement on Maritime Delimitation between the Republic of Ecuador and the Republic of Costa Rica (21 April 2014), (2017) 93 *LoSB* 16

2015
Agreement on the delimitation of the maritime boundary in the Sea of Oman between the Islamic Republic of Iran and the Sultanate of Oman (26 May 2015), registered in accordance with Article 102 of the Charter of the United Nations on 21 February 2017, No. 54173

Bilateral Treaties establishing some Form of Inter-state Co-operation for the Exploitation of Transboundary Resources
(in chronological order by date of conclusion)

1976
Agreement between the United Kingdom of Great Britain and Northern Ireland and the Kingdom of Norway relating to the Exploitation of the Frigg Field Reservoir and the Transmission of Gas therefrom to the United Kingdom (10 May 1976), UKTS No. 113 (1977)

1979
Agreement between the United Kingdom of Great Britain and Northern Ireland and the Kingdom of Norway relating to the Exploitation of the Murchison Field Reservoir and Offtake of Petroleum therefrom (16 October 1979), 1249 UNTS 173

Agreement between the United Kingdom of Great Britain and Northern Ireland and the Kingdom of Norway relating to the Exploitation of the Statfjord Field Reservoir and Offtake of Petroleum therefrom (16 October 1979), 1254 UNTS 380

2001
Treaty between the Federal Republic of Nigeria and the Democratic Republic of Saõ Tomé and Principe on the Joint Development of Petroleum and other Resources in respect of Areas of Exclusive Economic Zone of the two States (21 February 2001), (2003) 50 *LoSB* 42

Memorandum of Understanding between the Royal Government of Cambodia and the Royal Thai Government regarding the Area of their Overlapping Maritime Claims to the Continental Shelf (18 June 2001), in DA Colson and RW Smith (eds.), *International Maritime Boundaries* (Martinus Nijhoff, 2005) vol. V, 3735

Agreement between the Republic of the Congo and the Republic of Angola approving Offshore Unitization Prospects 14 K and A-IMI (10 September 2001), in DA Colson and RW Smith (eds.), *International Maritime Boundaries* (Martinus Nijhoff, 2011) vol. VI, 4281

2002

Protocol on Implementation of Article 6.2 of the Treaty between the Federal Republic of Nigeria and the Republic of Equatorial Guinea concerning their Maritime Boundary (2 April 2002), 2220 UNTS 410

Timor Sea Treaty between the Government of East Timor and the Government of Australia (20 May 2002), 2258 UNTS 3

2005

Framework Agreement between the United Kingdom of Great Britain and Northern Ireland and the Kingdom of Norway concerning Cross-boundary Petroleum Co-operation (4 April 2005), 2491 UNTS 3

2007

Framework Treaty relating to the Unitisation of Hydrocarbon Reservoirs that extend across the Delimitation Line between Trinidad and Tobago and Venezuela (20 March 2007), 2876 UNTS (I-50196)

Agreement on the Exploration and Production of Hydrocarbons in the Common Interest Maritime Zone between the Democratic Republic of the Congo and the Republic of Angola (30 July 2007), in DA Colson and RW Smith (eds.), *International Maritime Boundaries* (Martinus Nijhoff, 2011) vol. VI, 4270

2008

Agreement between Norway and Iceland concerning Transboundary Hydrocarbon Deposits (3 November 2008), 2888 UNTS (I-50378)

2010

Unitisation Agreement for the Exploitation and Development Hydrocarbon Reservoirs of the Loran-Manatee that extends across the Delimitation Line between Trinidad and Tobago and Venezuela (16 August 2010), 2876 UNTS (I-50197)

2012

Agreement between the United States of America and Mexico concerning Transboundary Hydrocarbon Reservoirs in the Gulf of Mexico (20 February 2012), US TIAS 14-718

Treaty concerning the Joint Exercise of Sovereign Rights Over the Continental Shelf in the Mascarene Plateau Region between the Government of the Republic of Mauritius and the Government of the Republic of Seychelles (13 March 2012), (2013) 79 *LoSB* 26

Treaty Concerning the Joint Management of the Continental Shelf in the Mascarene Plateau Region between the Government of the Republic of Mauritius and the Government of the Republic of Seychelles (13 March 2012), (2013) 79 *LoSB* 41

BIBLIOGRAPHY
(in alphabetical order by author)

YE Acikgonul, 'Reflections on the Principle of Non-Cut Off: A Growing Concept in Maritime Boundary Delimitation Law' (2016) 47 *Ocean Development and International Law* 52.

YE Acikgonul, 'Equitable Delimitation of Maritime Boundaries: The Uncontested Supremacy of Coastal Geography in Case Law' (2017) 31 *Ocean Yearbook* 173.

M Akehurst, 'The Hierarchy of the Sources of International Law' (1974–1975) 47 *British Yearbook of International Law* 273.

M Al-Qahtani, 'The Role of the International Court of Justice in the Enforcement of its Judicial Decisions' (2002) 15 *Leiden Journal of International Law* 781.

D Anderson, 'Negotiating Maritime Boundary Agreements: A Personal Perspective' in R Lagoni and D Vignes (eds.), *Maritime Delimitation* (Martinus Nijhoff, 2006) 121.

D Anderson, 'Grisbådarna Revisited' in D Anderson (ed.) *Modern Law of the Sea – Selected Essays* (Martinus Nijhoff, 2008) 477.

D Anderson, 'Maritime Delimitation in the *Black Sea* Case (Romania v. Ukraine)' (2009) 8 *Law and Practice of International Courts and Tribunals* 305.

D Anderson, 'Delimitation of the Maritime Boundary in the Bay of Bengal (Bangladesh/Myanmar): Case No. 16' (2012) 106 *American Journal of International Law* 817.

M-C Aquarone, 'The 1985 Guinea/Guinea-Bissau Maritime Boundary Case and its Implications' (1995) 26 *Ocean Development and International Law* 413.

J-M Arbour, 'Le Limites du Plateau Continental et de la Zone Économique Exclusive: les Fondements du Titre de l'Etat sur les Espaces Maritimes et ses Rapports avec l'Opération de Délimitation' in D Pharand and U Leanza (eds.), *The Continental Shelf and the Exclusive Economic Zone: Delimitation and Legal Regime* (Martinus Nijhoff, 1993) 13.

D Arrow, 'Seabed, Sovereignty and Objective Regimes' (1984) 7 *Fordham International Law Journal* 169.

H Ascensio, 'Les Actes Unilatéraux Etatiques en Droit de la Mer' in M Forteau and J-M Thouvenin (eds.), *Traité de Droit International de la Mer* (Pédone, 2017) 190.

D Attard, *The Exclusive Economic Zone in International Law* (Oxford University Press, 1987).

A Azar, *L'Exécution des Décisions de la Cour Internationale de Justice* (Bruylant, 2003).

L Balmond, 'Le Plateau Continental jusqu'à 200 milles marins' in *Le Processus de Délimitation Maritime – Étude d'un Cas Fictif* (Pédone, 2004) 98.

J Barboza, 'The Beagle Channel Dispute: Reflections of the Agent of Argentina' (2014) 13 *Chinese Journal of International Law* 147.

R Barnes, 'Objective Regimes Revisited' (2000) 9 *Asian Journal of International Law* 97.

JL Batongbacal, 'Extended Continental Shelf Claims in the South China Sea: Implications for Future Maritime Boundary Delimitations' (2015) 29 *Ocean Yearbook* 21.

KA Baumert, 'The Outer Limits of the Continental Shelf under Customary International Law' (2017) 111 *American Journal of International Law* 827.

M Becker and C Rose, 'Investigating the Value of Site Visits in Inter-State Arbitration and Adjudication' (2017) 8 *Journal of International Dispute Settlement* 219.

V Becker-Weinberg, *Joint Development of Hydrocarbon Deposits in the Law of the Sea* (Springer, 2014).

R Beckman and C Sim, 'Maritime Boundary Disputes and Compulsory Dispute Settlement: Recent Developments and Unresolved Issues' in MH Nordquist et al. (eds.), *Legal Order of the World's Oceans – UN Convention on the Law of the Sea* (Martinus Nijhoff, 2018) 228.

J Beer-Gabel, 'Variations sur la Notion de Frontière Maritime' in *Droit de la Mer – Études dédiées au Doyen Claude-Albert Colliard* (Pédone, 1992) 10.

J Beer-Gabel, 'Les Accords de Délimitation Maritime, la Pratique des Etats' in *Le Processus de Délimitation Maritime: Étude d'un Cas Fictif* (Pédone, 2004) 323.

J Bell, 'Sources of Law' (2018) 77 *Cambridge Law Journal* 40.

M Bennouna, 'Le Droit International entre la Lettre et l'Esprit' (2017) 383 *Recueil des Cours* 9.

R Bernhardt, 'Custom and Treaty in the Law of the Sea' (1987) 205 *Recueil des Cours* 247.

S Besson, 'State Consent and Disagreement in International Law-Making: Dissolving the Paradox' (2016) 29 *Leiden Journal of International Law* 289.

B Bix, *Law, Language and Legal Indeterminacy* (Oxford University Press, 1993).

N Bobbio, *La consuetudine come fatto normativo* (Giappichelli, 2010).

D Bodansky, '*Non Liquet* and the Incompleteness of International Law' in L Boisson de Chazournes and P Sands (eds.), *International Law, the International Court of Justice and Nuclear Weapons* (Cambridge University Press, 1999) 153.

L Boisson de Chazournes and A Angelini, 'Regard sur la Mise en Œuvre des Décisions de la Court internationale de Justice' (2016) 40 *L'Observateur des Nations Unies* 63.

DW Bowett, 'The Arbitration between the United Kingdom and France concerning the Continental Shelf Boundary in the English Channel and South-Western Approaches' (1978) 49 *British Yearbook of International Law* 1.

DW Bowett, *The Legal Regime of Islands in International Law* (Oceana, 1978).

DW Bowett, 'Islands, Rocks, Reefs, and Low-Tide Elevations in Maritime Boundary Delimitations' in JI Charney and LM Alexander (eds.), *International Maritime Boundaries* (Martinus Nijhoff, 1991) vol I, 131.

DW Bowett, 'The Dubai/Sharjah Boundary Arbitration of 1981' (1995) 65 *British Yearbook of International Law* 103.

DW Bowett, '*Res Judicata* and the Limits of Rectification of Decisions by International Tribunals' (1996) 8 *African Journal of International and Comparative Law* 577.

A Boyle and C Chinkin, *The Making of International Law* (Oxford University Press, 2007).

J Briscoe, 'Islands in Maritime Boundary Delimitation' (1989) 7 *Ocean Yearbook* 14.

J Brotton, *A History of the World in Twelve Maps* (Penguin, 2013).

C Brown, 'Article 59' in A Zimmermann et al. (eds.), *The Statute of the International Court of Justice – A Commentary* 2nd edn (Oxford University Press, 2012) 1416.

ED Brown, 'The *Anglo-French Continental Shelf Case*' (1979) 16 *San Diego Law Review* 461.

I Brownlie, 'International Law at the Fiftieth Anniversary of the United Nations' (1995) 255 *Recueil des Cours* 9.

I Brownlie, 'The Sources of the Law Governing Maritime Delimitation' in M Rama Montaldo (ed.), *El Derecho Internacional en un Mundo en Transformación: Liber Amicorum en Homenaje al Profesor Eduardo Jiménez de Aréchaga* (FCU, 1995) vol. II, 733.

RR Bundy, 'State Practice in Maritime Delimitation' in GH Blake (ed.), *Maritime Boundaries* (Routledge, 1994) 18.

N Burke, '*Nicaragua v. Colombia* at the ICJ: Better the Devil you Don't?' (2012) 2 *Cambridge Journal of International and Comparative Law* 314.

L Caflisch, 'Lez Zones Maritimes sous Juridiction Nationale, leurs Limites et leur Délimitation' in D Bardonnet and M Virally (eds.), *Le Nouveau Droit International de la Mer* (Pédone, 1983) 35.

L Caflisch, 'La Délimitation des Espaces entre Etats dont les Côtes se font face ou sont adjacentes' in R-J Dupuy and D Vignes (eds.), *Traité du Nouveau Droit de la Mer* (Bruylant, 1985) 374.

P Cahier, 'Le Problème des Effets des Traités à l'égard des Etats Tiers' (1974) 143 *Recueil des Cours* 589.

P Cahier, 'Les Sources du Droit relatif à la Délimitation du Plateau Continental' in *Le Droit International au Service de la Paix, de la Justice et du Développement – Mélanges Michel Virally* (Pédone, 1991) 175.

H Caminos, 'Les Sources du Droit de la Mer' in R-J Dupuy and D Vignes (eds.), *Traité du Nouveau Droit de la Mer* (Bruylant, 1985) 27.

H Caminos, 'The Legal Regime of Straits in the 1982 United Nations Convention on the Law of the Sea' (1987) 205 *Recueil des Cours* 9.

B Cardozo, *The Nature of the Judicial Process* (Yale University Press, 1921).

C Carleton, 'Maritime Delimitation in Complex Island Situations: A Case Study on the Caribbean Sea' in R Lagoni and D Vignes (eds.), *Maritime Delimitation* (Martinus Nijhoff, 2006) 153.

E Castellarin, 'La sentence partielle du 30 juin 2016 dans l'affaire du différend territorial et maritime entre la Croatie et la Slovénie' (2016) 62 *Annuaire Français de Droit International* 129.

G Cataldi, 'L'Italia e la Delimitazione degli Spazi Marini' (2004) 87 *Rivista di Diritto Internazionale* 621.

G Cataldi, 'La Mise en Œuvre des Décisions des Tribunaux Internationaux dans l'Ordre Interne' (2016) 386 *Recueil des Cours* 267.

H Charlesworth, 'Law-making and Sources' in J Crawford and M Koskenniemi (eds.), *The Cambridge Companion to International Law* (Cambridge University Press, 2012) 187.

JI Charney, 'Disputes implicating the Institutional Credibility of the Court: Problems of Non-appearance, Non-participation, and Non-performance' in LF Damrosch (ed.), *The International Court of Justice at a Crossroads* (Transnational Publishers, 1987) 289.

JI Charney, 'The Delimitation of Ocean Boundaries' (1987) 18 *Ocean Development and International Law* 497.

JI Charney, LM Alexander, DA Colson, RW Smith and C Lathrop (eds.), *International Maritime Boundaries* (Martinus Nijhoff 1991) vols. I–VII.

JI Charney, 'Progress in International Maritime Boundary Delimitation Law' (1994) 88 *American Journal of International Law* 227.

JI Charney and GM Danilenko, 'Consent and the Creation of International Law' in L Fisler Damrosch et al. (eds.), *Beyond Confrontation – International Law for the Post-Cold War Era* (Westview Press, 1995) 23.

BS Chimni, 'Customary International Law: A Third World Perspective' (2018) 112 *American Journal of International Law* 1.

C Chinkin, *Third Parties in International Law* (Oxford University Press, 1993).

RR Churchill, 'Maritime Delimitation in the Jan Mayen Area' (1985) 10 *Marine Policy* 16.

RR Churchill, 'Fisheries Issues in Maritime Boundary Delimitation' (1993) 17 *Marine Policy* 44.

RR Churchill, 'The Greenland-Jan Mayen Case and its Significance for the International Law of Maritime Boundary Delimitation' (1994) 9 *International Journal of Marine and Coastal Law* 1.

RR Churchill and AV Lowe, *The Law of the Sea* (Manchester University Press, 1999).

RR Churchill, 'Dispute Settlement under the UN Convention on the Law of the Sea: Survey for 2006' (2007) 22 *International Journal of Marine and Coastal Law* 463.

RR Churchill, 'Dispute Settlement under the UN Convention on the Law of the Sea: Survey for 2007' (2008) 23 *International Journal of Marine and Coastal Law* 601.

RR Churchill, 'Dispute Settlement under the UN Convention on the Law of the Sea: Survey for 2009' (2010) 25 *International Journal of Marine and Coastal Law* 457.

RR Churchill, 'The *Bangladesh/Myanmar* Case: Continuity and Novelty in the Law of Maritime Boundary Delimitation' (2012) 1 *Cambridge Journal of International and Comparative Law* 137.

RR Churchill, 'Dispute Settlement under in the Law of the Sea: Survey for 2012' (2013) 28 *International Journal of Marine and Coastal Law* 564.

RR Churchill, 'Dispute Settlement under in the Law of the Sea: Survey for 2014' (2015) 30 *International Journal of Marine and Coastal Law* 585.

RR Churchill, 'Dispute Settlement in the Law of the Sea: Survey for 2015, Part II and 2016' (2017) 32 *International Journal of Marine and Coastal Law* 379.

MC Ciciriello, 'L'Effetto delle Isole nella Delimitazione degli Spazi Marini' (1989) 91 *Il Diritto Marittimo* 675.

MC Ciciriello, *Le Formazioni Insulari e la Delimitazione degli Spazi Marini* (Editoriale Scientifica, 1990).

MC Ciciriello, 'Le Rapport entre le Plateau Continental et la Zone Économique Exclusive dans la Jurisprudence Internationale la plus récente' in D Pharand and U Leanza (eds.), *The Continental Shelf and the Exclusive Economic Zone: Delimitation and Legal Regime* (Martinus Nijhoff, 1993) 379.

VP Cogliati-Bantz, 'The *South China Sea Arbitration (The Republic of the Philippines v. The People's Republic of China)*' (2016) 31 *International Journal of Marine and Coastal Law* 759.

J Colombos, 'Territorial Waters' (1924) 9 *Transactions of the Grotius Society* 89.

J Colombos, *The International Law of the Sea* 6th edn (Longman, 1967).

D Colson, 'The Legal Regime of Maritime Boundary Agreements' in JI Charney and LM Alexander (eds.), *International Maritime Boundaries* (Martinus Nijhoff, 1991) vol. I, 41.

D Colson, 'The Delimitation of the Outer Continental Shelf between Neighboring States' (2003) 97 *American Journal of International Law* 91.

L Condorelli, 'L'Autorité de la Décision des Juridictions Internationales Permanentes' in *La Juridiction Internationale Permanente – Colloque de Lyon* (Pédone, 1987) 277.

B Conforti, 'L'Arrêt de la Cour Internationale de Justice dans l'Affaire de la Délimitation du Plateau Continental entre la Libye et Malte' (1986) 90 *Revue Générale de Droit International Public* 313.

J Cooper, 'Delimitation of the Maritime Boundary in the Gulf of Maine Area' (1986) 16 *Ocean Development and International Law* 59.

J-P Cot, 'The Dual function of Base Points' in H Hestermeyer et al. (eds.), *Coexistence, Cooperation and Solidarity – Liber Amicorum Rüdiger Wolfrum* (Martinus Nijhoff, 2012) 807.

T Cottier, *Equitable Principles of Maritime Boundary Delimitation* (Cambridge University Press, 2015).

P Couvreur, *The International Court of Justice and the Effectiveness of International Law* (Brill, 2017).

J Crawford and T Viles, 'International Law on a Given Day' in J Crawford (ed.), *International Law as an Open System* (Cameron May, 2002) 69.

J Crawford, *Brownlie's Principles of Public International Law* 8th edn (Oxford University Press, 2012).

J Crawford and M Koskenniemi (eds.), *The Cambridge Companion to International Law* (Cambridge University Press, 2012).

J Crawford, 'Chance, Order, Change: the Course of International Law' (2013) 365 *Recueil des Cours* 9.

JH Currie, 'Maritime Boundary Delimitation in a Federal Domestic Setting: The *Newfoundland and Labrador v. Nova Scotia* Arbitration' (2004) 17 *Leiden Journal of International Law* 155.

P Dailler, 'Le Processus de Délimitation Maritime: la Convention de Montego Bay' in *Le Processus de Délimitation Maritime: Étude d'un Cas Fictif* (Pédone, 2004) 264.

P d'Argent, 'Des Frontières et des Peuples: l'Affaire de la Frontière Terrestre et Maritime entre le Cameroun et le Nigéria (Arrêt sur le Fond)' (2003) 48 *Annuaire Français de Droit International* 281.

J d'Aspremont, 'The Idea of "Rules" in the Sources of International Law' (2014) 84 *British Yearbook of International Law* 103.

E David, 'La Sentence Arbitrale du 14 Février 1985 sur la Délimitation de la Frontière Maritime Guinée-Guinée Bissau' (1986) 31 *Annuaire Français de Droit International* 350.

JL de Azcárraga, *La Plataforma Submarina y el Derecho Internacional – La Zona Nerítica Epijurisdiccional* (Instituto Francisco de Vitoria, 1952).

E De Brabandere, 'The Use of Precedent and External Case Law by the International Court of Justice and the International Tribunal for the Law of the Sea' (2016) 15 *Law and Practice of International Courts and Tribunals* 24.

E Decaux, 'L'Arrêt de la Cour Internationale de Justice dans l'Affaire du Plateau Continental (Tunisie/Libye): Arrêt du 24 Février 1982' (1982) 28 *Annuaire Français de Droit International* 357.

E Decaux, 'Arrêt de la Chambre de la Court Internationale de Justice sur l'Affaire de la Délimitation de la Frontière Maritime dans le Golfe du Maine (Canada/Etats-Unis): Arrêt du 12 Octobre 1984' (1984) 30 *Annuaire Français de Droit International* 304.

E Decaux, 'L'Arrêt de la Cour Internationale de Justice dans l'Affaire du Plateau Continental (Libye/Malte): Arrêt du 3 Juin 1985' (1985) 31 *Annuaire Français de Droit International* 294.

E Decaux, 'Affaire de la Délimitation Maritime dans la Région située entre le Groenland et Jan Mayen (Danemark c. Norvège)' (1993) 39 *Annuaire Français de Droit International* 495.

E Decaux, 'Affaire de la Délimitation Maritime et des Questions Territoriales entre Qatar et Bahreïn (Fond) Arrêt du 16 Mars 2001' (2001) 47 *Annuaire Français de Droit International* 177.

V-D Degan, 'Internal Waters' (1986) 17 *Netherlands Yearbook of International Law* 3.

V-D Degan, 'Consolidation of Legal Principles on Maritime Delimitation: Implications for the Dispute between Slovenia and Croatia in the North Adriatic' (2007) 6 *Chinese Journal of International Law* 601.

L Delabie, 'Le fragile Équilibre entre Prévisibilité Juridique et Opportunité Judiciaire en Matière de Délimitation Maritime: l'Arrêt de la Cour Internationale de Justice dans l'Affaire du *Différend Territorial et Maritime (Nicaragua c. Colombie)*' (2012) 58 *Annuaire Français de Droit International* 223.

DJ Devine, 'Base Points, Baselines in Median-line Delimitation' (2002) 27 *South African Yearbook of International Law* 223.

I Diaité, 'Le Règlement du Contentieux entre la Guinée-Bissau et le Sénégal relatif à la Délimitation de leur Frontière Maritime' (1996) 41 *Annuaire Français de Droit International* 700.

Y Dinstein, 'The Interaction between Customary International Law and Treaties' (2007) 322 *Recueil des Cours* 243.

H Dipla, 'Arrêt de la Cour Internationale de Justice en l'Affaire de la Délimitation Maritime dans la Région située entre le Groenland et Jan Mayen' (1994) 98 *Revue Générale de Droit International Public* 899.

E Doussis, 'Îles, Îlots, Rochers et Hauts-Fonds Découvrants' in *Le Processus de Délimitation Maritime – Étude d'un Cas Fictif* (Pédone, 2004) 134.

P-E Dupont and A Solomou, 'Provisional Measures in Maritime Delimitation Cases' in J Crawford et al. (eds.), *The International Legal Order: Current Needs and Possible Responses – Essays in Honour of Djamchid Momtaz* (Brill, 2017) 312.

R-J Dupuy, 'La Mer sous Compétence Nationale' in R-J Dupuy and D Vignes (eds.), *Traité du Nouveau Droit de la Mer* (Bruylant, 1985) 219.

R Dworkin, *Taking Rights Seriously* (Duckworth, 1977).

R Dworkin, 'On Gaps in the Law' in P Amselek and N MacCormick (eds.), *Controversies about Law's Ontology* (Edinburgh University Press, 1991) 84.

R Dworkin, *Law's Empire* (Hart, 1998).

TO Elias, 'The Doctrine of Intertemporal Law' (1980) 74 *American Journal of International Law* 285.

T Endicott, *Vagueness in Law* (Oxford University Press, 2000).

MD Evans, *Relevant Circumstances and Maritime Delimitation* (Oxford University Press, 1989).

MD Evans, 'Maritime Delimitation and Expanding Categories of Relevant Circumstances' (1991) 40 *International and Comparative Law Quarterly* 1.

MD Evans, 'Delimitation and the Common Maritime Boundary' (1993) 64 *British Yearbook of International Law* 283.

MD Evans, 'Less Than an Ocean Apart: The St. Pierre et Miquelon and Jan Mayen Islands and the Delimitation of Maritime Zones' (1994) 43 *International and Comparative Law Quarterly* 678.

MD Evans, 'Intervention, the International Court of Justice and the Law of the Sea' (1995) 48 *Revue Hellénique de Droit International* 73.

MD Evans, 'Maritime Delimitation after *Denmark* v. *Norway*: Back to the Future?' in GS Goodwin-Gill and S Talmon (eds.), *The Reality of International Law – Essays in Honour of Ian Brownlie* (Oxford University Press, 1999) 153.

MD Evans, 'The Maritime Delimitation between Eritrea and Yemen' (2001) 14 *Leiden Journal of International Law* 141.

MD Evans, 'Case concerning *Maritime Delimitation and Territorial Questions between Qatar and Bahrain* (*Qatar* v *Bahrain*)' (2002) 51 *International and Comparative Law Quarterly* 709.

MD Evans, 'Maritime Boundary Delimitation: Where Do We Go From Here?' in D Freestone et al. (eds.), *Law of the Sea – Progress and Prospects* (Oxford University Press, 2006) 137.

MD Evans, 'The Law of the Sea' in MD Evans, *International Law* (Oxford University Press, 2014) 651.

MD Evans, 'Maritime Boundary Delimitation' in DR Rothwell et al. (eds.), *The Oxford Handbook of the Law of the Sea* (Oxford University Press, 2015) 254.

MD Evans, 'Maritime Boundary Delimitation: Whatever Next?' in J Barrett and R Barnes (eds.), *Law of the Sea – UNCLOS as a Living Treaty* (BIICL, 2016) 41.

MD Evans, 'Relevant Circumstances' in A Oude Elferink et al. (eds.), *Maritime Boundary Delimitation – The Case Law: Is It Consistent and Predictable?* (Cambridge University Press, 2018) 222.

J Evensen, 'Working Methods and Procedures in the Third United Nations Conference on the Law of the Sea' (1986) 199 *Recueil des Cours* 415.

MB Feldman, 'The Tunisia-Libya Continental Shelf Case: Geographic Justice or Judicial Compromise?' (1983) 77 *American Journal of International Law* 219.

S Fietta and R Cleverly, *A Practitioner's Guide to Maritime Boundary Delimitation* (Oxford University Press, 2016).

RE Fife, 'La Négociation de l'Accord de Délimitation Maritime: une Perspective Norvégienne' in *Le Processus de Délimitation Maritime: Étude d'un Cas Fictif* (Pédone, 2004) 336.

RE Fife, 'Le Traité du 15 Septembre 2010 entre la Norvège et la Russie relatif à la Délimitation et à la Coopération Maritime en Mer de Barents et dans l'Océan Arctique' (2010) 56 *Annuaire Français de Droit International* 399.

G Fitzmaurice, 'Some Problems Regarding the Formal Sources of International Law' in *Symbolae Verzijl* (Martinus Nijhoff, 1958) 153.

G Fitzmaurice, 'The Problem of *Non Liquet*: Prolegomena to a Restatement' in *Mélanges Offerts à Charles Rousseau – La Communauté Internationale* (Pédone, 1974) 89.

S Forlati, '"Interesse di Natura Giuridica" ed Effetti per gli Stati Terzi delle Sentenze della Corte Internazionale di Giustizia' (2002) 85 *Rivista di Diritto Internazionale* 99.

G Francalanci, 'La Ligne d'Équidistance' in D Pharand and U Leanza (eds.), *The Continental Shelf and the Exclusive Economic Zone: Delimitation and Legal Regime* (Martinus Nijhoff, 1993) 57.

W Friedmann, 'The *North Sea Continental Shelf Cases*: A Critique' (1970) 64 *American Journal of International Law* 229.

J Gardner, 'Concerning Permissive Sources and Gaps' (1988) 8 *Oxford Journal of Legal Studies* 457.

S Garfield, *On the Map – Why the World Looks the Way It Does* (Profile Books, 2013).

P Gautier, 'Le Plateau Continental de la Belgique et sa Délimitation: quelques Réflexions sur la Notion d'Accord implicite' (1995) 28 *Revue Belge de Droit International* 108.

P Gautier, 'Conduite, Accord Tacite et Délimitation Maritime' in *Droit des Frontières Internationales – The Law of International Borders* (Pédone, 2016) 145.

G Gidel, 'La Mer Territoriale et la Zone Contiguë' (1934) 48 *Recueil des Cours* 133.

G Giraudeau, 'La remarquable Entrée en Scène du TIDM dans le Contentieux de la Délimitation Maritime: l'Arrêt du 14 Mars 2012 relatif au Différend entre le Bangladesh et le Myanmar dans le Golfe du Bengale' (2012) 17 *Annuaire du Droit de la Mer* 93.

C Gray, *Judicial Remedies in International Law* (Oxford University Press, 1987).

C Gray, 'The 2014 Judicial Activity of the International Court of Justice' (2015) 109 *American Journal of International Law* 583.

C Gray, 'The 2016 Judicial Activity of the International Court of Justice' (2017) 111 *American Journal of International Law* 415.

D Gray, 'Seaward Limits of the Continental Shelf and EEZ: Technical Concerns' in D Pharand and U Leanza (eds.), *The Continental Shelf and the Exclusive Economic Zone: Delimitation and Legal Regime* (Martinus Nijhoff, 1993) 19.

DW Grieg, 'Third Party Rights and Intervention before the International Court' (1991–1992) 32 *Virginia Journal of International Law* 285.

H Grotius, *De Jure Belli ac Pacis* W Whewell (ed.) (Cambridge University Press, 1853).

G Guillaume, 'De l'exécution des Décisions de la Cour internationale de Justice' (1997) 7 *Swiss Review of International and European Law* 431.

G Guillaume, 'Les Hauts-Fonds Découvrants en Droit International' in *La Mer et Son Droit – Mélanges Offerts à Laurent Lucchini et Jean-Pierre Quéneudec* (Pédone, 2003) 287.

J Harrison, *Making the Law of the Sea – A Study in the Development of International Law* (Cambridge University Press, 2011).

HLA Hart, *The Concept of Law* 2nd edn (Oxford University Press, 1994).

HLA Hart, *The Concept of Law* 3rd edn (Oxford University Press, 2012).

KJ Heller, 'Specially-Affected States and the Formation of Custom' (2018) 112 *American Journal of International Law* 191.

T Henriksen and G Ulfstein, 'Maritime Delimitation in the Arctic: The Barents Sea Today' (2011) 42 *Ocean Development and International Law* 1.

LL Herman, 'The Court Giveth and the Court Taketh Away: An Analysis of the Tunisia-Libya Continental Shelf Case' (1984) 33 *International and Comparative Law Quarterly* 825.

GI Hernández, *The International Court of Justice and the Judicial Function* (Oxford University Press, 2014).

R Higgins, 'Some Observations on the Inter-Temporal Rule in International Law' in J Makarczyk (ed.), *Theory of International Law at the Threshold of the 21st Century – Essays in Honour of Krzysztof Skubiszewski* (Kluwer, 1996) 173.

L Huang and X Liao, 'Natural Prolongation and Delimitation of the Continental Shelf Beyond 200 nm: Implications of the *Bangladesh/Myanmar* Case' (2014) 4 *Asian Journal of International Law* 281.

C Hurst, 'The Continental Shelf' (1949) 34 *Transactions of the Grotius Society* 153.

R Ida, 'The Role of Proportionality in Maritime Delimitation Revisited: The Origin and Meaning of the Principle from the Early Decisions of the Court' in N Ando et al. (eds.), *Liber Amicorum Judge Shigeru Oda* (Martinus Nijhoff, 2002) vol. II, 1037.

MT Infante-Caffi, '*Peru* v. *Chile*: The International Court of Justice Decides on the Status of the Maritime Boundary' (2014) 13 *Chinese Journal of International Law* 741.

G Jaenicke, 'The Role of Proportionality in the Delimitation of Maritime Zones' in A Bos and H Siblesz (eds.), *Realism in Law-Making – Essays on International Law in Honour of Willem Riphagen* (Martinus Nijhoff, 1986) 51.

SP Jagota, 'Maritime Boundary' (1982) 171 *Recueil des Cours* 81.

SP Jagota, *Maritime Boundary* (Martinus Nijhoff, 1985).

RY Jennings, 'General Course on Principles of International Law' (1967) 121 *Recueil des Cours* 323.

RY Jennings, 'The Limits of Continental Shelf Jurisdiction: Some Possible Implications of the *North Sea Case* Judgment' (1969) 18 *International and Comparative Law Quarterly* 819.

RY Jennings, *The Acquisition of Territory in International Law* (Manchester University Press, 2007).

RY Jennings and A Watts, *Oppenheim's International Law* 9th edn (Longman, 1992).

Ø Jensen, *The Commission on the Limits of the Continental Shelf – Law and Legitimacy* (Martinus Nijhoff, 2014).

Ø Jensen, 'Maritime Boundary Delimitation Beyond 200 Nautical Miles: The International Judiciary and the Commission on the Limits of the Continental Shelf' (2015) 84 *Nordic Journal of International Law* 580.

PC Jessup, 'Intervention in the International Court' (1981) 75 *American Journal of International Law* 903.

BB Jia, 'International Case Law in the Development of International Law' (2015) 382 *Recueil des Cours* 175.

E Jouannet, 'L'impossible Protection des Droits des Tiers par la Cour Internationale de Justice dans les Affaires de Délimitation Maritime' in *La Mer et son Droit – Mélanges offerts à Laurent Lucchini et Jean-Pierre Quéneudec* (Pédone, 2003) 315.

M Kaldunski, 'A Commentary on Maritime Boundary Arbitration between Bangladesh and India concerning the Bay of Bengal' (2015) 28 *Leiden Journal of International Law* 799.

M Kaldunski and T Wasiliewski, 'The International Tribunal for the Law of the Sea on Maritime Delimitation: The *Bangladesh v. Myanmar* Case' (2014) 45 *Ocean Development and International Law* 123.

J Kammerhofer, 'Uncertainty in the Formal Sources of International Law: Customary International Law and Some of its Problems' (2004) 15 *European Journal of International Law* 523.

M Kamto, 'Le Contentieux de la Frontière Maritime entre la Guinée-Bissau et le Sénégal' (1997) 101 *Revue Générale de Droit International Public* 695.

M Kamto, 'Considérations actuelles sur l'inexécution des Décisions de la Cour internationale de Justice' in TM Ndiaye and R Wolfrum (eds.), *Law of the Sea, Environmental Law and Settlement of Disputes – Liber Amicorum Judge Thomas A. Mensah* (Martinus Nijhoff, 2007) 215.

M Kamto, 'Sur Quelques Questions Techniques liées à la Détermination du Tracé d'une Frontière Maritime Délimitée' in R Casado-Raigón and G Cataldi (eds.), *L'Evolution et l'Etat actuel du droit international de la mer – Mélanges offerts à Daniel Vignes* (Bruylant, 2009) 481.

M Kamto, 'Considérations actuelles sur la méthode de délimitation maritime devant la Cour internationale de Justice. De Charybde en Scylla?' in J Crawford et al. (eds.), *The International Legal Order: Current Needs and Possible Responses – Essays in Honour of Djamchid Momtaz* (Brill, 2017) 383.

S Kaye, 'The Use of Multiple Boundaries in Maritime Boundary Delimitation: Law and Practice' (1998) 19 *Australian Yearbook of International Law* 49.

S Kaye, 'Lessons Learned from the *Gulf of Maine* Case: The Development of Maritime Boundary Delimitation Jurisprudence since UNCLOS III' (2008) 14 *Ocean and Coastal Law Journal* 73.

H Kelsen, 'Théorie du Droit International Public' (1953) 84 *Recueil des Cours* 1.

D Kennedy, 'The *Nuclear Weapons* Case' in L Boisson de Chazournes and P Sands (eds.), *International Law, the International Court of Justice and Nuclear Weapons* (Cambridge University Press, 1999) 462.

HJ Kim, 'La Délimitation de la Frontière Maritime dans le Golfe du Bengale: Courir deux Lièvres à la Fois avec Succès dans le Règlement de la Délimitation Maritime' (2012) 58 *Annuaire Français de Droit International* 443.

F Kirgis, 'Custom on a Sliding Scale' (1987) 81 *American Journal of International Law* 146.

J Klabbers, *International Law* 2nd edn (Cambridge University Press, 2017).

N Klein, *Dispute Settlement in the UN Convention on the Law of the Sea* (Cambridge University Press, 2005).

N Klein, 'Provisional Measures and Provisional Arrangements in Maritime Boundary Disputes' (2006) 21 *International Journal of Marine and Coastal Law* 489.

M Kohen, *Possession Contestée et Souveraineté Territoriale* (PUF, 1997).

M Kohen, 'La Relation Titre/*Effectivités* dans le Contentieux Territorial à la Lumière de la Jurisprudence Récente' (2004) 108 *Revue Générale de Droit International Public* 561.

R Kolb, *Case Law on Equitable Maritime Delimitation: Digest and Commentaries* (Martinus Nijhoff, 2003).

N Krisch, 'The Decay of Consent: International Law in an Age of Public Goods' (2014) 108 *American Journal of International Law* 1.

A Kulick, 'From Problem to Opportunity?: An Analytical Framework for Vagueness and Ambiguity in International Law' (2016) 59 *German Yearbook of International Law* 257.

B Kunoy, 'A Geometric Variable Scope of Delimitations: The Impact of a Geological and Geomorphological Title to the Outer Continental Shelf' (2006) 11 *Austrian Review of International and European Law* 49.

B Kunoy, 'The Admissibility of a Plea to an International Adjudicative Forum to Delimit the Outer Continental Shelf Prior to the Adoption of Final Recommendations by the Commission on the Limits of the Continental Shelf' (2010) 25 *International Journal of Marine and Coastal Law* 237.

B Kunoy, 'Establishment of the Outer Limits of the Continental Shelf: Is Crossing Boundaries Trespassing?' (2011) 26 *International Journal of Marine and Coastal Law* 313.

B Kunoy, 'The Delimitation of an Indicative Area of Overlapping Entitlement to the Outer Continental Shelf' (2012) 83 *British Yearbook of International Law* 61.

B Kwiatkowska, 'Equitable Maritime Boundary Delimitation: A Legal Perspective' (1988) 3 *International Journal of Estuarine and Coastal Law* 287.

B Kwiatkowska, 'Equitable Maritime Boundary Delimitation, as exemplified in the Work of the International Court of Justice during the Presidency of Sir Robert Yewdall Jennings and Beyond' (1997) 28 *Ocean Development and International Law* 91.

B Kwiatkowska, 'The Eritrea/Yemen Arbitration: Landmark Progress in the Acquisition of Territorial Sovereignty and Equitable Maritime Boundary Delimitation' (2001) 32 *Ocean Development and International Law* 1.

B Kwiatkowska, 'The *Qatar v Bahrain* Maritime Delimitation and Territorial Questions Case' (2002) 33 *Ocean Development and International Law* 227.

B Kwiatkowska, 'The Contribution of the 2002 (Cameroon v. Nigeria; Equatorial Guinea intervening) Land and Maritime Boundary between Cameroon and Nigeria Judgment of the International Court of Justice to Equitable Maritime Boundary Delimitation' (2005) 17 *Hague Yearbook of International Law* 95.

B Kwiatkowska, 'The 2006 UNCLOS Annex VII Barbados/Trinidad and Tobago Award: Landmark Progress in Compulsory Jurisdiction and Equitable Maritime Boundary Delimitation' (2007) 19 *Hague Yearbook of International Law* 33.

S Lalonde, 'The Role of the "Uti Possidetis" Principle in the Resolution of Maritime Boundary Disputes' in F Baetens and C Chinkin (eds.), *Sovereignty, Statehood and State Responsibility – Essays in Honour of James Crawford* (Cambridge University Press, 2015) 248.

M Lando, 'Compliance with Provisional Measures Indicated by the International Court of Justice' (2017) 8 *Journal of International Dispute Settlement* 22.

M Lando 'Delimiting the Continental Shelf Beyond 200 Nautical Miles at the International Court of Justice: The *Nicaragua v Colombia* Cases' (2017) 16 *Chinese Journal of International Law* 137.

M Lando 'Judicial Uncertainties concerning Territorial Sea Delimitation under Article 15 of the United Nations Convention on the Law of the Sea' (2017) 66 *International and Comparative Law Quarterly* 589.

M Lando 'The *Croatia/Slovenia* Arbitral Award of 29 June 2017: Is there a Common Method for Delimiting All Maritime Zones under International Law?' (2017) 100 *Rivista di Diritto Internazionale* 1184.

C Lathrop, 'Newfoundland and Labrador-Nova Scotia: The latest "International" Maritime Boundary' (2003) 34 *Ocean Development and International Law* 83.

C Lathrop, 'Why Litigate a Maritime Boundary? Some Contributing Factors' in N Klein (ed.), *Litigating International Law Disputes: Weighing the Options* (Cambridge University Press, 2014) 230.

E Lauterpacht, *Aspects of the Administration of International Justice* (Cambridge University Press, 1991) 125.

H Lauterpacht, 'Sovereignty over Submarine Areas' (1950) 27 *British Yearbook of International Law* 376.

H Lauterpacht, 'Some Observations on the Prohibition of "*Non Liquet*" and the Completeness of the Law' in *Symbolae Verzijl* (Martinus Nijhoff, 1958) 196.

H Lauterpacht, *The Development of International Law by the International Court* (Oxford University Press, 1982).

H Lauterpacht, *The Function of Law in the International Community* (Oxford University Press, 2011).

R Lavalle, 'Not Quite a Sure Thing: The Maritime Areas of Rocks and Low-Tide Elevations Under the UN Law of the Sea Convention' (2004) 19 *International Journal of Marine and Coastal Law* 43.

R Lavalle, 'The Rights of States over Low-Tide Elevations: A Legal Analysis' (2014) 29 *International Journal of Marine and Coastal Law* 457.

R Le Bœuf, '*Différend en Mer de Chine Méridionale (Philippines c. Chine) – Sentence arbitrale du 12 juillet 2016*' (2016) 62 *Annuaire Français de Droit International* 159.

LH Legault and B Hankey, 'From Sea to Seabed: The Single Maritime Boundary in the Gulf of Maine Case' (1985) 79 *American Journal of International Law* 961.

J-P Lévy, *La Conférence des Nations Unies sur le Droit de la Mer – Histoire d'une Négociation Singulière* (Pédone, 1983).

X Liao, 'Evaluation of Scientific Evidence by International Courts and Tribunals in the Continental Shelf Delimitation Cases' (2017) 48 *Ocean Development and International Law* 136.

X Liao, 'Is There a Hierarchical Relationship between Natural Prolongation and Distance in the Continental Shelf Delimitation?' (2018) 33 *International Journal of Marine and Coastal Law* 79.

V Lowe, 'Uniform Interpretation of the Rules of International Law Governing Innocent Passage' (1991) 6 *International Journal of Estuarine and Coastal Law* 73.

V Lowe, *International Law* (Oxford University Press, 2007).

L Lucchini and M Vœlckel, *Droit de la Mer* (Pédone, 1990).

L Lucchini, 'L'Etat Insulaire' (2000) 285 *Recueil des Cours* 251.

L Lucchini, 'Le Juge et l'Équidistance: Sense or Sensibility?' in F Alabrune et al. (eds.), *L'Etat Souverain dans le Monde d'Aujourd'hui – Mélanges en l'Honneur de Jean-Pierre Puissochet* (Pédone, 2008) 175.

L Lucchini, 'Plaidoyer pour une ligne unique de délimitation' in R Casado-Raigón and G Cataldi (eds.), *L'Evolution et l'Etat actuel du droit international de la mer – Mélanges offerts à Daniel Vignes* (Bruylant, 2009) 561.

BM Magnússon, 'Judgment in the *Dispute Concerning Delimitation of the Maritime Boundary between Bangladesh and Myanmar in the Bay of Bengal* (14 March 2012)' (2012) 27 *International Journal of Marine and Coastal Law* 623.

BM Magnússon, 'Is there a Temporal Relationship between the Delineation and the Delimitation of the Continental Shelf beyond 200 Nautical Miles?' (2013) 28 *International Journal of Marine and Coastal Law* 465.

BM Magnússon, 'The Rejection of the Theoretical Beauty: The Foot of the Continental Slope in Maritime Boundary Delimitations Beyond 200 Nautical Miles' (2014) 45 *Ocean Development and International Law* 41.

BM Magnússon, *The Continental Shelf Beyond 200 Nautical Miles – Delineation, Delimitation and Dispute Settlement* (Martinus Nijhoff, 2015).

J-G Mahinga, 'La Délimitation de la Frontière Maritime entre la Roumanie et l'Ukraine dans la Mer Noire' (2010) 137 *Journal du Droit International* 1157.

J-G Mahinga, *Le Tribunal International du Droit de la Mer – Organisation, Compétence et Procédure* (Larcier, 2013).

V Marotta Rangel, 'Le Plateau Continental dans la Convention de 1982 sur le Droit de la Mer' (1985) 194 *Recueil des Cours* 269.

NS Marques Antunes, 'The 1999 Eritrea-Yemen Maritime Delimitation Award and the Development of International Law' (2001) 50 *International and Comparative Law Quarterly* 299.

NS Marques Antunes, *Towards a Conceptualisation of Maritime Delimitation: Legal and Technical Aspects of a Political Process* (Martinus Nijhoff, 2003).

N Marques Antunes, 'Entitlement to Maritime Zones and their Delimitation – In the Doldrums of Uncertainty and Unpredictability' in A Oude Elferink et al. (eds.), *Maritime Boundary Delimitation – The Case Law: Is It Consistent and Predictable?* (Cambridge University Press, 2018) 62.

G Marston, 'Low-Tide Elevations and Straight Baselines' (1972–73) 46 *British Yearbook of International Law* 405.

G Marston, 'Delimitation of Maritime Zones: Recent Commonwealth Decisions' (1980) 51 *British Yearbook of International Law* 263.

G Marston, 'St. Pierre–Miquelon Arbitration: Canada–France Maritime Delimitation Award' (1993) 17 *Marine Policy* 155.

A Matine-Daftary, 'Cours Abrégé sur la Contribution des Conférences de Genève au Développement Progressif du Droit International de la Mer' (1961) 102 *Recueil des Cours* 635.

T McDorman et al., 'The Gulf of Maine Boundary: Dropping Anchor or Setting a Course?' (1985) 9 *Marine Policy* 90.

T McDorman, 'The Continental Shelf' in DR Rothwell et al. (eds.), *The Oxford Handbook of the Law of the Sea* (Oxford University Press, 2015) 181.

D McRae, 'Adjudication of the Maritime Boundary in the Gulf of Maine' (1979) 17 *Canadian Yearbook of International Law* 292.

D McRae, 'The Single Maritime Boundary: Problems in Theory and Practice' in ED Brown and RR Churchill (eds.), *The UN Convention on the Law of the Sea: Impact and Implementation* (Law of the Sea Institute, 1987) 225.

M Mendelson, 'The Formation of Customary International Law' (1998) 272 *Recueil des Cours* 155.

M Mendelson, 'On the Quasi-normative Effect of Maritime Boundary Agreements' in N Ando et al. (eds.), *Liber Amicorum Shigeru Oda* (Martinus Nijhoff, 2002) vol. II, 1069.

JG Merrills, 'Land and Maritime Boundary between Cameroon and Nigeria (Cameroon v. Nigeria; Equatorial Guinea intervening), Merits, Judgment of 10 October 2002' (2003) 52 *International and Comparative Law Quarterly* 788.

H Miller, 'The Hague Codification Conference' (1930) 24 *American Journal of International Law* 674.

R Mishra, 'The "Grey Area" in the Northern Bay of Bengal: A Note on a Functional Cooperative Solution' (2016) 47 *Ocean Development and International Law* 29.

M Miyoshi, 'Considerations of Equity in Maritime Boundary Cases before the International Court of Justice' in N Ando et al. (eds.), *Liber Amicorum Shigeru Oda* (Martinus Nijhoff, 2002) vol. II, 1087.

G Morelli, 'La Théorie Générale du Procès International' (1937) 61 *Recueil des Cours* 257.

G Morelli, *La Sentenza Internazionale* (CEDAM, 1931).

G Morelli, *Studi sul Processo Internazionale* (Giuffrè, 1963).

G Morelli, *Nuovi Studi sul Processo Internazionale* (Giuffrè, 1972).

MW Mouton, 'The Continental Shelf' (1954) 85 *Recueil des Cours* 343.

D Müller, 'Les Limites Extérieures des Espaces Marins' in M Forteau and J-M Thouvenin (eds.), *Traité de Droit International de la Mer* (Pédone, 2017) 529.

SD Murphy, 'International Law relating to Islands' (2016) 386 *Recueil des Cours* 9.

TM Ndiaye, 'Le Juge et la Délimitation Maritime: Modes d'Emploi' in JN Van Dyke et al. (eds.), *Governing Ocean Resources: New Challenges and Emerging Regimes – A Tribute to Judge Choon-Ho Park* (Martinus Nijhoff, 2013) 139.

TM Ndiaye, 'The Judge, Maritime Delimitation and the Grey Areas' (2015) 56 *Indian Journal of International Law* 493.

LMD Nelson, 'Equity and the Delimitation of Maritime Boundaries' (1978) 11–12 *Revue Iranienne de Relations Internationales* 197.

K Neri, 'L'Arrêt de la Cour Internationale de Justice du 27 Janvier 2014 dans l'Affaire du *Différend Maritime (Perou c. Chili)*' (2014) 60 *Annuaire Français de Droit International* 91.

O Nilufer, 'International Court of Justice: Case concerning *Maritime Delimitation in the Black* Sea *(Romania v. Ukraine)* – Judgment of 3 February 2009' (2010) 25 *International Journal of Marine and Coastal Law* 63.

LN Nguyen, 'UNCLOS Tribunals and the Development of the Outer Continental Shelf Regime' (2018) 67 *International and Comparative Law Quarterly* 425.

MH Nordquist (ed.), *United Nations Convention on the Law of the Sea 1982 – A Commentary* (Martinus Nijhoff, 1993).

DP O'Connell, *The International Law of the Sea* (Oxford University Press, 1984).

S Oda, 'The Continental Shelf' (1957) 1 *Japanese Annual of International Law* 15.

S Oda, 'The International Court of Justice Viewed from the Bench' (1993) 244 *Recueil des Cours* 9.

R O'Keefe, 'Palm-Fringed Benefits: Island Dependencies in the New Law of the Sea' (1996) 45 *International and Comparative Law Quarterly* 408.

R O'Keefe, 'Legal Title versus *Effectivités*: Prescription and the Promise and Problem of Private Law Analogies' (2011) 13 *International Community Law Review* 147.

F Olorundami, 'The ICJ and its Lip-service to the Non-priority Status of the Equidistance Method of Delimitation' (2015) 4 *Cambridge Journal of International and Comparative Law* 53.

F Olorundami, 'Revisiting the *Libya/Malta* Decision and Assessing its Relevance (or otherwise) to the East China Sea Dispute' (2016) 15 *Chinese Journal of International Law* 717.

F Olorundami, 'Objectivity versus Subjectivity in Maritime Boundary Delimitation' (2017) 32 *International Journal of Marine and Coastal Law* 36.

F Orrego-Vicuña, 'La Zone Économique Exclusive: Regime et Nature Juridique dans le Droit International' (1986) 199 *Recueil des Cours* 9.

F Orrego-Vicuña, 'The Contribution of the Exclusive Economic Zone to the Law of Maritime Delimitation' (1989) 31 *German Yearbook of International Law* 120.

F Orrego-Vicuña, *The Exclusive Economic Zone: Regime and Legal Nature under International Law* (Cambridge University Press, 1989).

F Orrego-Vicuña, 'La Limite Intérieure de la Limite Extérieure : le Chevauchement de Revendications et la Délimitation du Plateau Continental Étendu' in R Casado-Raigón and G Cataldi (eds.), *L'Evolution et l'Etat actuel du Droit International de la Mer – Mélanges offerts à Daniel Vignes* (Bruylant, 2009) 691.

F Orrego-Vicuña, 'Le Rôle de la Jurisprudence Internationale' in M Forteau and J-M Thouvenin (eds.), *Traité de Droit International de la Mer* (Pédone, 2017) 77.

A Oude Elferink, 'Does Undisputed Title to a Maritime Zone Always Exclude its Delimitation: The Grey Area Issue' (1998) 13 *International Journal of Marine and Coastal Law* 143.

A Oude Elferink, 'Maritime Delimitation between the United Kingdom and Denmark/Faroe Island' (1999) 14 *International Journal of Marine and Coastal Law* 541.

A Oude Elferink, 'The Impact of the Law of the Sea Convention on the Delimitation of Maritime Boundaries' in D Vidas and W Østreng (eds.), *Order of the Oceans at the Turn of the Century* (Martinus Nijhoff, 1999) 457.

A Oude Elferink, 'International Law and Negotiated and Adjudicated Maritime Boundaries: A Complex Relationship' (2015) 58 *German Yearbook of International Law* 231.

A Oude Elferink, 'ITLOS's Approach to the Delimitation of the Continental Shelf beyond 200 Nautical Miles in the *Bangladesh/Myanmar* Case: Theoretical and Practical Difficulties' in R Wolfrum et al. (eds.), *Contemporary Developments in International Law – Essays in Honour of Budislav Vukas* (Martinus Nijhoff, 2016) 231.

A Oude Elferink, 'Relevant Coast and Relevant Area' in A Oude Elferink et al. (eds.), *Maritime Boundary Delimitation – The Case Law: Is It Consistent and Predictable?* (Cambridge University Press, 2018) 173.

BH Oxman, 'La Troisième Conférence des Nations Unies sur le Droit de la Mer' in R-J Dupuy and D Vignes (eds.), *Traité du Nouveau Droit de la Mer* (Bruylant, 1985) 143.

BH Oxman, 'On Rocks and Maritime Delimitation' in MH Arsanjani et al. (eds.), *Looking to the Future: Essays on International Law in Honour of W. Michael Reisman* (Martinus Nijhoff, 2010) 893.

J-H Paik, 'The Role of Proportionality in Maritime Delimitation: State of the Jurisprudence' in HP Hestermeyer et al. (eds.), *Coexistence, Cooperation and Solidarity – Liber Amicorum Rüdiger Wolfrum* (Martinus Nijhoff, 2012) 199.

P Palchetti, 'Opening the International Court of Justice to Third States: Intervention and Beyond' (2002) 6 *Max Planck Yearbook of United Nations Law* 139.

P Palchetti, 'La Protection des Intérêts d'Etats Tiers par la Cour Internationale de Justice: l'Affaire de la Frontière Terrestre et Maritime entre le Cameroun et le Nigéria' (2003) 107 *Revue Générale de Droit International Public* 865.

I Papanicolopulu, *Il Confine Marino: Unità o Pluralità?* (Giuffrè, 2005).

I Papanicolopulu, 'Some Thoughts on the Extension of Existing Boundaries for the Delimitation of New Maritime Zones' in R Lagoni and D Vignes (eds.), *Maritime Delimitation* (Martinus Nijhoff, 2006) 143.

I Papanicolopulu, 'A Note on Maritime Delimitation in a Multizonal Context: The Case of the Mediterranean' (2007) 38 *Ocean Development and International Law* 381.

C Parry, *The Sources and Evidences of International Law* (Manchester University Press, 1965).

C Paulson, 'Compliance with Final Judgments of the International Court of Justice since 1987' (2004) 98 *American Journal of International Law* 434.

S Pawlak, 'Some Reflections on Factors exerting Influence on Maritime Boundary Delimitation' in H Hestermeyer et al. (eds.), *Coexistence, Cooperation and Solidarity – Liber Amicorum Rüdiger Wolfrum* (Martinus Nijhoff, 2012) 223.

N Peiris, 'Ghana v. Ivory Coast. Case No. 23' (2018) 112 *American Journal of International Law* 88.

A Pellet, 'The Normative Dilemma: Will and Consent in International Law-making' (1988–1989) 12 *Australian Yearbook of International Law* 22.

A Pellet, 'Article 38' in A Zimmermann et al. (eds.), *The Statute of the International Court of Justice – A Commentary* 2nd edn (Oxford University Press, 2012) 731.

A Pellet and B Samson, 'La Délimitation des Espaces Marins' in M Forteau and J-M Thouvenin (eds.), *Traité de Droit International de la Mer* (Pédone, 2017) 565.

N Petersen, 'The Role of Consent and Uncertainty in the Formation of Customary International Law' in BD Lepard (ed.), *Reexamining Customary International Law* (Cambridge University Press, 2017) 111.

HD Phan and LN Nguyen, 'The *South China Sea Arbitration*: Bindingness, Finality, and Compliance with UNCLOS Dispute Settlement Decisions' (2017) 7 *Asian Journal of International Law* 36.

MCW Pinto, 'Maritime Boundary Issues and their Resolution' in N Ando et al. (eds.), *Liber Amicorum Shigeru Oda* (Martinus Nijhoff, 2002) vol. II, 1115.

MCW Pinto, 'Article 76 of the UN Convention on the Law of the Sea and the Bay of Bengal Exception' (2013) 3 *Asian Journal of International Law* 215.

R Pistorelli, 'La Piattaforma Continentale: un Istituto ancora vitale?' (1978) 60 *Rivista di Diritto Internazionale* 496.

R Platzöder, *Third United Nations Conference on the Law of the Sea: Documents* (Oceana, 1986).

GP Politakis, 'The 1993 Jan Mayen Judgment: The End of Illusions?' (1994) 41 *Netherlands International Law Review* 1.

J-S Ponroy, 'Le Plateau Continental au-delà des 200 milles marins' in *Le Processus de Délimitation Maritime – Étude d'un Cas Fictif* (Pédone, 2004) 108.

M Pratt, 'The Role of the Technical Expert in Maritime Delimitation Cases' in R Lagoni and D Vignes (eds.), *Maritime Delimitation* (Martinus Nijhoff, 2006) 79.

J-F Pulvenis, 'Zone Économique et Plateau Continental: Unité ou Dualité ?' (1978) 11–12 *Revue Iranienne des Relations Internationales* 103.

J-F Pulvenis, 'Le Plateau Continental, Définition et Regime' in R-J Dupuy and D Vignes (eds.), *Traité du Nouveau Droit de la Mer* (Bruylant, 1985) 275.

J-P Quéneudec, 'L'Arbitrage relatif à la Détermination de la Frontière Maritime entre la Guinée-Bissau et le Sénégal' (1990) 35 *Annuaire Français de Droit International* 325.

J-P Quéneudec, 'Les Principes dégagés par le Juge et le Rôle des Circonstances Pertinentes en Matière de Délimitation Maritime' in *Le Processus de Délimitation Maritime: Étude d'un Cas Fictif* (Pédone, 2004) 279.

JJ Quintana, 'The International Court of Justice and the Formulation of International Law: The Law of Maritime Delimitation as an Example' in AS Muller and D Rai (eds.), *The International Court of Justice: Its Future Role after Fifty Years* (Martinus Nijhoff, 1997) 367.

NM Rajkovic, 'The Visual Conquest of International Law: Brute Boundaries, the Map, and the Legacy of Cartogenesis' (2018) 31 *Leiden Journal of International Law* 267.

R Ranjeva, 'Le Règlement des Différends' in R-J Dupuy and D Vignes (eds.), *Traité du Nouveau Droit de la Mer* (Bruylant, 1985) 1105.

PS Rao, 'The Nature and Function of International Law: An Evolving International Rule of Law' (2015) 55 *Indian Journal of International Law* 459.

J Raz, 'Legal Reason, Sources and Gaps' in J Raz (ed.), *The Authority of Law* (Oxford University Press, 1979) 53.

P Reuter, 'Une Ligne Unique de Délimitation des Espaces Maritimes' in *Mélanges Georges Perrin* (Diffusion Payot, 1984) 251.

S-M Rhee, 'Equitable Solutions to the Maritime Boundary Dispute between the United States and Canada in the Gulf of Maine' (1981) 75 *American Journal of International Law* 590.

N Ridi, 'Precarious Finality? Reflections on *Res Judicata* and the *Question of the Delimitation of the Continental Shelf* Case' (2018) 31 *Leiden Journal of International Law* 383.

WM Riesman and GS Westerman, *Straight Baselines in Maritime Boundary Delimitation* (St. Martin's Press, 1992).

WM Riesman and MH Arsanjani, 'Some Reflections on the Effect of Artisanal Fishing on Maritime Boundary Delimitation' in TM Ndiaye et al. (eds.), *Law of the Sea, Environmental Law and Settlement of Disputes – Liber Amicorum Judge Thomas A. Mensah* (Martinus Nijhoff, 2007) 629.

F Rigaldies, 'La Délimitation du Plateau Continental entre Etats voisins' (1976) 14 *Canadian Yearbook of International Law* 116.

F Rigaldies, 'La Zone Économique Exclusive dans la Pratique des Etats' (1998) 35 *Canadian Yearbook of International Law* 3.

JA Roach, 'Base Points and Baselines in Maritime Boundary Delimitation' in MH Nordquist and JN Moore (eds.), *Maritime Border Diplomacy* (Martinus Nijhoff, 2012) 269.

A Roberts, 'Traditional and Modern Approaches to Customary International Law: A Reconciliation' (2001) 95 *American Journal of International Law* 757.

N Ronzitti, 'Le Droit Humanitaire applicable aux Conflits Armés en Mer' (1993) 242 *Recueil des Cours* 9.

N Ros, 'Au-delà de la Borne 602: la Frontière Maritime entre l'Espagne et la France en Mer Méditerranée' (2014) 141 *Journal du Droit International* 1099.

S Rosenne, *League of Nations Conference for the Codification of International Law* (Oceana, 1975).

S Rosenne, 'Article 59 of the Statute of the International Court of Justice Revisited' in *Liber Amicorum Eduardo Jiménez de Aréchaga* (FCU, 1994) 1129.

S Rosenne, 'The Perplexities of Modern International Law' (2001) 291 *Recueil des Cours* 9.

DR Rothwell and T Stephens, *The International Law of the Sea* 2nd edn (Hart, 2016).

F Salerno, 'Treaties establishing Objective Regimes' in E Cannizzaro (ed.), *The Law of Treaties beyond the Vienna Convention* (Oxford University Press, 2011) 225.

J Salmon and I Sinclair, 'Special Features of the Qatar v. Bahrain Case before the ICJ – Affaire de la Délimitation Maritime et de Questions Territoriales entre Qatar et Bahreïn: Arrêt de la CIJ du 16 Mars 2001' in *Studi di Diritto Internazionale in Onore di Gaetano Arangio-Ruiz* (Editoriale Scientifica, 2004) vol. II, 1167.

LI Sanchez Rodriguez, 'L'Uti Possidetis: Application à la Délimitation Maritime' in *Le Processus de Délimitation Maritime: Étude d'un Cas Fictif* (Pédone, 2004) 303.

G Scelle, *Plateau Continental et Droit International* (Pédone, 1955).

O Schachter, 'Linking Equity and Law in Maritime Delimitation' in N Ando et al. (eds.), *Liber Amicorum Shigeru Oda* (Martinus Nijhoff, 2002) vol. II, 1163.

C Schulte, *Compliance with Decisions of the International Court of Justice* (Oxford University Press, 2004).

SM Schwebel, *Justice in International Law – Further Selected Writings of Stephen M. Schwebel* (Cambridge University Press, 2011).

I Scobbie, '*Res Judicata*, Precedent and the International Court: A Preliminary Sketch' (1999) 20 *Australian Yearbook of International Law* 299.

T Scovazzi, 'The Evolution of the International Law of the Sea: New Issues, New Challenges' (2000) 286 *Recueil des Cours* 39.

T Scovazzi, *Elementi di Diritto Internazionale del Mare* 3rd edn (Giuffrè, 2002).

T Scovazzi, 'Recent Developments as regards Maritime Delimitation in the Adriatic Sea' in R Lagoni and D Vignes (eds.), *Maritime Delimitation* (Martinus Nijhoff, 2006) 189.

T Scovazzi, 'Baselines' in R Wolfrum (ed.), *Max Planck Encyclopedia of Public International Law* (Oxford University Press, 2012) vol. I, 852.

M Shahabuddeen, *Precedent in the World Court* (Cambridge University Press, 1996).

SP Sharma, 'The Single Maritime Boundary Regime and the Relationship between the Continental Shelf and the Exclusive Economic Zone' (1987) 2 *International Journal of Estuarine and Coastal Law* 203.

M Shaw, 'The Beagle Channel Arbitration Award' (1978) 6 *International Relations* 415.

M Shaw, *Rosenne's Law and Practice of the International Court 1920–2015* 5th edn (Martinus Nijhoff, 2015).

D Silvestre, 'Le Processus de Délimitation Maritime: les Intérêts en Matière de Pêche et d'Environnement' in *Le Processus de Délimitation Maritime: Étude d'un Cas Fictif* (Pédone, 2004) 186.

B Simma, 'The Antarctic Treaty as a Treaty Providing for an "Objective Regime"' (1986) 19 *Cornell International Law Journal* 189.

L Siorat, *Le Problème des Lacunes en Droit International* (LGDJ, 1958).

M Sørensen, *Les Sources du Droit International* (Einar Munksgaard, 1946).

J Stone, '*Non Liquet* and the Function of Law in the International Community' (1959) 35 *British Yearbook of International Law* 124.

S Suarez, *The Outer Limits of the Continental Shelf – Legal Aspects of their Establishment* (Springer, 2008).

S Subedi, 'The Doctrine of Objective Regimes in International Law and the Competence of the United Nations to Impose Territorial or Peace Settlements on States' (1994) 37 *German Yearbook of International Law* 162.

C Sun, 'Comments on the Three-stage Approach of Maritime Delimitation' in MH Nordquist et al. (eds.), *Challenges of the Changing Arctic – Continental Shelf, Navigation, and Fisheries* (Martinus Nijhoff, 2016) 613.

CR Symmons, 'Article 15' in A Proelss (ed.), *United Nations Convention on the Law of the Sea – A Commentary* (Hart, 2017) 149.

J Symonides, 'Delimitation of Maritime Areas between the States with Opposite or Adjacent Coast' (1984) *Polish Yearbook of International Law* 19.

S Talmon, 'Determining Customary International Law: The ICJ's Methodology between Induction, Deduction and Assertion' (2015) 26 *European Journal of International Law* 417.

Y Tanaka, 'Reflections on the Concept of Proportionality in the Law of Maritime Delimitation' (2001) 16 *International Journal of Marine and Coastal Law* 433.

Y Tanaka, 'Reflections on Maritime Delimitation in the Cameroon/Nigeria Case' (2004) 53 *International and Comparative Law Quarterly* 369.

Y Tanaka, 'Quelques Observations sur deux Approches Jurisprudentielles en Droit de la Délimitation Maritime: l'Affrontement entre Prévisibilité et Flexibilité' (2004) 37 *Revue Belge de Droit International* 419.

Y Tanaka, 'Low-Tide Elevations in International Law of the Sea: Selected Issues' (2006) 20 *Ocean Yearbook* 189.

Y Tanaka, *Predictability and Flexibility in the Law of Maritime Delimitation* (Hart, 2006).

Y Tanaka, 'Case concerning the Territorial and Maritime Dispute between Nicaragua and Honduras in the Caribbean Sea (8 October 2007)' (2008) 23 *International Journal of Marine and Coastal Law* 327.

Y Tanaka, 'Reflections on Maritime Delimitation in the Nicaragua-Honduras Case' (2008) 68 *Zeitschrift für ausländisches öffentliches Recht und Völkerrecht* 903.

Y Tanaka, 'Reflections on Maritime Delimitation in the Romania/Ukraine Case before the International Court of Justice' (2009) 56 *Netherlands International Law Review* 397.

Y Tanaka, *The International Law of the Sea* 2nd edn (Cambridge University Press, 2015).

Y Tanaka, 'Article 74' in A Proelss (ed.), *United Nations Convention on the Law of the Sea – A Commentary* (Hart, 2017) 563.

Y Tanaka, 'Article 83' in A Proelss (ed.), *United Nations Convention on the Law of the Sea – A Commentary* (Hart, 2017) 651.

Y Tanaka, 'Reflections on the Interpretation and Application of Article 121(3) in the South China Sea Arbitration (Merits)' (2017) 48 *Ocean Development and International Law* 365.

Y Tanaka, *The Peaceful Settlement of International Disputes* (Cambridge University Press, 2018).

Y Tanaka, 'The Disproportionality Test in the Law of Maritime Delimitation' in A Oude Elferink et al. (eds.), *Maritime Boundary Delimitation – The Case Law: is it Consistent and Predictable?* (Cambridge University Press, 2018) 291.

GJ Tanja, *The Legal Determination of International Maritime Boundaries: the Progressive Development of Continental Shelf, EFZ and EEZ Law* (Kluwer, 1990).

J Tasioulas, 'In Defence of Relative Normativity: Communitarian Values and the *Nicaragua* Case' (1996) 16 *Oxford Journal of Legal Studies* 85.

VJM Tassin, 'L'Exploration et l'Exploitation des Ressources Naturelles du Plateau Continental à l'Heure de l'Extension au-delà des 200 milles marins' (2010) 15 *Annuaire du Droit de la Mer* 87.

P Tavernier, 'Observations sur le Droit Intertemporel dans l'*Affaire de l'Île de Kasikili/Sedudu (Botswana/Namibie)* Cour internationale de Justice: Arrêt du 13 décembre 1999' (2000) 104 *Revue Générale de Droit International Public* 429.

M They, 'Les suites du différend maritime opposant le Nicaragua et la Colombie: les arrêts rendus par la Cour internationale de Justice le 17 mars 2016 (exceptions préliminaires)' (2016) 62 *Annuaire Français de Droit International* 1.

H Thirlway, 'The Law and Procedure of the International Court of Justice 1960–1989 – Part Six' (1994) 65 *British Yearbook of International Law* 1.

H Thirlway, 'The Law and Procedure of the International Court of Justice 1960–1989 – Supplement, 2007: Parts Four, Five and Six' (2007) 78 *British Yearbook of International Law* 17.

H Thirlway, *The Sources of International Law* (Oxford University Press, 2014).

H Thirlway, *The International Court of Justice* (Oxford University Press, 2016).

H Thirlway, 'Territorial Disputes and Their Resolution in the Recent Jurisprudence of the International Court of Justice' (2018) 31 *Leiden Journal of International Law* 117.

S Torres Bernárdez, 'Provisional Measures and Interventions in Maritime Delimitation Disputes' in R Lagoni and D Vignes (eds.), *Maritime Delimitation* (Martinus Nijhoff, 2006) 33.

S Touzé, 'Affaire relative à la Délimitation Maritime en Mer Noire (Roumanie c. Ukraine): Une Clarification Didactique de la Règle de l'Équidistance-Circonstances Pertinentes' (2009) 55 *Annuaire Français de Droit International* 221.

T Treves, 'La Limite Extérieure du Plateau Continental: Evolution Récente de la Pratique' (1989) 35 *Annuaire Français de Droit International* 724.

T Treves, 'Codification du Droit International et Pratique des Etats dans le Droit de la Mer' (1990) 223 *Recueil des Cours* 9.

T Treves, 'What Have the United Nations Convention and the International Tribunal for the Law of the Sea to Offer As Regards Maritime Delimitation Disputes?' in R Lagoni and D Vignes (eds.), *Maritime Delimitation* (Martinus Nijhoff, 2006) 63.

T Treves, 'La Communauté Internationale et la Délimitation du Plateau Continental au-delà des 200 milles marins' in F Alabrune et al. (eds.), *L'Etat Souverain dans le Monde d'Aujourd'hui – Mélanges en l'Honneur de Jean-Pierre Puissochet* (Pédone, 2008) 311.

T Treves, 'Maritime Delimitation and Offshore Features' in S Jayakumar et al. (eds.), *The South China Sea Disputes and the Law of the Sea* (Edward Elgar, 2014) 121.

FA Vallat, 'The Continental Shelf' (1946) 23 *British Yearbook of International Law* 333.

C Van Bynkershoek, *Quaestionum Juris Publici Libri Duo* (Clarendon, 1930).

JM Van Dyke, 'Judge Shigeru Oda and Maritime Boundary Delimitation' in N Ando et al. (eds.), *Liber Amicorum Shigeru Oda* (Martinus Nijhoff, 2002) vol. II, 1197.

G Vega-Barbosa, 'The Admissibility of Outer Continental Shelf Delimitation Claims Before the ICJ Absent a Recommendation by the CLCS' (2018) 49 *Ocean Development and International Law* 103.

S Veierud Busch, 'The Delimitation of the Continental Shelf beyond 200 nm: Procedural Issues' in A Oude Elferink et al. (eds.), *Maritime Boundary Delimitation – The Case Law: Is It Consistent and Predictable?* (Cambridge University Press, 2018) 319.

D Vidas, 'Consolidation or Deviation? On Trends and Challenges in the Settlement of Maritime Delimitation Disputes by International Courts and Tribunals' in N Boschiero et al. (eds.), *International Courts and the Development of International Law – Essays in Honour of Tullio Treves* (Asser Press, 2013) 325.

D Vidas, 'The Delimitation of the Territorial Sea, the Continental Shelf, and the EEZ: A Comparative Perspective' in A Oude Elferink et al. (eds.), *Maritime Boundary Delimitation – The Case Law: Is It Consistent and Predictable?* (Cambridge University Press, 2018) 33.

M Virally, 'Panorama du Droit International Contemporain' (1983) 183 *Recueil des Cours* 9.

P Von Mühlendhal, 'L'Arrêt de la Cour Internationale de Justice dans l'Affaire de la Délimitation Maritime en Mer Noire (Roumanie c. Ukraine): l'Aboutissement d'un Processus vieux de Quarante Ans?' (2009) 22 *Revue Québécoise de Droit International* 1.

P Von Mühlendhal, 'Tiny Land Features in Recent Maritime Delimitation Case Law' (2016) 31 *International Journal of Marine and Coastal Law* 1.

P Von Mühlendahl, *L'Équidistance dans la Délimitation des Frontières Maritimes* (Pédone, 2016).

B Vukas, 'Maritime Delimitation in a Semi-enclosed Sea: The Case of the Adriatic Sea' in R Lagoni and D Vignes (eds.), *Maritime Delimitation* (Martinus Nijhoff, 2006) 205.

H Waldock, 'The Legal Basis of Claims to the Continental Shelf' (1951) 36 *Transactions of the Grotius Society* 115.

JS Warioba, 'Monitoring Compliance with and Enforcement of Binding Decisions of International Courts' (2001) 5 *Max Planck Yearbook of United Nations Law* 41.

P Weil, 'Vers une Normativité Relative en Droit International?' (1982) 86 *Revue Générale de Droit International Public* 5.

P Weil, *Perspectives du Droit de la Délimitation Maritime* (Pédone, 1988).

P Weil, 'Délimitation Maritime et Délimitation Terrestre' in Y Dinstein (ed.), *International Law at a Time of Perplexity – Essays in Honour of Shabtai Rosenne* (Martinus Nijhoff, 1989) 1021.

P Weil, 'Des Espaces Maritimes aux Territoires Maritimes: Vers un Conception Territorialiste de la Délimitation Maritime' in *Le Droit International au Service de la Paix, de la Justice et du Développement – Mélanges Michel Virally* (Pédone, 1991) 501.

P Weil, 'A propos la Double Fonction des Lignes et Points de Base dans le Droit de la Mer' in EG Bello and BA Ajibola (eds.), *Essays in Honour of Judge Taslim Olawale Elias* (Martinus Nijhoff, 1992) 145.

P Weil, 'Le Droit International en Quête de son Identité' (1992) 237 *Recueil des Cours* 9.

P Weil, '"The Court cannot Conclude Definitively ... " Non Liquet Revisited' (1998) 36 *Columbia Journal of Transnational Law* 109.

P Weil, 'Les Hauts-Fonds Découvrants dans la Délimitation Maritime' in N Ando et al. (eds.), *Liber Amicorum Shigeru Oda* (Martinus Nijhoff, 2002) vol. I, 307.

M Xiouri, 'Towards the Acceptance of the Equidistance Rule in the Delimitation of the Continental Shelf and the Exclusive Economic Zone' in P Pazartzis et al. (eds.), *Reconceptualising the Rule of Law in Global Governance, Resources, Investment and Trade* (Hart, 2016) 243.

C Yallourides, 'Calming the Waters in the West African Region: The Case of Ghana and Côte d'Ivoire' (2018) 26 *African Journal of International and Comparative Law* 507.

S Yanai, 'International Law concerning Maritime Boundary Delimitation' in M Fitzmaurice and NA Martínez Gutiérrez (eds.), *The IMLI Manual on International Maritime Law – Volume I: The Law of the Sea* (Oxford University Press, 2014) 304.

E Zoller, 'L'Affaire de la Délimitation du Plateau Continental entre la République Française et le Royaume-Uni de Grande Bretagne et d'Irlande du Nord (Décision du 30 Juin 1977)' (1977) 23 *Annuaire Français de Droit International* 359.

E Zoller, 'Recherche sur les Méthodes de Délimitation du Plateau Continental: à Propos de l'Affaire Tunisie-Libye (Arrêt du 24 Février 1982)' (1982) 86 *Revue Générale de Droit International Public* 645.

INDEX

Adjustment, 235–44
Advisory Committee of Jurists (1920), 301, 305
  Non liquet, 302
  Root-Phillimore Plan, 302
Alleged Violations of Sovereign Rights and Maritime Spaces in the Caribbean Sea, 56, 320
Angle-bisector, 21, 39, 50, 129, 163, 267, 316
Anglo/French Arbitration, 18, 146, 147
  Effect of islands, 178, 186
  Navigation, 204
  Proportionality, 261
  Security, 207
Archipelagic baselines, 55, 144
Arcs of circle, 73

Bangladesh v. India, 22, 23, 28, 41, 42, 44, 47, 48, 52, 71, 77, 79, 84, 129, 133, 136, 146, 151, 250
  Adjustment of the provisional equidistance line, 178, 234, 239
  Angle-bisector, 163, 316
  Application of radial projections, 79
  Coastal instability, 163–5
  Commission on the Limits of the Continental Shelf, 95
  Cut-off effect, 172, 177, 225
  Disproportionality, 279
  Dissenting opinion by PS Rao, 140
  Exceptional character of, 139
  Grey Area, 135, 140
  Joint development zone, 143
  Low-tide elevations, 149, 164
  Most natural prolongation argument, 223
  Relevant area, 82
  Site visit, 164

Bangladesh/Myanmar, 22, 42, 44, 46, 48, 49, 52, 53, 86, 90, 100, 128, 133, 135, 143, 168, 250, 311, 312
  Adjustment of the provisional equidistance line, 177, 234, 239
  Angle-bisector, 316
  Commission on the Limits of the Continental Shelf, 95
  Compliance, 319
  Cut-off effect, 172, 177, 225
  Disproportionality, 279
  Exceptional character of, 139
  Geomorphology, 222
  Grey Area, 135, 140
  Identification of relevant area by parallels and meridians, 91
  Joint development zone, 143
  Most natural prolongation argument, 223
  Relevant area, 82
  Rights of third states, 220
  St Martin's Island, 146, 153, 184
Barbados v. Trinidad and Tobago, 20, 76, 249
  Access to natural resources, 199
  Coastal length disparity, 176
  Conduct, 214
  Cut-off effect, 170
  Effect of islands, 189
  Pleadings, 314
  Proportionality, 264
Base points, 122
  Appropriateness of, 145
  Islands as, 24, 150–6
  Low-tide elevations, 144, 147–50, 164
  Relevant coast, relationship to, 156–65

Base points (cont.)
    Selection of, 6, 24, 47, 109, 123, 133, 144–50
    Subjectivity in the selection of, 145
Basis of title, 6, 7, 30–2
    As a means to ensure objectivity, 32
    As the foundation of the three-stage approach, 32
    Connection with delimitation, 30, 108
    Continental shelf, 4, 103, 105–9
    Continental shelf beyond 200 nm, 41, 42, 103, 130–5
    Distance from the coast, 41, 42, 105, 106, 108, 109, 131
    Exclusive Economic Zone, 4, 103, 104–5
    Land boundary demarcation, 31
    Natural prolongation, 106, 107, 115
    Relationship with *effectivités*, 31
    Relevant circumstances, 167, 168
    Territorial sea, 4
    Tunisia/Libya, 82
    Uti possidetis juris, 31
Beagle Channel Arbitration, 241
Navigation, 202
Black Sea, 1, 21, 28, 29, 34, 41, 48, 52, 59, 62, 63, 79, 84, 121, 249, 311
    Adjustment of the provisional equidistance line, 236
    Base points, 145, 153
    Coastal length disparity, 176
    Cut-off effect, 170
    Difference from *Gulf of Maine*, 59
    Disproportionality, 246, 264, 274
    Internal waters, 61, 62
    Karkinits'ka Gulf, 59, 62, 63, 79
    Pleadings, 315
    Rights of third states, 219
    Security, 209
    Serpents' Island, 153, 155, 184
    Straight baselines, 61

Cameroon v. Nigeria, 20, 39
    Coastal length disparity, 176
    Compliance, 318, 321
    Conduct, 213
    Cut-off effect, 170
    Pleadings, 314
    Proportionality, 264
    Rights of third states, 219
Channel Islands, 19, 178
Charter of the United Nations, 305
Coastal instability, 21, 122, 156, 161–5
Coastal length disparity
    Relationship to Disproportionality, 280–7
Commission on the Limits of the Continental Shelf, 95, 96, 98, 131, 139, 279
    Relationship between delineation and delimitation, 95–8
Completeness of international law, 294
    Fitzmaurice, 296
    Hart, 295
    Kelsen, 297
    Lauterpacht, 297
    Non liquet, 294
    Not 'complete' but 'completed', 298
    Role of international tribunals, 298
    Siorat, 300
    Weil, 295
Compliance, 25
    Conclusion of delimitation treaty, 317
    Creation of an *ad hoc* commission, 318
Continental shelf, 2
    Basis of title, 105–9
    Basis of title beyond 200 nm, 131
    Beyond 200 nm, 41–3, 95–8, 128–43
    Effet utile of, 112
    Existence *ipso facto* and *ab initio*, 112, 114, 131, 138
    Incorporation into the Exclusive Economic Zone, 109, 114
    Ipso jure rights over the, 105
    Relationship to the Exclusive Economic Zone, 103, 109–21, 140
    Treaties delimiting the, 116–21
    Truman Proclamation (1945), 105, 206

INDEX

Convention on the Continental Shelf (1958), 9
  Article 1, 105, 106, 107
  Article 2, 105
  Article 3, 114
  Article 6, 13, 14, 18, 20, 102, 175, 186, 202, 204, 261, 314
Convention on the Territorial Sea and the Contiguous Zone (1958), 102
Corn Islands
  Costa Rica v. *Nicaragua*, 153, 188
  Nicaragua v. *Colombia* (2012), 46, 156
Costa Rica v. *Nicaragua*, 5, 47, 49, 54, 63, 69–72, 92, 100
  Area of overlapping entitlements, 69
  Base points, 153
  Compliance, 319
  Cut-off effect, 171
  Effect of islands, 188
  Implicit acceptance of radial projections, 76
  Land boundary terminus, 195
  Nicoya Gulf, 63
  Nicoya Peninsula, 70
  Objective treaty regimes, 87
  Radial projections, 69
  Santa Elena Peninsula, 171
Croatia/Slovenia, 4
Customary international law, 2, 7, 14, 20, 43, 107

Delimitation
  Absence of a 'right answer', 233
  Academic commentary, 27–8
  Adjacent coasts, 14, 71
  Agreement, primacy of, 17
  As a process, 24–6
  As a single operation, 24
  Case-by-case approach, 17, 24
  Common law of, 26
  Convention on the Continental Shelf (1958), 13
  Definition of, 34
  Equitable principles, 9, 10, 15, 16, 18, 102

Equitable solution, 25, 27, 30, 64, 81, 103, 109, 121, 233, 243
  Lack of customary rules of international law, 293
  Opposite coasts, 13, 71
  Relationship to delineation, 97, 138
  Straits, 11
  Territorial sea, 2–5, 21, 102
  Three time periods, 17
  Three-stage approach, 21–3, 24
    Presumption in favour of, 23
  Treaties, 116, 136
  Two-stage approach, 20–1, 24
Dhalaks, 151, 191
Disproportionality, 3, 7, 21, 24, 26, 30, 65, 81, 173, 198
  As a delimitation method, 252–3
  As a discretionary assessment, 274
  As a relevant circumstance, 261
  As a test of equitableness, 262, 263–7
  Assessment by international tribunals, 267–75
  Coastal configuration, impact of, 7, 275–80
  Continental shelf beyond 200 nm, 259–60, 278
  Criticism to its application between opposite coasts, 277
  De Azcárraga, 252
  Difference from proportionality, 248–52
  Function in maritime delimitation, 7, 260–7
  In angle-bisector delimitations, 268–70
  Inapplicability as between adjacent coasts, 276
  Independent of coastal length disparity, 286
  Legal basis, 7
  Link to natural law doctrine, 258
  Mathematical assessment, 270–5
  Modest calling of, 288
  Original lack of legal basis, 253–9
  raison d'être, 275
  Relationship to coastal length disparity, 7, 280–7
  Vallat, 252

Draft Articles on the Law of the Sea
 (1956), 12, 106, 114, 197
Dubai/Sharjah
 Effect of islands, 181
Dumbarton Oaks Conference, 305, 306

*El Salvador/Honduras (Nicaragua
 intervening)*, 307
Enclaving, 19, 124
Envelope of arcs method, 73
Equidistance, 14
 As a starting point in delimitation,
  32, 109, 115
 Base points, selection of, 6, 24,
  47, 109
 Basis of title, connection with,
  103, 104
 Basis of title, consistency with, 109
 Coastal configuration, effect of, 103
 Coastal instability, effect of, 161–5
 Compelling reasons not to use, 23,
  109, 121, 126, 161
 Continental shelf, 13
 Continental shelf beyond 200 nm,
  128–43
 Definition of, 102
 Draft Articles on the Law of the Sea
  (1956), 12
 Grey Area, 135–43
 Innapropriateness of, 23
 League of Nations Codification
  Conference (1930), 11, 102
 Modified equidistance line, 308
 Simplified equidistance line, 308
 Strict equidistance line, 308
 Third United Nations Conference on
  the Law of the Sea
  (1973–1982), 15
Equitable principles, 9, 10, 15, 16,
 18, 102
Equitable solution, 25, 27, 30, 64, 81,
 103, 109, 121, 127
Eritrea/Yemen, 20, 71, 151, 249
 Effect of islands, 183, 191
 Relevant area, 82
 Rights of third states, 218
Exclusive Economic Zone, 2
 Basis of title, 104–5, 109

 Declaration of, 105, 109
 Incorporation of the Continental
  shelf, 109, 114
 Relationship to the Continental shelf,
  103, 109–21, 140
 Treaties delimiting the, 116–21

Fishery Zone, 20, 119, 175, 200
Frontal projections, 62, 63, 73, 190
 General direction of the coast, 77
 Implemented by parallels of
  latitude, 91
 Tracé parallèle, 74
Function of maritime zones, 7
 Continental shelf, 4
 Exclusive Economic Zone, 4
 Relevant circumstances, 168, 195
 Territorial sea, 4

Georges Bank, 197
Ghana/Côte d'Ivoire, 3, 42, 47, 90, 91,
 98, 126, 127, 130, 312
 Angle-bisector, 316
 Coastal instability, 164
 Commission on the Limits of the
  Continental Shelf, 95
 Compliance, 319
 Conduct, 214
 Cut-off effect, 170
 Land boundary terminus, 194
 Pleadings, 316
 Grey Area, 135–43
 Judicial function, effect on, 141
 Relationship between the Exclusive
  Economic Zone and the
  continental shelf, 140–3
Grisbådarna Arbitration, 197
Guinea/Guinea-Bissau, 18, 39
 Access to natural resources, 198
 Effect of islands, 182, 190
 Land boundary terminus, 193
 Proportionality, 261, 269
 Security, 208
Gulf of Maine, 41, 56, 61, 63, 79,
 146, 248
 Access to natural resources, 197
 Bay of Fundy, 56, 57, 62, 63, 64, 79
 Coastal length disparity, 173

INDEX

Compliance, 318
Conduct, 212
Difference from *Black Sea*, 61
Effect of islands, 187
Internal waters, 57, 62
Land boundary terminus, 193
Pleadings, 313
Proportionality, 262
Relationship between proportionality and coastal length disparity, 280
Security, 208
Straight baselines, 62
Guyana v. Suriname, 20, 241
Land boundary terminus, 194
Navigation, 202
Pleadings, 314
Proportionality, 264

International Court of Justice, 1, 5, 14, 20, 21, 25, 30, 34, 37, 39, 42, 45, 46, 48, 54, 56, 59, 63, 66, 69, 74, 77, 81, 83, 84, 87, 97, 100, 103, 106, 114, 122, 145, 148, 152, 157, 162, 167, 171, 174, 179, 182, 183, 187, 193, 202, 207, 212, 217, 227, 239, 246, 254, 261, 293, 306
Benin/Niger Chamber, 31
El Salvador/Honduras Chamber, 307
Gulf of Maine Chamber, 56, 63, 146, 173, 187, 194, 198, 208, 248, 262
International Law Commission, 12, 87, 106, 197, 201, 253, 292
International Tribunal for the Law of the Sea, 3, 22, 42, 44, 46, 49, 53, 66, 86, 90, 95, 100, 128, 134, 135, 140, 146, 153, 168, 172, 177, 185, 220, 222, 239, 307
Special Chamber, 3, 42, 47, 90, 91, 95, 126, 130, 164, 194, 214
International tribunals
Filling the gaps left by states, 294
Interaction with states, 321–2
Law-making function, 7, 17, 290, 291–308
Non liquet, 294
Irrelevant circumstances, 7

Jan Mayen, 20, 24, 40, 45, 48, 66, 67
Access to natural resources, 200
Coastal length disparity, 174
Compliance, 318
Conduct, 212
Effect of islands, 190
Pleadings, 313
Proportionality, 263
Security, 209
Separate opinion of Judge Schwebel, 232
Separate opinion of Judge Shahabuddeen, 284–6
Joint development zone, 143
Jurisdictional Immunities of the State, 293

Kerkennah Islands, 187

Lacunae in international law, 300
League of Nations, 301
League of Nations Codification Conference (1930), 9, 10–12, 102
Libya/Malta, 30, 40, 42, 45, 114, 249
Adjustment of the provisional equidistance line, 239
Basis of title, 230
Coastal length disparity, 174
Compliance, 318
Effect of islands, 188
Intervention by Italy (1984), 217
Navigation, 202
Pleadings, 313
Proportionality, 262
Relationship between proportionality and coastal length disparity, 280
Rights of third states, 217
Security, 209
Separate opinion of Judge ad hoc Valticos, 277
Low-tide elevations, 144, 164

Median line. *See* Equidistance
Meeting of the states parties to UNCLOS, 311, 312
Modus vivendi, 211, 212

INDEX

Newfoundland and Labrador/Nova Scotia Arbitration, 282
Nicaragua v. Colombia (2012), 22, 25, 40, 46, 48, 52, 66, 70, 79, 83, 84, 121, 124–5, 126
   Adjustment of the provisional equidistance line, 240
   Base points, 146, 152, 156
   Coastal length disparity, 176
   Commission on the Limits of the Continental Shelf, 96
   Conduct, 215
   Cut-off effect, 171
   Disproportionality, 250, 287
   Effect of islands, 179
   Lack of compliance, 319
   Pleadings, 315, 316
   Preliminary objections (2007), 215
   Punta de Perlas, 79
   Relevant coast, 156
   Rights of third states, 220
   Security, 209
   Separate opinion of Judge Abraham, 159–61
   Weighing relevant circumstances, 234
Nicaragua v. Colombia (2016)
   Commission on the Limits of the Continental Shelf, 96
Nicaragua v. Honduras, 20, 28, 72, 77, 121, 122–4, 126
   Coastal instability, 161–3
   Land boundary terminus, 194
   Pleadings, 314
   Proportionality, 267
   Rights of third states, 219
Non liquet, 294, 296, 297, 298
North Sea Continental Shelf, 1, 7, 9, 14–15, 29, 37, 55, 103, 106, 107, 167, 227
   Compliance, 318
   Cut-off effect, 169
   Navigation, 202
   Proportionality, 254, 261
   Security, 207
   Weighing relevant circumstances, 232
Nova Scotia, 187

Objectivity, 19, 25, 27, 125, 127
Open texture, 295

Pact of Bogotá, 320
Permanent Court of International Justice, 301
Peru v. Chile, 28, 72, 74, 83, 90, 92, 249
   Compliance, 319
   Conduct, 216
   Disproportionality, 265, 270
   Envelope of arcs, 76
   Implicit acceptance of radial projections, 76
   Land boundary terminus, 194
   Peru's second submission, 76
   Presence of an 80-nm agreed boundary, 92
   Tacit agreement, 216
   Tracé parallèle, 74
Predictability. *See* Objectivity
Proportionality. *See* Disproportionality
Provisional equidistance line, 3, 6, 20, 25
   Adjustment of, 26, 30, 64, 123, 124, 127, 235–44
   As an objective exercise, 30
   Base points, selection of, 133, 144–50
   Coastal configuration, impact of, 6
   Construction of, 6, 143–65
   Continental shelf beyond 200 nm, 6
   Islands as base points, 24, 150–6

Qatar v. Bahrain, 20, 56, 148, 152, 231
   Compliance, 319
   Effect of islands, 183, 189
   Pleadings, 314
   Proportionality, 264
   Rights of third states, 219

Radial projections, 40, 62, 63, 69, 73
   Application by international tribunals, 76–81
   Arcs of circle, 73
   Bangladesh v. India, 80
   Effect on predictability in delimitation, 80
   Envelope of arcs, 73

Implicit acceptance of, 76
Limits of, 80
Practical justification of, 73
Rare endorsement by international tribunals, 76
Use in identifying the limits of the relevant area, 93
Relevant area, 6, 24, 25
  Area of overlapping claims, 66
  Area of overlapping entitlements, 66
  As an objective exercise, 30
  Coastal configuration, effect of, 71
  Coasts facing the open sea, 90–3
  Costa Rica v. *Nicaragua*, 69–72
  Delimitation beyond 200 nm, 95–8
  Discretion in the identification of, 72
  Disproportionality, effect on, 81
  Elusive definition of, 65–9
  Fourth stage, 6, 99
  Identification by parallels and meridians, 91
  Identity with the area of overlapping entitlements, 71
  Impact of existing delimitation treaties, 86
  Inconsistency in the identification of, 65
  Lack of objectivity in the definition of, 69
  Limits imposed by UNCLOS, 81
  Objective treaty regimes, 87–90
  Objectivity in the identification of, 70
  Outer limits, 82
  Pre-existing boundaries as limits of, 84–90
  Radial projections, 73
  Subjectivity in the identification of, 72
  Tracé parallèle, 91
  Tripartite distinction in *Jan Mayen*, 66, 71
Relevant circumstances, 3, 4, 5, 6, 18, 25, 26, 109, 125
  Access to natural resources, 25, 195–201
    Catastrophic repercussions test, 198, 199, 200
    Test for overall equitableness of the boundary, 198
  Adjustment of the provisional equidistance line, 235–44
    Arbitrariness of, 236
    Limited character of, 240
    Methods of adjustment, 239–44
  Basis of title, 167, 168
  Coastal length disparity, 24, 50, 64, 65, 173–8
    Adjacent coasts, 176, 177
    Delimitation beyond 200 nm, 177
    Opposite coasts, 177
  Conduct, 211–17
  Cut-off effect, 168–73
    Concavity, 169
    Delimitation beyond 200 nm, 172
    Non-encroachment, 169
    Opposite coasts, 171
    Relationship to enclavement of islands, 170
  Double function of, 229
  Dual 'title-function' basis, 7, 168, 230, 232, 233
  Effect of islands, 24, 178–92
    Enclavement, 178–81
    Full effect, 188–92
    Human geography factors, 179, 181, 191
    Island as part of the coast, 190
    Island states, 188
    Islands far from mainland, 189
  Effect of Islands, 24, 178–92
    No effect, 181–6
  Function of maritime zones, 168, 195
  Geomorphology, 221–7
    Approach of states to delimitation beyond 200 nm, 226
    Most natural prolongation argument, 223
  Identification of, 227–32
    Evans, 227
    Limiting the list of relevant circumstances, 227
    Tanaka, 229
    Weil, 229
  Irrelevant circumstances, 210–27

Relevant circumstances (cont.)
  Land boundary terminus, 193–5
  Navigation, 201–5
  Continental shelf, 203, 205
  Exclusive Economic Zone, 204, 205
  International Law Commission, 201
  Rights of third states, 217–21
  Security, 25, 205–10
  Weighing process, 232–5
  Dual 'title-function' basis, 233
  Irrelevant in practice, 235
  Remnant of case-by-case approach, 235
  Subjectivity of, 232
  Tanaka, 233
Relevant coast, 6, 24, 25
  Angle-bisector boundaries, 39
  Approximation, 48–56
  Approximation by reference to straight baselines, 52, 82
  As an objective exercise, 30
  Coast of bays and inlets, 56–65
  Coast of third states, exclusion of, 38
  Coastal length disparity, effect on, 38, 50, 64
  Consistency with the basis of title, 40
  Continental shelf beyond 200 nm, 41
  Discretion to approximate, 49, 50, 56
  Disproportionality, effect on, 38, 50
  Fourth stage, 6, 99
  Identification of, 43–65
  Land boundary terminus, 45
  Margin of appreciation in identifying the, 80
  Most distant base points, 44–8
  Natural configuration, 48
  Numerical value, 38
  Objective standard for identification, 44
  Radial projections, 40
  Reduction to a single point, 64
  Selection of base points, effect on, 38, 156–65
  Source of maritime entitlements, 37
Res inter alios acta, 86, 88
Res judicata, 88, 306

San Francisco Conference. *See* United Nations Conference on International Organization (1945)
Scilly Isles, 19, 186
Seal Island, 187
Somalia v. Kenya
  Merits (pending), 323
  Relationship between delineation and delimitation, 97, 139
Sources of international law, 7
  Article 38 of the ICJ's Statute, 8, 23
  Customary international law, 290, 292
    Delimitation by convenience, 293
    Drafting history of delimitation treaties, 293
    Lack of evidence of *opinio juris* on the delimitation process, 293
  Judicial decisions, 8
  Treaties, 290
South China Sea Arbitration, 150
Special circumstances, 20
  Continental shelf, 12, 13, 175, 186
  Territorial sea, 3, 4, 5, 123, 125
St Pierre et Miquelon, 77, 249
  Access to natural resources, 199
  Cut-off effect, 169
  Dissenting opinion of Prosper Weil, 77
  Effect of islands, 189, 191
  Proportionality, 262
  Use of frontal projections, 77
States, 7, 116
  Approach to the delimitation process, 308–21
    Compliance with judicial decisions on delimitation, 317–21
    Delimitation treaties, 308–10
    Pleadings, 312–17
    Statements in multilateral fora, 311–12
  Compliance with judicial decisions on delimitation, 8, 25
  Delimitation treaties, 8, 136
  Interaction with international tribunals, 321–2

INDEX

Judicial development, sanction of, 8, 26, 291
Pleadings, 8, 136
Statements on the international plane, 8
Statute of the International Court of Justice
  Article 38, 8, 23, 291, 297, 301, 306
  Article 59, 220, 304, 306
  Drafting history, 301–8
Statute of the International Tribunal for the Law of the Sea
  Article 33, 220
Straight baselines, 52, 55, 61, 147, 151, 152, 155
  Basis of title, consistency with, 56
  Legal coast and natural coast, 52, 61
  Objections to, 53, 54
Straits, 11, 102

Territorial sea, 2, 11
  Two-stage approach, 3, 125
The land dominates the sea, 35, 37, 105
Third United Nations Conference on the Law of the Sea (1973–1982), 9, 10, 15–17, 102, 138, 139, 257, 322
Tracé parallèle, 74
Tripolitanian Furrow, 224
Truman Proclamation (1945), 105, 206, 252
Tunisia/Libya, 18, 57, 81
  Compliance, 318
  Conduct, 211
  Effect of islands, 182, 187
  Gulf of Gabes, 57
  Inconsistency with the basis of title, 82
  Internal waters, 82
  Land boundary terminus, 193
  Proportionality, 262
  Special agreement, 313

UNCLOS, 1, 9
  Article 7, 52, 53, 54, 55, 56, 61, 82, 147, 149, 151, 152, 155
  Article 11, 145
  Article 13, 144, 147, 149
  Article 15, 2, 3, 102, 123, 144, 241
  Article 17, 203
  Article 47, 55, 145
  Article 56, 104, 110, 111–12, 116
  Article 57, 83, 104, 132
  Article 58, 113, 205
  Article 60, 113, 205
  Article 74, 2, 3, 16, 23, 25, 27, 103, 136, 211, 216, 217, 228, 233, 235, 241, 243, 289, 298, 300, 312
  Article 76, 41, 42, 83, 96, 97, 107, 108, 111, 113, 130–1, 132, 134, 138, 139, 140, 223, 224, 239, 259, 279
  Article 78, 114, 205
  Article 80, 113, 114, 205
  Article 83, 2, 3, 16, 23, 25, 27, 103, 136, 211, 216, 217, 222, 224, 228, 233, 235, 241, 243, 289, 298, 300, 312
  Article 111, 205
  Article 121, 179, 188, 231, 239
  Customary international law, 43
  Drafting history, 16–17, 102, 108, 112, 206
UNCLOS I. *See* United Nations Conference on the Law of the Sea (1958)
UNCLOS III. *See* Third United Nations Conference on the Law of the Sea (1973–1982)
United Nations Conference on International Organization (1945), 304, 305
United Nations Conference on the Law of the Sea (1958), 12–14
Ushant, 186

Vagueness, 17, 23, 103, 136, 290
  Article 74 UNCLOS, 7
  Article 83 UNCLOS, 7
Vienna Convention on the Law of Treaties, 86, 88

CAMBRIDGE STUDIES IN INTERNATIONAL AND
COMPARATIVE LAW

Books in the Series

145 *Comparative Reasoning in International Courts and Tribunals*
    Daniel Peat
144 *Maritime Delimitation as a Judicial Process*
    Massimo Lando
143 *Prosecuting Sexual and Gender-Based Crimes at the International Criminal Court: Practice, Progress and Potential*
    Rosemary Grey
142 *Narratives of Hunger in International Law: Feeding the World in Times of Climate Change*
    Anne Saab
141 *Sovereignty in China: A Genealogy of a Concept Since 1840*
    Adele Carrai
140 *Narratives of Hunger: Climate-Ready Seeds and International Law*
    Anne Saab
139 *Victim Reparation under the Ius Post Bellum: An Historical and Normative Perspective*
    Shavana Musa
138 *The Analogy between States and International Organizations*
    Fernando Lusa Bordin
137 *The Process of International Legal Reproduction: Inequality, Historiography, Resistance*
    Rose Parfitt
136 *State Responsibility for Breaches of Investment Contracts*
    Jean Ho
135 *Coalitions of the Willing and International Law: The Interplay between Formality and Informality*
    Alejandro Rodiles
134 *Self-Determination in Disputed Colonial Territories*
    Jamie Trinidad
133 *International Law as a Belief System*
    Jean d'Aspremont
132 *Legal Consequences of Peremptory Norms in International Law*
    Daniel Costelloe
131 *Third-Party Countermeasures in International Law*
    Martin Dawidowicz

130 *Justification and Excuse in International Law: Concept and Theory of General Defences*
   Federica Paddeu
129 *Exclusion from Public Space: A Comparative Constitutional Analysis*
   Daniel Moeckli
128 *Provisional Measures before International Courts and Tribunals*
   Cameron A. Miles
127 *Humanity at Sea: Maritime Migration and the Foundations of International Law*
   Itamar Mann
126 *Beyond Human Rights: The Legal Status of the Individual in International Law*
   Anne Peters
125 *The Doctrine of Odious Debt in International Law: A Restatement*
   Jeff King
124 *Static and Evolutive Treaty Interpretation: A Functional Reconstruction*
   Christian Djeffal
123 *Civil Liability in Europe for Terrorism-Related Risk*
   Lucas Bergkamp, Michael Faure, Monika Hinteregger and Niels Philipsen
122 *Proportionality and Deference in Investor-State Arbitration: Balancing Investment Protection and Regulatory Autonomy*
   Caroline Henckels
121 *International Law and Governance of Natural Resources in Conflict and Post-Conflict Situations*
   Daniëlla Dam-de Jong
120 *Proof of Causation in Tort Law*
   Sandy Steel
119 *The Formation and Identification of Rules of Customary International Law in International Investment Law*
   Patrick Dumberry
118 *Religious Hatred and International Law: The Prohibition of Incitement to Violence or Discrimination*
   Jeroen Temperman
117 *Taking Economic, Social and Cultural Rights Seriously in International Criminal Law*
   Evelyne Schmid
116 *Climate Change Litigation: Regulatory Pathways to Cleaner Energy*
   Jacqueline Peel and Hari M. Osofsky
115 *Mestizo International Law: A Global Intellectual History 1842–1933*
   Arnulf Becker Lorca
114 *Sugar and the Making of International Trade Law*
   Michael Fakhri

113 *Strategically Created Treaty Conflicts and the Politics of International Law*
Surabhi Ranganathan
112 *Investment Treaty Arbitration As Public International Law: Procedural Aspects and Implications*
Eric De Brabandere
111 *The New Entrants Problem in International Fisheries Law*
Andrew Serdy
110 *Substantive Protection under Investment Treaties: A Legal and Economic Analysis*
Jonathan Bonnitcha
109 *Popular Governance of Post-Conflict Reconstruction: The Role of International Law*
Matthew Saul
108 *Evolution of International Environmental Regimes: The Case of Climate Change*
Simone Schiele
107 *Judges, Law and War: The Judicial Development of International Humanitarian Law*
Shane Darcy
106 *Religious Offence and Human Rights: The Implications of Defamation of Religions*
Lorenz Langer
105 *Forum Shopping in International Adjudication: The Role of Preliminary Objections*
Luiz Eduardo Salles
104 *Domestic Politics and International Human Rights Tribunals: The Problem of Compliance*
Courtney Hillebrecht
103 *International Law and the Arctic*
Michael Byers
102 *Cooperation in the Law of Transboundary Water Resources*
Christina Leb
101 *Underwater Cultural Heritage and International Law*
Sarah Dromgoole
100 *State Responsibility: The General Part*
James Crawford
99 *The Origins of International Investment Law: Empire, Environment and the Safeguarding of Capital*
Kate Miles
98 *The Crime of Aggression under the Rome Statute of the International Criminal Court*
Carrie McDougall

97 *'Crimes against Peace' and International Law*
   Kirsten Sellars
96 *Non-Legality in International Law: Unruly Law*
   Fleur Johns
95 *Armed Conflict and Displacement: The Protection of Refugees and Displaced Persons under International Humanitarian Law*
   Mélanie Jacques
94 *Foreign Investment and the Environment in International Law*
   Jorge E. Viñuales
93 *The Human Rights Treaty Obligations of Peacekeepers*
   Kjetil Mujezinović Larsen
92 *Cyber Warfare and the Laws of War*
   Heather Harrison Dinniss
91 *The Right to Reparation in International Law for Victims of Armed Conflict*
   Christine Evans
90 *Global Public Interest in International Investment Law*
   Andreas Kulick
89 *State Immunity in International Law*
   Xiaodong Yang
88 *Reparations and Victim Support in the International Criminal Court*
   Conor McCarthy
87 *Reducing Genocide to Law: Definition, Meaning, and the Ultimate Crime*
   Payam Akhavan
86 *Decolonising International Law: Development, Economic Growth and the Politics of Universality*
   Sundhya Pahuja
85 *Complicity and the Law of State Responsibility*
   Helmut Philipp Aust
84 *State Control over Private Military and Security Companies in Armed Conflict*
   Hannah Tonkin
83 *'Fair and Equitable Treatment' in International Investment Law*
   Roland Kläger
82 *The UN and Human Rights: Who Guards the Guardians?*
   Guglielmo Verdirame
81 *Sovereign Defaults before International Courts and Tribunals*
   Michael Waibel
80 *Making the Law of the Sea: A Study in the Development of International Law*
   James Harrison
79 *Science and the Precautionary Principle in International Courts and Tribunals: Expert Evidence, Burden of Proof and Finality*
   Caroline E. Foster

78 *Transition from Illegal Regimes in International Law*
   Yaël Ronen
77 *Access to Asylum: International Refugee Law and the Globalisation of Migration Control*
   Thomas Gammeltoft-Hansen
76 *Trading Fish, Saving Fish: The Interaction between Regimes in International Law*
   Margaret A. Young
75 *The Individual in the International Legal System: Continuity and Change in International Law*
   Kate Parlett
74 *'Armed Attack' and Article 51 of the UN Charter: Evolutions in Customary Law and Practice*
   Tom Ruys
73 *Theatre of the Rule of Law: Transnational Legal Intervention in Theory and Practice*
   Stephen Humphreys
72 *Science and Risk Regulation in International Law*
   Jacqueline Peel
71 *The Participation of States in International Organisations: The Role of Human Rights and Democracy*
   Alison Duxbury
70 *Legal Personality in International Law*
   Roland Portmann
69 *Vicarious Liability in Tort: A Comparative Perspective*
   Paula Giliker
68 *The Public International Law Theory of Hans Kelsen: Believing in Universal Law*
   Jochen von Bernstorff
67 *Legitimacy and Legality in International Law: An Interactional Account*
   Jutta Brunnée and Stephen J. Toope
66 *The Concept of Non-International Armed Conflict in International Humanitarian Law*
   Anthony Cullen
65 *The Principle of Legality in International and Comparative Criminal Law*
   Kenneth S. Gallant
64 *The Challenge of Child Labour in International Law*
   Franziska Humbert
63 *Shipping Interdiction and the Law of the Sea*
   Douglas Guilfoyle
62 *International Courts and Environmental Protection*
   Tim Stephens

61 *Legal Principles in WTO Disputes*
   Andrew D. Mitchell
60 *War Crimes in Internal Armed Conflicts*
   Eve La Haye
59 *Humanitarian Occupation*
   Gregory H. Fox
58 *The International Law of Environmental Impact Assessment: Process, Substance and Integration*
   Neil Craik
57 *The Law and Practice of International Territorial Administration: Versailles to Iraq and Beyond*
   Carsten Stahn
56 *United Nations Sanctions and the Rule of Law*
   Jeremy Matam Farrall
55 *National Law in WTO Law: Effectiveness and Good Governance in the World Trading System*
   Sharif Bhuiyan
54 *Cultural Products and the World Trade Organization*
   Tania Voon
53 *The Threat of Force in International Law*
   Nikolas Stürchler
52 *Indigenous Rights and United Nations Standards: Self-Determination, Culture and Land*
   Alexandra Xanthaki
51 *International Refugee Law and Socio-Economic Rights: Refuge from Deprivation*
   Michelle Foster
50 *The Protection of Cultural Property in Armed Conflict*
   Roger O'Keefe
49 *Interpretation and Revision of International Boundary Decisions*
   Kaiyan Homi Kaikobad
48 *Multinationals and Corporate Social Responsibility: Limitations and Opportunities in International Law*
   Jennifer A. Zerk
47 *Judiciaries within Europe: A Comparative Review*
   John Bell
46 *Law in Times of Crisis: Emergency Powers in Theory and Practice*
   Oren Gross and Fionnuala Ní Aoláin
45 *Vessel-Source Marine Pollution: The Law and Politics of International Regulation*
   Alan Khee-Jin Tan
44 *Enforcing Obligations Erga Omnes in International Law*
   Christian J. Tams

43 *Non-Governmental Organisations in International Law*
    Anna-Karin Lindblom
42 *Democracy, Minorities and International Law*
    Steven Wheatley
41 *Prosecuting International Crimes: Selectivity and the International Criminal Law Regime*
    Robert Cryer
40 *Compensation for Personal Injury in English, German and Italian Law: A Comparative Outline*
    Basil Markesinis, Michael Coester, Guido Alpa and Augustus Ullstein
39 *Dispute Settlement in the UN Convention on the Law of the Sea*
    Natalie Klein
38 *The International Protection of Internally Displaced Persons*
    Catherine Phuong
37 *Imperialism, Sovereignty and the Making of International Law*
    Antony Anghie
35 *Necessity, Proportionality and the Use of Force by States*
    Judith Gardam
34 *International Legal Argument in the Permanent Court of International Justice: The Rise of the International Judiciary*
    Ole Spiermann
32 *Great Powers and Outlaw States: Unequal Sovereigns in the International Legal Order*
    Gerry Simpson
31 *Local Remedies in International Law (second edition)*
    Chittharanjan Felix Amerasinghe
30 *Reading Humanitarian Intervention: Human Rights and the Use of Force in International Law*
    Anne Orford
29 *Conflict of Norms in Public International Law: How WTO Law Relates to Other Rules of International Law*
    Joost Pauwelyn
27 *Transboundary Damage in International Law*
    Hanqin Xue
25 *European Criminal Procedures*
    Edited by Mireille Delmas-Marty and J. R. Spencer
24 *Accountability of Armed Opposition Groups in International Law*
    Liesbeth Zegveld
23 *Sharing Transboundary Resources: International Law and Optimal Resource Use*
    Eyal Benvenisti

22 *International Human Rights and Humanitarian Law*
   René Provost
21 *Remedies against International Organisations*
   Karel Wellens
20 *Diversity and Self-Determination in International Law*
   Karen Knop
19 *The Law of Internal Armed Conflict*
   Lindsay Moir
18 *International Commercial Arbitration and African States: Practice, Participation and Institutional Development*
   Amazu A. Asouzu
17 *The Enforceability of Promises in European Contract Law*
   James Gordley
16 *International Law in Antiquity*
   David J. Bederman
15 *Money Laundering: A New International Law Enforcement Model*
   Guy Stessens
14 *Good Faith in European Contract Law*
   Reinhard Zimmermann and Simon Whittaker
13 *On Civil Procedure*
   J. A. Jolowicz
12 *Trusts: A Comparative Study*
   Maurizio Lupoi and Simon Dix
11 *The Right to Property in Commonwealth Constitutions*
   Tom Allen
10 *International Organizations before National Courts*
   August Reinisch
9 *The Changing International Law of High Seas Fisheries*
   Francisco Orrego Vicuña
8 *Trade and the Environment: A Comparative Study of EC and US Law*
   Damien Geradin
7 *Unjust Enrichment: A Study of Private Law and Public Values*
   Hanoch Dagan
6 *Religious Liberty and International Law in Europe*
   Malcolm D. Evans
5 *Ethics and Authority in International Law*
   Alfred P. Rubin
4 *Sovereignty over Natural Resources: Balancing Rights and Duties*
   Nico Schrijver

3   *The Polar Regions and the Development of International Law*
    Donald R. Rothwell
2   *Fragmentation and the International Relations of Micro-States: Self-Determination and Statehood*
    Jorri C. Duursma
1   *Principles of the Institutional Law of International Organizations*
    C. F. Amerasinghe

For EU product safety concerns, contact us at Calle de José Abascal, 56–1°, 28003 Madrid, Spain or eugpsr@cambridge.org.

www.ingramcontent.com/pod-product-compliance
Ingram Content Group UK Ltd.
Pitfield, Milton Keynes, MK11 3LW, UK
UKHW020504090825
461507UK00002B/20